On Prejudice

On Prejudice

A GLOBAL PERSPECTIVE

Edited and with an Introduction by

Daniela Gioseffi

Anchor Books
DOUBLEDAY
New York London Toronto Sydney Auckland

AN ANCHOR BOOK
PUBLISHED BY DOUBLEDAY
a division of Bantam Doubleday Dell Publishing Group, Inc.
1540 Broadway, New York, NY 10036

ANCHOR BOOKS, DOUBLEDAY, and the portrayal of an anchor
are trademarks of Doubleday, a division of Bantam Doubleday
Dell Publishing Group, Inc.

Acknowledgments for individual works appear on pages 702–16

Book design by Claire Vaccaro

Library of Congress Cataloging-in-Publication Data

On prejudice: a global perspective / edited and with an introduction
by Daniela Gioseffi. — 1st Anchor Books ed.
    p. cm.
    Includes bibliographical references and index.
    1. Prejudices. 2. Prejudices in literature. I. Gioseffi,
    Daniela.
BF575.P906 1993
303.3'85—dc20   93-12594
                                                      CIP

ISBN 0-385-46938-1
FIRST ANCHOR BOOKS EDITION: September 1993
10 9 8 7 6 5 4 3 2 1

With profound gratitude to the Ploughshares Fund, an independent world peace foundation, Fort Mason, California, for an award grant which allowed me to complete the initial research and proposal for this global compendium, and with sincere admiration for Sally Lilienthal, its president, for her tireless and brave commitment to world peace and human decency.

To my beloved daughter, nieces, nephews, stepchildren, and all the children of Earth who need to believe in empathy, equality, tolerance, and unity among all peoples in order to survive into the future. And with special thanks to my husband for his helpful intellectual camaraderie through the long labor of this project.

While I drew and wept along with the terrified children I was drawing, I really felt the burden I am bearing. I felt that I have no right to withdraw from the responsibility of being an advocate. It is my duty to voice the sufferings of humankind, the never-ending sufferings heaped mountain-high. This is my task, but it is not an easy one to fulfill.

FROM *DIARIES* OF KÄTHE KOLLWITZ, 1920

Hear my cry, O God the Reader; vouchsafe that this my book fall not still-born into the world-wilderness. Let there spring, Gentle One, from out its leaves vigor of thought and thoughtful deed to reap the harvest wonderful. Let the ears of guilty people tingle with truth, and seventy millions sigh for the righteousness which exalteth nations, in this drear day when human brotherhood is mockery and a snare. Thus in Thy good time may infinite reason turn the tangle straight, and these crooked marks on a fragile leaf be not indeed.

FROM *THE SOULS OF BLACK FOLKS,* W. E. B. DU BOIS, 1903

A Note to the Reader About This Book

To give an integrated global perspective representative of all issues of *prejudice* and its related *genocide, racism, ethnocentrism, sexism* or *androcentrism, monoculturalism* versus *multiculturalism* and *interculturalism,* and the newer, more vital issue *environmental racism* is a daunting task, yet I attempt it here in order that a communality be represented, impressionistic of the many differing voices of humanity. *On Prejudice: A Global Perspective* encompasses the many oppressed peoples of the Earth, as prior texts on such issues, though good in heart and true in mind, have tended to be from one voice or cultural orientation. In our time of cultural inclusion, it is important that insights be gained anew from a variety of perspectives so that we learn from our collective folly and our past, in hopes that we heed many prophets of the past and present who have warned us of the need for all like-minded ethical people to come together, everywhere, across political boundaries and cultures, against oppression of the few or the weak by the many or the powerful. Our current predicament is one of global demise, and great minds, East and West, South and North, are warning us that the planet's salvation can be accomplished only through world unity and the end of wasteful war economies that use our human potential, our earthly resources, and our intelligence and knowledge for a rapidly advancing *omnicide.*

Though every aspect of every situation of prejudice obviously cannot be included in the scope of one book, this text, made of many voices from differing cultural backgrounds, assembles an overview of the issue. Though all genocides and histories of slavery cannot be represented in one book, a combination of analogies throughout time and place yields an impression and expression of the vastness of the subject. One selection leads to another, or revolves around a point made in the preceding or following one, but the logic is, in effect, *circular* more than linear, as poetry and fiction create a balance of *pathos, ethos,* and *logos,* with polemic in a variety of forms, historical commentary, psychological analysis, essay, or memoir. What is true of the tactics used to create a genocide against a given group, or slavery in one instance, is analogous to another. Prejudice, wherever and whenever it is felt or acted upon, whether in the form of individual or collective biased crime, has similar aspects and psychological dynamics. The reader or educator can use one situation for comparison with another, one instance as a metaphor for another, one cultural destruction or affirmation as analogous to another, in order to deepen understanding of the sociopolitical dynamics involved.

The advantage of this book over others, on the issues of xenophobia, ethnocentrism, the nature of prejudice in many manifestations, aside from its obvious multiple ethnicities and viewpoints, is that the texts assembled for Part One can help to create historical understanding for what is occurring in the present and build empathy for all situations of oppression and human conflict, toward future hopes and aspirations for pluralistic human unity. The reader is sensitized by a reading of Part One, "On Xenophobia and Genocide: The Past and the Present," to understand the meanings of Part Two, "Cultural Destruction and Cultural Affirmation," dealing with language and cultural interaction in terms of colonization, media influence, educational needs and curriculum debates, and pride versus prejudice concerning one's roots and those of others. Parts One and Two ready the general reader or student to thereby accept the suggestions for achieving tolerance and understanding presented in Part Three, "Beyond Culture and Prejudice," and the Human Rights Appendix, where one is led beyond prejudgmental positions of cultural worth to a worldly view of open-mindedness and tolerance. Part Three also provides examples of successful intercultural communication, empathy, tolerance, and understanding, to counteract the horrors of prejudice and genocide presented in Part One. The reader travels from despair and disillusionment to hope and survival, an affirmation of humanity and its aspirations to world peace and planetary salvation. The head and the heart, creative writing and polemic, come together herein as the selections in Part One are designed to lead the reader through the realizations of empathetic understanding of the horrors prejudice has wrought throughout history.

Using the Table of Contents with its often self-explanatory titles and authors, the reader can browse the subject at will, as much as read along in a linear fashion. Each selection is independent of every other and affords some measure of understanding on the overall theme. Reading the selections in any order, at will, can yield useful realizations.

There are *biographical notes,* with bibliographic information, on contributing authors in alphabetical order at the close of the text. These offer suggestions for further reading in a meaningful context, where biographical data on a given author is also present. Books excerpted in the text are named in the contributors' notes or in the acknowledgment of copyright holders at the back of the book. (Reprint permission for individual selections must be obtained from copyright holders, as they are acknowledged on those pages.)

A brief *resource list* of prominent organizations, for citizen activists and educators, is presented at the end, with the idea that this list will be different for each country or language in which the book might be read. An alphabetical *index of authors* helps in the location of each contributor's work.

The *Appendix* containing human rights declarations and statements on race is a useful tool. The statements crystallize our task for the future and orient the reader to what has been done and decided as a basis for future action against prejudice. They offer the educator or seminar leader a model for affirmative statement.

Of course, Part One can offer only a suggestion of the enormity of the history of prejudice, slavery, and genocide, but one can garner a full realization of the economic, political, and psychological causes involved in xenophobia's myriad forms. The selections in Part One prepare the groundwork for response to Part Two. When fully digested, Parts One and Two motivate one to reach *beyond culture* to the inspiration groundwork of Part Three, on intercultural understanding and nonviolent action—toward the "human ecology" needed if there is to be a future on Earth. And what better place to begin than with Anne Hebért's litany of "The Offended," in our journey toward understanding? If *empathy* is the mother of love, then *understanding* is its finest component.   *Daniela Gioseffi, 1993*

Introduction

History counts its skeletons in round numbers.
A thousand and one stays at a thousand,
as though the one had never existed:
an imaginary embryo, an empty cradle,
an ABC unread, . . . no one's place in the line. . . .
We stand in the meadow made of dead flesh,
and the meadow is silent as a false witness . . .
where corpses once sang with their mouths full of earth.
                                    —Wislawa Szymborska, Poland

Racism and ethnic conflict are again playing an intensified role in our dangerously overmilitarized world, just as in 1944 when W. E. B. Du Bois wrote "Prospect of a World without Race Conflict." Du Bois knew what was happening to the Jews in Hitler's Germany, and he drew analogies between the dynamics of prejudice operating in that supertragedy and others, such as the genocide committed by eighteenth-century slave traders—in which more than five million Africans were estimated to have died in bondage en route to just the Caribbean Islands alone. Du Bois knew what all twentieth-century humanist sociologists concerned about the bogus science of Nazi *"eugenics"* were attempting to demonstrate. There is no primary physical or biological difference between Jew and German, African, European, or Asian, as all so-called races of humankind are inextricably mixed, stemming from the same genetic pool originating somewhere over 250,000 years ago in the heart of Africa. We were all born of the same natural creation. Without earth and without water in combination, in short, without *mud* from which all seeds and living creatures grow, there would be no life anywhere on Earth. This is, of course, not an "Afrocentric" view, but biogenetic fact, having nothing to do with cultural values from any particular nation or with value judgments of any kind. It is ironic that neo-Nazi skinheads or Ku Klux Klan defamers talk of "mud people" as a pejorative term, since without the fertile mud of creation, no life could exist on Earth.

Indeed, scientists across the biosphere are now warning us that all global sustenance for life of every kind is imminently threatened, while huge amounts of resources, money, human intelligence, and potential are wasted on greater and increasing endeavors at war. Research dollars spent by superpower nations on biological, or germ, warfare increased one hundredfold over the past two decades—while at the same time nuclear and chemical weapons were stockpiled to mind-boggling proportions. To give a global perspective on the subject of *prejudice* in all its many manifestations—*racism, sexism, ethnocentrism, androcentrism, xenophobia*—can be a daunting task, as prejudice is a most significant part of humankind's story on the planet. Its persistence still fuels the war economies of xenophobic nations, which must now, in unity, turn themselves to the hard ameliorating tasks of planetary citizenship and eco-sanity if any life is to survive on the intricately connected biosphere.

As Du Bois explained in his aforementioned essay, humanists, readers, leaders, and thinkers everywhere—to avert global disaster—have a duty to disseminate the findings of biological science on the issues of "race." It takes a long time for scientific truth to reach the masses unless definite efforts are made. Just as public health everywhere is still handicapped by superstitions long disproved by science, so fallacies concerning race are still taken as truth, even taught in schools, textbooks, social conversation, newspapers, novels, movies, and other media and used to scapegoat subgroups or out-groups of various cultures worldwide.

Since the turn of the century, social scientists, field anthropologists, biologists, and paleontologists have abandoned the useless classification of humankind into "Mongoloid, Negroid, Caucasoid," as if each stemmed from separate entities with individually different gestations. We know that we all crawled, fishy-tailed, from mud and that we all stem from the same gene pool. The word *race* need be used only to specify the human race in all its manifest cultural diversity. We are all inextricably mixed, as for example in the United States, where 80 percent or more of American Blacks are estimated to have so-called white blood in their veins. The mixing of so-called races throughout the world has been going on since the very beginning of life on Earth. The human population everywhere is hybrid and becoming increasingly so. This researcher, for one example, is a mixture of many cultures, Italian, Polish, Russian, Jewish, Greek, Albanian, and Ethiopian among them. Just as many who trace their family history back a few generations discover they are a mixture of many cultures, so nation-states have ancient multicultural tribal elements and interracial beginnings.

Indeed, *biological diversity* is understood, in our time, to be an important and necessary quality for the survival of a given species. Biogeneticists are concerned about the diversity of rapidly declining species, as organisms with more diverse strains are ensured against biological weaknesses and have a better chance of surviving plagues or ecological disasters. Though the full understanding of such a complex concept requires a study of microbiology, to put it simply in lay terms, we've learned that so-called pedigrees of any species tend to be weaker and less resistant to disease than more diversified strains. "Aryan" concepts are misguided in more ways than one.

In order to help disseminate the truths science had discovered about the concept of "race" through the first half of the century, a team of UNESCO scholars* and experts, conferring and pooling their knowledge in Paris in 1950, drafted the first of four statements the United Nations would issue to dispel what Dr. Du Bois called "race fiction." These four "Statements on Race," drafted around midcentury after the horrors of two world wars by UNESCO scholars from around the world, have given us succinct tools for a continuing educational process. They conclude that scientists had long reached general agreement in recognizing humankind as one species, *Homo sapiens*. Differences among peoples that exist in secondary physical characteristics of skin tone or variable features or shapes have nothing to do with "race." These variables of humankind are merely cultural, national, religious, linguistic, and geographic. Such cultural differences, bred by geographic location, do not necessarily coincide with so-called racial groups. The old-fashioned classification of humankind into Mongoloid, Negroid, and Caucasoid by physical anthropologists was stated to be *dynamic,* not static, but ever-changing. Such classifications could not be designated as "races" but were artificially subdivided in the past. In short, there are no innate or inherited characteristics of "intelligence" or intelligence potential common to such ever-changing and already long ago mixed subdivisions.

---

* Sociologists and biologists Ashley Montagu of the United States, Claude Lévi-Strauss of France, Gunnar Myrdal of Sweden, Ernest Beaglehold of New Zealand, Costa Pinto of Brazil, Juan Comas of Mexico, Humayun Kabir of India, and Morris Ginsberg and Julian S. Huxley of Britain were among them. (Statements One and Two are summarized here. See the Appendix for the two final statements.)

"Any common psychological attribute within a given cultural group is due to a common historical or social background and such attributes may obscure the fact that, within different populations consisting of many human types, one will find approximately the same range of temperament and intelligence." So the UNESCO scholars concluded, adding more eminent scientists to their subsequent drafting of three more statements in Paris, Moscow, and New York through 1967. Though only a summary can be offered here, they went on to say: "All normal human beings are capable of learning to share in a common life, to understand the nature of mutual service and reciprocity, and to respect social obligations and contracts. Such biological differences as exist between members of different ethnic groups have no relevance to problems of social and political organization, moral life, and communication between human beings. Biological studies lend support to the ethic of universal brotherhood [and sisterhood]. [Humankind] is a social being who can reach his [or her] fullest potential only through interaction. Every person is, in effect, his [or her] brother's [or sister's] keeper for all are a part of humankind."

Variables of intelligence are the same within all groups. As anthropologist Ruth Benedict declared, there is only one race, and that race is "the human race." All else was mere *"Patterns of Culture,"* consisting of explicit and implicit behaviors acquired and transmitted by symbols. Such cultural symbols, including their embodiment in artifacts, constitute the distinctive achievement of human groups. Culture consists of traditional values and symbols derived from a common geographic history. Cultural systems are acquired—not innate—as products of action and are at the same time conditioned elements for further action.

While economic theory still struggles, after the bloodbath of history, to talk straight on colonial imperialism, psychological testing as a science has not yet recovered from the shame of its racist and sexist use of "intelligence tests." Stephen Jay Gould, in his 1986 book *The Mismeasure of Man,* summarizes the misadventures that occurred in the study of the human mind through the twentieth century. He demonstrates that IQ tests were used to oppress minorities and women and other socially disadvantaged groups. As many educational psychologists have also done, he shows that intelligence is a complex of many qualities upon which social and political forces impact with great effect. Gould's indispensable book and Ashley Montagu's *The Fallacy of Race:*

Man's Most Dangerous Myth are important studies on the subject of prejudice which have international implications. They deal with an aspect of *biological determinism*—the claim regarding the measurability of human intelligence—which Gould demonstrates is based on innumerable fallacies. One false hypothesis concerns the measuring of intelligence so that several varied capabilities are valued as one entity located wholly in the brain, uninfluenced by the varieties of cultural values and attitudes surrounding an individual. The second fallacy ranks an individual's intelligence according to numerical "intelligence quotients." These IQ scores, or numerical ratings, were misused in a way in which French psychologist Dr. Alfred Binet, their creator, never intended—as unalterable, unerring, unchanging quotients not influenced by sociological factors and conditioning. A true measure of intellectual capacities or abilities cannot be accurately achieved without reference to cultural conditioning and advantages, and certainly cannot be found to predict the future achievements or learning potentials of individuals. As Gould concludes, "Few tragedies can be more extensive than the stunting of life, few injustices deeper than the denial of an opportunity to strive or even to hope, by a limit imposed from without but falsely identified as lying within."

Since all humans are of one race, what are the basic dynamics of prejudice or xenophobia and its converse phenomenon, ethnocentrism, which continues to keep national economies fueled for war and global efforts divided at this dangerous juncture when unity is required for our survival on Earth? Psychologists the world over who have closely studied the nature of prejudice find that self-hatred is at its core. The self-hating bigots among us hate the exotic other being as a projection of their own shortcomings. *Projection,* the psychological term for visiting upon others what we find or imagine—deep down—lacking in ourselves, is the basis of prejudice in the human psyche. Confucius or Buddha, Jesus Christ in his Sermon on the Mount, Muhammad in his teachings of tolerance, but psychologists everywhere—Freud as a seminal thinker of the modern movement of psychology in the West, or Australian-born Dorothy Rowe of Britain, or Robert Coles of the United States, twentieth-century shamans, spiritual leaders, tribal sages and healers of every sort, across the burgeoning disciplines—all, all have told us that we loathe most in others what we hate subconsciously in ourselves. This penchant for *projection* of our own secret murderous drives and greed upon our "enemies" has been the bane and waste of our existence and has brought us to the faltering brink of a militarized world economy, so overstocked with nuclear weapons alone that we could kill every one of the many of us fifty times over with one enormous explosion. What an irony, Hell on Earth more surreal than any poem or rock video!

As William James explained at the beginning decade of our century, in his well-known essay "The Moral Equivalent of War":

> War-taxes are the only ones men never hesitate to pay, as the budgets of all nations show us. History is a bath of blood. The *Iliad* (which we still celebrate in our classical literary studies) is one long recital of how Diomedes and Ajax, Sarpedon and Hector killed. No detail of the wounds they made is spared us, and the . . . mind fed upon the story. Greek history, all history, is a panorama of jingoism and imperialism—war for war's sake, all the citizens being warriors. It is horrible reading, because of the irrationality of it all—save for the purpose of making "history"—and the history is that of the utter ruin of a civilization. . . . Those wars were purely piratical. Pride, gold, women, slaves, excitement, were their only motives. . . . "The powerful exact what they can," said Athenians, "and the weak grant what they must."

Homer himself sang his epics throughout ancient Greece to teach the idiocy and waste of war, yet the fallacies and fictions of race prejudice still operate around the globe to deflect attention from our real enemies: *disease, natural disaster, hunger, and ecological destruction,* even after the work of three generations of scientists has sought to defuse and explain them.

In dealing with prejudice, one must first constantly remind oneself of an old adage indigenous to many cultures worldwide: "Two wrongs do not make a right." For example, both the U.S. and Japanese majority cultures have committed human rights violations against "minority" cultures by projecting evil and guilt into them. The U.S. internment of Japanese Americans in concentration camps during World War II was a crime, exposed as a ploy of land and property grabbers—and not recognized by the U.S. government as a violation of human rights until quite recently. By the same token, a Japanese

"Aryan" attitude still causes Koreans living in Japan to suffer the degradation and oppression which goes with the denial of citizenship and the right to vote.

Prejudice is a worldwide phenomenon and the dynamics of every instance of it—throughout human history—are analogous. White European bigotry toward native American peoples is analogous to prejudice against Jews in Hitler's Germany, against Armenians in Turkey, or against Blacks in South Africa, to name a few examples in which hatred has been understandably returned, making the philosophical axiom "Hate begets hate" undeniably true. The fact is that no nation hands are free of crimes of prejudice, despite the fact that superpowers are capable of spreading genocide on a more vast and technocratic scale than ever before. The student in search of truth must be extremely wary of the censorship of his or her nation's history to discover the extent of its ethnocentric behavior. Each nation attempts to bury the aggression it is responsible for in a jingoistic patriotism elemental to ethnocentrism. Just as individuals will rationalize their hostile behaviors, projecting their own selfishness into imagined enemies, so nations do also.

The danger is that past violations of human rights by the United States in the Philippines, Haiti, Vietnam, Nicaragua, El Salvador; by the Turks in Armenia; by the French in Vietnam and Algiers; by the English in India and Africa; by the former U.S.S.R. in Afghanistan; by China in Tibet and Cambodia; and by the Japanese in Korea can soon be forgotten, censored, or de-emphasized—just as each of us tends to submerge the memory of our own selfish behaviors.

> The bloody massacre in Bangladesh quickly covered over the memory of the Russian invasion of Czechoslovakia, the assassination of Allende drowned out the groans of Bangladesh, the war in the Sinai Desert made people forget Allende, the Cambodian massacre made people forget Sinai, and so on and so forth until ultimately everyone lets everything be forgotten,

wrote Milan Kundera in *The Book of Laughter and Forgetting*. His statement demonstrates the raison d'être for studying history, if we are not to be condemned to repeating our folly and if we are to awaken from the "nightmare of history" wrought by the dynamics of prejudice.

Insistent clinging to outmoded ideas of "race" or genetic superiority or inferiority continue to give rise to new and intensified levels of biased crime. In addition to this increase in "hate crimes," the Earth's ecosystems are faltering on the deficit investments of militarized economies and their polluting industries, driving all toward self-annihilation as we rapidly approach the year 2000. There is increasing fear that all the genocides in our history will culminate in *omnicide,* as outmoded ideas of ethnocentricity and prejudice continue to fuel the profit motives of industrialist nations—dominated by war deficits—even as the ozone layer continues to disappear and plagues such as AIDS and incurable tuberculosis need our efforts and human resources, which are overextended on stockpiled armaments.

As W. E. B. Du Bois said in 1944: "This careless ignorance of the facts of race is precisely the refuge where antisocial economic reaction flourishes." He could be speaking today. Race and ethnic wars and the chilling concept of "ethnic cleansing" are renewing themselves in a post–cold war world of failing overmilitarized technocracies, and it is a known fact—a vicious cycle—that racial and ethnic tensions increase wherever economic structures falter. Experts agree that the depleted world economy, wasted on war efforts, is in great measure the reason for renewed ethnic and religious strife. "Haves" fight with "have-nots" for the smaller piece of the pie that must go around. One need only observe living creatures at a feeding tray to understand the situation. As long as all have some fair measure of sustenance, things are peaceful, but when the food supply drops, skirmishes, sometimes deadly, develop. Still, there is a reluctance to talk straight on the economics of imperialism, as the superpowers pretend their expansionist policies had no part in the wars still raging in Somalia, Bosnia, Burma, Azerbaijan, Angola, Afghanistan, Palestine, El Salvador, South Africa, Korea, and Cambodia.

Nazi-inspired crimes are again occurring worldwide. For one example, in Portland, Oregon, in 1988 an Ethiopian man was beaten to death by "skinheads." The neo-Nazi burning of a fifty-three-year-old Jewish man near Bonn, reported at the end of 1992, is another example. There's a chilling rise in incidents on college campuses, too. The infamous "Hitler Caper" at Dartmouth University in the United States, in 1990—in which a saboteur inserted a passage from *Mein Kampf* into the masthead of *The Dartmouth Review* on the eve of Yom Kippur—is only one of many worse such happenings worldwide.

There have been numerous biased attacks and beatings, killings, and defacing of cemeteries, synagogues, and churches in cities and towns everywhere. From Azerbaijan to Bosnia, Los Angeles to Paris, London to New Delhi, Tokyo to New York, Burma to Tibet, crimes of prejudice, ethnic purges, even death camp atrocities and mass rapes are happening in the wake of decaying boundaries and outmoded technocracies.

Surely there isn't a soul left who hasn't understood that human rights and democratic ideals, for example, had little to do with the Gulf massacres called "Desert Storm." The world knows that Geneva protocols were violated in every direction during that destructive charade, fought to protect an emirate and for oil profits invested in stock exchanges. The dictator, Saddam Hussein, was a media-manufactured "Butcher of Baghdad" even though his might came from the very allied nations who—when oil as a commodity was threatened—decided to declare war against him. His multibillion-dollar military aid, his chemical and other armaments and bunkers came from the very nations who opposed him—in their prior desire to help him ward off their enemy Iran. Now that he refused to behave as they wished, "hateful" greed was projected onto him, though he'd always been the same vindictive and dictatorial personality. But could the U.S. administration have rallied U.S. citizenry to such a flag-waving degree for the profits of arms dealers if Americans were not easily led to believe that Moslems or Middle Easterners—or Arabic-looking peoples of any kind—are less human than Christians?

Though the situation had other complexities, involving the assets of the Imir of Kuwait, crimes against humanity are allowed because of false ideas of "race" and nationhood. Ethnocentrism, the bonding of people around their nationhood, makes it easier to project evils onto scapegoated enemies in times of war. Prejudice and xenophobia throughout human history have been easily rallied into use by leaders for their own imperialist schemes. There is a deep need for humans, social creatures by nature, to bond together with those whom they feel are more like themselves, as "difference" constitutes a threat. Those people who look and talk and move and dress differently than "we" do can't be trusted, we tell ourselves. Their different ways threaten our ways and, in effect, tell us our ways are no good. This is the false assumption operable in ethnocentrism—as if people cannot be different yet equally human.

Hitler, thought of as the mastermind of "eugenics" or Aryan breeding, knew himself that concepts of "race" were bogus science and that he was using ethnocentrism and prejudice as a means to rally the German people for his greedy imperialist designs on Europe. In a conversation reported by Hermann Rauschning in *The Voice of Destruction,* Hitler said:

> I know perfectly well, just as well as those tremendously clever intellectuals, that in the scientific sense there is no such thing as race. But a farmer, and cattle breeder, cannot get his breeding successfully achieved without the conception of race. And I, as a politician, need a conception which will enable the order, which has before now existed on an historic basis, to abolish itself and an entirely new and anti-historic concept needs to be enforced and given an intellectual basis. . . . With creation and use of the conception of race, our German Nationalism will be able to carry its revolution far and wide and reshape the world!

Hitler's own admission that the idea of an Aryan nation was merely propaganda—along with the fact that biological diversity is actually a necessary and desirable quality for our species' survival—should be enough to convince the most fanatic neo-Nazi that he or she is blinded by the projection of his or her own self-hatred and is simply scapegoating others. Ralph Ginzburg, author of *100 Years of Lynchings* (Black Classic Press, 1988), in studying the case histories of the lynching of minority populations, particularly Blacks, throughout U.S. history, came to hold one overriding conviction. After spending several years documenting case history after case history, he agreed with psychologists and sociologists from Gordon Allport *(The Nature of Prejudice,* Doubleday, 1954) to William H. Grier and Price M. Cobbs *(Black Rage,* Basic Books, 1992) that the *projection of self-hatred* caused by guilt or feelings of inadequacy lies at the root of race hatred. He found, for one example, that a slothful and sex-mad white rapist had led the mob that lynched an innocent Black man for the alleged crime of rape in a 1936 incident in the southern United States. Often, a race-hater was seen to ascribe to his target the greed or criminality, or guilt, he secretly hated or felt most within himself. This was a means of his ego survival.

As psychologist Dorothy Rowe of Britain explains, our egos require that we have enemies. Freud, among others, discovered the psychological process of creating enemies—which requires that for our ego survival and sanity we deflect our own aggression or self-hatred outward onto others. Our superegos, or civilized behaviors keep us from murdering each other over our projections of greed and jealousy, but when the id or ego is released from all civilized bonds, as in war or hate crimes, violence and aggression ensue. Since we have seen how self-hatred is at the root of race hatred and projection is the means of prejudice, it has become a popular idea that those who "love" themselves make the best "lovers." Many new age psychologists as well as gurus and shamans of every kind, worldwide, also are explaining the interconnectedness of our sexual self-hatred projected upon others. Those who practice projection to the extent of torturing others for the evils they hate in themselves are found, according to eminent psychologists everywhere, to be overly disciplined and repressed, not only in their sexuality but in their self-expression. No doubt those who use sexual tortures upon others are imbued with a deep self-hatred of their own sexual natures.

Prejudice is learned behavior. The judgmental parent fosters the judgmental child. Small children are color-blind toward others until taught to hate. When we are told too often that we are bad and wrong and our sexuality "dirty," such pronouncements become self-fulfilling. Abuse is passed on from generation to generation within a family until someone breaks the cycle. The dynamics of prejudice hold true for nations as for individuals.

The need to project our failing economics upon others can be seen in the struggle of xenophobic pronouncements between U.S. and Japanese businesspeople. The U.S. media has been full of anti-Japanese sentiments of late, and U.S. citizens, ignorant of the real cause of the demise of their own economy, have picked up these hateful sentiments commercialized by failing business executives. They want to blame the failure of U.S. business upon the Japanese rather than accept military overkill spending on nuclear armaments as a major culprit. Top-heavy, self-aggrandizing management, as well as legislative corruption in banking scandals, is involved in the causes of the U.S. economic demise, but it is advantageous for powerful and corrupt forces to project greed onto an enemy—especially an exotic one toward whom much xenophobia has prevailed throughout U.S. history. The Japanese become scapegoats of U.S. failure, instead of examples of homogeneous unity and successful industry. Never mind that for years after World War II, Japan was not allowed to indulge in military buildup as the United States and U.S.S.R. were during the cold war and therefore concentrated all their efforts on consumer products. Without a militarized industry, their consumer-oriented economy soared. Meanwhile, superpower legislative and bureaucratic corruption, coupled with overkill military spending, caused the demise of U.S. and U.S.S.R. peacetime industrial efforts.

The other side of projecting evil onto others for our failures, as mentioned earlier, is the tendency to bond together for strength in ethnocentric partnerships, or patriotic nationhood—derived from the basic family tribal mentality which sees survival as dependent upon one's blood relations. As Albert Einstein explained: "A human being is part of the whole, called by us the universe. A part limited in time and space. He experiences himself, his thoughts and feelings, as something separate from the rest, a kind of optical delusion of his consciousness. This delusion is a kind of prison for us, restricting us to our personal desires and to affection for a few persons nearest to us. Our task must be to free ourselves from this prison by widening our circle of compassion to embrace all living creatures."

In the case of individuals such as Arthur Kirk, an Iowa farmer described by Osha Gray Davidson in his book *Broken Heartland: The Rise of the American Rural Ghetto* (Anchor, 1990), the need to project feelings of personal economic failure can also result in "race" hatred. Like many U.S. farmers of the 1980s, Kirk had fallen deeply into debt during the huge farm crisis of the Reagan years. Agrarian populations worldwide still procreate according to old customs of peopling the farm with field hands. In the United States, for example, the Midwest heartland of farming communities produces more people than can be sustained by the land. As family farmers met their demise because of administration policies which favored corporate farms, the starving, overflowing populations of farmlands either moved to urban centers where they were met with more unemployment or created rural ghettos with jobless, disenfranchised workers easily sucked into a right-wing neo-Nazi mentality. Since there are few people of varying color or ethnos in these areas, it is easy to blame the "exotic other" for all the ills visited upon the community. In such predominantly "white" areas, imaginary enemies are easily manufactured of Semites or Blacks or Latins who have rarely been experienced as neighbors—as ordinary, feeling, thinking, struggling people like anyone else. The jobless and disenfranchised are always the most fertile ground for the corruption of prejudice and xenophobic racism.

Rather than see the administration in Washington, controlled by the rich corporate farmer, as the cause of his demise, Arthur Kirk, a desperate, failed farmer of the American heartland, projected all of his feelings of failure and inadequacy onto some far-off Jewish bankers of the city whom he imagined to have caused all his troubles. He joined with others in neo-Nazi organizations that misinterpret "Christian" scripture—written by ancient Jews—ironically, to blame "Jews" for all their troubles. In this way Kirk could unload—or project—his feelings of guilt at "failing" his family upon an imagined, dehumanized target. Kirk, a broken man full of hostility for the failure of his family farm, ended up misdirecting his anger in a tragic shoot-out with state police. Before he died, he was heard to yell: ". . . damned Jews! They destroyed everything I ever worked for . . . for 49 . . . years. By God, I ain't puttin' up with . . . [it]. Farmers fought the Revolutionary War and we'll fight [Jewish bankers] . . . we'll take [them] on their own terms!" His language needs expurgation as it was full of the worst curses and bigotry imaginable. The report to the governor by Judge Van Pelt concluded that by the time of Kirk's death, he had reached such a state of paranoia—misdirected fears and hostility—that it was difficult to hold him responsible for his actions. He had been reduced to the mentality of a cornered animal. His pitiable story is documented in detail in Davidson's book.

Many generations of humanist social scientists have been and are still forced to set their sights on debunking myths and fallacies of the "races" of humankind as genetically separate from one another. They are still trying to explain the dynamics of projection and scapegoating. They know that those in power deliberately used the social sciences, at first, as instruments to prove the inferiority of vast populations of people in order to exploit them as slave labor and confiscate their lands, worldy goods, and rights.

Cultural institutions can also serve the need for collective scapegoating and greed. Western culture, for example, in its need to exploit Africa and her people seemed to declare, by the force of omission, that Blacks had no history before Europeans arrived to pillage Africa. Protestant fundamentalists or Catholic fundamentalists tend to conveniently forget that Jesus Christ was himself a Jew, by culture, and a product of Hebrew Old Testament moral conviction. Bogus biology and false interpretations of scripture have been used to exaggerate the physical differences among peoples of every color, classifying them into subgroups. Yet robbery of the land and belongings of subgroups or out-groups is behind the use of racist propaganda.

Another dynamic gleaned from the accurate study of history shows that "haves" tend to divide and conquer "have-nots" in a desire to maintain their own, superior status quo. The rich get the poorer masses of people to kill each other in order to divert attention from their own greed and thievery. The Los Angeles riots in 1992 are a case in point. Even though instigated by the verdict in the Rodney King case, they occurred around the same period in U.S. history as disclosure of the monumental S&L scandal and corrupt military overspending. It is tragic to realize that poor Los Angeles neighborhoods were burned in race riots which targeted hardworking small-business owners—predominantly minority Koreans and Blacks divided against each other—while rich majority executives involved in destroying and exploiting the U.S. economy—and costing taxpayers billions—went unprosecuted.

Jews in Nazi Germany were burned in ovens and lamp shades were manufactured from their human skin, as much to confiscate what bit of worldly goods they might have had as to "purify" the "Aryan" race. Again, the myth of "ethnic purification" was used by paranoid leaders and imperialist thieves for the purposes of psychological projection and "divide and conquer" tactics—just as it was used upon Armenians for the same purposes in Turkey. It was easy to get the people of Germany, suffering post–World War I economic failure, to follow paranoid fascists like Hitler by using projection as a weapon of propaganda. Fascist greed was projected onto innocent Poles, Jews, and other subgroups. Japanese Americans were interned in U.S. concentration camps because they had good farmland that others coveted. Always, the enemy is created by psychological projection and dehumanizing generalization. Japanese Americans were accused of bonding with a far-off enemy, and American xenophobia toward Asians, an old story, was exploited for the purpose of confiscating goods and land. Always there are the gold wedding bands and gold teeth stolen from the corpses, from Cambodian killing fields back to the Rape of Nanking. From the bombing of civilian cities like Dresden, Hiroshima,

Nagasaki, Beirut and Baghdad to the taking of native lands everywhere throughout history, there is the greed motive, along with a projection of the greed motive onto the enemy.

Pilgrim settlers had to imagine Native Americans as subhuman savages in order to kill and rob them of their very sustenance and rightful use of their own lands and hunting grounds. They easily projected all their greed, guilt, and self-hatred, wrought by an overly strict and judgmental Puritan ethic, into the "savage" enemy. Colonial wars upon indigenous population are always in the service of exploitation—to take what the enemy, manufactured by the process of projection, possesses. Thus the ego survives while robbing "the enemy" of his or her rights. History details how often friendliness of native peoples is betrayed by treachery and ethnocentrism on the part of their conquerors. William Penn was one writer among the U.S. colonists who appreciated the integrity of indigenous tribal customs, honor, bravery, and justice among the Leni Lenape of Pennsylvania, whom he encountered and with whom he managed relatively peaceful relations. Penn was an exception—for a colonialist of his day in his open-minded approach to a culture so different from his own. "Purifying" the "race" as Puritans and others have talked of it—in ethnocentric fashion—is always a propaganda ploy, as the race is already, as biogeneticists have discovered, inextricably mixed and needs no purification, biological diversity being an important means of its survival.

These truths must be faced by all as survival of the entire human race depends on its blending in unity. We might many years from now all be the same lovely tawny, yellowish reddish brownish pinkish tan colors that the decadent pale and wealthy languishers on resort beaches seek, even as they are served cool drinks by darker-skinned natives who have been disenfranchised from their lands through the dynamics of prejudice. It is not just an ironic joke to realize the wasted human potential that litters our beaches with plastic suntan oil containers under a depleted ozone layer radiant with radioactivity as citizens of blotted and crumbling technocracies covet the suntanned look of toiling "minorities" who must labor in the out of doors.

"Me! I'm not prejudiced! I don't need to study prejudice! I'm free of it, or I suffer from it, so what do I need to learn about it?" We might protest. We might tell ourselves: "All women and men are created equal. Prejudice is terrible! I already know that!" But we should be very wary of the belief that there is nothing more to learn about the nature of prejudice. It's clear, as psychology explains, that none of us can be perfectly free of social prejudices, those subtle stereotypical reactions to surnames or cultural backgrounds or skin tones or eye slant or nose width and breadth or sexual orientation that are jumbled in the haunted attic of our psyches, causing us to prejudge people before any evidence is in. As Charles Lamb, a nineteenth-century anti-Semitic English essayist admitted in *Imperfect Sympathies:* "For myself, earth-bound and fettered to the scene of my activities, I confess that I do feel the differences of mankind, national and individual. . . . I am, in plainer words, a bundle of prejudices—made up of likings and dislikings—veriest thrall to sympathies, apathies, antipathies."

Indeed, one of the most common themes of literature through the ages has been that of prejudice from Leo Tolstoy's *Anna Karenina* to Isaac Babel's *Karl Yankel* or Chekhov's *Rothschild's Fiddle,* from James Baldwin's *Notes of a Native Son* to Toni Morrison's *The Bluest Eye* and *Beloved.* World literature is replete with examples to support the theme of prejudice and no culture holds a monopoly on it. The vague unspoken suspicions we live with concerning each other cause us to visit "the sins of the fathers" upon each other. We are certainly aware of the human rights crimes committed upon Blacks by whites and on Jews by Gentiles, but are we aware that prejudice goes the other way too and destroys much human potential—especially now, when all humanitarians of every culture and background need to unite to save Earth from imminent destruction?

Are you a Jew who is suspicious of all Germans? Or a Black suspicious of all whites? Or a woman who feels superior to all men? Or a homosexual who feels superior to heterosexuals? Are you an Asian who feels Europeans, especially all Americans descended from them, are inferior? Are you a person of African descent who hates or envies mulattoes? These are subtler reactionary prejudices less explored or articulated by the media, yet each requires a dissertation in itself.

Say that you never subtly suspect all Irishman of drinking too much; all Blacks of being better rhythmic dancers or having more savage libidos; all Latins of harboring intense animal sexuality and being "hot-tempered"; all Jews of being industriously stingy and overly bookish; all Italians of being connected to syndicated crime; all Japanese of being suspiciously unctuous or superintelligent; all blonds of being dumber or having more fun; and all brunettes of being capable of more manipulative evil—and one can conclude you weren't born on this planet. We need to face the fact that we all have stereotypical reactions *in subtle ways,* more subtle than these examples, but they exist because the human mind must generalize in order to think and name things and thusly things become symbols of themselves.

Count Alfred Korzibski pointed out, long ago, that "Cow 1 is not Cow 2" with his "Structural Differential" and science of "General Semantics," but we cannot ever completely free ourselves of making subliminal generalizations about the "otherness" of the other. Language communication depends on generalizing concepts into denotative words. My friend is a Lithuanian German woman, and a brunette, and I am a Slavic Jewish Greek Italian with Ethiopian ancestry and a blond; but without seeing us, most people would guess our hair color to be the opposite. Some whites have large noses and full lips and some Blacks have small noses and thin lips. Some Jews look like Germans or Spaniards or Arabs or Italians, and Koreans and Vietnamese do not want to be mistaken for Japanese or Chinese. There are subtle differences in every being, unique from every other being, and still, despite the many mixtures in all our roots, we generalize about our nationhood or cultures or see ourselves as separate from others of other skin tones. We even manage to get "Coloreds" and "Blacks" separated and divided from each other in hierarchies of privilege in South Africa, in order that those possessed of the laws and the land might rule those who are dispossessed of their birthright. Blacks complain, too, that they discriminate among themselves according to skin shades, and ethnic Jews complain that overassimilated "Waspy" Jews look down on them. Italians in America have come to be suspicious of each other because of media sensationalizing of "Mafia connections" and are afraid to congregate to defend themselves against this cruel stereotyping. Such stereotyping of ethnic groups as criminals, aided by the media, is a means to divide and conquer them, as Indian scouts of one tribe were recruited by European settlers to help defeat other native tribes, and Black African slave traders of differing tribes sold their own people to European slave traders. A few assimilated Jews sold information about ethnic Jews to Nazi sympathizers in order to save their own skins during the Holocaust, just as Italian American male novelists and screenwriters have learned to profit from Mafia stereotyping in a culture which will buy nothing else from them about their own people. These are desperate acts of the disenfranchised that are the equivalent of self-destructive race riots that burn down the neighborhoods of the disenfranchised.

Stephen Jay Gould wrote of an interestingly subtle form of prejudice in *The Mismeasure of Man:*

> After extensive ghetto riots during the summer of 1967 [in the United States], three [white] doctors wrote a letter to the prestigious *Journal of the American Medical Association:* "It is important to realize," the doctors said, "that only a small number of the millions of slum dwellers have taken part in the riots, and that only a subfraction of these rioters have indulged in arson, sniping and assault. Yet, if slum conditions alone determined and initiated riots, why are the vast majority of slum dwellers able to resist the temptations of unrestrained violence? Is there something peculiar about the violent slum dweller that differentiates him from his peaceful neighbor?" We all tend to generalize from our own areas of expertise. These doctors are psychosurgeons. But why should the violent behavior of some desperate and discouraged people point to a specific disorder of their brain while the corruption and violence of some congressmen and presidents provokes no similar theory? Human populations are highly variable for all behaviors; the simple fact that some do and some don't provides no evidence for specific pathology mapped upon the brain of the doers. Shall we concentrate upon an unfounded speculation for the violence of some— one that follows the determinist philosophy of blaming the victim—or shall we try to eliminate the oppression that builds ghettos and saps the spirit of their unemployed in the first place?

Such subtleties of *determinist* attitudes operate even in the most civilized and educated circles, proving that the need for disseminating the truth about race and racial attributes persists even among the educated, though those who have a wide understanding of world history and culture are generally found to harbor less prejudice toward people of other cultures. This recent wisdom is causing some U.S. cities to require urban police to be trained in liberal arts. Studies show that education can succeed in helping us develop sensitivity and empathy for those of other backgrounds and cultures. Courses in conflict resolution and intercultural communication as well as a new multicultural approach to education are now being instituted worldwide in response to such studies.

Also, the need to foster the truth about racial attitudes is giving rise to a heated debate over multicultural curricula in the schools, as ethnic strife renews itself everywhere and the disenfranchised rise up out of their pain and claim the pride of their cultural accomplishments and the history of their resistance to oppression. Yet how many white children the world over have actually read Black slave narratives and understood the depth and breadth of slaveholding brutality as history? How many have experienced narratives by cruelly colonized indigenous people telling of their lot—and their respect for the land and its resources—as actual history?

The raging debate among Eurocentrists and Afrocentrists and educators who helped to pioneer multicultural studies is a ridiculous example of particularist exclusionism. Multiculturalists are considered too extreme by those conservatives who are angry Eurocentrists or those avengers who are justifiably angry Afrocentrists. For an interesting revelation of culture and history, one might look at Martin Barnal's *Black Athena,* a controversial but factual view on the issues. In 1987 Barnal helped to revive much forgotten and censored Black history,* during the same period that Diane Ravitch, an educator who has taught at Columbia Teachers College and served as a government official in education, was attacked by Afrocentrists and Eurocentrists alike. Ravitch presents a moderate view for all sides, though the difficulty for such views is that they cannot correct heinous wrongs with enough passionate intensity to satisfy wounded avengers, even as they may cause less conflict in the present. And so the heated argument between the Afrocentrists—with their justifiable anger—and "threatened" Eurocentrists continues. But the debate does not change the truth of what W. E. B. Du Bois said at the outbreak of World War I about the pillaging of Africa being an important element of the roots of European imperialism.

---

* A history revived and resurrected for years by eminent Black scholars like W. E. B. Du Bois, Frederick Douglass, Zora Neal Hurston, Langston Hughes, Lerone Bennett, and others.

To understand the problems involved in the curriculum debate, imagine—just for one example—a young person seated in a classroom, and imagine if that young person happens to be Jewish and he or she is forced to read the following description of a Jewish ghetto of the Lower East Side of Manhattan by Henry James:

> I recall the intensity of the material picture in the dense Yiddish quarter. . . . There is no swarming like that of Israel when once Israel has got a start, and the scene here bristled, at every step, with the signs and sounds, immitigable, unmistakable, of a Jewry that had burst all bounds. That it has burst all bounds in New York, almost any combination of figures or of objects taken at hazard sufficiently proclaims; but I remember how the rising waters, on this summer night, rose, to the imagination, even above the housetops and seemed to sound their murmur to the pale distant stars. It was as if we had been thus, in the crowded, hustled roadway, where multiplication, multiplication of everything, was the dominant note, at the bottom of some vast sallow aquarium in which innumerable fish, of over-developed proboscis, were to bump together, for ever, amid heaped spoils of the sea. . . . The children swarmed above all—here was multiplication with a vengeance; and the number of very old persons, of either sex, was almost equally remarkable; the very old person being in equal vague occupation of the doorstep, pavement, curbstone, gutter, roadway, and every one, alike using the street for overflow. . . . There are small strange animals, known to natural history, snakes or worms, I believe, who, when cut into pieces, wriggle away contentedly and live in the snippet as completely as in the whole. So the denizens of the New York Ghetto, heaped as thick as the splinters on the table of a glass-blower. . . . The advanced age of so many figures, the ubiquity of the children, carried out in fact this analogy; they were all there for race, and not, as it were, for reason: that excess of lurid meaning, in some of the old men's and old women's faces in particular, would have been absurd, in the conditions, as a really directed attention—it could only be the gathered past of Israel mechanically pushing through.

The Italians, "Negroes," and other "Aliens" described by Henry James in his essays on New York do not fare any better, and this is only one example of bigotry in the English canon of American literature, James is just one of the many bigoted writers—like Ezra Pound, T. S. Eliot, Céline, and Heidegger—that "minority" children are forced to study in schools across the world that teach them nothing of their own cultural contribution to humankind. Indeed, even as authors Mark Twain and William James (Henry James's brother) were decrying the U.S. war policy of genocide against Filipinos, Henry James was writing his bigoted descriptions of Blacks, Italians, and Jews of Manhattan, whom he called "aliens." We continue to use the phrase "illegal alien" today to describe people who are forced to our shores by colonial imperialist war crimes on the part of our own governments. Culture is always a mixed bag, but what good is a literary canon, as a symbol of "the humanities," if it is full of bigotry and is not humanizing but merely decadent? These are the questions that need to be asked. Isn't a Black, Jewish, Latino, Italian, Cherokee, or Sioux child better off reading one of the considered classic literatures of his or her own people—to gain the strength and pride in self that will serve him or her well through life? One can't help but agree with Amiri Baraka, African American writer and educator, and numerous others who have opposed the teaching of bigoted or narrowly cultured writers in the classroom in favor of writers who bring self-respect to children of all backgrounds. Their position is especially well taken since self-hatred or lack of self-respect, as has been discussed, leads to prejudice. The use of "divide and conquer" tactics based on color, creed, national origin, more than any other conquering vice, has served throughout history to oppress minority populations who are set at each other's throats while the controlling group maintains its wealth.

As an example, it was easy for Charles Stuart, a white middle-class wife murderer in Boston in 1989, to claim falsely that an anonymous Black man had shot his wife in their family car in a Black ghetto area. Stuart played upon white middle-class xenophobia toward Blacks, as much as Hitler played on German xenophobia toward Jews. The Stuart case became a white media "racist soap opera" which deeply offended the Black community. A murder of a Black man that very same night in the same area went unnoticed by the media. An innocent Black man was initially charged with the crime because of projection of race hatred. There are many ways in which the media help to manipulate and intensify prejudicial stereotyping, as the history of Hollywood movie making shows. Some recent antiracist Hollywood movies about Black troops in the Civil War *(Glory)* or the integrity of Native American cultures *(Dances with Wolves)* or Latin American peoples *(El Norte)* have begun in some measure to undo the damage of biased images of the past. But the Hollywood industry still bears many blights in its history. *Birth of a Nation,* an anti-Semitic film glorifying the Ku Klux Klan, is still considered a classic. Hollywood often still stereotypes Blacks as athletes and entertainers, women as "sexpots," Italians as Mafiosi, and all ethnics as criminals.

Still it's useless to blame some newly born white Afrikaner child for the crimes of apartheid as it was conceived by generations of whites who came before, and there is no reason for Serbs of today to murder Croats of today—and involve Muslims and Macedonians in the carnage besides—because Croats of yesteryear massacred Serbs. Should some young person who has worked for what he or she has today be disenfranchised to pay for the sins of slavery perpetrated by his or her forebears? The problem is that the sins of the past are not easily made good again, and the vestiges of slavery live on in the unjust present and are the cause of the unjust present. And who shall pay? The answer as Margaret Duras puts it in *The War* is that "we must all share the crime" and try to know enough history to avoid the prejudgments that constitute prejudice. All of us are responsible for the fairness of our society and must take responsibility for fairness upon ourselves. The truth is that if we all do, we will stop wasting an investment in war and human potential, and, with cooperation, there will be—there can be—enough to go around to all. No one need be disenfranchised and everyone is morally enriched. This is not a sentimental truth but a moral clarity.

For too long humanity has based economic systems on competition rather than cooperation. *Symbiosis* (the principle of cooperative survival), stressed by renowned microbiologist Lynn Margulis in her groundbreaking book *Symbiosis and Cell Evolution,* 1981, as an alternative to Darwinian *survivalism,* is a new ideal prevalent in feminist spirituality. It is also found in prehistoric tribal ways, respectful of resources and human life, and it can work. The Seville Statement on Violence (See Appendix), drawn up by psychologists from around the globe, has concluded that violence need not be present in human society in order for humankind to survive. Cooperation can work. It's the only way that civilization can truly move progressively forward.

The Earth needs to be viewed as from outer space, a spiral of interlocking systems owned by all peoples, in order for any people to survive. We must think in terms of growth, oscillation, overshoot, and limits to the growth of sustainable systems. This sort of view makes control of Earth's population, or planned parenthood, and eradication of environmental racism—or waste dumping on the disenfranchised—two of the most important issues related to our survival. We can see how these issues—along with the dynamics of prejudice—concern the problems of hazardous nuclear, biological, and chemical waste disposal and ozone depletion. We must focus on the interconnection of dynamic patterns to see that the economy and the environment are indeed one system inseparable from our concepts for survival as a species. Freeing ourselves from the wasted potentials of wars encouraged by xenophobia and prejudice is necessary for this to happen, but according to the World Commission on Environmental Development: "Humanity has the ability to make development sustainable—to ensure that it meets the needs of the present without compromising the ability of future generations to meet their own needs." The need today is for all peoples of Asia or Europe, Africa or the Americas to address themselves to the human situation. We need to talk about human destiny, not geographic or cultural or racial destiny.

UN Secretary-General U Thant wrote in *The Limits to Growth* more than twenty years ago:

> I do not wish to seem overdramatic, but I can only conclude from the information that is available to me as Secretary-General, that the Members of the United Nations have perhaps ten years left in which to subordinate their ancient quarrels and launch a global partnership to curb the arms race, to improve the human environment, to defuse the population explosion, and to supply the required momentum to development efforts. If such a global partnership is not forged within the next decade, then I very much fear that the problems I have mentioned will have reached such staggering proportions that they will be beyond our capacity to control.

Approximately three decades ago, Martin Luther King, Jr., concurred: "In a world facing the revolt of ragged and hungry masses . . . of children; in a world torn between the tensions of East and West, white and colored, individuals and collectivists; in a world whose cultural and spiritual power lags so far behind her technological capabilities that we live each day on the verge of nuclear . . . annihilation; in this world, nonviolence is no longer an option for intellectual analysis, it is an imperative for action." Now, global ecologists agree that three decades is likely all the time left to save the children and all life on Earth from the plunge toward human self-extinction. Still, the Center for Defense Information in Washington, D.C.— founded and run by former U.S. navy officers to educate the public about how the military economy is destroying the country—says through its *Defense Monitor* that the Pentagon alone will spend $38 billion in 1993, plus $350 billion over the next ten years on war industry. U.S. nuclear policy is still driven, even post–cold war, by outdated policies and desires to buy new weapons systems such as B-2 bombers and nuclear missiles and submarines. The world has more than 48,000 nuclear warheads today with total explosive power equaling 90,000 Hiroshima bombs—to say nothing of its germ warfare and chemical weapons stockpiles. Even if all planned nuclear weapons cuts were implemented, in the year 2003 the world would still have as many as 20,000 nuclear weapons containing the explosive power of more than 200,000 Hiroshima bombs. If cuts planned as of January 1993 are implemented, the U.S. nuclear arsenal—among the biggest of the superpowers—will be reduced but will still contain from 20,000 to 8,500 warheads and more than 3,500 strategic and 5,000 stored and deployed tactical nuclear weapons.

Economic hardship and political turmoil in the former Soviet Union combined with U.S. reluctance to abandon old policies and weapons dealings may undermine agreements to reduce the chances of omnicide. Troubled superpowers are selling their outmoded weaponry, out of control, to "third world" dictatorships everywhere— creating a dangerous unchecked policy of proliferation, in defiance of attempts by the United Nations or other more progressive international organizations to stop them. Race hatred and ethnocentrism are still used as ploys to justify military spending. The United States in 1993 is responsible for approximately 59 percent of the world's war weapons sales, while the former U.S.S.R. sells approximately 39 percent of all weapons. The profit motive of arms dealers is driving corporate-controlled states at breakneck speed into the brick wall of oblivion for all. It remains to be seen if good intentions can serve leaders like the newly elected William Jefferson Clinton of the United States quickly enough to save the human species from omnicide.

Much pressure from the world's peoples, in unison and intercultural, nonviolent unity, must be brought to bear upon world leaders and world bodies like the UN—too influenced in the past by U.S. foreign policy to be fully effective. A global citizenry and global mentality—devoid of ethnocentrism, prejudice, and race hatred—have been growing by leaps and bounds as a counterforce to the greed of the war industrialists. If we are to survive, race prejudice and nationalism must give way to international cooperation. It is time for all to count themselves planetary citizens in nonviolent civil disobedience against outmoded military technocracies everywhere across the biosphere. But despite the lessons of slavery and the Holocaust and numerous genocides from the Rape of Nanking to Armenia to Babi Yar and the bombings of Hiroshima and Nagasaki, ethnocentric ideas still govern our political decisions and stifle our ability to rise above human folly.

A Damocles sword is already falling over Somalia and southern Africa, even as it falls over the former Yugoslavia, even as it falls over all of us and between Soviet Armenia and Azerbaijan, in Germany where neo-Nazis riot against Romanian gypsies, in Los Angeles where Blacks and Koreans are ironically pitted against each other in a white supremacist society. In the inner cities of the United States or in the streets of London and Paris, racial and ethnic strife is renewed among disenfranchised ethnic youths, some of whom join street gangs or the Ku Klux Klan or neo-Nazi skinhead groups to battle in deadly earnest. A white truck driver is dragged from his vehicle and pummeled nearly to death by a group of angry Black youths in retaliation for a white police gang's brutal beating of a Black man, witnessed by an entire nation on videotape. Neo-Nazism in all its manifestation is aided and abetted by an old Nazi cartel left over from World War II. People of Madrid give a fascist salute to Franco's memory to celebrate his birthday in retaliation for a peace march of immigrants and others against neo-Nazism. Immigrants are wanted nowhere on the globe, not even in developed nations, except as disenfranchised cheap labor, devoid of human rights. Native populations falter in their economic breakdowns and the loss of jobs. Everywhere we reap the legacy of Hitler and Stalin and the U.S./U.S.S.R. cold war which has left the ethnic populations of the world at each other's throats.

Indeed, most of the criminals of Hitler's and Stalin's regimes were never brought to trial for their crimes against humanity, despite the Nuremburg trials and Geneva protocols—just as the United States has never truly accepted admonition for its xenophobic crimes in mining Nicaraguan harbors or in bombing Japan's civilian targets. Perhaps William Jefferson Clinton can be convinced that to accept World Court admonition for such war crimes—an important symbolic act—would strengthen world government. Still, decades after World War II, neo-Nazis and Klansmen run for office in the United States and Germany and other countries of the world, amassing large amounts of votes.

Looking closely at peoples of different backgrounds, we soon learn that they do not really look alike and are individuals with every manner of attribute and variety not unlike our own. Mostly each is human and deserving of respect, and there are good and not so good people of every kind and variety. Avoiding generalizations isn't easy, but we can sensitize ourselves against them and refuse to let our leaders blind us to any group's humanity. Most readers would never murder because of their prejudices or deprive another of his or her human rights because of xenophobia, but everyday, somewhere in the world, many are being murdered because of their color, race, ethnos, sexual orientation, or religion.

Inga Thorson of the Ministry of Foreign Affairs of Sweden explains: "Despite the fact that we live in a global community, political leaders of the superpowers have displayed an attitude of arrogance in their international relations, based on short sighted, narrow and egoistic [read: ethnocentric] thinking. Hopefully, there are now some signs of new possibilities to create more of an equilibrium in world affairs, perhaps even a restoration of real influence of the United Nations" (The Gaia Peace Atlas, 1988). Since she said these words, we have begun to see signs of her hopes on the horizon, as, for example, the United States moved into Somalia to help feed the starving rather than instigate a civil war, even if it is past cold war policy that helped to create the present situation there. Nations are again looking with renewed interest to world government and law to solve global problems. The media are helping to unearth the truth, even if they helped in the past to build stereotypical and prejudicial attitudes. National Public Radio, for example, is clearly editorializing that U.S. foreign policy—and superpower war policy in general—has had too much power over the United Nations in past.

Militarized societies throughout history were always accompanied by increased levels of violence against people on the domestic level because of their race, ethnicity, religion, sex, sexual orientation, or class. Since all types of biased crimes are based on the idea of domination—which assumes that differences necessitate a dynamic of superior and inferior, dominant and dominated—sexually biased crimes must be seen as part of the dynamics of prejudice also.

Though ethnic and racial violence is recognized by sophisticated societies, the gender-based crime, specifically violence against females, is just beginning to be recognized—even though violations of women's human rights are among the most pervasive biased crimes worldwide. The rape of women in Bosnia is beginning to receive international attention as of this writing, but at the start of the decade, one rape every six minutes was occurring in the United States while France was reporting 95 percent of its victims of violence to be women, about 51 percent of those at the hands of a lover or spouse. Other countries found between 30 to 65 percent of female homicides to be committed by male family members. Domestic violence, brides burned for dowry, female sexual mutilation, gang rapes on campuses, sexual torture of political prisoners, and the exchange of food rations for sex in refugee camps are only some of the many forms that violence against women takes. More female than male children die of malnutrition worldwide, according to the World Health Organization, and domestic battery is the leading cause of injury to women worldwide.

Even in 1993, gender-based crimes of violence are considered to be private matters, not political issues, and in many countries such crimes are still sanctioned by laws and customs. If one group of ethnics was so systematically maimed and frequently killed by another, we would see it as an attempt at genocide or a state of war against that group's human rights. Violence against women needs to be addressed as both a local and a global issue, as Robin Morgan and her international team of women authors have expressed in her still current *Sisterhood Is Global* (Anchor, 1990). More than 50 percent of children worldwide witness violence to their mothers or themselves on the part of their "protectors," and greater numbers watch it every day on television. It therefore becomes, as society teaches it, natural and inevitable to live amidst violence toward women and domination and subjugation between people who are different. Discussing the connection between militarism and "third world" distress, Lucille Mair, UN secretary-general for the 1980 World Conference on Women, wrote: "This cultural violence follows an ideological continuum—starting from the domestic sphere where it is tolerated, if not positively accepted. It then moves to the public political arena where it is glamorized and even celebrated; it becomes part of the national ethic and threatens to become the norm of international conduct. Women and children, above all, are the prime victims of this cult of aggression." Violence against women is an aspect of militarism! Unless we end the cult of silence and complacency toward the violence at the domestic core of our civilizations, we can't hope to end the biased crime and violence against races, religious groups, and nations.

As Carl Sagan has said: "What has evolved on our planet is not just life, not just grass or mice or beetles or microbes, but being with a great intelligence, with a capacity to anticipate the future consequences of present actions. . . . What a waste it would be if, after four billion years of tortuous biological evolution, the dominant organism on the planet contrived its own annihilation. No species is guaranteed its tenure on this planet. And we've been here for only about a million years, we, the first species that has devised the means for its self-destruction."

Since human waste of essential resources and generation of pollutants have surpassed sustainable rates, unless there are significant reductions in material and energy flows, the world faces an uncontrolled decline in per capita food output, energy availability, and industrial production. Even as this decline begins to occur, prejudice toward others rises, everywhere, exacerbated by the destabilizing collapse of superpower nations—as, for example, in the Balkans today. To avoid this decline, growth in material consumption and use of resources on armaments must be curtailed and population must be eased down at the same time as we develop a rapid and drastic increase in efficiency of material energy use. That efficiency requires an end to the growth of war economies worldwide and the xenophobia that sustains them. Ecologists, poets, social scientists, and indigenous tribal peoples everywhere are offering a similar message, as a world movement toward planetary citizenship grows with the notion of successful intercultural cooperation at its core.

One phenomenon of this movement is a growing and pioneering study of how people communicate across cultures and how they need to do so successfully in the shrinking global village. That field study, known as "Intercultural Communication" offers some hope, on a human scale, for world peace. Pioneers of the study, such as Edward T. Hall, explain that we need to go beyond our own cultural orientation and close-minded, judgmental attitudes toward other cultural practices or styles to forge human interaction without conflict and condescension. Each culture has its own style of communication and this can cause serious misunderstandings. Differing styles of *proxemics* (the use of space) and *chronemics* (the use of time)—two elements of Intercultural Communication—can be illustrated by a brief excursion through various modes of greeting in varying societies. These offer recognizable examples of differing nonverbal styles across cultures: Russians greet with "bear hugs"; Spaniards and Italians kiss on both cheeks; some French still exchange three kisses; Japanese bow and do not look superiors in the eyes; English and Germans shake hands; some Native American tribes show an open palm free of weaponry as a gesture of friendship; African Americans with southern roots tend not to stare strangers in the eyes except as a challenge and to be more animated in greeting than whites; Arabic peoples stare intently into the faces and eyes of others as a matter of course; Eskimos rub noses instead of kissing; Blacks of Jamaica, Barbados, Trinidad, and other Caribbean islands tend to be more soft-spoken and relaxed in style about time than brusque white or Black native northeasterners; Jewish New Yorkers tend to be more open and direct with strangers. Such differences, if not taken into account, can cause miscommunication, offense, and even violent conflict.

A subtler example is offered by the miscommunication, based on varying proxemics, between Haitians and Koreans in a recent New York City store boycott sensationalized by the media. Few people are aware that apart from the political forces which motivated Haitians to boycott the Korean store, there is a very different style in Korean and Haitian cultures which contributed to the conflict: it's considered very impolite for a Korean to touch the hand of a stranger or nonintimate. Haitians communicate with friendly body language and are apt to touch hands or arms in conversation. Korean storekeepers will often abruptly place change on the counter, making Haitians feel they are racist in keeping their distance and not wanting to have any physical contact. Because Haitian commerce in the homeland functions with a system of bartering, goods are allowed to be handled in the market-place and their quality debated until a price is settled upon. Korean shopkeepers create an inviolate display of goods, carefully arranged for aesthetic effect and appeal. These cultural differences in style contrib-uted to the conflicts between the two ethnic groups and added to their stereotyping of each other as thieves and racists. Understanding differ-ences like these between cultures can help greatly to avert misunder-standing, race hatred, and violence.

But studying aspects of Intercultural Communication, now widely taught in colleges, to become mindful and nonjudmental of other cultures can lead us to a dangerous edge, if we do not maintain a proper perspective. Though the humanist views all cultures as impor-tant and integral to their own value systems and the knowledgeable person must view contributions from every quarter of the world as equally worthy and important, the issue of planetary citizenship is to ask which nation upholds human rights for all? Which is guilty in the violation of the United Nations' Declaration of Human Rights and requires discipline by a world court? Which guarantees life, liberty, and the pursuit of happiness to all? It is not completely valid to quote Shakespeare, as a student of Intercultural Communication, and say: "Nothing is either good or bad, but thinking makes it so." It is also necessary to ask whether a specific nation upholds human rights for all within its society. There's a huge difference between "propriety" in the study of culture, and the insanity of overlooking murderous crimes against humanity, such as genocide or slavery or the withholding of equal rights from any group or the subversion of a culture's accom-plishments, history, language, or literature. In appreciating the differ-ences between cultures, one cannot go to the extreme of simply decid-ing, "Who are we to judge? This is not so where human rights are involved!"

Though such a point may seem obvious, with the growth of intercultural studies, multiculturalism, and field anthropology of hu-mane purpose and view, there has also grown a tendency for some students to take a nonjudgmental attitude toward human rights abuses and to simply call such abuses "different," rather than utterly wrong, racist, prejudiced, or sexist.

If the wasted human potential in the battle of the color line continues into the twenty-first century—as Du Bois warned that it would be the main battle line of the twentieth century—no one will prosper. Asians have their horrors to remember from the Rape of Nanking to the colonization of Korea and the holocausts of Vietnam and Cambodia, and their internal human rights struggles as in China today. There is also a monstrous past history of Eurocentric pillaging of China that most in the West today are ignorant of. Westerners, too, have an offensive tendency to jumble separate Asian cultures—each with its own integrity and intricate histories, languages, and traditions —into one called generally "Chinese." If one knew the history of Asia, would he or she dare to call a Korean Vietnamese or a Japanese Chinese, or vice versa?

The economic factors involved in the strife in the Balkans, or the crumbling Soviet commonwealth, or the disintegration of Yugoslavia, or the civil strife in Somalia or Los Angeles and other decaying urban centers of the world cannot be overlooked or underestimated. Dr. Helen Caldicott, Australian pediatrician and antinuclear activist, has said in her chapter "First World Greed and Third World Debt," in her book *If You Love This Planet:* "When I think of malnutrition and of more than forty thousand children around the world dying daily from starvation-related disease, I am brought brutally face to face with the affluent countries. The gap between the 20 percent rich and the 80 percent poor is not decreasing but increasing. In 1987, the average income in the First World was $12,070, while it was $670 . . . in the third world." Other globally conscious scientists and economists worldwide have explained the concept of "have" and "have-not" nations as an issue of "third world" nations incurring bigger debts because of superpower xenophobia and ethnocentricism. Lesser developed nations often increase their debts based upon the pillaging and depletion of their resources and labor by foreign nations. We have seen how, for example, South Korean students have demonstrated against the use of their labor force for U.S. gain. It is true—as these students claimed—that South Korea had by the 1980s become a cheap labor camp for U.S.-bought goods—despite South Korean dictators who claimed economic growth for themselves.

Humankind continues to succeed in dividing itself into particularist omnicidal portions, though coming events could be worse than all the genocides in our history. If the global economy and planetary ecosystems continue to crumble unchecked on the biosphere of a dying planet, the scramble for a piece of the crumbling pie could become more fierce. Race fiction could intensify to create scapegoats for financial failings. Already we hear "welfare queens" being blamed for all ills. Romanian Gypsies—once massacred—living in sanctuary in East Germany amidst jobless, disenfranchised German youths, are targeted by angry skinheads. It is difficult to fathom that the *entire* food stamp program, devised to feed hungry people of the United States, *does not* cost even the markup overhead on one nuclear bomber.* It is impossible for those not taught the truth to understand that the real reason for their economic demise is an overinvestment in nuclear, biological, and chemical warfare and its multibillion-dollar research, testing, and development. The federal budget in the U.S.—to use one superpower example—has over the past two decades devoted only 20 percent to all human services (education, health care, social entitlements), while xenophobic wars have cost more than 60 percent of the pie.

Many citizens of military technocracies think they are living in equal opportunity democracies. In their gas-guzzling lives full of electric gadgetry and plastic and chemical waste dumping, they can't imagine that the freedom of all to breathe air everywhere is threatened by their pollutants. Can they see that the success of frugal indigenous peoples attempting to sustain themselves on their threatened lands or among their exploited forests is linked to the destiny of all air and water and the lives of all on the biosphere? Can they come to realize that so-called primitive tribal ways are more intelligently in tune with Earth, in terms of saving Earth's resources, than those of obscenely exploitative nation-states which call themselves "civilized"? *Can humankind come, at last, to realize that the real enemy of all is disease, starvation, prejudice, and war?* That *is* the question!

For a global supertragedy to be avoided, the past must be remembered and the young—who have not lived through world wars—need to be sensitized to the heinous crimes against humanity that have been committed by nation-states in the past. "Genocidal Studies" needs to go hand in hand with "Peace Studies" in order for either to be meaningful. The conflict resolution taught in "Peace Studies" requires an

---

* According to the Council on Economic Priorities and Betty Lall, foremost arms control expert.

understanding of the dynamics of prejudice, along with the insights of course studies in "Intercultural Communication." Democracy with a common ethics of human rights needs to be instituted in a powerful, cooperative world government for our planet to survive. Spheres of differing, contradictory, even seemingly conflicting ethics can cease to exist and a powerful world court—across all ethnocentric lines, truly representative of East and West and all continents and countries—must be allowed to develop into a world society with values, ideals, and goals that uniformly and globally uphold human rights. *For all human-kind is endowed by natural creation with certain unalienable rights, and among these rights are life, liberty, and the pursuit of happiness.* Planetary citizen-ship needs to be governed by a system of ethics that includes *all* the people. Such a democratic world system is the only way to keep hu-mankind from perishing from the earth, at this juncture in its history, as all ecosystems are straining beyond their limits.

Baha'i, Buddhist, Confucian, Christian, Hindu, Jew, Muslim, Shintoist, Sikh, Zoroastrian and others came together out of a com-mon concern for peace at a World Conference of Religions in 1970 in Kyoto, Japan, to try to articulate a concrete universal basic ethic of all religions in the service of world society. They concluded that all shared a conviction of the fundamental unity of the human family, of the equality and dignity of all human beings; a sense of the sacredness of the individual conscience, and of the values of an interracial human community; a recognition that might is not right, that national power is not self-sufficient and absolute; a belief that love, compassion, un-selfishness, and the force of inner truth and spirit have ultimately greater power than hate, prejudice, enmity, and self-interest; a sense of obligation to stand on the side of the poor and the oppressed as against the rich and the oppressors; and a profound hope that goodwill finally prevail. They agreed with Martin Luther King, Jr., who stated with moral clarity: "The doctrine of black supremacy is just as dangerous and evil as the doctrine of white supremacy [or yellow or red suprem-acy]. . . . God is not interested in only the freedom of black people or brown people or yellow people or white people, but of ALL peo-ple."

The United Nations' Universal Declaration of Human Rights, adopted and proclaimed by the General Assembly in December 1948, is not yet fifty years old, and its member countries have not fully begun to realize the original plan to publish and disseminate, display, and expound it in schools and educational institutions everywhere, regardless of the political status of countries or territories. Neither has the World Court been powerful enough to make superpower nations heed the declaration, and the Geneva Conventions Protocols. The Nuremburg trials have never fully brought war criminals either to trial or to discipline. Yet, these documents and efforts have given us the basis for a world constitution which embodies the Golden Rule, to which all great world religions subscribe: "Do unto others as you would have them do unto you"—in whatever language it is phrased— was meant by Buddha, Muhammad, Christ, Lao-tse, Gandhi, Tolstoy, Martin Luther King, Jr., and Malcolm X to cross national and racial boundaries. Neither the Bible of the Hebrew people nor the Koran of the prophet Muhammad was meant to be interpreted, as it has been, by fanatics of prejudice and hate who use the scripture to bolster their ideas of racial or religious supremacy. Yet, in fact, organized religions have committed and are responsible for much of the killing that has happened in the names of their prophets, all of whom would be appalled by the murderous behavior of some of their professed followers. Contemporary "ecofeminist" spirituality understands this. It revives the idea of indigenous peoples everywhere finding Earth, herself, the great corn or wheat or rice goddess, the mother of all peoples. Newer religious associations, like the one adhered to by Thomas Jefferson, Unitarian Universalism, are based on the tenet of religious tolerance. Founded in Central Europe, Unitarianism is a spiritual system which accepts humanists of any creed—Islamic or Christian, atheist or agnostic, Jewish, Buddhist, Confucian, or tribal native—into its unifying fold.

In its often self-aggrandizing attempt to convert and amass power in its competitive hierarchies and sustain its own population against other religions, patriarchal religion has been a major cause of war, used by militarists as an excuse for massacre, down through the ages from the Crusades to the reign of Bloody Mary to the "born again" Christian, Jewish, and Islamic fundamentalist wars, and mass killings and suicides of our time. The dogmas of various faiths have not transcended greedy wars and heinous crimes, from inquisition to censorship, torture, murder, massacre of the innocents, and imprisonment in the name of this or that god or gods. Yet fundamentalists go on extolling their own way as the *only* good and proper way to human empathy and truth, even as they spit hatred in the face of any humanity different from their own or refuse to see that the population explosion —if continued unchecked by sex education and voluntary contraception—will absolutely result in the death of all humankind. Planetary citizens everywhere are standing up for the scientific truths of our survival needs. They tell us that church, state, and world government must remain separate if humankind is to survive.

In viewing the Armenian massacres of 1915, Adolf Hitler, in his plan to exterminate the Jews of Germany and Poland, decided that his plan would succeed because "No one remembers what the Turks did to the Armenians." Dr. Rosalie Bertell of Canada and Robert Jay Lifton and Eric Markusen of the United States are among those scientists who have explained the phenomenon of *psychic numbing,* an element of *avoidance* and *apathy.* It is a psychic malaise which prepares us to accept genocide and omnicide. Psychic numbing is a conditioned response to a glut of horror, as if one had been forced to drink the bitter hemlock of knowledge of man's inhumanity to man, and woman, so often that he or she can no longer feel or taste bitter outrage, sorrow, or pathos but only numbness—as if experiencing a psyche put to sleep. Humane feelings which might bring action are so utterly drenched in blood, so to speak, that one can no longer see "red" or feel the outrage or emotional pain that might motivate action. When one actually studies the "nightmare of history" or even watches the ever-present murder and violence on television and in the other media and learns how much death and torture and cruelty have been dealt by prejudice to human by human—or could be again—one might wring one's hands and weep and sob real tears of sorrow and remorse and feel depression, but say, "How could *they?*" As long as we say "they" instead of "we" and feel we would never commit such crimes, we may be doomed to repeat them.

If we look closely at our separate governments, we might find that we are complicitous with all sorts of horrors committed abroad and internally in our "minority" ghettos, simply by not speaking up or not realizing or knowing the truth of the xenophobic past. We need to remember all the genocides and slaveries in our human history and to be aware that the dynamics of prejudice operate the same way in all of them. The powerful group in charge, whoever or from whatever culture they be, will try to divide and conquer the subculture(s) or out-group(s) against each other. The majority fearing the demise of its position always persecutes and colonizes or enslaves the minority, unless mindful of their equal humanity. Elie Weisel wrote in *One Generation After:*

> Spring 1945: emerging from its nightmare, the world discovers the camps, the death factories. The senseless horror, the debasement: the absolute reign of evil. Victory tastes of ashes. Yes, it is possible to defile life and creation and feel no remorse. To tend one's garden and water one's flowers but two steps away from barbed wire. To experiment with monstrous mutations and still believe in the soul and immortality. To go on vacation, be enthralled by the beauty of a landscape, make children laugh—and still fulfill regularly, day in and day out, the duties of killer. . . . Many held degrees in philosophy, sociology, biology, general medicine, psychiatry, and fine arts. There were lawyers among them. And—unthinkable but true—theologians. And aristocrats. . . . Adolf Eichmann was an ordinary man. He slept well, he ate well. He was an exemplary father, a considerate husband . . . I was shaken by his normal appearance.

Very ordinary people, like you and me, Dear Reader, are capable of prejudice, but more, we are capable of what psychologists call apathy, avoidance, and psychic numbing. We can turn away, simply not be bothered, as we are too busy with earning our own living and searching for the beloved or sustaining the beloveds. We often compromise ourselves, or neglect the knowledge that would help us vote wisely, because we need to keep our jobs or pay our war taxes, even when those jobs or taxes are ultimately genocidal or omnicidal in nature. But, as Pastor Martin Niemoller said concerning the question of how the Nazis were able to take over an entire society: "In Germany the Nazis came first for the Communists, and I didn't speak up because I wasn't a Communist. Then they came for the Jews, and I didn't speak up because I wasn't a Jew. Then they came for the trade unionists, and I didn't speak up because I wasn't a trade unionist. Then they came for the Catholics, and I didn't speak up because I was a Protestant. Then they came for me, and by that time there was no one left to speak for me."

Robert Jay Lifton and Eric Markusen explain in *The Genocidal Mentality* that when the Nazi doctors wanted to "purify" the "Aryan" strain they invented the bogus science of "eugenics" to rid the chosen race first of the mentally infirm and physically disabled; when that task was complete, they turned to ethnic strains that they saw as a blight upon their kind—the Jews, Gypsies, Blacks, Poles, homosexuals, AWOL* Italian soldiers, and finally even very "German" Germans who did not agree with their purges. For we must remember that millions of a majority culture end up—because of apathy—dying in wars also.

As nation-statehood forced upon East and West by totalitarian communism and corrupt capitalism meet their demise and the walls tumble down, old hatreds are rekindled, and again blood feuds arise out of newfound freedoms and disputed boundaries. Rape and abuse and murder of women and children are on the rise, as men massacre each other in wars and boundary skirmishes, committing heinous human rights violations everywhere. Yet there are hopeful signs on the horizon of our common despair over these renewed insanities—a growing awareness of the preciousness and precariousness of all human life, regardless of skin color, ethnos, religion, nationality, culture—a desire to come together as one human race to save Earth. Concepts of intercultural tolerance are born anew, even as bigotry is rekindled within threatened and shrinking economies. We need to understand that though Nazi crimes and demonstrations are on the rise, with 40,000 known neo-Nazi sympathizers reported living in the newly unified Germany, 40,000 German citizens of goodwill toward all have organized themselves in a mass demonstration against neo-Nazism and marched against it and for human rights. Hundreds of thousands of U.S. citizens marched in opposition to the xenophobic bombing of ancient Baghdad's civilians and cultural treasures. Hundreds of thousands paid for bus trips and car rides to Washington, D.C., from around the United States to march in massive demonstrations against nuclear weaponry and nuclear testing.

The demonstrations organized in Tiananmen Square or Prague, Washington or Moscow, and many cities of Europe, East and West, North and South, give us great hope that an international corps of citizens in every country have seen the light—beyond all prejudice and

---

* Absent Without Official Leave, or classified as deserters.

psychic numbing—and are united in nonviolent actions, legacies of Tolstoy, Gandhi, Martin Luther King, Jr., Dorothy Day, the Women's Pentagon Action. They are united in the hope that this new century will see the end of all wars on the globe and therefore a salvation of Earth's faltering ecosystems through world democracy. The image of the blue marbled swirling globe as seen from outer space has become a flag of planetary citizenship everywhere and organizations like Greenpeace and Worldwatch have gained in popularity far and wide. Science is showing us, irrevocably, worldwide, that the best chance for saving our common planet Earth, our human sustenance everywhere, is true democracy that enfranchises the people of the land with the land of their origins—not false or imperfect striving democracy, such as we admittedly have in the developed nations. The nonaligned nations have been investing their economies in self-defense mechanisms against biological, chemical, and nuclear warfare and have literally developed the technical means for detecting and verification needed to establish world peace between the crumbling superpowers which must now disarm themselves to survive. World economists have shown how economic conversion from war industries will profit and save the Earth and are viable means for future productivity.

Indigenous people everywhere hold the true wisdom of our common race, our Earth, inhabited by one human species from the same roots, in all its wondrous variety. Within this one common pool of humanity, many cultures and differing cultural truths, all with their good and not so good sides, have developed over the centuries of life on our planet, now seen as a ball of blue water common to all of us, a Gaia system all one, a Great Grain Goddess of Fertility to all Her children of all colors. "Perhaps for the first time, world leaders can move from responding to the cold war to shaping environmentally healthy societies. The environment can then move to the center of economic decision making, where it belongs," says the Worldwatch Institute.

This is why the issues of prejudice are so vital today. There is no time to waste human potential and resources on ethnocentric war, hatred and violence while Earth hangs in the balance. Yet as the world economy falters, we turn to look our neighbors in the face and eye their piece of bread, hungrily. We want to blame those a little different from ourselves in skin tone or eye slant or sexuality or culture or language for our problems. The unemployed, drunken husband who beats his wife and children because he is so ashamed of his failure to provide for them is a microcosm of the world, as much as is the disenfranchised youth, out of a job, without an education, who beats a darker- or lighter-skinned man or burns a Jew to death out of self-hatred. His biased crime is a microcosm of Holocaust genocide. The need to find a scapegoat, someone or a group of someones to blame for his feelings of inadequacy, is the root of prejudice and the violence that ensues.

In the need to preserve the pride of differing cultures and validate their integrity without fostering their prejudice toward one another, there is a delicate balance between pride and ethnocentric foolery. As of this writing, in 1993, the population of the Earth with Her delicate ecosystems stands at 5.4 billion and is due to double rapidly within the next thirty to forty years, if the human race can sustain itself. If nothing is done to check the population growth now threatening the quality of life everywhere, we are bound to see issues of prejudice constantly on the rise—because of the shrinking resources and land areas available within disintegrating and outmoded nations—unless people of moral conviction, with knowledge of the dynamics of prejudice, rise up everywhere in nonviolent resistance. Yet, at this dangerous juncture, as we near the year 2000, after more than eighty centuries of art and human creativity, philosophy, music, poetry, social and biological science—we humans, considered the *paragon of animals in our ability to think,* named *Homo sapiens,* meaning wise or knowing animal, persist, brutishly, in hating and killing each other for the colors of our skin, the shapes of our features, our places of origin on our common terra firma, our styles of culture or language, and most ironically of all our "religious" beliefs—despite the fact that all the great religions of the Earth teach the same basic golden rule: *"Do unto others as you would have them do unto you."* Along with love and death, our literatures remain full of expressions of the experience of repression and oppression known as *prejudice,* the prejudgment of the worth of people and things based upon insufficient or erroneous evidence lacking in objectivity and factual data. Prejudice in all its manifestations—xenophobia, ethnocentrism, sexism, androcentrism, genocidal politics and militarism, environmental and social racism, cruel colonization and cultural destruction, crimes of cultural exclusionism and expansionism, imperialism, ethnic wars and hatred of each other—is still the major focus of our literatures, our history-making events, and our nightly news in the global village as the stars of our common galaxy, light-years old, and our satellites, new since mid century, beam down into homes everywhere in the global village and teach us, daily, that we are all of *one* race, the only one we've found in the galaxy, *the human race.*

Daniela Gioseffi, New York/New Jersey, 1993

Contents

A Note to the Reader About This Book   vii
Introduction by the Author/Editor   xi

Part One   *On Xenophobia and Genocide:*
The Past and the Present

1. The Past Revisited: Against Forgetting

The Offended, Anne Hebért, translated by Al Poulin, Jr.   1

From *Candide* ("The slave he met . . ."), Voltaire   1

From *The Congo:* "An Outpost of Progress," Joseph Conrad   3

The World of the Slaves, Jan Rogoziński   6

Sweating and Whipping, Nicolás Guillén, translated by
    Daniela Gioseffi and Enildo A. García   25

Africa, Abused Continent: The Roots of War and Imperialism,
    W. E. B. Du Bois   26

The Song of the Slaves, Yevgeny Yevtushenko, translated by
    Daniela Gioseffi with Sophia Buzevska   37

The Pilgrim Invasion, William Apes of the Pequod Nation   40

Germ Warfare Against the Indians, Chief Blackbird of the
    Ottawa Nation   43

A Friend of the Indians, Joseph Bruchac of the
    Abenaki Nation   44

Fighting the Mexicans, Geronimo, Chief of the
    Apache Nation   45

Memoir of a Sauk Warrior, Black Hawk   48

To John Brown, A. Frances Ellen Watkins Harper   54

Bury Me in a Free Land, A. Frances Ellen Watkins Harper   55

From *Narrative of the Life of Frederick Douglass,*
Frederick Douglass   56

Toward a Personal History, Rochelle Ratner   64

A Visit to Belzec, William Heyen   65

The Yellow Star and the Pink Triangle: Sexual Politics in the Third
Reich, Jack Nusan Porter   67

Men in History, William Heyen   73

I Am a Child of the Holocaust, Merle Hoffman   75

We Must Share the Crime, Marguerite Duras, translated by
D. G. Luttinger   83

Ravages of War, Jose Emilio Pacheco, translated by
Katherine Silver   84

The Armenian Experience of Genocide, The Zoryan Institute   86

Songs of Bread, Diana Der-Hovanessian   98

An Armenian Looking at Newsphotos of the Cambodian Deathwatch,
Diana Der-Hovanessian   99

Massacre and Murderous Butchery: U.S. Conquest of the Philippines,
Mark Twain and Others   99

Hitler and the Gypsies: A Genocide That Must Be Remembered,
Dora E. Yates   103

Hiroshima Was a War Crime, Shigetoshi Iwamatsu   110

A Brief History of Women in a Man's World,
Marilyn French   115

Women's Brains, Stephen Jay Gould   118

The Witch Hunts, Barbara Ehrenreich and Deirdre English   125

Nuclear Bomb Testing on Human Guinea Pigs: Bikini, Rongelap,
Utirik, Kwajalein, Darlene Keju-Johnson   129

2. The Present Reflected in the Past Remembered

Everything Is Wonderful, Jayne Cortez   134

The Race Factor in International Politics, Hugh Tinker   135

Genocide Is a New Word for an Old Crime,
Jack Nusan Porter   143

Watching Human Rights: Mass Denationalizations,
Aryeh Neier   153

A Nation of Nations: "We the People . . ."
Daniel Patrick Moynihan   155

The American Neo-Nazi Movement, Elinor Langer   159

In the Face of Hatred, James Wright   169

Germany's Right-Wing Revival: Bashers, Frank Thaler   170

The Hitler Spring, Eugenio Montale, translated by
Daniela Gioseffi   174

In Europe, Immigrants Are Needed, Not Wanted,
Alan Riding   175

Extreme Prejudice Toward Polish Americans, Rachel Toor   177

From *Blood of My Blood:* "An Extraordinary Bigotry,"
Richard Gambino   180

From *The Japanese Today:* "Race Prejudice Pervades the World,"
Edwin O. Reischauer   182

From *Turning Japanese:* "The Resentment Americans Have Toward the
Rising Asian Economic Powers . . ." David Mura   188

From *Tales from the Bazaar,* Robert D. Kaplan   189

Racism and the Australian Aborigines, Julian Burger   195

And Then the Perfect Truth of Hatred, Philip Appleman   196

From *Sentenced to Silence:* "Religion Is Known to Be a Dangerous Topic
for Writers . . ." Siobhan Dowd   197

Drama in Cell 1081, Lilia Quindoza-Santiago, translated by
Daniela Gioseffi   199

Justifiable Anger: Excerpts from Public Speeches,
Malcolm X   199

Three Days and a Question, Grace Paley   203

From *Second Class Citizen:* "Sorry, No Coloureds,"
Buchi Emecheta   205

Right Now, Milton Kessler   213

Racism and the War on Drugs, Clarence Lusane   215

Reading Poems in Public, Maurice Kenny of the
    Mohawk Nation   220

Central America: Vanishing Forests, Endangered Peoples,
    Alan Weisman and Sandy Tolan   221

The United Fruit Co., Pablo Neruda, translated by
    Daniela Gioseffi   225

The Americans, Tran Thi Nga and
    Wendy Wilder Larsen   226

Prejudice Against the Handicapped, Chris Gillespie   227

The Small Mute Boy *and* The Small Mad Boy, Federico Garcia Lorca,
    translated by Daniela Gioseffi   235

From "Looking to the Future [of the Former U.S.S.R.],"
    Elena Bonner   236

The Disintegration of Yugoslavia, Lenard J. Cohen   244

Chinese Seizure of Tibet, Julian Burger   259

Burma: A Nation of Prisoners; Paula Green   260

The Sexualization of Racism, Calvin C. Hernton   266

On Being Crazy, W. E. B. Du Bois   271

Racism and Homophobia, Phillip Brian Harper   273

Genocidal Ideology: Trauma and Cure, Robert J. Lifton with
    Eric Markusen   281

Man Is Endowed with a Strong Aggressive Nature, Sigmund Freud,
    translated and adapted by D. G. Luttinger   288

Baby Villon, Philip Levine   291

Our Need for Enemies, Dorothy Rowe   292

The Need for Scapegoats, Robert Coles   298

Lampshades of Human Skin, Daniela Gioseffi   301

Our Earth Is a Vulnerable Abused Place, Maurice F. Strong   305

From *Earth in the Balance*, Al Gore   306

Amazon Rain Forest: Missing the People for the Trees, Susanna Hecht and Alexander Cockburn   312

From the Garden of Eden, Stanley Barkan   315

From "Planetary Feminism: The Politics of the 21st Century," Robin Morgan   316

My Country Is the World, Virginia Woolf   338

Ain't I a Woman, Sojourner Truth   339

"Ethnically Cleansed" or Cleaning Women, Lucia Maria Perillo   339

Sky Woman and Her Sisters, Paula Gunn Allen of the Laguna/Lakota Nation   343

Part Two   *Cultural Destruction and Cultural Affirmation*

Colonization, Education, Language, History, Folk Art, Religion, Literary Art, Tradition, Media Stereotyping and Media Control, Cultural Collapse, Cultural Reaffirmation, Pride or Prejudice, Ethnocentrism, Fascist Bigotry, Democracy, and Tolerance

Language, Bei Dao, translated by Bonnie S. McDougall   355

From *The Language of Oppression,* Haig A. Bosmajian   356

Teotihuacán, Carole Stone   372

"If Black English Ain't a Language, Then Tell Me What Is?," James Baldwin   372

From *The Gaia Atlas of First Peoples:* "Cultural Collapse," Julian Burger   376

From *The Gaia Atlas of First Peoples:* "Missionary Childhood," Sharon Venne of the Cree Nation   378

African Language Writing, Phyllis Bischof   379

From "Breaking the Silence: Strategic Imperatives for Preserving Culture," Robert Viscusi   381

The Old Italians Dying, Lawrence Ferlinghetti   385

English Revisited, Carolyne Wright   388

From *Make-Believe Media:* "Make-Believe History,"
    Michael Parenti   394

The Colonisation of Our Pacific Islands, Chailang Palacios   399

Trumpets from the Island of Their Eviction,
    Martin Espada   401

White Earth Land Struggle: Omissions and Stereotypes,
    Winona La Duke of the Chippewa Nation   402

Reporting "Terrorism": The Experience of Northern Ireland,
    Brian Hamilton-Tweedale   404

Name in Print!, Langston Hughes   409

say french, D. H. Melhem   411

Beyond Belief: The Press and the Holocaust,
    Deborah E. Lipstadt   412

Invisible Victims, Martin A. Lee and Gloria Channon   415

An Ocean Away, a World Apart: The Same Old Hatreds,
    Andrei Codrescu   418

Brought Up on Right-Wing Anthologies, Amiri Baraka, interviewed by
    Bertrand Mathieu   427

From "Literary Hegemonies," Helen Barolini   429

Orange: Hiring, Harriet Zinnes   431

Strangers in the Village, David Mura   434

Modern Secrets: "Last Night I Dreamt in Chinese . . ."
    Shirley Geok-Lin Lim   450

What Means Switch, Gish Jen   451

The Souls of Black Folks, W. E. B. Du Bois   468

Blacks with a Capital B, Gwendolyn Brooks, interviewed by
    D. H. Melhem   470

Critical Thinking: Racism and Education in the U.S. "Third World,"
    Sharon Spencer   471

Justice Denied in Massachusetts, Edna St. Vincent Millay   479

Immigrant Education: From the Transcripts of the Sacco and
    Vanzetti Trial, Nicolo Sacco   480

Public School No. 18: Paterson, New Jersey,
    Maria Mazziotti-Gillan   483

The Wife's Story, Bharati Mukherjee   484

Multiculturalism: E Pluribus Plures, Diane Ravitch   498

Part Three   *Beyond Culture and Prejudice,
Toward Pride and Tolerance*

*Problems and Solutions for Interculturalism and Understanding, Cross-
Cultural and Intercultural Communication, Nonviolent Activism Toward
True Democracy, Ecological Sanity, and Planetary Citizenship*

Proxemics in a Cross-Cultural Context: Japan and the Arab World,
    Edward T. Hall   521

Against Stereotyping: The Native Irishman, A Converted Saxon
    (Anonymous)   535

The Leaders of the Crowd, W. B. Yeats   536

America: The Multinational Society, Ishmael Reed   537

The Law of Love and Nonviolent Action, Leo Tolstoy   541

From *Science and Liberty*, Aldous Huxley   542

Satyagraha, Mahatma Gandhi   545

"I Am Against Fanatics," A Dialog Between Elie Wiesel and
    Merle Hoffman   546

Nationalism Is Always Oppressive, Amiri Baraka, interviewed by
    D. H. Melhem   559

Meeting in Jerusalem, Mona Elaine Adilman   561

A Forgiving Land; Postwar Vietnam, Lady Borton   562

To Hannah Vo-Dinh, a Young Poet of Vietnam, Fran Castan   565

From *The Gaia Atlas of First Peoples*: "A Global Voice,"
    Julian Burger   567

From "Speech to the U.S. Congress," Nelson Mandela   569

"Yes, Mandela," Dennis Brutus   572

Breaking the Chains, Bishop Desmond Tutu   573

Still I Rise, Maya Angelou   574

From "On Loving Your Enemies" and "Declarations of Independence,"
Martin Luther King, Jr.   575

Caria, Yannis Ritsos, translated by Edmund Keeley   582

From "Fourth of July Speech to a White Audience, 1852,"
Frederick Douglass   583

From "A Bench by the Side of the Road," Toni Morrison   584

There's Been a Misunderstanding About the Sixties,
Lerone Bennett, Jr.   585

For Medgar Evers, David Ignatow   588

Coalitions of Indigenous Peoples: Will the White Man Understand?,
Julian Burger and Paulinho Paiakan, Kayapo Chief   589

What Treaty That the Whites Have Kept Has the Red Man Broken?,
Sitting Bull, Chief of the Sioux Nation   590

From *Man's Most Dangerous Myth: The Fallacy of Race,*
Ashley Montagu   591

From *Leaves of Grass:* "I Sing the Body Electric,"
Walt Whitman   602

From "Democracy": A Public Speech, Barbara Jordan   605

True Democracy Demands Moral Conviction, Vacláv Havel, translated
and adapted by Daniela Gioseffi with Sophia Buzevska   606

The Riot of Colors, Tess Onwueme   608

Children Are Color-Blind, Genny Lim   609

From "Poem of the End": "Poets of Truth," Marina Tsvetayeva,
translated and adapted by Daniela Gioseffi with
Sophia Buzevska   611

Worldwide and *Awake,* Fazil Hüsnü Dağlarca, translated by
Talât Sait Halman   612

Appendix: Selected Human Rights Declarations and
   Statements on Race   615

The Seville Statement on Violence, UNESCO International Scholars
(Seville, 1986)   617

Two Statements on Race, UNESCO International
Scholars   621
   III.   Proposals on the Biological Aspects of Race (Moscow,
   1964)   621
   IV.   Statement on Race and Racial Prejudice (Paris,
   1967)   626

Women's Pentagon Action *Unity Statement*, Collectively Written,
April 1982   633

Disabled People's Bill of Rights, American Coalition of Citizens with
Disabilities   637

The United Nations Universal Declaration of Human
Rights   638

Bibliographical Biographies of Contributors   644

Resource List of Organizations   700

Acknowledgments of Copyright   702

Index of Authors   717

Cain slew Abel, and Romulus slew Remus; violence was the beginning and, by the same token, no beginning could be made without using violence, without violating. The first recorded deeds in our biblical and our secular tradition, whether known to be legendary or believed in as historical fact, have traveled through the centuries with the force which human thought achieves in the rare instances when it produces cogent metaphors or universally applicable tales. The tale spoke clearly: whatever brotherhood human beings may be capable of has grown out of fratricide, whatever political organization men may have achieved has its origin in crime.

—HANNAH ARENDT, *WAR AND REVOLUTION*

If the arrangement of society is bad (as ours is), and a small number of people have power over the majority and oppress it, every victory over Nature will inevitably serve only to increase that power and that oppression. This is what is actually happening.

—ALDOUS HUXLEY

The only thing necessary for the triumph of evil is for good men to do nothing.

—EDMUND BURKE

PART ONE

On Xenophobia
and Genocide:

The Past and the Present

Käthe Kollwitz, *The Survivors*, Kl.184.
Courtesy Galerie St. Etienne, New York.

1.
The Past
Revisited:
Against
Forgetting

The Offended

ANNE HEBÉRT

Translated by Al Poulin, Jr.

The poor were lined up in famine's order
The seditious were examined in anger's order
The masters were judged in good conscience's order
The humiliated were interrogated in offense's order
The crucified were considered in mutilation's order
In this extreme misery the mutes came to the front lines
A whole nation of mutes stayed on the barricades
Their desire for the word was so urgent
That the Verb came through the streets to meet them
The burden it was charged with was so heavy
That the cry "fire" exploded from its heart
Disguised as a word.

From Candide
("The slave he met . . .")

VOLTAIRE

My friend, you see how perishable are the riches of this world;
nothing is steadfast but virtue and the happiness of seeing Miss
Cunegonde again."

"I admit it," said Cacambo, "but we still have two sheep with
more treasures than ever the King of Spain will have, and in the
distance I see a town I suspect is Surinam, which belongs to the

Dutch. We are at the end of our troubles and the beginning of our happiness."

As they drew near the town they met a negro lying on the ground wearing only half his clothes, that is to say, a pair of blue cotton drawers; this poor man had no left leg and no right hand.

"Good Heavens!" said Candide to him in Dutch, "what are you doing there, my friend, in this horrible state?"

"I am waiting for my master, the famous merchant Mr. Vanderdendur."

"Was it Mr. Vanderdendur," said Candide, "who treated you in this way?"

"Yes, sir," said the negro, "it is the custom. We are given a pair of cotton drawers twice a year as clothing. When we work in the sugar-mills and the grind-stone catches our fingers, they cut off the hand; when we try to run away, they cut off a leg. Both these things happened to me. This is the price paid for the sugar you eat in Europe. But when my mother sold me for ten patagons on the coast of Guinea, she said to me: 'My dear child, give thanks to our fetishes, always worship them, and they will make you happy; you have the honour to be a slave of our lords the white men and thereby you have made the fortune of your father and mother.' Alas! I do not know whether I made their fortune, but they certainly did not make mine. Dogs, monkeys and parrots are a thousand times less miserable than we are; the Dutch fetishes who converted me tell me that we are all of us, whites and blacks, the children of Adam. I am not a genealogist, but if these preachers tell the truth, we are all second cousins. Now, you will admit that no one could treat his relatives in a more horrible way."

"O Pangloss!" cried Candide. "This is an abomination you had not guessed; this is too much, in the end I shall have to renounce optimism."

"What is optimism?" said Cacambo.

"Alas!" said Candide, "it is the mania of maintaining that everything is well when we are wretched."

And he shed tears as he looked at his negro; and he entered Surinam weeping.

From The Congo:
"An Outpost of Progress"

JOSEPH CONRAD

S lavery is an awful thing," stammered out Kayerts in an unsteady voice.

"Frightful—the sufferings," grunted Carlier with conviction.

They believed their words. Everybody shows a respectful deference to certain sounds that he and his fellows can make. But about feelings people really know nothing. We talk with indignation or enthusiasm; we talk about oppression, cruelty, crime, devotion, self-sacrifice, virtue, and we know nothing real beyond the words. Nobody knows what suffering or sacrifice mean—except, perhaps the victims of the mysterious purpose of these illusions. . . .

"At last we opened a reach. A rocky cliff appeared, mounds of turned-up earth by the shore, houses on a hill, others with iron roofs, amongst a waste of excavations, or hanging to the declivity. A continuous noise of the rapids above hovered over this scene of inhabited devastation. A lot of people, mostly black and naked, moved about like ants. A jetty projected into the river. A blinding sunlight drowned all this at times in a sudden recrudescence of glare. 'There's your company's station,' said the Swede, pointing to three wooden barrack-like structures on the rocky slope. 'I will send your things up. Four boxes did you say? So. Farewell.'

"I came upon a boiler wallowing in the grass, then found a path leading up the hill. It turned aside for the boulders, and also for an undersized railway truck lying there on its back with its wheels in the air. One was off. The thing looked as dead as the carcass of some animal. I came upon more pieces of decaying machinery, a stack of rusty rails. To the left a clump of trees made a shady spot, where dark things seemed to stir feebly. I blinked, the path was steep. A horn tooted to the right, and I saw the black people run. A heavy and dull detonation shook the ground, a puff of smoke came out of the cliff, and that was all. No change appeared on the face of the rock. They were building a railway. The cliff was not in the way or anything; but this objectless blasting was all the work going on.

"A slight clinking behind me made me turn my head. Six black men advanced in a file, toiling up the path. They walked erect and slow, balancing small baskets full of earth on their heads, and the clink kept time with their footsteps. Black rags were wound round their loins, and the short ends behind waggled to and fro like tails. I could see every rib, the joints of their limbs were like knots in a rope; each had an iron collar on his neck, and all were connected together with a chain whose bights swung between them, rhythmically clinking. Another report from the cliff made me think suddenly of that ship of war I had seen firing into a continent. It was the same kind of ominous voice; but these men could by no stretch of imagination be called enemies. They were called criminals, and the outraged law, like the bursting shells, had come to them, an insoluble mystery from the sea. All their meager breasts panted together, the violently dilated nostrils quivered, the eyes stared stonily uphill. They passed me within six inches, without a glance, with that complete, deathlike indifference of unhappy savages. Behind this raw matter one of the reclaimed, the product of the new forces at work, strolled despondently, carrying a rifle by its middle. He had a uniform jacket with one button off, and seeing a white man on the path, hoisted his weapon to his shoulder with alacrity. This was simple prudence, white men being so much alike at a distance that he could not tell who I might be. He was speedily reassured, and with a large, white, rascally grin, and a glance at his charge, seemed to take me into partnership in his exalted trust. After all, I also was a part of the great cause of these high and just proceedings.

"Instead of going up, I turned and descended to the left. My idea was to let that chain gang get out of sight before I climbed the hill. You know I am not particularly tender; I've had to strike and to fend off. I've had to resist and to attack sometimes—that's only one way of resisting—without counting the exact cost, according to the demands of such sort of life as I had blundered into. I've seen the devil of violence, and the devil of greed, and the devil of hot desire; but, by all the stars! these were strong, lusty, red-eyed devils, that swayed and drove men—men, I tell you. But as I stood on this hillside, I foresaw that in the blinding sunshine of that land I would become acquainted with a flabby, pretending, weak-eyed devil of a rapacious and pitiless folly. How insidious he could be, too, I was only to find out several months later and a thousand miles farther. For a moment I stood appalled, as though by a warning. Finally I descended the hill, obliquely, towards the trees I had seen.

"I avoided a vast artificial hole somebody had been digging on the slope, the purpose of which I found it impossible to divine. It wasn't a quarry or a sandpit, anyhow. It was just a hole. It might have been connected with the philanthropic desire of giving the criminals something to do. I don't know. Then I nearly fell into a very narrow ravine, almost no more than a scar in the hillside. I discovered that a lot of imported drainage pipes for the settlement had been tumbled in there. There wasn't one that was not broken. It was a wanton smashup. At last I got under the trees. My purpose was to stroll into the shade for a moment; but no sooner within than it seemed to me I had stepped into the gloomy circle of some inferno. The rapids were near, and an uninterrupted, uniform, headlong, rushing noise filled the mournful stillness of the grove, where not a breath stirred, not a leaf moved, with a mysterious sound—as though the tearing pace of the launched earth had suddenly become audible.

"Black shapes crouched, lay, sat between the trees leaning against the trunks, clinging to the earth, half coming out, half effaced within the dim light, in all the attitudes of pain, abandonment, and despair. Another mine on the cliff went off, followed by a slight shudder of the soil under my feet. The work was going on. The work! And this was the place where some of the helpers had withdrawn to die.

"They were dying slowly—it was very clear. They were not enemies, they were not criminals, they were nothing earthly now, nothing but black shadows of disease and starvation, lying confusedly in the greenish gloom. Brought from all the recesses of the coast in all the legality of time contracts, lost in uncongenial surroundings, fed on unfamiliar food, they sickened, became inefficient, and were then allowed to crawl away and rest. These moribund shapes were free as air —and nearly as thin. I began to distinguish the gleam of the eyes under the trees. Then, glancing down, I saw a face near my hand. The black bones reclined at full length with one shoulder against the tree, and slowly the eyelids rose and the sunken eyes looked up at me, enormous and vacant, a kind of blind, white flicker in the depths of the orbs, which died out slowly. The man seemed young—almost a boy—but you know with them it's hard to tell. I found nothing else to do but to offer him one of my good Swede's ship's biscuits I had in my pocket. The fingers closed slowly on it and held—there was no other movement and no other glance. He had tied a bit of white worsted round his neck—Why? Where did he get it? Was it a badge—an ornament—a charm—a propitiatory act? Was there any idea at all connected with it? It looked startling round his black neck, this bit of white thread from beyond the seas."

The World of the Slaves

JAN ROGOZIŃSKI

Sugar enriched many planters as well as their European creditors and suppliers—and sugar made slavery necessary. The labor of black slaves was the basis for life on the sugar islands from the 17th century. Economically, socially, and politically, slavery dominated the islands to an extent never matched in human history. By the 1750s, almost nine out of ten men and women were slaves on all the islands where sugar was grown. Never before in human history had so high a proportion of a population been slaves.

Slavery tended to change over time as the island economies developed. At first, most slaves worked as hands on cane estates. By the end of the 18th century, slaves did every conceivable type of task—thus creating an entire range of situations from total bondage to comparative freedom. Blacks condemned to gang labor on sugar estates had the least control over their own lives. White overseers and black drivers controlled every minute of their day. Slaves doing other sorts of work could exercise more initiative and set their own pace. The greatest autonomy was enjoyed by skilled craftsmen and slaves living in towns—for example, in the seaports of the Virgin Islands, Curaçao, or the Bahamas.

In the Caribbean slave societies, sugar and human misery went together. On an individual basis, some slaves may have lived decent lives—as good as or better than those of European laborers during the same centuries. Urban slaves and those on islands without sugar fared the best. Slaves endured the harshest labor and most rigid controls during the early years of development, as planters set up estates. During these years, life on the islands was brutal and rough for both owners and slaves. As their masters prospered, some slaves enjoyed better treatment, and governments strove to improve or "ameliorate" slave conditions from about 1770.

Overall, the sugar islands failed the most basic test of slave well-being—the ability to survive and multiply. Before about 1800, death rates among Caribbean slaves always were much higher than birth rates. Perhaps the most telling indictment of the sugar islands is the happier fate of Africans carried to North America. While island blacks died out, the slave population rapidly multiplied in British North America and the United States. Since Caribbean slaves died without reproducing themselves, the sugar estates could operate only by constantly importing enormous numbers of new slaves. Moreover, the high death rate among slaves in the Caribbean does not tell the entire story. Millions more died while they were being brought across the Atlantic to the sugar islands. The slaughter started during the dread "Middle Passage."

The Slave Trade Booms During the 18th Century

Except for the Spanish, all the colonial powers encouraged and were directly involved in the Atlantic slave trade. Until the 1680s, the Dutch West India Company dominated Atlantic commerce, including the slave trade. The British and French then destroyed Dutch commercial power during the Second (1665–1667) and Third (1672–1678) Dutch Wars. Great Britain henceforth flourished as the supreme slaving nation in the Atlantic world. Between 1690 and 1807, British traders exported some 2,500,000 slaves to the Caribbean and Spanish America. Envying British success, the French government tried to foster participation by its own nationals. But French entry into the slave trade was slow and ineffective. During the 18th century, French slavers exported from Africa only half as many slaves as British traders.

Because of the peculiar nature of the slave trade, European governments believed they needed to garrison fortified settlements and warehouses along the coast of West Africa. These forts provided a safe haven where their nationals received and stored slaves provided by African rulers and slave dealers. And the forts also protected them from attack by hostile European powers (especially, at first, the Dutch). These trading posts were enormously expensive, and private capital was not at first ready to enter the business. During the 17th century, the Dutch, French, British, and Danish governments thus set up privileged state companies for Africa. In return for maintaining the African forts, these were granted legal monopolies over the slave trade.

None of these monopoly companies made money or brought over enough slaves to satisfy the Caribbean planters, and all countries turned to free trade. The British government allowed the charter of the Royal Africa Company to expire in 1712. In France, a royal decree in 1716 largely opened the trade to all Frenchmen who fitted out their ships in any of five major ports. Further reforms effectively opened the slave trade to almost all French merchants by 1741. Moreover, the government further encouraged the trade by exempting slaves from certain export and import duties and collecting only a modest tax on slaves imported into its colonies.

The Major Slave Routes to the Caribbean

Under the free trade regime, the British and French slave trades dramatically expanded. At their high point in the 1790s, British traders, many headquartered in Liverpool, brought almost 50,000 slaves each year to the Caribbean. At first, they carried most slaves to Barbados. From 1720, Jamaica took the lion's share of British slave exports. The acquisition of the Ceded Islands and especially Grenada opened up new markets after 1763. Although British America also imported slaves, the Caribbean plantations were the main consumer of slaves. The thirteen mainland colonies purchased only half as many slaves as the one small island of Jamaica.

After the Portuguese and the British, the French were the most important slave dealers. French slavers brought in about 150,000 slaves during the 17th century and more than one million during the 18th. However, the sugar plantations on Saint-Domingue consumed slaves so rapidly—especially after 1763—that French traders never met their needs. Between 1701 and 1810, French merchants supplied only two-thirds of the French West Indian market, with British, Dutch, and North American merchants making up the deficit.

French ships invariably stopped first at Martinique, their first landfall out of Africa. A few ships occasionally went to Guadeloupe, but most either sold their cargo on Martinique or continued on to Saint-Domingue. After 1730, Saint-Domingue became the preferred destination, receiving more than three-quarters of all French slaves in the 1780s. Before going on to Saint-Domingue, traders rested the slaves on Martinique or on one of the tiny islands nearby. After the deadly Middle Passage, most needed a few days of rest to regain the appearance of good health.

The Dutch, whose small and arid islands were only minor sugar producers, primarily brought in slaves for sale on the British and French islands and on the Spanish mainland. Although Dutch merchants lost their dominance of the trade during the 1680s, they remained highly competitive carriers. Dutch slave imports actually grew during the 18th century, but their cargoes now formed only a dwindling proportion of an immensely larger trade. Altogether the two West India companies carried about 225,000 slaves to the Caribbean and Spanish America, while Dutch free traders imported another 50,000 into the West Indies between 1734 and 1803. Curaçao flourished as a slave depot into the 1720s. In later years, most Dutch slavers headed for Sint Eustatius to supply the French market.

The Danish West India Company also built forts and factories on the African coast. The company colonized Saint Thomas for use as a slave depot, and the Danish slave trade expanded after it purchased Saint Croix in 1733. Following the Dutch example, the Danish government abolished the company's monopoly in 1734, opening the trade to all Danish merchants. Saint Croix received substantial numbers of Africans for use on its own plantations. As a free port, it also developed into a major center for the inter-island or secondary market in slaves. Generally, larger ships from Africa docked at Christiansted, while smaller vessels from the West Indies used the lesser port at Frederiksted.

The Slave Trade in Africa

The Africans brought to the Caribbean already were slaves in Africa, and they were sold to European traders by their African owners. Almost all came from western Africa, usually from tribes living within 200 miles of the coast. Over the centuries, the slave trade tended to move slowly down the coast of West Africa, from the Senegambian region down to the Congo and Angola. During the 1800s, Biafra and the west-central regions contributed most slaves, with perhaps 10 percent coming from Mozambique on the eastern coast.

Slavery always was widespread in West Africa, often taking in one-third or more of the population. However, some scholars believe that African slavery during earlier eras usually involved smaller groups in face-to-face relationships. Thus, traditional African forms of slavery presumably were less harsh than slavery on Caribbean sugar estates.

In precolonial Africa, no one really was a free individual, and the family, kinship grouping, or lineage was the dominant political and economic institution. African kinship groups sought to assimilate newly bought slaves into their circle—although in a subordinate position or status. Over several generations, the descendants of these slaves might come to belong to the tribe. Many slave villages might then work under their own management, paying a tribute something like that owed by serfs in medieval Europe.

But only settled and assimilated slaves belonged to the tribe. Most new slaves were taken in war, kidnapped on raids disguised as wars, or convicted as criminals. Immediately after capture or trial, a new slave's life was forfeit, and his master could treat him as he liked. Usually the master tried to sell new slaves as far away as possible from the region where they were taken. This prevented them running away to their own kinship group.

Since African societies contained many slaves, an extensive internal slave trade had developed. When the Portuguese landed on the West African coast in 1450, they found that a complex system of trade routes already crossed the continent. Since the 600s, organized intercontinental slave trades had transported millions of Africans north and east to the slave-holding Islamic states. A northern route carried perhaps seven to ten million slaves across the Sahara to North Africa and Egypt. An eastern network took some five million slaves north to Egypt and the Middle East, or across the Red Sea to Arabia.

After the Europeans arrived, Africans continued to control the supply of slaves to the transatlantic trade. Because they had no immunity to malaria and yellow fever, Europeans (and North Africans) literally could not live in West Africa. Moreover, African warriors were equal or superior to Europeans, and their weapons were as effective until the end of the 19th century. European traders visited the slave coast at the sufferance of its African rulers. They did not create trade networks. They simply set up forts along the coast that tapped into the routes of Africa's already existing slave trade.

African slave dealers charged high prices in trade goods. As more and more slave ships came to the West African coast, prices rose sharply during the 18th century. Obviously, selling prices could vary between widely separated African ports. Overall, the average price of a male slave probably doubled from about £10 in the 1700s to £20 in 1740. It then dipped before rising again in the 1780s, to an average of £25 on the Gold Coast.

European purchasers, who competed for supplies with both the internal and Middle East trades, had to take what African sellers offered them. Thus we cannot identify the precise origins of Caribbean blacks. European traders named slaves after the port where they purchased them, even though many had been captured hundreds of miles away. With rare exceptions, Europeans knew little about the political or cultural origins of the slaves they bought.

Because of the strong African demand, sellers tended to offer Europeans only the "least indispensable" slaves. African owners valued female slaves more highly than males. Thus fewer women than men showed up at slave markets, and the European slave traders mainly shipped adult males. Overall, European slavers carried twice as many men as women to the Americas, and children under ten years of age made up less than 10 percent of their cargoes.

The Middle Passage

Slave traders often spent several months purchasing slaves at various ports. As soon as they accumulated their cargo, they sailed for the Americas with their captives on the notorious Middle Passage. Most followed a direct route due west to near the Ascension Islands and then turned north toward the West Indies and Martinique or Barbados. Tropical storms or the doldrums near the equator could delay the voyage, which might take as little as one month or as long as half a year.

As the trade boomed during the 18th century, slavers of all nations carried, fed, and treated slaves in similar ways. Slave ships tended to be small and narrow. Into their limited cargo space, their captains packed an average of three hundred captives and a relatively large crew of thirty-five to control the slaves. On average they allotted each captive only half the amount of room afforded convicts, emigrants, or soldiers transported during the same years.

All traders used temporary platforms between decks to provide sleeping space. Male slaves, but not women or children, were shackled together in pairs—left leg to right leg, left wrist to right wrist. Some captains removed the shackles once the ship was at sea, others took them off during the day, and some left their captives chained throughout the voyage. Most fed the slaves on dried beans, rice, corn, yams, and palm oil—with meat a rare treat.

The Middle Passage took a heavy toll of Europeans as well as Africans. All told, 13 percent of the slaves carried aboard French ships during the 18th century died before reaching the West Indies. And almost one out of five seamen sailing out of Nantes did not return to France. During the early years, outbreaks of smallpox, measles, or other highly communicable diseases caused astronomical death rates on some voyages. At all times, anemic dysentery and scurvy were the biggest killers. Contrary to legend, overcrowding or "tight packing" was not the major cause of death on board. Since the risk of dysentery increases with time at sea, the death rate instead rose with the length of the voyage, the quality of food and water during the passage, and epidemics and health conditions at the time of departure in Africa.

Slaves were expensive. Since they could not resell dead or diseased slaves, all captains had a strong economic motive to minimize losses. Most ships carried surgeons, but their medical efforts did the sick little good. Death rates dropped after 1750 because Europeans used faster ships, learned more about hygiene and diet, and introduced crude forms of vaccination against smallpox. On average, about 20 percent of the slaves died during the Middle Passage before 1700, compared to some 5 percent around 1800.

Although it killed fewer victims as slavers improved their techniques, the Middle Passage deserves the universal condemnation it has received. Whether it was caused by cruelty or by ignorance, even a 5 percent death rate (in 1800) is extraordinary among young adults during a two to three month voyage. Moreover, many additional slaves died on the way to the ships before leaving Africa. No precise accounting is possible. But as many as eight million Africans may have died to bring four million slaves to the Caribbean islands.

The Unique Nature of Caribbean Slavery

Slavery is difficult to define precisely. Individual freedom, the logical opposite of slavery, is a modern concept. Before the 19th century, hardly anyone was free in our sense of the word. Ties and obligations, which they could not unilaterally dissolve, constrained most persons and limited their freedom of action. Every individual belonged to one or more communities and was bound by family traditions, village customs, obligations to lords, or craft regulations. Even today, it is questionable whether we can accurately describe as "free" the many men and women laboring at jobs they dislike in order to purchase food, clothing, and housing.

What made slavery on tropical plantations unusual was the master's total freedom of control over his or her slaves. In most agricultural societies, serfs were members of a village governed by communal traditions. Their lord usually could not interfere with the customary ways of doing things. By contrast, Caribbean sugar plantations resembled factories in a modern capitalist society. To meet the demands of the world market, the owner and his agents had to manage rigorously all steps of production. Until the end of the 18th century, most sugar estates used the "gang" system. The owner treated dozens or hundreds of slaves literally as units of production. He organized their labor from day to day and even hour to hour. And he used physical force to ensure that, like cogs in a well-oiled machine, the slaves performed their assigned tasks on time.

Slaves working on cane estates always suffered the harshest conditions and labored under the most rigorous controls. The very nature of the sugarcane industry partially explains the master's need for total control. The weight and bulk of harvested cane are enormous compared to other grasses. (As a rule of thumb in the 18th century, planters needed 20 pounds of cane to make 1 pound of sugar.) Thus growers can not export cane unless they first concentrate the sugar by milling it. In this process, machines squeeze out the cane juice, which then is boiled to evaporate excess water, producing crystalline sugar and a by-product called molasses.

Milling is crucial and must be done quickly. Laborers must cut sugar as soon as it is ripe and then take it to the mill within 24 hours or it will ferment. For this reason, immediate access to a sugar mill is essential. From the 1860s, most notably in Cuba, several dependent farmers *(colonos)* brought their cane to a large mill *(central)* owned by a dominant planter or corporation. During the 18th century, however, every planter thought it necessary to have his own mill under his total control.

A sugar plantation—a "factory set in a field"—thus combined agriculture and manufacturing. It was a novel social, economic, and political organization, which brought together large amounts of capital and human labor and combined them on tropical soils. To make a profit, a planter had to manage and coordinate a complex series of tasks. For the slaves, most of these tasks involved intense and monotonous labor.

Island Laws Give Planters Unlimited Power over Their Slaves

Planters, especially on cane estates, had to exercise close control over their slaves. At least through the 18th century, island laws granted them the unlimited powers they needed, and the courts seldom bothered with the relationships between slaves and masters. Since slavery now was rare in western Europe, the colonies had to develop new laws regulating slavery. The legislature of each British island made its own laws—with the consent of the governor and Crown—for and peculiar to that colony. Laws were harshest where slaves greatly outnumbered their owners (Jamaica) and less severe in islands without sugar plantations (the Bahamas).

French, Dutch, Danish, and Spanish islands in theory enjoyed less local initiative, since they were governed by royal laws. In 1685 the Crown proclaimed one single Code Noir (Black Code) governing the treatment of slaves in all French colonies. However, although it was drawn up in the mother country, French jurists based the Code Noir on practices and precedents in the Antilles. Thus, it was at least as oppressive in many areas as the laws passed by legislatures on the British islands.

All islands sought to protect the planter and not the slave. Whether British, French, Spanish, Dutch, or Danish, all courts savagely punished slaves who rebelled or struck their masters. In these cases, the penalties included slow death by torture and the loss of an ear, hand, or leg. Early slave codes also authorized mutilation for persistent runaways and theft.

Except for the Spanish, slave codes treated the slaves as property and thus allowed planters to do as they pleased with their slaves. British slave laws often did not mention slave marriages, families, education, or religious conversion. The French Code Noir did recognize marriage and required slaves to be baptized. But slaves could not marry without their master's consent, and owners did not have to provide time off for religious education or worship.

The differences between these slave laws mattered little in practice. The sugar planters and their agents dominated colonial society and controlled local affairs. London, Paris, Copenhagen, and The Hague sent governors to the islands under their flags. But these governors could act effectively only with the support of the colonial planters. On all islands, slavery was regulated by local courts and customary law.

The French Code Noir and Spanish colonial laws were more generous than British laws in their treatment of manumission (the gaining of free status). By prohibiting manumission without the owner's consent, the British colonies made it almost impossible to gain freedom. More slaves became free in the Spanish colonies, such as Cuba. Courts in these colonies frequently allowed slaves to own personal property, make contracts, and buy their freedom with their own savings. To a more limited extent, self-purchase also became part of the customary law in the French islands. French (and Spanish) courts also permitted marriage between white males and freed female slaves, whose children thus became free as well.

French law gave freed slaves full legal rights of citizenship. But British colonies usually denied freed slaves all legal privileges except that of a jury trial. Even if free, blacks and persons of color in British colonies could not vote or hold political office, and laws forbade them to enter certain trades. Thus freedmen were both more numerous and more powerful in the French colonies. They were especially influential in the South and West provinces of Saint-Domingue, where they took a major part in the revolution of 1791.

The Harsh Life of a Field Slave

By the 18th century, sugarcane estates could not function without the labor of African slaves, who were bound to the soil by strict laws. The slave in turn became bound up in a rhythm of unceasing labor determined by the needs of the sugar plant itself. Work routines fell into a fixed and unvarying pattern. In a set sequence of steps, the slaves prepared and manured the soil, then planted, weeded, harvested, crushed, cured, boiled, and sometimes distilled the cane. As soon as they had completed one task, another demanded the attention of the planter and slaves.

Before land could be used for sugarcane, slaves with axes removed and burned the existing trees and brush. Once they cleared the land, owners laid out sugar plantations in patterns that made crop rotation easier, saved on transportation costs, and simplified slave management. Most planters divided their property into three to five large cane fields. Each year they harvested canes from one part of the land, with the other fields divided among growing canes and fallow. On the larger islands of Jamaica and Saint-Domingue, a sugar plantation usually took up about four times the amount of land given to cane. The cane mill and the boiling and refining houses occupied a central location in the middle of the fields. The remaining acres were taken up by food plots ("provision grounds"), grazing land, the planter's house, slave quarters, workshops, and animal pens.

The Plantation as Farm: Planting and Harvesting Sugarcane

Planters generally harvested cane about eighteen months after it was planted. They timed planting and harvesting to coincide with the island's rainy and dry seasons. During the rainy season—May/June to December/January—the slaves dug holes and dunged, planted, fertilized, and weeded the growing plants. During the dry season, from

January to May/June, they harvested and processed the mature crop, cutting the canes and carrying them to the mill to be ground.

Sugarcane is propagated through cuttings from the tops of mature plants. Originally these were planted in long trenches. From the 1720s, most planters adopted holing to prevent soil erosion and conserve moisture. Using hand-held hoes, the slaves dug holes 5 to 6 inches deep and about 5 foot square. They then laid one or two cane tops in the center of each hole and covered them with about two inches of soil. As the plant sprouted and grew taller, the slaves filled the hole with mold and dung until the field was level. During the following weeks, they weeded and thinned the growing plants and inserted new cuttings to replace any failing to grow. After five or six months, the canes were large enough to keep down the weeds.

This method of planting involved extremely heavy labor. Particularly on clay soils baked hard by the sun, holing is arduous work, and only the fittest of the slaves could endure it. Because the land was cut up by the cane holes, slaves had to spread dung by hand. Long files of slaves, usually women, carried the heavy dung baskets to the fields.

To spread out the harvest, planting was staggered over several months early in the rainy season. Cane planted in July was ready to be harvested 18 months later in January. Thus, the slaves performed one difficult task after another during the entire period from July through March. The heavy labor of holing, dunging, and weeding had barely ended, when it was time to begin cutting, hauling, and milling the mature cane.

Harvesting the cane was as difficult as holing. Using machetes, cutlasses, or long heavy "bills," the slaves chopped off the canes close to the ground. They then stripped the canes of leaves and cut them into shorter pieces 3 or 4 feet in length. These heavy bundles were then carried to the mills by the slaves, on pack animals, or in carts drawn by cattle or mules.

The Plantation as Factory: Sugar Milling and Refining

At the mill the slaves crushed the cane to remove the liquid or juice, which boiled and clarified until it crystallized into sugar. As a final step, they might distil molasses (the residue remaining after the cane is clarified) into rum at the still house. The first step, crushing or milling the cane, used a vertical three-roller mill. Wind, water, slaves, or cattle turned the middle roller. Through interconnecting cogs and teeth, it turned the two rollers on either side.

Two slaves fed the newly cut canes into this mill. One in front of the rollers inserted the canes. The other behind the rollers received the crushed stalks and passed them back to extract the rest of the liquid. The cane juice from the rollers ran off into a series of as many as seven copper vats of decreasing size. Slaves added lime water to the boiling cane syrup, and they removed the gross matter with a long-handled skimmer. From the last boiler, the liquid sugar was emptied into wooden troughs or coolers. If the boiling was successful, the liquid cooled into a mixture of crystals and molasses. After thirteen or fourteen hours, a plug at the bottom of each trough was removed, permitting the molasses to drain off.

This first stage of grinding and boiling produced a coarse brownish product known as *muscovado,* from a Portuguese word meaning "less finished." Many planters shipped the sugar in this state, but some went on to make a semi-refined grade known as clayed sugar. Slaves placed the muscovado into cone-shaped clay molds, and covered the top of each mold with a whitish clay. This helped to purge the sugar of molasses as the water drained down through the sugar toward a small hole in the bottom of the cone. Work in the sugar mill, where the boiling process raised the temperature above 120 degrees, was as demanding as field labor. It also demanded considerable skill. The slave supervising the boiling operations had an especially demanding job. More than any one else his judgment could mean the difference between a profit or loss.

On most islands, cattle, horses, mules, or even the slaves themselves turned the sugar mill's rollers. On low-lying islands open to the trade winds—especially Barbados but also on Antigua, Saint Kitts, and lowland Guadeloupe—planters introduced windmills during the 18th century. Water mills primarily were found in the French islands. Many plantations on Saint-Domingue introduced water mills in the 1740s and 1750s. To a lesser extent, planters also built water mills on Guadeloupe, Martinique, and Jamaica.

Refining represents the third and last stage in sugar making. The raw product was reheated, and egg whites, white vinegar, or bullock's blood was added. This solution was clarified by the removal of scum, reboiled, and cooled in molds with a layer of wet clay to separate the crystals. Almost all sugar was refined in Europe or in North America. Some Martinique and Guadeloupe planters built their own refineries at the end of the 17th century, but the government forced them to close to protect the French refining industry.

Besides muscovado and clayed sugar, many plantations sold several liquid by-products of the milling process. They produced the coarsest—known as *garapa* by the Portuguese and *grappe* by the French—by collecting cane juice skimmed from the boiling syrup and allowing it to ferment. This produced an inexpensive but very strong liquor popular among slaves and poor whites. From the molasses left by the boiling and claying processes, the planters distilled a milder and smoother liquor known in French as *tafia* and in English as rum. All of the colonists enjoyed rum, but the British colonies in North America and the Caribbean formed the largest market. Thus the French sold most of their rum to foreigners, contrary to both British and French law.

Slave Gangs, Slave Tasks

During all periods, slavery was harshest on sugar estates under the "gang system." Sugar gangs enjoyed the least personal freedom, suffered the worst conditions, and endured frequent physical punishments. These slaves worked under close control at repetitive tasks, with each member of the gang doing the same work. Throughout the 1700s, planters rigorously standardized the gang system to increase production. Under the supervision of drivers, large gangs dug cane holes, weeded the growing plants, and cut mature cane. A long line of slaves moved down the field in order, urged on by the whips of the drivers. At other times—when the slaves carried dung baskets, cane, or grass on their heads—the gang marched in a file, with the drivers in the rear.

Many planters divided their field slaves into three or more gangs. They assigned slaves by age and strength, trying to match the strongest slaves to the hardest tasks. The drivers put mature men and women into the first or "great" gang, which they trained to do the hard work of holing and harvesting. The second gang—youths from twelve to eighteen and elderly men and women—was given lighter field work. Children six to twelve went into the third gang, and the drivers put them to work weeding or gathering grass. Women as well as men formed part of the first gang. Indeed, more women than men worked in the fields. Since men held almost all the skilled jobs as drivers and craftsmen, women filled up the field gangs, even though men usually outnumbered women overall.

These gangs worked from dawn to dark, six days a week and more than 300 days a year. Although they usually did not work on Sundays, owners expected field slaves to spend their spare time growing food on their provision grounds. The slaves marched to the fields about 5 A.M. in the summer and a little later during the winter months. They continued to labor until dusk, with two breaks to cook their meals. The normal workday thus lasted ten to twelve hours. But it was much longer during the sugar harvest, when milling and boiling continued around the clock and slaves worked sixteen or eighteen hours a day.

The harsh gang system was most prevalent on the sugar estates. Slaves in towns or on smaller farms worked under the "task system." This meant that their owner or a driver assigned them a set amount of work to accomplish within a certain time limit. Skilled craftsmen— carpenters, barrel makers, masons, bricklayers, women spinners and weavers—always worked by the task. Moreover, tasking was employed in growing products other than sugar—including arrowroot, cocoa, coffee, long-staple cotton, pimento, rice, and lumber. Some sugar estates also switched from gang to tasking from the late 18th century. On the British islands, tasking replaced ganging as part of a policy of "amelioration" that sought to keep slaves alive as prices for new slaves increased.

Field Slaves Must Fend for Themselves

On large plantations, owners and managers cared about the slaves only as laborers and only during working hours. After the days' gang labor was done, whites left the slaves to do as they pleased. In most cases, they expected the slaves to feed, clothe, and house themselves. As a result, estate slaves lived under miserable conditions, and they also had little contact with whites. These two facts are related. On a large cane plantation, eight to ten whites managed hundreds of slaves. To these white managers, the slaves literally were faceless "hands" working in anonymous "gangs."

Field hands and most skilled slaves lived away from their owners in what often were miniature African villages. Estate slaves usually constructed their own houses out of straw and mud, thatching them with guinea grass, cane tops, or palmetto fronds. Rarely larger than 12 feet square, slave huts typically contained only two rooms, without floors or windows. Other than a few wooden bowls, a water-jug, and an iron pot for boiling their meals, most slaves had no furniture and slept on the floor.

These flimsy slave huts have disappeared without a trace. Old maps show that they often were set close to the sugar mill and within sight of the overseer's house. In the French West Indies, slave huts usually were constructed in a circle around a common open area. On some estates they were laid out in rows, with the huts of the headmen and drivers closer to the more solid houses of the managers.

Estate owners also took little responsibility for slave clothing and food. In most colonies, laws required owners to give every slave clothes each year. On the British islands, these laws became more generous during the period of amelioration after 1770. But most owners simply gave out rolls of coarse cloth and expected the slave women to make it into clothes. As late as 1800, travelers described slaves— both male and female—as working naked or nearly so in both the fields and sugar factory. For Sunday and holidays, slaves might dress up in better clothes that they had bought or made for themselves. House servants and town slaves were more decently dressed, though often barefoot.

The wholly inadequate housing and clothing of the field slaves contributed to their high death rate. Caribbean evenings and mornings can be quite cool, particularly in the winter months. West Africans have relatively little tolerance for cold. Already weakened by overwork and malnourishment, slaves easily fell victim to the "fevers" that killed so many.

More than anything else, however, plantation slaves suffered from a lack of adequate food. Planters used two methods to feed their estate slaves. Those on Barbados and the Leewards (and later Cuba) devoted all their land to sugar. To feed the slaves, they imported corn from North America and beans from England. On Jamaica, Saint-Domingue, Puerto Rico, and some of the Windward Islands, land remained more abundant. Here owners assigned the slaves "provision grounds" and expected them to grow their own food when they could.

Slaves often went hungry between June and September, the very months in which heavy work digging cane holes exhausted their energies. Many starved following hurricanes or during war-time naval blockades. At the best of times, a slave's diet was limited and monotonous. Most slaves lived on gruels or stews of cornmeal, rice, millet, and kidney beans ("pigeon peas"). To these they added the root plants —yams, potatoes, cassava, sweet potatoes—that formed the main diet of many West Africans. Some slaves also raised greens and fruit as well as hogs and chickens. However, they often sold both produce and animals, using their earnings to buy a few innocent pleasures, such as clothing, liquor, and tobacco.

Field slaves were seriously malnourished because they consumed little protein or fat. Planters rarely supplied fresh meat and fed their slaves from imported supplies of dried and salted fish, pork, and beef. Few slaves got as much as a pound a week, and the imported meat and fish often turned putrid before they received it. A diet low in meat and fat condemned field slaves to poor health and low fertility. The lack of these essential elements led to high death rates—among newly born children and infants as well as adults. Planters did not deliberately set out to starve their slaves. However, most planters—especially during the 18th century—did not provide a diet that could maintain health or even an efficient work force.

Overwork and underfeeding rather than deliberate cruelty were the main causes of high slave mortality. There is little reliable information about whipping and other punishments during the course of everyday life on rural estates. Occasional anecdotes describe cases of exceptional brutality, especially during the earlier years. In the British colonies at least, punishments apparently became less frequent and brutal toward the end of the 18th century. Most owners were sane enough not to deliberately destroy the expensive species of human machinery that provided their income. However, many planters—out of greed, carelessness, or mere stupidity—did allow their slaves to die of hunger and disease. . . .

The Sugar Plantation as a Killing Machine

On all the sugar islands, death rates for black slaves were always higher than birth rates. Africans sold to Caribbean cane estates suffered a much harsher fate than those carried farther north to America. In contrast to the remarkable natural decrease (excess of deaths over births) in the Caribbean, the American slave population rapidly increased. Since the slaves in both cases came from the same regions of West Africa, this difference provides perhaps the harshest indictment of Caribbean slavery. In 1825, both the United States and the islands had an African population of about two million. But slave traders had carried (through 1810) about 3,500,000 slaves to the islands and only some 375,000 to British North America.

It sometimes is said that Latin or Roman Catholic countries enjoyed a milder or more humane form of slavery compared to the Dutch or English. The survival rates do not support this belief. African slaves fared as badly in the French colonies as in the British. In the Greater Antilles, it is possible to compare British Jamaica to French Saint-Domingue (today Haiti). From 1655 through 1807, Jamaica imported about 750,000 slaves. In 1834, only 310,000 slaves were freed. Saint-Domingue took in about 800,000 slaves prior to the slave rebellion in 1791. A census in 1789 counted only 435,000. The death rate was even higher on the smaller Leeward Islands. Although Barbados received 387,000 slaves, the planters only freed 81,000 in 1834. From 1635, Martinique imported 366,000 slaves; only 100,000 Africans remained in 1848, when the French abolished slavery.

The record is slightly better for Spanish Cuba and Puerto Rico. On these islands, the African population did not increase over time; but at least the slaves did not die off as rapidly as on the French and British islands. Cuba, for example, imported about 700,000 slaves from 1761 through 1870. The census of 1877 counted 480,000 Africans.

Because the slaves died without reproducing themselves, the sugar estates could operate only by constantly importing new workers from Africa. A vicious cycle existed. The slave traders brought in new slaves, many of whom soon died—making it necessary to bring in yet more slaves to die. We could continue this catalog of human misery for every island (except the Bahamas and Curaçao). As with the extermination of the Arawak in the 1500s, the word *genocide* precisely describes the fate of Africans carried to the sugar islands as field slaves.

This "natural decrease" continued for some two centuries. Contemporary critics blamed cruel masters, poor food and housing, intense work schedules, disease, and the rigors of the Middle Passage. All of these worked together to make the tropical sugar plantation a true killing machine. Caribbean slaves suffered from both high death rates and low birth rates, and both factors hindered population growth. Very high infant mortality provided the most important check on the slave population. A low-protein and low-fat diet reduced births and also made adults more susceptible to disease.

There is an obvious connection between sugar plantations and high death rates. Slave deaths increased as agriculture intensified after 1700. At least in the British colonies, death rates fell toward the end of the century. Slavery thus was most deadly during the early years when planters rapidly developed sugar estates and introduced the factory-type discipline of gang slavery. The population decline slowed in the older colonies as the economy matured and more slaves worked away from the fields.

Overall, the natural decrease averaged about 3 percent per year in Jamaica and 4 percent a year in the Leeward and Windward islands. By the 19th century, the African population fell only 1 percent a year or less in the older colonies. The French colonies may have had a worse record. Some planters on Saint-Domingue had to replace 10 percent of their hands every year.

African slaves (and white immigrants) died most rapidly during their first three years in the islands, when they were said to be undergoing "seasoning." During these first years, at least 15 to 20 percent died and sometimes as many as one in three. Already weakened by confinement and malnutrition during the Middle Passage from Africa, many perished from the sudden exposure to a new disease environment. Dysentery (the "bloody flux") killed many new arrivals. Others succumbed to tuberculosis, typhoid, and varieties of malaria and yellow fever to which they had not been exposed in Africa.

Slaves also died rapidly during their first years of life. Three out of every four babies died before the age of five. Thus, the effective birth rate was very low. Abolitionists and other critics accused planters of believing that it was "better to buy than to breed." Since both pregnant women and young children ate without working, these critics

charged, planters did not encourage slave births. However, most planters probably favored births—at least in principle. Yet, as one planter
said, despite all he did, "the children do not come."

Recurrent epidemics continued to kill off both creole slaves living past childhood and Africans that outlasted the seasoning process. A
few lived into their sixties or seventies. But the average life expectancy,
among those surviving infancy, probably was less than forty years. A
field hand's chance of survival to middle age finally began to increase
after 1800. Second and third-generation creoles adapted to the West
Indian disease environment. When the slave trade ended in 1807, it
brought a halt to epidemics introduced by the constant influx of new
Africans. The number of creole slaves actually began to increase in
Barbados by about 1810, in Jamaica from the 1840s. The development
of natural immunities and better food probably helped the most—
18th-century medical care the least.

Sweating and Whipping

NICOLÁS GUILLÉN

Translated by Daniela Gioseffi and
Enildo A. García

The whip,
sweat and the whip!

The sun rose early
and found the Black barefoot
and his wounded body naked,
collapsed on the field.

The wind passed wailing:
—What black flowers lie in your hands!
His blood commanded, Let's go!
He demanded of his blood: Let's go!
He fled bleeding, barefoot.
The trembling sugarcane
opened a path for him.

Afterwards, the sky was calm,
and under the sky, the slave
bled darkly in the blood of his master.

The whip,
sweat and the whip,
dark red as the blood of the master;
the whip,
sweat and the whip,
dark red in the blood of his master,
dark red as the blood of the master.

Africa, Abused Continent: The Roots of War and Imperialism

W. E. B. DU BOIS

"*Semper novi quid ex Africa,*" cried the Roman proconsul; and he voiced the verdict of forty centuries. Yet there are those who would write world history and leave out this most marvelous of continents. Particularly today most men assume that Africa lies far afield from the centers of our burning social problems, and especially from our present problem of World War.

Yet in a very real sense Africa is a prime cause of this terrible overturning of civilization which we have lived to see; and these words seek to show how in the Dark Continent are hidden the roots, not simply of war today but of the menace of wars tomorrow.

Always Africa is giving us something new or some metempsychosis of a world-old thing. On its black bosom arose one of the earliest, if not the earliest, of self-protecting civilizations, and grew so mightily that it still furnishes superlatives to thinking and speaking men. Out of its darker and more remote forest fastnesses, came, if we may credit many recent scientists, the first welding of iron, and we know that agriculture and trade flourished there when Europe was a wilderness.

Nearly every human empire that has arisen in the world, material and spiritual, has found some of its greatest crises on this continent of

Africa, from Greece to Great Britain. As Mommsen says, "It was through Africa that Christianity became the religion of the world." In Africa the last flood of Germanic invasions spent itself within hearing of the last gasp of Byzantium, and it was again through Africa that Islam came to play its great role of conqueror and civilizer.

With the Renaissance and the widened world of modern thought, Africa came no less suddenly with her new old gift. Shakespeare's Ancient Pistol cries,

> *A foutre for the world, and worldings base!*
> *I speak of Africa, and golden joys.*

He echoes a legend of gold from the days of Punt and Ophir to those of Ghana, the Gold Coast, and the Rand. This thought had sent the world's greed scurrying down the hot, mysterious coasts of Africa to the Good Hope of gain, until for the first time a real world commerce was born, albeit it started as a commerce mainly in the bodies and souls of men.

So much for the past; and now, today: the Berlin Conference to apportion the rising riches of Africa among the white peoples met on the fifteenth day of November, 1884. Eleven days earlier, three Germans left Zanzibar (whither they had gone secretly disguised as mechanics), and before the Berlin Conference had finished its deliberations they had annexed to Germany an area over half as large again as the whole German Empire in Europe. Only in its dramatic suddenness was this undisguised robbery of the land of seven million natives different from the methods by which Great Britain and France got four million square miles each, Portugal three quarters of a million; and Italy and Spain smaller but substantial areas.

The methods by which this continent has been stolen have been contemptible and dishonest beyond expression. Lying treaties, rivers of rum, murder, assassination, mutilation, rape and torture have marked the progress of Englishman, German, Frenchman, and Belgian on the Dark Continent. The only way in which the world has been able to endure the horrible tale is by deliberately stopping its ears and changing the subject of conversation while the devilry went on.

It all began, singularly enough, like the present war, with Belgium. Many of us remember Stanley's great solution of the puzzle of Central Africa when he traced the mighty Congo sixteen hundred miles from Nyangwe to the sea. Suddenly the world knew that here lay the key to the riches of Central Africa. It stirred uneasily, but Leopold of Belgium was first on his feet, and the result was the Congo Free State—God save the mark! But the Congo Free State, with all its magniloquent heralding of peace, Christianity, and commerce, degenerating into murder, mutilation and downright robbery, differed only in degree and concentration from the tale of all Africa in this rape of a continent already furiously mangled by the slave trade. That sinister traffic, on which the British Empire and the American Republic were largely built, cost black Africa no less than 100,000,000 souls, the wreckage of its political and social life, and left the continent in precisely that state of helplessness which invites aggression and exploitation. "Color" became in the world's thought synonymous with inferiority, "Negro" lost its capitalization, and Africa was another name for bestiality and barbarism.

Thus the world began to invest in color prejudice. The "color line" began to pay dividends. For indeed, while the exploration of the valley of the Congo was the occasion of the scramble for Africa, the cause lay deeper. The Franco-Prussian War turned the eyes of those who sought power and dominion away from Europe. Already England was in Africa, cleaning away the debris of the slave trade and half-consciously groping toward the new imperialism. France, humiliated and impoverished, looked toward a new northern African empire sweeping from the Atlantic to the Red Sea. More slowly Germany began to see the dawning of a new day, and, shut out from America by the Monroe Doctrine, looked to Asia and Africa for colonies. Portugal sought anew to make good her claim to her ancient African realm; and thus a continent where Europe claimed but a tenth of the land in 1875 was in twenty-five more years practically absorbed.

Why was this? What was the new call for dominion? It must have been strong, for consider a moment the desperate flames of war that have shot up in Africa in the last quarter of a century: France and England at Fashoda, Italy at Adua, Italy and Turkey in Tripoli, England and Portugal at Delagoa Bay, England, Germany and the Dutch in South Africa, France and Spain in Morocco, Germany and France in Agadir, and the world at Algeciras.

The answer to this riddle we shall find in the economic changes in Europe. Remember what the nineteenth and twentieth centuries have meant to organized industry in European civilization. Slowly the divine right of the few to determine economic income and distribute the goods and services of the world has been questioned and curtailed. We called the process revolution in the eighteenth century, advancing democracy in the nineteenth, and socialization of wealth in the twentieth. But whatever we call it, the movement is the same: the dipping of more and grimier hands into the wealth-bag of the nation, until today only the ultrastubborn fail to see that democracy in determining income is the next inevitable step to democracy in political power.

With the waning of the possibility of the big fortune, gathered by starvation wage and boundless exploitation of one's weaker and poorer fellows at home, arose more magnificently the dream of exploitation abroad. Always, of course, the individual merchant had at his own risk and in his own way tapped the riches of foreign lands. Later, special trading monopolies had entered the field and founded empires overseas. Soon, however, the mass of merchants at home demanded a share in this golden stream; and finally, in the twentieth century, the laborer at home is demanding and beginning to receive a part of his share.

The theory of this new democratic despotism has not been clearly formulated. Most philosophers see the ship of state launched on the broad, irresistible tide of democracy, with only delaying eddies here and there; others, looking closer, are more disturbed. Are we, they ask, reverting to aristocracy and despotism—the rule of might? They cry out and then rub their eyes, for surely they cannot fail to see strengthening democracy all about them?

It is this paradox which has confounded philanthropists, curiously betrayed the socialists, and reconciled the imperialists and captains of industry to any amount of "democracy." It is this paradox which allows in America the most rapid advance of democracy to go hand in hand in its very centers with increased aristocracy and hatred toward darker races, and which excuses and defends an inhumanity that does not shrink from the public burning of human beings.

Yet the paradox is easily explained: the white workingman has been asked to share the spoil of exploiting "chinks and niggers." It is no longer simply the merchant prince, or the aristocratic monopoly, or even the employing class, that is exploiting the world: it is the nation, a new democratic nation composed of united capital and labor. The laborers are not yet getting, to be sure, as large a share as they want or will get, and there are still at the bottom large and restless excluded classes. But the laborer's equity is recognized, and his just share is a matter of time, intelligence, and skillful negotiation.

Such nations it is that rule the modern world. Their national bond is no mere sentimental patriotism, loyalty, or ancestor-worship. It is increased wealth, power, and luxury for all classes on a scale the world never saw before. Never before was the average citizen of England, France, and Germany so rich, with such splendid prospects of greater riches.

Whence comes this new wealth and on what does its accumulation depend? It comes primarily from the darker nations of the world —Asia and Africa, South and Central America, the West Indies and the islands of the South Seas. There are still, we may well believe, many parts of white countries like Russia and North America, not to mention Europe itself, where the older exploitation still holds. But the knell has sounded faint and far, even there. In the lands of darker folk, however, no knell has sounded. Chinese, East Indians, Negroes, and South American Indians are by common consent for governance by white folk and economic subjection to them. To the furtherance of this highly profitable economic dictum has been brought every available resource of science and religion. Thus arises the astonishing doctrine of the natural inferiority of most men to the few, and the interpretation of "Christian brotherhood" as meaning anything that one of the "brothers" may at any time want it to mean.

Like all world schemes, however, this one is not quite complete. First of all, yellow Japan has apparently escaped the cordon of this color bar. This is disconcerting and dangerous to white hegemony. If, of course, Japan would join heart and soul with the whites against the rest of the yellows, browns, and blacks, well and good. There are even good-natured attempts to prove the Japanese "Aryan," provided they act "white." But blood is thick, and there are signs that Japan does not dream of a world governed mainly by white men. This is the "Yellow Peril," and it may be necessary, as the German Emperor and many white Americans think, to start a world crusade against this presumptuous nation which demands "white" treatment.

Then, too, the Chinese have recently shown unexpected signs of independence and autonomy, which may possibly make it necessary to take them into account a few decades hence. As a result, the problem in Asia has resolved itself into a race for "spheres" of economic "influence," each provided with a more or less "open door" for business opportunity. This reduces the danger of open clash between European nations, and gives the yellow folk such chance for desperate unarmed resistance as was shown by China's repulse of the Six Nations of Bankers. There is still hope among some whites that conservative North China and the radical South may in time come to blows and allow actual white dominion.

One thing, however, is certain: Africa is prostrate. There at least are few signs of self-consciousness that need at present be heeded. To be sure, Abyssinia must be wheedled, and in America and the West Indies Negroes have attempted futile steps toward freedom; but such steps have been pretty effectually stopped (save through the breech of "miscegenation"), although the ten million Negroes in the United States need, to many men's minds, careful watching and ruthless repression.

Thus the white European mind has worked, and worked the more feverishly because Africa is the Land of the Twentieth Century. The world knows something of the gold and diamonds of South Africa, the cocoa of Angola and Nigeria, the rubber and ivory of the Congo, and the palm oil of the West Coast. But does the ordinary citizen realize the extraordinary economic advances of Africa and, too, of black Africa, in recent years? E.D. Morel, who knows his Africa better than most white men, has shown us how the export of palm oil from West Africa has grown from 283 tons in 1800, to 80,000 tons in 1913, which together with by-products is worth today $60,000,000 annually. He shows how native Gold Coast labor, unsupervised, has come to head the cocoa-producing countries of the world with an export of 89,000,000 pounds (weight *not* money) annually. He shows how the cotton crop of Uganda has risen from 3,000 bales in 1909 to 50,000 bales in 1914; and he says that France and Belgium are no more remarkable in the cultivation of their land than the Negro province of Kano. The trade of Abyssinia amounts to only $10,000,000 a year, but it is its infinite possibility of growth that is making the nations crowd to Addis Ababa.

All these things are but beginnings; "but tropical Africa and its peoples are being brought more irrevocably each year into the vortex of the economic influences that sway the western world." There can be no doubt of the economic possibilities of Africa in the near future. There are not only the well-known and traditional products, but boundless chances in a hundred different directions, and above all, there is a throng of human beings who, could they once be reduced to the docility and steadiness of Chinese coolies or of seventeenth and eighteenth-century European laborers, would furnish to their masters, a spoil exceeding the gold-haunted dreams of the most modern of imperialists.

This, then, is the real secret of that desperate struggle for Africa which began in 1877 and is now culminating. Economic dominion outside Africa has, of course, played its part, and we were on the verge of the partition of Asia when Asiatic shrewdness warded it off. America was saved from direct political dominion by the Monroe Doctrine. Thus, more and more, the imperialists have concentrated on Africa.

The greater the concentration the more deadly the rivalry. From Fashoda to Agadir, repeatedly the spark has been applied to the European magazine and a general conflagration narrowly averted. We speak of the Balkans as the storm center of Europe and the cause of war, but this is mere habit. The Balkans are convenient for occasions, but the ownership of materials and men in the darker world is the real prize that is setting the nations of Europe at each other's throats today.

The present world war is, then, the result of jealousies engendered by the recent rise of armed national associations of labor and capital whose aim is the exploitation of the wealth of the world mainly outside the European circle of nations. These associations, grown jealous and suspicious at the division of the spoils of trade-empire, are fighting to enlarge their respective shares; they look for expansion, not in Europe but in Asia, and particularly in Africa. "We want no inch of French territory," said Germany to England, but Germany was "unable to give" similar assurances as to France in Africa.

The difficulties of this imperial movement are internal as well as external. Successful aggression in economic expansion calls for a close union between capital and labor at home. Now the rising demands of the white laborer, not simply for wages but for conditions of work and a voice in the conduct of industry, make industrial peace difficult. The workingmen have been appeased by all sorts of essays in state socialism, on the one hand, and on the other hand by public threats of competition by colored labor. By threatening to send English capital to China and Mexico, by threatening to hire Negro laborers in America, as well as by old-age pensions and accident insurance, we gain industrial peace at home at the mightier cost of war abroad.

In addition to these national war-engendering jealousies there is a more subtle movement arising from the attempt to unite labor and capital in worldwide freebooting. Democracy in economic organization, while an acknowledged ideal, is today working itself out by admitting to a share in the spoils of capital only the aristocracy of labor—the more intelligent and shrewder and cannier workingmen. The ignorant, unskilled, and restless still form a large, threatening, and, to a growing extent, revolutionary group in advanced countries.

The resultant jealousies and bitter hatreds tend continually to fester along the color line. We must fight the Chinese, the laborer argues, or the Chinese will take our bread and butter. We must keep Negroes in their places, or Negroes will take our jobs. All over the world there leaps to articulate speech and ready action that singular assumption that if white men do not throttle colored men, then China, India, and Africa will do to Europe what Europe has done and seeks to do to them.

On the other hand, in the minds of yellow, brown, and black men the brutal truth is clearing: a white man is privileged to go to any land where advantage beckons and behave as he pleases; the black or colored man is being more and more confined to those parts of the world where life for climatic, historical, economic, and political reasons is most difficult to live and most easily dominated by Europe for Europe's gain.

What, then, are we to do, who desire peace and the civilization of all men? Hitherto the peace movement has confined itself chiefly to figures about the cost of war and platitudes on humanity. What do nations care about the cost of war, if by spending a few hundred millions in steel and gunpowder they can gain a thousand million in diamonds and cocoa? How can love of humanity appeal as a motive to nations whose love of luxury is built on the inhuman exploitation of human beings, and who, especially in recent years, have been taught to regard these human beings as inhuman? I appealed to the last meeting of peace societies in St. Louis, saying, "Should you not discuss racial prejudice as a prime cause of war?" The secretary was sorry but was unwilling to introduce controversial matters!

We, then, who want peace, must remove the real causes of war. We have extended gradually our conception of democracy beyond our social class to all social classes in our nation; we have gone further and extended our democratic ideals not simply to all classes of our own nation, but to those of other nations of our blood and lineage—to what we call "European" civilization. If we want real peace and lasting culture, however, we must go further. We must extend the democratic ideal to the yellow, brown, and black peoples.

To say this, is to evoke on the faces of modern men a look of blank hopelessness. Impossible! we are told, and for so many reasons—scientific, social, and what not—that argument is useless. But let us not conclude too quickly. Suppose we have to choose between this unspeakably inhuman outrage on decency and intelligence and religion which we call the World War and the attempt to treat black men as human, sentient, responsible beings? We have sold them as cattle. We are working them as beasts of burden. We shall not drive war from this world until we treat them as free and equal citizens in a world democracy of all races and nations. Impossible? Democracy is a method of doing the impossible. It is the only method yet discovered of making the education and development of all men a matter of all men's desperate desire. It is putting firearms in the hands of a child with the object of compelling the child's neighbors to teach him, not only the real and legitimate uses of a dangerous tool but the uses of himself in all things. Are there other and less costly ways of accomplishing this? There may be in some better world. But for a world just emerging from the rough chains of an almost universal poverty, and faced by the temptation of luxury and indulgence through the enslaving of defenseless men, there is but one adequate method of salvation—the giving of democratic weapons of self-defense to the defenseless.

Nor need we quibble over those ideas—wealth, education, and political power—soil which we have so forested with claim and counterclaim that we see nothing for the woods.

What the primitive peoples of Africa and the world need and must have if war is to be abolished is perfectly clear:

First: land. Today Africa is being enslaved by the theft of her land and natural resources. A century ago black men owned all but a morsel of South Africa. The Dutch and England came, and today 1,250,000 whites own 264,000,000 acres, leaving only 21,000,000 acres for 4,500,000 natives. Finally, to make assurance doubly sure, the Union of South Africa has refused natives even the right to *buy* land. This is a deliberate attempt to force the Negroes to work on farms and in mines and kitchens for low wages. All over Africa has gone this shameless monopolizing of land and natural resources to force poverty on the masses and reduce them to the "dumb–driven–cattle" stage of labor activity.

Secondly: we must train native races in modern civilization. This can be done. Modern methods of educating children, honestly and effectively applied, would make modern, civilized nations out of the vast majority of human beings on earth today. This we have seldom tried. For the most part Europe is straining every nerve to make over yellow, brown, and black men into docile beasts of burden, and only an irrepressible few are allowed to escape and seek (usually abroad) the education of modern men.

Lastly, the principle of home rule must extend to groups, nations, and races. The ruling of one people for another people's whim or gain must stop. This kind of despotism has been in later days more and more skillfully disguised. But the brute fact remains: the white man is ruling black Africa for the white man's gain, and just as far as possible he is doing the same to colored races elsewhere. Can such a situation bring peace? Will any amount of European concord or disarmament settle this injustice?

Political power today is but the weapon to force economic power. Tomorrow, it may give us spiritual vision and artistic sensibility. Today, it gives us or tries to give us bread and butter, and those classes or nations or races who are without it starve, and starvation is the weapon of the white world to reduce them to slavery.

We are calling for European concord today; but at the utmost European concord will mean satisfaction with, or acquiescence in, a given division of the spoils of world dominion. After all, European disarmament cannot go below the necessity of defending the aggressions of the whites against the blacks and browns and yellows. From this will arise three perpetual dangers of war. First, renewed jealousy at any division of colonies or spheres of influence agreed upon, if at any future time the present division comes to seem unfair. Who cared for Africa in the early nineteenth century? Let England have the scraps left from the golden feast of the slave trade. But in the twentieth century? The end was war. These scraps looked too tempting to Germany.

Secondly: war will come from the revolutionary revolt of the lowest workers. The greater the international jealousies, the greater the corresponding costs of armament and the more difficult to fulfill the promises of industrial democracy in advanced countries. Finally, the colored peoples will not always submit passively to foreign domination. To some this is a lightly tossed truism. When a people deserve liberty they fight for it and get it, say such philosophers; thus making war a regular, necessary step to liberty. Colored people are familiar with this complacent judgment. They endure the contemptuous treatment meted out by whites to those not "strong" enough to be free. These nations and races, composing as they do a vast majority of humanity, are going to endure this treatment just as long as they must and not a moment longer. Then they are going to fight and the War of the Color Line will outdo in savage inhumanity any war this world has yet seen. For colored folk have much to remember and they will not forget.

But is this inevitable? Must we sit helpless before this awful prospect? While we are planning, as a result of the present holocaust, the disarmament of Europe and a European international world police, must the rest of the world be left naked to the inevitable horror of war, especially when we know that it is directly in this outer circle of races, and not in the inner European household, that the real causes of present European fighting are to be found?

Our duty is clear. Racial slander must go. Racial prejudice will follow. Steadfast faith in humanity must come. The domination of one people by another without the other's consent, be the subject people black or white, must stop. The doctrine of forcible economic expansion over subject peoples must go. Religious hypocrisy must stop. "Bloodthirsty" Mwanga of Uganda killed an English bishop because they feared that his coming meant English domination. It did mean English domination, and the world and the bishop knew it, and yet the world was "horrified"! Such missionary hypocrisy must go. With clean hands and honest hearts we must front high heaven and beg peace in our time.

In this great work who can help us? In the Orient, the awakened Japanese and the awakening leaders of New China; in India and Egypt, the young men trained in Europe and European ideals, who now form the stuff that revolution is born of. But in Africa? Who better than the twenty-five million grandchildren of the European slave trade, spread through the Americas and now writhing desperately for freedom and a place in the world? And of these millions first of all the ten million black folk of the United States, now a problem, then a world salvation.

Twenty centuries before Christ a great cloud swept over sea and settled on Africa, darkening and well-nigh blotting out the culture of the land of Egypt. For half a thousand years it rested there until a black woman, Queen Nefertari, "the most venerated figure in Egyptian history," rose to the throne of the Pharaohs and redeemed the world and her people. Twenty centuries after Christ, black Africa, prostrate, raped, and shamed, lies at the feet of the conquering Philistines of Europe. Beyond the awful sea a black woman is weeping and waiting with her sons on her breast. What shall the end be? The world-old and fearful things, war and wealth, murder and luxury? Or shall it be a new thing—a new peace and new democracy of all races: a great humanity of equal men? *"Semper novi quid ex Africa!"*

The Song of the Slaves

YEVGENY YEVTUSHENKO

Translated by Daniela Gioseffi with
Sophia Buzevska

We're the slaves . . . we're slaves . . . we are slaves . . .
our hands are coarse as the earth.
Our hovels are graves.
Our bent backs are hardened,
we're bred like animals for mowing,
thrashing, and even the erection
of pyramids—in order to exalt
the Pharaohs' arrogant foreheads.
You laugh at our fate, merrymaking
swaggering in the midst of women, wine.
While the slave carries pillars
and the rock-heavy boulders of pyramids.
Is it possible there's no strength left to rear up
in the battle of revolt?
Surely, in the eyes of poor people it's not possible that
this destiny is repeated eternally.
We're slaves. . . . We are slaves.
            The Pyramid lasts
And later the slaves arose
against the Pharaohs to avenge all,

flinging kings under the feet of the mob . . .
But is there any meaning made?
I,
        Egyptian Pyramid,
inform you,
        the Bratsk Station,
how many slaves were slaughtered in uprisings
but still I see no miracles.
They're saying
            that slavery is abolished.
I dispute:
        it's strong as ever,
the slavery of race prejudice,
slavery of money,
            slavery of possessions.
Yes,
    there are no outmoded chains.
The people wear new chains—
chains of corrupt politics,
                of churches,
and the subtle paper chains of news.
Here lives a little person,
a clerk, let's say . . .
He has his own small home on mortgage.
He has a wife and daughter.
In bed he berates the authorities,
all very well, but in the morning he brings reports,
scrapping and bowing: "Yes" . . .
Is he free,
        Bratsk Station?
Poor fella!
Don't judge him too harshly.
            He's a slave to his family.
Very well. But seated
            in the presidential chair
is a different sort of man,
and if,
    let's suppose,
            he's not even a scoundrel,

what good can he do?
As you know, apart from innovations
the chair is like the Pharaoh's throne—
                    enslaved by its own feet.
Its feet support it
and necessarily restrain it.
It's tiresome for the president
that someone's demand hangs over *him,*
but it's too late to fight;
                    fists are bound
in the dough of flattery.
Wearily, the president sniffs:
                    "Oh, go to the devil!
Noble passions die in him . . .
Who is he?
He's the slave of his own power.

Imagine,
        Bratsk Station,
how many people are living
                    with oppression, fear!
People,
        where is your touted progress?
People, people, how deluded you are!
I observe with squared edges
and cracked sphinxes,
your many projects under construction,
your snouting around like a pig,
                    and I see
                        the spirit of man is weak.
It's impossible not to lose faith
                    in man.
Man—by nature is a slave.
        Man will never change.
No,
        I flatly refuse
to wait for something to show up . . .
I'm telling you
            frankly

straight out,
          Bratsk Station,
I, the Egyptian Pyramid.

The Pilgrim Invasion

WILLIAM APES of the Pequod Nation

December, 1620, the Pilgrims landed at Plymouth, and without asking liberty from any one, they possessed themselves of a portion of the country, and built themselves houses, and then made a treaty, and commanded them [the Indians] to accede to it. This, if now done, would be called an insult, and every white man would be called to go out and act the part of a patriot, to defend their country's rights; and if every intruder were butchered, it would be sung upon every hilltop in the Union, that victory and patriotism was the order of the day. And yet the Indians, though many were dissatisfied, without the shedding of blood, or imprisoning any one, bore it. And yet for their kindness and resignation towards the whites, they were called savages, and made by God on purpose for them to destroy. It appears that a treaty was made by the Pilgrims and the Indians, which treaty was kept during forty years; the young chiefs during this time, was showing the Pilgrims how to live in their country, and find support for their wives and little ones; and for all this, they were receiving the applauses of being savages. The two gentlemen chiefs were Squanto and Samoset, that were so good to the Pilgrims.

The next we present before you are things very appalling. We turn our attention to dates, 1623, January and March, when Mr. Weston['s] Colony, came very near starving to death; some of them were obliged to hire themselves to the Indians, to become their servants, in order that they might live. Their principal work was to bring wood and water; but not being contented with this, many of the whites sought to steal the Indian's corn; and because the Indians complained of it, and through their complaint, some one of their number being punished, as they say, to appease the savages. Now let us see who the greatest savages were; the person that stole the corn was a stout athletic man, and because of this, they wished to spare him, and take an old man who was lame and sickly, and that used to get his living by weaving, and because they thought he would not be of so much use to them, he was, although innocent of any crime, hung in his stead. Oh, savage, where art thou, to weep over the Christian's crimes. Another act of humanity for Christians, as they call themselves, that one Capt. Standish, gathering some fruit and provisions, goes forward with a black and hypocritical heart, and pretends to prepare a feast for the Indians; and when they sit down to eat, they seize the Indians' knives hanging about their necks, and stab them to the heart. The white people call this stabbing, feasting the savages. We suppose it might well mean themselves, their conduct being more like savages than Christians. They took one Wittumumet, the Chief's head, and put it upon a pole in their fort; and for aught we know, gave praise to God for success in murdering a poor Indian; for we know it was their usual course to give praise to God for this kind of victory, believing it was God's will and command, for them to do so.

But we have more to present; and that is, the violation of a treaty that the Pilgrims proposed for the Indians to subscribe to, and they the first to break it. The Pilgrims promised to deliver up every transgressor of the Indian treaty, to them, to be punished according to their laws, and the Indians were to do likewise. Now it appears that an Indian had committed treason, by conspiring against the king's life, which is punishable with death, and Massasoit makes demand for the transgressor, and the Pilgrims refuse to give him up, although by their oath of alliance they had promised to do so. Their reasons were, he was beneficial to them. This shows how grateful they were to their former safeguard, and ancient protector. Now, who would have blamed this venerable old chief if he had declared war at once, and swept the whole colonies away? It was certainly in his power to do it, if he pleased; but no, he forbore, and forgave the whites. But where is there a people, called civilized, that would do it? we presume, none; and we doubt not but the Pilgrims would have exerted all their powers to be avenged, and to appease their ungodly passions. But it will be seen that this good old chief exercised more Christian forbearance than any of the governors of that age, or since. It might well be said he was a pattern for the Christians themselves; but by the Pilgrims he is denounced, as being a savage.

In this history of Massasoit we find that his own head men were not satisfied with the Pilgrims; that they looked upon them to be intruders, and had a wish to expel those intruders out of their coast. A false report was made respecting one Tisquantum, that he was murdered by an Indian, one of Coubantant's men. Upon this news, one Standish, a vile and malicious fellow, took fourteen of his lewd Pilgrims with him, and at midnight, when a deathless silence reigned throughout the wilderness. At that late hour of the night, meeting a house in the wilderness, whose inmates heard—Move not, upon the peril of your life. At the same time some of the females were so frightened, that some of them undertook to make their escape, upon which they were fired upon. Now it is doubtless the case that these females never saw a white man before, or ever heard a gun fired. It must have sounded to them like the rumbling of thunder, and terror must certainly have filled all their hearts. And can it be supposed that these innocent Indians could have looked up them as good and trusty men? Do you look upon the midnight robber and assassin as being a Christian, and trusty man? These Indians had not done one single wrong act to the whites, but were as innocent of any crime, as any beings in the world. But if the real sufferers say one word, they are denounced, as being wild and savage beasts.

The history of New England writers say, that our tribes were large and respectable. How then, could it be otherwise, but their safety rested in the hands of friendly Indians. In 1647, the Pilgrims speak of large and respectable tribes. But let us trace them for a few moments. How have they been destroyed, is it by fair means? No. How then? By hypocritical proceedings, by being duped and flattered; flattered by informing the Indians that their God was a going to speak to them, and then place them before the cannon's mouth in a line, and then putting the match to it and kill thousands of them. We might suppose that meek Christians had better gods and weapons than cannon. But let us again review their weapons to civilize the nations of this soil. What were they: rum and powder, and ball, together with all the diseases, such as the small pox, and every other disease imaginable; and in this way sweep off thousands and tens of thousands.

Germ Warfare Against the Indians

CHIEF BLACKBIRD of the Ottawa Nation

The Ottawas were greatly reduced in numbers on account of the small-pox which they brought from Montreal during the French war with Great Britain. This small-pox was sold to them shut up in a tin box, with the strict injunction not to open their box on their way homeward, but only when they should reach their country; and that this box contained something that would do them great good, and their people! The foolish people believed really there was something in the box supernatural, that would do them great good. Accordingly, after they reached home they opened the box; but behold there was another tin box inside, smaller. They took it out and opened the second box, and behold, still there was another box inside the second box, smaller yet. So they kept on this way till they came to a very small box, which was not more than an inch long; and when they opened the last one they found nothing but mouldy particles in this last little box! They wondered very much what it was, and a great many closely inspected to try to find out what it meant. But alas, alas! pretty soon burst out a terrible sickness among them. The great Indian doctors themselves were taken sick and died. The tradition says it was indeed awful and terrible. Every one taken with it was sure to die. Lodge after lodge was totally vacated—nothing but the dead bodies lying here and there in their lodges—entire families being swept off with the ravages of this terrible disease. The whole coast of Arbor Croche, or Waw-gaw-naw-ke-zee, where their principal village was situated, on the west shore of the peninsula near the Straits, which is said to have been a continuous village some fifteen or sixteen miles long and extending from what is now called Cross Village to Seven-Mile Point (that is, seven miles from Little Traverse, now Harbor Springs), was entirely depopulated and laid waste. It is generally believed among the Indians of Arbor Croche that this wholesale murder of the Ottawas by this terrible disease sent by the British people, was actuated through hatred, and expressly to kill off the Ottawas and Chippewas because they were friends of the French Government or French King, whom they called "Their Great Father." The reason that today we see no full-grown trees standing along the coast of Arbor Croche, a mile or more in width along the shore, is because the trees were entirely cleared away for this famous long village, which existed before the small-pox raged among the Ottawas.

A Friend of the Indians

JOSEPH BRUCHAC of the Abenaki Nation

A man who was known
as a friend of the Indians
spoke to Red Jacket one day
about the good treatment
the Senecas enjoyed
from their white neighbors.

Red Jacket walked with him
beside the river, then suggested
they should sit together
on a log next to the stream.

They both sat down.
Then Red Jacket slid closer
to the man and said, "Move Over."

The man moved over, but when he did
Red Jacket again slid closer.
"Move Over," he said.

Three times this happened
until the man had reached
the end of the log near the water.
Then, once more, he was told, "Move Over."

"But if I move further
I shall fall in the water,"
the man pleaded,
teetering on the edge.

Red Jacket replied,
"And even so you whites
tell us to move on when
no place is left to go."

Fighting the Mexicans

GERONIMO, Chief of the Apache Nation

In the summer of 1858, being at peace with the Mexican towns as well as with all the neighboring Indian tribes, we went south into Old Mexico to trade. Our whole tribe went through Sonora toward Casa Grande, our destination, but just before reaching that place we stopped at another Mexican town called by the Indians "Kas-ki-yeh." Here we stayed for several days, camping just outside the city. Every day we would go into town to trade, leaving our camp under the protection of a small guard so that our arms, supplies, and women and children would not be disturbed during our absence.

Late one afternoon when returning from town we were met by a few women and children who told us that Mexican troops from some other town had attacked our camp, killed all the warriors of the guard, captured all our ponies, secured our arms, destroyed our supplies, and killed many of our women and children. Quickly we separated, concealing ourselves as best we could until nightfall, when we assembled at our appointed place of rendezvous—a thicket by the river. Silently we stole in one by one: sentinels were placed, and, when all were counted, I found that my aged mother, my young wife, and my three small children were among the slain. There were no lights in camp, so without being noticed I silently turned away and stood by the river. How long I stood there I do not know, but when I saw the warriors arranging for a council I took my place.

That night I did not give my vote for or against any measure; but it was decided that as there were only eighty warriors left, and as we were without arms or supplies, and were furthermore surrounded by the Mexicans far inside their own territory, we could not hope to fight successfully. So our chief, Mangus-Colorado, gave the order to start at once in perfect silence for our homes in Arizona, leaving the dead upon the field.

I stood until all had passed, hardly knowing what I would do—I had no weapon, nor did I hardly wish to fight, neither did I contemplate recovering the bodies of my loved ones, for that was forbidden. I did not pray, nor did I resolve to do anything in particular, for I had no purpose left. I finally followed the tribe silently, keeping just within hearing distance of the soft noise of the feet of the retreating Apaches. During the march as well as while we were camped I spoke to no one and no one spoke to me—there was nothing to say.

Within a few days we arrived at our own settlement. There were the decorations that Alope [Geronimo's wife] had made—and there were the playthings of our little ones. I burned them all, even our tepee. I also burned my mother's tepee and destroyed all her property. [This was in accordance with Apache custom, which required that the property of deceased relatives be destroyed.]

I was never again contented in our quiet home. I had vowed vengeance upon the Mexican troopers who had wronged me, and whenever I saw anything to remind me of former happy days my heart would ache for revenge upon Mexico.

As soon as we had again collected some arms and supplies Mangus-Colorado, our chief, called a council and found that all our warriors were willing to take the warpath against Mexico. I was appointed to solicit the aid of other tribes in this war.

When I went to the Chiricahua Apaches, Cochise, their chief, called a council at early dawn. Silently the warriors assembled at an open place in a mountain dell and took their seats on the ground, arranged in rows according to their ranks. Silently they sat smoking. At a signal from the chief I arose and presented my cause as follows:

"Kinsmen, you have heard what the Mexicans have recently done without cause. You are my relatives—uncles, cousins, brothers. We are men the same as the Mexicans are—we can do to them what they have done to us. Let us go forward and trail them—I will lead you to their city—we will attack them in their homes. I will fight in front of the battle—I only ask you to follow me to avenge this wrong done by these Mexicans—will you come?

"It is well—you will all come."

I returned to my own settlement, reported this success to my chieftain, and immediately departed to the southward into the land of the Nedni Apaches. Their chief, Whoa, heard me without comment, but he immediately issued orders for a council, and when all were ready gave a sign that I might speak. I addressed them as I had addressed the Chiricahua tribe, and they also promised to help us.

It was in the summer of 1859, almost a year from the date of the massacre of Kaskiyeh, that these three tribes were assembled on the Mexican border to go upon the warpath. Their faces were painted, the war bands fastened upon their brows, their long scalp-locks ready for the hand and knife of the warrior who could overcome them.

When all were ready the chieftains gave command to go forward. None of us were mounted and each warrior wore moccasins and also a cloth wrapped about his loins. This cloth could be spread over him when he slept, and when on the march would be ample protection as clothing. In battle, if the fight was hard, we did not wish much clothing. Each warrior carried three days' rations, but as we often killed game while on the march, we seldom were without food.

I acted as guide into Mexico, and we followed the river courses and mountain ranges because we could better thereby keep our movements concealed. We entered Sonora and went southward past Quitaco, Nacozari, and many smaller settlements.

When we were almost at Arispe we camped, and eight men rode out from the city to parley with us. These we captured, killed, and scalped. This was to draw the troops from the city, and the next day they came. The skirmishing lasted all day without a general engagement, but just at night we captured their supply train, so we had plenty of provisions and some more guns.

That night we posted sentinels and did not move our camp, but rested quietly all night, for we expected heavy work the next day. Early the next morning the warriors were assembled to pray—not for help, but that they might have health and avoid ambush or deceptions by the enemy.

As we had anticipated, about ten o'clock in the morning the whole Mexican force came out. There were two companies of cavalry and two of infantry. I recognized the cavalry as the soldiers who had killed my people at Kaskiyeh. This I told to the chieftains, and they said that I might direct the battle.

I was no chief and never had been, but because I had been more deeply wronged than others, this honor was conferred upon me, and I resolved to prove worthy of the trust. I arranged the Indians in a hollow circle near the river, and the Mexicans drew their infantry up in two lines, with the cavalry in reserve. We were in the timber, and they advanced until within about four hundred yards, when they halted and opened fire. Soon I led a charge against them, at the same time sending some braves to attack their rear. In all the battle I thought of my murdered mother, wife, and babies—of my vow of vengeance, and I fought with fury. Many fell by my hand, and constantly I led the advance. Many braves were killed. The battle lasted about two hours.

At the last four Indians were alone in the center of the field—myself and three other warriors. Our arrows were all gone, our spears broken off in the bodies of dead enemies. We had only our hands and knives with which to fight, but all who had stood against us were dead. Then two armed soldiers came upon us from another part of the field. They shot down two of our men and we, the remaining two, fled toward our own warriors. My companion was struck down by a saber, but I reached our warriors, seized a spear, and turned. The one who pursued me missed his aim and fell by my spear. With his saber I met the trooper who had killed my companion and we grappled and fell. I killed him with my knife and quickly rose over his body, brandishing his saber, seeking for other troopers to kill. There were none. Over the bloody field, covered with the bodies of Mexicans, rang the fierce Apache war-whoop.

Still covered with the blood of my enemies, still holding my conquering weapon, still hot with the joy of battle, victory, and vengeance, I was surrounded by the Apache braves and made war chief of all the Apaches. Then I gave orders for scalping the slain.

I could not call back my loved ones, I could not bring back the dead Apaches, but I could rejoice in this revenge. The Apaches had avenged the massacre of Kaskiyeh.

Memoir of a Sauk Warrior

BLACK HAWK

> *Brothers,—You see this vast country before us, which the Great Spirit gave to our fathers and us; you see the buffalo and deer that now are our support.—Brothers, you see these little ones, our wives*

and children, who are looking to us for food and raiment; and you now see the foe before you, that they have grown insolent and bold; that all our ancient customs are disregarded; the treaties made by our fathers and us are broken, and all of us insulted; our council fires disregarded, and all the ancient customs of our fathers; our brothers murdered before our eyes, and their spirits cry to us for revenge. Brothers, these people from the unknown world will cut down our groves, spoil our hunting and planting grounds, and drive us and our children from the graves of our fathers, and our council fires, and enslave our women and children.

—Chief of the Pequod

The whites were settling the country fast. I was out one day hunting in a bottom, and met three white men. They accused me of killing their hogs. I denied it, but they would not listen to me. One of them took my gun out of my hand and fired it off—then took out the flint, gave back my gun, and commenced beating me with sticks, and ordered me off. I was so much bruised that I could not sleep for several nights.

Some time after this occurrence, one of my camp cut a bee-tree, and carried the honey to his lodge. A party of white men soon followed, and told him that the bee-tree was theirs, and that he had no right to cut it. He pointed to the honey, and told them to take it. They were not satisfied with this, but took all the packs of skins that he had collected during the winter, to pay his trader and clothe his family in the spring, and carried them off!

How could we like such people, who treated us so unjustly? We determined to break up our camp, for fear that they would do worse —and when we joined our people in the spring, a great many of them complained of similar treatment.

This summer our agent came to live at Rock Island. The trader explained to me the terms of the treaty that had been made [a treaty signed in 1804 by four drunken Indians without any authority from their tribe], and said we would be obliged to leave the Illinois side of the Mississippi, and advised us to select a good place for our village and remove to it in the spring.

We started to our hunting grounds, in good hopes that something would be done for us. During the winter, I received information that three families of whites had arrived at our village, and destroyed some of our lodges, and were making fences and dividing our cornfields for their own use—and were quarrelling among themselves about their lines in the division! I immediately started for Rock River, a distance of ten days' travel, and on my arrival, found the report to be true. I went to my lodge, and saw a family occupying it.

What *right* had these people to our village, and our fields, which the Great Spirit had given us to live upon? My reason teaches me that land cannot be sold. The Great Spirit gave it to his children to live upon, and cultivate, as far as is necessary for their subsistence; and so long as they occupy and cultivate it, they have the right to the soil—but if they voluntarily leave it, then any other people have a right to settle upon it. Nothing can be sold but such things as can be carried away.

The white people brought whisky into our village, made our people drunk, and cheated them out of their horses, guns, and traps! Consequently, I visited all the whites and begged them not to sell whisky to my people. One of them continued the practice openly. I took a party of my young men, went to his house, and took out his barrel and broke in the head and turned out the whisky. I did this for fear some of the whites might be killed by my people when drunk.

It was ascertained that a great war chief [General E. P. Gaines], with a large number of soldiers, was on his way to Rock River. The war chief arrived, and convened a council at the agency. He said: "I hope you will consult your own interest and leave the country you are occupying, and go to the other side of the Mississippi."

I replied: "That we had never sold our country. We never received any annuities from our American father! And we are determined to hold on to our village!"

The war chief said: "I came here, neither to beg nor hire you to leave your village. My business is to remove you, peaceably if I can, but forcibly if I must! I will now give you two days to remove in—and if you do not cross the Mississippi within that time, I will adopt measures to force you away!"

The war chief appointed the next day to remove us. We crossed the Mississippi during the night and encamped some distance below Rock Island. The great war chief convened another council, for the purpose of making a treaty with us. In this treaty, he agreed to give us corn in place of that we had left growing in our fields. I touched the goosequill to this treaty, and was determined to live in peace.

The corn that had been given us was soon found to be inadequate to our wants; when loud lamentations were heard in the camp, by our women and children, for their roasting-ears, beans, and squashes. To satisfy them, a small party of braves went over, in the night, to steal corn from their own fields. They were discovered by the whites, and fired upon. Complaints were again made of the depredations committed by some of my people, *on their own corn fields!*

[Invited by the Winnebagoes to plant corn in their territory, Black Hawk and his people crossed the Mississippi. When warned by General Atkinson that this act was contrary to the treaty, he decided to return.]

I received news that three or four hundred white men, on horseback, had been seen about eight miles off. I immediately started three young men, with a white flag, to meet them and conduct them to our camp, that we might hold a council with them and descend Rock River again. I directed them, in case the whites had encamped, to return, and I would go and see *them*. After this party had started, I sent five young men to see what might take place. The first party went to the encampment of the whites and were taken prisoners. The last party had not proceeded far before they saw about twenty men coming towards them in full gallop! They stopped, and finding that the whites were coming so fast, in warlike attitude, they turned and retreated, but were pursued, and two of them overtaken and killed! The others made their escape. When they came in with the news, I was preparing my flags to meet the war chief. The alarm was given. Nearly all my young men were absent, about ten miles off. I started with what I had left (about forty), and had proceeded but a short distance before we saw a part of the army approaching. I raised a yell, and said to my braves: "Some of our people have been killed!—wantonly and cruelly murdered! We must revenge their death!"

In a little while we discovered the whole army coming towards us in full gallop! We were now confident that our first party had been killed. I immediately placed my men in front of some bushes, that we might have the first fire, when they approached close enough. They made a halt some distance from us. I gave another yell, and ordered my brave warriors to charge upon them—expecting that we would all be killed. They did charge! Every man rushed and fired, and the enemy retreated in the utmost confusion and consternation before my little, but brave band of warriors!

After pursuing the enemy some distance, I found it useless to follow them, as they rode so fast, and returned to my encampment with a few of my braves. I lighted my pipe, and sat down to thank the Great Spirit for what we had done. I had not been long meditating, when two of the three young men I had sent out with the flag to meet the American war chief entered. My astonishment was not greater than my joy to see them living and well.

I had resolved upon giving up the war—and sent a flag of peace to the American war chief, expecting, as a matter of right, reason, and justice that our flag would be respected. Yet instead I was forced into war, with about five hundred warriors, to contend against three or four thousand.

Finding that all was safe, I made a dog feast [a ceremony in which a dog was sacrificed and eaten]. Before my braves commenced feasting, I took my medicine bags, and addressed them in the following language:

"Braves and Warriors: These are the medicine bags of our forefather, Muk-a-ta-quet, who was the father of the Sac nation. They were handed down to the great war chief of our nation, Na-na-ma-kee, who has been at war with all the nations of the lakes and all the nations of the plains, and have never yet been disgraced! I expect you all to protect them!"

Ne-a-pope, with a party of twenty, remained in our rear, to watch for the enemy whilst we were proceeding to the Ouisconsin, with our women and children. We arrived, and had commenced crossing them to an island, when we discovered a large body of the enemy coming towards us. We were now compelled to fight, or sacrifice our wives and children to the fury of the whites. I met them with fifty warriors about a mile from the river, when an attack immediately commenced. I was mounted on a fine horse, and was pleased to see my warriors so brave. I addressed them in a loud voice, telling them to stand their ground, and never yield it to the enemy. At this time I was on the rise of a hill, where I wished to form my warriors that we might have some advantage over the whites. But the enemy succeeded in gaining this point, which compelled us to fall back into a deep ravine, from which we continued firing at them and they at us, until it began to grow dark. My horse having been wounded twice during this engagement, and fearing from his loss of blood that he would soon give out, I ordered my warriors to return.

In this skirmish, with fifty braves, I defended and accomplished my passage over the Ouisconsin, with a loss of only six men, though opposed by a host of mounted militia. I would not have fought there, but to gain time for my women and children to cross to an island. A warrior will duly appreciate the embarrassments I labored under—and whatever may be the sentiments of the white people, in relation to this battle, my nation, though fallen, will award to me the reputation of a great brave in conducting it. We returned to the Ouisconsin, and crossed over to our people. Here some of my people left me, and descended the Ouisconsin, hoping to escape to the west side of the Mississippi, that they might return home. I had no objection to their leaving me, as my people were all in a desperate condition—being worn out with travelling, and starving from hunger.

A party of whites, being in advance of the army, came upon our people, who were attempting to cross the Mississippi. They tried to give themselves up—the whites paid no attention to their entreaties—but commenced *slaughtering* them! In a little while the whole army arrived. Our braves, but few in number, finding that the enemy paid no regard to age or sex, and seeing that they were murdering helpless women and little children, determined to *fight until they were killed.* As many women as could, commenced swimming the Mississippi, with their children on their backs. A number of them were drowned, and some shot, before they could reach the opposite shore.

The massacre, which terminated the war, lasted about two hours. Our loss in killed, was about sixty, besides a number that were drowned. The loss of the enemy could not be ascertained by my braves, exactly; but they think that they killed about sixteen, during the action.

After hearing this sorrowful news, I started, with my little party, to the Winnebago village at Prairie La Cross. On my arrival there, I entered the lodge of one of the chiefs, and told him that I wished him to go with me to his father—that I intended to give myself up to the American war chief, and die, if the Great Spirit saw proper. I then started, with several Winnebagoes, and went to their agent, at Prairie du Chien, and gave myself up.

1833

To John Brown

A. FRANCES ELLEN WATKINS HARPER

Kendalville, Indiana
November 25, [1859]

Dear Friend: Although the hands of Slavery throw a barrier between you and me, and it may not be my privilege to see you in your prison-house, Virginia has no bolts or bars through which I dread to send you my sympathy. In the name of the young girl sold from the warm clasp of a mother's arms to the clutches of a libertine or a profligate,—in the name of the slave mother, her heart rocked to and fro by the agony of her mournful separations,—I thank you, that you have been brave enough to reach out your hands to the crushed and blighted of my race. You have rocked the bloody Bastile; and I hope that from your sad fate great good may arise to the cause of freedom. Already from your prison has come a shout of triumph against the giant sin of our country. The hemlock is distilled with victory when it is pressed to the lips of Socrates. The Cross becomes a glorious ensign when Calvary's page-browed sufferer yields up his life upon it. And, if Universal Freedom is ever to be the dominant power of the land, your bodies may be only her first stepping stones to dominion. I would prefer to see Slavery go down peaceably by men breaking off their sins by righteousness and their iniquities by showing justice and mercy to the poor; but we cannot tell what the future may bring forth. God writes national judgments upon national sins; and what may be slumbering in the storehouse of divine justice we do not know. We may earnestly hope that your fate will not be a vain lesson, that it will intensify our hatred of Slavery and love of freedom, and that your martyr grave will be a sacred altar upon which men will record their vows of undying hatred to that system which tramples on man and bids defiance to God. I have written to your dear wife, and sent her a few dollars, and I pledge myself to you that I will continue to assist her. May the ever-blessed God shield you and your fellow-prisoners in the darkest hour. Send my sympathy to your fellow-prisoners; tell them to be of good courage; to seek a refuge in the Eternal God, and lean upon His everlasting arms for a sure support. If any of them, like you, have a wife or children that I can help, let them send me word.

Bury Me in a Free Land

A. FRANCES ELLEN WATKINS HARPER

Make me a grave where'er you will,
In a lowly plain or a lofty hill;
Make it among earth's humblest graves,
But not in a land where men are slaves.

I could not rest, if around my grave
I heard the steps of a trembling slave;
His shadow above my silent tomb
Would make it a place of fearful gloom.

I could not sleep, if I heard the tread
Of a coffle-gang to the shambles led,
And the mother's shriek of wild despair
Rise, like a curse, on the trembling air.

I could not rest, if I saw the lash
Drinking her blood at each fearful gash;
And I saw her babes torn from her breast,
Like trembling doves from their parent nest.

I'd shudder and start, if I heard the bay
Of a bloodhound seizing his human prey;
And I heard the captive plead in vain,
As they bound, afresh, his galling chain.

If I saw young girls from their mother's arms
Bartered and sold for their youthful charms,
My eye would flash with a mournful flame,
My death-pale cheek grow red with shame.

I would sleep, dear friends, where bloated Might
Can rob no man of his dearest right;

My rest shall be calm in any grave
Where none can call his brother a slave.

I ask no monument, proud and high,
To arrest the gaze of the passers by;
All that my yearning spirit craves
Is—*Bury me not in a land of slaves!**

From Narrative of the Life of Frederick Douglass

FREDERICK DOUGLASS

Chapter One

I was born in Tuckahoe, near Hillsborough, and about twelve miles from Easton, in Talbot county, Maryland. I have no accurate knowledge of my age, never having seen any authentic record containing it. By far the larger part of the slaves know as little of their ages as horses know of theirs, and it is the wish of most masters within my knowledge to keep their slaves thus ignorant. I do not remember to have ever met a slave who could tell of his birthday. They seldom come nearer to it than planting-time, harvest-time, cherry-time, spring-time, or fall-time. A want of information concerning my own was a source of unhappiness to me even during childhood. The white children could tell their ages. I could not tell why I ought to be deprived of the same privilege. I was not allowed to make any inquiries of my master concerning it. He deemed all such inquiries on the part of a slave improper and impertinent, and evidence of a restless spirit. The nearest estimate I can give makes me now between twenty-seven and twenty-eight years of age. I come to this, from hearing my master say, some time during 1835, I was about seventeen years old.

* Harper included a copy of this poem in a letter that she wrote to one of John Brown's men who was awaiting execution for his part in the raid on Harpers Ferry. Published in *Liberator,* January 14, 1864.

My mother was named Harriet Bailey. She was the daughter of Isaac and Betsey Bailey, both colored, and quite dark. My mother was of a darker complexion than either my grandmother or grandfather.

My father was a white man. He was admitted to be such by all I ever heard speak of my parentage. The opinion was also whispered that my master was my father; but of the correctness of this opinion, I know nothing; the means of knowing was withheld from me. My mother and I were separated when I was but an infant—before I knew her as my mother. It is a common custom, in the part of Maryland from which I ran away, to part children from their mothers at a very early age. Frequently, before the child has reached its twelfth month, its mother is taken from it, and hired out on some farm a considerable distance off, and the child is placed under the care of an old woman, too old for field labor. For what this separation is done, I do not know, unless it be to hinder the development of the child's affection toward its mother, and to blunt and destroy the natural affection of the mother for the child. This is the inevitable result.

I never saw my mother, to know her as such, more than four or five times in my life; and each of these times was very short in duration, and at night. She was hired by a Mr. Stewart, who lived about twelve miles from my home. She made her journeys to see me in the night, travelling the whole distance on foot, after the performance of her day's work. She was a field hand, and a whipping is the penalty of not being in the field at sunrise, unless a slave has special permission from his or her master to the contrary—a permission which they seldom get, and one that gives to him that gives it the proud name of being a kind master. I do not recollect of ever seeing my mother by the light of day. She was with me in the night. She would lie down with me, and get me to sleep, but long before I waked she was gone. Very little communication ever took place between us. Death soon ended what little we could have while she lived, and with it her hardships and suffering. She died when I was about seven years old, on one of my master's farms, near Lee's Mill. I was not allowed to be present during her illness, at her death, or burial. She was gone long before I knew any thing about it. Never having enjoyed, to any considerable extent, her soothing presence, her tender and watchful care, I received the tidings of her death with much the same emotions I should have probably felt at the death of a stranger.

Called thus suddenly away, she left me without the slightest intimation of who my father was. The whisper that my master was my father, may or may not be true; and, true or false, it is of but little consequence to my purpose whilst the fact remains, in all its glaring odiousness, that slaveholders have ordained, and by law established, that the children of slave women shall in all cases follow the condition of their mothers; and this is done too obviously to administer to their own lusts, and make a gratification of their wicked desires profitable as well as pleasurable; for by this cunning arrangement, the slaveholder, in cases not a few, sustains to his slaves the double relation of master and father.

I know of such cases; and it is worthy of remark that such slaves invariably suffer greater hardships, and have more to contend with, than others. They are, in the first place, a constant offence to their mistress. She is ever disposed to find fault with them; they can seldom do any thing to please her; she is never better pleased than when she sees them under the lash, especially when she suspects her husband of showing to his mulatto children favors which he withholds from his black slaves. The master is frequently compelled to sell this class of his slaves, out of deference to the feelings of his white wife; and, cruel as the deed may strike any one to be, for a man to sell his own children to human flesh-mongers, it is often the dictate of humanity for him to do so; for, unless he does this, he must not only whip them himself, but must stand by and see one white son tie up his brother, of but few shades darker complexion than himself, and ply the gory lash to his naked back; and if he lisp one word of disapproval, it is set down to his parental partiality, and only makes a bad matter worse, both for himself and the slave whom he would protect and defend.

Every year brings with it multitudes of this class of slaves. It was doubtless in consequence of a knowledge of this fact, that one great statesman of the south predicted the downfall of slavery by the inevitable laws of population. Whether this prophecy is ever fulfilled or not, it is nevertheless plain that a very different-looking class of people are springing up at the south, and are now held in slavery, from those originally brought to this country from Africa; and if their increase will do no other good, it will do away the force of the argument, that God cursed Ham, and therefore American slavery is right. If the lineal descendants of Ham are alone to be scripturally enslaved, it is certain that slavery at the south must soon become unscriptural; for thousands are ushered into the world, annually, who, like myself, owe their existence to white fathers, and those fathers most frequently their own masters.

I have had two masters. My first master's name was Anthony. I do not remember his first name. He was generally called Captain Anthony—a title which, I presume, he acquired by sailing a craft on the Chesapeake Bay. He was not considered a rich slaveholder. He owned two or three farms, and about thirty slaves. His farms and slaves were under the care of an overseer. The overseer's name was Plummer. Mr. Plummer was a miserable drunkard, a profane swearer, and a savage monster. He always went armed with a cowskin and a heavy cudgel. I have known him to cut and slash the women's heads so horribly, that even master would be enraged at his cruelty, and would threaten to whip him if he did not mind himself. Master, however, was not a humane slaveholder. It required extraordinary barbarity on the part of an overseer to affect him. He was a cruel man, hardened by a long life of slaveholding. He would at times seem to take great pleasure in whipping a slave. I have often been awakened at the dawn of day by the most heart-rending shrieks of an own aunt of mine, whom he used to tie up to a joist, and whip upon her naked back till she was literally covered with blood. No words, no tears, no prayers, from his gory victim, seemed to move his iron heart from its bloody purpose. The louder she screamed, the harder he whipped; and where the blood ran fastest, there he whipped longest. He would whip her to make her scream, and whip her to make her hush; and not until overcome by fatigue, would he cease to swing the blood-clotted cowskin. I remember the first time I ever witnessed this horrible exhibition. I was quite a child, but I well remember it. I never shall forget it whilst I remember any thing. It was the first of a long series of such outrages, of which I was doomed to be a witness and a participant. It struck me with awful force. It was the blood-stained gate, the entrance to the hell of slavery, through which I was about to pass. It was a most terrible spectacle. I wish I could commit to paper the feelings with which I beheld it.

This occurrence took place very soon after I went to live with my old master, and under the following circumstances. Aunt Hester went out one night,—where or for what I do not know,—and happened to be absent when my master desired her presence. He had ordered her not to go out evenings, and warned her that she must never let him catch her in company with a young man, who was paying attention to her belonging to Colonel Lloyd. The young man's name was Ned Roberts, generally called Lloyd's Ned. Why master was so careful of her, may be safely left to conjecture. She was a woman of noble form, and of graceful proportions, having very few equals, and fewer superiors, in personal appearance, among the colored or white women of our neighborhood.

Aunt Hester had not only disobeyed his orders in going out, but had been found in company with Lloyd's Ned; which circumstance, I found, from what he said while whipping her, was the chief offence. Had he been a man of pure morals himself, he might have been thought interested in protecting the innocence of my aunt; but those who knew him will not suspect him of any such virtue. Before he commenced whipping Aunt Hester, he took her into the kitchen, and stripped her from neck to waist, leaving her neck, shoulders, and back, entirely naked. He then told her to cross her hands, calling her at the same time a d——d b——h. After crossing her hands, he tied them with a strong rope, and led her to a stool under a large hook in the joist, put in for the purpose. He made her get upon the stool, and tied her hands to the hook. She now stood fair for his infernal purpose. Her arms were stretched up at their full length, so that she stood upon the ends of her toes. He then said to her, "Now, you d——d b——h, I'll learn you how to disobey my orders!" and after rolling up his sleeves, he commenced to lay on the heavy cowskin, and soon the warm, red blood (amid heart-rending shrieks from her, and horrid oaths from him) came dripping to the floor. I was so terrified and horror-stricken at the sight, that I hid myself in a closet, and dared not venture out till long after the bloody transaction was over. I expected it would be my turn next. It was all new to me. I had never seen any thing like it before. I had always lived with my grandmother on the outskirts of the plantation, where she was put to raise the children of the younger women. I had therefore been, until now, out of the way of the bloody scenes that often occurred on the plantation.

Appendix to Narrative of the Life of Frederick Douglass

I find, since reading over the foregoing Narrative, that I have, in several instances, spoken in such a tone and manner, respecting religion, as may possibly lead those unacquainted with my religious views to suppose me an opponent of all religion. To remove the liability of such misapprehension, I deem it proper to append the following brief explanation. What I have said respecting and against religion, I mean strictly to apply to the *slaveholding religion* of this land, and with no possible reference to Christianity proper; for, between the Christianity of this land, and the Christianity of Christ, I recognize the widest possible difference—so wide, that to receive the one as good, pure, and holy, is of necessity to reject the other as bad, corrupt, and wicked. To be the friend of the one, is of necessity to be the enemy of the other. I love the pure, peaceable, and impartial Christianity of Christ: I therefore hate the corrupt, slaveholding, women-whipping, cradle-plundering, partial and hypocritical Christianity of this land. Indeed, I can see no reason, but the most deceitful one, for calling the religion of this land Christianity. I look upon it as the climax of all misnomers, the boldest of all frauds, and the grossest of all libels. Never was there a clearer case of "stealing the livery of the court of heaven to serve the devil in." I am filled with unutterable loathing when I contemplate the religious pomp and show, together with the horrible inconsistencies, which every where surround me. We have men-stealers for ministers, women-whippers for missionaries, and cradle-plunderers for church members. The man who wields the blood-clotted cowskin during the week fills the pulpit on Sunday, and claims to be a minister of the meek and lowly Jesus. The man who robs me of my earnings at the end of each week meets me as a class-leader on Sunday morning, to show me the way of life, and the path of salvation. He who sells my sister, for purposes of prostitution, stands forth as the pious advocate of purity. He who proclaims it a religious duty to read the Bible denies me the right of learning to read the name of the God who made me. He who is the religious advocate of marriage robs whole millions of its sacred influence, and leaves them to the ravages of wholesale pollution. The warm defender of the sacredness of the family relation is the same that scatters whole families,—sundering husbands and wives, parents and children, sisters and brothers,—leaving the hut vacant, and the hearth desolate. We see the thief preaching against theft, and the adulterer against adultery. We have men sold to build churches, women sold to support the gospel, and babes sold to purchase Bibles for the *poor heathen! all for the glory of God and the good of souls!* The slave auctioneer's bell and the church-going bell chime in with each other, and the bitter cries of the heart-broken slave are drowned in the religious shouts of his pious master. Revivals of religion and revivals in the slave-trade go hand in hand together. The slave prison and the church stand near each other. The clanking of fetters and the rattling of chains in the prison, and the pious psalm and solemn prayer in the church, may be heard at the same time. The dealers in the bodies and souls of men erect their stand in the presence of the pulpit, and they mutually help each other. The dealer gives his blood-stained gold to support the pulpit, and the pulpit, in return, covers his infernal business with the garb of Christianity. Here we have religion and robbery the allies of each other—devils dressed in angels' robes, and hell presenting the semblance of paradise.

> "Just God! and these are they,
>   Who minister at thine altar, God of right!
> Men who their hands, with prayer and blessing, lay
>   On Israel's ark of light.
>
> "What! preach, and kidnap men?
>   Give thanks, and rob thy own afflicted poor?
> Talk of thy glorious liberty, and then
>   Bolt hard the captive's door?
>
> "What! servants of thy own
>   Merciful Son, who came to seek and save
> The homeless and the outcast, fettering down
>   The tasked and plundered slave!
>
> "Pilate and Herod friends!
>   Chief priests and rulers, as of old, combine!
> Just God and holy! is that church which lends
>   Strength to the spoiler thine?"

The Christianity of America is a Christianity, of whose votaries it may be as truly said, as it was of the ancient scribes and Pharisees, "They bind heavy burdens, and grievous to be borne, and lay them on men's shoulders, but they themselves will not move them with one of their fingers. All their works they do for to be seen of men.—They love the uppermost rooms at feasts, and the chief seats in the synagogues, ... and to be called of men, Rabbi, Rabbi.—But woe unto you, scribes and Pharisees, hypocrites! for ye shut up the kingdom of heaven against men; for ye neither go in yourselves, neither suffer ye them that are entering to go in. Ye devour widows' houses, and for a pretence make long prayers; therefore ye shall receive the greater damnation. Ye compass sea and land to make one proselyte, and when he is made, ye make him twofold more the child of hell than yourselves.—Woe unto you, scribes and Pharisees, hypocrites! for ye pay tithe of mint, and anise, and cumin, and have omitted the weightier matters of the law, judgment, mercy, and faith; these ought ye to have done, and not to leave the other undone. Ye blind guides! which strain at a gnat, and swallow a camel. Woe unto you, scribes and Pharisees, hypocrites! for ye make clean the outside of the cup and of the platter; but within, they are full of extortion and excess.—Woe unto you, scribes and Pharisees, hypocrites! for ye are like unto whited sepulchres, which indeed appear beautiful outward, but are within full of dead men's bones, and of all uncleanness. Even so ye also outwardly appear righteous unto men, but within ye are full of hypocrisy and iniquity."

Dark and terrible as is this picture, I hold it to be strictly true of the overwhelming mass of professed Christians in America. They strain at a gnat, and swallow a camel. Could any thing be more true of our churches? They would be shocked at the proposition of fellowshipping a *sheep*-stealer; and at the same time they hug to their communion a *man*-stealer, and brand me with being an infidel, if I find fault with them for it. They attend with Pharisaical strictness to the outward forms of religion, and at the same time neglect the weightier matters of the law, judgment, mercy, and faith. They are always ready to sacrifice, but seldom to show mercy. They are they who are represented as professing to love God whom they have not seen, whilst they hate their brother whom they have seen. They love the heathen on the other side of the globe. They can pray for him, pay money to have the Bible put into his hand, and missionaries to instruct him; while they despise and totally neglect the heathen at their own doors.

Such is, very briefly, my view of the religion of this land; and to avoid any misunderstanding, growing out of the use of general terms, I mean, by the religion of this land, that which is revealed in the words, deeds, and actions, of those bodies, north and south, calling themselves Christian churches, and yet in union with slaveholders. It is against religion, as presented by these bodies, that I have felt it my duty to testify. . . .

Sincerely and earnestly hoping that this little book may do something toward throwing light on the American slave system, and hastening the glad day of deliverance to the millions of my brethren in bonds —faithfully relying upon the power of truth, love, and justice, for success in my humble efforts—and solemnly pledging my self anew to the sacred cause,—I subscribe myself, FREDERICK DOUGLASS
LYNN, *Mass., April 28, 1845.*

Toward a Personal History

ROCHELLE RATNER

(for Marc)

The Jews always knew to travel light

just a few books,
the clothes on their backs,
provisions for two or three days
(it might not be unleavened bread,
but then they expected this).

Husband, wife, and children
running from pogrom to pogrom,
keeping up conversation:

Lord, I do not see why, I accuse You
but bless You anyway.

If only the man returned home
finding possessions destroyed
his family nowhere in sight
he did not dare speak.

A Visit to Belzec

WILLIAM HEYEN

I.

This is Belzec,
in the East of Poland,
in the Lublin region
where the fumes of Sobibor,
Maidenek, and Treblinka still
stain the air:
smell the bodies
in the factories' smoke,
smell the sweet gas
in the clover and grass.
This is Belzec
where the death compound's gate
proclaims in Hebrew,
"Welcome to the Jewish State."
This is Belzec.
This is SS humor.
Curse them forever
in their black Valhalla.

II.

"At 7:20 a.m. a train arrived from Lemberg with 45 wagons holding more than 6,000 people. Of these, 1,450 were already dead on arrival. Behind the small barbed-wire windows, children, young ones, frightened to death, women and men. As the train drew in, 200 Ukrainians detailed for the task tore open the doors and, laying about them with their leather whips, drove the Jews out of the cars. Instructions boomed from a loudspeaker, ordering them to remove all clothing, artificial limbs, and spectacles. . . .

"They asked what was going to happen to them. . . . Most of them knew the truth. The odor told them what their fate was to be. They walked up a

small flight of steps and into the death chambers, most of them without a word,
thrust forward by those behind them.''

III.

Listener, you have walked
into the smoke-streaked mirror
of my dream, but I can't,
or won't remember.
Did my jackboots gleam?
Did I fill out quotas?
Was it before, or after?
Did I close those doors,
or did I die?

I can still feel
iron and cold water on my fingers.
I remember running
along the bank of a river,
under trees with full summer
stars in their branches,
the sky lit up with flares
and the slight murderous arcs of tracers,
the night air wet
with the sugary odors of leaves.
Dogs barked.
Were they mine?
Were they yours?
Was I running from,
or after?

IV.

"Inside the chambers SS men were crushing the people together. 'Fill them up
well,' [Hauptsturmführer Christian] Wirth had ordered, '700 or 800 of them
to every 270 square feet.' Now the doors were closed. . . .

"The bodies were tossed out, blue, wet with sweat and urine, the legs soiled
with feces and menstrual blood. A couple of dozen workers checked the mouths

of the dead, which they tore open with iron hooks. Other workers inspected anus and genital organs in search of money, diamonds, gold, dentists moved around hammering out gold teeth, bridges and crowns. . . ."

V.

Listener, all words are a dream.
You have wandered into mine.
Now, as workers rummage among the corpses,
we will leave for our affairs.

This happened only once, but happened:
one Belzec morning, a boy in deathline
composed a poem, and spoke it.
The words seemed true, and saved him.
The guard's mouth fell open to wonder.

We have walked together
into the smoke-streaked
terror of Belzec,

and have walked away.
              Now wind,
and the dawn sun,
       lift our meeting

to where they lift the human haze

         above that region's pines.

The Yellow Star and the Pink Triangle: Sexual Politics in the Third Reich

JACK NUSAN PORTER

In the 1930s there began in Germany a persecution of male homo-sexuals that was, as with the Jews, the worst in their history. (Lesbians, since they could "breed" children, presented no practical reproductive problems to the Nazi state and, therefore, were spared.) While "gay" is so American and "New Yorky," the term "homosexual" better describes the victims of this genocide, and the modern plague of AIDS only heightens interest in "gay genocides" throughout history. "Gay" was not used by the Nazis; hard, steely terms like "arse-flicker" replaced the gentle word "gay." Only in Yiddish, mother-tongue to millions of shtetl-*Yidden,* was there a soft, motherly expression—*faygelach*—"little birds"—used.

Yet AIDS would have fitted in beautifully with the distorted Nazi ideology that homosexuals were a "contragenic" group (to use Richard Plant's clinical term) or "sexual vagrants" (to use the Grand Inquisitor himself, Heinrich Himmler's term).

It all started with the murder of Ernst Röhm and other SA leaders in the famous blood purge that began June 30, 1934. The first Nazi pogrom against the Jews, on the other hand, was the infamous *Kristallnacht* of November 9–10, 1938, four years later, and the actual extermination of the Jews did not begin until after the Wannsee Conference, until the summer of 1941. Thus, it could be argued that the murder of the homosexuals started earlier than that of the Jews.

While hundreds of books and articles have been written on the Final Solution to the "Jewish Problem," the "gay genocide" has been either a taboo subject too delicate to touch upon or a topic too often obscured by other issues. In fact, to most Holocaust scholars like Yehuda Bauer, Raul Hilberg, or the late Lucy Dawidowicz, it is not even considered a "genocide," let alone part of the Holocaust.

Books that have appeared on homosexuals in Germany have either been good books put out by obscure publishers—for example, John Lauritsen and David Thorstad, *The Early Homosexual Rights Movement: 1864–1935* (New York: Times Change Press, 1974); Heinz Heger, *The Men with the Pink Triangle* (Boston: Alyson, 1980); plus works by the Gay Men's Press of London—or, if more widely circulated, flamboyantly written books with little regard for historical accuracy or good taste, yet published by some large, well-known publishers —for example, Frank Rector, *The Nazi Extermination of Homosexuals* (New York: Stein & Day, 1981); Martin Sherman, *Bent* (New York: Avon Books, a Bard Book, 1979); Adriaan Venema, *The Persecution of Homosexuals by the Nazis* (Los Angeles: Urania Manuscripts, 1979). However, a recent book of Richard Plant, *The Pink Triangle: The Nazi War against Homosexuals* (Henry Holt, 1986), is cause for celebration. Plant, a survivor of the Holocaust and a teacher at the New School for

Social Research in New York City, has written a very fine book on the subject and it stands with some of the best literature on the Holocaust.

Controversy surrounds every aspect of this genocide, even the label "genocide." For example, we do not accurately know the number of homosexuals incarcerated and killed. Figures like 250,000 to 500,000, even a million, are thrown about wildly as if to say that the greater the numbers, the more tragic the event. This obsession with numbers is a legacy of the Holocaust. Why are 20,000 killed less tragic than 20 million? In the aftermath of the Holocaust, even numbers themselves lose their significance.

Three of the most renowned and respected scholars of gay history —Professor Vern L. Bullough, Professor Erwin Haeberle, and Professor Rüdiger Lautmann—all agree with Mr. Plant that not more than 20,000 homosexuals were ever killed, even though the figures range from 5,000 to 15,000. Gay prisoners, who were forced to wear pink triangles, often did not survive long in the camps because they were isolated from one another and harassed by guards and other prisoners. Of those committed to the camps, 60% of the homosexuals, 41% of the political prisoners, and 35% of the Jehovah's Witnesses died. Of course, Jews and Gypsies (over 500,000 victims) had much higher death rates.

Other questions also arise concerning the sexual politics of the Third Reich. Was Hitler homophobic? If so, how could he have tolerated Ernst Röhm and other homosexual Nazis for so many years? It is clear that Röhm and the SA were decimated not because they were gay but because of powerful power conflicts within the Third Reich. After Hitler came to power, the *Wehrmacht* made him aware that the SA posed a threat to them. In truth, Hitler no longer needed the SA. For external forces he had a professional army; for internal force a disciplined police corps (the SS) that questioned none of his policies. Röhm and the SA, their antics and their politics of continuous national socialist revolution, embarrassed Hitler. Furthermore, the palace intrigues of the SS under Himmler to gain an upper hand were proving successful. Hitler had tolerated the sexual excesses of the SA in his climb to power, but after 1934, when he had obtained it, Röhm and his cohorts proved to be a political liability. Hitler, ever the pragmatist, knew that the SA was very unpopular with the conservative circles of Franz von Papen, the Prussian aristocracy, the *Wehrmacht* and the industrial elite, all of whom were threatened by this so-called "people's army." In this political trade-off Röhm had to go.

Hitler's July 13, 1934, speech to the Reichstag justified the blood purge as due largely to the necessity of "burning out" the "plague-boil" of "perversion." Hitler lied in that speech when he said he did not know the extent to which gays were in command of the SA; he did *not* lie, however, in his condemnation of this "perversion." Hitler did despise homosexuality; his homophobia was rooted in his own fears about his sexuality and his masculinity. He was determined that no one would ever suspect *him* of sexual inadequacy, femininity, or homosexuality. Yet, as in so many other aspects of his life, Hitler felt ambivalent toward homosexuality. He feared it and detested it, yet was fascinated by it. He was at the same time a pragmatic political being and a homophobe. Now that he had disposed of Röhm and the SA, he could freely express his true feelings on the subject from an invulnerable position. Hitler could now attack homosexuals for political reasons as well as psychosexual reasons.

A significant homosexual civil-rights movement had existed in Germany since 1897, supported strongly by both the Social Democratic and, later, the Communist parties. Led by the renowned sexual reformer Dr. Magnus Hirschfeld, director of the Berlin Institute of Sexology, this movement had worked for the abolition of Paragraph 175 of the German Criminal Code, a sodomy statute adopted in 1871 when the German Empire (the "second Reich") was created under Bismarck. This movement was allied with the growing feminist movement in Germany and with left-wing causes.

Hirschfeld himself was a Jew, an antimilitarist, a socialist, and a homosexual. A petition drawn up by Hirschfeld's Scientific Humanitarian Committee was signed by thousands of German writers and intellectuals including Albert Einstein, Thomas Mann, and Martin Buber. In the 1920s, during the Weimar Republic, prospects for reform looked excellent, but in 1928, when letters were sent to German political parties asking for their position on reform, the Nazi reply was as follows:

Munich, May 14, 1928

Community before Individual:
It is not necessary that you and I live, but it is necessary that the German people live. And they can live only if they can fight, for life

means fighting. And they can fight only if they maintain their masculinity. They can only maintain their masculinity if they exercise discipline, especially in matters of love. . . . Anyone who even thinks of homosexual love is our enemy. We reject anything which emasculates our people and makes them a plaything for our enemies, for we know that life is a fight, and it is madness to think that men will ever embrace fraternally. Natural history teaches us the opposite. Might makes right. And the stronger always win over the weak. Let's see to it that we once again become strong! . . .

In 1929 a Reichstag committee voted by the close margin of 15 to 13 to introduce a penal reform bill that would decriminalize private homosexual acts. The crisis provided by the 1929 stock market crash caused the bill to be shelved, however, just when success appeared imminent.

The antihomosexual nature of Nazism became evident in 1933, along with its anti-Semitism, when the Nazis vandalized and closed Hirschfeld's Institute. Hirschfeld himself watched the burning of his library on newsreels at a movie theater in France. He had left Germany in 1930 for a trip around the world; he never returned. Hirschfeld represented all that the Nazis despised; his humanitarianism was the antithesis of everything for which they stood. He died in Nice on May 14, 1935, at age 67.

The Nazi purge of homosexuals from their own ranks was only beginning. On June 23, 1935, the anniversary of the Röhm killings, the Nazis began a legal campaign against homosexuals by adding to paragraph 175 another law, 175a, which created ten new criminal offenses including kisses between men, embraces, and even homosexual fantasies. Arrests jumped from about 800 to 8,000 per year; more important, the Gestapo, under the notoriously antihomosexual leadership of Heinrich Himmler, entered the picture. Himmler is quoted as follows:

Just as we today have gone back to the ancient Germanic view of the question of marriage mixing [sic] different races, so too in our judgment of homosexuality—a symptom of degeneracy that could destroy our race—we must return to the guiding Nordic principle: extermination of degenerates.

The Nazi persecution of gays cut short two other phenomena: the homosexual-rights movement led by Dr. Hirschfeld and the sexual research movement, which was also led largely by Jews. Thus, to be Jewish, sexually tolerant, and liberal was to be *ipso facto* an enemy of Nazism. Sexual freedom, religious freedom, and intellectual freedom, including sexual research, seems to go hand in hand in a democratic society; conversely, a fascist state seems to have little room for any of these freedoms.

It is good that research on this subject appears on the scene at this time. There is a new Holocaust Museum being erected in Washington, DC, and it will commemorate not only the six million Jews murdered by Hitler but also other victims of genocide such as Armenians and Gypsies.

Jewish "exclusivists" will argue that the Holocaust was unique to Jews. They do not wish to share the museum with any other victims. Other Jews oppose sharing on the grounds that some of the minorities acted as informers, collaborators, and guards, or even murdered Jews—venting their frustrations at prejudice against them in anti-Semitism.

The Jewish "universalists," on the other hand, who have won the deciding round on the questions, agree to share the sacred memory of an experience so devastating (two-thirds of the Jews in Europe died) and in which Jews so clearly predominated numerically, with all the people who were murdered. Thus, the museum is expected to commemorate homosexuals as well as Gypsies, Jehovah's Witnesses, POWs (mostly Russians and Poles), and anti-Nazi political prisoners from many nations including Polish and Ukrainian citizens. The Holocaust *was* unique and the Jews were unique victims, but the other victims must be honored and given a place of respect.

Men in History

WILLIAM HEYEN

I.

Keitel *still* expected the secret weaponry
of deliverance, and maniacal Goering
even *now* angled for power.
Eva Braun, shadowy queen
of this black bower, resigned herself
to long hours of waiting
for cyanide, or one more night's love,

but over the Fuehrer's last days,
as Berlin crumbled above him
and a fine dust seemed
to cloud his bunkers, he moved
divisions of ghosts across maps,
and others around him
kept asking themselves
if this was all a dream.

Shriveled, insubstantial, unreal
even to himself, he walked
with an old peasant's stoop
in a uniform stained by food
dropped by his shaking hands.
Above him, his Reich's burnished eagle
lay in rubble, flew downward into flame.

II.

But now it was mid-April,
his birthday, his fifty-sixth
year to heaven,
and since it was his last, and since
he knew, he left for the last time
his shelter and eventual tomb—

sixteen feet of concrete and six of earth—
for the Chancellery's upper rooms,

where walls peeled, drapes were down,
and paintings he'd insisted on
were long since packed away.
A hat lay in an easy chair,
old newspapers haunted the corridors.
This man shook hands, blustered,
passed out signed photographs of himself
framed in silver. Often nostalgia

floated him back twenty years until
his eyes brimmed with tears quickly
wiped away with the back of his hand.

III.

Then it was over.
He took his leave, wound
back down to his bunker
to finish the war,
to wait for God to open
the iron gate of the sun
for one more soldier soon
to die. This architect, this

messiah, this man in history
would die just once,
would flame just once into a darkness
far past our spit and curses.
As he said to Albert Speer:
"Believe me, it is easy for me
to end my life. A brief moment
and I'm freed of everything."

IV.

Born in Brooklyn of German parents,
I remember lines scratched on our doors,

the crooked swastikas my father cursed
and painted over. And I remember
the *Volksfest* at Franklin Square
on Long Island every summer—
stands of smoked eel, loaves
of dark bread, raffles, shooting galleries,
beer halls, bowling alleys,
boys in *lederhosen*
flooded by an ocean of guttural German
they never learned, or learned to disavow.
I remember hourly parades under the lindens,
the elders' white beards, the sad depths of their eyes.

I remember their talk of the North Sea,
the Rhine of Lorelei, Cologne's
twin towers, the Black Forest, the mountains,
the Hamelin piper who led everyone's children to nowhere.
But I, too, was a child: all those years
there was one word I never heard,
one name never mentioned.

I Am a Child of the Holocaust

MERLE HOFFMAN

I am a child of the Holocaust, a survivor of sorts, a kind of surrogate sufferer. I have never smelled the burning flesh or felt the pain of my kidneys close to bursting—my legs turned to leadened fatigue as I stood crushed against others in the trains bound for Auschwitz or Treblinka or Dachau. I have never eaten out of the bowl I was forced to shit in, nor had my children torn out of my arms as I stood in an interminable line waiting for the selection process. Nor have I cowered in some corner clutching what was important to me, my mouth dry with terror as I listened for the sound of the S.S. boots outside my door, wondering if it was me they had finally come for. Nor have I felt the mounting panic of the bodies surrounding me as they struggled helplessly for air, gasping and gagging, tearing desperately at each other as the gas slowly entered the chambers.

No, I have not been there, yet it is always with me. I am a child of the Holocaust, a survivor who was not personally threatened, yet cannot forget.

It comes to me at odd times. I remember once, a magnificent evening in the Islands, warm, sensuous breezes, a sky full of light, a smell of flowers and expectation, and suddenly I smelled the fires. Or, often in the midst of self-doubt and deep despair, I have stopped to step out of myself and wonder at my absolute gall for daring depression when I had survived, had escaped by the mere arbitrary factor of time and place of birth.

Strangely, I can't remember a time when I didn't know about the holocaust—I can't recall when I heard about it for the first time, it was just there—always. I do remember my teacher's arm. How, one summer, when I came early for my weekly piano lesson and caught him unexpectedly in the garden without a shirt, I saw the numbers. Instinctively I knew I should not have looked, should not have seen, but then I did. He caught my furtive, surprised glance, murmured something about being a part of the Resistance during the war, and it was never mentioned again.

And then there were my friends, children of the real survivors. The ones who had lost aunts, uncles, sisters, brothers, mothers, friends. The survivors whose children had now become the one hope and the one light in the darkness of lost generations. These were the children upon whose shoulders salvation and guilt lay. The children who had to make up to everyone for everything, who lived in a particular paranoid reality that separated and branded them at the same time, who always seemed to be excusing themselves for having survivors for parents.

But I was not thinking of any of these things when I stood at the Wall. I had arrived in Berlin on New Year's Day 1990. The night before there had been a massive joyous celebration—400,000 people dancing, drinking, awash with the heady joy of a newfound freedom and historical imperative. But that day there was only the routine of new tourists who had come as ritual pilgrims to look, worship, laugh, touch and despise.

It was cold, gray and icy on the Kurfastendaam (the main thoroughfare), a kind of German Champs Elysee that separated both Berlins with two great monuments on either side, the Brandenburg Gate on the east and the Goddess of Peace on the west. At first it was difficult to make out the strange phallic structure with its gold forms, thrusting itself into the sky. Upon questioning my guide I was told this was the "Goddess of Peace" and those gold domed cylinders were to symbolize the weapons of the enemy taken in war. On top of the structure was the Goddess, a winged victory, an idealized woman granting her powers of fertility and nurture to the power and the glory of German militarism.

A strange parade it was that marched towards the Wall that day. Families, youths, foreigners, children sliding on the icy city streets, laughingly falling to the ground as their parents playfully scooped them up in their arms. Dogs too, pulling their owners towards the Wall which stood like some great fractured totem imposing and ridiculous at the same time. A massive concrete Rorschach test, changing definitions by the minute. And the sound of the chipping—the constant chipping away at the Wall. The entrepreneurs selling graffitied pieces for $3, the students ready to loan you a chisel for a few marks, the two East German soldiers standing on the top with slightly bemused smiles, as if they knew they would be part of everyone's memory bank. And I, too, was swept away by the energy and the faces of joy and expectation around me. As I walked through the Brandenburg Gate, I was struck by the references to Gorbachev. The graffiti that read "Long live Gorby"; "Viva Gorby." And the crosses—these were near the Reichstag—the Reichstag that was the centerpiece of the Nazi regime where the machinery, the bureaucracy of the Third Reich and the final solution was played out.

Behind the imposing buildings (there were seven of them) white wooden crosses were attached to a wire fence with a name or the word "anonymous." These were the martyrs to German separation, those who were killed trying to cross over. The last death was in May, 1989, merely months before the falling of the Wall. I remember a conversation with a West German student who told me how surreal this separation had become. How he had been eating in a cafe when he heard someone had been shot trying to escape from the East. "You get used to it," he said shrugging.

There is a special history here, one not often spoken of, of the martyrs of this place—of the Gandhi follower who was given a 13-month jail sentence for merely holding a sign that read "Freedom for the Political Prisoners." Of the Indian, T. N. Zutshi, who travelled to East Berlin in March 1960 wearing a placard which read: "The first step toward freedom: Get rid of your fear and speak the truth!"

According to Zutshi, "At East Berlin's Alexanderplatz Station, policemen tried to wrest my poster from me. There ensued a scuffle with the police, as hundreds of spectators looked on. I refused to be led away, clung to my poster and shouted my slogan." Zutshi's action caused a sensation; he was released after five days of custody and interrogation. His courage, along with the tradition of creative non-violence expressed by others, and the sacrifice of Pastor Oskar Bruesewitz who burned himself to death in front of the Church at Zeist in protest, moved me to a poignant rage.

The story is that upon reaching the square in front of the church, Bruesewitz unfolded the posters he brought along in his car and then proceeded to douse himself with gasoline. A group of people rushed forward with outstretched arms to extinguish the flames engulfing him. However, two policemen lunged immediately for the posters and removed them on the spot. To this day it is not known what was written on them, but they are rumored to have contained the phrase "DO NOT CORRUPT THESE YOUNG PEOPLE."

They are all my comrades. They are beyond nation, beyond nationalism. Yet, they are German. "German unity is a German question," said Helmut Kohl in the *NY Times*. "There is a difference between understandable misgivings and fears and what is disguised as fear but is really economic jealousy."

Disguised as fear? Repeated reports of the rise of anti-Semitism in Germany and, increasingly, in Russia, belie the minimization of appropriate and understandable anxiety at the so-called "German Question"—the issue of German reunification. A. M. Rosenthal, writing in his weekly *NY Times* column, "On My Mind," says "I search through the endless newspaper columns about the German wave rolling toward unification, but I cannot find any of the words I am looking for.

"I cannot hear them in the drone of the experts mustered up for TV nor in the Sunday talk shows. . . . These are some of the words: Auschwitz, Rotterdam, Polish untermenschen, Leningrad, slave labor, crematorium, Holocaust, Nazi."

A German question? Rosenthal argues that "to keep the words

hidden is to kill the murdered twice, this time with the forgetting mind." Rosenthal, it seems, is also a survivor.

November 8, 1989 marked the 50th anniversary of the Nazi pogrom known as Kristallnacht (the Night of the Broken Glass), a night when the white heat of fire mixed with the brilliance of the shattered glass of Jewish homes and shops to give prophetic form to the coming of the "FINAL SOLUTION."

Fifty years later these fires still burn. Anti-Semitism, as Eli Weisel has said, is a "light sleeper." East Germany, which until very recently has never publicly accepted any responsibility for Nazi crimes, has spurned the growth of violent right-wing activity. According to an article in the *NY Times* "hundreds of skinheads goose-stepped through Leipzig shouting "Seig Heil" as they smashed windows and disrupted a regular weekly demonstration for German unity. Like Hitler's brownshirts, the skinheads fought with bystanders shouting "To hell with the Jews."

And, as the world watches the cataclysmic changes in the Soviet Union with bated breath and shouts of "Viva Gorby" fill the international air-waves, thousands of Soviet Jews are attempting to escape the personal results of Glasnost. Reporter Joel Brinkley writes of fleeing Russian Jews who tell of "physical attacks against themselves, relatives or friends. One man said his brother had been murdered and thrown into the river, bound head and foot, just because he was a Jew."

Will they come to America? According to a Mr. Eikel of Kiev, interviewed by the *New York Observer* in February, "I always felt anti-Semitism in the Soviet Union, but I've also read that there's anti-Semitism in the United States." Speaking of his decision to emigrate to Israel, Eikel states that "now I want to live in a country with Jews."

Unfortunately, Eikel's appraisal of anti-Semitism in the United States is correct. According to the Anti-Defamation League of B'nai B'rith, "anti-Semitic incidents in the United States increased 12 percent in 1989, reaching the highest level since the organization started keeping track 11 years ago. The greatest number of attacks occurred in New Jersey and New York." *(New York Observer)* Oddly enough, Middlesex County, NJ seems to be a hot bed for growing anti-Jewish hatred. An anonymous advertisement appeared in the student newspaper at North Brunswick Township High School which read "The ovens are in the kitchen. Rope them up. I'm hungry and need a lampshade."

It is not that the Nazi regime had a patent on anti-Semitism, not as if the roots of this ancient prejudice and scapegoating did not travel deep and wide into the past of most European nations, not as if the majority of the world's population looked away when the first reports of the unbelievable parameters of the Holocaust began to leak into consciousness, not that the concept of collective guilt does not embrace all of us, but when analyzing and comparing the calculated evils of state-initiated genocide, the Holocaust stands unparalleled in human history. An event so unbearably evil that its remembrance is, in a sense, best left to the survivors, for even the best analytic, intellectual, philosophical or political attempts to explain it will fall hollow and short. Indeed, recent attempts to deny its existence is the most insidious form of what Rosenthal would call "killing the murdered twice."

Yet look we must, hear the voices of the survivors, read the accounts of the camps, look at the numbers burned into flesh and remember, even if memory itself is an untrustworthy instrument. For it is just these memories that give form to the mirror that we must hold up to our souls. It is a reflection that should claim no ownership in human consciousness, yet it lives on in all hate-inspired violence and racial prejudice.

"That's the difficulty in these times. Ideas, dreams and cherished hopes rise within us, only to meet the horrible truth and be shattered. It's a wonder I haven't dropped all my ideals, because they seem so absurd and impossible to carry out. Yet, I keep them because in spite of everything I still believe that people are really good at heart.

"I see the world gradually being turned into a wilderness. I hear the ever-approaching thunder, which will destroy us too. I can feel the sufferings of millions and yet, if I look up into the heavens I think it will come out all right and that peace and tranquility will return again." Anne Frank—The Diary.

The consistent arguments for a speedy reunification of Germany are based on an expressed belief that a strong, economically powerful, unified fatherland (Germany), controlled by NATO and the Soviet Union, will indeed bring a kind of peace and tranquility to post World War II Germany. As the G.D.R. loses over 2,000 of its citizens daily to the West, and the Eastern economy crumbles, the political and economic necessity of a United Germany is being posited as both necessary and unstoppable.

Max Lerner of the *NY Post* writes that "If we could order history according to our memories of trauma, I would continue to fight against any further enhancement of the power of a Germany that gave us Adolf Hitler. Nothing can extirpate the fact of the Holocaust." Patrick J. Buchanan, also writing for the *NY Post,* believes that "a strong, united, free Germany in the heart of Europe will be as great a triumph for America as a strong free Japan in the Far East."

Buchanan also compares the treatment of the East Germans by the Allies at the end of the war with the annihilation of the Jews during the Holocaust. In this, Buchanan is a political comrade of Heidegger's, who in response to a letter demanding that he be accountable for his support and reinforcement of Nazi ideology, wrote: "I can only add that instead of the "Jews" one should put "East Germans," with the difference that everything that happened since 1945 is known to all the world, while the bloody terror of the Nazi reality was kept secret from the German people."

Going even further in apologia for a new unified Germany, Henry Ashby Turner *(NY Times,* February 11, 1990) believes that fears of an economically powerful and militaristic Germany are for the most part unfounded.

"Some people think the Germans bear a hereditary taint that predisposes them to aggressive, even criminal, behaviors as a nation. Surely no one conversant with the record of humanity can seriously entertain the hackneyed notion of indelible national character."

Perhaps not. Perhaps not an indelible national character, but if history teaches us anything it is the indelibility and undeniability of anti-Semitism, a trait which goes beyond nation and national character, yet is, at the same time, ultimately expressed through both.

It also teaches us that each generation must struggle anew, and ofttimes start the process of remembrance again, if liberty and freedom are to be maintained. Indeed, since World War II our own country has witnessed great achievements in civil and human rights, while the last nine years under Reagan and Bush have shown us a precipitous slide backwards. Aided by a conservatively loaded Supreme Court, we have witnessed the roll back of both civil liberties and reproductive freedom.

Losing constitutional rights and privileges that we once thought to be sacrosanct has taught a new generation of Americans that there are no safe political harbors. Turner asks his readers, "How can Germans born since 1945 be held culpable for what happened before them?" Those in our own country who fight against any type of affirmative action program use just those types of arguments. Why, indeed, should I have to bear the burden of my ancestors 100 years ago who held Blacks as slaves?

Although each generation is, in a sense, a new beginning, we do not begin in a vacuum. We are all our parents children and have with us all the individual and collective societal baggage that attends it. Just as Americans must bear the burdens of a history that was based on the inhumanity of slavery, so must this generation of Germans deal with the reality of their past.

"Children of killers are not killers. They are children," according to Eli Weisel. I would only add that they have the responsibility of not forgetting that many of their parents, grandparents or other relatives were killers. Likewise, they must be sure not to fall victim to that seductive, pervasive disease of spiritual and historical amnesia that seems to afflict so much of the German population.

Primo Levi in *The Drowned and the Saved* speaks eloquently to the issue of German responsibility: "Let it be clear that to a greater or lesser degree all were responsible, but it must be just as clear that behind their responsibility stands that great majority of Germans who accepted in the beginning out of mental laziness, myopic calculation, stupidity and national pride the 'beautiful words' of Corporal Hitler, followed him, were swept away by his ruin, afflicted by deaths, misery and remorse and rehabilitated a few years later as the result of an unprincipled political game."

There is, of course, always the danger that by defining ultimate evil as German, we allow ourselves to pale in terms of our own individual responsibility. If the heart and head of the virus of anti-Semitism rests on the Kurfurstendaam, then the trunk and the limbs spread worldwide.

To posit that the German youth of today bear no direct responsibility for the Second World War and the Holocaust is true, but to then deny them any moral responsibility for dealing with its residual effects is moral cowardice.

Anti-Semitism may "sleep lightly" around the world, but it was in Germany that it awakened most fully. The children of the holocaust are everywhere.

We Must Share the Crime

MARGUERITE DURAS

Translated by D. G. Luttinger

There's an awesome amount of them. There's really monumental numbers of dead. Seven million Jews have been exterminated—carried in cattle cars, then gassed in specifically engineered death factories, then burned in specially built ovens. In Paris, people don't talk about the Jews as yet. Their babies were handed over to female officials responsible for strangling Jewish infants and experts in the art of execution by putting pressure on the carotid arteries. They smiled and said it was painless. This new countenance of death has been invented in Germany—organized, rationalized, manufactured before it met with outrage. You're amazed. . . . Some people will always be overcome by it, inconsolable. One of the grandest civilized nations in the world, the age-long capital of music, has just systematically murdered eleven million human beings with the absolute efficiency of a national industry. The whole world looks at the mountain, the mass of death dealt by God's creature to his fellow humans. Someone quotes the name of some German man of letters who's been very upset and become extremely depressed and to whom these matters have given much fodder for thought. If Nazi crime is not seen in world terms, if it isn't understood collectively, then that man in the concentration camp at Belsen who died alone but with the same communal soul and class cognition that made him undo a bolt on the railroad one night somewhere in Europe, without a leader, without a uniform, without a witness, has been betrayed. If you give a German and not a collective interpretation to the Nazi horror, you reduce the man in Belsen to regional dimensions. The only possible answer to this crime is to turn it into a crime committed by all humanity. To share it. Just as the idea of equality and brotherhood. In order to bear it, to stomach the idea of it, we must share the crime.

Ravages of War

JOSE EMILIO PACHECO

Translated by Katherine Silver

During recess we used to eat those kinds of cream tarts that no longer exist. We played in two gangs: Arabs and Jews. Israel had just been established and there was a war against the Arab League. The children who really were Jews and Arabs only insulted each other or fought when they spoke. Our professor, Bernardo Mondragón, said to them: You were born here. You are as Mexican as your fellow students. Don't pass on the hatred. After all that has happened (the endless massacres, the extermination camps, the atomic bomb, the millions and millions of deaths), the world of tomorrow, the world in which you will grow up and be men, should be a peaceful place, without crime, without vileness. A short laugh rang out from the back row. Mondragón watched us sadly, probably asking himself what will become of us over the years, how many evils and catastrophes are we yet to witness.

The extinguished brilliance of the Ottoman Empire still persisted like the light of a long-dead star. For me, a child of the Roman Quarter, both Jews and Arabs were "Turks." The "Turks" didn't seem as strange as Jim, who was born in San Francisco and spoke two languages without an accent; or Toru, who was brought up in a concentration camp for Japanese; or Peralta and Rosales. They did not pay tuition; they were on scholarship; they lived in the run-down neighborhood called the Doctors Quarter. The Highway of Piety—not yet renamed Cuauhtémoc Avenue—and Urueta Park formed the borderline between the Roman Quarter and Doctors. Little Rome was another town altogether. The Bag Man lurks there. The Great Kidnapper. If you go to Little Rome, my son, they will kidnap you, scratch your eyes out, cut off your hands and your tongue, then throw you out into the streets to beg, and the Bag Man will take everything you get. During the day he is a beggar; at night he is an elegant millionaire, thanks to the exploitation of his victims. The fear of being near Little Rome. The fear of riding the streetcar over the Coyoacán Avenue bridge: only rails and girders. Underneath runs the dirty River of Piety, which sometimes overflows when it rains.

Before the war in the Middle East, our class's main sport revolved around giving Toru a hard time. Slant eyes, Chinaman, ate the shit and away he ran. Watch out, Toro, I'm going to nail you up by the horns. I never joined in with the jeers. I thought about how I would feel if I were the only Mexican in a school in Tokyo; about how Toru must suffer when he sees those movies that portray the Japanese as gesticulating monkeys who died by the thousands. Toru was the best student in the class. He excelled in every subject. Always studying, with a book in his hands. He knew jujitsu. One time he got sick of it and almost tore Domínguez to pieces. He forced him to get down on his hands and knees and beg for forgiveness. Nobody messed with Toru after that. Today he manages a Japanese factory and employs four thousand Mexican slaves.

I am from the Irgun. I will kill you: I am from the Arab League. The battles in the desert began. We called it that because it was a courtyard of red earth—brick and volcanic rock dust—without any plants or trees, just a cement box in the back. It was built over a passageway leading from the house on the corner to the street across the way that was used as an escape route during the times of religious persecution. We thought this underground area was a vestige of some prehistoric era. Nevertheless, the Cristero war was closer to us at that time than our infancy is to us now. This was the religious war against reform in which many members of my mother's family participated as more than just sympathizers. Twenty years later she continued to worship martyrs like Father Pro and Anacleto González Flores. No one, on the other hand, remembered the thousands of dead peasants, the agrarian reform advocates, the rural professors, the press gangs.

I did not understand anything: war, any war, seemed to me to be the stuff of which movies are made. Sooner or later the good guys win (who are the good guys?). Fortunately, there had been no wars in Mexico since General Cárdenas squelched the Saturnino Cedillo uprising. This was difficult for my parents to believe, because their childhood, adolescence, and youth were spent against a background of constant battles and executions. But things seemed to be going well that year. Classes were constantly being called off so they could take us to the inaugurations of highways, avenues, sports arenas, dams, hospitals, ministries, enormous buildings.

As a rule, they were nothing more than a pile of rocks. The president inaugurated enormous unfinished monuments to himself. Hours and hours under the sun without so much as a sip of water— hey, Rosales, bring some lemons, they're great to quench your thirst, pass one over here—waiting for Miguel Alemán to arrive. Young, smiling, simpatico, shining, waving from aboard a cattle truck surrounded by his retinue. Applause, confetti, paper streamers, flowers, girls, soldiers (still wearing their French helmets), gunmen, the eternal little old lady who breaks through the military barricade and is photographed with El Señor Presidente as she hands him a bouquet of roses.

I had many friends, but my parents did not like any of them: Jorge because he was the son of a general who fought against the Cristeros; Arturo because his parents were divorced and he was looked after by an aunt who charged people to read their fortunes; Alberto because his widowed mother worked in a travel agency, and a decent woman should never work outside the home. That year Jim and I became friends. During these inaugurations, which had become a natural part of life, Jim would say: Today my father is going to come. And then: Do you see him? He is the one with the sky-blue tie. There he is, standing next to President Alemán. But nobody could distinguish him from all those other heads plastered with linseed oil or cream. But yes, they often published pictures of him. Jim carried the clippings around in his knapsack. Did you see my dad in *El Excélsior?* How strange: you don't look like him at all. Well, they say I look like my mother. I'm going to look like him when I grow up.

The Armenian Experience of Genocide

THE ZORYAN INSTITUTE

Mass murder of civilians and genocide—the organized extermination of an entire people—are often used by repressive regimes as tools of political intimidation and conflict resolution. Armed with increasingly sophisticated weapons as well as the means to legitimate their bloody exploits, governments have annihilated whole populations with impunity, confident that they can dictate the writing of history. Authoritarian rulers are also certain that the public forgets such tragedies easily and quickly. As militarism increases, worldwide resources become scarcer, and their distribution grows more unequal, "final solutions" become more attractive to governments in crisis.

The genocide of the Armenian people during the First World War was the final act in the long history of repression of Armenians by the Ottoman Turkish government. Along with other groups, Armenians were turned into an exploited and oppressed people by an increasingly repressive regime. To improve the lot of the largely peasant Armenian population, Armenian political parties had struggled long for a new social order based on equality between the various religious and ethnic groups as well as on political and economic justice. That vision contradicted the ideology of Turkish elites, both imperial and republican, which sought the solution to social problems in extreme nationalism, militarism, and turkification of subject peoples and lands.

The Genocide perpetrated by the Ittihad ve Terakke (Union and Progress) government beginning in 1915 is, in this context, significant for world history as well as the victim people. It is the first genocide in the twentieth century, the best documented, the most successful, and the least remembered. This event brought to an end three millennia of collective existence for Western Armenians in their homeland. Yet, for "strategic" considerations, it is justified and covered up by the current Turkish government as well as some of its allies.

Calculated Policies

In his *The Tragedy of Armenia* (1918) U.S. Ambassador to the Ottoman Empire and eyewitness to the tragedy Henry Morgenthau expresses his firm conviction that Armenians were the victims of a preconceived plan of annihilation. He cites numerous sources of information about the massacres, their nature, and their scope:

> *During the spring of 1914 they [the Ottoman government] evolved their plan to destroy the Armenian race.*
>
> *Now, as four of the Great Powers were at war with them and the two others were their allies, they thought the time opportune.*
> *. . . They concluded that, once they had carried out their plan,*

the Great Powers would find themselves before an accomplished fact and that their crime would be condoned. . . .

The facts contained in the reports received at the Embassy from absolutely trustworthy eyewitnesses surpass the most beastly and diabolical cruelties ever before perpetrated or imagined in the history of the world. The Turkish authorities had stopped all communication between the provinces and the capital in the naive belief that they could consummate this crime of ages before the outside world could hear of it. But the information filtered through the Consuls, missionaries, foreign travelers, and even Turks.

Renowned sociologist Irving L. Horowitz of Rutgers University points out the significance of the genocide of the Armenians by the Ittihadists as a precedent-setting case. In his study *Taking Lives: Genocide and State Power* (1980) Horowitz describes the Genocide as an act without parallel in any earlier era and "the fate of the Armenians as the essential prototype of genocide in the twentieth century." The civilized world, according to Horowitz, was too absorbed in its own horrors of the First World War to recognize the uniqueness of the destruction of the Armenian people.

Historian Howard Sachar of the George Washington University devotes considerable space to the Genocide in his *Emergence of the Middle East, 1914–1924* (1969). He argues that the Ittihadist regime viewed deportations and massacres as merely effective diplomacy, the realization of Sultan Abdul Hamid II's injunction that "the best way to finish with the Armenian Question is to finish with the Armenians." Sachar concludes, "By any standards this was surely the most unprecedented, indeed the most unimaginable racial annihilation, until then, in modern history."

In his history of the First World War, *The World Crisis* (1929), Winston S. Churchill describes the Armenian massacres:

In 1915, the Turkish Government began, and ruthlessly carried out, the infamous general massacre and deportation of Armenians in Asia Minor. . . . The clearance of the race from Asia Minor was about as complete as such an act, on a scale so great, could well be. It is supposed that about one and a quarter millions of Armenians were involved, of whom more than half perished. There is no rea-

sonable doubt that this crime was planned and executed for political reasons.

In her *Accounting for Genocide* (1979), political sociologist Helen Fein recounts Germany's perception of their allies' policy during the First World War. Count Wolf-Metternich, German Ambassador to the Ottoman Empire, understood that the Ittihadists sought to exterminate the Armenian people as an end in itself even though such a policy inhibited the war effort. He wrote the Reich Chancellor in June 1916:

> *I have discussed with Talaat Bey and Hallil Bey the deportation of the Armenian workers from Amanus stretch, which deportation hampers the conduct of the war. These measures, I told the ministers, among other things, gave the impression as if the Turkish government were itself bent on losing the war. . . . But no one any longer has the power to control the many-headed hydra of the Committee, to control the chauvinism and the fanaticism . . . there is not much to gain from the Armenians. . . . Turkification means to expel or kill everything non-Turkish.*

Helen Fein agrees with historian Ulrich Trumpener of Princeton University who, in his *Germany and the Ottoman Empire, 1914–1918* (1968), asserts that Germany was aware of and indifferent to the Ottoman policy of mass extermination.

Genocide as Radical Solution

The Genocide involved several premeditated steps, beginning with the disarming and emasculation of the Armenian population. In the early part of 1915, Armenian soldiers in the Ottoman army were removed from combat positions, disarmed, and transformed into road laborers. They were driven by the whips and bayonets of Turkish soldiers into the mountains, where they were murdered en masse.

At the same time Armenian civilians, who since the 1908 Young Turk revolution had the right to bear arms for their own protection, were ordered by the government to disarm. Most Armenians understood what their fate would be if they did not have the means to defend themselves—the disarming of Armenians before the Hamidian massacres of 1894–1896 was still an integral part of their collective consciousness. Many, nonetheless, surrendered their arms rather than provoke the hostility of the authorities. The arms they gave up were taken as evidence that a revolution was planned; the bearers were thrown into prison on charges of treason, tortured, and massacred shortly thereafter. The punishment of those suspected of concealing arms or discovered to be concealing arms was even more dreadful.

After the disarming of the population, the men in villages and towns throughout the Empire were issued official deportation orders by public criers and proclamations. The men were led away from their homes by Turkish soldiers and shot at the first desolate place.

Leo Kuper, a sociologist at the University of Southern California, describes the genocidal process in his study *Genocide:*

> *The emasculation of the Armenian population was completed by the culling of Armenian leaders. Throughout the country, the government arrested and deported the elite, the educated, the deputies, the publicists, the writers, the poets, the jurists, the advocates, the notaries, the civil servants, the doctors, the merchants, the bankers and generally all those with substantial means and influence. This measure was presumably designed to deprive Armenians of leadership and representation so that the deportations might be completed without public clamor and without resistance. The effect was to leave the Armenian population a defenseless and easy prey for the next stage, that of deportation.*

The Genocide continued throughout 1915 and 1916 with the elimination of the women, children, old men, and sick, who suffered a harsher fate than that of the young men. They were organized into caravans by the government and forced by Turkish soldiers to walk endlessly along prearranged routes. Their destination was the deserts of Syria and Mesopotamia, but few made it that far. Denied provisions for survival, many faced slow and painful deaths by thirst, hunger, exposure, and exhaustion. Others were killed outright by local Turks, Kurds, and Turkish soldiers, who attacked the caravans with regularity and impunity.

After Armenians were removed from their homes, the Ittihadists resettled non-Armenians, including many of the Turks who were driven out of Western Thrace during the Balkan wars, on Armenian land. In *Armenia: The Survival of a Nation,* Christopher Walker notes, "Government resettlement of Turks, Kurds, or Circassians was from this time onwards a central feature of the process of killing Armenians. Resettlement of refugees is too complicated a process to be conjured out of the air; the frequency with which it occurs in 1915 highlights again the deliberateness of government policy."

Eyewitness to Horror

By focusing on statements dealing with the overwhelming fact of the Genocide, its premeditated nature, and its numerical or geographical scope, there is a danger of losing sight of the individual human suffering referred to by such phrases as "untold horrors," "unparalleled brutality," "hellish massacres," "lethal savagery," and "unimaginable racial annihilation."

The following brief excerpts from the official British Blue Book, compiled by historian Arnold Toynbee at the direction of Lord Bryce, provide an idea of the inhumanity embodied in the Genocide:

> In Harpoot and Mezre the people have had to endure terrible tortures. They had their eyebrows plucked out, their breasts cut off, their nails torn off; their torturers hew off their feet or else hammer nails into them just as they do in shoeing horses. This is all done at nighttime, and in order that the people may not hear their screams and know their agony, soldiers are stationed round the prisons, beating drums and blowing whistles. . . . Harpoot has become the cemetery of the Armenians. [From a statement by a German eyewitness, communicated by the American Committee for Armenian and Syrian Relief]
>
> At the first large station a sight burst upon my view which, although I knew and was prepared for it, was nevertheless a shock. There was a mob of a thousand or more people huddled about the station and environs, and long strings of cattle-trucks packed to suffocation with human beings. It was the first glimpse of the actual

deportation of the Armenians. . . . There was no confusion, no wailing, no shouting, just a mob of subdued people, dejected, sad, hopeless, past tears. [From a narrative of a physician who had resided in Empire for ten years]

In volume 3 of the seven-volume *Source Records of the Great War* (1931), in which Talaat Pasha's infamous extermination orders are reprinted, appears a statement by Dr. Martin Niepage, the leader of the German missionary movement within the Ottoman Empire. He recorded the horror witnessed by German missionaries:

When I returned to Aleppo in September, 1915, from a three months' holiday at Beirut, I heard with horror that a new phase of Armenian massacres had begun which were far more terrible than the earlier massacres under Abdul-Hamid, and which aimed at exterminating, root and branch, the intelligent, industrious, and progressive Armenian nation, and at transferring its property to Turkish hands.

Herr Greif, of Aleppo, reported corpses of violated women lying about naked in heaps on the railway embankment at Tell-Abiad and Ras-el-Ain. Another, Herr Spiecker, of Aleppo, had seen Turks tie Armenian men together, fire several volleys of small shot with fowling pieces into the human mass, and go off laughing while their victims slowly perished in frightful convulsions. Other men had their hands tied behind their back and were rolled down steep cliffs. Women were standing below, who slashed those who had rolled down with knives until they were dead.

A German I know saw hundreds of Christian peasant women who were compelled, near Ourfa, to strip naked by the Turkish soldiers. For the amusement of the soldiers they had to drag themselves through the desert in this condition for days together in a temperature of 40° centigrade, until their skins were completely scorched. Another witness saw a Turk tear a child out of its Armenian mother's womb and hurl it against the wall.

As did many eyewitness survivors, Rev. Abraham Hartunian recorded his own experiences during the Genocide. His son, Rev. Vartan Hartunian, translated these memoirs as *Neither to Laugh Nor to Weep* (1968). The clergyman writes:

Many of our teachers, professors, and doctors—those of the educated class—were captured and with the words "So you are the intellect of this people!" had their heads placed in vises and squeezed till they burst.

Many children were herded out of the deserts, thrown alive into ditches, and covered over with dirt and sand, to smother beneath the earth. Many were thrown into rivers or dashed to the ground. Many were killed by ripping their jaws and tearing their faces in half. Many women were stripped naked and lined up, and, their abdomens slashed one by one, were thrown in ditches and wells to die in infinite agony. The Kaymakam [mayor] of Der-el-Zor, holding a fifteen-year-old girl before him, directed his words to a murderous band and then, throwing her to the ground, clubbed her to death with the order "So you must kill all Armenians, without remorse."

The atrocities witnessed by missionaries, relief workers, and survivors are confirmed by officials of the United States government, who were stationed at consulates throughout the Empire. American consuls sent numerous reports and dispatches between 1915 and 1918 to their superiors at the American embassy in Constantinople and the State Department in Washington, D.C.

Jesse B. Jackson, American consul at Aleppo for over a decade, described the Genocide in detail as he and his aides witnessed it:

One of the most terrible sights ever seen in Aleppo was the arrival early in August 1915 of some 5,000 terribly emaciated, dirty, ragged, and sick women and children. . . . These people were the only survivors of the thrifty and well-to-do Armenian population of Sivas, carefully estimated to have originally been over 300,000 souls!

From these camps the gendarmes took several hundred almost daily and pushed them on towards the desert beyond the reach of help, going from Aleppo first to Meskene, then to Hamam, Rakka, Sebha, Abou-Harari, and finally to Deir-el-Zor and the surrounding villages, about half way between Aleppo and Bagdad on the Euphrates river. At Meskene they died in such numbers that one of my employees who was sent there to distribute relief to the sufferers late in 1916 said that he had seen more than 150 long mounds where the dead had been buried in trenches (dug by themselves), wherein from 100 to 300 bodies had been buried. . . . He also told of having seen many hundreds of skeletons lying strewn along the highways between Aleppo and Deir-el-Zor and Aleppo and Ourfa at which no effort whatever had been made to bury.

It is without doubt a carefully planned scheme to thoroughly extinguish the Armenian race.

In a June 1915 report to the State Department the American consul general in Beirut conveyed his sense of the Ittihadist government's brutality:

Women with little children in their arms, or in the last days of pregnancy were driven along under the whip like cattle. Three different cases came under my knowledge where the woman was delivered on the road, and because her brutal driver hurried her along she died of hemorrhage. . . . Some women became so completely worn out and hopeless that they left their infants beside the road. Many women and girls have been outraged. At one place the commander of gendarmerie openly told the men to whom he consigned a large company, that they were at liberty to do what they choose with the women and girls.

Leslie A. Davis, American consul at Harput, explained the reality of the deportations in his communications:

I have visited their encampment a number of times and talked with some of the people. A more pitiable sight cannot be imagined. They are almost without exception ragged, filthy, hungry and sick. That is not surprising in view of the fact that they have been on the road for nearly two months with no change of clothing, no chance to wash, no shelter and little to eat. . . .

As one walks through the camp mothers offer their children and beg one to take them. In fact, the Turks have been taking their choice of these children and girls for slaves, or worse. . . .

There are very few men among them, as most of them have been killed on the road. All tell the same story of having been attacked and robbed by the Kurds. Most of them were attacked over and over again and a great many of them, especially the men, were killed. Women and children were also killed. Many died, of course, from sickness and exhaustion on the way and there have been deaths each day that they have been here. . . . Those who have reached here are only a small portion, however, of those who started. By continuing to drive these people on in this way it will be possible to dispose of all of them in a comparatively short time. . . .

Not many men have been spared, however, to accompany those who are being sent into exile, for a more prompt and sure method has been used to dispose of them. Several thousand Armenian men have been arrested during the past few weeks. These have been put in prison and each time that several hundred had been gathered up in that way they were sent away during the night. . . . There have been frequent rumors that all of these were killed and there is little doubt that they were. . . . The fate of all the others has been pretty well established by reliable reports of a similar occurrence on Wednesday, July 7. . . . On Wednesday morning they were taken to a valley a few hours' distant where they were all made to sit down. Then the gendarmes began shooting them until they had killed nearly all of them. Some who had not been killed by bullets were then disposed of with knives and bayonets. A few succeeded in breaking the rope with which they were tied to their companions and running away, but most of these were pursued and killed. A few succeeded in getting away. . . .

The entire movement seems to be the most thoroughly organized and effective massacre this country has ever seen.

The Terror of the State

From the Turkish government's point of view, the genocide of Armenians was the final solution to one aspect of a fundamental set of problems. Such problems also included the need to democratize political institutions, to implement agrarian reform, and to recognize Kurdish aspirations—problems which remain to be resolved. From the Armenian point of view, the Genocide constituted the violent end to a long and oppressive Ottoman rule which lacked respect for life and liberty. The Genocide also brutally stopped a process of development which had once promised a renewed life in a just and democratic society.

Before 1914, more than two million Armenians lived in the Ottoman Empire. By the end of the First World War no more than 100,000 Armenians remained in what is now Turkey. About a half million homeless refugees fled to Russian Armenia, other areas of the Middle East, Europe, and the Americas. Thus, at least 1.5 million Armenian lives were claimed by the Genocide. Survivors who live with tragic memories and their descendants who share the suffering are found in a score of countries today.

The fate of Armenians, according to Irving Horowitz, illustrates that different forms of state authority and different power elites can generate the appropriate ideology and mobilize the machinery of death necessary to exterminate a people. The Sultan began the destruction of the Armenian minority in the name of the Ottoman Empire. The Young Turks continued the process in the name of Turkish nationalism. The Kemalists, who replaced the defeated Young Turks in 1923, completed this process in the name of development and hegemonic integration. Horowitz concludes, "Hence, between 1893 and 1923 roughly 1,800,000 Armenians were liquidated, while another 1,000,000 were exiled, without a single political or military elite within the state assuming responsibility for the termination of the slaughter. . . ."

Helen Fein places the Genocide within its political context:

> The victims of twentieth-century premeditated genocide—the Jews, the Gypsies, the Armenians—were murdered in order to fulfill the state's design for a new order. War was used in both cases to transform the nation to correspond to the ruling elite's formula by eliminating groups conceived of as alien, enemies by definition.

In their joint study of Armenians for the Minority Rights Group, entitled *The Armenians* (1981), David Lang and Christopher Walker conclude as well that the Genocide was systematic and ably executed from the highest government level to meet pan-Turkic political aims. They write:

> The mass-murder was not just a matter of "isolated incidents." It was carefully thought out and planned months, if not years, in advance. Nor did it result from religious intolerance, though the Young Turks mobilized the innate fanaticism of the village Mullahs

and the greed of Turkish have-nots. There were in fact Muslim leaders who were shocked by the measures taken and protested against them.

Rejecting Genocide

For many, including the recognized and community-supported political parties in the Diaspora, accounting for the unpunished Genocide constitutes a fundamental aspect of Armenian aspirations for a free and collective national existence. That vision remains relevant; Armenians refuse to be relegated to the dustbin of history either through genocide or by its denial, even if that means being a burden on the conscience of humanity.

The Genocide, which ended three thousand years of Armenian life in Armenia, generated new claims, sanctioned in international law by the UN Convention on the Prevention and Punishment of Genocide. These include the recognition of the Genocide and the application of elementary justice. By international law, the present Turkish government bears responsibility for the crimes committed by its predecessors even if republican Turkey had repudiated those crimes—something it has consistently failed to do.

Unless principles of justice are called upon to prevail in relations between nations, mass extermination as a tool of political dominance may become more common in the future than it has been up to now. If Armenians and other victims of genocide do not do everything in their power to pursue their battle against genocide, they will have failed in their responsibility toward future generations. Then not only genocide, but the total destruction of humanity, will be looked upon with indifference.

Songs of Bread*

DIANA DER-HOVANESSIAN

You think I wrote from love.
You think I wrote from ease.
You imagine me singing as I walked
through wheat praising bread.
You imagine me looking from my window
at my children in the grass, my wife
humming, my dog running, my sun still
warm. But this notebook is drenched
in blood. It is written in blood
in a wagon rolling past yellow, amber,
gold wheat. But in the dark, in
the smell of sweat, urine, vomit.
The song of blue pitchers filled
with sweet milk, the song of silver
fountains welcoming home students,
the song of silo, barn, harvest,
tiller and red soil, all written
in the dark. The Turks allowed it.
What harm in a pen soon to be theirs,
a notebook to be theirs, a coat,
theirs, unless too much blood splattered.
You read and picture me in
a tranquil village, a church, on
the Bosporus, on a hillside, not
in anguish, not in fury, not wrenching
back the dead, holding the sun still
for a few more hours, making bread
out of words. This notebook you ransomed
dear friend, postponed, delayed my storm.
You see only its calm.

* Title of a group of poems written in prison in 1915 by the Armenian poet Daniel Varoujan
before his execution.

An Armenian Looking at Newsphotos of the Cambodian Deathwatch

DIANA DER-HOVANESSIAN

My sack of tiny
bones, bird
bones, my baby
with head so large
your thin neck bends,
my flimsy bag of breath,
all my lost cousins
unfed
wearing your pink flesh
like cloth
my pink rag doll
with head that grows
no hair,
eyes that cannot close,
my unborn past,
heaving your dry tears.

Massacre and Murderous Butchery: U.S. Conquest of the Philippines

MARK TWAIN AND OTHERS

Mark Twain commented on the Philippine war:[1]

> We have pacified some thousands of the islanders and buried
> them; destroyed their fields; burned their villages, and turned their
> widows and orphans out-of-doors; furnished heartbreak by exile to
> some dozens of disagreeable patriots; subjugated the remaining ten
> millions by Benevolent Assimilation, which is the pious new name

of the musket; we have acquired property in the three hundred concubines and other slaves of our business partner, the Sultan of Sulu, and hoisted our protecting flag over that swag.

And so, by these Providences of God—and the phrase is the government's, not mine—we are a World Power.

American firepower was overwhelmingly superior to anything the Filipino rebels could put together. In the very first battle, Admiral Dewey steamed up the Pasig River and fired 500-pound shells into the Filipino trenches. Dead Filipinos were piled so high that the Americans used their bodies for breastworks. A British witness said: "This is not war; it is simply massacre and murderous butchery."[2]

In November 1901, the Manila correspondent of the Philadelphia *Ledger* reported:

> *The present war is no bloodless, opera bouffe engagement; our men have been relentless, have killed to exterminate men, women, children, prisoners and captives, active insurgents and suspected people from lads of ten up, the idea prevailing that the Filipino as such was little better than a dog. . . . Our soldiers have pumped salt water into men to make them talk, and have taken prisoners people who held up their hands and peacefully surrendered, and an hour later, without an atom of evidence to show that they were even insurrectos, stood them on a bridge and shot them down one by one, to drop into the water below and float down, as examples to those who found their bullet-loaded corpses.*

Secretary of War Elihu Root responded to the charges of brutality: "The war in the Philippines has been conducted by the American army with scrupulous regard for the rules of civilized warfare. . . . with self-restraint and with humanity never surpassed."

In Manila, a Marine named Littletown Waller, a major, was accused of shooting eleven defenseless Filipinos, without trial, on the island of Samar. Other marine officers described his testimony:

> *The major said that General Smith instructed him to kill and burn, and said that the more he killed and burned the better pleased he would be; that it was no time to take prisoners, and that he was*

to make Samar a howling wilderness. Major Waller asked General Smith to define the age limit for killing, and he replied "Everything over ten."

In the province of Batangas, the secretary of the province estimated that of the population of 300,000, one-third had been killed by combat, famine, or disease. . . .

Racism, paternalism, and talk of money mingled with talk of destiny and civilization. In the Senate, Albert Beveridge spoke, January 9, 1900, for the dominant economic and political interests of the country:

> *Mr. President, the times call for candor. The Philippines are ours forever. . . . And just beyond the Philippines are China's illimitable markets. We will not retreat from either. . . . We will not renounce our part in the mission of our race, trustee, under God, of the civilization of the world. . . .*
>
> *The Pacific is our ocean. . . . Where shall we turn for consumers of our surplus? Geography answers the question. China is our natural customer. . . . The Philippines give us a base at the door of all the East. . . .*
>
> *No land in America surpasses in fertility the plains and valleys of Luzon. Rice and coffee, sugar and cocoanuts, hemp and tobacco. . . . The wood of the Philippines can supply the furniture of the world for a century to come. At Cebu the best informed man on the island told me that 40 miles of Cebu's mountain chain are practically mountains of coal. . . .*
>
> *I have a nugget of pure gold picked up in its present form on the banks of a Philippine creek. . . .*
>
> *My own belief is that there are not 100 men among them who comprehend what Anglo-Saxon self-government even means, and there are over 5,000,000 people to be governed.*
>
> *It has been charged that our conduct of the war has been cruel. Senators, it has been the reverse. . . . Senators must remember that we are not dealing with Americans or Europeans. We are dealing with Orientals. . . .*

From the Philippines, William Simms wrote:

I was struck by a question a little Filipino boy asked me, which ran about this way: "Why does the American Negro come . . . to fight us where we are much a friend to him and have not done anything to him. He is all the same as me and me all the same as you. Why don't you fight those people in America who burn Negroes, that make a beast of you . . . ?"

Early in 1901 an American general returning to the United States from southern Luzon, said:

One-sixth of the natives of Luzon have either been killed or have died of the dengue fever in the last few years. The loss of life by killing alone has been very great, but I think not one man has been slain except where his death has served the legitimate purposes of war. It has been necessary to adopt what in other countries would probably be thought harsh measures.

NOTES

1. For a history of the U.S. in the Philippines, Theodore Roosevelt's bigotry, and William James's and Mark Twain's part in the anti-imperialist movement of the times (c. 1901), where these quotations and others are assembled with linking commentary, see *A People's History of the United States,* Howard Zinn, Harper & Row, 1980, pp. 293–309 of "The Empire and the People."
2. "It was a time of intense racism in the United States. In the years between 1889 and 1903, on the average, every week, two Negroes were lynched by mobs—hanged, burned, mutilated. The Filipinos were brown-skinned, physically identifiable, strange-speaking and strange-looking to Americans. To the usual indiscriminate brutality of war was thus added the factor of racial hostility."—Howard Zinn

Hitler and the Gypsies:
A Genocide That Must Be Remembered

DORA E. YATES

It is more than time that civilized men and women were aware of the Nazi crime against the Gypsies, as well as the Jews. Both bear witness to the fantastic dynamic of the 20th-century racial fanaticism. For these two peoples shared the horror of martyrdom at the hands of the Nazis for no other reason than that they *were*—they *existed*.

The Gypsies, like the Jews, stand alone in the history of the world as an isolated race; both are, seemingly, miraculous survivals. Each of them has handed down its customs and traditions from generation to generation, as well as an ancient mother-tongue unknown to other peoples: the Jews, Hebrew, and the Gypsies, Romani. Throughout the ages both these peoples have been persecuted unmercifully: the Jews ostensibly because of the steadfastness with which they clung to their faith and because of their economic successes, and the Gypsies for exactly opposite reasons: because of their supposed want of religion and their aloofness and poverty.

In the Dark Ages both groups were subjected to the rack and wheel for preserving their own traditions and refusing to intermarry with the Gentiles. Anti-Gypsy legislation existed from about 1500 to 1800 CE in several countries of Europe (except Hungary and the Southeast), but in Spain and France it became a dead letter, and in England and Italy was seldom enforced. In point of severity there is little to choose between these laws, though those promulgated in Germany were more numerous than in other countries and perhaps somewhat more barbarous. By the 18th century, however, we are told (*Journal of the Gypsy Lore Society,* Third Series), "even the German conscience began to prick German writers: one was at great pains to justify inhumanity, another could not think without shuddering about 'the old, helpless, perhaps quite innocent Gypsy woman who was buried alive;' and a third asks, 'What judge would without judgment and right send a man to be hung who was guilty of no particular crime, but simply because he belonged to a particular race?' "

Before the close of the 18th century, such specific anti-Gypsy legislation had come to an end. The Romanis in Europe were left, more or less, to pursue their normal nomadic life, unharassed by any restrictions except the vagrancy laws and frontier regulations. Throughout the 19th and the first three decades of the 20th centuries, they earned their living by their own traditional occupations and handicrafts. In Bulgaria Gypsy men plied the trades of tinkers, comb-makers, iron-workers, gimlet-makers, spoon-makers, sieve-makers, and carpet-weavers, or reared the buffaloes by which their traveling carts were drawn. In Serbia smithcraft was considered the noblest oc-cupation for the Romani; while in Turkey Turkish Gypsies sank so low in the social scale that they accepted employment as common hangmen. Many sedentary Gypsies in Albanian towns were occupied as porters, donkey-drivers, brick- and tile-makers and scavengers, and their women-folk found employment as charwomen. In other coun-tries Gypsy fiddlers played at village weddings and dances; Gypsy horse-dealers and blacksmiths carried on a prosperous trade; old Gypsy women put their extensive medical knowledge and herbal lore at the service of the country folk among whom they dwelt; young Gypsy girls sold flowers in the streets of Bucharest and thereby gave to that capital much of its color and gaiety; and everywhere Gypsy fortune-tellers advised all and sundry as to their future fate.

After the First World War some of the more progressive countries of Eastern Europe tried out various cultural experiments to fit the Gypsies into modern life. At Uzhorod in Czechoslovakia, for instance, a special open-air school was started for Gypsy children, surrounded by a playground enclosed with trees, and the curriculum included drawing, handicrafts, and violin instruction—with the result that this institution became a general cultural center for the entire Gypsy col-ony and was able to produce a Gypsy theatrical company which was invited to tour the whole of Southern Czechoslovakia. Long before 1939 Gypsies had their own Romani newspapers in Rumania, Yugo-slavia, and Soviet Russia, and already there were Gypsy doctors, law-yers, teachers, engineers, priests, and authors of considerable ability.

No exact statistics are obtainable on the distribution of the Gyp-sies in Europe before the two world wars—their ceaseless migrations from one country to another within Europe itself, and from Europe to Australia and North and South America, make an accurate estimate impossible. But at the beginning of the 20th century Arthur Thesleff and other investigators gave the rough total of 1,422,000. For the present we have no accurate information as to how many have survived Hitler's New Order; but we do know that their losses were extremely heavy.

Hitler revived and exceeded the savagery of the old 17th and 18th century laws against the "Ziguener." He decreed the wholesale massacre of Gypsies in Central, Eastern, and Southern Europe, for the sole reason that they *were* Gypsies, a race of free men and women. In Germany, before he came into power, tribes of Sinti, Ungri, and Gelderari had wandered peacefully from one village to another, peddling their small wares, mending the kettles and pots and pans of the villagers, and providing the music at their festivities.

The precise date at which Hitler decided on the extermination of Gypsies is unknown to us, but it is obvious that the men and women of this dark-skinned, black-eyed race were not "Nordics." At first Hitler tried to persuade the German professors of ethnography and anthropology to declare that the Gypsies were non-Aryans, and many men of learning were interned for refusing to deny the Indo-Aryan origin of the Romani people and their language. So Hitler and his gangsters then chose to classify the whole race as "asocial"—i.e., a nomadic people who did not fit into his New Order, and a proper object for genocide.

Of the hideous deeds of barbarity towards the Gypsies in Germany itself, we possess no written testimony. But from trustworthy interviews with "Ziguener" whose relatives were liquidated at the Belsen and other concentration camps, it has been estimated that of the five thousand nomadic Gypsies who roamed the roads of the Reich in 1939, less than seven hundred are alive today.

Reliable data on what actually happened in Nazi-occupied countries during the war are naturally difficult to secure. But from the evidence supplied by survivors I will quote two typical examples given by literate Gypsies from Latvia and Czechoslovakia respectively. The first of these is an account written by the Lettish Gypsy, Vanya Kochanowski, a university student who managed eventually to escape into France, "a living skeleton, with no flesh on my bones, but with feet swollen to the size of an elephant's paws."

"Before 1940," he writes, "life in Latvia was very wonderful. We Gypsies enjoyed absolute freedom and we could live and study as we wished. Anyone who wanted to work could earn a good livelihood, but work was not compulsory. Everyone carried on his own life according to his wishes. Then in 1940 our 'liberators' appeared from the East. Free discussion came to an end . . . but the Soviet government treated us Gypsies well, and although we were obliged to work hard and to attend school or university the Tziganes were satisfied with their regime. . . . But that stage did not last long. The new 'liberators'—the Nazis—were a hundred times worse than any medieval oppressors, and deportations and tortures became the order of the day. All Jews were herded into ghettos and soon the forests near Riga became a veritable charnel-house. . . ."

In Eastern Latvia all the Gypsies were assembled in three towns, Rezekne, Ludza, and Vilane. At Ludza they were locked up in a large synagogue where they died, in hundreds, of hunger and disease. When Kochanowski succeeded in telephoning to Ludza, the only reply he received was: "The Gypsies have already been reported to the forests" —the Nazi code phraseology for "murdered." The bitter protest he then lodged with official Nazi headquarters was met with the retort: "If you cannot prove to me that an adequate number of Gypsies are decent, hard-working folk, you will every one of you be exterminated."

So, with the collaboration of the chief of the Latvian Gypsies, Janis Lejamanis, this young student set to work to compile a register of *"Tziganes honnetes."* Then, in accordance with the ironic cruelty of the Nazi authorities, who thought the boy had had no education, he was ordered to write a dissertation proving that the Gypsies were Aryans. This, however, he accomplished satisfactorily and in scholarly fashion, giving as his source Miklosich's *Mundarten der Ziguener in Europa.* At last there came a decree that the Gypsies were not to be liquidated. But the "order of release" was diabolically delayed until it was too late: it arrived at 2 a.m., exactly two hours after fifteen to twenty-five hundred Gypsies had been massacred. Kochanowski himself, then a youth of strong physique, was spared, and in 1943 with other Lettish students sent to work for the Nazis, often for thirty-six hours on end under deadly fire from Russian troops, outside Leningrad. He was later imprisoned in a gruesome underground cell at Kaunas (Kovno), from the effects of which experience he still suffers in a sanitorium in France.

The second piece of evidence was contained in a letter written by Antonin Daniel to S. E. Mann of the British Ministry of Information, who before the war was lecturer in English at the Masaryk University in Brno and knew this Gypsy student well. In Czechoslovakia, in pre-war days, there was at Oslavany a flourishing colony of some one hundred and fifty Gypsy men, women, and children who contentedly followed their own trades and had made themselves acceptable to the country folk in that district by their skill as basket-makers, their exceptional knowledge of horses, and above all by the magic of their music. After the war Mr. Daniel wrote to Mr. Mann: "The whole Oslavany colony was taken a few years ago by the Nazis to Oswiecim, where they were done to death. There were only five survivors, among them myself, my sister, and my mother."

The Belgian review *Message* of November 13, 1942, reported a crime in Serbia more horrible than any in the three centuries of anti-Gypsy legislation: "One of the most recent crimes of the Germans seems to us to surpass by far all the others, because in addition to the suffering it gave rise to, it destroyed gentleness and beauty: all the Gypsies of Serbia have been massacred! . . . These merchants of po-etry, prognostications, lies, and songs were hunted down on the roads over which they fled, mounted on their galloping scarecrows of horses, their rolling caravans full of cries, color, and mystery."

At that date it was impossible to get any confirmation of this tale of terror, but since then the following authentic evidence has been collected by the Gypsy Lore Society (of England) from eyewitnesses, Gypsies and others, who had survived these holocausts. From Sarajevo Professor Rade Uhlik, whose carefully corroborated evidence is indisputable, writes:

"Before the war no Gypsy settlements had ever been more prosperous and self-supporting: today they are utterly derelict, and the Gypsy survivors have fled to Northeast Bosnia. . . . In so-called 'Independent' Croatia some twenty-eight thousand Gypsies were mercilessly butchered, and this computation, if not strictly reliable, is certainly underestimated. For the few children of fortune who did manage to escape from the hell of concentration camps and crematoria relate with horror that it was among a hundred thousand or so candidates for death that they witnessed the most awful and heart-rending scenes, when these barbarians tore Gypsy children from their mothers and fathers and hurled them into the crematory ovens. . . . The whole of Gypsydom in Croatia between the rivers Sava and Drava have been exterminated. They were massacred chiefly as 'Non-Aryans' —what a terribly ironic fate for the oldest Indo-Aryan race in existence!—being so designated on racial-political grounds, but also because they professed the Greek Orthodox faith. . . . I have to report with deep distress that their splendid, unique dialect of Romani has now become extinct. Only a few adult men, who at the outbreak of hostilities happened to be in prison, have survived the wholesale massacre. And since this remnant (perhaps one per cent of the whole number of Gypsies), having become nervous wrecks, are also useless from the biological point of view, owing to the total extermination of the women and children, there can be no Gypsy posterity for them— or for the world."

M. Frederic Max, of the French Embassy, early in 1946 sent us a first-hand account of the treatment of the Gypsies in Nazi concentration camps. Though himself never at Auschwitz "where thousands of Gypsies were interned and where whole tribes were sent to the gas chamber," he received faithful reports from a convoy of surviving Gypsies who came to Buchenwald in May 1944, which reports he confirmed by information from non-Gypsies, chiefly Jews, who had the rare good luck to return from that camp of death.

At Buchenwald the Gypsies from Germany, Bohemia, and Poland, he says, were lodged together in a block of "Blacks," so called because the inmates of this part of the camp were branded on the chest with a black triangle, to distinguish them as "asocials" from political prisoners, German law-breakers, and religious adversaries, who bore respectively a red, green, or violet stigma.

At Birkenau camp, the antechamber to Auschwitz itself, the Gypsies from Slovakia and the South of Poland were subjected to unspeakable tortures before being consigned to the gas chambers. "Many Gypsy women were selected for the 'experimental pavilion,' where German doctors experimented with artificial impregnation followed by abortion." In January 1945, before the approach of the Russian Army, the Auschwitz camp was evacuated, and the prisoners were driven westward by long forced marches without food, so that many of them died of cold and hunger or exhaustion or were suffocated in the barns into which they were crowded at night. Others were beaten to death by the SS or murdered in the forests by the Volkssturm. Very few survived.

In Dr. Bendell's evidence, given in the Belsen trial at Luneberg (as reported in the London *Daily Telegraph* of October 2, 1945), the information supplied by M. Max is confirmed by the statement that "of 11,000 Gypsies in a special camp at Auschwitz all were killed except 1,500 selected for working parties," i.e., slave labor. But no further corroboration of this cold-blooded mass murder is needed beyond the callous sworn testimony of the Nazi commandant of Auschwitz himself, Rudolf Franz Ferdinand Hoess, as published by William S. Shirer in *End of a Berlin Diary.*

Throughout the war young Gypsies who regained their freedom, together with hundreds of others who had never come under the Nazi heel, devoted their liberty to helping the Maquis and other resistance groups in their fight against Hitler, and more than one escaped prisoner-of-war has had reason to thank his Gypsy hosts who passed him from camp to camp till a neutral country was reached. No wonder that a young Gypsy writer recently suggested that "the United Nations institute an enquiry into the source of those monstrous Nazi orders to exterminate our race . . . so that the Gypsy martyrs at Auschwitz be avenged, like those of France or Poland, not by the fury of barbarism but by the hand of Justice."

It would be proper, also, for the nations to see that the Gypsy survivors who may find a refuge among them are treated with decency and respect, and allowed to lead their own lives in their own way, unharassed by the authorities. Since peace came to the world, many hidebound government officials seem to regard the Gypsies as an "anachronism." There are protection societies for wild birds, wild flowers, and other rarities—but there is no protection, even in America, for wild Gypsies.

"What we Gypsy survivors desire," declared Mateo Maximoff, a talented Romani author now with his people in Montreuil-sous-Bois, in France, "is complete liberty—that is the right to travel freely in the pursuit of our various trades, which would mean that facilities to cross frontiers should be extended to all Gypsies. . . . Just as no one could prevent the flower from budding or the bird from making his nest in the spring, so no one should stop the Gypsy from wandering over the face of the globe. For our race is a part of nature. We bring joy and gaiety to the villages through which we pass, because wherever we go we carry with us that element of mystery that intrigues the whole world."

History has proved again and again that the well-meaning but misguided attempts of philanthropists and missionaries to cure the Gypsies of their nomadism will never succeed. Though they may settle down contentedly in their winter quarters and send their children to school regularly during six months of the year, as soon as spring returns, "wanderlust" will attack them and the urge to take to the road prove irresistible. If Gypsies are freed from public interference, they will find their own way of fitting into the modern world and contributing their own unique value to their fellowmen.

Hiroshima Was a War Crime

SHIGETOSHI IWAMATSU

An Eyewitness Account

I, myself, suffered from the atomic bomb in Nagasaki on August 9, 1945. Since then, having reflected upon my own experience, I have been appealing continuously to the world for an understanding of the effects of nuclear weapons and for eliminating nuclear arms and energy from the world.

I was a student at the time of the burning of Hiroshima and Nagasaki. To assist the war effort, all students in Japan worked in factories except those who went to the battlefield. My own work was at the Mitsubishi Ordinance Factory making torpedoes for Japanese military use.

After the bombing of Hiroshima, Japanese military headquarters announced that the city had suffered slight damage; nothing very serious. But on the morning of August 9, when I was at the torpedo factory, there was an air-raid warning. A few American planes flew over without dropping bombs and soon the "all clear" signal sounded. We went back to the factory, but later, at 11:02 a.m., I saw an extremely bright flash of light through the window.

At that moment, there was only time to think: What happened? Electrical trouble? And then, all around me, the slate roof and walls, and the windows were smashed, with fragments flying everywhere. Many of the people in the factory were killed instantly or died that night or a few days later as a result of burns from heat rays, shock waves or radiation. The factory was located eight-tenths of a mile from the epicenter of the blast.

I ran from the site toward a northern suburb, fearing a second attack. The fence surrounding the factory as well as the houses nearby had been instantly destroyed. Many other survivors were also running in the same direction, under the strange, dark sky covered by the mushroom cloud generated by the atomic bomb blast.

The scene was like hell. Wounded people were running with torn-off skin hanging down like old rags, with bloodied heads and faces blackened from the blast.

About an hour later, in the garden of a doctor's house, I saw a nurse who had come from a nearby town to look after the people. She was crying after she glanced at the sufferers, because she could not bear to look at the seriously wounded. Wanting to make my way to my home, I returned to a bridge near the factory, but the fire was still burning so fiercely that I could not get through. I decided to stay at a railway bridge, where I saw a lot of school girls who lay on the ground, with eyes shut and breathing faintly but without visible hurt. They must have died shortly thereafter because of the invisible radio-activity.

The Victims Remember

I remember feeling a tremendous sense of despair and hopelessness, thinking about the war and the fate of Japan. I thought very little about myself and the miracle that my life had been spared.

After several hours, I was carried to a city far from Nagasaki by the rescue train which came from the north and stopped some distance from Nagasaki station. I saw a lot of dead or dying victims lying on the floor of the train like hurt animals.

After spending the night in a hall of the primary school I returned by train and walked through the completely devastated streets of Nagasaki. I saw many charred corpses which, I believe, nobody could bear to look at. At this point I was exposed to a great quantity of induced radioactivity and nuclear fallout in addition to the instantaneous radioactivity at the time of explosion.

Since that time, those who suffered from the bombing have been earnestly appealing to the world to take heed of their pain, agony, bitter life, anger, rage, despair and sorrow. These appeals have been almost in vain. . . .

Whenever I lecture to my class about the atomic bombs which the United States dropped on two inhabited cities in Japan, I first illustrate various Japanese war crimes, before and during World War II, which are much more grave than was generally adjudged by the International Military Tribunal. This is because I believe that the suffering inflicted by the atomic bomb, however incredibly tragic that was, must be protested to the world only after Japanese war crimes have been severely criticized by the Japanese themselves.

My own historic field of vision is not shared by the majority of atomic bomb victims. They forget the people who were murdered, shot, tortured, enslaved, plundered, burned and violated by the ferocious Japanese imperialist army of the Tenno Emperor system. Only a minority remembers. . . .

Both Sides Guilty

Japanese war crimes are not effaced by the bitter aftermath of the atomic bombing, even though the devastation might be termed genocide and the resulting diseases of the sufferers are incurable forever. Japanese crimes were another type of genocide, which can be atoned for only by Japanese efforts toward peace and international friendship.

What can we learn from all of this? The American crime of dropping atomic bombs on two Japanese cities is without parallel in world history. But the imperialist Japanese attacks on Korea, China, Southeast Asia, the United States, the United Kingdom and Holland were extremely serious war crimes, which cannot be nullified by the U.S. crime of dropping atomic bombs.

But the U.S. crime is not nullified because of previous Japanese war crimes. Americans have guilt to bear even though the Japanese committed serious war crimes. The war crimes of both countries do not cancel each other out. The only right approach is to judge by criteria composed of humanistic, social, international and global viewpoints. According to this method, it must be concluded that Japanese aggression and atrocities were serious crimes and, at the same time, the

American dropping of the atomic bombs was a grave outrage. Each nation should consider its own crimes, apologize to each other, atone, and try to build a peaceful world through new and higher steps. . . .

The brutal mass murder and destruction wrought by atomic bombs at Hiroshima and Nagasaki has been underestimated. They have been labeled infants' toys compared with the far more powerful weapons in the world's expanding nuclear stockpile.

This underestimation has generated not only the low estimation of the meaning of the U.S. atomic bombing of Japan, but also the opinion that the nuclear arms race is necessary as a deterrent.

But in truth, use of atomic bombs was the supreme offense against humanity which must not be repeated. I know this not only because of my own experience but also because of what I can see of the political, military, racial and other factors that contributed to the dropping of bombs:

· The United States dropped the genocide weapons on Hiroshima and Nagasaki, even though there was no need to do so. President Truman's explanation was only an awkward excuse. By that time Japan's war potential had decreased to a minimum. It had practically no defending force left.

· The United States decided to use the atomic bombs not on Germany but on Japan in the autumn of 1944, when the Allies already knew the surrender of both Japan and Germany was imminent. The selection of Japan might well have been motivated by the racism which regards the yellow Asian with contempt.

· The United States raced to complete the bombs as soon as possible —before the Japanese could surrender, which would have been in the near future. The rush to complete the bombs was not to achieve Japanese submission but for another aim.

An Unnecessary Deed

What was this aim? In choosing the cities upon which the bombs were to be dropped, U.S. authorities preferred those with many munitions factories and laborers, but no defense forces. Tokyo, where the Tenno, the political and military leaders, lived, and Kyoto, a traditional city, were excluded. The majority of the laborers had been drafted for active military service during the war, and the people who were working in the factories were old farmers, tradespeople or office workers, women and young students. There were also Koreans, who had been violently taken from their homeland, and prisoners of war. There were many houses and schools surrounding the factories. Most of the people who were killed or injured by the genocide weapons were not soldiers but civilians—the elderly, women and children, Koreans and unarmed prisoners.

The atomic bombing did not aim at—nor did it bring about—Japanese submission. The Tenno and other Japanese top leaders decided to surrender not because Hiroshima and Nagasaki were destroyed but because of Soviet entry into the Pacific war on August 8.

The devastation of two cities did not cause Japan's top leaders to surrender to the Allies because they did not care that much about the people's distress and sorrow. Because they cherished the Tenno system Soviet participation was the largest and final shock to them. They discussed the "enemy's" guarantee that the Japanese could retain the Tenno system. This was the deciding factor.

• Atomic bombs were the product of the energetic collaboration of eminent scientists, including many Nobel Prize winners. In Japan, an example of collaboration of scientists to devise cruel weapons is that of Ishii's group, which worked on biological weapons. But the military-university-industrial complex was established in the United States after the Manhattan Project.

• The United States occupation policy in Japan should be seen as an extension of the brutality of the atomic bombing. The United States suppressed freedom of discussion, speech and writing, especially on the part of atomic bomb survivors. They could not relate their own experience and appeal against further fission explosions. Letters and newspapers were checked for a time. U.S. authorities prohibited publication of the experience of survivors and the photographing of the devastation.

Cameramen of the Japan Cinema Company, working in collaboration with the academic investigation team sponsored by the Education Ministry of Japan, were captured in Nagasaki by the U.S. Military Police on October 17, 1945. All members of the camera team were forced to return to Tokyo and were confined in a room of the building that served as American military General Headquarters. There they edited their films of the devastated Hiroshima and Nagasaki. Those films were then all sent to the U.S. Army. But the camera team dared to make a secret copy, at the risk of death, for the future use of the Japanese people.

A Brief History of Women in a Man's World

MARILYN FRENCH

1. Mesopotamia

For three and a half million years of human life on earth, women were central in society. They did not lose status and rights until states began to form: a state is by definition dominated by an elite which always gains power through war. The city-states of Sumer rose in Mesopotamia around 3500 B.C.E. At first, women held power as queens and priestesses, but within a millennium, a priest–warrior elite had made innovations that degraded them. It invented prostitution by forcing female slaves to sell sex to earn money for the temple; few Sumerian women retained rights over their own bodies: royal women and priestesses were required to be chaste; female slaves' bodies were at their owners' disposal. The Reforms of Urukagina introduced a double standard, laws that apply only to women. One read, if a woman speaks in an (illegible) way to a man, her mouth shall be crushed with a fired brick. They named a new crime, adultery, which only women could commit.

Around 1300 B.C.E. the Assyrians conquered Mesopotamia and carried the degradation of women to its ultimate. Assyrian laws refer to women as if they were animals raised by a male owner: men could buy, sell, punish, or kill them. Girls never inherited and were sold into marriage. Virginity was required: brides found nonvirgins could be returned to their fathers or killed. A man could repudiate his wife without compensating her father. Men could legally fornicate with any woman unowned by another man, but the husband of an unfaithful wife could kill her and her lover or take the lover to court. Punishment was usually private, and courts entrusted it to the husband with the condition that if he killed her lover, he must also kill his wife. A wife who took property from a husband who was ill or died was killed.

Privately, an Assyrian husband could scourge his wife, pull out her hair, bruise and destroy her ears, but if he wanted to flog her, tear out her breasts, or cut off her nose or ears, he had to do it in public. Infanticide, legal and common, was a male prerogative—fathers decided which baby daughters would live or be killed. But women who aborted themselves or others were subject to the severest punishment in the Middle Assyrian code: they were impaled. Only women could commit abortion, just as only women could commit adultery. For a woman to make such a decision was a crime against the state as grave as high treason or assault on the king. The punishment is so savage because abortion subverted the power of the patriarchal father, surrogate for the patriarchal ruler, who alone has the right to kill.

2. Athens

Athenian law of the 6th century B.C.E. permitted infanticide by abandonment. Some fathers chose to raise more than one son; few raised more than one daughter. Some killed all daughters or raised them to be family servants. Babies left in conspicuous places were found and raised as slaves in brothels; if a baby was hidden, she died. Girls were fed little (and almost no protein) and were married at twelve to fourteen to men over thirty. Once married they spent the rest of their lives at work, confined in the home-workshop. Citizen men did not work. Athens had to pass laws to force men to marry: many were homosexual and married only to obey the law. But all men married late and many were killed in the frequent wars. Most were dead by 45, leaving young widows to be passed on to another husband to bear more children. Despite high war casualties, women had shorter lives: men averaged 45 years, women 36, from poor diet, giving birth before the body was fully formed, and poor living conditions.

Athens's founding myth was the war between Greek heroes and the Amazons, a society of women soldiers, brave, strong, and skilled. After the ninth century B.C.E., Athenian art and literature abound with portrayals of Greek men stabbing and clubbing naked Amazons, and carrying them off for rape—over 800 depictions survive in its art. Athenian men were obsessed with rape: major Olympian gods commit 395 rapes in the Greek myths. Several early myths depict rape-marriage, giving social sanction to force. Men used force even during sex with prostitutes, as shown in paintings on drinking cups used in symposia. The symposia immortalized by Plato were drinking and sex parties held in the men's quarter of private homes. The men's quarter, the largest and most luxurious part of the house, often the only room in the house with a mosaic floor, was a dining room with platforms for couches, entered directly from the street. Wives cleaned it and provided food, then withdrew. Men entertained other men with women hired for the evening. Their drinking cups are decorated with scenes of anal copulation with prostitutes forced to bend over for men with knives, men beating prostitutes, and older prostitutes forced to perform fellatio. The women are always naked, the men clothed. Men with complete control over women still needed to beat them.

3. The body is the ultimate contact point of power. —Michel Foucault

4. The feminist revolution has eased laws and customs constraining women in many parts of the world, but the patriarchal division of power and responsibility has not changed. To alter it, everyone, women and men, must have the basic power over their own bodies. We have a natural right to bodily integrity. Men's right is violated when they are raped, assaulted, or forced to go to war. Women may also die or be injured in war, but women's bodies are *systematically* violated by men.

Nature decrees that only women give birth; bearing the responsibility and burden of procreation, women and women alone have the right to decide whether or not to procreate. But Nature does not decree that only women raise children. The burden of producing the human race should not be borne entirely by half of it. The very people who deny women the power to choose whether or not to reproduce insist a child is each woman's personal responsibility after it is born. Society as an entity makes no effort to make childrearing possible. Individuals may choose not to be parents, but all of us are responsible for creating a world in which reproduction is not the heavy burden it is now, one in which a woman can have a child and support it at the same time.

To create a world fit for human life, everyone, women and men, must take responsibility for the necessary. We must build a society centered on reproduction because children are the most fragile of the three necessities: children, the human future, need a safe, healthy, felicitous environment or they grow warped or sick or die. They must be centers: not of obsessive attention, laden with material possessions, but of human concern. All our acts should be directed at creating a society in which all children would receive food, medical care, and education, and live on a healthy planet, in safe neighborhoods with a continuity of community, art and learning and delight. A society that provided a safe, healthy world for children, female bodily autonomy, and shared power and responsibility would be one in which we would not be spending most of our resources on weapons to kill our children, relations between the sexes would be reliably mutual and affectionate, and every child would be a wanted child.

Women's Brains

STEPHEN JAY GOULD

In the prelude to *Middlemarch,* George Eliot lamented the unfulfilled lives of talented women:

> Some have felt that these blundering lives are due to the inconve-
> nient indefiniteness with which the Supreme Power has fashioned
> the natures of women: if there were one level of feminine incompe-
> tence as strict as the ability to count three and no more, the social lot
> of women might be treated with scientific certitude.

Eliot goes on to discount the idea of innate limitation, but while she wrote in 1872, the leaders of European anthropometry were trying to measure "with scientific certitude" the inferiority of women. Anthropometry, or measurement of the human body, is not so fashionable a field these days, but it dominated the human sciences for much of the nineteenth century and remained popular until intelligence testing replaced skull measurement as a favored device for making invidious comparisons among races, classes, and sexes. Craniometry, or measurement of the skull, commanded the most attention and respect. Its unquestioned leader, Paul Broca (1824–80), professor of clinical surgery at the Faculty of Medicine in Paris, gathered a school of disciples and imitators around himself. Their work, so meticulous and apparently irrefutable, exerted great influence and won high esteem as a jewel of nineteenth-century science.

Broca's work seemed particularly invulnerable to refutation. Had he not measured with the most scrupulous care and accuracy? (Indeed, he had. I have the greatest respect for Broca's meticulous procedure. His numbers are sound. But science is an inferential exercise, not a catalog of facts. Numbers, by themselves, specify nothing. All depends upon what you do with them.) Broca depicted himself as an apostle of objectivity, a man who bowed before facts and cast aside superstition and sentimentality. He declared that "there is no faith, however respectable, no interest, however legitimate, which must not accommodate itself to the progress of human knowledge and bend before truth." Women, like it or not, had smaller brains than men and, therefore, could not equal them in intelligence. This fact, Broca argued, may reinforce a common prejudice in male society, but it is also a scientific truth. L. Manouvrier, a black sheep in Broca's fold, rejected the inferiority of women and wrote with feeling about the burden imposed upon them by Broca's numbers:

> *Women displayed their talents and their diplomas. They also invoked philosophical authorities. But they were opposed by* numbers *unknown to Condorcet or to John Stuart Mill. These numbers fell upon poor women like a sledge hammer, and they were accompanied by commentaries and sarcasms more ferocious than the most misogynist imprecations of certain church fathers. The theologians had asked if women had a soul. Several centuries later, some scientists were ready to refuse them a human intelligence.*

Broca's argument rested upon two sets of data: the larger brains of men in modern societies, and a supposed increase in male superiority through time. His most extensive data came from autopsies performed personally in four Parisian hospitals. For 292 male brains, he calculated an average weight of 1,325 grams; 140 female brains averaged 1,144 grams for a difference of 181 grams, or 14 percent of the male weight. Broca understood, of course, that part of this difference could be attributed to the greater height of males. Yet he made no attempt to measure the effect of size alone and actually stated that it cannot account for the entire difference because we know, a priori, that women are not as intelligent as men (a premise that the data were supposed to test, not rest upon):

> We might ask if the small size of the female brain depends exclusively upon the small size of her body. Tiedemann has proposed this explanation. But we must not forget that women are, on the average, a little less intelligent than men, a difference which we should not exaggerate but which is, nonetheless, real. We are therefore permitted to suppose that the relatively small size of the female brain depends in part upon her physical inferiority and in part upon her intellectual inferiority.

In 1873, the year after Eliot published *Middlemarch*, Broca measured the cranial capacities of prehistoric skulls from L'Homme Mort cave. Here he found a difference of only 99.5 cubic centimeters between males and females, while modern populations range from 129.5 to 220.7. Topinard, Broca's chief disciple, explained the increasing discrepancy through time as a result of differing evolutionary pressures upon dominant men and passive women:

> The man who fights for two or more in the struggle for existence, who has all the responsibility and the cares of tomorrow, who is constantly active in combating the environment and human rivals, needs more brain than the woman whom he must protect and nourish, the sedentary woman, lacking any interior occupations, whose role is to raise children, love, and be passive.

In 1879, Gustave Le Bon, chief misogynist of Broca's school, used these data to publish what must be the most vicious attack upon women in modern scientific literature (no one can top Aristotle). I do not claim his views were representative of Broca's school, but they were published in France's most respected anthropological journal. Le Bon concluded:

> In the most intelligent races, as among the Parisians, there are a large number of women whose brains are closer in size to those of gorillas than to the most developed male brains. This inferiority is so obvious that no one can contest it for a moment; only its degree is worth discussion. All psychologists who have studied the intelligence of women, as well as poets and novelists, recognize today that they represent the most inferior forms of human evolution and that they are closer to children and savages than to an adult, civilized man. They excel in fickleness, inconstancy, absence of thought and logic, and incapacity to reason. Without doubt there exist some distinguished women, very superior to the average man, but they are as exceptional as the birth of any monstrosity, as, for example, of a gorilla with two heads; consequently, we may neglect them entirely.

Nor did Le Bon shrink from the social implications of his views. He was horrified by the proposal of some American reformers to grant women higher education on the same basis as men:

> A desire to give them the same education, and, as a consequence, to propose the same goals for them, is a dangerous chimera. . . . The day when, misunderstanding the inferior occupations which nature has given her, women leave the home and take part in our battles; on this day a social revolution will begin, and everything that maintains the sacred ties of the family will disappear.

Sound familiar?*

I have reexamined Broca's data, the basis for all this derivative pronouncement, and I find his numbers sound but his interpretation ill-founded, to say the least. The data supporting his claim for increased difference through time can be easily dismissed. Broca based

---

* When I wrote this essay, I assumed that Le Bon was a marginal, if colorful, figure. I have since learned that he was a leading scientist, one of the founders of social psychology, and best known for a seminal study on crowd behavior, still cited today (*La psychologie des foules*, 1895), and for his work on unconscious motivation.

his contention on the samples from L'Homme Mort alone—only seven male and six female skulls in all. Never have so little data yielded such far ranging conclusions.

In 1888, Topinard published Broca's more extensive data on the Parisian hospitals. Since Broca recorded height and age as well as brain size, we may use modern statistics to remove their effect. Brain weight decreases with age, and Broca's women were, on average, considerably older than his men. Brain weight increases with height, and his average man was almost half a foot taller than his average woman. I used multiple regression, a technique that allowed me to assess simultaneously the influence of height and age upon brain size. In an analysis of the data for women, I found that, at average male height and age, a woman's brain would weigh 1,212 grams. Correction for height and age reduces Broca's measured difference of 181 grams by more than a third, to 113 grams.

I don't know what to make of this remaining difference because I cannot assess other factors known to influence brain size in a major way. Cause of death has an important effect: degenerative disease often entails a substantial diminution of brain size. (This effect is separate from the decrease attributed to age alone.) Eugene Schreider, also working with Broca's data, found that men killed in accidents had brains weighing, on average, 60 grams more than men dying of infectious diseases. The best modern data I can find (from American hospitals) records a full 100-gram difference between death by degenerative arteriosclerosis and by violence or accident. Since so many of Broca's subjects were elderly women, we may assume that lengthy degenerative disease was more common among them than among the men.

More importantly, modern students of brain size still have not agreed on a proper measure for eliminating the powerful effect of body size. Height is partly adequate, but men and women of the same height do not share the same body build. Weight is even worse than height, because most of its variation reflects nutrition rather than intrinsic size—fat versus skinny exerts little influence upon the brain. Manouvrier took up this subject in the 1880s and argued that muscular mass and force should be used. He tried to measure this elusive property in various ways and found a marked difference in favor of men, even in men and women of the same height. When he corrected for what he called "sexual mass," women actually came out slightly ahead in brain size.

Thus, the corrected 113-gram difference is surely too large; the true figure is probably close to zero and may as well favor women as men. And 113 grams, by the way, is exactly the average difference between a 5 foot 4 inch and a 6 foot 4 inch male in Broca's data. We would not (especially us short folks) want to ascribe greater intelligence to tall men. In short, who knows what to do with Broca's data? They certainly don't permit any confident claim that men have bigger brains than women.

To appreciate the social role of Broca and his school, we must recognize that his statements about the brains of women do not reflect an isolated prejudice toward a single disadvantaged group. They must be weighed in the context of a general theory that supported contemporary social distinctions as biologically ordained. Women, blacks, and poor people suffered the same disparagement, but women bore the brunt of Broca's argument because he had easier access to data on women's brains. Women were singularly denigrated but they also stood as surrogates for other disenfranchised groups. As one of Broca's disciples wrote in 1881: "Men of the black races have a brain scarcely heavier than that of white woman." This juxtaposition extended into many other realms of anthropological argument, particularly to claims that, anatomically and emotionally, both women and blacks were like white children—and that white children, by the theory of recapitulation, represented an ancestral (primitive) adult stage of human evolution. I do not regard as empty rhetoric the claim that women's battles are for all of us.

Maria Montessori did not confine her activities to educational reform for young children. She lectured on anthropology for several years at the University of Rome, and wrote an influential book entitled *Pedagogical Anthropology* (English edition, 1913). Montessori was no egalitarian. She supported most of Broca's work and the theory of innate criminality proposed by her compatriot Cesare Lombroso. She measured the circumference of children's heads in her schools and inferred that the best prospects had bigger brains. But she had no use for Broca's conclusions about women. She discussed Manouvrier's work at length and made much of his tentative claim that women, after proper correction of the data, had slightly larger brains than men. Women, she concluded, were intellectually superior, but men had prevailed heretofore by dint of physical force. Since technology has abolished force as an instrument of power, the era of women may soon be upon us: "In such an epoch there will really be superior human beings, there will really be men strong in morality and in sentiment. Perhaps in this way the reign of women is approaching, when the enigma of her anthropological superiority will be deciphered. Woman was always the custodian of human sentiment, morality and honor."

This represents one possible antidote to "scientific" claims for the constitutional inferiority of certain groups. One may affirm the validity of biological distinctions but argue that the data have been misinterpreted by prejudiced men with a stake in the outcome, and that disadvantaged groups are truly superior. In recent years, Elaine Morgan has followed this strategy in her *Descent of Woman,* a speculative reconstruction of human prehistory from the woman's point of view —and as farcical as more famous tall tales by and for men.

I prefer another strategy. Montessori and Morgan followed Broca's philosophy to reach a more congenial conclusion. I would rather label the whole enterprise of setting a biological value upon groups for what it is: irrelevant and highly injurious. George Eliot well appreciated the special tragedy that biological labeling imposed upon members of disadvantaged groups. She expressed it for people like herself—women of extraordinary talent. I would apply it more widely —not only to those whose dreams are flouted but also to those who never realize that they may dream—but I cannot match her prose. In conclusion, then, the rest of Eliot's prelude to *Middlemarch:*

> *The limits of variation are really much wider than anyone would imagine from the sameness of women's coiffure and the favorite love stories in prose and verse. Here and there a cygnet is reared uneasily among the ducklings in the brown pond, and never finds the living stream in fellowship with its own oary-footed kind. Here and there is born a Saint Theresa, foundress of nothing, whose loving heartbeats and sobs after an unattained goodness tremble off and are dispersed among hindrances instead of centering in some long-recognizable deed.*

The Witch Hunts

BARBARA EHRENREICH AND DEIRDRE ENGLISH

The extent of the witch craze is startling: in the late fifteenth and early sixteenth centuries there were thousands upon thousands of executions—usually live burnings at the stake—in Germany, Italy, and other countries. In the mid-sixteenth century the terror spread to France, and finally to England. One writer has estimated the number of executions at an average of six hundred a year for certain German cities—or two a day, "leaving out Sundays." Nine hundred witches were destroyed in a single year in the Würzburg area, and a thousand in and around Como. At Toulouse, four hundred were put to death in a day. In the Bishopric of Trier, in 1585, two villages were left with only one female inhabitant each. Many writers have estimated the total number killed to have been in the millions. Women made up some 85 per cent of those executed—old women, young women, and children.

The charges leveled against the "witches" included every misogynist fantasy harbored by the monks and priests who officiated over the witch hunts: witches copulated with the devil, rendered men impotent (generally by removing their penises—which the witches then imprisoned in nests or baskets), devoured newborn babies, poisoned livestock, etc. But again and again the "crimes" included what would now be recognized as legitimate medical acts—providing contraceptive measures, performing abortions, offering drugs to ease the pain of labor. In fact, in the peculiar legal theology of the witch hunters, healing, on the part of a woman, was itself a crime. As a leading English witch hunter put it:

> *For this must always be remembered, as a conclusion, that by Witches we understand not only those which kill and torment, but all Diviners, Charmers, Jugglers, all Wizards, commonly called wise men and wise women . . . and in the same number we reckon all good Witches, which do no hurt but good, which do not spoil and destroy, but save and deliver . . . It were a thousand times better for the land if all Witches, but especially the blessing Witch, might suffer death.*

The German monks Kramer and Sprenger, whose book *Malleus Maleficarum,* or *The Hammer of Witches,* was the Catholic Church's official text on witch-hunting for three centuries, denounced those "notoriously bad" witches, "such as use witch's medicines and cure the bewitched by superstitious means." They classed witches in "three degrees": "For some both heal and harm; some harm, but cannot heal; and some seem only able to heal, that is, to take away injuries." Kramer and Sprenger showed no sympathy for those who consulted the witch-healers:

> *For they who resort to such witches are thinking more of their bodily health than of God, and besides that, God cuts short their lives to punish them for taking into their own hands the vengeance for their wrongs.*

The inquisitors reserved their greatest wrath for the midwife, asserting:

> *The greatest injuries to the Faith as regards the heresy of witches are done by midwives; and this is made clearer than daylight itself by the confessions of some who were afterwards burned.*

In fact, the wise woman, or witch, as the authorities labeled her, did possess a host of remedies which had been tested in years of use. *Liber Simplicis Medicinae,* the compendium of natural healing methods written by St. Hildegarde of Bingen (A.D. 1098–1178) gives some idea of the scope of women healers' knowledge in the early middle ages. Her book lists the healing properties of 213 varieties of plants and 55 trees, in addition to dozens of mineral and animal derivatives. Undoubtedly many of the witch-healers' remedies were purely magical, such as the use of amulets and charms, but others meet the test of modern scientific medicine. They had effective painkillers, digestive aids, and anti-inflammatory agents. They used ergot for the pain of labor at a time when the Church held that pain in labor was the Lord's just punishment for Eve's original sin. Ergot derivatives are still used today to hasten labor and aid in the recovery from childbirth. Belladonna—still used today as an anti-spasmodic—was used by the witch-healers to inhibit uterine contractions when miscarriage threatened. Digitalis, still an important drug in treating heart ailments, is said to have been discovered by an English witch.

Meanwhile, the male, university-trained physicians, who practiced with the approval of the Church, had little to go on but guesswork and myth. Among wealthier people, medicine had achieved the status of a gentlemanly occupation well before it had any connection to science, or to empirical study of any kind. Medical students spent years studying Plato, Aristotle, and Christian theology. Their medical theory was largely restricted to the works of Galen, the ancient Roman physician who stressed the theory of "complexions" or "temperaments" of men, "wherefore the choleric are wrathful, the sanguine are kindly, the melancholy are envious," and so on. Medical students rarely saw any patients at all, and no experimentation of any kind was taught. Medicine was sharply differentiated from surgery, which was almost everywhere considered a degrading, menial craft, and the dissection of bodies was almost unheard of.

Medical theories were often grounded more in "logic" than in observation: "Some foods brought on good humours, and others, evil humours. For example, nasturtium, mustard, and garlic produced reddish bile; lentils, cabbage and the meat of old goats and beeves begot black bile." Bleeding was a common practice, even in the case of wounds. Leeches were applied according to the time, the hour, the air, and other similar considerations. Incantations and quasi-religious rituals mingled with the more "scientific" treatments inherited from ancient Greece and Rome. For example, the physician to Edward II, who held a bachelor's degree in theology and a doctorate in medicine from Oxford, prescribed for toothache writing on the jaws of the patient, "In the name of the Father, the Son, and the Holy Ghost, Amen," or touching a needle to a caterpillar and then to the tooth. A frequent treatment for leprosy was a broth made of the flesh of a black snake caught in a dry land among stones.

Such was the state of medical "science" at the time when witch-healers were persecuted for being practitioners of satanic magic. It was witches who developed an extensive understanding of bones and muscles, herbs and drugs, while physicians were still deriving their prognoses from astrology and alchemists were trying to turn lead into gold. So great was the witches' knowledge that in 1527, Paracelsus, considered the "father of modern medicine," burned his text on pharmaceuticals, confessing that he "had learned from the Sorceress all he knew."

Well before the witch hunts began, the male medical profession had attempted to eliminate the female healer. The object of these early conflicts was not the peasant healer but the better-off, literate woman healer who competed for the same urban clientele as that of the university-trained doctors. Take, for example, the case of Jacoba Felicie, brought to trial in 1322 by the Faculty of Medicine at the University of Paris, on charges of illegal practice. She was a literate woman and had received some unspecified "special training" in medicine. That her patients were well off is evident from the fact that (as they testified in court) they had consulted well-known university-trained physicians before turning to her. The primary accusations brought against her were that

> . . . she would cure her patient of internal illness and wounds or of external abscesses. She would visit the sick assiduously and continue to examine the urine in the manner of physicians, feel the pulse, and touch the body and limbs.

Six witnesses affirmed that Jacoba had cured them, even after numerous doctors had given up, and one patient declared that she was wiser in the art of surgery and medicine than any master physician or surgeon in Paris. But these testimonials were used against her, for the charge was not that she was incompetent, but that—as a woman—she dared to cure at all.

Along the same lines, English physicians sent a petition to Parliament bewailing the "worthless and presumptuous women who usurped the profession" and asking the imposition of fines and "long imprisonment" on any woman who attempted to "use the practyse of Fisyk." By the fourteenth century, the medical profession's campaign against urban, educated women healers was virtually complete throughout Europe. Male doctors had won a clear monopoly over the practice of medicine among the upper classes (except for obstetrics, which remained the province of female midwives even among the upper classes for another three centuries). They were ready to take on an important role in the campaign against the great mass of female healers—the "witches."

Physicians were asked to distinguish between those afflictions which had been caused by witchcraft and those caused by "some natural physical defect." They were also asked to judge whether certain women were witches. Often the accused would be stripped and shaved and examined by doctors for "devil's marks." Through the witch hunts, the Church lent its authority to the doctor's professionalism, denouncing non-professional healing as equivalent to heresy: "If a woman dare to cure *without having studied* she is a witch and must die." (Of course, there wasn't any way for a woman to attend a university and go through the appropriate study.)

The witch trials established the male physician on a moral and intellectual plane vastly above the female healer. It placed him on the side of God and Law, a professional on par with lawyers and theologians, while it placed her on the side of darkness, evil, and magic. The witch hunts prefigured—with dramatic intensity—the clash between male doctors and female healers in nineteenth-century America.

Nuclear Bomb Testing on Human Guinea Pigs: Bikini, Rongelap, Utirik, Kwajalein

DARLENE KEJU-JOHNSON

One important date that I never forget was in the year 1946. In that year the navy official from the U.S. government came to Bikini Island. He came and told the chief Juda—and I quote—"We are testing these bombs for the good of mankind, and to end all world wars."

In 1946 very few of us Marshallese spoke English or even understood it. The chief could not understand what it all meant, but there was one word that stuck in his mind and that was "mankind." The only reason why he knows the word "mankind" is because it is in the Bible. So he looked at the man, the navy official, and he says, "If it is in the name of God, I am willing to let my people go."

When the navy official came, it was too late. There were already thousands of soldiers and scientists on the atoll and hundreds of airplanes and ships in the Bikini lagoon. They were ready to conduct the tests. The Bikinians had no choice but to leave their islands, and they have never returned. The navy official did not tell the chief that the Bikinians would not see their home again. Today Bikini is off limits for

30,000 years. In other words Bikini will not be safe for these Bikinian people ever again.

The Bikinians were promised that the United States only wanted their islands for a short time. The chief thought maybe a short time is next week, maybe next month. So they moved to Rongerik.

Rongerik is a sandbar island. There are no resources on it. It was too poor to feed the people. We live on our oceans—it's like our supermarket—and from our land we get breadfruit and other foods. But on Rongerik there was nothing. The United States put the Bikinians on this island and left them there. After a year they sent a military medical official to see how they were. When he got there he found out that they were starving. Imagine; move someone else from their own home, by your power. Dump them on a little sand. And don't even bother to go back and see how they are doing for a year.

The people of Bikini have been moved, or relocated, three times. The people of Enewetak Atoll were also relocated. You cannot imagine the psychological problems that people have to go through because of relocation.

In 1954 the United States exploded a hydrogen bomb, code named BRAVO, on Bikini. It was more than 1,000 times stronger than the Hiroshima bomb. The Marshallese were never told about this bomb. We were never even warned that this blast was about to happen on our islands. Instead we experienced white fallout. The people were frightened by the fallout. The southern area of our islands turned yellow. And the children played in it. But when the fallout went on their skins, it burnt them. People were vomiting.

The people of Rongelap and Utirik were not picked up until three days after the explosion. It was horrible. Some American soldiers came and said, "Get ready. Jump in the ocean and get on the boat because we are leaving. Don't bring any belongings. Just go in the water." That's your home and you have to decide, with your husband and children, whether you are going to leave or not: But there was no time. People had to run fast. There was no boat to get the people, not even the children and the old people, to the ship. People had to swim with their children. It was very rough. When they got to the ship each family was given one blanket. Some families had 10 or 12 children, and they had to share one blanket.

They were taken to Kwajalein. It took one night to get there. They didn't even give people a change of clothing, so it meant they had to sleep in their contaminated clothing all the way. You imagine. They are burnt, they are vomiting. When they got to Kwajalein they were given soap and were told to wash in the lagoon. The soap and salt water was supposed to wash off the radiation. They were not told what had happened, why it had happened, what was wrong with them. Their hair was falling out, fingernails were falling off . . . but they were never told why.

The people of Rongelap and Utirik were on Kwajalein for three months before they were moved again. The people of Utirik went back to their contaminated island. The people of Rongelap didn't return to Rongelap for three years: it was too contaminated.

Twenty-eight American men who were on Rongerik monitoring the tests and the crew of a nearby Japanese fishing boat were also contaminated. We are in touch with one of these men who were studying the test. He has told us that the United States knew that the wind was blowing towards islands where people lived, but that they went ahead and tested anyway. It was not a mistake. It is interesting that the United States government moved the Marshallese in the 1940s when the small bombs were being tested, and then when the biggest bomb ever was tested the Marshallese were not even warned. This is why we believe that we have been used as guinea pigs.

Since the testing there has been a tremendous increase in health problems. The biggest problem we have now, especially among women and children, is cancers. We have cancers in the breast. We have tumour cancers. The women have cancers in their private places. Children are being deformed. I saw a child from Rongelap. It is an infant. Its feet are like clubs. And another child whose hands are like nothing at all. It is mentally retarded. Some of the children suffer growth retardation.

Now we have this problem of what we call "jellyfish babies." These babies are born like jellyfish. They have no eyes. They have no heads. They have no arms. They have no legs. They do not shape like human beings at all. But they are being born on the labour table. The most colourful, ugly things you have ever seen. Some of them have hairs on them. And they breathe. This ugly "thing" only lives for a few hours. When they die they are buried right away. A lot of times they don't allow the mother to see this kind of baby because she'll go crazy. It is too inhumane.

Many women today are frightened of having these "jellyfish babies." I have had two tumours taken out of me recently and I fear that if I have children they will be "jellyfish babies" also. These babies are being born not only on the radioactive islands but now throughout the thirty-five atolls and five islands of the Marshalls. I've interviewed hundreds of Marshallese women in the northern islands and this is their story I am telling you. The health problems are on the increase. They have not stopped.

It is not just the people who have been affected but also our environment. . . .

The United States is only leasing the islands but can you imagine if it owned them? That is why in 1982 the people of Kwajalein decided to take direct action. They sailed in to take over eleven off-limits islands and lived there for four months. A thousand people. They were saying to the United States, "You are not going to treat us like second-class citizens in our own islands!" They shut the base down. The missile testing was stopped.

The United States government, after all these years, has never conducted an epidemiological survey. The Department of Energy sends their medical team. But they will only go to the two islands that the United States recognises as affected by the fallout from the 1954 bomb—Rongelap and Utirik. But there are many others. And it is interesting that they will not check the children. They will only check those people who were on Rongelap and Utirik in 1954. . . .

Marshallese are fed up with the DOE and the United States government. We are asking for an independent radiological survey. We want to do it outside of the United States government.

This is what happened with the Rongelap people. They said, "We have had enough! You are not going to treat us like animals, like nothing at all! We are moving." So they moved from Rongelap with the Greenpeace ship, *Rainbow Warrior*. The whole island, 350 people, moved to live on Mejato, which is a small island in Kwajalein Atoll. Kwajalein landowners gave them that island. But the United States wouldn't help. Instead they did a campaign to discredit the Rongelapese.

By doing this the Rongelap people said that they don't want to be part of this whole nuclear craziness. And that their bottom line is, "We care about our children's future." Because they know that they are contaminated. They had to come to a very hard decision. Leaving your island in the Marshalls is not easy. So they decided that their children came first. They know they'll be dying out soon. They are dying now—slowly.

We are only small—very few thousand people out there on tiny islands, but we are doing our part to stop this nuclear madness. And although we are few we have done it! Which means you can do it too! But we need your support. We must come together to save this world for our children and the future generations to come.

2.

The Present Reflected
in the Past Remembered

Everything Is Wonderful

JAYNE CORTEZ

Under the urination of astronauts
and the ejaculation of polluted sparrows
and the evacuation of acid brain matter
everything is wonderful
except for the invasion and occupation
of Grenada
except for the avalanche of blood coagulating
in El Salvador
except for the brutal apartheid system
raging in South Africa
except for the threat of intervention
in Nicaragua
except for the war of repression
in Namibia
except for Pinochet creaming again
this very day
from the killing floor of Allende and Neruda
except for that
and the torrential rainfall
of cluster bombs falling in Beirut
everything is everything
wonderful and wonderful

The Race Factor in International Politics

HUGH TINKER

Western writers on international relations have tacitly ignored race as a factor in world conflicts. While acknowledging the existence of a gulf between 'North' and 'South' they feel more comfortable describing this as an economic gap, almost as a technical difficulty, which can be characterized by labelling the deprived countries of the Third World as less developed countries (LDCs). The peoples of the Third World are in no doubt about the causes of the basic division between white affluence and black and brown poverty and the continuing determination of the whites to preserve this division by reference to their innate superiority. As one Asian commentator declares: 'The West is still hamstrung by the anachronistic idea that White can always do things (including, of course, rule) better than Black, Brown or Yellow, whatever its Ideological commitment to human freedom and equality.'[1]

Whenever Western writers are brought to consider race as a problem in international politics they like to make the point that racial tensions are as serious among the Third World peoples as they are between white and black. They point to the hostility of the indigenous peoples to the overseas Chinese in Southeast Asia or to Indians and Pakistanis in East Africa. We may agree that these tensions are very real, but they do not create the global divisions which can be ascribed to white racial dominance. To the Third World, white racism is a continuing legacy of white imperialism and an aspect of the still pervasive force of neocolonialism. (Incidentally, the black-brown tensions mentioned above may also be attributed to a kind of subimperialism in which until very recently Indians and Chinese were agents of white imperialism.)

How far are we all prisoners of the past: both the recent past, in which the world was, effectively, the stage for Western expansion, and that remote past, in which the light-skinned Aryans foisted upon the dark-skinned Negritoid, Veddoid, and other subjugated races the syndrome of values which equated 'light' and 'fair' with good, and 'dark' and 'black' with evil? For this is where the racial factor begins; with a primordial sense of the superiority of white over black. Formerly,

students of race relations employed as a key concept the idea of prejudice. It was assumed that because of unfamiliarity, or social distance,
or merely lack of adequate education, individuals and groups were
'prejudiced', while rational, informed people were absolutely or relatively unprejudiced. Through more complete knowledge, the incidence of prejudice could be reduced and better race relations would
follow.

When this approach was seen to be wholly inadequate, students
of race relations embraced the 'problem' explanation. Hostility to
those of another race arose out of environmental shortcomings: poor
housing in short supply, educational inequalities, competition for jobs,
institutional inflexibility (such as police suspicion of the wanderer, the
displaced). Even when this explanation was in the context of liberalism
—involving a declared intention to make good these shortcomings—
there was a clear understanding that the problem arose from the inser-
tion of what one eminent English judge called 'an alien wedge' into
the 'host' society.[2]

The problem was caused by the arrival of black and brown groups
within white society: almost nobody (except a few radicals) saw the
problem as that of white racism. Any acknowledgement that there is
an innate hostility to 'lesser breeds without law' among almost all the
whites of the world is slow to arrive. A kind of rearguard action is still
being fought. During the twilight of the British Empire, progressives
might agree that right-wing imperial administrators were guilty of
colour prejudice; but not themselves. Today, British intellectuals (or
some of them) might agree that the British working class, the alleged
supporters of Enoch Powell and the National Front, are racialists; but
not of course themselves. The idea that deep in the white subcon-
scious there is the conviction that White is Wonderful and Black is
Beastly is resisted and rejected by all right-thinking (white) people.
Hence, the proposition that black and brown people are on one side
and white are on the other would be dismissed as obscurantist—indeed, racist—by right-thinking (white) people.

The proposition, in terms of international configurations, was
advanced long ago by non-white thinkers. The black American sociologist W. E. B. Du Bois insisted that 'the problem of the 20th century would be the problem of the colour line—the relation of the
darker to the lighter men in Asia and Africa, in America, and the
islands of the sea.'[3] The Indian poet, Rabindranath Tagore, told an

international conference: 'I regard the race and colour prejudice which barricades human beings against one another as the greatest evil of modern times.' The World Conference for International Peace through Religion, held in Geneva in 1928, identified causes of race friction in different areas of the world arising from migration, economic imperialism ('the crushing wealth of the West'), religious imperialism, the rising tide of nationalism in the East, and 'international discourtesy' displayed by the Western nations.[4] The conference was asked to recommend that the League of Nations establish a court of racial justice.

The conference achieved nothing, of course, and was followed shortly after by yet another long series of wars in which whites destroyed blacks, including the Italian invasion of Ethiopia. Although this invasion aroused worldwide censure, it was condemned by white critics as an ideological deviation, a manifestation of fascism. It was left to folk who were then almost invisible and inaudible on the world stage —the blacks of the United States and the Caribbean and young African intellectuals such as Kwame Nkrumah—to protest against the racist implications of the invasion: the extinction of the last independent black nation, the last symbol of black dignity.

When an international issue was belatedly recognized as having racial elements it was the Nazi persecution of the German Jews (the oppression of whites by fellow whites) which aroused the conscience of the Western world. The Nazi extermination policy led to the coining of the term genocide, and the adoption by the United Nations General Assembly of the Convention on the Prevention and Punishment of the Crime of Genocide (1948). The equally devastating extermination of black and brown peoples, such as the wiping out of the North American Indian tribes or the Herero tribe of South-West Africa, had aroused no such international concern.

The Nazi treatment of the Jews remains the reference point for any consideration of race as a factor in international conflict. It was this terrible crime against humanity which caused the infant United Nations to press on with the Universal Declaration of Human Rights (1948). These acknowledged rights represent the freedoms slowly acquired in Western liberal societies: equality before the law, freedom of thought, conscience, and religion, freedom of opinion and expression, freedom of assembly, and so on.

Because the application of this code was qualified by the members accepting it, in that the United Nations should not intervene in matters of domestic jurisdiction, the Declaration has remained little more than a statement of ideals. The same applies to the conventions which flowed from that declaration, including the International Convention on the Elimination of All Forms of Racial Discrimination (1965). This convention states that racial discrimination is 'any distinction, exclusion, restriction or preference based on race, colour, descent or national or ethnic origin'. This apparently sweeping definition of forms of racial discrimination is modified by the provision that the convention does not apply to 'distinctions, exclusions, restrictions or preferences made . . . between citizens and non-citizens'; another evocation of the 'domestic jurisdiction' principle. The Convention calls for the encouragement of 'integrationist multi-racial organizations and movements' and sets up a committee of experts to whom complaints about non-observance of the Convention may be referred to. Thus far the committee and the Convention have made only a limited impact upon international peace questions and the channels of the United Nations have been largely used as pressure points in the overall confrontation between the superpowers and their allies and clients.

Meanwhile, the Third World states have increasingly to be reckoned with in the United Nations. A mere dozen at the time of the organization's foundation, the march forward into independence increased their number to 75 by December 1964 and to over 100 by 1979.[5] These new states represent every kind of interest, and these interests are frequently in competition or conflict. There is no coherent Afro-Asian bloc and their priorities are often mutually divergent. But they unite when issues seen as originating in white dominance are before them. One issue, now recognized by all the world, is the prolongation of white dominance in southern Africa, a continent otherwise liberated from white imperial domination. The second issue, increasingly identified as racial by Afro-Asian nations, is thought by the West to lack such a connotation: this is Israel's occupation of the lands of the Palestinians.

South Africa is now so isolated as a global pariah that it is easy to forget how, until recently, the West was prepared to condone the system of white dominance as a part of the natural order. During the early years of the United Nations, whenever any questions concerning South Africa—including South-West Africa (now Namibia)—was brought into the international arena, the West either opposed intervention or abstained from taking sides. Britain, Australia, New Zealand, the United States, the Netherlands, and even the Scandinavian states, were quite clear that South Africa should not be put on trial for its internal policies towards non-whites. It was only after the entry of black African states into the United Nations in 1960 and immediately thereafter that the West began to reconsider its approach. South Africa remained secure in its economic strength and in its ties with the multinationals and seemed still able to ride out the storm.

The United Nations passed resolution after resolution, by the combined voting strength of the Third World and the communist bloc, without any practical effect. The climax was the adaptation by the General Assembly of a resolution establishing an International Convention on the Suppression and Punishment of the Crime of Apartheid (1973). This was ratified by 38 countries, none belonging to the West. The convention refers specifically to racial oppression and envisages the setting up of an international tribunal to try those guilty of the crimes enumerated.[6] This massive condemnation by world opinion seemed to leave the South African government unmoved; especially as the British government of the day announced that it could not accept the legality of the Convention.

However, when Portugal withdrew from Angola and the Popular Movement for the Liberation of Angola (MPLA) with Cuban military support, took over that country, South Africa began to revise its policies. South-West Africa was the most vulnerable terrain, and, having stonewalled for 30 years over its future, the government of B. J. Vorster unexpectedly indicated that it was prepared to negotiate with the United Nations. Within a few months, the whole apparatus of apartheid was demolished in South-West Africa/Namibia. The prohibition upon interracial marriages, the confinement of Africans to separate residential locations from whites, the classification of jobs on racial lines, the separate educational systems: all this was (in law) brought to an end. How, philosophically, South African whites could reconcile the contradiction between accepting multiracial practices in one of their territories alongside apartheid elsewhere must be a mystery! Negotiations then began for an agreement on the transfer of power to a new multiracial Namibian administration. At this point, the Western powers (the United States, Britain, France, West Germany, Canada) came forward as mediators between South Africa and the United Nations. All of them had investments in Namibia, some of massive proportions, and doubtless the move was to provide for a smooth transfer which would safeguard these investments. The plan does not seem to have worked out. At the time of writing it is still not clear whether Third World opposition to racialism or white solidarity will finally determine how Namibia emerges; whether through acceptance of African claims or by armed struggle. What has become clear is that the last ideological bastion of white exclusiveness has been breached, and South Africa's white friends have been compelled to recognize that the view of the Third World must prevail.

It may be argued that South Africa is a special case, a kind of historical accident, a fossil of white colonialism preserved when all the rest had dissolved away. Doubtless, the West would like to treat the South African case as an unpleasant inconvenience; but one that will not recur to be categorized as a special kind of 'problem', and that, given special treatment by the West, may, perhaps, eventually go away.

The emergence of Israel as another global outsider provides uneasy evidence that the introduction of race into international relations is not just a will-o'-the-wisp, as Western experts would like to say; it is a strategy promising a vigorous response. To mobilize Third World support, the Palestine Liberation Organization (PLO) and other Arab spokesmen have portrayed Israel as a paradigm of South Africa, and Zionism as a manifestation of racism. In 1975 came the United Nations resolution describing Zionism 'as a form of racism and racial discrimination'. The 72 states which voted for this resolution included most of the Afro-Asian world, as well as the Soviet bloc. (It was one issue which united the Soviet Union and China.) Only 35 states, led by the United States, voted against the resolution with another 32 abstaining.

Perhaps less dramatic but equally significant in its way, was the 1978 resolution directed against Israeli policies and practices which proclaimed 'the inalienable right of the peoples of Namibia, South Africa and Zimbabwe, of the Palestinian people and of all peoples under colonial or alien domination . . . to self-determination, national independence, territorial integrity . . . without external interference'. It has been a regular feature of conferences of non-aligned states to make these connections between southern Africa and Israel as areas of foreign (that is, white) occupation of essentially brown and black lands.

In consequence of these developments the former Israeli strategy of building friendships in Asia and Africa by providing advice and expertise on practical development now lies in ruins. Israel has been compelled to rely almost exclusively upon Western support, especially that of the United States. Prime Minister Begin worked hard at convincing his friends that his opponents are terrorists, comparing the PLO to the Nazis. Paradoxically, the Arabs and their communist allies hurl the same charge at Begin and accuse Israel of Nazi methods towards prisoners and the subject Arab population. It appears as though the agreed measurement for racism remains the treatment by whites (Germans) of fellow whites (Jews).

It seems inevitable that the problems created by white hegemony in South Africa and by Arab resistance to Israeli expansion will continue to haunt the international community right into the twenty-first century. Increasingly, the West will be forced to make a choice: to support its 'natural' partners (those on top) or to acquiesce in the Third World's assessment of these situations as unacceptable. Even those as skilled in international finesse as the French may find that the price of enjoying international influence is to make a definite choice. The choice may still be taken in terms of the realities of power; the Third World remains powerless. The consequences will be the increasing polarization of forces between those who dominate and those who are dominated: a division line which the white 'North' will seek to minimize while the black 'South' maximizes what is one of its moral advantages. For the international morality of the late twentieth century is agreed that racism is deplorable.

If race does become a dominant feature of international politics it will emerge as in the subtle undertones of the Israeli-Arab confrontation and not in the dramatic form of a race war. Two probable areas where racial undertones may become more pronounced are the Caribbean and the Pacific. The Caribbean is recognized as potentially dangerous for the West's protagonist, the United States, and the Pacific could also be a danger area under vastly different circumstances for both the United States and Australia. They still have memories of fighting for survival in this area. In both these vast areas the factor of race stems from historical experience: from the forcible transportation of black, brown, and yellow peoples to labour in the interests of whites. The plural societies thus created still perpetuate white dominance.[7] This dominance is closely tied in with the economic dominance of multinationals owned by and controlled from the West. Attempts to create a New International Economic Order will involve the emergence of a new racial order. In some aspects the confrontation between the races will be internal, as in Australia, New Zealand and Hawaii, and on much reduced scale in Puerto Rico, Bermuda, and the Bahamas. These internal confrontations will also, in certain cases, be between non-white rivals, as in Sri Lanka, Guyana and Fiji.[8] But, just as 'racial' differences escalated in Palestine/Israel from internal group conflict into international confrontation, so there is the prospect of local, internal conflicts being escalated until they become involved in international politics.

In the Caribbean, there is already a focus for this process: this is Cuba, which has now established cordial relations with most of its neighbours and has been declared by Castro to be an Afro-Latin culture. At present there is no such catalyst in the Pacific. Japan, which created this role in the past, is too firmly an honorary member of the white world, and perhaps its coming leader. As yet, the possible contenders are still under Western influence; but somewhere there may be a 'Pacific Castro', already studying at university or working for a trade union.

Along with the prospects of confrontation between whites and non-whites there are many potential conflicts between different brown and black peoples who see each other in terms of racial differences.[9] As the image of classical Western imperialism begins to fade, so we may expect its emotional power to be transferred to the image of racism: a power so much older than the oldest empire and (alas) likely to retain its potency until the end of time.

NOTES

1. *Asia Week,* 25 November 1977, in a review of the present writer's book, *Race, Conflict and the International Order.* The reviewer concluded: 'What this portends is the increasing polarisation of the world along racial lines.' By contrast, a review of the same book in the British Labour weekly, *Tribune,* on 14 October 1977, dismissed its 'unconvincing final prophecies of global polarisation along race rather than class division'.
2. Lord Radcliffe, 'Immigration and Settlement: Some General Considerations', *Race,* July 1969.
3. It was Du Bois who first declared that there is 'Beauty in Black'.
4. C. F. Andrews, 'Racial Influences', in Arthur Porritt (ed.). *The Causes of War:*

Economic, Industrial, Racial, Religious, Scientific and Political. London: 1932, pp. 63–113.

5. What or who constitute the Third World? Somewhat arbitrarily, the present body count does not include the countries of Latin America but does include those of the Caribbean.

6. The crime of apartheid includes, inter alia: 'Denial to a member or members of a racial group or groups of the right of life and liberty of persons' by murder, bodily or mental harm, infringement of freedom or dignity, torture, arbitrary arrest and illegal imprisonment, or deliberate imposition of living conditions calculated to cause the physical destruction of a racial group or groups, and 'any legislative and other measures calculated to prevent a racial group or groups from participating in the political, social, economic and cultural life of the country'.

7. Except perhaps in Fiji, where British colonial policy established the Fijian aristocracy as the powerholders, with Indians, Fijian commoners, and other groups as the governed. In 1987, we have seen this chiefly dominance challenged—but to the further detriment of the Indian majority still seen as intruder by the 'sons of the soil'.

8. The tension between Sinhalese and Tamils in Sri Lanka escalated into virtual civil war. Because there are 30 million Tamils in India, the Indian government intervened, introducing a military 'peace keeping force' into northern Sri Lanka in 1987. An example of how an internal racial conflict may be internationalized.

9. Tom Mboya was taken by the Australians to visit Papua New Guinea when it was still a trust territory. He is supposed to have observed, after meeting the Papuans, 'If I had realised that they were black I would never have agreed to Indonesia taking over West Irian.'

Genocide Is a New Word for an Old Crime

JACK NUSAN PORTER

Genocide is a new word for an old crime. The originator of the term was Raphael Lemkin, a Polish legal scholar. The word first appeared in 1944 in his *Axis Rule in Occupied Europe* (1973 reprint). Lemkin coined a hybrid word consisting of the Greek prefix *genos* (nation, tribe) and the Latin suffix *-cide* (killing). He felt that the destruction of the Armenians during World War I and of the Jews during World War II called for the formulation of a legal concept that would accurately describe the deliberate killing of entire human groups. Lemkin was more than a scholar. He inspired and promoted action on the international level to outlaw genocide. It was largely due to his efforts that the United Nations decided to debate the issue of genocide, to organize a convention to discuss it, and to eventually include it as a part of international law in 1948.

Before 1944 no dictionary, encyclopedia, or textbook used the term genocide, and even after 1944 there have been some glaring omissions. For example, there is no mention of the term in *Webster's International Dictionary* until 1961. All three major sociology dictionaries have also ignored the term (Gould and Kolb, 1964; Theodorson and Theodorson, 1969; and Hoult, 1969). Both the earlier *Encyclopedia of the Social Sciences* (Seligman and Johnson, 1933) and the *International Encyclopedia of the Social Sciences* (Sills, 1968) have no separate descriptive and analytical listing for "genocide." The Sills' encyclopedia does mention genocide but only under the heading of "international crimes" where genocide is defined in the context of international law, not sociologically or historically (Sills, 1968: Vol. 7:515–519).

On the other hand, the encyclopedias written by minority groups affected by genocide (Armenians and Jews are two examples) have excellent coverage of the topic. For example the new *Encyclopedia Judaica* has a long and comprehensive account of the Holocaust in Europe by Jacob Robinson, yet, ironically, even in this Jewish publication the actual term "genocide" cannot be found as a major listing. Only "genocide convention" is mentioned.

The United Nations General Assembly, during its first session in 1946, carried out the mandate proposed by Raphael Lemkin and adopted two resolutions: the first affirmed the principles of the charter of the International Military Tribunal in Nuremberg, Germany (the so-called Nuremberg Trials of Nazi leaders) and the second affirmed that genocide was a crime under international law and, if committed, would be punished. The U.N. asked for international cooperation in preventing and punishing genocide and invited member states to enact necessary national legislation.

In a final provision the Assembly called for studies aimed at creating an international legal instrument to deal with the crime. That was the origin of the Convention on the Prevention and Punishment of the Crime of Genocide which was unanimously adopted by the Assembly on December 9, 1948. The Convention, which in international law means an agreement among sovereign nations pledging them to specified obligations, went into effect on January 12, 1951. By January 1973, seventy-six governments had ratified the Convention. The United States, however, has never ratified the agreement, claiming that it has existing legislation that covers genocide; that the wording of the Convention is vague in certain areas; that the Convention violates national sovereignty in its provision for an international tribunal; and that an entire nation cannot be charged with the crime of genocide because of the acts of a few individual citizens. These issues have been raised by United States senators, and the Senate has successfully rejected any efforts to ratify the Convention.

Controversy has arisen over several sections of the Genocide Convention. Article II reads as follows:

> *In the present Convention, genocide means any of the following acts committed with intent to destroy, in whole or in part, a national, ethnical [sic], racial or religious groups [sic], as such:*
>
> *(a) Killing members of the group;*
> *(b) Causing serious bodily harm to members of the group;*
> *(c) Deliberately inflicting on the group conditions of life calculated to bring about its physical destruction in whole or in part;*
> *(d) Imposing measures intended to prevent births within the group;*
> *(e) Forcibly transferring children of the group to another group.*

Sections (b) and (d) have generated the most controversy in the United States Senate. The senators who voted against the United States' ratifying the Convention were mindful that American blacks had charged the United States with genocide, basing their accusations on sections (a), (b), (c), and (d) of the United Nations Convention. Furthermore America was being charged with genocide in Vietnam in the late 1960s and early 1970s; this was another reason why some senators were extremely reluctant to ratify and support the Convention.

While the U.N. does provide for enforcement of the Genocide Convention by the use of international courts, the actual implementation has been limited. In essence the U.N. Convention is more of a symbolic than a legislative contract, and those U.S. senators who voted against it have little to fear of the United States ever being brought before a tribunal. Claims of genocide have been made, *inter alia,* to the United Nations with regard to blacks in Southern Sudan, Kurds in Iraq, Nagas in India, Communists and Chinese in Indonesia, Ibos in Nigeria, and Beharis in Pakistan, but no formal decision in these cases has been reached by the United Nations. Because of political pressures and lack of real opportunity for enforcement, the United Nations has never formally applied the Convention to any genocide in the postWorld War II period, though numerous private citizens and groups have.

Furthermore the U.N. Convention is not retroactive. Therefore the United States could not be charged with genocide against the American Indians, the blacks, or the Vietnamese. The legal scholar Cherif Bassiouni maintains that the U.S. cannot be charged with genocide regarding the Indian massacres or the Vietnam war because it has never ratified the U.N. Genocide Convention. He also argues that because the Convention states that only individuals can be charged with genocide, it would require an extremely loose interpretation of the Convention text to charge a government with a crime. And, finally, Bassiouni contends that in both the Vietnam and Indian frontier situations, the requisite and specific intent of the United States government to commit genocide has never been established.

The problems of intent and application of the term genocide to specific cases will be discussed in the next section, but, in summary, the following points should be emphasized. First, the U.N. Convention on Genocide has been charged with controversy from its very inception, and it has never enforced specific punishment for cases of genocide. Secondly, there is a difference between the legal and the sociological definitions of genocide. Genocide has taken place in the past (e.g., the persecution of American Indians), but legally the United States cannot be charged with genocide. There can thus be a number of responses to genocide: the act is committed but the victimizer is never found; the act is committed but the victimizer is never charged; the act is defined as genocide by the victims, but the victimizer does not concur that it is in fact genocide, and therefore will not be charged with the crime. From both a theoretical and a practical point of view, the problem of genocide is confusing and frustrating in definition, application, and enforcement.

My definition of genocide is slightly broader than that of the United Nations. I include the deliberate extermination of political and sexual groups as well as racial, religious, tribal, or ethnic groups. Thus the attempt to exterminate homosexuals in Nazi Germany could be labeled genocide. In the early 1950s, under pressure from Soviet Russia, extermination of groups for political persuasion or beliefs did not fall under the rubric of genocide in the U.N. definition. Thus the elimination of anti-Communist Poles or Ukrainians in the USSR in the 1930s and 1940s and, in recent times, the massacre of anti-Communist Cambodians could not be labeled genocide. Annihilation based on political beliefs is not considered genocide according to the legal definition of the United Nations Convention.

The U.N.'s exclusion of political and sexual groups from its Convention proves that we do not have the conceptual categories to describe *all* forms of mass violence and murder we have seen in this century. Our sociological concepts are inadequate to cope with the phenomena. The term "massacre" describes mass killings without the intent to kill *all* members of the groups in question. Since the popular and classical definition of genocide implies the murder or attempted murder of an *entire* group (be it racial, religious, tribal, sexual, or ethnic), then the killing of anti-Communist Cambodians or Ukrainians would not technically be genocide, because the aim of the victimizers was not to kill *all* Cambodians or Ukrainians, just those with a particular set of political beliefs. I disagree with this narrow definition and believe genocide can include the extermination of groups for strictly political beliefs.

The Problem of Application and Intention

Recently there has been heated debate about the use and abuse of the terms "racism" and "racist." The term "genocide" has been similarly abused. Since "genocide" has become such a powerful catch-word, it is often used in political and cultural rhetoric. It is at least understandable that the term has been abused by political activists. However, even professional scholars have misused the concept. Because of the vague wording in some sections of the U.N. Genocide Convention, some scholars have applied the term genocide to the wrong phenomena.

For example genocide has been applied to all of the following: "race-mixing" (integration of blacks and non-blacks); drug distribution; methadone programs; the practice of birth control and abortions among Third World people; sterilization and "Mississippi appendectomies" (tubal ligations and hysterectomies); medical treatment of Catholics; and the closing of synagogues in the Soviet Union. In other words when one needs a catch-all term to describe "oppression" of one form or another, one often resorts to labeling it "genocide." The net result is a debasement of the concept.

Often the concept is applied to phenomena that are total opposites: integration and lack of integration; drug abuse and programs to curb such abuse. The following are examples of this linguistic abuse:

• The Nazi Party of America, demonstrating in Milwaukee in February 1976, argued at a schoolboard meeting that "integration is genocide for the white race." Before the meeting the Nazis distributed literature that charged the Jews with genocide against whites in America. One handbill read: "Deport Blacks to Africa and Jews to Israel or some other island [sic] except . . . those Jews who are suspected of treasonable activities such as genocide against whites." Such activities were defined as "race-mixing" and the distribution of obscene movies and magazines by "pornographic Jews." The handbills also condemned those "sick, depraved Jews who monopolize the motion picture industry [and who] can hardly wait to turn America into a mongrel cesspool" because these Jews promote racial integration and harmony.

• Regarding government-sponsored methadone programs, Black Panther Party leader Ericka Huggins said: "We don't need methadone. We don't need the government making any more good citizens. Methadone is just genocide, mostly against Black people. What we need is political education."

• At an anti-abortion rally in Washington, D.C. in 1978, Senator Orrin G. Hatch (R-Utah) stated: "I call (abortion) an epidemic and it has to be stamped out now." He noted that federal payments for abortion make it "possible for genocidal programs as were practiced in Nazi Germany." (From literature distributed by the National Abortion Rights Action League, 1979)

• Weisbord cites numerous instances of blacks viewing birth control as a "diabolical plot." His examples include reaction to the sterilization of the Relf sisters in South Carolina in June 1973, which Black Muslims and other black organizations called "a deliberate act of genocidal sterilization."

· Sociologist Rona Fields (1976), in a study of medical treatment of Catholics in Northern Ireland, charged the Protestants with "psychological genocide." She identified social control mechanisms which produce a mixture of chaos and docility and argued that such mechanisms were established in order to destroy the cultural identity of Catholics.

These examples point out the many ways the term has been used. Which applications of the term can be considered legitimate and which not? To some extent that depends on which definition one follows. Naturally some applications, such as those used by the American Nazis, are blatant distortions of reality. Other applications, however, that may sound exaggerated rest on the definition of genocide used in the United Nations Convention. Rona Fields' application of the term, for example, is based on the clause ". . . causing serious bodily or mental harm" [Article II, section (b)]. This vague and controversial clause has led to several uses or abuses of the term genocide. To Fields (1976) "psychological genocide" can occur if such "mental harm" is present. The question is what constitutes mental harm? How much mental harm is necessary in order to label it genocidal?

Some sociologists have expressed an abhorrence of the abuse that some terms and concepts take within sociology and in the general society. Dennis Wrong (1976) has called the abuse of the term genocide an example of the "banalization and trivialization of a subject and its exploitation for partisan purposes." He is especially vehement about using the concept of genocide to describe the treatment of blacks in the United States: "Slavery and color castes were evil institutions to be sure, but by no stretch of the imagination can they be compared to the extermination of 10,000 Jews a day in the death camps of Auschwitz." (Wrong, 1976, personal communication to author)

The issue of intent has also generated controversy. The United Nations Convention specifically uses the phrase "intent to destroy, in whole or in part, a national ethnical [sic], racial or religious groups [sic] . . ." (Article II). However, it would seem that it is not enough for there to be an intention to destroy, but that the intent be acted upon and in great measure carried out. Thus in the case of the American blacks, there was no intent to commit mass extermination. While repressive acts did occur, mass genocide was not one of them. On the other hand, in the case of the American Indians, there was both the intent to commit genocide and its execution.

In the area of intent and in the area of "causing serious . . . mental harm," the United Nations definition seems too broad or too vague. The problem confronting scholars in the field will be whether to use a narrow or a broad definition at this stage of research. Will the concept be used so broadly that its meaning and application will become useless? Or will it be used in such a narrow manner that certain genocides will be overlooked because they do not fall within the parameters of the definition? Furthermore should sociologists use only a legal definition of genocide such as that of the United Nations, or should they formulate their own definition? In short do we want definitional precision or phenomenological inclusion at this juncture? I would like to find a golden mean between these extremes if in fact that is possible—that is, to reject overly broad applications while remaining flexible. The next section will attempt to develop this kind of definition.

What Is Genocide?

Genocide is the deliberate destruction, in whole or in part, by a government or its agents, of a racial, sexual, religious, tribal, ethnic, or political minority. It can involve not only mass murder, but also starvation, forced deportation, and political, economic, and biological subjugation. Genocide involves three major components: ideology, technology, and bureaucracy/organization.

Ideology. A key element in the act of genocide is an ideology that the victimizer utilizes in order to exterminate the victim. This ideology, usually based on racial or religious grounds, serves to legitimize any acts, no matter how horrendous. Racist or religious propaganda is used to spread the ideology. Such propaganda defines the victim as outside the pale of human existence and therefore vulnerable to attack. Words such as "sheep," "savages," "vermin," "subhumans," "gooks," and "lice" are commonly used, especially during war or colonialization, to reduce the victims to the level of nonhumans, thus making it easier to annihilate them.

Helen Fein has added immensely to theory building in genocide studies by emphasizing this key element of ideology. She describes the role of myth, or what Gaetano Mosca would call a "political formula," which legitimizes the existence of a state of *volk* as a vehicle for the destiny of the dominant group and, by definition, excludes the victim-group as being outside the realm of the "sanctified universe."

Fein presents a theory to explain the genocide of Jews, Armenians, and Gypsies. Historically these groups have been the victims of repeated collective violence—Jews for nearly 2,000 years; Armenians for 500 years of Turkish Ottoman domination; and Gypsies for nearly a thousand years. For Fein, genocide is a rational, premeditated action with particular goals. She notes that the liberal ideal of 19th-century nationalism justified removing authorities who were deemed illegitimate because they did not represent the people. The 20th-century "formula" justified eradicating people to assure the legitimation of the state's authority. One way to eradicate groups that did not fit into a nation-state was to assimilate them; another way was to expel them; a third was to exterminate them.

Fein also describes the process of placing people "outside the sanctified universe." One example she uses is that of the Armenians. The Muslim Turks regarded the Christian Armenians as *dimmis* or infidels. For many years the latter were tolerated and protected in exchange for their accommodation to discrimination, subordination, powerlessness, and oppression. Armenians were also labeled *rayah* or sheep who could be fleeced. The Young Turk movement before and during World War I attempted to establish power and authority in order to fulfill its ideal of forging a new Turkish identity and destiny. In their scheme there was no place for large distinct minorities like the Armenians.

The genocide of Jews and Gypsies during World War II was also based on this "formula." Nazism utilized a pseudoscientific, neo-Darwinian, racist ideology which identified the German people (*volk*) as possessing a distinct identity and destiny. This identity was based on "blood." Jews and Gypsies (as well as homosexuals) were formally defined as not *volk,* but aliens to whom the Germans or Aryans would owe no obligation at all. While the Germans belonged to the "greatest, highest race" of Aryans, the Jews and Gypsies belonged to no human race. By definition they were nonhuman.

Jews were to be annihilated because they were "vermin," "lice," "bloodsuckers," "parasites," and "bacilli"; Gypsies, because they were "filthy animals," "rodents," etc. Both were seen as racial "polluters" because they were racially "deformed" and "degenerate" in the first place. Thus laws were passed making illegal sexual relations between Jews and Aryans.

In this ideological schema the Aryan *volk* had a messianic right to prevail over others and to use any means from war to political deception to do so. The *volk* demanded not only equality with other nations but room to expand and colonialize (the concept of *lebensraum*). In its expansion it could subjugate and annihilate any "inferior" races who might "pollute" the *volk*. As Fein concludes about Armenians and Jews:

> . . . in both cases the victims had earlier been decreed outside the universe of obligation by Koranic injunction and by Christian theodicy. However, churches holding out the possibility of conversion to all must assume a common humanity and, therefore, may not sanction unlimited violence. But a doctrine which assumes people do not belong to a common species imposes no limits inhibiting the magnitude of crime permissible.

An ideology based on racism or the "new formula" that Fein describes is a prerequisite for genocide; it stigmatizes and isolates the victims while mobilizing the victimizers in their genocidal pursuits.

Technology. Once the victim is labeled by the prevailing propaganda as being outside the universe of moral obligation, the killing can take place. The technology of death has become more efficient as modern nation-states have become more technologically sophisticated. While primitive means like clubs, spears, and gunbutts have been used in poorly developed nations (for example, the genocide in Burundi-Rwanda in the 1960s), more sophisticated methods like gas chambers, crematoriums, and "killing vans" were used by the Nazis to kill Gypsies and Jews. Today, of course, with modern nuclear systems we have the capacity to kill many more human beings in a shorter time than even the Nazi regime was able to do. Thus technology is an obvious component of genocide.

Bureaucracy. Hilberg has detailed the enormous state apparatus that was necessary to undertake genocide in Germany and the conquered territories. Just as technology has become more sophisticated, so too have organizational and logistic skills. The carrying out of genocide necessitates some minimum organization; optimally effective genocide such as in Germany necessitated an enormously complex organization. Coordination of various military and civilian groups, rail transportation, the courts, and the like is essential. Fein and Horowitz have noted that modern premeditated genocide must first be recognized as organized state murder, and such murder requires a complex bureaucracy. The human victim is reduced to a nonhuman entity and, like any merchandise, must be assembled, evaluated, selected, stored, and ultimately disposed of as efficiently as possible.

Watching Human Rights: Mass Denationalizations

ARYEH NEIER

Writing in these pages recently, historian Eric Hobsbawm warned of the dangers in the current trend to establish "ethnic-linguistic nation states." . . . One such danger is that, as between the two world wars, minorities in many countries may be deprived of their nationality and become stateless. Some could be forced to leave the lands where they were born and have lived all their lives, with no place to go.

Hobsbawm cited what may be the most extreme proposal that has yet emerged: that of President Zviad Gamsakhurdia of Georgia to limit citizenship to those whose ancestors lived in the territory prior to 1801, when Georgia was incorporated into the Russian Empire. Nothing may come of this, but proposals to limit citizenship for the sake of ethnic purity are also being debated intensely in the newly independent Baltic States. The most restrictive legislation could be adopted in Latvia, which is only 52 percent ethnic Latvian, a fact that has caused this part of the population to fear they could become a minority in their own country. A proposed law, which cleared the first hurdle toward passage on October 9, requires that those who were not born in Latvia prior to June 17, 1940, or are not descended from such persons, must have been permanent residents of Latvia for sixteen years and must possess a conversational knowledge of Latvian to qualify for citizenship. Among the excluded are soldiers demobilized in Latvia who had not been permanent residents prior to their military service, as well as those "sent into Latvia after June 17, 1940, as USSR Communist Party and Komsomol personnel." But exclusion would also apply to those convicted of various crimes, registered drug addicts or alcoholics and those living without legal financial sources. All these and others would be barred from voting and from jobs, housing and other benefits that may be restricted to citizens. At a later date the law could also subject those denied the possibility of becoming citizens—for example, an alcoholic or an unemployed person in his 30s who was born in Latvia but whose parents migrated there after 1940—to deportation. But to where? Presumably, the Russian Republic is envisioned as the dumping ground, though not all those who may be deported by the Baltic States are ethnic Russians and, burdened with its own economic problems, Russia may not want such deportees.

That is the situation now facing a minority in another part of the world: the Palestinians of Kuwait. Although many were born in Kuwait or have resided there for decades, they are victims of the postwar nationalist purification of the country. Typically, those Palestinians who originated in the West Bank, or whose families moved to the West Bank following the establishment of Israel in 1948, carry Jordanian papers and are able to go to Jordan. Their situation is often dire, since they leave behind their jobs, schools and property, and there are few opportunities for them in Jordan. Yet at least they have a haven. The 18,000 to 20,000 Palestinians in Kuwait whose roots are in Gaza, or whose families fled to Gaza from elsewhere in what had been Palestine, have a more desperate plight. When Egypt administered Gaza, it did not annex the territory and, accordingly, the residents never acquired Egyptian citizenship. Unless Israel allows these Palestinians to repatriate to Gaza, or unless Egypt grants them visas, probably their only choice is to go to Iraq. My colleagues at Middle East Watch have established that since liberation, Kuwaiti authorities have forced about 2,000 Palestinians across the Iraqi border, while thousands of others have left for Iraq on their own, seeing no alternative.

When new nation-states were being established in Europe as part of the peace settlement following World War I, it was widely feared that they would deal with their minorities in just this fashion. As a consequence, the League of Nations promulgated a series of Minority Treaties, which were imposed on the new states as a condition of recognition and membership. The Baltic States—which until then had been territories of the Russian Empire—were among those required to sign these declarations acknowledging that their inhabitants had a right to citizenship and protection regardless of birth, nationality, language, race or religion. The League itself was to enforce these treaties and declarations. Unfortunately, the weakness of the League of Nations was reflected in its failure to fulfill this role.

Since it was not one of the newly created states, Germany was not required to sign such a treaty. Accordingly, even if the League had been inclined to do so, it could not have invoked a treaty to protest the cancellation of citizenship for all naturalized Germans of Jewish origin when the Nazis came to power in 1933. That event, among the first mass denationalizations on grounds of race or ethnic identity, was not unique in Europe. Fascist Italy denationalized the Croat and Slovene minorities it had absorbed after World War I and, in 1936, even Greece canceled naturalizations, a move directed against Armenian refugees, many of whom had fled there decades earlier to escape pogroms in Turkey.

In *The Origins of Totalitarianism,* Hannah Arendt pointed out that in the 1930s "mass denationalizations were something entirely new and unforeseen. They presupposed a state structure which, if it was not yet fully totalitarian, at least would not tolerate any opposition and would rather lose its citizens than harbor people with different views." It is a great irony that states such as Latvia and Kuwait should celebrate their liberation from the totalitarian rule of the Soviet Union and Iraq by setting out on the road of ethnic purification, which, as Arendt saw, is one that leads directly toward totalitarianism.

A Nation of Nations: "We the People . . ."

DANIEL PATRICK MOYNIHAN

The Constitution of the United States begins: "We the People of the United States. . . ." Yet, as we know, the United States is not made up of a single group of people. It is made up of many peoples. Immigrants from Europe, Asia, Africa, and Central and South America settled in North America seeking a new life filled with opportunities unavailable in their homeland. Coming from many nations, they forged one nation and made it their own. More than 100 years ago, Walt Whitman expressed this perception of America as a melting pot: "Here is not merely a nation, but a teeming Nation of nations."

Although the ingenuity and acts of courage of these immigrants, our ancestors, shaped the North American way of life, we sometimes take their contributions for granted. . . .

Immigrants did not abandon their ethnic traditions when they reached the shores of North America. Each ethnic group had its own customs and traditions, and each brought different experiences, accomplishments, skills, values, styles of dress, and tastes in food that lingered long after its arrival. . . .

Millions of immigrants from scores of homelands brought diversity to our continent. In a mass migration, some 12 million immigrants passed through the waiting rooms of New York's Ellis Island; thousands more came to the West Coast. At first, these immigrants were welcomed because labor was needed to meet the demands of the Industrial Age. Soon, however, the new immigrants faced the prejudice of earlier immigrants who saw them as a burden on the economy. Legislation was passed to limit immigration. The Chinese Exclusion Act of 1882 was among the first laws closing the doors to the promise of America. The Japanese were also effectively excluded by this law. In 1924, Congress set immigration quotas on a country-by-country basis. . . .

The remarkable ability of Americans to live together as one people was seriously threatened by the issue of slavery. It was a symptom of growing intolerance in the world. Thousands of settlers from the British Isles had arrived in the colonies as indentured servants, agreeing to work for a specified number of years on farms or as apprentices in return for passage to America and room and board. When the first Africans arrived in the then-British colonies during the 17th century, some colonists thought that they too should be treated as indentured servants. Eventually, the question of whether the Africans should be viewed as indentured, like the English, or as slaves who could be owned for life, was considered in a Maryland court. The court's calamitous decree held that blacks were slaves bound to lifelong servitude, and so were their children. . . .

Yet the court ruling that set blacks apart from other races fanned flames of discrimination that burned long after slavery was abolished—

and that still flicker today. The concept of racism had existed for centuries in countries throughout the world. For instance, when the Manchus conquered China in the 13th century, they decreed that Chinese and Manchus could not intermarry. To impress their superiority on the conquered Chinese, the Manchus ordered all Chinese men to wear their hair in a long braid called a queue.

By the 19th century, some intellectuals took up the banner of racism, citing Charles Darwin. Darwin's scientific studies hypothesized that highly evolved animals were dominant over other animals. Some advocates of this theory applied it to humans, asserting that certain races were more highly evolved than others and thus were superior.

This philosophy served as the basis for a new form of discrimination, not only against nonwhite people but also against various ethnic groups. Asians faced harsh discrimination and were depicted by popular 19th-century newspaper cartoonists as depraved, degenerate, and deficient in intelligence. When the Irish flooded American cities to escape the famine in Ireland, the cartoonists caricatured the typical "Paddy" (a common term for Irish immigrants) as an apelike creature with jutting jaw and sloping forehead.

By the 20th century, racism and ethnic prejudice had given rise to virulent theories of a Northern European master race. When Adolf Hitler came to power in Germany in 1933, he popularized the notion of Aryan supremacy. "Aryan," a term referring to the Indo-European races, was applied to so-called superior physical characteristics such as blond hair, blue eyes, and delicate facial features. Anyone with darker and heavier features was considered inferior. Buttressed by these theories, the German Nazi state from 1933 to 1945 set out to destroy European Jews, along with Poles, Russians, and other groups considered inferior. It nearly succeeded. Millions of these people were exterminated.

The tragedies brought on by ethnic and racial intolerance throughout the world demonstrate the importance of North America's efforts to create a society free of prejudice and inequality.

A relatively recent example of the New World's desire to resolve ethnic friction nonviolently is the solution the Canadians found to a conflict between two ethnic groups. A long-standing dispute as to whether Canadian culture was properly English or French resurfaced in the mid-1960s, dividing the peoples of the French-speaking Quebec Province from those of the English-speaking provinces. Relations grew tense, then bitter, then violent. The Royal Commission on Bilingualism and Biculturalism was established to study the growing crisis and to propose measures to ease the tensions. As a result of the commission's recommendations, all official documents and statements from the national government's capital at Ottawa are now issued in both French and English, and bilingual education is encouraged. . . .

The year 1980 marked a coming of age for the United States's ethnic heritage. For the first time, the U.S. Census asked people about their ethnic background. Americans chose from more than 100 groups, including French Basque, Spanish Basque, French Canadian, Afro-American, Peruvian, Armenian, Chinese, and Japanese. The ethnic group with the largest response was English (49.6 million). More than 100 million Americans claimed ancestors from the British Isles, which includes England, Ireland, Wales, and Scotland. There were almost as many Germans (49.2 million) as English. The Irish-American population (40.2 million) was third, but the next largest ethnic group, the Afro-Americans, was a distant fourth (21 million). There was a sizable group of French ancestry (13 million), as well as of Italian (12 million). Poles, Dutch, Swedes, Norwegians, and Russians followed. These groups, and other smaller ones, represent the wondrous profusion of ethnic influences in North America.

Canada, too, has learned more about the diversity of its population. Studies conducted during the French/English conflict showed that Canadians were descended from Ukrainians, Germans, Italians, Chinese, Japanese, native Indians, and Eskimos, among others. Canada found it had no ethnic majority, although nearly half of its immigrant population had come from the British Isles. Canada, like the United States, is a land of immigrants for whom mutual tolerance is a matter of reason as well as principle.

The people of North America are the descendants of one of the greatest migrations in history. And that migration is not over. Koreans, Vietnamese, Nicaraguans, Cubans, and many others are heading for the shores of North America in large numbers. This mix of cultures shapes every aspect of our lives. To understand ourselves, we must know something about our diverse ethnic ancestry.

The American Neo-Nazi Movement

ELINOR LANGER

The story you are about to read is an ugly one. If it were a film, it would be rated "R." On television, a solicitous commentator would warn parents to urge children from the room. It is the story of something secret becoming public; of something forbidden becoming permitted; of the long, slow re-emergence of racial thinking in the United States from its retreat after World War II to the point where it can once again energize action; of the gradual, tentative crystallization of a political movement openly aimed at white hegemony. The problems of understanding this phenomenon are many. Composed of elements ranging from the Ku Klux Klan of Connecticut to the skinheads of California, the racial movement is scattered and diverse, and on matters as important as its relationship to American society in general and American racism in particular, observers disagree.

I want to make it plain from the outset that I am not an authority on the neo-Nazi movement. I live in Portland, Oregon, where in November 1988 three skinheads murdered an Ethiopian man, and like many of my friends and neighbors, I was startled to see how—literally —close to home it had come. The murder took place in a neighborhood very near where my husband and I had lived when we first moved to Portland years before. Of the three assailants, one was a neighbor, living a few blocks away in a building in which I had just considered taking an office; the second was a rock musician and all-round counterculture personage who moved in circles close to those of our baby sitter as well as, at some points, close to mine; and the third was a recent homecoming king of a local high school with some of whose friends and schoolmates my own acquaintances also overlapped.

Originally, the boys were to have been tried jointly and, my attention having been caught, I arranged to write about the trial for this magazine [*The Nation*]. It then transpired that the cases were severed, and ultimately, because the defendants all pleaded guilty, there were no trials at all. But in the meantime, as you will see, the trail had led directly from the Portland skinheads, members of a local gang called East Side White Pride, to a California-based neo-Nazi organization called White Aryan Resistance (WAR) and to its youth arm, the Aryan Youth Movement (A.Y.M.), headed, respectively, by a man named Tom Metzger and his son, John, and my article on the Portland case had become this special issue of *The Nation* on the movement as a whole.

In introducing to *Nation* readers a subject that until recently I knew little about, I feel a certain diffidence; my chief comfort in doing so is that one of the things I have realized during this period is how little is generally known. Unlikely as it seems, there appears to be only a handful of scholars at work on specialized aspects of the movement, and as far as I have been able to learn there is no ongoing research of a general sociological nature. The books that are available have been written mostly by journalists, invariably as a result of having covered some local occurrence, but these, though useful, tend to suffer from an excess of anecdote and an absence of documentation. There are organizations that at first glance appear to know everything and without which no one looking at the neo-Nazi movement would get very far, but their interests also are specialized, and it soon becomes apparent that though their facts are indispensable their assumptions are arguable, and it is necessary to weigh their interpretations against one's own.

In writing about a subject that carries with it the automatic weight of its association with Nazi Germany, I find myself uncomfortable for another reason, suspended between caution and alarm. Especially about a movement as underreported as this one, you do not write, in the first place, merely to observe "This too will pass away"; you write to sound an alert. At the same time, you know that the tests of time are different and that historians of another generation will consider the evidence and say either that it was all simply part of another "Brown Scare" in which people, as usual, lost their heads, and some their civil liberties, or that a dangerous movement was on the rise and that we failed to discern it early enough and help stamp it out. I do not know where along the spectrum the truth of the neo-Nazi movement lies. I do know that it is among us, that it is violent and mean, and that it is time to open up the subject for further investigation and discussion so that out of a broader base of information and variety of perspectives there can possibly be fashioned a sound response.

. . .

In using the term "neo-Nazi," I am referring roughly to an array of groups and individuals, including:

· Nazis: old-line groups principally descended from the American Nazi Party founded by George Lincoln Rockwell in 1959, whose members still appear in uniform, as well as other small Nazi-identified parties and groupings whose members usually do not.

· The skinheads: youth gangs in various cities with names like Youth of Hitler and the Confederate Hammerskins—some, like San Francisco's American Front, openly connected with Metzger's WAR, and some not; skinheads are the fastest-growing wing of the movement today.

· The Ku Klux Klan: no longer the centralized Klan of previous eras, but three separate and rival Klan federations and innumerable splinter groups; it is a government-infiltrated and at times government-manipulated Klan, a shadow of its former self, many of whose units are, however, "Nazified" in that they cooperate freely with the Nazi groups (something that was unthinkable in the past, when the Klan's patriotism and the Nazis' Germanophilism invariably clashed) and share many of the same ideas.

· The Posse Comitatus: a decentralized, antistate and largely rural movement, which also appears as the Christian Patriots or American Freemen Association, whose adherents believe, among other things, that all government should be rooted at the county level and that cooperating with any higher authority, including the I.R.S. or, indeed, even the state Department of Motor Vehicles, is wrong.

· The Christian Identity movement: an Aryan-inspired religious denomination descended from a nineteenth-century movement known as Anglo-Israelism or British Israelism, which holds that the "chosen people" of the Bible are white Anglo-Saxons, that Jews are descended from Satan and that all nonwhites are "pre-Adamic" "mud people," a lower species than whites; it is a religious movement that, as in the case of Idaho's Aryan Nations-Church of Jesus Christ, Christian (as opposed to Jesus Christ, Jew), is often indistinguishable from a political one.

The Nature of the Movement

In the phrase "neo-Nazi movement," both the terms "neo-Nazi" and "movement" require further discussion, and they have to be argued together. . . . the Klanwatch Project of the Southern Poverty Law Center (S.P.L.C.) in Montgomery, Alabama . . . uses the overall heading "white supremacist" and reserves "neo-Nazi" for the groups that had their genesis with Rockwell. The term "white supremacist" is also used by another major monitoring organization, the Center for Democratic Renewal in Atlanta. The problem with this usage, it seems to me, is not that it is wrong but that it does not go far enough, retaining an old-fashioned, unduly Southern and narrowly political flavor that fails to reflect the modern racialism that comes to us directly from the Nazi era and that I think is the essential characteristic these groups share. The neo-Nazi label does have varying degrees of applicability. James Farrands, Imperial Wizard of The Invisible Empire, Knights of the Ku Klux Klan, with whom I spoke a few months ago, was indignant at being associated with neo-Nazis and at pains to assure me that "you don't have to be a Nazi to be an anti-Semite," and to find a member of the Posse Comitatus with the same revulsion would not be difficult. But for the most part these organizations have no enemies to the right. If there are those within the movement who object to their Nazi bedfellows, they do not generally make themselves heard.

More important than any differences among the groups is the fact that the individuals within them function together as a movement and know that they are one—a point on which the two monitoring organizations mentioned above, as well as the Anti-Defamation League of B'nai B'rith (A.D.L.), largely agree. Klan and Nazi units have worked together at least since their combined assault on anti-Klan demonstrators at a rally in Greensboro, North Carolina, in 1979, in which five were killed, three of them members of the Communist Workers Party. Klan/neo-Nazi joint appearances on occasions such as an annual gathering in Pulaski, Tennessee, honoring the founding of the Klan—this year also attended by Aryan Nations pastor Richard Butler—have become routine. . . . the Klan . . . near Spokane, in eastern Washington . . . [is headed by] Kim Badynski, who recently relocated to the Northwest from Chicago, where his Klan faction was closely associated with various Nazi groups. He is now close to pastor Butler and the Aryan Nations group in Idaho, at whose compound he has often appeared with . . . Rick Cooper,* publisher of a newsletter called "National Socialist Vanguard Report," who is proud to call himself a Nazi and would probably satisfy anyone's definition. Other visitors to the Idaho compound, whose annual Aryan Nations congress has been one of the central gathering points of the movement for several years, have included skinheads, Identity Christians, Posse associates and so on. An Aryan martyrs list saluted throughout the movement would include not only Robert Mathews, founder of the violent brotherhood called "The Order," whose death in a 1984 shootout with the F.B.I. on Whidbey Island, Washington, is commemorated by an annual vigil, but also Gordon Kahl, a North Dakota Posse farmer convicted of tax evasion who killed two federal marshals attempting to serve a warrant for probation violation in 1983, and was himself killed in an F.B.I. shootout in Arkansas a few months later. The mail-order catalogues of the Christian Patriots, a Posse group, and of the National Vanguard, a West Virginia Nazi group begun by Rockwell-follower William Pierce, not only offer many selections in their specialized areas (roughly, European prehistory and myth, in the case of the Nazis; the monetary system, in the case of the Patriots) but often overlap, featuring not only such classics as Carleton Putnam's *Race and Reason* (which is still winning converts) and Henry Ford's *The International Jew* (ditto) but such newer and highly influential tracts as *The Hoax of the Twentieth Century* by Arthur Butz and *Did Six Million Really Die?* by Richard Harwood. If there is a household of an adherent of any wing of the movement that does not have a copy of *The Turner Diaries,* Pierce's fantasy of the violent overthrow of the U.S. government by patriotic guerrillas, I would be surprised. . . .

To the readers of these books, Jews are the force controlling your life, blacks are genetically inferior and race mixing is the nearest thing to the end of the world this side of Armageddon. Although one group may start with the Jews and end with the blacks and another may start with the blacks and end with the Jews, they are linked by the newer idea that blacks are the latest woe that the Jews are heaping on the world. These are not the only convictions held in common, of course. Hostility to homosexuals and aliens, to name only two other groups, is

[* Rick Cooper is located east of Portland.]

also universal, though reflected less in the current ideological libraries than in the streets. But it is above all else the centrality of the Jew, even in the wake of the Holocaust, that makes me believe that "neo-Nazi" is the proper label for the movement in question. The quality of its hate and the direction of its intentions go beyond what we have seen in America before. As anomalous as it seems in a country in which blacks are not only the primary historical but also the primary daily victims of racism of every description, the Jew is, increasingly, the ultimate target; and lest the logic elude you, it is that, out of fear of being recognized as a race themselves, the Jews have conceived and implemented a variety of political strategies, of which integration is only the most offensive, designed to minimize racial differences in general. The significance of the historic shift on the far right from the dominance of the Klan to the dominance of the Nazi-influenced skinheads and others is in fact precisely the linkage of blacks and Jews in an explicitly genocidal context. [Racist] cartoons . . . , a WAR video that opens with a laugh track over a scene of bulldozers burying bodies at Auschwitz, the words of Rick Cooper ("When the people can no longer tolerate the Jews, those people who don't believe in the Holocaust will want one; and those who do believe in the Holocaust will want another one. . . . The next Holocaust won't be a hoax"), emanating from the same source, have got to give one pause. However much some Jews, and some blacks, may now wish to part company, from the neo-Nazi viewpoint they are part of the same problem, as are gays and every other minority as well.

The reader would undoubtedly like to know how many people are involved, a point on which the available data are unfortunately not very good. Estimates made by the three monitoring organizations mentioned above range from about 10,000 to about 20,000 members of these groups nationally, with the organizations agreeing on a rule of thumb of about ten passive supporters for every hard-core member—and thus a possible total of up to 200,000—and agreeing as well that the numbers are conservative. The larger number, which by some counts includes an additional 30,000 Christian Identity followers, is also presumed to include the 100,000 or so subscribers to a Washington, D.C.–based newspaper called *The Spotlight,* published by an ideologically similar but stylistically dissimilar far-right organization, the

Liberty Lobby, founded in 1957 by Willis Carto, who also founded the revisionist Institute for Historical Review and the contemporary Populist Party, as well as the 44,000 people who voted for the 1988 Populist presidential candidate, David Duke.

As uncertain as the number of adherents is the number of incidents of hate-motivated violence that we read about in our papers every day; everyone agrees they are dramatically increasing, but there are no reliable figures. With the exception of the A.D.L., which issues an annual audit of anti-Semitic incidents (1,432 in 1989, a 12 percent increase over the previous year), most national organizations prefer not to quantify, believing that with the violence and the reporting apparently increasing simultaneously, the situation is not only a social but also a statistical mess; and with a monitoring agency in the Northwest alone reporting a 400 percent overall increase during the same year, this seems a reasonable inference. The Hate Crimes Statistics Act recently signed by President Bush requires the Justice Department to begin keeping national statistics for the first time, but since participation by state and local police agencies is voluntary—and certain acts, such as cross burnings, may in some cases be arbitrarily excluded—it is questionable how comprehensive they will be.

More important than the number either of members or of incidents, however, is the relationship between the two—a matter that has scarcely begun to be discussed. While it appears that most hate crimes are committed by individuals who are not associated with any organized group, the impulses of the member and the nonmember appear to be much the same. If it is an exaggeration to say that every hate criminal is a potential neo-Nazi, certainly they give the leaders reason to hope. At the least, there appears to be a kind of multiplier effect whereby one thing leads to another, and the mere existence of the movement acts as an enabling force for the open expressions of racism that, until recently, have tended to be underground. There is a dynamism at work here that any static accounting, whether of "members" or "incidents," cannot reflect.

Epilogue: "Can It Happen Here?"

In historical writing about racism there is a tradition in which the author acknowledges the inevitable incompleteness of his or her treatment of so large and unending a subject. Thus David Chalmers, in his 1965 history of the Klan, *Hooded Americanism,* quotes the Klan's first historian, Walter Fleming, who wrote in 1905, "There is still much that is obscure about the Ku Klux Klan and I shall be glad to obtain additional information . . . and to receive notices of mistakes and errors in this account." George Mosse, in his history of European racism, *Toward the Final Solution,* titles his last chapter, "A Conclusion That Does Not Conclude." . . . With the neo-Nazi movement continuing to unfold in both the United States and Europe, there is more—much more—to be said. From questions about the internal character of the movement to its external connections, my own list of topics untouched here is long, and readers will undoubtedly have many questions of their own.

Anyone approaching the movement with the seriousness it deserves is immediately faced with another dilemma also remarked on by historians: maintaining intellectual perspective, a problem shared by virtually every Klan-watch organization and individual Klan watcher today. As someone who has spent the last year and a half flooded with materials from and about the movement, I have to say that, again, I am no exception. When the *Protocols of the Elders of Zion* arrives in your mailbox in a plain wrapper and you have grasped its currency in the minds of people at the other mailboxes where it is also arriving in a plain wrapper, you tend to forget that is just about the only way to get it these days. When you have listened enough to the British band Skrewdriver playing and singing "Race and Nation," "White Power" and "Tomorrow Belongs to Me," it is hard to remember the Rolling Stones. Once you have learned that you can celebrate Hitler's birthday by buying, among other things, a teddy bear ("The Dolf Bear has the Fuhrer's famous mustache and you can even comb his black hair"), you forget that with less rigmarole you can walk into any toy store and buy Shakesbeare, Paddington or Pooh. Apart from the sheer quantity of material, there is something about its character that is spellbinding. I know that I looked forward to the biweekly showings of *Race and Reason* in Portland and I believe that other observers with whom I was in contact around the country did too. There is even a kind of excited trade in these materials—"I'll trade you Baxter for Monique," or, more accurately, "You can copy my Baxter if I can copy your Monique"—as researchers and activists share a sense of mutual astonishment: What will they say next? It is hard to avoid the feeling that the neo-Nazis are everywhere, embedded in everything, Tomorrow the World.

In addition to the problem of intellectual perspective, there is also a problem of political perspective, which is in many respects the reverse: namely, a tendency to minimize or marginalize the neo-Nazis by defining them as "extremists" and denying their relationship to racial issues as a whole. Civil rights activists point out that the Reagan Administration, for example, prosecuted violent, racially motivated crimes such as The Order's while simultaneously endorsing one of the racial movement's essential premises, that it is time for black preference programs to end. Again, the historians can be helpful. In his book, *The Old Christian Right,* about William Pelley, Gerald Winrod and Gerald L. K. Smith in the 1930s, Leo Ribuffo makes the case that the " 'extremism' of the far right often converged with the cultural and political mainstream," a point also made by historians of racism in other places and times. "The theory segregating far right villainy from the mainstream obscures the sources of indecency," Ribuffo goes on.

As unexceptional as such a proposition may appear when applied to the past, however, when applied to the present it becomes controversial. The Anti-Defamation League—the government's principal adviser on these matters—prefers a line of reasoning that labels the neo-Nazis as "extremists," an approach that, in the A.D.L.'s view, leads to effective prosecution, which in turn diminishes the force of the movement—fewer overt acts, fewer models to follow—and puts it in a category with both far-left and black anti-Semitism, which is where the organization feels the neo-Nazis belong. The implications of one's definition of the problem are extremely important, both in interpreting the racial movement and in deciding on courses of action. In assessing the extent of anti-Semitic feeling in the Midwest during the farm crisis of the early 1980s, a period of heightened Posse Comitatus activity, almost all observers, including The American Jewish Committee, reported more anti-Semitism than did the A.D.L., which was particularly concerned lest a majority of American farmers be branded anti-Semitic when they were not. In considering whether to support a demonstration against the Aryan Nations in Idaho last year, nearly all local and regional grass-roots antiracist groups, including the Rainbow Coalition, agreed to do so; the A.D.L. did not, citing the burden on local law enforcement authorities of keeping the racist and antiracist demonstrators apart. The general position of the A.D.L. is that the problem is serious but not too serious, and that the authorities have it well in hand.

Knowing only too well that in criticizing the A.D.L. one can find oneself in undesirable company, it seems to me, nonetheless, that its strategy of containment rests on a fallacy. The neo-Nazis' ideology and activities are certainly "extreme," but they exist along a racist continuum on which it is difficult to draw a line. Granted that the situation could be a lot worse, but with the rising number of hate crimes occurring simultaneously with the rise in influence of the neo-Nazi movement, can it really be described as being in hand? As a Jew with my own reading of history, the combination of minimizing the problem and trusting authority makes me uneasy. If the problem were limited to "extremists," prosecutions would, in fact, suffice; but if it is general, nothing short of a painful national self-assessment will be required. Since we do not know under what circumstances the present movement could become something more, I for one am glad that in addition to the cautious accountings of the A.D.L. we have the broad-based, antiracist organizing of the Center for Democratic Renewal, the aggressive litigation of the S.P.L.C., the militance of the John Brown Anti-Klan Committee and the activities of countless other organizations and individuals throughout the United States, because we need every one. The premature consolidation of a monolithic viewpoint about a movement we still understand so little is not in anyone's interest.

I want to return one final time to the words of a historian, again George Mosse. Anyone writing on Nazis or anything connected with Nazis is invariably asked the one question everyone always wonders about, the dread question, the Sinclair Lewis question, "Can it happen here?" and in being confronted with this several times in the course of this work, I came to see that the key word in the question is obviously "it." If "it" means another Hitler, the answer is probably no, if only because history does not literally repeat. But there are subtler forms of repetition. In a period of declining national authority manifested everywhere from our weakening social structure to our worsening economic position, a movement is stirring that explains it all, and people are starting to listen. In following the course of racism and anti-Semitism from the fringes to the center of German thought, and from theory to practice, Mosse remarks, "In 1930 . . . in Germany [the] left [and] the center had to argue on the terrain occupied by the racist right . . . one of the Nazis' principal victories before seizing power." That much, I now think, can happen here and is, indeed, beginning to happen; and that is the problem already posed by the American neo-Nazi movement today.

In the Face of Hatred

JAMES WRIGHT

I am frightened by the sorrow
Of escaping animals.
The snake moves slowly
Beyond his horizon of yellow stone.
A great harvest of convicts has shaken loose
And hurries across the wall of your eyes.
Most of them, all moving alike,
Are gone already along the river.
Only two boys,

Trailed by shadows of rooted police,
Turn aimlessly in the lashing elderberries.
One cries for his father's death,
And the other, the silent one,
Listens into the hallway
Of a dark leaf.

Germany's Right-Wing Revival: Bashers

FRANK THALER

On Thursday, October 3, 1991, Germans marked the one-year anniversary of reunification. Some celebrated with a rampage of neo-Nazi violence against foreign workers and asylum-seekers. Over that weekend the violence spread. Arson attacks, stabbings, and beatings swept over the country—not to mention the subterranean undertone, unreported in crime statistics, of threats and racial slurs. The terror's main victims are people whose skin color most obviously identifies them as non-German, yet whites fall victim too, particularly Poles. Not only asylum-seekers and foreign workers but foreign students and plain tourists are fair game for German xenophobes.

Anti-foreign violence had been on an upswing ever since the opening of East German borders in November 1989. The initial euphoria of the approaching German unity, combined with Chancellor Kohl's success in steamrolling foreign opposition to the forced pace of reunification, gave many Germans a surge of national pride. "We are here again" (*"Wir sind wieder da"*) rang the slogan of a new self-assertion. At the same time, the insecurities and mass stress of social and economic restructuring in East Germany provided the classic breeding grounds for violent scapegoating. The West Germans themselves had only recently emerged from a difficult restructuring process, carried out in the early and mid-'80s, which strengthened the economy while driving millions of young people and older workers to the margins of society. Their dilemma was intensified by a severe housing shortage—brought about in part by the practical elimination of public housing construction—and increasing homelessness. In the context of aroused national emotions, these difficulties have produced a toxic social brew.

For more than a year West German politicians had easy explanations. In proportion to population, there had been many more anti-foreign incidents in East Germany than in the West, whose leaders could attribute the violence to forty years of GDR socialism, and to its alleged deficits of civilization. However, by the end of September such evasion was no longer possible. From September 17 to 22 a pogrom took place in the Saxon city of Hoyerswerda, just north of Dresden. Neo-Nazi youths hurled rocks and Molotov cocktails at buildings housing foreign workers and asylum-seekers. A large crowd stood by and cheered—particularly when a bus convoy transporting foreigners out of the city was attacked. Hoyerswerda set off a chain reaction, as the brutality spread west. The university city of Freiburg in Baden-Württemberg was the scene of repeated assaults. The quantitative center of violence was Germany's most populous state, North Rhine-Westphalia, where thirteen attacks were recorded against asylum-seeker housing during the "weekend of German unity."

The connection between bad times and feelings of social threat at the hands of foreign groups is not unique to Germany. The United States, Britain, and France have had their share of racism. But none of the other leading NATO democracies has a *völkisch* concept of citizenship. In Germany what counts for citizenship is blood. A Pole who scarcely speaks German but can prove German blood by showing evidence of his grandfather's membership in the Nazi Party is not only bestowed German citizenship but is showered with subsidies to aid transition into German society. A 25-year-old resident of Berlin, born of Turkish parents in Germany, where he has lived all his life, is by blood a Turk and therefore always a Turk, with no practical hope of obtaining a fraction of the rights granted to the Pole with a Nazi grandfather.

In times of economic distress, this underlying rejection of foreigners takes its toll. And for all the official optimism, the signs are that the slump in East Germany is not going to dissipate soon. Officially, East German unemployment through October stood at 11.9 percent; economists estimate the real rate at around 30 percent, maybe more. The difference is concealed by definitional casuistry, early retirement, and dead-end jobs that expire after two years. Economic rationalization will in the first instance lead to further job loss. Billions invested in equipment under a two-year special incentive program will make industry more productive but will not relieve unemployment. Increasing rents will contribute to a relative, if not an absolute, impoverishment of the "loser" population.

Moreover, even an improvement in material conditions will not repair the psychological damage of the precipitate dissolution of East Germany. Many East Germans will have more money in their pockets. But aside from a small number of enterprises purchased by foreign investors, privatization has put former state industrial companies almost exclusively in the hands of West Germans. The near-term hope of East Germans is to become well-paid helots: they will enjoy a decent standard of creature comfort but will remain second-class citizens, held largely in contempt by the dominant Westerners. The more unfortunate East Germans, consigned to life on welfare, will count for even less. For people in both groups, one clear avenue for maintaining self-esteem will be to take pride in being German. People who otherwise feel worthless can at least feel superior to "lesser" breeds.

Meanwhile, a recent opinion survey commissioned by *Der Spiegel* newsmagazine showed 38 percent of West German respondents expressing "understanding" for right-wing radical tendencies arising from the "foreigner problem." The Republican and National People's Union parties, taken for dead in 1990, have revived at the polls in Bremen and Lower Saxony. Together they won 7.7 percent in Bremen, a 67 percent increase in their previous share. Worse, the Bremen SPD and CDU had themselves pandered to anti-foreign popular sentiment, both playing up their resistance to further settlement of asylum-seekers in Bremen.

Even the strength of the West German economy is now suspect. It has long thrived on low inflation and solid public finances. But massive public deficits—politically required to finance reunification in the face of Western sullenness over tax hikes—and spiraling wage settlements have undermined these traditional strengths. Underlying inflation has increased. Large unemployment and welfare expenditures in East Germany have pushed up social security taxes and made West German labor—already the most expensive in the industrialized world —still more costly. The hard-won competitive edge that Germany gained as a result of the CDU consolidation policy during the '80s could erode.

Germany will have an increasingly difficult time holding its competitive ground. The Germans do well in manufacturing goods of the second industrial revolution—chemicals, machines, automobiles. However, as for high-technology industries of the future—personal computers, microchips, semiconductors, telecommunications, biotechnology, materials technology—they are not in the running. Germany is already on the way to becoming a technological dependent of America and Japan.

In this context, as in places as diverse as Birmingham, England, and Louisiana, far-right extremism is a useful political tool. For Helmut Kohl, "the Chancellor of German unity," the barbarism has emerged at a good time. Kohl's false promises of instant prosperity for the East (at no cost to the West) could not be fulfilled. At first he blamed non-fulfillment on forty years of GDR socialism, coupled with Communist conspirators. But then the foreigners became a handy political theme. No more "abuse" can be permitted of the right to asylum, guaranteed in Article 16 of the Federal German Basic Law. Kohl has called for changes in Article 16. His position is sheer demagogy. Asylum-seekers are not responsible for housing shortages or any other problem in Germany. By making asylum law a central, burning issue of German politics, he implies that alleged asylum abusers *are* a source of ills, and that by getting rid of them, those ills will be cured. It does not seem to bother Kohl that he might be inciting further Hoyerswerda-style violence.

The opposition SPD is afraid of losing votes over the foreigner issue. In so-called resistance to changes in Article 16, it proposes accelerating the asylum procedure so that cases can be decided more quickly and rejected applicants expelled immediately. The national leadership has agreed to the erection of central "collection points," where asylum applicants would be gathered into ghettos pending decision of their cases.

One of the few politicians speaking any sense is the federal president, Richard von Weizsäcker. He has demonstratively visited the lodgings of asylum-seekers, and he has pointed out the sham nature of the controversy over changes in Article 16. The big problem, he asserts, will come with prospective mass migration from Eastern Europe. Literally millions could be streaming West. How can anyone seriously think that changing a couple of sentences in Article 16 will have practical bearing on a problem of that dimension? He is right, and his remarks invite another question: If the foreigner "problem" evokes wild reactions now, what happens if mass migration actually occurs? Political and economic collapse in the Soviet Union, civil war in Yugoslavia, rising unemployment and political uncertainty even in more

fortunate Eastern European states—all these factors make such an occurrence more likely than not. If it does, will Germany's democracy
have the stamina to cope?

The Hitler Spring

EUGENIO MONTALE

Translated by Daniela Gioseffi

A dense white cloud of mayflies madly
whirls around pale streetlamps and over rooftops,
spreading a blanket like scattered sugar
upon which the sole grinds.
Summer looms now and releases
the night frosts it once held captive
in secret caves of the dead season.

Suddenly, an infernal messenger flies through the passageway.
The murderers salute; a mystic chasm, fired
and flagged with swastikas, has grabbed and swallowed us!
The shop windows, humble and unobtrusive, are closed,
though they, too, are armed
with toy cannons of war;
and the butcher has stuffed dressings of flowers and berries
in the mouths of slaughtered goats.
The ritual of a gentle hangman, once innocent of blood,
is changed to a spastic dance of shattering wings;
the mayflies' little deaths whiten the pier's edge
and water continues to eat at the shoreline,
and now, no one is blameless.

All for nothing, now? —the Roman candles at San Giovanni,
which whitened the horizon, the oaths,
and the lingering farewells with the strength of a baptism
in sad expectation of the horde (but a bud exploded in air,
dispersing on the ice and rivers of your country
messengers of Tobias, the seven, the seeds of the future)

and a heliotrope born of burned hands is sucked dry
by a pollen that weeps like fire and is winged with ice and salt.
      Oh, ulcerated
springtime will go on with her festival, and freeze
in death that death! Look, again beyond, Clizia,
you preserve your destiny by a love which doesn't change
until the blind sun you carry inside yourself
blinds itself in the other, and confounds itself and all in God.
Maybe the sirens and holy bells
which salute the monsters of the night
at their warlock's sabbath are already damned with celestial sound
released, descending to conquer with its breath
a dawn which may yet reappear, tomorrow, white
without wings of terror, to the dried lit horizons of the south.

In Europe, Immigrants Are Needed, Not Wanted

ALAN RIDING

A brief walk along any street in downtown London, Paris, Frankfurt or Milan immediately shows how immigration from the third world has turned many Western European cities into melting pots. But 30 years after this process began, a surge of racist incidents, smoldering hostility toward immigrants and new moves to keep out poor foreign workers show how Western Europe still has to come to terms with this change.

With new prosperity making Western Europe the most powerful magnet for poor immigrants after the United States, plans by the 12-nation European Community to eliminate its internal borders after 1992 have suddenly turned immigration into the region's most explosive social issue. In country after country, polls show that the public is strongly opposed to new immigration and, in some cases, even favors repatriation of some of the 12 million immigrants now in the region.

Yet, as the United States has discovered in trying to curb the influx of undocumented aliens, economic forces—the flight from poverty and the chance of a relatively well-paid job—are invariably more effective in attracting new immigrants than border controls and hostility are in keeping them out.

The appeal of moving to Western Europe is steadily growing, not only to those without hope in the traditional emigrant countries of North Africa, but also to those newly unemployed in Eastern Europe. Today, just as young Moroccans risk their lives to reach Spain in small boats, the railroad stations of Berlin and Vienna are crowded with Poles, Romanians and others seeking a new life farther west. "You don't have to be a visionary to predict that the Turks in Germany will be pushed into France and Spain or that Italy will soon face grave difficulties," a French commentator, Yann de l'Ecotais, wrote in *L'Express* magazine, referring to the 1.4 million Turks in West Germany and the growing numbers of North Africans in Italy.

In some places, immigrants have become the scapegoats for high unemployment, although they often do manual or low-paid jobs that natives refuse. And nonwhite or non-Christian immigrants are often seen as a threat to ethnic, religious and cultural traditions.

In the medium term, another force may come into play. With a slump in birth rates and a jump in life expectancy, experts believe that by the turn of the century Western Europe will need immigration to sustain its growth. "In the coming years, Western Europe will have to coexist with hostility toward immigrants and a demand for immigrants," said Jean-Claude Chesnais, a population expert at France's National Institute of Demographic Studies.

But for today's politicians, the immediate priority is clear: to be seen to be addressing the immigration problem in such a way as to reassure electorates that their national identities are not about to be transformed by alien influences.

For example, in France, where anti-immigration feelings are feeding the growth of the extreme rightist National Front, the Socialist Government recently dropped plans to allow immigrants to vote in local elections, fearing it would lose more French votes than it would win immigrant votes. In Spain and Italy, countries with long traditions of emigration, governments are trying to reduce illegal immigration from North Africa. Similarly, London has ruled that no more than 250,000 Hong Kong Chinese will be granted British passports before the colony reverts to China in 1997.

When a single regional market is formed at the end of 1992,

foreigners entering one European Community country could travel freely to the 11 others. Finding a common policy involves not only deciding which outsiders will require visas to enter the Community, but also insuring that illegal immigrants, political refugees, drug traffickers and terrorists do not profit from the borderfree region. London, for example, insists on the right to check citizens from non-Community countries who enter from another Community country. Bonn favors a more liberal visa policy for Eastern Europe than France and Britain favor. Spain is alarmed at the prospect of having to demand visas of citizens from its former colonies in Latin America.

Aware that even stricter measures may be insufficient to neutralize the pull of prosperity and the push of poverty, the Community is also turning its focus toward aiding countries that export most migrants—although in Eastern Europe it is also motivated by the need to encourage democracy and capitalism.

In the case of North Africa, Spain, Italy, Portugal and France have decided to sponsor a more ambitious initiative. If successful, the planned Conference on Security and Development in the Mediterranean would not only address the relationship between immigration and North Africa's problems of poverty, population growth and unemployment, but would also tackle questions of security and economic development throughout the Mediterranean area.

Long-term programs of this kind, though, seem unlikely to alleviate the social tensions currently being stirred by the immigration problem. Rather, many politicians believe the only real answer lies in fully integrating existing immigrant communities. But most Western European countries still seem reluctant to accept that they have already become multi-ethnic societies.

Extreme Prejudice Toward Polish Americans

RACHEL TOOR

In addition to the strain of everyday life, Polish Americans contended with another, sometimes more vexing, problem: prejudice. It seemed to be everywhere. Many of their neighbors viewed Poles as rowdy, disorganized, ignorant, filthy, and prone to drunkenness and sloth. In the early 20th century, even President Woodrow Wilson, who had been a professor of law and economics at Princeton University, as well as the institution's president, publicly commented that Poles came from "the ranks where there was neither skill nor energy nor any initiative of quick intelligence." The impetus for these kinds of attack is unclear. Most cultures single out scapegoats to be the butt of unflattering jokes. The French take cheap shots at the Belgians and Irish Americans and Italian Americans trade frequent barbs, as do the English and the Scotch.

In any case, the stereotyping of Polish Americans has been reinforced by films, television, and plays. Perhaps the best-known fictional Polish American is Stanley Kowalski, the brutish character created by Tennessee Williams in his classic drama, *A Streetcar Named Desire,* first staged in 1948. For many Americans, Kowalski stood for all Polish Americans: violent, crude, poorly educated, and a heavy drinker. Since the late 1960s Polish—or "Polak"—jokes have enjoyed a great vogue. Many television comedians routinely tell jokes deprecating Poles, and these jokes gain momentum in the retelling. In the 1970s, television's "lovable bigot," Archie Bunker—the main character in the hit show "All in the Family"—reinforced prejudice against Polish Americans by calling his Polish-American son-in-law "meathead." Books like *It's Fun to Be a Polak* helped keep this prejudice alive. Even worse, Polish jokes have reached the highest levels of American society. When Ronald Reagan was running for president in 1980 he asked reporters, "How do you know who the Polish guy is at a cockfight?" He answered himself, "He's the one with the duck."

These "humorous" slights perpetuated the image of the "dumb Polak" by focusing on the lower-class backgrounds and peasant heritage of many Poles and fanning the flames of what some scholars perceive as an inferiority complex within the Polish-American community. To combat these attacks, in 1973 Edward J. Piszek, president of Mrs. Paul's Kitchens, a frozen-food manufacturer, launched a massive advertising campaign to stamp out Polish jokes. Working with the Orchard Lake Schools of Michigan, "Project Pole" was a half-million-dollar affair. It featured literate and intelligent ads, such as the one that showed a picture of celebrated novelist Joseph Conrad (1857–1924, née Jozef Korzeniowski) and read: "One of the greatest storytellers in the English language was a Pole. He changed his name, his language and the course of English literature." A lawsuit brought against the American Broadcasting Company (ABC) by the Polish American Congress charged the network with refusing to allow equal airtime for a response to jokes viewed by many as "personal attacks on the character, intelligence, hygiene or appearance" of Americans of Polish descent. And Polish Americans took exception to an insulting skit on the "Carol Burnett Show," sending in bags of critical mail and forcing an apology on the air.

The issue of Polish stereotypes took a curious turn in November 1987, when a lengthy letter to the editor appeared in the *New York Times Book Review*. It was written by Stanislaus A. Blejwas, a Polish-American historian, and the subject of the letter was remarks made by another Polish American, Czeslaw Milosz, one of the leading Polish-language authors of the 20th century. Milosz, who had labored in obscurity for many years, rose to international celebrity in 1980, when he won the Nobel Prize for literature. He quickly became a source of enormous pride to the Polish-American community, which demanded his presence at a host of cultural events. But Milosz objected to acting as a spokesman for a community that had long neglected him. Indeed, the poet recently told an interviewer that he resents being invited to give public readings before "a lot of Poles, who come to see a famous Pole to lessen their own feeling of inferiority." Milosz went on to criticize the "incredible cultural crudeness" of many Polish Americans, a condition he traces to the "ghetto" mentality the community brought over from the homeland.

These opinions incensed Blejwas, who in his letter to the *Times* explained the feelings of Polish Americans in these words:

> *After a decade of Polish jokes in the national media, jokes which even Mr. Milosz disliked, Polish-Americans took satisfaction in the recognition accorded to Mr. Milosz by the Nobel Prize, and we applauded him. . . . Like any other ethnic group [the Polish Americans] . . . have both good and negative points. Furthermore, their diversity and socioeconomic and cultural integration into American society belies crude (there is that word again!) generalizations and stereotyping. . . . What are the . . . roots of the contempt of some Polish intellectuals for their Polish cousins? Is it due to a political culture still heavily encrusted with gentry contempt*

*for those of lower social origin and rank? Is it simply the arrogance
that many intellectuals, regardless of their national identity, felt for
the masses? Or, in America, is it that sense of "alienation" our
culture provokes which causes [some] . . . to stoop to the level of
those who indulge themselves in Polish jokes?*

From Blood of My Blood: "An Extraordinary Bigotry"

RICHARD GAMBINO

Writing in the autumn 1969 issue of *The American Scholar,* Michael Lerner examined the bigotry toward Italian-Americans fashionable among upper-class liberals. His points are telling.

> *An extraordinary amount of bigotry on the part of elite, liberal
> students goes unexamined at Yale and elsewhere. Directed at the
> lower middle class, it feeds on the unexamined biases of class per-
> spective, the personality predilections of elite radicals and academic
> disciplines that support their views. . . . The radical may object
> that he dislikes the lower middle class purely because of its racism
> and its politics. But that is not sufficient explanation: Polish jokes
> are devoid of political content. . . . Hip radicals are often amused
> by the Italian defamation league bumper sticker: "A.I.D.-Ameri-
> cans of Italian descent." Poles, Italians, Mayor Daley and the
> police are safe objects for amusement, derision or hatred.*

Lerner's observations bring to mind comments that greeted me in response to an experience of mine in 1972. During a trip to Sicily, thieves in the city of Catania broke into the trunk of my automobile and stole my luggage. Upon hearing of this, a college-educated engineer in New York commented, "There are no criminals in Sicily, only the natives." Another educated middle-class New Yorker said, "Catania? That's where crime was invented, wasn't it? No, it was Palermo." Yet three years before, when my car was burglarized on the very street where I live in New York City, the incident elicited no comments at all. The widespread crime in American cities is simply regarded as a fact of life. But crimes committed by Italians or Italian-Americans are cause for sensation-mongering.

The fact is that Italian-Americans have become the scapegoat of comfortable, educated, influential Americans. In the 1970 edition of *Beyond the Melting Pot* (M.I.T. Press), Nathan Glazer and Daniel Moynihan commented:

> During the 1960's the mass media, and the *non-Italian politicians,* combined to make the Mafia a household symbol of evil and wrongdoing. Television ran endless crime series, such as *The Untouchables,* in which the criminals were, for all purposes, exclusively Italian. Attorneys Generals, of whom Robert F. Kennedy was the archetype, made the "war against organized crime" a staple of national politics. . . . This is rather an incredible set of facts. Ethnic sensitivities in New York, in the nation, have never been higher than during the 1960s. To accuse a major portion of the population of persistent criminality would seem a certain course of political or commercial disaster. But it was not. The contrast with the general "elite" response to Negro crime is instructive. Typically, the latter was blamed on white society. Black problems were muted, while Italian problems were emphasized, even exaggerated. Why?
>
> We do not know. There may have been some displacement of antiblack feeling to Italians, possibly as a consequence of the association of the Mafia with drug traffic, and the latter's association with high rates of black crime. It may be that society needs an unpopular group around, and the Italians were for many reasons available. Democratic reformers, in largest number Jews but also including among them political figures who had come from Irish Catholic and white Protestant groups, were able to use the Italian association with crime to topple any number of Italian political leaders and, perhaps more important, to prevent others from acquiring any ascendancy. Many political figures thus gained advantage.

Similarly, Lerner observed:

> In general, the bigotry of a lower-middle class policeman
> toward a ghetto black or of a lower-middle-class mayor
> toward a rioter is not viewed in the same perspective as the
> bigotry of an upper-middle-class peace matron toward a
> lower-middle-class mayor; or of an upper-class university
> student toward an Italian, a Pole or a National Guardsman
> from Cicero, Illinois—that is, if the latter two cases are
> called bigotry at all.

The long-standing bigotry against Italian-Americans has in recent
years become respectable also because many white Americans find in
the Italian-American a scapegoat for their own guilt about the sufferings of blacks. The constant association of the Mafia with ghetto
crime, especially crime involving drugs, affords the guilt-laden liberal
villains with whom to relieve his overwrought conscience. The Mafia,
linked with or supported by their racist ethnic kin, is to blame and not
the white upper middle class whose historic unconcern for blacks now
pricks their conscience.

From The Japanese Today: "*Race Prejudice Pervades the World*"

EDWIN O. REISCHAUER

We often think of racial prejudice as being a special problem
. . . of the white race in relations with other races, but it
actually pervades the world. . . . Because the Japanese have merged
their feelings about race, culture, and nation together, they have probably made their attitudes toward race all the stronger. It is almost as if
they regarded themselves as a different species from the rest of humanity.

Before World War II few Japanese had ever had any significant
contacts with Westerners, and they still reacted with some of the shock
they felt when they first encountered the Portuguese in the sixteenth

century and the more numerous Englishmen and Americans in the nineteenth century. They found them positively revolting with their blue eyes and "red" hair—the attributes of goblins in Japan—and their sweaty bodies clothed in hot woolen clothes and inadequately bathed according to more fastidious Japanese standards. A strong body odor resulting from a diet richer in animal fats made them still smellier. *Bata-kusai,* "stinking of butter," is still a term used for obnoxiously Western things. Styles in clothes, food, and bathing have changed since then, but the hairy bodies of Caucasian men are still somewhat revolting to Japanese, and the sense of racial difference still runs deep in Japan. In the many cases of interracial marriages I have known, if family objections were raised, it was almost always the Japanese family that protested the most.

Japanese attitudes toward the black or darkly colored races are worse than toward Caucasians, whose blue eyes and "red" hair are now much admired. Having had almost no contacts with blacks before the coming of the American army of occupation, Japanese still tend to view them with some wonderment and revulsion. During the civil rights movement of the 1960s in the United States, most Japanese unconsciously looked at the problem from the point of view of the majority whites. The long injustices that the blacks had undergone impressed them less than the difficulty the whites faced in dealing with such a large and very distinct minority.

One would assume that Koreans and Chinese, who in physical characteristics are usually indistinguishable from Japanese, would be racially more accepted than Westerners, but this is not the case. Probably more Japanese parents today would tolerate an American son-in-law or even a daughter-in-law than they would a Korean or Chinese. "Racial" prejudice is severe against the roughly 700,000 Koreans who remain in Japan from among those imported for forced labor there during World War II. Despite the fact that more than forty years have passed and most of these so-called Koreans have become Japanese in language and living style, they are prevented as much as the laws permit from acquiring Japanese citizenship. Most Japanese still feel that marriage with the child of a Korean or Chinese immigrant, as with the surviving 2 percent of Japanese irrationally designated as outcasts (*burakumin*), would sully their "pure" Japanese blood. Prejudice against darker-skinned Southeast and South Asians is even stronger. During the past two decades of disturbances in Southeast Asia, only a few hundred Southeast Asians have been granted permanent domicile in nearby Japan. . . .

Attitudes in Japan toward racially similar peoples contrast sharply with those of Europe, where international marriages have always been common, particularly among the aristocracy, and where class has been more important than nationality or minor physical differences. The British royal family is predominantly German, even though family names have been changed from Hannover to Windsor and Battenberg to Mountbatten. Wilhelm II, the last of the kaisers, and Nicholas II, the last of the czars, were both grandchildren of Queen Victoria and spoke to each other in English. In East Asia mixed marriages occurred only between the . . . [lower classes] of port cities.

The racist attitudes of East Asia are clearest in the treatment of children of mixed marriages. In Korea and Vietnam the offspring of American soldiers and native women, usually of low social status, have normally been rejected by the local society or subjected to severe discrimination. The situation has been worse for the half-blacks than for the half-whites. The best hope for either group was to be adopted into racist America. Somewhat the same situation existed in postwar Japan. A worthy Japanese lady, who was much praised for her orphan-age for such children, could only hold out the hope that they might in time find a new life for themselves on the frontiers of civilization in the Amazon. Biracial children of better family background have com-monly achieved normal careers, but most of them have done so not in Japanese society but in the United States. . . .

If it is extremely difficult for other East Asians living in Japan to cross over the imaginary "racial line" and actual "culture line" into full membership in Japanese society, it is all but impossible for a West-erner. Occidentals are treated with amazing kindness and hospitality, though rarely invited to a Japanese home simply because of the embar-rassing lack of space. Only in a few specialized situations are Western-ers subjected to unpleasant discrimination, as, for example, when they are excluded from certain bars because of fear of their rowdiness or the uneasiness they would cause other patrons. Usually the treatment they receive is so generous as to make them seriously embarrassed when it comes to reciprocating.

But such kind treatment is based on the assumption that they will remain merely visitors or at least outsiders. It is very difficult for a Westerner to be accepted as truly one of the group. As an external adornment he or she may be lionized, but no one wants him as a full member. A Westerner who becomes very well informed about Japan may even be resented. To the extent that he becomes accustomed to Japanese habits of thought and ways of life he may come to be considered a *hen na gaijin,* a "foreigner with a screw loose," who makes the Japanese feel ill at ease. True fluency in Japanese may raise feelings bordering on hostility, though a few outrageously mispronounced phrases will produce enthusiastic praise. The Japanese feel that foreigners should never forget that they are foreigners.

Many Americans living in Japan are infuriated by their ultimate rejection and irritated by the unconsciously pejorative overtones of words used for foreigners. In my childhood clearly insulting words, such as *ijin,* "strange people," or *keto,* "hairy barbarian," were sometimes heard, but neutral terms won out, such as *Seiyojin,* "Westerner," for all Caucasians and the official word *gaikokujin* for all foreigners. *Gaikokujin* still remains in official use but has been shortened for informal use to *gaijin,* "outsiders." This term emphasizes the exclusiveness of Japanese attitudes and has picked up pejorative overtones that many Westerners resent. Interestingly, it is not used for Koreans, Chinese, and some of Japan's other near neighbors, who are differentiated by their national origins. But such more specific names usually carry even more derogatory overtones than *gaijin.* . . .

Feelings of inferiority seem to have been a natural breeding ground for nationalism throughout the world. The first stirrings of modern nationalism in northern Europe were probably inspired by feelings of backwardness relative to the older lands of the Mediterranean. Early American spread-eagle patriotism was obviously linked to the country's position as a raw and weak frontier land on the edges of the Western world. Nationalism throughout the non-Western world seems clearly to have been a reaction to Western domination.

The Japanese experience is particularly reminiscent of the British, whose early and strong sense of nationalism may derive from the same sources as those of Japan. Overrun repeatedly by foreign military and cultural invasions, the British developed the same irrational pride and sense of distinctiveness. Their island position probably contributed to the similarities. The Japanese often refer to their distinctive attitudes as *shimaguni-konjo,* "the feelings of an island people." In time, as people began to realize the undesirability of such attitudes, the term developed the same negative overtone as "insularity" for the British.

In Japan the early expressions of nationalism were largely made in response to a Japanese sense of inferiority to China. China might be huge, old, and the home of the Confucian sages, but only Japan was "the home of the gods." The long period of intensive learning from China from the sixth to the ninth centuries left a deeply ingrained sense of inferiority in Japan that only slowly wore away as the Japanese assimilated what they had borrowed and turned it into their own distinctive civilization. Not until the nineteenth century did Japanese attitudes toward China change to a sense of superiority because of their newly developed power, wealth, and greater success in handling modern problems, and even then Japan's superiority complex was tempered by a lingering respect for what China once had been. . . .

Such attitudes of inferiority and superiority are scarcely unique to Japan. Inferiority and superiority complexes seem to be closely related: one flips easily into the other. . . .

Japanese sometimes claim that their sense of distinctiveness from the rest of the world has nothing to do with feelings of superiority or inferiority, but this is difficult to accept in a society that has always been so conscious of hierarchic order. The Japanese among themselves are an extraordinarily egalitarian people today, but the terms *Nihon-ichi,* "first in Japan," and *sekai-ichi,* "first in the world," are constantly heard. One of the most popular T-shirt symbols written in *kanji* that Americans have imported from Japan is *ichiban,* "number one." . . .

The strong Japanese sense of nationalism has at times been of great benefit to Japan. In the middle of the nineteenth century, though gripped by a severe struggle for power among themselves, no Japanese dreamed of making common cause with the foreigners against the best interests of Japan as a whole. Unlike the leaders of many more recently created states, Japanese leaders did not attempt to stash away personal riches in foreign lands. Every one of them remained entirely committed to Japan and its national fortunes. As the country began to surmount the crisis and achieve its objectives, individual Japanese were not averse to harvesting riches and honors for themselves, but they all continued to put national interests first.

Nationalism again came to the aid of the Japanese in the catastrophe of World War II and its aftermath. Most Japanese were forced to struggle desperately to survive, but few of them tried to do this at the expense of national interests. Again many in time became affluent, but they prospered as part of a bigger effort to bring prosperity back to Japan. Again none of them sought to sequester their own riches abroad to escape some possible future national calamity at home. In much of the developing world today, such unsullied nationalism is more the exception than the rule.

. . . At first all modern technology was defined as being Western, leaving very little untouched by it that could be defined as Japanese or Eastern. But in actuality modern technology is Western not by nature but only by time sequence. There is very little in the contemporary West that has not been profoundly changed by modern technology. We are about as far from our seventeenth-century forebears as the Japanese are from theirs. Modern technology started in the West, to be sure, but technology by its nature belongs to all people. The spread of agriculture and the use of iron and bronze did not make all cultures part of the ones where these innovations started. The spread of Chinese inventions such as paper, printing, gunpowder, porcelain, and even the bureaucratic system did not make other lands culturally Chinese. Modern technology and industrial society belong as much to the Japanese as to the peoples of the West. The Japanese have operated steam engines two thirds as long as Westerners, and the time gap in later technological innovation has become steadily shorter until it has now disappeared entirely. Subtract technological change, and the Japanese are still every bit as much Japanese as Americans are American.

Cultural differences often remain as sharp as ever. Nothing is more central to historical Western culture than Christianity, but less than 2 percent of Japanese are professing Christians today—probably a smaller percentage, as we have seen, than in 1600. In institutions influenced by technology, both Japan and the West have gravitated in the same direction. Educational systems, political institutions, industrial organization, and a myriad other things are remarkably similar. For contemporary Japanese, particularly younger ones, there is no longer any sharp sense of differences, and those that exist lose their significance except to give each country an intriguing sense of identity.

Since World War II both the Japanese government and people have sought to minimize nationalism in every way they could. Most of them, not without reason, see themselves as being one of the most internationalized people in the world. Japanese schools probably teach more about the world than do those of any other nation. The history and culture of the West and Chinese antiquity form major elements of Japanese education together with ample teaching about Japan itself. Does the educational system of any other country embrace so fully three different cultures? In the West, the content of most education usually gets little beyond the confines of the Occident, and in former colonial lands, what is taught about the former colonial masters is likely to be offset by inadequacies in education about the country itself. Education in Japan does ignore vast areas of the world, but not as egregiously so as elsewhere.

Life in Japan is as international as in any other country.

From Turning Japanese: *"The Resentment Americans Have Toward the Rising Asian Economic Powers . . ."*

DAVID MURA

The resentment Americans have toward the rising Asian economic powers is based on racism: there's no way the slant eyes could beat us if everyone played fair; there's no way they could ever be better than America, than a nation of whites. American racism is revealed by America's ignorance of how Japanese culture has fit into the Japanese postwar surge, in the inability to distinguish differences within Japanese society, either between particular groups or between individuals. Nor do Americans have much sense of how the Japanese look at them. They seem unable to think of the Japanese as a completely human Other, with all the complexities that Americans grant themselves.

As an American, even after my time in Japan, I share some of these limitations. And yet I also know that when white Americans look at Japanese-Americans today, they still see us through the gauze of stereotypes they possess about the Japanese; we too are still somehow Other.

Because of this position, I find it impossible to share the picture of Japan presented by Lee Iacocca or Richard Gephardt. They fear Japan's success. For me, Japan's changed status became part of its attraction, part of my desire to identify with the Japanese.

I realize that my feelings about my Japanese background would be less positive if I had returned to a less prosperous land of origin. Japan also possesses an incredibly well-preserved and complex indigenous culture. This makes it very different from a country like the Philippines; there the combined colonialism of the Spanish and the Americans has served to obliterate much of the native culture. When I went to the Philippines, there were no equivalents of Noh, Kabuki, Bashō, or Lady Murasaki, no museum filled with scrolls and ink-block prints. What would have resisted or modified the influx of culture from the West had disappeared. Half the television programs were broadcast in English.

From Tales from the Bazaar

ROBERT D. KAPLAN

As individuals, few American diplomats have been as anonymous as the members of the group known as Arabists. And yet as a group, no cadre of diplomats has aroused more suspicion than the Arab experts have. Arabists are frequently accused of romanticism, of having "gone native"—charges brought with a special vehemence as a result of the recent Gulf War and the events leading up to it. Who are the Arabists? Where did they come from? Do they deserve our confidence?

For Jack McCreary, it was a moment of sweet satisfaction. A self-described "child of the sixties," who had spent nearly two decades of his life in the Arab world, McCreary was the U.S. embassy's press and culture officer in Iraq in January of 1988, when the doors of the new American Cultural Center, on Mansour Street in Baghdad, opened for the first time. At last, McCreary thought, there was one place under Saddam Hussein's rule where ordinary Iraqis and Americans could talk to each other in the same room. "The great thing about living for long stretches in an awful country," McCreary said during an evening I spent with him and his wife, Carol, at their home in Virginia, "is that the smallest victory, no matter how pathetic and inconsequential, gives you an incredibly big boost."

Life in Baghdad for the McCrearys and their young daughters, Kate and Joanna, was made up of a number of such boosts. If anyone can squeeze a little water from an ugly regime's monolithic stone, it is McCreary.

After graduating from the University of California at Berkeley in 1968, McCreary entered the Peace Corps, serving in Marrakech, Morocco, where he and Carol met and were married. At the American University of Cairo, McCreary perfected his Arabic. He then joined the U.S. Foreign Service, working as a political officer at American embassies in Qatar, Saudi Arabia, and Yemen. In Yemen, where I first met him, McCreary was becoming frustrated. Doing his job properly, he felt, ought to mean immersing himself in Arabic with Arabs. "I still marvel at the physical beauty of Arabic script. I'm shocked at people who come to Arab countries and can't read the signs." But Yemen, like Qatar and Saudi Arabia, was politically closed and sterile. Embassy officers were denied regular, official contact with Yemenis. McCreary, who has a "4" rating in Arabic, on a Foreign Service test scale of 5— meaning he speaks and reads Arabic fluently—was meeting nobody except other diplomats. So he gave up the job of political officer in order to run the embassy's press and culture division. As far as his career was concerned, this was an unorthodox move. But McCreary's life changed. "Suddenly I was with Yemenis all the time."

Hume Horan, a former ambassador to Saudi Arabia and Sudan, observes, "It's the embassy cultural officers who get the real internist's-eye view of a difficult country. They have fewer restrictions placed on their movements. Since Arab writers and artists are in a terrible financial situation and nobody cares about their work, they come cheap: for the price of a meal and a bit of appreciation they'll pour their souls out to you, providing the kind of psychological clues to the workings of a system that a political officer will never get from his Foreign Ministry contacts."

In the summer of 1987, after finishing his assignment in Yemen, McCreary was posted to Iraq. "On a strictly political level, nothing was happening," McCreary explained. "The embassy people knew nobody at the palace. We had no access to the Baath Party. We'd invite Iraqis to receptions and they were too frightened to show up. For us to claim we knew Baghdad would have been like a Third World diplomat claiming to know Washington because there was one desk officer at the State Department who returned his phone calls. But on the cultural level in Iraq there was tremendous hope."

Western secular culture was a bone that Saddam tossed to his affluent urban subjects. Among other things, Baghdad was the lone Arab capital offering classical piano and violin recitals and a degree program in European music. McCreary's daughters took ballet lessons at an Iraqi government school. McCreary became involved in a jazz club, Al-Ghareeb ("The Stranger"), in downtown Baghdad, where he played the saxophone and Joseph Wilson, the embassy's deputy chief of mission, sang, while McCreary's daughter Kate—along with a crowd of Iraqi artists—made charcoal sketches of the performances. "It was a marvelous place: jazz at night, me playing, Kate and the Iraqis drawing away. From the point of view of my job, the Iraqis' interest in classical music and jazz was certainly to be encouraged."

The jazz club and his daughters' ballet lessons bought McCreary and his wife rare entrée to the homes of numerous Iraqi families. "It was an artsy crowd of ancien régime types and politically neutered intellectuals. Carol and I worked constantly to give these people a sense of American values, to demonstrate how free people think and behave: to show them *it was possible*. But they were cowed. The big crisis in one family was the teenage daughter, whose beauty had attracted one of Saddam's Takriti goons." (Takrit is Saddam Hussein's birthplace, and that of many of his closest associates.)

The United States Information Agency helped arrange for an American singer, Billy Stephens, to give a concert in Baghdad. Stephens sang "We Shall Overcome" and John Lennon's "Imagine." But when the singer asked the crowd of English-speaking Iraqis to join in, there was silence. "Nobody dared," Carol McCreary remembered.

"But there was such hope, things really were getting better," Carol went on. She described the lifting of internal travel restrictions after the Iran-Iraq War was over, and the end of rationing. The American diplomatic community in Baghdad assumed that there was a thin wedge of opportunity it could exploit, especially after the revolution in Romania. *Maybe it could happen here.* The diplomats all knew it wasn't much of a hope, but it was enough to keep them going.

Jack McCreary said, "Of course, considering all that has happened, this must sound silly to you. I'm embarrassed to talk about it. They were building chemical and nuclear weapons while they let a few diplomats open a library and play in a jazz club. It all seems so stupid and misguided."

Pekinese Orchids

The McCrearys, whom a right-wing observer might be tempted to ridicule as "liberal, multicultural, Peace Corps types," have in fact tested a canon of neoconservative interventionism—"the export of democracy"—on a deeply personal level under the worst possible conditions, and have the emotional scars to prove it. "The Arab world can be a nasty place," says a key State Department official currently engaged in Middle East diplomacy. "But the Arabist is someone who doesn't have the luxury to theorize from the sidelines. He must actually live there and work solo with this intractable reality."

McCreary and his colleagues are, of course, aware that "Arabist" is among the most loaded words in America's political lexicon. In the Middle Ages an Arabist was a physician who had studied Arab medicine, which was then more advanced than the kind practiced in Europe. In the late nineteenth and early twentieth centuries an Arabist was a student of the language, history, and culture. With the birth of Israel, in 1947, the word gained another meaning. "It became a pejorative for 'he who intellectually sleeps with Arabs,'" said Richard Murphy, a former assistant secretary of state for Near East affairs, during a recent interview. Murphy's wife, Anne, nodded sadly. "If you call yourself an Arabist," she said, "people may think you're anti-Semitic."

Along with that suspicion come suspicions of "clientitis" and elitism. I was told a story about one U.S. diplomat's wife in Cairo during the 1956 Sinai war who innocently said of the Egyptians, then fighting a British-French-Israeli alliance: "We're so proud of them." The head of a conservative foundation in Washington once lectured me along these lines: "Spanish—because of our intimate contact with the Latin world—connotes a non-elite, drug-lord, 7-Eleven-store culture. Arabic is a distant, difficult, and thus mysterious language, and fluency in it suggests erudite entry to a ruling class where Jews and other ethnic Americans are not welcome."

In the wake of Iraq's August, 1990, invasion of Kuwait, which most Arabists did not anticipate, the term "Arabist" became even more negative. Francis Fukuyama, then a Reagan Administration appointee on the State Department's Policy Planning Staff, and now a consultant for the Rand Corporation, commented after the invasion, "Arabists are more systemically wrong than other area specialists in the Foreign Service. They were always sending cables, and coming into the [Planning Staff] office, saying things about Saddam being a potential moderate that now they're claiming they never said."

The more it gained ascendancy as a term of political abuse, the more indiscriminately "Arabist" came to be applied. During the Gulf crisis the *New York Times* columnist William Safire and the *Washington Post* columnist Jim Hoagland frequently described John Kelly, who was then the assistant secretary of state for Near Eastern and South Asian affairs, as an Arabist, even though Kelly, with his limited Middle East experience, was distrusted by real Arabists as a politically imposed outsider. By war's end anyone who was vaguely sympathetic toward Arabs was being called an Arabist, even if he or she didn't speak the language and had never lived in the Arab world. I asked a senior Arabic-speaking diplomat at the State Department about the word "Arabist," and he frowned, his chin slumping to his chest, as he muttered, "The word has become poison; nobody uses it around here anymore."

But people do. One reason is sheer convenience. Terms like "Arabic-speaking officers" and "Middle East specialists" are simply too cumbersome. Another reason is prickly pride. "NEA [Near Eastern Affairs] is the best bureau at State," says one State Department Arab hand. "It attracts the best people because Arabists are always exposed to crises." Another NEA type says, "Any fool can learn Spanish in order to serve in Latin America." "The Eastern Europe people never had a riot on their hands until 1989," says Carleton Coon Jr., a former ambassador with wide experience in the Middle East. "They never had an ambassador killed. Near East hands know what it's like to be shot at and in the media hot seat." The attacks on Arabists notwithstanding, these people are a self-assured breed, for whom the word "Arabist" implies a tight-knit fraternity within the diplomatic corps, united by their ability to speak a "superhard" language and by a vivid, common experience abroad that, as one Arabist told me, "we can't even properly explain to our relatives." "We Arabists," says Hume Horan, in a whimsical, self-mocking tone, "are the Pekinese orchids begot by an American superpower. I suppose only a rich and powerful nation has a justification for us."

Horan knows that that is an overstatement. Arabists, or something like them, would be needed by the United States in the Arab world even if America were to abandon the internationalist assumptions of its foreign policy and its overreaching hopes for a new world order. Leaving the question of Israel aside, American businesses have economic interests in the Middle East worth many billions of dollars. It is important to know what is going on in the region. Then, too, there is the obvious matter of the Middle East's oil, on which much of the world economy depends. Though it should stop well short of the role of policeman, the United States clearly needs to maintain a significant presence of some sort.

And yet, even during the hottest moments of recent history in the Middle East, few diplomats have been more anonymous than the Arabists have. With the exception of April Glaspie, the recent U.S. ambassador to Iraq, Arabists are just an opaque "them," even to many of their worst enemies. Arabists, I found, are privately talkative, publicly shy. Like other bureaucrats and civil servants, they don't call attention to themselves. They don't pontificate on talk shows or op-ed pages. Peter Rodman, a fellow at the Johns Hopkins Foreign Policy Institute, who ran the Policy Planning Staff in the Reagan Administration, believes that the breadth, depth, and texture of the Arabists' knowledge of the Arab world may work to immobilize their analytical thinking about it. . . .

Racism and the Australian Aborigines

JULIAN BURGER

We are not all equal in the eyes of the law, and it is indigenous people who suffer most. The rate of imprisonment for Canadian Indians is three times that for whites. In parts of New Zealand, Maoris make up 50 per cent of prisoners, even though they are only 9 per cent of the population. Australian jails have an Aboriginal intake 14 times the national average. And a disturbing number of Aborigines die in custody.

Aborigines suffered from European settlement: tens of thousands were shot, tortured, and poisoned as they resisted invasion. The violence continues as protective legislation for Aborigines has been ignored and as the police deal with the victims of acculturation.

Between 1980 and 1988, 103 Aborigines died in custody, according to a Royal Commission. Some died from natural causes, but nearly two-thirds of those under 30 who died were found hanged. Two or more Aborigines are now dying in custody every month. Aborigines allege that police or prison officers have been negligent or, in some cases, directly caused a death. The beating and subsequent death of 16-year-old John Pat at the hands of the police was witnessed in 1983. During the inquest, one detective admitted that police had falsified records. Five policemen charged with manslaughter were acquitted by an all-white jury.

Whether suicides or victims of violence, the root cause lies in the loss of Aboriginal land, citizenship, culture, and dignity. At the same time that white Australia celebrated 200 years of settlement Aboriginal deaths in custody became the country's biggest human rights issue. Most are found hanged. Since the invasion by Europeans, Aboriginal families have been forced from their lands, their rights and laws disregarded.

And Then the Perfect Truth of Hatred

PHILIP APPLEMAN

There was a preacher in our town
whose Sunday text was the Prince of Peace,
but
when he looked out at the Monday world—
at the uppity blacks and pushy Jews
and sassy wives and sneaky heathen—blood
scalded his face as purple as if
he'd hung by his heels. Then
his back-yard, barber-shop, street-corner sermons
scorched us with all the omens of siege:
our roofs aflame, tigers at the gates,
hoodlums pillaging homes, ravaging
wives and daughters, the sky
come crashing down,
and we gazed into his blazing truth
of Onward Christian Soldiers,
A Mighty Fortress Is Our God,
Soldiers of the Cross. No question now
of sissy charity, this
was the Church Militant, burning
its lightning bolts across
our low horizons.

It's been a while since that preacher went off
to the big apartheid in the sky,
and the only hint of eternal life
is the way he resurrects each week
to sell salvation on the screen.
He's younger after all these years,
in designer suits and toothy smiles,
but we know him by the cunning eyes
where he harbors his old stooges,
Satan, Jehovah. He calls them up,
and across the country, glands begin

pumping bile into our lives:
sleet storms in the voice,
cords in the neck like bullwhips,
broken promises, broken bones—
the wreckage of his deep
sincerity.

From Sentenced to Silence: *"Religion Is Known to Be a Dangerous Topic for Writers . . ."*

SIOBHAN DOWD

Religion is known to be a dangerous topic for writers: no one needs to be reminded of the continuing plight of Salman Rushdie, who remains in hiding more than three years after the late Ayatollah Khomeini delivered his notorious death threat. Another novelist, Alaa Hamed of Egypt, also lives in constant danger. Convicted, on charges of blasphemy, to eight years' imprisonment, Hamed is free pending the confirmation of his sentence. He receives frequent death threats, however, has lost his job, and has had all his property confiscated and his books banned. In Pakistan, an eminent sociologist and noted poet is also facing a death sentence on charges of blasphemy. Akhtar Hamed Khan has recently been charged with "insulting the Holy Prophet," based on a fable in verse he wrote entitled *Sher aur Ahmak* (*The Lion and Ahmak*). The fable tells of a man, Ahmak, who brings up a lion cub that becomes so spoiled that it refuses to return to the jungle and instead turns on Ahmak and eats him. Under section 253c of the penal code, which sentences to death anyone who "by words, either spoken or written, or by visible representation, or by any imputation, innuendo, or insinuation, directly or indirectly, defies the sacred name of the Holy Prophet," Khan has been accused of blaspheming the Holy Prophet and the fourth caliph of Islam, who is referred to as the Lion of Allah.

Another sensitive topic is the role of women. Mariam Ferouz of Iran, whom LaMarche mentioned two years ago, is no longer in prison but still under house arrest. The editor of a magazine called *Jahan-e-Zanan* (*Women's World*), she has been detained since 1983 and, now, aged seventy-seven, she has lost her hearing in one ear, reportedly as a result of torture. Another writer from Iran, Shahrnush Parsipour has been banned and has a case pending against her because of her short story collection *Zanan-e Bedoun-e Mardan* (*Women without Men*).

Arguably the most sensitive topic for writers to broach just now, however, is ethnicity. The war in what was formerly Yugoslavia—a conflict without clearly delineated front lines, so that journalists often unwittingly find themselves in no-man's land—accounted for no less than thirty percent of the deaths this past year and for many other instances of censorship. But ethnic tensions can be found in other places, such as Ecuador, Ethiopia, the Commonwealth of Independent States, Guatemala, Burma, Sri Lanka, Nigeria, and Somalia. The mushrooming of these conflicts no doubt is partially due to the domino effect of the fall of communism, but the roots lie deeper—often in the artificial borders left over by Western colonial powers that aimed to divide peoples, not unify them, so that suppression could be easier. Within these borders, ethnic minorities have commonly been given short shrift by those in power. Writers who try to probe the causes of the conflict, or who try to defend those peoples who find themselves under attack, are increasingly becoming victims themselves.

To cite just two examples, Myrna Mack is a Guatemalan author of social anthropology whose brutal murder in September 1990 was, her colleagues believe, a direct result of her exposure of the injustices inflicted on the indigenous population by the Latino government. Ismail Besikci, a Turkish author whose books on the plight of the Kurds in Turkey have caused him to spend much of his adult life behind prison bars, was fined the equivalent of over $100,000 for a recent publication.

Drama in Cell 1081

LILIA QUINDOZA-SANTIAGO

Translated by Daniela Gioseffi

Then, I awakened and could hear
Blows pounding your jaws and breast.
Your captain managed such ferocity after a drink,
when he found you asleep on the job.

We share the same skin, absolutely—
You slave, I prisoner.
If by chance I finally disappear from your sight,
You'll take my place in cell 1081.

So then keep my ration of rice and fish.
You need it even more than I.
Why is my miserable fish all there is for you;
hasn't your captain just received a bonus?

But, I forget you're merely my ignorant guard,
Why not let me escape, instead;
So I can help you resolve our humanity, forever.
Together, we'll create our own freedom.

Justifiable Anger:
Excerpts from Public Speeches

MALCOLM X

I was born in Omaha, Nebraska, back in 1925—that period when
the Ku Klux Klan was quite strong in that area at that time—and
grew up in Michigan, partially.
. . . Shortly after I was born—the Ku Klux Klan gave my father
an ultimatum—or my parents an ultimatum—about remaining there,
so they left and went to Lansing.

My father was a Garveyite, and in those days, you know, it wasn't the thing for a black man to be outspoken or to deviate from the accepted stereotype that was usually considered the right image for Negroes to fulfill or reflect. . . .

He was both a Garveyite and a minister, a Baptist minister. In those days you know how it was and how it still is; it has only changed in the method, but the same things still exist: whenever a black man was outspoken, he was considered crazy or dangerous. And the police department and various branches of the law usually were interwoven with that Klan element, so the Klan had the backing of the police, and usually the police had the backing of the Klan, same as today . . .

. . . They burned the house that we lived in in Omaha, and I think this was in 1925, and we moved to Lansing, Michigan, and we ran into the same experience there. We lived in an integrated neighborhood, by the way, then. And it only proves that whites were as much against integration as they are now, only then they were more openly against it. And today they are shrewd in saying they are for it, but they still make it impossible for you to integrate. So we moved to Michigan and the same thing happened: they burned our home there. And he was—like I say—he was a clergyman, a Christian; and it was Christians who burned the home in both places—people who teach, you know, religious tolerance and brotherhood and all of that. . . .

My light color is the result of my mother's mother having been raped by a white man. I hate every drop of white blood in me. Before I am indicted for hate again, sir—is it wrong to hate the blood of a rapist? But to continue: My father was a militant follower of Marcus Garvey's "Back to Africa" movement. The Lansing, Michigan, equivalent of the Ku Klux Klan warned him to stop preaching Garvey's message, but he kept on and one of my earliest memories is of being snatched awake one night with a lot of screaming going on because our home was afire. But my father got louder about Garvey, and the next time he was found bludgeoned in the head, lying across streetcar tracks. He died soon and our family was in a bad way. We were so hungry we were dizzy and we had nowhere to turn. Finally the authorities came in and we children were scattered about in different places as public wards. . . .

I started my life in crime. I was in all of it that the white police and the gangsters left open to the black criminal, sir. I was in numbers, bootleg liquor, "hot" goods, women. I sold the bodies of black women to white men, and white women to black men. I was in dope, I was in everything evil you could name. The only thing I could say good for myself . . . was that I did not indulge in hitting anybody over the head. . . . I went to prison for what I did, and the reason that I don't have any hesitation or reluctance whatsoever to point out the fact that I went to prison: I firmly believe that it was the Christian society, as you call it, the Judaic-Christian society, that created all of the factors that send so many so-called Negroes to prison. And when these fellows go to prison there is nothing in the system designed to rehabilitate them. There's nothing in the system designed to reform them. All it does is—it's a breeding ground for a more professional type of criminal, especially among Negroes. Since I saw, detected, the reluctance on the part of penologists, prison authorities, to reform men and even detected that—noticed that after a so-called Negro in prison tries to reform and become a better man, the prison authorities are more against *that* man than they were against him when he was completely criminally inclined, so this is again hypocrisy. Not only is the Christian society itself religious hypocrisy, but the court system is hypocrisy, the entire penal system is hypocrisy. Everything is hypocrisy. . . . We must stop drinking, we must stop smoking, we must stop committing fornication and adultery, we must stop gambling and cheating and using profanity, we must stop showing disrespect for our women, we must reform ourselves as parents so we can set the proper example for our children. Once we reform ourselves of these immoral habits, that makes us more godly, more godlike, more righteous. That means we are qualified then, to be on God's side, and it puts God on our side. God becomes our champion then, and it makes it possible for us to accomplish our own aims. . . .

I'm going to tell you a secret: the black man is a whole lot smarter than white people think he is. The black man has survived in this country by fooling the white man. He's been dancing and grinning and white men never guessed what he was thinking. . . . While everybody else is sharing the fruit, the black man is just now starting to be thrown some seeds. It is our hope that through the Honorable Elijah Muhammad, we will at last get the soil to plant the seeds in. You talk about the progress of the Negro—I'll tell you, mister, it's just because the Negro has been in America while *America* has gone forward that the Negro appears to have gone forward. The Negro is like a man on a luxury commuter train doing ninety miles an hour. He looks out of the window, along with all the white passengers in their Pullman chairs, and he thinks *he's* doing ninety, too. Then he gets to the men's room and looks in the mirror—and he sees he's not really getting anywhere at all. His reflection shows a black man standing there in the white uniform of a dining-car steward. He may get on the 5:10, all right, but he sure won't be getting off at Westport.

. . . The black masses are learning for the first time in four hundred years the real truth of how the white man brainwashed the black man, kept him ignorant of his true history, robbed him of his self-confidence. The black masses for the first time are understanding that it's not a case of being anti-white or anti-Christian, but it's a case of seeing the true nature of the white man. We're anti-evil, anti-oppression, anti-lynching. You can't be anti- those things unless you're also anti- the oppressor and the lyncher. You can't be anti-slavery and pro-slavemaster; you can't be anti-crime and pro-criminal. . . . The brainwashed black man can never learn to stand on his own two feet until he is on his own. We must learn to become our own producers, manufacturers and traders: we must have industry of our own, to employ our own. The white man resists this because he wants to keep the black man under his thumb and jurisdiction in white society. He wants to keep the black man always dependent and begging—for jobs, food, clothes, shelter, education. The white man doesn't want to lose somebody to be supreme over. He wants to keep the black man where he can be watched and retarded. . . .

As soon as the white man hears a black man say he's through loving white people, then the white man accuses the black man of hating him. . . .

The white man has brainwashed himself into believing that all the black people in the world want to be cuddled up next to him. When he meets what we're talking about, he can't believe it, it takes all the wind out of him. When we tell him we don't want to be around him, we don't want to be like he is, he's staggered. It makes him re-evaluate his three-hundred-year myth about the black man. What I want to know is how the white man, with the blood of black people dripping off his fingers, can have the audacity to be asking black people do they hate him. That takes a lot of nerve. . . .

. . . Any Negro who teaches other Negroes to turn the other cheek is disarming that Negro. Any Negro who teaches Negroes to turn the other cheek in the face of attack is disarming that Negro of his God-given right, of his moral right, of his natural right, of his intelligent right to defend himself. Everything in nature can defend itself, and is right in defending itself.

Three Days and a Question

GRACE PALEY

On the first day I joined a demonstration opposing the arrest in Israel of members of Yesh Gvul, Israeli soldiers who had refused to serve in the occupied territories. Yesh Gvul means: *There Is a Limit*.

TV cameras and an anchorwoman arrived and *New York Times* stringers with their narrow journalism notebooks. What do you think? the anchorwoman asked. What do *you* think, she asked a woman passerby—a woman about my age.

Anti-Semites, the woman said quietly.

The anchorwoman said, But they're Jewish.

Anti-Semites, the woman said, a little louder.

What? One of our demonstrators stepped up to her. Are you crazy? How can you . . . Listen what we're saying.

Rotten anti-Semites—all of you.

What? What What, the man shouted. How you dare to say that —all of us Jews. Me, he said. He pulled up his shirtsleeve. Me? You call me? You look. He held out his arm. Look at this.

I'm not looking, she screamed.

You look at my number, what they did to me. My arm . . . you have no right.

Anti-Semite, she said between her teeth. Israel hater.

No, no, he said, you fool. My arm—you're afraid to look . . . my arm . . . my arm.

On the second day Vera and I listen at PEN to Eta Krisaeva read her stories that were not permitted publication in her own country, Czechoslovakia. Then we walk home in the New York walking night, about twenty blocks—shops and lights, other walkers talking past us. Late-night homeless men and women asleep in dark storefront doorways on cardboard pallets under coats and newspapers, scraps of blanket. Near home on Sixth Avenue a young man, a boy, passes—a boy the age a younger son could be—head down, bundles in his arms, on his back.

Wait, he says, turning to stop us. Please, please wait. I just got out of Bellevue. I was sick. They gave me something. I don't know . . . I need to sleep somewhere. The Y, maybe.

That's way uptown.

Yes, he says. He looks at us. Carefully he says, AIDS. He looks away. Oh. Separately, Vera and I think: A boy—only a boy. Mothers after all, our common trade for more than thirty years.

Then he says, I put out my hand. We think he means to tell us he tried to beg. I put out my hand. No one will help me. No one. Because they can see. Look at my arm. He pulls his coatsleeve back. Lesions, he says. Have you ever seen lesions? That's what people see.

No. No, we see a broad fair forehead, a pale countenance, fear. I just have to sleep, he says.

We shift in our pockets. We give him what we find—about eight dollars. We tell him, Son, they'll help you on 13th Street at the Center. Yes, I know about that place. I know about them all. He hoists the bundle of his things to his back to prepare for walking. Thank you, ladies. Goodbye.

On the third day I'm in a taxi. I'm leaving the city for a while and need to get to the airport. We talk—the driver and I. He's a black man, dark. He's not young. He has a French accent. Where are you from? Haiti, he answers. Ah, your country is in bad trouble. Very bad. You know that, miss.

Well, yes. Sometimes it's in the paper.

They thieves there. You know that? Very rich, very poor. You believe me? Killing—it's nothing to them, killing. Hunger. Starving people. Everything bad. And you don't let us come. Starving. They send us back.

We're at a red light. He turns to look at me. Why they do that? He doesn't wait for me to say, Well . . . because . . . He says, Why, hard.

The light changes. We move slowly up traffic-jammed Third Avenue. Silence. Then, Why? Why they let the Nicaragua people come?

Why they let Vietnamese come? One time American people want to kill them people. Put bomb in their children. Break their head. Now they say, Yes Yes, come come come. Not us. Why?

Your New York is beautiful country. I love it. So beautiful, this New York. But why, tell me, he says, stopping the cab, switching the meter off. Why, he says, turning to me again, rolling his short shirt-sleeve back, raising his arm to the passenger divider, pinching and pulling the bare skin of his upper arm. You tell me—this skin, this black skin—why? Why you hate this skin so much?

Question: Those gestures, those arms, the three consecutive days thrown like a formal net over the barest unchanged accidental facts. How? Why? In order to become—probably—in this city one story told.

From Second Class Citizen: "*Sorry, No Coloureds*"

BUCHI EMECHETA

Thinking about her first year in Britain, Adah could not help wondering whether the real discrimination, if one could call it that, that she experienced was not more the work of her fellow-countrymen than of the whites. Maybe if the blacks could learn to live harmoniously with one another, maybe if a West Indian landlord could learn not to look down on the African, and the African learn to boast less of his country's natural wealth, there would be fewer inferiority feelings among the blacks.

In any case, Francis and Adah had to look for another place to live. If it had been possible for them to find a new place, they would have moved within weeks of her arrival in London. But it had not been. During the days and weeks that followed, she had asked people at work if they knew of anywhere. She would read and reread all that shop windows had to advertise. Nearly all the notices had "Sorry, no coloureds" on them. Her house-hunting was made more difficult because she was black; black, with two very young children and pregnant with another one. She was beginning to learn that her colour was something she was supposed to be ashamed of. She was never aware of this at home in Nigeria, even when in the midst of whites. Those whites must have had a few lessons about colour before coming out to the tropics, because they never let drop from their cautious mouths the fact that, in their countries, black was inferior. But now Adah was beginning to find out, so did not waste her time looking for accommodation in a clean, desirable neighbourhood. She, who only a few months previously would have accepted nothing but the best, had by now been conditioned to expect inferior things. She was now learning to suspect anything beautiful and pure. Those things were for the whites, not the blacks.

This had a curious psychological effect on her. Whenever she went into big clothes stores, she would automatically go to the counters carrying soiled and discarded items, afraid of what the shop assistants might say. Even if she had enough money for the best, she would start looking at the sub-standard ones and then work her way up. This was where she differed from Francis and the others. They believed that one had to start with the inferior and stay there, because being black meant being inferior. Well, Adah did not yet believe that wholly, but what she did know was that being regarded as inferior had a psychological effect on her. The result was that she started to act in the way expected of her because she was still new in England, but after a while, she was not going to accept it from anyone. She was going to regard herself as the equal of any white. But meanwhile she must look for a place to live.

Every door seemed barred against them; nobody would consider accommodating them, even when they were willing to pay double the normal rent. She searched all she could, during her lunch hours and on her way home from work. Francis would then take a turn. They had one or two hopeful experiences, but they were rejected as soon as it was known that they had children. . . .

One of the peculiarities of most Nigerian languages is the fact that one could make a song of everything. Native housewives used this method a lot. If an older wife of a polygamous marriage wanted to get even with a younger rival who was the favourite of the husband, she would make up all sorts of songs about the younger woman. Many women would go as far as to teach their children these songs, which were meant as a kind of psychological pressure on the young woman.

Of course, at Ashdown Street, neighbours would start singing as soon as they saw Adah coming. Most of the songs were about the fact that she and her husband would soon have to make their home in the street. What use would her education be then? the songs would ask. To whom would she show her children off then? It was all so Nigerian. It was all so typical.

Matters came to a new head when the landlord got so fed up with them that he decided not to accept their rent. Only someone who had been in a similar situation would know what an emotional torture this could be. Adah and Francis had the solicitor's letters pouring in every week, counting down the number of their days for them, just like a blast-off day for astronauts. They knew they were not wanted, because they were Ibos, because they had their children with them, because Adah worked in a library and because they found it difficult to conform to the standard which they were expected to live by.

Meanwhile the songs and the laughs took a much more direct form. "I can't wait to see them pack their brats and leave our house," the landlady would say loud and clear along the hallway, to nobody, just like a mad woman roaming about in an open asylum. At the end of her proclamation, she would then burst into one of her improvised songs, sometimes dancing to them in a maniacal sort of way. All this jarred on Adah's consciousness, almost driving her crazy. She had to bear it without responding in kind because, having lived most of her formative years in a mission fee-paying school, she had long forgotten the art of hurling abusive songs at others. Sometimes, though, she would scream "The Bells of Aberdovey" or "The Ash Grove" at the top of her voice, but her listeners did not understand what she was singing about. And even if they had, the songs were as inappropriate as wearing a three-piece suit on a sunny afternoon in Lagos. This went on so much that Adah started to doubt her senses. She would laugh loudly at nothing, just to show her neighbours how happy she was. The funny thing about the whole situation was that she was not unaware of the fact that her showy behaviour was really uncalled for. But it seemed that, like Francis, she had lost control of the situation. Just like a person living with a madman would. You come to behave and act like a mad person if you are surrounded by mad people. Was that what people call adaptation? she wondered.

Two weeks later, on the noticeboard in front of the post office at Queen's Crescent, she read on a blue card of a vacant room. There was no "Sorry, no coloureds" on it. Adah could not believe her eyes. And the vacant room was not very far from where they lived: just around the corner, in Hawley Street. To make sure the room would be kept for them, she decided to phone the landlady as soon as she got to the library. She would make sure she phoned when the other assistants were out of earshot, otherwise they would think her mad or something. She had it all planned in her head. She had worked and talked for almost six months in London, so she was beginning to distinguish the accents. She knew that any white would recognise the voice of an African woman on the phone. So to eradicate that, she pressed her wide tunnel-like nostrils together as if to keep out a nasty smell. She practised and practised her voice in the loo, and was satisfied with the result. The landlady would definitely not mistake her for a woman from Birmingham or London, yet she could be Irish, Scots or an English-speaking Italian. At least, all these people were white.

It was stupid of her though, because the landlady would find out eventually. She was simply counting on human compassion. When the landlady found out that they were blacks, she'd beg her, plead with her to give them a place to stay, at least till after her baby was born. Adah was sure her plea would move anybody, forgetting that her plight had failed to move her countrymen.

The voice that answered the phone was that of a middle-aged woman. She sounded busy and breathless. Not a very cultured voice, rather like the voices of the shrieking women who sold cabbages at Queen's Crescent market.

Yes, the two rooms were still available. The rent was the exact amount Francis and Adah were paying at Ashdown Street. Yes, she would keep the rooms for them. No, she did not mind children. She was a grandmother herself, but her grandchildren were somewhere in America. Was Adah an American, the voice wanted to know? She sounded like one, went on the voice. She'd be very glad to have them, to keep her house alive.

It was all so friendly, so humane. But what would happen when the landlady was faced with two black faces? Adah told herself that it would be better to postpone this discovery to the last minute. One could never tell, she consoled herself, the woman might not even mind their being black. Hadn't she thought she was American? Adah realised that perhaps she made a little mistake there. She ought to have jumped at the woman's suggestion and claimed to be American. After all, there were black and white Americans!

Meanwhile she walked, as it were, on air. The woman had invited her and Francis to come and that was all there was to it. Why expect refusal, when the woman had sounded so jubilant? On her way home on the platform at Finchley tube station, it seemed to her ears and mind that the train that curled gracefully into view was singing with her. Sharing her happiness and optimism. It was going to be all right, the silent passengers seemed to be saying to her with their eyes, not their mouths. In fact everywhere and everything seemed saturated with happiness.

It was nearing the end of summer. The wind that blew carried an autumnal nip. The leaves were still on the trees, but were becoming dry, perched like birds ready to fly off. Their colour was yellow approaching brown. One or two eager leaves had fallen already, but those were isolated ones, too few to matter. As far as Adah was concerned, it was still summer. The trees still had leaves on them. And that was all she cared about.

She banged at their front door impatiently. Francis came out, in his loose, unbuttoned pale green cardigan, his belly bulging like that of his pregnant wife. The tail-ends of his shirt were hanging untidily out of his grey trousers. He peered at Adah over the top of his rimless glasses, blinking angrily, wondering what it was that had taken hold of her to make her behave so audaciously in a house where they were still like beggars.

"Don't look at me like that," she cried with joy. "We've got a room—no, two rooms. She advertised for one room, but when I phoned, she said she had two vacant. And, guess what, we will have to pay only the same four pounds we pay here. Two rooms for us in London!"

All this was too much for Francis. He had either been reading and concentrating hard, or he was sleeping before Adah's bang on the front door woke him. Either way, he was like somebody in a daze and it was taking him quite a while to come out of it. He succeeded in jolting himself into wakefulness.

"Who, er . . . what, er . . . ? Just wait a minute. Who is this person offering us a room, er, er . . . two rooms. Is she all right? This woman. I mean . . . she's all right, isn't she?"

"Of course she is all right. We're going to see the rooms this evening. I told her we would come at nine. Janet will look after the children for us. We must take the rooms," Adah explained, her voice ringing musically.

But Francis maintained that there was a catch in it somewhere. He went on probing Adah. "You said you spoke to her. So she heard your voice, then? It's amazing, I must say."

Adah hoped very much that the woman would take them. The joy on Francis's face was like that of a little boy. He always reminded her of their little Vicky when he was pleased. She did not delude herself into expecting Francis to love her. He had never been taught how to love, but he had an arresting way of looking pleased at Adah's achievements. Adah hoped she would never stop achieving success. Maybe that would keep the marriage together until they got back to Nigeria.

Children used to be one of the great achievements Francis appreciated, but in London, the cost, the inconvenience, even the shame of having them, had all eroded his pride in them. As long as Adah could bring home little triumphs like this one, he would go on looking pleased.

Adah did not tell him that she had held her nose when talking to the woman, neither did she tell him that she chose nine o'clock because it would be dark and the woman might not realise in time that they were black. If only they could paint their faces; just until the first rent had been paid. She dismissed this idea, mainly because she knew that Francis would not play. There was nothing she could do but to hope for the best. Even if it all failed in the end, she was thankful for the temporary happiness they were experiencing. Francis started calling her "darling", talking to her just like ordinary husbands did to their wives. He even volunteered to get the kids from the nursery, so that Adah could do the cooking. It was like a stolen hour. She was even beginning to think that Francis might be in love with her after all. All she need do was to bring up surprises like this once in a while. She did not allow herself to think that they might fail to get the rooms. The disappointment would be too heavy to bear.

Janet, now very friendly with Adah, did not need much persuasion to come and baby-sit for them. She was as excited as Adah, and they spent the time before their departure speculating on how nice Adah's flat was going to look. For, said Janet, two rooms made a flat. Didn't Adah know?

The night air was nippy, but Hawley Street was only ten minutes' walk from Ashdown Street. At first, they walked quickly, burning with hope. But when they came near to Hawley Street, Francis started to blow his nose, lagging behind as if he were going to face castration.

He looked round him, the excitement of the evening still with him, and exclaimed, "Good Lord, the place looks like a burial ground."

Adah had to laugh. The laughter of relief. Yes, the house was in a tumble-down area with most of the surrounding houses in ruins, and others in different stages of demolition. The area had a desolate air like that of an unkempt cemetery. Some of the houses had their roofs ripped off, leaving the walls as naked as Eve with no fig leaf for cover. The bare walls could be tombstones or the ruins of houses bombed by Hitler.

Adah did not mind the ruins and demolition, because the more insalubrious the place was, the more likely the landlady would be to take blacks.

They knocked at the door. A woman's small head popped out of a window, like that of a tortoise sunning itself. The head was like a mop being shaken at them. The voice was high and sounded strained, as it had been when it talked to Adah in the morning. She could not tell the age of the woman from the small head, full of loose-hanging curls. But there was something she could tell: the owner of that head could either not see properly or was colour-blind. Or maybe she actually did not mind their colour. Adah started to shake, not from the nippy air but from that sort of cold that comes from the heart.

"The rooms—the advertisement on the noticeboard," Francis yelled at the quivering head.

"Yes, shan't be a minute. Be down soon to show them to you. Just wait a minute."

Then the head disappeared. It was looking as if they were going to be given the rooms. *God, please let it be so,* Adah prayed. The two of them were too astounded for words. Adah put both hands in her coat pockets, to cover her bulging middle. She remembered she had not told the woman that, in less than four months, there was going to be another little Obi added to the group. That would be a problem for the future. For the moment, she must cover the baby up.

They could hear the light steps racing down the stairs. Even Francis was beginning to be confident. The woman did not mind blacks living in her house. The steps tapped down the hallway and the light sprung on. Now the day of reckoning had arrived, thought Adah. The lights would certainly show them up for what they were. Niggers.

The door was being opened . . .

At first Adah thought the woman was about to have an epileptic seizure. As she opened the door, the woman clutched at her throat with one hand, her little mouth opening and closing as if gasping for air, and her bright kitten-like eyes dilated to their fullest extent. She made several attempts to talk, but no sound came. Her mouth had obviously gone dry.

But she succeeded eventually. Oh, yes, she found her voice, from wherever it had gone previously. That voice was telling them now that she was very sorry, the rooms had just gone. Yes, both rooms. It was very stupid of her, she condescended, because she ought to have told them from the upstairs window. She would put their name down, though, because she was sure another room was going to be vacant down the road. She pointed to some of the waste land further down. If there were any houses in the direction of her pointed finger, only she could see them. All that Adah and Francis could see was tumbled-down ruins. She hoped they would understand. The room had just gone. She was breathlessly nervous and even frightened as she explained.

Francis and Adah said nothing as the flood of words poured out. Adah had never faced rejection in this manner. Not like this, directly. Rejection by this shrunken piece of humanity, with a shaky body and moppy hair, loose, dirty and unkempt, who tried to tell them that they were unsuitable for a half derelict and probably condemned house with creaky stairs. Just because they were blacks?

They stood there, as if rooted to the spot. The frightened woman hoped they would go. She begged them once more to understand that the rooms were gone. Her little eyes darted in Francis's direction, and Adah was sure the woman was going to scream, for the look on his face was ugly. All the letters that formed the word "hatred" seemed to be working themselves indelibly into it, like carvings on a stone. He was staring at this woman, and he seemed to be looking beyond her. She started to close the door, firmly. She was expecting opposition, but none came. Adah could not even utter the plea she had rehearsed. The shock was one she would never forget.

"Let's go," Francis said.

They walked away in silence. Adah could not bear it. She had either to start screaming or talking; anything that came into her head. She started telling Francis the story of Jesus. She went on and on, how they were turned out of all the decent houses and how Mary had the baby in the manger.

Francis looked as if he was in another world, not listening to her. There was nothing Adah could do but to keep talking and try to keep up with Francis, though he was now walking fast, as if chased by demons. Then, all of a sudden, he stopped. Adah was startled. Was he going to kill her now, she wondered?

But he did not touch her. All he said was, "You'll be telling the world soon that you're carrying another Jesus. But, if so, you will soon be forced to look for your own Joseph."

"But Jesus was an Arab, was he not? So, to the English, Jesus is coloured. All the pictures show him with the type of pale colour you have. So can't you see that these people worship a coloured man and yet refuse to take a coloured family into their home?"

Right Now

MILTON KESSLER

I see children with faces unravelling into balls of shreds of cries.
I see children whose fathers are specks of disappearing red dust.
I see children eaten by the president's Dracula-smirk helicopter-
    armpit wave.
I see children whose parents sell them away to strangers for a buck
or bucket of plastic chicken because you have to sell or sacrifice.
I see children wetnursed by minimum-wage slaves.
I see fetuses punished as if they were senile grandfathers.
I see children hugging their crumbling parents who hang on their
    tiny clavicles,

huge smothering dolls stuffed with the poisons of the time.
I see children shot by accident and backed over by accident
and failed by accident and falling out of windows by accident
and robbed off the streets too small standing to reach the deranged
    hand
of some American citizen with a velour sofa for a car.
I see children drowning suicided on white powder in gift condos.
Check high school public drug telephone at 68th and 2nd.
I see children whose male adult is every booze violent knock on
    the door.
I see children iron masked by assistant principals.
I see children scanned by the lewd blue monocular of network TV.
I see geniuses packing immortal bags full of grocery insecticides.
I see the terror at the locked school door and the doorless school
    toilet.
I see shy children restrained for singing to themselves.
I see children fire-bombed to death by the police of Philadelphia.
I see boarder babies shrieking for every mammal's rights.
I see college infants auctioned into sports by born again elders.
I see children chained by corpse parents insane after a week of
    worthless work.
I see tiny human hands and feet laced with hell roaches and lead.
I see movies vomiting reels of rat-perfed frames of demon-children.
Beat the fear of God into them. Scare the devil out of them.
Crack babies scream and scratch.
Twelve year old wives too undeveloped to drive the shotgun
    pickup.
Fetuses fished out on educational TV.
Infants living alone with a telephone.
I see baby-porn selling tires and A.T. & T.
I see right now in central New York, a boy of ten walking miles
    alone
to the cancer corridor, his mother's only visitor.
And then what, America, and then what?

Racism and the War on Drugs

CLARENCE LUSANE

The dreams of thousands of African Americans are rapidly going up in smoke. The twisted curls of smoke emanating from pipes filled with crack, heroin, PCP, ice, and other deadly substances symbolize the blurred nightmares that are strangling community after community. While Blacks and other people of color in the United States comprise less than 15 percent of all drug users, the damage and havoc caused by substance abuse and by the destructive impact of the federal government's drug war is felt much more deeply in those communities. An FBI study notes the fact that while Blacks represent only 12 percent of all illegal drug users, Blacks are 41 percent of all those arrested on cocaine and heroin charges.

From the jungles of Bolivia to the high plains of Laos, from the dingy and rank basements of the inner cities and rural United States to the executive suites of the largest U.S. corporations, from the White House and beyond, the drug crisis has linked tens of millions across the globe.

The national and international illegal drug crisis is both rooted in and the expression of deeply troubled economic, political, and social relations. As this crisis of race, class, and global politics unfolds, the battle against illegal drugs has taken on a character not unlike the religious crusades of medieval Europe.

The U.S. government's "war on drugs," at best, obscures all of these relationships and, at worst, perpetuates them. The potential long-term harm of the drug war is not that it won't end illegal and deadly drug trafficking and abuse. The real danger is that it will mask the brutal social realities that must be addressed if suffering and destruction caused by the drug crisis is to stop.

The government, in engaging its drug war at home and abroad, has aimed its weapons overwhelmingly at people of color. Despite the fact that Whites are the majority of users and traffickers, Blacks, Latinos, and third world people are suffering the worst excesses of a program that violates civil rights, human rights, and national sovereignty.

At the same time, there is an urgent need to address the harm caused by the explosion of drug trafficking and abuse, particularly in communities of color. The drug crisis and its underlying causes are very real indeed. As the National Urban League wrote in *The State of Black America 1989,* "Substance abuse is the single major leading social, economic, and health problem confronting the African-American community."

The economic and political policies of the United States, particularly during Ronald Reagan's Presidency, fettered the opportunities for advancement for millions around the world and in the United States. Reagan was determined to halt the development of progressive governments in Nicaragua and Grenada with anti-communist, pro-militarist foreign policy initiatives. His program was funded by the shift of federal dollars from sorely needed social programs to the military budget and, perhaps more disastrous, by massive, unprecedented deficit spending.

The U.S. government uses the drug war to obscure the collusion of U.S. intelligence agencies with major international trafficking networks. In the past, anti-communist foreign policy aims have served as justification for the CIA and other agencies to knowingly allow traffickers to import illegal drugs into the United States. One critical question that has been conspicuously avoided by the Bush administration and the media monopolies is: "Has the CIA escalated the drug crisis in the United States by assisting the efforts of known drug traffickers?"

The end of the Cold War has meant a shift in foreign policy rhetoric. The new international enemy of humankind has been transformed from a communist to a drug dealer/terrorist or "narco-terrorist." Although new enemy images are being created, the ends have remained the same. Opening up and protecting markets for U.S. corporations and waging low-intensity/high-death military and political campaigns against third world liberation movements continue to be the *real* reasons for U.S. intervention abroad. . . .

The flood of illegal narcotics into the Black community has led more than a few to speculate that a "conspiracy" exists to destroy the African American community through drugs. Many believe that either a section of the government or a group of White racists is carrying out a plan of Black genocide via drugs. Ample historic evidence points to a correlation between high levels of Black activism followed by the increased presence of illegal drugs in the Black community. Most notably, as the Civil Rights and Black Power movements of the Sixties gained momentum and after the urban rebellions in the major cities, more illegal drugs entered the Black community than at any other time in history. Prior to today's crisis, the greatest amount of heroin use in Black American history occurred between 1965 and 1970.

Whether or not there is a conspiracy, Black people's need for money and consequent desire for psychological escape, exacerbated by the alienating and inequitable environment of poor communities, go a long way in explaining the drug crisis. That this situation would be exploited by those within and without these communities is not only a logical response under the capitalist system, but a rational one. The structures and institutional mechanisms of capitalism, and the systemic levers of racism accompanying it, are in themselves explanation enough.

Capitalist power determines not only who has jobs and who doesn't, but also what type of job and where. The lack of a viable economic life in the Black community is the result of a conscious decision to locate businesses, industries, and services elsewhere. The structure of the national economy is similarly controlled to the degree that people of color are disproportionately channelled into the lowest paying and most back-breaking jobs. Further, economic underdevelopment takes place in the social context of (de facto) segregated schools, political disempowerment, and a racist cultural milieu.

The fact is that judges, politicians, police officers, the CIA, and other authorities, as well as organized racists, *are* involved in drug trafficking, money laundering, or payoffs. It's virtually impossible, in fact, to have the magnitude of drugs that flow into the Black community without official and semi-official complicity. Federal narcotics agents have been charged and arrested on numerous occasions for such crimes.

The Black community has been the market of choice for drug traffickers. While traffickers do not discriminate in whom they sell to, they, like all astute capitalists, chase the easiest profit to be gained with the least risk. Again, we do not have to identify a conspiracy. Pure and simple profit is enough motivation. . . .

In the late Seventies, the conservative challenge to domestic and foreign policy began to take hold. Conservative spokespeople on a variety of issues, from anti-Sovietism to anti-abortion, found new life and energy. At the center of this revitalized political movement was the attack on working people and people of color. Republican Party and right-wing think tanks began to propagate the message that for all intents and purposes racism was no longer a serious factor in U.S. public life.

This view bullied its way into public policy with the election of Ronald Reagan in 1980. It was not, however, limited to just a fringe wing of the Republican Party. Mass defections of Whites from the Democratic Party indicated that a significant number of Whites believed that the gains and battles of the Sixties and Seventies in effect had eliminated racism from the American reality. Most Whites believed that Black faces in high places meant that racism was dead.

A poll by the National Opinion Research Center at the University of Chicago, conducted between February and April 1990, found that most Whites still harbor extremely negative and racist views about Blacks, Latinos, and Asians. In the poll, 62 percent of Whites said they believe Blacks are more likely than Whites to be lazy, 51 percent believe that Blacks are not patriotic, 53 percent believe Blacks are less intelligent than Whites, and 78 percent said they believe Blacks would rather live off welfare. Similar views were held of Latinos and Asians. Seventy-four percent of Whites felt that Latinos prefer welfare and 56 percent thought Latinos were lazy. Asians were seen as less patriotic by 55 percent of Whites and less intelligent by 36 percent.

Reagan's view that racism had disappeared neatly fit into his political objective of "getting government off the backs of the American people." In fact, what he really meant was to lift all regulations on corporations. Money spent on unnecessary social programs and overly strict government regulations, the Reagan backers argued, were the reasons that the U.S. economy was faltering. If America was to be economically strong again, they continued, the rich must be allowed to develop in whatever way they saw fit, unburdened by labor unions, health regulations, and affirmative action programs.

Right-wing ideologues, such as Defense Secretary Caspar Weinberger, Attorney General Edwin Meese III, Office of Management and Budget Director David Stockman, Secretary of HUD Samuel Pierce, and CIA Director William J. Casey, were brought in to carry out conservative policies, which they did with vicious enthusiasm, gross incompetence, and, in too many instances, blatant corruption. Under Reagan's men, environmental safeguards, workplace health and safety standards, banking regulations, and other hard-won protections were thrown out. At the same time, they also shifted billions of dollars from badly needed social programs to the military. . . .

Meanwhile, the inner cities were left to decay. As factories and other businesses folded, the tax base of cities declined, and employees at city service agencies found themselves unable to serve those most in need. Worse, the demand for low-skilled Black labor, which had been the base for building nearly every major city in the United States, virtually disappeared. Low-skilled and unskilled jobs were lost by the tens of thousands in cities and towns across the country. In Los Angeles, more than 80,000 low-skilled industrial jobs in auto assembly, tires, and similar occupations were lost.

Reagan slashed billions from social programs that had a direct and immediate impact on the health, education, housing, and employment opportunities of poor people and people of color. By the middle of Reagan's second term, his Medicaid cuts meant an 18 percent drop in the number of poor individuals who were eligible for coverage, from 64 percent in the mid-1970s to 46 percent in 1986. After eight years of Reagan's housing cuts, the homeless population grew from about 500,000 in 1980 to more than two million by 1990. Reaganomics meant that close to 200 rural health community hospitals closed between 1981 and 1990.

Meanwhile, Reagan's support for non-democratic governments abroad in South Korea, the Philippines, Haiti, Turkey, Chile, and many other nations mirrored increasingly anti-democratic sentiments at home. As Reagan happily built on the military budget of $1.9 trillion, the consequences of domestic government priorities destroyed the hopes of millions of people. For people of color, this was only the beginning. Overt racial violence and incidents surged in the Reagan years. From the rise of skinhead racists to the gestures and actions of Ronald Reagan himself, public acts of racial violence and racism saw a revitalization in the Eighties.

According to a report that reviewed the incidence of hate crimes in the Eighties issued by the Klanwatch Project of the Southern Poverty Law Center, at least 230 organized hate groups—including the Ku Klux Klan, skinheads, Nazis, and other White supremacist groups—operated throughout the United States. The report, titled *Hate Violence and White Supremacy,* documents dozens of hate crimes from the past decade. This includes eleven murders, sixty cross-burnings, and nearly 100 documented shootings and assaults taking place in forty states and

the District of Columbia. While the visibility of the KKK has declined, according to the report, many other groups are growing in
numbers and influence.

Reading Poems in Public

MAURICE KENNY of the Mohawk Nation

I stand on a stage and read poems,
poems of boys broken on the road;
the audience tosses questions.

I tell of old chiefs swindled of their daughters,
young braves robbed of painted shields,
Medicine Man hitting the bottle;
I chant old songs in their language
of the Spirit in wind and water . . .
they ask if Indians shave.

I recite old stories,
calendar epics of victory battles,
and calvary dawn massacres on wintered plains,
villages where war ponies are tethered to snow . . .
and they want to know
how many Indians commit suicide.

I read into the microphone,
I read into the camera,
I read into the printed page,
I read into the ear . . .
and they say what a pretty ring you wear.
The tape winds, the camera reels,
the newspaper spins
and the headlines read:
Ruffian, the race horse, dies in surgery.

At the end of the reading they thank me;
go for hamburgers at McDonalds
and pick up a six-pack to suck

as they watch the death
of Geronimo on the late show.

I stand on a stage and read poems,
and read poems, and read . . .

Central America: Vanishing Forests, Endangered Peoples

ALAN WEISMAN AND SANDY TOLAN

An old Indian stands in the rain in northern Argentina, amid the charred ruins of his village. His name is Pa'i Antonio Moreira. Over his thin sweater two strings of black beads crisscross his chest like bandoliers, signifying that he is a *ñanderú,* a shaman of his people. They are among the last few Guaraní Indians in this country, part of a cultural group that once inhabited a forest stretching from Argentina to the Amazon. Now only remnants of that forest and its creatures and people are left.

The night before, government men in forest-service uniforms torched the community's village. The 1,500-acre tract of semitropical woodland where they lived is only a few miles from Iguazú Falls, the biggest waterfall in South America. Once sacred to the Guaraní, Iguazú is now overwhelmed by tourists. Moreira's village was burned to make way for yet another hotel. The next Indian village to the south is also gone, swallowed by the waters of a new reservoir. The villages beyond that are no longer surrounded by black laurel and ceiba trees, which sheltered the deer and tapir the Guaraní once hunted, but by silent forests of Monterey pine, imported from California and planted by a nearby paper company for its superior fiber content.

The old shaman's kinsmen huddle around a fire, while the embers of their homes hiss and sizzle in the rain. The people descend from a stubborn band of Guaraní who refused to be evangelized when Jesuits arrived here 400 years ago. Moreira tells us that these ills curse the Guaraní's world because white men ignore the true way of God. Only the Indian, he says, remembers how God intended the world to be.

Then why, we ask, has God allowed the white man to triumph, and the Indian to suffer?

He gazes at us from beneath heavy-lidded eyes filled with loss and compassion. "The white man hasn't triumphed," he says softly. "When the Indians vanish, the rest will follow."

Throughout the Americas, great changes fueled by visions of progress have swept away the habitats of countless plants and animals. But entire human cultures are also becoming endangered. During the past two years, we traveled to 15 American countries, from the United States to Chile, to document this swift, often irreversible destruction.

Nations with growing, impoverished populations strike a Faustian bargain with the developed world: To create jobs and electricity for industry, they borrow hundreds of millions of dollars from foreign banks. They build huge dams that flood their richest lands and displace thousands of rural poor. To repay the massive debt, they invite foreign companies to mine their timber, gold, oil, and coal, or convert their farmlands to produce luxury crops for consumers in North America, Europe, and Japan. To ease pressures on overcrowded lands, they allow poor settlers to slash and burn their way into virgin forests, where they clash with the indigenous people already living there—including some of the last uncontacted tribes in the hemisphere.

For centuries the Yuquí Indians of the Bolivian Amazon roamed naked through jungles so remote they thought no one else existed. Their word for *world* translates simply as *leaves*.

"When we first saw the white people, we thought they were the spirits of our dead ancestors," recalled Ataiba, the last of the Yuquí chiefs. He recalled how his people had begun to encounter strange things in the jungle—fresh fish hung from trees, sacks of sugar, cooking pots, machetes—all laid beside new trails. One day, at the end of one of these gift trails, Ataiba saw light-skinned people watching him. After many months, the pale strangers, evangelicals from the Florida-based New Tribes Mission, convinced Ataiba that they could offer safe haven from the growing violence of confrontations with loggers and settlers. One morning late in 1989, Ataiba led his people out of the forest forever, to become permanent wards of the mission village.

Often, on the heels of the missionaries, come the forces of development. In Ecuador during the early 1970s, the government contracted with Texaco to build an oil industry in the Ecuadorian Amazon and help bring the country into the global economy. Until then, many natives there had never even heard of a nation called Ecuador, let alone petroleum.

"We didn't know the sound of a motor," explained Toribe, a young Cofán leader. The Cofán, who live along Ecuador's Río Aguarico, were still hunting peccaries and monkeys with blowguns. "We couldn't figure out what animal could be making those noises." The sounds were Texaco's helicopters. Soon settlers streamed down the oil-company roads, changing life irrevocably for the Cofán.

"With the petroleum companies came epidemics," recalled Toribe. "We didn't know flu, measles, and these other illnesses. Many fled from here. Those that stayed were finished. It was all contaminated. There were fifteen thousand of us on this side of the Río Aguarico. Now we are only four hundred."

Oil from Ecuador, hardwoods from Bolivia, and from Honduras to Costa Rica to Brazil, beef cattle raised for export where forests once stood: We had stumbled onto another kind of gift trail, this one leading back to the United States. The savanna surrounding Bogotá, Colombia, with some of the finest soil in Latin America, produces not food but bargain-priced roses, chrysanthemums, and carnations to sell on street corners and in supermarkets in the United States and beyond. To meet the high standards of the international marketplace, the blossoms, along with the women who tend them inside plastic-covered hothouses, are regularly gassed with pesticides. The chemicals leak into the Bogotá savanna's streams and aquifers, which are also being depleted as business grows and more flowers must be watered.

In Honduras, mangrove forests lining the Gulf of Fonseca's estuaries are threatened by modern mariculture. Huge shrimp farms restrict local fishermen's access to the crabs, mollusks, and small fish they have netted for generations.

In Brazil, the biggest dam in the Amazon, Tucurui, has displaced thousands of people and created such mosquito infestations that thousands more are leaving. Tucurui was built to power aluminum smelters owned by U.S., European, and Japanese companies. The ore comes from the Amazon's largest mine, which strips away hundreds of acres of jungle each year to provide foil and cans.

In eastern Panama, the Bayano Dam was part of a master plan to bring new industry to the capital and, via its new road, open jungle frontiers. Settlers quickly turned the jungle into cattle pasture, threatening the survival of the forest-dwelling Kuna Indians and creating massive soil erosion. So much loose soil washes into Bayano's reservoir that the dam's manager says eventually its turbines will stop functioning.

On South America's second-biggest river, the Parana, we watched men building the longest dam in the world: Yacyreta, along the Argentina-Paraguay border. More than $1 billion in World Bank and Inter-American Development Bank loans was allegedly diverted from the dam project to finance things like Argentina's Falklands war. Now there's not enough money to relocate the 40,000 people whose cities and farms will be flooded. As much as $30 million *was* spent, however, on an elevator to carry fish like dorado, a prized local species, upstream to spawn. Unfortunately, the elevator, built by North American dam contractors, was designed for salmon, which go upstream, spawn, and die. Dorado need to return. And there's no down elevator.

While these huge projects often collapse under their own weight, even small, well-intended plans can falter if they don't transcend conventional models of commerce. The notion that a "green" market solution will allow both consumption and conservation may be wishful thinking. In western Brazil we visited a cooperative founded to save both the rainforest and its people by harvesting replenishable Brazil nuts for candy. But when co-op members, who lack basic sanitation and electricity, voted to pay themselves a living wage, the price of their product rose above the world market rate. In order to keep costs competitive, Cultural Survival, the Boston-based nonprofit group that devised the scheme, now buys most Rainforest Crunch nuts from commercial suppliers who undercut the cooperative.

Our travels did reveal a few signs of hope: a land-recovery program run by villagers in southern Honduras, a proposal to put Kuna Indians in charge of protecting the watershed of Panama's Bayano Dam. But these projects are exceptions. Alone, they are not enough to halt the momentous effects of uncontrolled development. Sustainable development must be contoured to local needs rather than imposed from afar by economic forces.

When we reached the Strait of Magellan, residents of southern Chile showed us great inland sounds that soon will be dammed to power yet more aluminum smelters—this time, Australian. On Tierra del Fuego, they took us to ancient hardwood rainforests, scheduled to be turned into fax paper by Canadian and Japanese companies.

Finally, we stood with Professor Bedrich Magas of Chile's Magellan University at the tip of the Americas, looking out toward the growing polar ozone hole. Magas reminded us that the National Aeronautics and Space Administration had recently discovered destructive chlorine over the northern United States—just like that which was found over Antarctica only a few years earlier. It was a disturbing reminder of the warning of the Guaraní shaman: What we do to the lives and lands of others may ultimately determine the fate of our own.

The United Fruit Co.

PABLO NERUDA

Translated by Daniela Gioseffi

When the trumpets had sounded, and
all was prepared on the earth
and Jehova divided the world
to Coca-Cola Incs, Anaconda,
Ford Motors, and other entities:
the United Fruit Inc. reserved for itself
the succulent, central coast of my land,
the sweet waistline of America.
The executives baptized our lands
naming them "Banana Republics,"
and over the sleeping dead,
over the disquieted heroes,
who had conquered their greatness,
their liberty and flags,
established an *opera buffa:*
raped all industry,
awarded crowns like Caesar,
unleashed all greed, and created
the dictatorial "Reign of the Flies"—
the flies Trujillos, the flies Tachos,
the flies Carias, the flies Martinez,

the flies Ubico, the flies all of them
wet with the blood of their marmalade
extracts, drunken flies buzzing
over the tombs of the people,
flies circus flies, scholarly flies
trapped in tyranny.

Then in the bloody kingdom of the flies,
The United Fruit Company Incorporated
unloaded coffee and fruits;
cargo boats overflowed, trays of spoils
floated away from our drowning dominions.

And all the time, somewhere, in the sugar factory
purgatories of our seaports,
smothered by gases, a Native
fainted away in the fumes of the morning
an anonymous corpse, a numberless thing,
a spiraling number,
a branch of dead fruit
in the rotten vat steaming with carrion fruit.

The Americans

TRAN THI NGA AND WENDY WILDER LARSEN

The Americans came to Vietnam
and turned our country upside down
with their money and their army.

Their soldiers slept with our women.
Their generals patted our generals on the heads
as if they were children.

Bao and I had a successful business at first
selling Vietnamese handicrafts at the PX,
silver, ceramics, lacquerware.

Inflation rose higher and higher.
I thought we should get out.
Bao said no.

"America is so strong,
the richest, most powerful country in the world.

Number one in the world. She will never desert us.
She cannot. She is in too deep.

She will send more ammunition.
NBC and CBS say so.

She will bring more phantoms and battleships
and B 52s to bomb Hanoi."

Prejudice Against the Handicapped

CHRIS GILLESPIE

Throughout history, the disabled have been treated with varying amounts of respect and contempt. They were often regarded as a burden on society, as imperfect, or as symbolic of bad luck or sin. Some of the stigmatization experienced by the handicapped today can be traced back to the earliest moral lessons of Western society. In Greek mythology, for example, Hera's punishment for arguing with Zeus was that her son Hephaestus was born lame. Ashamed of his deformity, Hera threw her son out of heaven. Another character in Greek mythology, Philoctetes, was bitten by a serpent. When the stench from his wound grew too great to bear, his traveling companions abandoned him on a deserted island. These examples—both depicting the casting aside of the physically handicapped—are disturbing because they come from stories that were meant to embody the moral and cultural ideals of the culture that told them.

Much more disturbing is the harmful depiction of the disabled that can be found in both testaments of the Bible—the book whose tenets have shaped and reflected the thoughts and value systems of people across cultures and millennia. In it, disability is often equated with sin and divine justice. In the New Testament, Jesus heals a man before warning him, "Behold, thou art made whole. Sin no more lest a worse thing come unto thee" (John 5:13). As explained in Myron Eisenberg's ground breaking book, *Disabled People as Second-Class Citizens,* Jesus' statement defines the handicapped man as an incomplete person and defines both his present and possible future afflictions as divine retribution for his sins.

In the Old Testament, Moses relates what will happen to those who disobey God's new commandments: "He will send disease after disease on you . . . The Lord will strike you with infectious diseases, with swelling and fever . . . The Lord will send boils on you . . . He will make your body break out with sores. You will be covered with scabs, and you will itch, but there will be no cure. The Lord will make you lose your mind: he will strike you with blindness and confusion . . . the Lord will cover your legs with incurable, painful sores; boils will cover you from head to foot." This one passage from Deuteronomy associates almost every affliction known in Biblical times with punishment for disobedience to God. As long as such judgments are endowed with any credibility as truth, the handicapped will fail to achieve complete freedom from social stigmata. To illustrate, in 1952, Marie Killilea sought lodging for herself and her daughter. When the home owner learned that Killilea's daughter had cerebral palsy, she threw both mother and daughter out of her house, ranting that "only bad, dirty people would have a child like that!" (Eisenberg, et al., p6).

The Physically Handicapped

Such instances are rare today, as fewer and fewer people pay close *literal* attention to Biblical text or believe that the Bible is the actual "word of God." But stigmatization of people with disabilities lives on in our society in more subtle ways. For the physically handicapped, it has largely taken the form of neglect of both their needs and their abilities.

My own experience as a handicapped person came when I was a young child living in New York City. Just after finishing kindergarten, I was diagnosed with a hip disorder and was subsequently forced to wear a large metal and plastic prosthesis on my left leg for several years. My local elementary school in New York City lacked the proper facilities to accommodate me, so the city sent an instructor to my home for several hours two to three times per week, leaving me to watch public television much of the rest of the time. After three years, my mother sought to send me to a public school so I could grow up with children my age and receive the same school time that others were enjoying. The second nearest school to my home had something called a "health class," in which I was enrolled. Our motley crew consisted of first- through sixth-grade students with various disabilities: kidney problems, cerebral palsy, hearing impairment. There was a burn victim and several students whose disabilities I was never able to discern. Even the teacher was one of us, complete with her own handicap. When a fourth grader broke his leg, he was sent temporarily to the class for the same reason that I was there: the fourth grade was on the sixth floor and there was no way to get up there except the stairs. I remember a suggestion that I be carried up to the "normal" class. It was rejected for safety reasons. I could have walked up to the sixth floor the same way I walked up to the second floor for the health class, but again, I would have caused tie-ups on the stairway in an emergency.

I had no learning disability and was actually able to study above my own grade level both with the home instructor and in the health class, with its mixed age group. But my relegation to home tutoring and to a special class of handicapped students denied me the chance to grow up with my peers—to integrate fully with my own age group and be a part of the socialization process that shaped the "normal" students. I was going to school either across town or not at all, so I had few friends my age in the neighborhood. Part of the raison d'être for the class might have been to shield disabled children from the terrible cruelty often displayed by other children toward those that can be labeled outsiders, but it didn't stop anyone from calling me "peg leg" in the bathroom. Furthermore, it allowed all the other six to twelve year olds to grow up never experiencing our group of segregated misfits as part of their "normal" world. We were, rather, a group of others down on the second floor, who did not come for lunch in the cafeteria or play outside during recess. The plate on our door was a proclamation of our difference: We were not class 209 like any other class would have been, but HC-209.

It is a known aspect of prejudice that we tend to fear and hate those we know the least. Some of the most racist areas of the United States are those areas that have never been inhabited by minority groups. By contrast, in large cities—where circumstance forces people to live and interact more closely with the wide variety of people that cities attract—it is easy to find mixed-race or same-sex couples living largely unmolested, if not well tolerated. The "normal" kids that became temporary members of the health class while their skiing injuries healed had little trouble becoming friends with us regulars and remaining friends with us when they returned to the mainstream. Had he a chance to see that aside from some plastic and steel at the hip I was a regular person, the kid who called me "peg leg" might have been my friend instead.

This is not to say that all of the students of HC-209 could have prospered in regular classes, but many of them could have if provided with adequate facilities and a sense from the "normal" crowd that they belonged. Similarly, not all of the handicapped are capable of becoming what we call "productive members of society." But many of the handicapped—both mentally and physically—are quite capable of performing many jobs that are not hampered by their disabilities.

Society has been slow to make this integration possible. Such sluggishness can be blamed in part on the recent tremendous growth of the handicapped population. After World War II, a more modern medical establishment began for the first time to save the lives of many who were disfigured, crippled, or brain damaged either at birth or due to accidents, illness, or war injuries. This progress in the medical struggle against trauma and infection has resulted in much greater numbers of surviving handicapped people than our society has ever seen. This surge has created new problems and issues with which we have been slow to deal. Among the most important of these neglected issues have been accessibility and integration. Employers are still reluctant to hire people that might have special needs. A tremendous shortsightedness is only just being overcome in certain societies, but not without prodding. For example, in the United States, *The Americans with Disabilities Act*—which went into effect in 1992—mandated that certain public accommodations be accessible to the handicapped. But it is shocking to think that many medical facilities in the United States will require costly construction—mandated by the new law—just to become adequately accessible to those that traditionally need them most. This shortcoming, rather than an anomaly, is representative of the progress that has yet to be made.

The Mentally Handicapped and the Mentally Ill

During the renaissance, the mentally ill of Europe were turned into a travelling side show called the "Ship of Fools." They were loaded onto ships that traveled from port to port around Europe, where they were displayed like circus animals. The practice served the dual purpose of freeing cities from having to deal with or care for their mentally ill on a daily basis and of providing a periodic freak show for mass entertainment.

By the end of the 19th century, with the dawn of psychoanalysis, the medical establishment began to recognize insanity as an illness to be treated, rather than a curse to be demonized. The enlightenment of the general public, however, lagged far behind that of medicine. Society continues to this day to stigmatize not just those who are mentally ill, but even those who are known or suspected to have been treated for psychological problems in the past. This was clearly demonstrated during the United States 1988 presidential campaign when members of the Republican party—already adept at exploiting society's racial prejudices (eg, the infamous "Willie Horton" advertisement)—exploited North American prejudice against the mentally ill. Unfounded (and untrue) rumors were circulated that Democratic candidate Michael Dukakis had twice undergone psychiatric treatment. A week later, Dukakis had dropped eight percentage points in U.S. opinion polls.

Perhaps the most barbaric treatment perpetrated upon any disabled group in modern history was that received by the mentally handicapped in Nazi Germany in the 1930s. As pointed out by Lifton and Markusen in *The Genocidal Mentality,* the first stages of Nazi genocide began not against Jews, but against 100,000 of the mentally ill under the guise of *eugenics*—the bogus science of systematic purification of the gene pool. This genocide was all the more obscene because it took place long after psychoanalysis had dispelled any myths that the mentally ill are incurable, evil, or something less than human. There is a discomforting similarity between the Nazi view that the mentally ill were contaminating a potentially pure race and the Biblical stance that illness or disability was a form of punishment for the soul contaminated by sin.

In western society, perhaps the greatest contributor to the lingering fear of the mentally ill has been the mass media. In Europe and the United States, the fledgling mass newspaper industry of the 1880s learned quickly that great attention to stories about "Jack the Ripper" sold newspapers. A new "Ship of Fools" was launched and the disabled were once again being used as a side show for the public. If people were no longer to venture out and view society's freaks, they could at least have the same tastes satisfied by the press. Today, tremendous coverage is given to "psycho-murder" cases. The inordinate attention perhaps satisfies our continuing need to point out society's "freaks" and all that is different about them; we still thrill to the hint of danger posed by aberrations about which we know little. So the public is treated for weeks on end to headlines screaming about how nobody is safe from the "crazed killer" at large and speculating where the "madman" might strike next. When the tabloids land a story about a psychopath who kills at the behest of his neighbor's dog or one who eats his victims, the word smiths go crazy and the public buys newspapers. Thus the attention given these stories is far greater, proportionally, than that given to stories more directly affecting the reading public. Such sensationalism combined with heavy use of the "language of madness" eclipses the fact that murders involving the mentally ill are relatively rare, especially when compared with the number of murders involving "sane" people (despite the overuse of "temporary insanity" pleas employed by the lawyers of accused murderers).

Among the mass media in the United States, it is television that appears to have the greatest influence on perceptions. Americans, especially children, watch a startling amount of television. And while its exact effect in some areas—for example, its ability to promote violence —is hotly debated, there can be little doubt that it influences the perceptions people have about their environment and accept as "reality." At one extreme, many people even lose the ability to distinguish fictional television portrayals from reality. Ample evidence for this can be seen in the huge volumes of mail that television networks receive addressed not to actors, but to the fictional characters they portray on soap operas—programs unique in that they enter the lives of their viewers on a daily basis. Given such influence, it follows that when distorted views of reality are presented to viewers, they will acquire or reinforce misconceptions about the world around them. This especially applies to negative stereotypes about the mentally ill.

Despite the fact that most mentally ill persons have no propensity toward violence, they are by far the most likely characters on television both to commit violence and be the victims of violence. Studies conducted from 1969 to 1985 by Gerbner, Gross, Morgan, and Signorielli of the Cultural Indicators Project revealed some startling statistics about the portrayal of the mentally ill on television: Only 27.2% of the female characters in prime time programs commit violent acts, but 60% of mentally ill female characters commit violent acts. Only 8.7% of characters in general committed murder, but 21.6% of mentally ill characters committed murder. The mentally ill were also 68% more likely to be victims of violence than characters in general. Thus the association of mentally ill characters with violence on television—both as perpetrators and as victims—amounts to a gross distortion of reality. Increasing the danger of misperception is the typical story line's need both to create and resolve conflict within a half-hour or one-hour time slot, which leaves little room for any substantial character development. "Bad guys" are often defined only by their evil nature or, very often, by a closely related combination of evil and mental illness.

Due to its quest for commercial success and its status almost as a family member in the average American household, television has taken on a unique role in shaping our perceptions and misperceptions about the mentally ill. But it does not invent prejudices for us, and we as a society also have a long way to go before we can be said to have overcome them. Perhaps only when we have become better educated and more understanding of people we perceive as different will we stop willingly allowing the media to feed and to feed upon our fears and prejudices.

Both the physically handicapped and mentally handicapped are less often portrayed and less stigmatized on American television than the mentally ill. They, unlike the mentally ill, have begun to appear in more positive roles. Recently, they have even become a target of advertisers. One children's clothing store features a wheelchair-bound child dancing with other children. The McDonald's fast food chain has used persons with Down's syndrome in its commercials, attempting to show that the company is making an effort to hire capable people with handicaps at its restaurants. Two television movies—*Bill* and *Bill, on His Own*—starred Mickey Rooney as a retarded man who finds love and learns to live independently. For several years, Larry Drake has played Benny, a mentally handicapped man, on the dramatic series *LA Law*. The role depicts a caring person who, despite his handicap, successfully holds a job and lives independently. While centered on Benny's very tolerant coworkers, the show has also dealt with fear and misunderstanding of the mentally handicapped. In one moving episode, the harmless Benny must fight off a mistaken charge of attempted sexual assault. But the media giveth and the media taketh away: Larry Drake has become typecast. In late 1992, he played his second consecutive Hollywood movie starring role as a homicidal lunatic.

While the mentally ill face their own special problems and—whether permanently or temporarily—are often incapable of interacting "normally" with society, the case is different for both the mentally and physically handicapped. Many members of each group are capable of leading constructive and fulfilling lives, of holding jobs responsibly, and living with at least some degree of independence—but only if given a chance. A more active role played by the media in conveying this fact to a public that remains largely isolated from such people will certainly be beneficial. Such positive reinforcement, combined with incentives like *The Americans with Disabilities Act,* will lead to more and more people with disabilities playing successful roles in society.

It would be selling short the abilities of the handicapped, however, to suggest that success is entirely dependent on special accommodations being made by society. A desire to succeed and a belief in one's abilities are the first requirements for circumventing a handicap. John Milton wrote Paradise Lost and Paradise Regained after he had gone blind; Beethoven composed throughout his gradual 17-year descent into deafness and wrote his monumental Ninth Symphony in complete deafness; French painter Henri de Toulouse-Lautrec, whose growth was stunted by a childhood accident, nonetheless became a renowned 19th-century artist; Charles P. Steinmetz of the United States, whose work revolutionized electrical engineering, was a hunchback; and modern day theoretical physicist Stephen Hawking has established himself as one of the great thinkers of the 20th century, despite a body rendered useless by amyotrophic lateral sclerosis (Lou Gehrig's disease); Hellen Keller, blind and deaf from age two, not only learned to communicate but became an author, lecturer, and advocate; and Stevie Wonder and Ray Charles are just two of many successful, though blind, modern musicians. While many of these people may have had the advantage of genius as a weapon in their struggles, many others face difficulties every day with the talents of mere mortals but the courage of heroes. Thus, the success of any handicapped person must be a collaboration between themselves and a tolerant and adaptive society.

The Small Mute Boy and The Small Mad Boy

FEDERICO GARCIA LORCA
Translated by Daniela Gioseffi

The Small Mute Boy

The small boy went searching for his voice.
[The King of the Crickets stole it.]
In a drop of water,
the child was searching for his voice.

"I don't want to speak with it:
I'll make a ring with it
so that you may wear my silence
on your little finger."

In a drop of water,
the small boy kept searching for his voice.

[The far away imprisoned voice
donned cricket's clothes.]

The Small Mad Boy

I said: "Good Afternoon."
But it wasn't.
The afternoon was elsewhere
having already vanished.

(And the light shrugged
its shoulders like a young woman.)

"Good afternoon!" But it's useless!
This one's false, a half moon
made of lead.
The other won't appear.

[And the light, as it appeared to all others,
played with the mad boy at being a statue.]

"That other woman was little
and ate pomegranates.

This one's immense and green! I can't
take her in my arms or clothe her!
Won't she approach? What's she like?"

[And the light as it departed, teased
and divided the mad boy from his own shadow.]

From: "Looking to the Future [of the Former U.S.S.R.]"

ELENA BONNER

Ethnic Tensions Split the Commonwealth

The Commonwealth states have not been immune to ethnic tensions similar to those found in Georgia. Moldova's relationship with the CIS (particularly with Russia) is complicated by problems in the Trans-Dniester region. The sources of the conflict go back to the regime of Soviet President Mikhail Gorbachev, when Moscow, attempting to keep Moldova from declaring independence, provoked strikes in the region. (A similar tactic was used in the Baltics.) Russians living in Trans-Dniester demanded sovereignty or a high degree of autonomy, with guarantees that if Moldova and Romania reunited—they have long-standing ties—they would have the right to secede.

It is hard to judge the likelihood of reunification, or when reunification might occur if it takes place at all. But the conflict in Trans-Dniester has moved from the political to the military, aided by the appearance in the region of Russian Cossacks who say they are defending resident Russians and the speeches of Vice President Aleksandr Rutskoi and numerous deputies of the Russian parliament, as well as the presence of Russia's Fourteenth Army (Russian President Boris Yeltsin's decree ordering the removal of the army from the region has not been fulfilled).

The population of Trans-Dniester is mixed—23 percent Russian and the rest almost equally divided between Moldovans and Ukrainians. Ukraine's plan is to wait and watch. In Moldova itself, the party supporting reunification with Romania is strong. The question of federalizing the republic, recently raised in the Moldovan parliament, has not been decided, but this holds out the possibility of peace.

Azerbaijan joined the CIS along with the other republics in December 1991. But after the fall of President Ayaz Mutalibov the leaders of the Popular Front, who took control of the government, announced that Azerbaijan would not join the CIS. The new president, Abulfez Elchibey, has not disavowed that statement. Azerbaijan initiated military action against the Armenians of Nagorno-Karabakh, using arms received from the CIS and taking advantage of the fact that Armenia had not yet received its share of CIS weaponry. More than 5,000 people have died in the war over who will control the enclave (and perhaps as many more in fighting in June alone).

Azerbaijan's relations with the rest of the CIS and with Turkey and Iran depend on the position they take on Nagorno-Karabakh. The views of the Conference on Security and Cooperation in Europe (CSCE) are guarded, and aimed at preserving the enclave's previous status. But it is naive to think there are powers that can do this without genocide and wide-ranging warfare, which would involve not only Nagorno-Karabakh, Azerbaijan, and Armenia but also Turkey, Iran, and Russia. International recognition of Nagorno-Karabakh and the establishment of an internationally administered zone could be the path out of the war, but the CSCE must change its position for that to happen.

All the former republics of Central Asia are members of the CIS.

The majority are ruled by former leaders under the union who turned in their party tickets, and by the same party, which has changed its name. However, the stormy events of May and September in Tajikistan are a sign of instability. All the former republics (except Kyrgyzstan) signed an agreement on protecting their borders with Russia, Kazakhstan, and Armenia. Foreign policy is oriented more toward Turkey, Iran, Afghanistan, and the Arab East than the CIS, since there is little hope of aid from the latter.

When part of the Soviet Union, Central Asia had the widest gap between the living standards of its insignificant wealthy minority and the overwhelming majority who lived in poverty (a colonial picture). In Turkmenistan, Tajikistan, Uzbekistan, and Kyrgyzstan in the 1980s, over 50 percent of the population lived below the poverty line. Clan struggles complicate the job of governing in these states, as well as an entrenched narcotics mafia (which has become a serious problem for the countries in the region and threatens to become a problem for the CIS and the rest of the world). It looks as if Central Asia's development will not be a democratic one.

Kyrgyzstan is the exception. It is one of Central Asia's poorest states, the poverty there exacerbated by a recent earthquake. President Askar Akayev, a physicist, wants to hold to a democratic course. He insisted during the ratification process for the new constitution that an article declaring "the land, resources, and waters belong to the Kyrgyz people" be changed to "the land, resources, and waters belong to the people of Kyrgyzstan." An agreement with Russia guarantees the rights of Kyrgyzstan's Russian-speaking population. This new state could become a democratic model for the rest of Central Asia, but it will require the West's active support.

Kazakhstan, the second-largest former republic, has reasserted its ties and its equality with Russia through a treaty of friendship and cooperation that is in the spirit of President Nursultan Nazarbayev's proclamation that "Kazakhstan will never be anybody's underbelly." Nazarbayev apparently is skeptical about the future of the Commonwealth, and has said, "we don't need to drag anyone by the ears into the CIS." Kazakhstan is confidently developing relations with India, Pakistan, Turkey, South Korea, Japan, Europe, and the United States. In the process it has attracted foreign investment in mining and refining, with the hard currency received from these deals being used to improve other sectors of the economy.

Kazakhstan's domestic situation is more stable than Russia's, despite the fact that the city of Karaganda was one of the centers of the miners' strikes in 1989. Ethnic conflict has been minimal, but the growing Cossack movement could become a destabilizing factor since over 50 percent of the population is Russian-speaking. The project for a new constitution in which both the Kazakh and Russian languages have equal status and which stresses guarantees for human rights, has the approval of Western experts but has elicited protests from national organizations that want to create a single "Turkic space" composed of Kazakhstan, Central Asia, and the Transcaucasus (Georgia, Armenia, and Azerbaijan). I think the president, whose character is a mixture of pragmatism, an active desire for democracy, and authoritarianism (within limits), and who has the confidence of the people, can bring about reforms without social explosions. But it is important that no destabilizing impulses come from Russia.

Belarus has consistently supported Russia in the CIS but now seems to be planning to leave the Commonwealth, as manifested in decisions to create its own currency and army and in its refusal to sign the defense pact. This former republic, which suffered more than any other in World War II and was damaged by fallout from the nuclear accident at Chernobyl, is in extremely difficult economic and psychological straits. Its president, Stanislav Shushkevic, has managed to avoid conflicts with his neighbors in the CIS, but his situation in parliament is not simple. The republic is about to have a referendum on re-election to parliament, and it is not certain that Shushkevic will retain his post. Perhaps leaders of the Popular Front, with a more nationalistic platform, will come to power. If they do, the present foreign policy orientations on Ukraine and Belarus's European neighbors will hold, but the same cannot be said with certainty about ties to Russia.

Relations between Russia and Ukraine are already strained. Conflict began in August 1991 when the Russian parliament reclaimed the Crimea, a former Russian territory that had been annexed to the Ukraine during Soviet rule, and also expressed solidarity with Russians living in the eastern border regions of Ukraine. Tensions abated, but flared up again after the CIS was founded, the direct result of vague agreements on strategic forces, an undivided army, and continuing pretensions to the Crimea on the Russian side. These will not lead to war, but friendly relations have been lost for a long time.

Domestically, Ukraine suffers from fewer conflicts than Russia.

The presidency of Leonid Kravchuk, which has managed to cooperate both with the old nomenklatura and the leaders of Rukh, the opposition movement that brought him to power, remains stable. In foreign policy Ukraine is oriented toward Europe, chiefly Germany, and is improving relations with Belarus to the north. It takes a neutral position in the conflict between Russia and Moldova, although it could speak even more forcefully than Russia about its "fellow citizens" in the Trans-Dniester region (where there are more Ukrainians than Russians).

The Question of Russia

Russia, even after the disintegration of the Soviet Union, remains a great state of 150 million people, with a colossal territory and abundant natural wealth. But if we exclude the former republics now caught up in wars, it is torn by the sharpest contradictions—contradictions between Moscow and the autonomous republics, regions, and oblasts. There is also a struggle between the old nomenklatura and the new one in process of formation. (Moscow, like any capital, is a city of bureaucrats and nomenklatura, in this case from three systems—the state, party, and army. These people largely "determine the weather" for all Russia and have no intention of bowing out.)

There are contradictions between president and parliament because Yeltsin was elected a year after the parliament was seated, and under more democratic conditions. As a result, there is still no law on buying and selling land and no policy for attracting foreign investment. There are many contradictions in the economic reform program, which was begun late, with the liberation of prices before broad privatization, which instantly bankrupted 99 percent of the population.

The course of reform is paradoxical: as prices for consumer goods have jumped (some are up fiftyfold!), the markets have not filled with more goods but instead are almost empty. The main contradictions of the last year: conversion of the defense industry to the production of civilian goods apparently will not take place, and Russia will take over the arms market that was the Soviet Union's. The promised sharp reduction of the army will not take place, either. Troop strength is around 2.5 million, which means the military will continue to strain the budget, with all the concomitant consequences. Why is such a large army needed? To fight whom? Thus the fears of Kazakhstan, Belarus, and Ukraine—that once they give up their nuclear potential they will be defenseless before Russia—are not groundless. Social tensions in Russia are increasing wildly, extreme nationalistic tendencies are growing, and the Communists are active, uniting with the Christian Democrats and some of the old unions. There is fertile soil for this bloc in the rapid division of society into millions of beggars and a handful of millionaires, with no middle class; to this can be added the unemployment of many army officers.

Russia is losing friends (Armenia and perhaps Georgia) and gaining enemies (Ukraine, Moldova, Azerbaijan). The speaker of the parliament's statement that Ossetia could be annexed to Russia if its people so wish and in accordance with its policies in Trans-Dniester demonstrates the vagueness of Russian national policy, not the defense of the democratic principle of self-determination, because otherwise Russia would have to extend it to Nagorno-Karabakh and some of its own autonomous regions. The future will show what the country will become. But even if reform is not halted by a social explosion, peace and abundance will not come to Russia's citizens soon. This process will be more difficult than in the other CIS countries because Russia is large and made up of many ethnic groups, is unwilling to give up the dominance of the military in the budget, and has a messianic mentality.

A Plea for Armenia

It is hardest to write about Armenia. This former republic was cut off on all sides to suit the Leninist idea of socializing the entire Islamic world. Its geopolitical situation in a historically created hostile environment does not give it an outlet to the West. Poor in land and natural resources, especially fuels, only nuclear energy can give it economic independence. The country has been devastated by earthquakes, which caused it to shut down its only nuclear reactor, and by a three-year economic blockade by Azerbaijan, which is waging war with the Armenian enclave of Nagorno-Karabakh (which has been blockaded for four years).

Armenia is dying. Only people with bad intentions fail to see this. But the international organizations that were silent for four years, even though blockades against peaceful populations are forbidden by the Geneva Conventions, accused Armenia of aggression when its troops recently tried to create a corridor for delivering humanitarian aid to Nagorno-Karabakh. The West is silent about the fact that of the 130,000 tons of grain intended for the relief of Armenia, 126,000 ended up in Azerbaijan, or that the Finnish houses sent in 1989 to the earthquake-damaged area of the country have been used for Azerbaijani settlements. Pitted against the 200,000 Armenians in Nagorno-Karabakh is the full might of Azerbaijan, which was supported at first by the army of the Soviet Union and not of the CIS.

As I listened in June to reports from the World Ecology Forum and agreed with the points about the need to save the ecosphere, I thought about the need to save those who have been placed on the brink of extinction by fate and people, politics and ideology. All the humanistic ideas, all the words about a New Europe will be only empty demagogy if one morning we hear that there is no more Armenia, which was a cradle of civilization and Christianity. How does one write about the future of the country when there is a war going on to exterminate it? I do not know.

The End of Another Myth

We lived in myths for decades. Myths fell. Others were created. The myth of the CIS is dying. The process of signing bilateral agreements is beginning. God grant that they be more than mere fiction. The next stage will obviously be the formation of blocs. The Central Asian bloc: Uzbekistan, Tajikistan, Turkmenistan. Azerbaijan will lean toward it. The Western bloc: Ukraine, Belarus, and perhaps Moldova. And the Central bloc: Russia, Kazakhstan, and Kyrgyzstan. Of course things will not be absolutely clear-cut—Islam will have an effect on Kazakhstan and especially Kyrgyzstan, and there may be conflicts in the Central Asian and Western blocs. But the predicted and even announced · union has not come about.

The future of the countries of the former Soviet Union and Europe, their peace and world peace, no longer depend on the East-

West juxtaposition. Freed from the threat of a third world war, humanity still could choke on the blood of hundreds of small internecine wars. The experience of the last few years has shown that the struggle for self-determination is unstoppable, no matter what sacrifices it demands. Lithuania, Latvia, Turkmenistan, Yugoslavia, Ossetia, Nagorno-Karabakh, Trans-Dniester. The list can be extended, but this is enough to make my point: no matter how international organizations resist it, they will have to recognize the right of people to self-determination and to separate it irrevocably from the right to inviolable borders. Borders fall from outside the state. People determine themselves inside states.

Peace missions cannot keep repeating that conflicts must be settled peacefully. They must bring concrete proposals for compromise (compromise is movement by both sides). Federalization, demilitarized zones, zones of international supervision, protectorates, total independence—for each case there will be a different solution, but with complete guarantees for the rights of ethnic minorities remaining in the territories. The mechanisms for this process must be developed. We must change the tactics of peace missions, which now wait until blood has been shed and conflicts are resolved not by right but by might.

And still, what will happen to our country—excuse me, our many countries—caught up in the speeding process of disintegration and its strange bedfellow, the process of becoming? Which is stronger in our life today I do not know. On the level of daily life everything that was bad, still is. Even worse! Sometimes I ask myself, was there ever that August? Maybe it never happened.

But August 1991 did happen. It destroyed communism and the world's strongest bastion of communism—the Soviet Union. And from that moment began a new, post-August time in which hope appeared.

Revolutions are made quickly. But the process of creation is long and tedious; it takes many years of hard work. We must create our country and ourselves. As a Radio Liberty listener wrote: "We destroyed our prison, but for some reason we expect the jailers to keep bringing swill to our cells." That is an accurate description of our situation today.

The Disintegration of Yugoslavia

LENARD J. COHEN

Once again the vexatious political problems of the Balkans have resulted in regime breakdown, ethnic violence, and human suffering. Between the summer of 1991 and the spring of 1992 the Yugoslav federation designed by Josip Broz Tito's Communist regime completely disintegrated, and was replaced by several successor states. Three of the republics in the former federation—Croatia, Slovenia, and Bosnia and Herzegovina—established their independence through unilateral "disassociation" from the Yugoslav state and, despite the armed struggles that then ensued on their territories, were soon recognized by the international community.* A fourth republic, Macedonia, also proclaimed independence, but its recognition was postponed after Greece complained that a state with that name would have territorial aspirations to its northern province of Macedonia.

International acceptance also eluded the two remaining republics, Serbia and Montenegro, which endeavored to inherit the mantle of the former Yugoslav state. This "remodeled" Yugoslavia failed to obtain international recognition because of the widely held belief that Serbian President Slobodan Milosevic was masterminding military aggression against Croatia and Bosnia.

Why did Yugoslavia collapse, and why has that collapse generated so much violence and suffering? Answers to those questions abound, ranging from conventional observations that the state was doomed to disintegrate as a result of internal contradictions to recent arguments that the international community failed to prevent the spread of violence. Two other factors, however, are particularly significant for understanding the violent dissolution of the Yugoslav federation: one is the persistence and intensification of deep antagonisms among the country's diverse ethnic and religious groups. The second is the failure of political leaders, who came to power in multiparty elections in 1990, to agree on a new model of political and economic co-existence that could have preserved some form of Yugoslav state unity, but would have also permitted expanded "sovereignty" of the federation's

* In this article, Bosnia is used as the shortened form of the country's name.

territorial units and ethnic groups. The combined impact of heightened ethnic and religious animosities and failed political leadership not only contributed to the demise of Yugoslavia, but also unleashed the violent ethnic strife consuming the former federation.

In the "Prism of History"

Balkan society is known for its pronounced religious and ethnic diversity and for its intractable pattern of group antagonisms. Throughout much of Balkan history the region's heterogeneity has been nurtured to maintain authoritarian rule. For example, the contending Ottoman and Hapsburg empires, which asserted hegemony over the various South Slav ethnic groups between the late fourteenth and early sixteenth centuries, maintained political control until the early twentieth century through several divide-and-rule strategies, including the segmentation of religious communities.

Despite those imperial policies, some members of the nonruling intelligentsia sought to forge closer ties among different ethnically related communities. One such initiative, the "Yugoslav idea," elaborated by Croatian intellectuals during the first part of the nineteenth century, advocated closer cultural and political ties among the various South Slav peoples. Although it attracted considerable support among the South Slav intelligentsia, and provided an important option for political change as imperial rule waned just before and during World War I, the Yugoslav idea enjoyed little support from others in the region.

Its limited popular support notwithstanding, a unified Yugoslav state was created in 1918, bringing together several South Slav and non-Slav ethnic groups. While the state's Belgrade-based political regimes largely abandoned the earlier imperial policies of group division, their attempts to induce a pan-ethnic "Yugoslav" consciousness during most of the next 73 years only aggravated ethnic antagonisms. Whether under the Serbian dominated unitary state between the two World Wars, or the more ethnically balanced but oppositionless Communist federation established by Tito, ethnic grievances continued to accumulate. Short-lived periods of political contestation or liberalization—such as the fragmented multiparty system of the 1920s, and the factionalized one-party socialist pluralism Tito reluctantly permitted in the second part of the 1960s—proved to be episodes of ethnic and political rivalry that did not offer the opportunity for the reconciliation of group animosities. Pre-Communist and Communist political elites in Belgrade, just as earlier rulers in Constantinople, Vienna, and Budapest, managed to constrain widespread ethnic conflict for long periods of time, but deep-seated ethnic resentments persisted, simmering beneath the façade of stability and cohesion.

Historically, the potential for ethnic- and religious-based violence in the Balkans has been most evident during periods of regime crisis and breakdown (for example, the last phase of Ottoman control leading to the Balkan Wars, the final throes of Hapsburg rule, and the collapse and dismemberment of the Yugoslav state in 1941). Discussing his native Bosnian society in the period just before World War I, the Nobel Prize–winning author Ivo Andric captured how seemingly tranquil group relations have exploded into an orgy of mutual bloodletting when the political system has broken down. In an illustrative case, Andric describes the "Sarajevo frenzy of hate" that erupted among Muslims, Roman Catholics, and Orthodox believers following the assassination on June 28, 1914, of Archduke Franz Ferdinand in Sarajevo:

> Adherents of the three main faiths . . . hate one another from birth to death, senselessly and profoundly. . . . [O]ften, they spent their entire lives without finding an opportunity to express that hatred in all its facets and horror; but whenever the established order of things is shaken by some important event, and reason and law are suspended for a few hours or days, then this mob or rather a section of it, finding at last an adequate motive, overflows into the town . . . and, like a flame which has sought and has at last found fuel, these long-kept hatreds and hidden desires for destruction and violence take over the town, lapping, sputtering, and swallowing everything, until some force larger than themselves suppresses them, or until they burn themselves out and tire of their own rage.[1]

An even more widespread frenzy of hatred among nationalities and religious groups during World War II resulted in the loss of approximately one-tenth of Yugoslavia's population. The wartime atrocities and political polarization bequeathed a pattern of emotional scars that were masked by the Communist system's promising slogans ("Brotherhood and Unity," "Equality of Nations"), pan-ethnic strategies, and political uniformity.

The Politics of Intransigence

The important role played by tradition and other historical factors in the violent disintegration of Yugoslavia is closely linked to the country's recent political leadership. The future of the Yugoslav federation was profoundly affected during the late 1980s by the ascendance of nationalist political leaders devoted to the radical alteration or even dissolution of the state. Many of these nationalist leaders first appeared within the higher ranks of the ruling League of Yugoslav Communists (LCY), where their emergence was connected with the failure of Tito's heirs to find a way out of the country's serious economic and political crisis. Thus, as Yugoslavia's standard of living deteriorated sharply in the second half of the 1980s, quarrels among the country's regionally based and ethnically divided political elites intensified. Without the presence of a powerful figure such as Tito to maintain cohesion, regional leaders took advantage of the formally decentralized structure of both the LCY and the state in order to develop their own strategies for crisis management and reform.

In Serbia a relatively new figure on the political scene, Slobodan Milosevic, was able to quickly mobilize strong support in the second half of the 1980s by capitalizing on Serbian grievances regarding Albanian nationalism in the province of Kosovo, as well as Serbia's alleged lack of influence in the Yugoslav federation. As members of the nationality that had been the core force in the creation of the Yugoslav state in 1918, had been the predominant group in the wartime Communist movement, and also composed the largest ethnic group in the country, most Serbs believed their interests were inadequately recognized at the federal level.

Through his brash articulation of Serbia's political discontent, and particularly his populist mobilization of Serbian ethnic consciousness at mass rallies—sometimes referred to as "street democracy"—

Milosevic challenged the oligarchic Titoist style of managing the "national question" and also provoked a sharp nationalist backlash from Yugoslavia's other republics and ethnic groups. In Slovenia, for example, where popular support for enhanced regional and ethnic autonomy and opposition to the federal system had been growing for several years, reform Communists soon crossed swords with Milosevic on matters such as constitutional change, the reorganization of the LCY, and the problem of Kosovo. Citizens and leaders in Croatia and the other republics also watched the growing Serbian nationalism with trepidation, but until the disintegration of the LCY in early 1990 did little to advance their own ethnic or regional concerns.

As the aftershocks of the democratic earthquake that rocked eastern Europe in the fall of 1989 reached the Balkans, Yugoslavia's failed and fragmented Communist elites were forced to grudgingly embrace the concept of party pluralism. Unable to resolve the country's serious economic and political crises, or to even maintain the party's unity, Communist leaders could no longer defend the contradictory admixture of one-party monopoly and "self-management" that had been the hallmark of Yugoslav socialism. The result was the multiparty elections held throughout Yugoslavia's republics from April to December 1990 that marked a watershed in the country's political development. In several republics (Slovenia, Croatia, Bosnia, and Macedonia) the ruling Communists were defeated by non-Communist, center-right parties. In other areas (Serbia, Vojvodina, and Montenegro), former Communist elites and party organizations—reconfigured and sometimes newly labeled "socialist"—retained power, but were now forced to deal with a small but vocal parliamentary and extra-parliamentary non-Communist opposition. By the fall of 1990 over 200 political parties had been formed, the majority of which were small, regionally based organizations striving to advance specific ethnic interests.

Although the elections of 1990 were an impressive exercise in regime transition, the results left the country even more politically fragmented than it had been during the last days of Communist rule. Thus, whether born-again Communists or non-Communists, both the newly elected political authorities and the bulk of the opposition forces in all regions of Yugoslavia were committed to programs of regional and ethnic nationalism that seriously challenged the power of the federal system. Yugoslavia's prime minister, Ante Markovic, attempted to reorient the government's policy along post-Communist lines and carry out countrywide economic reforms, but his ability to implement these measures was persistently stymied by the policies of contending ethnic and regional groups. Moreover, the fact that the most influential republics (Serbia, Croatia, and Slovenia) were now governed by popularly elected political leaders devoted to sharply conflicting visions of the country's future constitutional organization, also undermined Markovic's efforts to introduce any long-term reforms.

In Croatia, for example, the new government led by Franjo Tudjman's Croatian Democratic Alliance supported—along with the new post-Communist government in Slovenia—the transformation of the existing Yugoslav federation into a "confederation of sovereign states." Leaders in both republics said they were prepared to unilaterally "disassociate" from the Yugoslav federal structure should planned negotiations in 1991 among the republican leaders on the country's future prove unsuccessful. In Serbia, Milosevic, who had finally consolidated his power in a competitive (albeit not fully democratic) election, remained strongly committed to what he termed a "modern federation," that is, an arrangement in which the country's dispersed Serbian population would remain united in a single state and would enjoy enhanced political influence. Milosevic's views on constitutional questions, and particularly his opposition to the idea of a confederation, were shared by the large Serbian contingent in the country's military establishment, as well as by top "Yugoslav-oriented" officers from other ethnic groups who—either because of their Communist political backgrounds or professional self-interests—strongly objected to proposals by new non-Communist elites advocating military depoliticization, cuts in the armed forces, and a further devolution of political power.

The Answer to the "Serbian Question"

It did not take long for the various positions concerning the constitutional transformation of the country to become entangled with the emotionally charged "Serbian question"—disputes concerning the rights and status of the 25 percent of Yugoslavia's Serbs living outside the Serbian republic. The majority of these dispersed Serbs—who were concentrated in Bosnia and in Croatia, where they had suffered

greatly at the hands of the Croatian fascist regime during World War II
—feared proposals by the newly elected nationalist government in
Croatia to divide the country into separate states, and also its suggestions that Croatia and Bosnia become more closely associated. Angst
among Croatia's Serbs intensified when the Tudjman regime adopted
new constitutional provisions in 1990 that referred to the republic as
the sovereign state of the Croats and other nations living in Croatia,
but no longer explicitly recognized the republic's Serbian community
(12.2 percent of Croatia's population in 1991) as a major ethnic group.
The constitutional provisions also designated the use of traditional
Croatian ethnic symbols (a coat of arms, flag, and national anthem) as
the republic's official insignia.

While the new symbolism was offensive to many of Croatia's
Serbs, their deeper fear was that Tudjman planned to sever Croatia
from the Yugoslav state—either by creating a loose confederation or by
outright secession—which would leave the Serbs at the political mercy
of a Croatian majority and nationalist government. The anxiety of the
Serb minority was particularly intense in the Krajina area, where it
constituted a majority of the population. Statements by Croatian authorities that minority rights in the republic would be respected were
deeply mistrusted in the Serb community, and were at odds with the
nationalist and anti-Serb rhetoric frequently adopted by President
Tudjman and certain quarters of his party's leadership. Serbian anxiety
was also fueled by the steady and sensational campaign of anti-Croatian
propaganda emanating from Serb nationalists in Belgrade.

For the Milosevic regime—obsessed with the idea of preserving
the federal state and enhancing Serbian influence—support for the
"unity" of the Serbs and particularly the protection of the large Serb
communities in Croatia and Bosnia, was a crucial bargaining chip in
discussions about Yugoslavia's future. Thus, Milosevic claimed that he
did not oppose the self-determination of Yugoslavia's nations, or even
legal secession by the republics, as long as those rights did not infringe
on the equal right of Serbs in a particular republic to exercise self-
determination. Accordingly, Milosevic maintained, if a majority of
citizens in Croatia or Bosnia, for example, desired their independence
from the Yugoslav state, the borders of those republics must be
changed in order to protect the interests of local Serb inhabitants.

Driven by his broader goal of assuring Yugoslav unity under Serbian influence, Milosevic encouraged the country's diasporic Serb

communities to push for self-determination while still carefully with-holding Serbia's full recognition of their political autonomy or accep-tance of their plans to become part of the Serbian republic. By keeping the Serbian question on the front burner and opening the issue of border changes, Milosevic and his allies in the Yugoslav People's Army (JNA) hoped they could prevent Croatia's Tudjman—and also the closely allied Croat and Muslim leaders of Bosnia—from making any hasty decisions about leaving the Yugoslav federation. Moreover, should negotiations collapse, Milosevic calculated that the Serbian question could serve as a pretext for federally sponsored armed inter-vention that would forestall either Croatia's or Bosnia's secession. The tactic of directing attention to the dispersed Serbs in Yugoslavia also suited Milosevic's domestic agenda: by turning a spotlight on the al-leged plight of the Serbs, Milosevic hoped to deflect attention from his socialist regime's authoritarian cast and also to appeal for political unity and support against the Serbs' putative internal and external enemies.

For Tudjman, if there was any real Serbian question at all worth considering, it was essentially whether the Serbs in Croatia—and par-ticularly the roughly one-quarter of that group living in the Krajina—would acknowledge the republic's sovereignty, or whether Croatia's authorities would have to take stronger measures to maintain law and order. Claiming that from August 1990 to March 1991 his government had refrained from using force against the armed Krajina Serbs who had blocked roads, seized control of local facilities, and established autonomous enclaves, an exasperated Tudjman threatened on April 4 that Croatia would no longer accept such behavior: "We have played democracy for long enough and it is high time to say that Croatia is a republic and that it has a right to establish order."

As talks among the leaders of the republics on Yugoslavia's future proceeded between January and June 1991, the Serbian question be-came a major impediment to any compromise between the advocates of federalism or confederalism. Progress was also obstructed by the inability of most republic leaders to move from fixed positions or retreat from maximum goals.

This intransigence created a vicious cycle of escalating tension and an inevitable drift toward disintegration and violence. Increasingly pessimistic that they could negotiate the creation of a confederation, and fearing they might have to fight their way out of the existing federation, the leaders of Slovenia and Croatia began to expand their own armed forces (including importing arms, which was technically illegal under federal laws). Meanwhile, the leaders of Serbia and their allies in the JNA, unwilling to compromise on their goal of preserving Yugoslavia as an only slightly remodeled federation, exerted unrelenting pressure on the new governments in Ljubljana and Zagreb to abandon their plans for sovereignty and to disband their budding armies.

Disputes concerning the question of imported arms and the buildup of military forces by the republics cast a shadow over the interrepublic summit meetings during the first half of 1991, with Slovenia and Croatia calling for the depoliticization of the JNA, and the JNA working both overtly and covertly to undermine the position of the non-Communist nationalist leaders in Zagreb and Ljubljana. For their part, Croatian authorities were particularly enraged over growing cooperation between federal military forces and local Serb militias, a relationship that had developed after JNA units had intervened in Croatian communities in which there had been outbursts of Serb-Croat violence.

When Serbia, together with its two provinces and Montenegro, connived in mid-May 1991 to block the planned rotation of the collective presidency's Croatian representative to the annual post of state president, Croatia became even more determined to leave the Yugoslav federation. Slovenia's problems with the JNA—which had focused on who would control the republic's Territorial Defense forces (a local militia established by the Tito regime in the late 1960s) and had led to several face-offs in 1991—also propelled that republic's nationalist leadership into a more intransigent position.

While most of the country's major civilian and military leaders recognized the danger of violence if they failed to reach agreement, they proved woefully inept in finding a way out of the looming disaster. The posturing on the seemingly intractable federation-confederation dispute, saber rattling by all sides, and leadership mishandling or outright manipulation of the explosive Serbian question hastened the destruction of an already fragile country. An awkward last-ditch Bosnian-Macedonian proposal, designed as a compromise between the contending federal and confederal options, was given short shrift by the negotiating parties and did nothing to halt Yugoslavia's slide toward disintegration. In late June, when Slovenia and Croatia finally made good on their frequent threats to unilaterally declare independence, the JNA responded with force and the country entered a new phase of military struggle and civil strife.

The Internationalization of the Crisis

The first armed conflict precipitated by the dissolution of the Yugoslav federation was a ten-day war in mid-1991 in which Slovenian forces defeated units of the JNA. That war was followed by more protracted hostilities, first in Croatia and then in Bosnia, involving remnants of the JNA, military and police units under the command of those states's new political authorities, as well as armed groups linked to various local ethnic communities (Serbs versus Croats in Croatia and Serbs versus Croats and Muslims in Bosnia). The military struggles in Croatia and Bosnia triggered the eruption of ethnic violence on a scale not seen in those regions since World War II. By the summer of 1992— after thousands of people had been killed and injured and more than 2.5 million people had been forced to flee their homes—the international community had become actively engaged in a frustrating effort to dampen hostilities, provide humanitarian relief, and negotiate a long-term political settlement among the region's new states.

The violent dismemberment of Yugoslavia occurred just as the cold war ended, but before new mechanisms for conflict management had been established to deal with a crisis of this proportion. As a result, the international response to the Yugoslav breakup has been incoherent and hastily contrived. For example, the European Community (EC) and the United States in June 1991 sent signals encouraging Yugoslavia's unity and strongly discouraging Slovenia's and Croatia's planned unilateral disassociation from the existing federation for fear it might set a dangerous precedent for the Soviet Union, which probably encouraged the Yugoslav federal government and the JNA to employ force against the two breakaway republics. While Secretary of State James Baker 3d may have evenhandedly expressed American opposition to secession by the republics and the use of armed force to settle political disputes during a visit to Belgrade on June 21, the JNA top command apparently chose to view Washington's emphatic support for Yugoslavia's cohesion as a green light for military intervention should secession occur.

Shortly after hostilities began in Slovenia, the EC successfully negotiated a cease-fire and an agreement that provided for a three-month moratorium on further moves toward independence by Croatia and Slovenia. The agreement also included EC-sponsored negotiations among the republics about their future, and an understanding that Stipe Mesic, the Croatian representative in the collective state presidency, would finally assume his post as state president.

However, when JNA forces subsequently retreated from Slovenia into Croatia a short time later, the EC, lacking its own joint military forces and internally divided about the best method for handling the crisis, proved helpless to prevent an escalation of the conflict. Divisions in the 12-member Community—a newly assertive Germany, for example, strongly advocated the immediate recognition of Croatia and Slovenia and expanded EC involvement, while Britain and France urged a more cautious policy and further negotiations among the former Yugoslav republics—sent mixed signals to the warring parties, who exploited the international disagreements to pursue their respective agendas. Other multilateral organizations also initially failed to manage the Yugoslav crisis. NATO rules said the crisis was an "out of area conflict"; the Conference on Security and Cooperation on Europe (CSCE) was untested, lacked military forces, and could take action only by consensus; while the Western European Union (WEU), perceived as a kind of EC security arm, had never undertaken a major venture.

As the war in Croatia intensified in late 1991, the Zagreb government pleaded for international intervention in the crisis, viewing the deployment of foreign troops in Croatia as the best chance for reasserting sovereignty in its war-torn multiethnic regions. For their part, the Serbian government, the JNA, and local Serb militias regarded the EC's immobility as a positive, providing their forces with an opportunity to crush Croatian independence or, at a minimum, expand the territory under Serb control.

As the international community floundered in its attempts to resolve the crisis, over a dozen EC negotiated cease-fire agreements collapsed in rapid succession. Meanwhile, EC-hosted negotiations at The Hague and later in Brussels concerning Yugoslavia's future also failed to devise a peaceful model of disassociation and cooperation among the parties. By early December, Croatia's Mesic, who had formally abandoned his post as Yugoslavia's last president, announced to the Croatian Assembly: "I have fulfilled my duty—Yugoslavia no longer exists." In January 1992, as the fighting continued, Germany decided to recognize the independence of Slovenia and Croatia, thereby prodding the EC and its member states to follow suit.

Having proved unsuccessful at peacemaking and peacekeeping, the EC turned its latter mission over to the United Nations, which previously had remained on the sidelines because of its own divisions about the propriety of intervening in a sovereign state's internal disputes. Exhausted by the war, having already seized considerable territory in Croatia, but now faced with the prospect of UN intervention and European support for the Zagreb government, Serbia and JNA leaders finally committed themselves to a cease-fire agreement that was negotiated by special UN envoy Cyrus Vance.

Leaders of the militant Serb community in the Krajina felt betrayed by the Belgrade government's decision to end hostilities and submit to the deployment of international troops in their region, but Milosevic rationalized his action by pointing to provisions of the agreement stipulating that Serb enclaves in Croatia would remain outside the direct control of Zagreb authorities. Milosevic and the remnants of the federal army had no intention of abandoning their efforts to settle the Serbian question on their own terms. For the moment, the venue of warfare would simply be transferred from Croatia to Bosnia.

War Comes to Bosnia

Bosnia, with its complicated mosaic of ethnic and religious communities, had long been recognized as the Balkan's most explosive powderkeg (in 1991 its population was 43.7 percent Muslim, 31.4 percent Serb, 17.3 percent Croat, and 5.5 percent Yugoslav—that is, those who did not consider themselves a member of any ethnic group). When, following a referendum held at the end of February 1992 in which Muslims and Croats voted overwhelmingly for Bosnia's independence (a vote in which the republic's Serbs abstained), Serb officials, working in close association with locally based JNA forces, proceeded to prepare for hostilities. Mistakenly believing that recognition of Slovenia and Croatia by the EC and UN in January had been the principal factor dampening hostilities in those republics, and still chafing from earlier criticism about its initial commitment to Yugoslav unity in mid-1991, the United States recognized in April the independence of Bosnia and Herzegovina along with that of Croatia and Slovenia.

Ironically, while criticism of Washington's overly cautious policy on secession in 1991 was warranted, the unique circumstances in Bosnia actually justified a prudent approach. The United States expectation that diplomatic recognition of Bosnia would calm matters seriously underestimated the history of ethnic and religious violence in that republic, the claims to the region by Serbs and Croats, and the tenuous authority of Alija Izetbegovic's Bosnian government. The fact that Bosnia's various ethnic and religious groups had coexisted during the authoritarian Tito era and that most inhabitants of the republic deplored ethnic rivalry, did not detract from the intense latent hatred and psychological distance existing among the various groups. Assessments of ethnic relations in Bosnia based on the cheerful atmosphere observed in Sarajevo during the 1984 Winter Olympic games, or other glib claims that the area had been an oasis of harmony for 500 years, seriously misjudged the real situation.

Faced with the growing possibility that the largest Serb community outside Serbia would become formally separated from it, the Belgrade government, Serbs in Bosnia, and JNA forces in the area decided to use whatever force necessary in order to forestall such an event. The war that ensued in Bosnia has led to even more casualties than the previous struggle in Croatia. Terrified at the prospect of being once again dominated by a Croatian-Muslim alliance strongly supported by Germany, Serb forces attempted to alter the demographic structure of the republic by brutally employing their superior military strength to forcibly oust Croat and Muslim inhabitants from Serb controlled territory—the notorious and internationally condemned policy of "ethnic cleansing." Croat and Muslim paramilitary forces often defended and advanced their own interests with equal brutality, re-creating an all too familiar pattern of violence and atrocities against civilians.

Angered by Belgrade's apparent role in the aggressive Serb onslaught against Croats and Muslims in Bosnia, the UN and EC imposed harsh economic sanctions against Serbia in May 1992. However, as unrelenting violence with tragic consequences for the civilian population continued throughout the summer and into this fall, the absence of an established international security force and political differences among members of the international community on how to resolve the crisis hampered peacekeeping efforts. Except for a small number of officers already posted in Sarajevo (as headquarters staff for the peacekeeping forces in Croatia), UN forces were not deployed in Bosnia until hostilities were well under way, and then only a small force was used to open the airport in Sarajevo.

Although NATO and the WEU altered their constitutions so they could provide military assistance to nonmilitary multilateral organizations (leading to the July deployment of Western naval forces in the Adriatic Sea to assist in the implementation of sanctions against Serbia), most leading members of the international community were extremely reluctant to become deeply enmeshed in what had become an exceptionally complex and bloody struggle. By July a dispute had even emerged between the UN's Security Council and UN Secretary General Boutros Boutros-Ghali about whether further resources should be expended on the Yugoslav case when so many other international conflicts and humanitarian crises deserved attention. As the violent consequences of Yugoslavia's disintegration continue unabated in Bosnia and threatens to spill over into other regions of the former federation (the predominantly ethnic Albanian province of Kosovo, which has been under Belgrade's tight control for several years, is the next most likely flashpoint), the international community continues its clumsy, albeit well-meaning, improvisation of a new "security architecture" for the post–cold war period.

In late August 1992, at a meeting in London sponsored by the UN and the EC, the belligerents and foreign states created a permanent conference in Geneva to deal with the Balkan crisis, but agreements reached to end the fighting were not implemented. The UN subsequently expelled the new Serbo-Montenegrin Yugoslavia, authorized sending additional troops to Bosnia, and created a War Crimes Commission in September to investigate atrocities, but hostilities and "ethnic cleansing" continued. As winter approached, it was feared that the trickle of humanitarian aid reaching Bosnia would be insufficient to avoid a heavy loss of civilian life.

Balkan Cooperation after Yugoslavia?

Developing a coordinated and consistent international response to Yugoslavia's collapse presents a major challenge as the fierce fighting and carnage continue. Apart from the immediate problem of containing the blood-letting, other significant issues also need to be addressed before there can be any long-term resolution of the crisis. In view of the decisive role played by Balkan political leaders in generating the present difficulties—especially the major actors from the two largest ethnic communities, Slobodan Milosevic and Franjo Tudjman—the question naturally arises whether political forces in Serbia and Croatia will be able to find new leaders who can transcend the politics of intransigence and find solutions to the serious problems faced by the region. For different reasons, Milosevic and Tudjman have been politically weakened by the war, and opposition forces in both their republics have been growing in strength, but neither leader appears ready to leave the scene.

Looking beyond the current warfare and disruption, it also remains unclear whether the various successor states to Yugoslavia can successfully resuscitate the extensive economic linkages that previously existed among the republics and regions. The imperatives of economic survival and geography suggest that such cooperation will eventually resume, even after the most recent episodes of violence. Determining how to do this will require considerable time and commitment, and will also require a change of political leadership. Thus, until the current frenzy of hate either subsides or is extinguished, and until a broader solution is found for resolving the conflict in Bosnia—possibly a radical decentralization of the region into three ethnic territorial enclaves, each closely associated with its preferred neighboring state—the violent aftermath of Yugoslavia's disintegration seems destined to continue.

NOTES

1. *Gospodjica* (Zagreb: Mladost, 1961), p. 77.

Chinese Seizure of Tibet

JULIAN BURGER

Military annexation by a powerful neighbour can overturn the social and spiritual fabric as well as the economy of an indigenous population. Tibet, a Buddhist state with a central belief in nonviolence, is in the grip of a superpower: military occupation by the Chinese.

Since the Chinese Red Army invaded Tibet 40 years ago, it has destroyed land through mismanagement and dismantled what the Chinese considered to be feudal social relations, archaic economic practices, and an oppressive religion. They forced farmers to grow wheat instead of the better adapted hill barley. They collectivized herders and their animals. The result has been crop failures, overgrazing, and the first famine in the country's history. Up to 40 per cent of China's mineral wealth and most of its timber lies in Tibet. Billions of US dollars-worth of timber have been trucked to China.

The Chinese destroyed nearly all the 6000 monasteries and holy shrines and more than half the libraries. In 1959 10,000 Tibetans, including the Dalai Lama, Tibet's political and spiritual leader, fled to India. There are now well over 100,000 Tibetan refugees. Chinese immigration escalated in 1983, when the government offered Tibetan land to immigrants. The Tibetans who remain have been pushed up into the hills.

Tibet, bordering India, is a key part of China's defences, and China now keeps one-quarter of its nuclear force in the area. Chinese military presence has increased: today there is one soldier for every ten Tibetans.*

---

* Little over half the original territory of Tibet is administered as the Tibetan Autonomous Region (TAR). The rest has been incorporated into four provinces of China. In Amdo, now part of Gansu, Sichuan, and Qinghai, there are 3.5 million Chinese to 700,000 Tibetans. In Lhasa, 75% of the people are Chinese.

Tibet's social, political and religious framework has been dismantled by the People's Republic of China since their invasion over 40 years ago, in 1950.

Burma: A Nation of Prisoners

PAULA GREEN

Burma is a Texas-sized nation of Southeast Asia located between the two population giants of Asia: China and India. Its 41 million people are 70% Burman and 30% indigenous minority groups. Burma shares long remote jungle borders with Thailand and China.

Over the centuries Burma was settled by tribal peoples migrating from Tibet, China, and other bordering areas. Theravadan Buddhism became firmly established in Burma in the 11th century and has been the religion of 85% of the people since that time. The people known as the Burmans (for whom the country is named) settled in the central, rice-producing lowlands while the many diverse indigenous groups occupied the peripheral high mountain jungle areas. Due to remoteness and primitive transportation there was limited contact between the ethnic minorities and the Burmese until the British entered in the 19th century.

In 1886 Burma lost its independence and was annexed as a province of British India. Colonialism was humiliating for the Burmese people. They were stripped of their power and replaced in their posts by imported Indians and British. The British favored the ethnic minorities of the peripheral areas who were less resistant to British rule and more responsive to conversion by Christian missionaries. This policy of divide and conquer created enormous dissension in Burma that is reflected in deep and unhealed Burman-ethnic conflicts today.

During World War II Burma became a battleground between the British and Japanese. In 1947 the British granted independence to Burma, and independence hero Aung San became its leader. Shortly after independence, however, Aung San and his close ministers were assassinated. His daughter, Burma's Nobel Prize winner, was then two years old. U Nu became Prime Minister, ruling until the military coup of 1962.

In 1962, Ne Win staged a coup and established himself and the military as the rulers of Burma. Ne Win began a policy of extreme isolation and xenophobia, rejecting outside investments and media, and nationalizing industry, banks, trade, and businesses. Proclaiming the "Burmese Way to Socialism," he instead achieved the Burmese way to one-party rule, economic collapse, social breakdown, and bankruptcy. Ne Win controlled and oppressed the Burmese people through intimidation, fear, disappearances, arrests, torture, and murder.

Nonviolent Rebellion

Prior to 1988 there was sporadic organized resistance to the military rule, but in 1988, facing severe economic conditions, a massive and stunningly courageous rebellion began. Led by students and monks who have traditionally been the spokespersons for dissent, the rebellion spread to all of Burma's cities and involved millions of people risking life and safety for the possibility of overthrowing the hated government. Universities and schools were closed, but the rebellion grew.

Ne Win resigned as head of the government, and a period of chaos among the ruling party members and the military ensued. No leader emerged immediately, but after a few months of massive daily demonstrations calling for elections, the military took control and determined to put down the uprising at any cost. The new government established itself as the State Law and Order Restoration Council (SLORC) in September 1988.

Lasting more than six months, the demonstrations were completely nonviolent, but the military response was violent and brutal in the extreme. Approximately 10,000 people, including children, monks, and the elderly, were shot down in the streets or hauled off to torture and death in prisons. Thousands more were jailed and tortured. During these bloody months, no cameras recorded the massacres, which preceded the widely witnessed and similar slaughter in China's Tiananmen Square a few months later.

In response to international pressure in the form of economic threats, SLORC allowed elections to be held in May 1990. The leader of the National League for Democracy (NLD), Aung San Suu Kyi, campaigned from SLORC-imposed house arrest, and there was no independent media covering the elections. Despite such electoral intimidation, the people again demonstrated their courage and gave 84% of the vote to Aung San Suu Kyi and the NLD. However, SLORC refused to relinquish power and responded instead by jailing most of the newly elected officials and initiating an even more stringent reign of terror and impoverishment upon the population.

SLORC's elaborate spy system has shattered trust between people. The military is the only source of news and media. Assembly and protest are illegal and the universities have remained shut since 1988. Anyone thought to be in opposition to SLORC risks arrest, torture, and imprisonment for years without trial.

Life is extremely harsh in the jungle peripheries of Burma. Since the time of independence from Britain, the ethnics have been at war with the Burmese government over issues of self-determination and recognition of their special status, languages, and cultures. No friend of the ethnics, SLORC relies for its monetary support on sales of teak, minerals, gems, and opium to be found in the minority areas. Burma now has the third highest deforestation rate in the world. Sophisticated military hardware makes life in the jungles more precarious each year and many ethnic groups face total obliteration in the near future. SLORC troops destroy villages by pillaging and burning homes and crops, capturing males to be used as porter slaves and human mine detectors, and capturing young women for the prostitution trade in Thailand.

Opposition Struggles

Living with the ethnics and sharing their precarious fate are approximately 3,000 university students from the cities of Burma, refugees of the military crackdown. The students are learning jungle survival strategies from the ethnics and forging alliances that will be necessary for Burma's political future. These students and others hiding in Bangkok have formed themselves into the All Burma Students Democratic Front (ABSDF).

Also in the jungles along the Thai border is the NCGUB, the National Coalition Government of the Union of Burma. This is the remnant of the prodemocracy movement, composed of both Burman and ethnic representatives. This government-in-exile is developing itself and building connections with the worldwide prodemocracy movement. However, it is living on a fragile thread in an impoverished jungle camp made of bamboo and thatch huts, likely the most improbable government headquarters in the world today.

There is no knowing when this stranglehold on the people of Burma will come to an end nor who will be left in Burma to celebrate its demise and form a new government. At the U.N. the SLORC delegation still holds the Burma seat although they do not represent the people of Burma. In a rare gesture in late 1991 the U.N. voted to censure the SLORC government, but criticism and verbal condemnation by foreign governments or organizations is ineffectual unless it is backed up by economic action.

Since the military takeover in 1962, Burma has largely been closed to foreigners and especially to the international press. Thus few people remember Burma. Aung San Suu Kyi remains the most important symbol of hope for the Burmese, but there is no indication as to when she will be freed. Burma received some much-needed media attention from the touching images of Suu Kyi's eighteen-year-old son accepting the Nobel Peace Prize on behalf of his imprisoned mother; from solidarity demonstrations in many cities worldwide; and from the November 1991 publication of a collection of essays (*Freedom from Fear*) written by Aung San Suu Kyi before her imprisonment. Over 1,000 university students in Burma demonstrated for freedom during the Nobel Prize awards, but they were promptly arrested and now face torture and death.

Time is of the essence. Each year the population and natural resources are further decimated. The "dry season offensive" by the military into the ethnic areas is particularly vicious this winter of 1991–92. Reports of widespread malnutrition and starvation, burned villages and abandoned rice paddies, and arrests and torture in many different ethnic areas along the peripheries of Burma give cause for outrage and alarm.

In a political situation receiving so little attention, and with the power of the Nobel Peace Prize waking the world up briefly, our efforts can make a significant difference. Change will come to Burma one day as it comes everywhere, and the terrible tragedy of Burma will someday heal. With the help of concerned citizens around the world, perhaps we can save precious lives and hasten that day.

Who's Involved?

The Government: A military regime has dominated the country since 1962, warring against its own people. The State Law and Order Restoration Council (SLORC) is the current regime which came to power in a 1988 coup. The dictatorship has renamed the country Myanmar, but since this name is against the will of the people, it is not used in the prodemocracy movement.

The opposition: National League for Democracy (NLD) which won the 1990 elections under its leader Aung San Suu Kyi, recipient of the 1991 Nobel Peace Prize. She is under house arrest and much of the opposition has been arrested, tortured, killed, or scattered. Organizing in the jungles along the Thai border are the All Burma Students Democratic Front (ABSDF) and the National Coalition Government of the Union of Burma (NCGUB).

Costs

Lives: Burma's population is 41 million. It has been called a land of "41 million prisoners." An estimated 10,000 people lost their lives during 1988 protests. Thousands more have been jailed, tortured, and murdered, others have been enslaved as porters for the military. Entire ethnic villages are wiped out by military attack. Approximately 7,000 students who fled to the Thai border are thought to have died of malaria, starvation, or military murder. 500,000 people have been forcibly relocated from their homes inside Burma to malarial swamps far from transportation, schools, and workplaces.

Freedom: There are no freedoms in Burma. SLORC dominates in every aspect. Amnesty International states that Burma has one of the worst human rights records in the world and that "in Burma torture follows arrest as night follows day."

Economy: The military government demonetized the currency several times. Formerly known as the "rice bowl of Asia," Burma is now the fourth poorest country in the world. It is estimated that the military budget is 50% of the country's current operating budget.

Land: The military is selling the natural resources of Burma at a prodigious rate to finance the war against its own people. Burma is rich in teak and other hardwoods, oil, fish, precious gems, tin, tungsten, and opium. Burma now has the third highest deforestation rate in the world.

Rationale

The military leaders seek power and wealth.

Outside Involvement

Asia: China sold $2 billion (U.S. dollars) worth of arms to Burma in 1991 and trades for teak. China trains Burmese fighter pilots for bombing raids on students and ethnic jungle villages. Japan gives substantial Overseas Development Aid (ODA) to Burma and purchases large supplies of teak and fish. Japan is the largest investor in Burma. Thailand is greatly implicated in teak trade, owning all the logging concessions in Burma. Thailand stopped logging in its own country due to deforestation and landslides and is now destroying Burma's forests. Thailand also refuses to give amnesty to Burmese refugees and ships them back to Burma knowing they will be imprisoned and possibly executed. Thailand, which had its own military coup in February 1991, cooperates with the Burmese government in treatment of ethnics along their shared border. The ASEAN nations refused to condemn Burma at their 1991 meeting, because all of them, especially Singapore, Thailand, and South Korea, are trading partners with SLORC.

Europe and North America: Major international corporations are involved in Burma including Pepsico, Amoco, Unocal, Shell, Petrol Canada, etc. A German company is a major arms supplier of the SLORC regime. International tourist, hotel, and mining interests are preparing for development in Burma. To eradicate opium fields the U.S. supplies SLORC with Agent Orange and 2-4-D which are instead sprayed over ethnic villages. From 1974–88 the U.S. gave the

Burmese military dictatorship more than $71 million in "anti-narcotics" equipment, mainly aircraft, which are used against the students and ethnics in the jungles. The U.S. also trains Burma's military leaders: 72% of Burma's current top military leadership was trained in the U.S.

Opium Trade: Illegal trading with governmental and nongovernmental interests worldwide. According to the U.S. State Department, "Burma is the world's largest producer of illicit opium and exporter of opium-based narcotics." Since SLORC took command in 1988, opium production and sales have increased. The amount of money pouring into the coffers of the Burmese dictatorship from the opium trade cannot be documented, but is said to be substantial.

Prospects for the Future

The fact that much of Burma's opposition leadership is dead or imprisoned bodes ill for Burma's future. The SLORC regime will collapse when international trade and investments with the SLORC government are brought to a halt. Until that time, prospects for peace and reconciliation are dim.

Peace movement interest in Burma has been small. However, in November 1991 two Burma activists (one of them this author) convened a working conference in Washington, D.C. to build a coalition of nongovernmental organizations, human rights, environment and peace activists, and Burmese expatriates to further the goals of freedom for Burma. The International Burma Campaign (IBC) was created.

The Sexualization of Racism

CALVIN C. HERNTON

More than two decades ago, a Swedish social scientist was invited to America for the purpose of conducting perhaps the most thorough study of the race problem ever undertaken. The social scientist was Gunnar Myrdal. As it turned out, he produced a monumental work entitled *An American Dilemma.*

One of the most interesting aspects of the race problem was formulated by Myrdal into a schema which he called "The Rank Order of Discrimination." When Myrdal asked white Southerners to list, in the order of importance, the things they thought Negroes wanted most, here is what he got:

1. Intermarriage and sex intercourse with whites
2. Social equality and etiquette
3. Desegregation of public facilities, buses, churches, etc.
4. Political enfranchisement
5. Fair treatment in the law courts
6. Economic opportunities[1]

The curious thing about this "Rank Order" was that when Myrdal approached the Negroes, they put down the same items as did the whites, but with one major change—they listed them in the direct *reverse* order!

Today the same reverse positions are still maintained with equal vigor by both whites and blacks. While I am not going to charge either group with being totally dishonest, I am going to assert that neither whites nor blacks were or are being completely honest with themselves. For, of the various facets of the race problem in America, there is no doubt that the sexual aspect is as much a "thorn in the side" to blacks as it is to whites. Both groups, for their own special reasons, are hideously concerned about it.

The white man, especially the Southerner, is overtly obsessed by the idea of the Negro desiring sexual relations with whites. The black man is secretly tormented every second of his wakeful life by the presence of white women in his midst, whom he cannot or had better not touch. Despite the severe penalties for associating with white women—lynching, castration, electrocution—blacks risk their lives for white flesh, and an occasional few actually commit rape. On the other hand, the white man, especially in the South, cannot seem to adhere to his own laws and customs prohibiting interracial intercourse—he insults, seduces, and rapes black women as if this were what they exist for. A preponderance of racial violence takes the form of sexual atrocities against not only black women but black men as well.

In the North, Midwest, and West, where there are few legal barriers against race mixing, many blacks and whites suffer social ostracism and castigation for engaging in interracial relations.

What does all of this mean? It means that the race problem is inextricably connected with sex. More and more in America, everything we make, sell, handle, wear, and do takes on a sexual meaning. Matters dealing with race relations are no exception. The Madison Avenue "hidden persuaders" and the "organization men" of the commercial world are functioning now in such an all-pervasive way that virtually no area of social reality, no facet of our psyches, can escape the all but total sexualization of American life. In nearly every television commercial, in every fashion magazine, on the "center pages" of our newspapers, on billboard, bus, and subway ads, in the tabloids of scandal, on the covers and pages of every "cheap" magazine—there is but one incessant symbol: the naked or half-naked white woman. The scantily clad white woman is irresistibly enticing as the ubiquitous sex symbol of our times. Sex pervades everything.

The sexualization of the race problem is a reality, and we are going to have to deal with it even though most of us are, if not unwilling, definitely unprepared.

A tall, dark black man boards the subway at 42nd Street in New York City. He takes a seat in the corner away from everybody. He pulls from his hip pocket a magazine; he looks around carefully, then opens the cover and instantly becomes engrossed. He turns the pages slowly, almost as if transfixed in and by some forbidden drug. There are naked women in various "naughty" poses on every page of the magazine. Their skin is white. A white man enters and stands beside the black man. Quickly the black man snaps the magazine shut, tucks it into his pocket, lays his head back and closes his eyes, probably to dream or to have a nightmare.

"I can't hardly sit by a Negro woman," said a white man who served as an informant for this book. "I can't be comfortable in their presence. I mean I get excited. They don't even have to be good-looking. I can't help but get erect no matter what kind of looking Negro she is."

I have before me the October (1963) issue of the *Science Digest*. There is a picture of a black man on the cover. The caption reads [italics mine]:

The Negro
HOW HE'S
DIFFERENT
WHY
WHITES
FEAR HIM

Inside, on one of the pages, it says that the thing whites fear most about blacks is that blacks have an uncontrollable urge to mate with the sisters and daughters of white men. White men, especially Southerners, are afraid of the so-called superior, savage sexuality of the black male, and they are dead set against any measures that will lift the African-American's status, because they are certain that such measures will bring the black man one step nearer to the white woman's bedroom. Meanwhile it is a common saying in the South among white males that "a man is not a man until he has slept with a nigger."

Listen to the advice a black woman in Mississippi gave reporter John Griffin, who she thought was a stranger to the way of white folks in the South.

> . . . well, you know you don't want to even look at a white woman. In fact, you look down at the ground or the other way . . . you may not know you're looking in a white woman's direction but they'll try to make something out of it. . . . If you pass by a picture show, and they've got women on the posters outside, don't look at them either. . . . Somebody's sure to say, "Hey, boy—what are you looking at that white gal like that for?"[2]

The white man's self-esteem is in a constant state of sexual anxiety in all matters dealing with race relations. So is the black man's, because his life, too, is enmeshed in the absurd system of racial hatred in America. Since racism is centered in and revolves around sex, the black man cannot help but see himself as at once sexually affirmed and negated. While the black man is portrayed as a great "walking phallus" with satyr-like potency, he is denied the execution of that potency, he is denied the most precious sexual image which surrounds him—the white woman. The myth of the sanctity of "white womanhood" is nothing more than a myth, but because this myth is acted upon *as if* it were real both by blacks and whites alike, then it *becomes* real as far as the behavior and sensitivities of those who must encounter it are concerned.

The sexualization of racism in the United States is a unique phenomenon in the history of mankind; it is an anomaly of the first order. In fact, there is a sexual involvement, at once real and vicarious, connecting white and black people in America that spans the history of this country from the era of slavery to the present, an involvement so immaculate and yet so perverse, so ethereal and yet so concrete, that all race relations tend to be, however subtle, *sex* relations.

It is important to see how the racism of sex in America has affected the sexual behavior of blacks and whites toward one another, and how black and white people perceive each other and themselves sexually as a result of living in a world of segregation and racial bigotry. As Negro and Caucasian, male and female, what do we mean to each other as sexual beings?

I am reminded of the way the policemen, during the historic march on Washington in 1963, constricted their eyes, tightened their faces, and fondled their sticks every time an interracial couple passed them in that mammoth parade. I am further reminded that when the marchers were yelling for F-R-E-E-E-E-DOM, for jobs, civil rights, equality of education, and the rest, a young black man leaped in the air and shouted out—"S-E-X!" Perhaps he was a "crackpot." Even so, can one be certain that he was not an omen for our times? I am not certain, for, I submit, that, secretly, for many blacks and whites, sexual liberty is as precious and sought-after as any other freedom. As the other barriers to freedom fall down, sexual liberty will become increasingly important in our society.

NOTES

1. Gunnar Myrdal, *An American Dilemma* (7th ed.; New York, London: Harper & Brothers, 1944), Vol. I, pp. 60–61.
2. John Griffin, *Black Like Me* (New York: Signet Books, 1963), p. 60.

On Being Crazy

W. E. B. DU BOIS

It was one o'clock and I was hungry. I walked into a restaurant, seated myself, and reached for the bill of fare. My table companion rose.

"Sir," said he, "do you wish to force your company on those who do not want you?"

No, said I, I wish to eat.

"Are you aware, sir, that this is social equality?"

Nothing of the sort, sir, it is hunger—and I ate.

The day's work done, I sought the theatre. As I sank into my seat, the lady shrank and squirmed.

I beg pardon, I said.

"Do you enjoy being where you are not wanted?" she asked coldly.

Oh no, I said.

"Well you are not wanted here."

I was surprised. I fear you are mistaken, I said, I certainly want the music, and I like to think the music wants me to listen to it.

"Usher," said the lady, "this is social equality."

"No, madame," said the usher, "it is the second movement of Beethoven's Fifth Symphony."

After the theatre, I sought the hotel where I had sent my baggage. The clerk scowled.

"What do you want?"

Rest, I said.

"This is a white hotel," he said.

I looked around. Such a color scheme requires a great deal of cleaning, I said, but I don't know that I object.

"We object," said he.

Then why, I began, but he interrupted.

"We don't keep niggers," he said, "we don't want social equality."

Neither do I, I replied gently, I want a bed.

I walked thoughtfully to the train. I'll take a sleeper through Texas. I'm a little bit dissatisfied with this town.

"Can't sell you one."

I only want to hire it, said I, for a couple of nights.

"Can't sell you a sleeper in Texas," he maintained. "They consider that social equality."

I consider it barbarism, I said, and I think I'll walk.

Walking, I met another wayfarer, who immediately walked to the other side of the road, where it was muddy. I asked his reason.

"Niggers is dirty," he said.

So is mud, said I. Moreover, I am not as dirty as you—yet.

"But you're a nigger, ain't you?" he asked.

My grandfather was so called.

"Well then!" he answered triumphantly.

Do you live in the South? I persisted, pleasantly.

"Sure," he growled, "and starve there."

I should think you and the Negroes should get together and vote out starvation.

"We don't let them vote."

We? Why not? I said in surprise.

"Niggers is too ignorant to vote."

But, I said, I am not so ignorant as you.

"But you're a nigger."

Yes, I'm certainly what you mean by that.

"Well then!" he returned, with that curiously inconsequential note of triumph. "Moreover," he said, "I don't want my sister to marry a nigger."

I had not seen his sister, so I merely murmured, let her say no.

"By God, you shan't marry her, even if she said yes."

But—but I don't want to marry her, I answered, a little perturbed at the personal turn.

"Why not!" he yelled, angrier than ever.

Because I'm already married and I rather like my wife.

"Is she a nigger?" he asked suspiciously.

Well, I said again, her grandmother was called that.

"Well then!" he shouted in that oddly illogical way.

I gave up.

Go on, I said, either you are crazy or I am.

"We both are," he said as he trotted along in the mud.

Racism and Homophobia

PHILLIP BRIAN HARPER

In 1845, the fugitive slave and abolitionist Frederick Douglass wrote the following words describing his experiences with Mrs. Sophia Auld, mistress of the Baltimore household in which Douglass lived and worked during the 1820s:

> My new mistress proved to be . . . a woman of the kindest heart and finest feelings. She had never had a slave under her control previously to myself. . . . But, alas! this kind heart had but a short time to remain such. The fatal poison of irresponsible power was already in her hands, and soon commenced its infernal work. . . . Slavery proved as injurious to her as it did to me. When I went there, she was a pious, warm, and tender-hearted woman. There was no sorrow or suffering for which she had not a tear. She had bread for the hungry, clothes for the naked, and comfort for every mourner that came within her reach. Slavery soon proved its ability to divest her of these heavenly qualities. Under its influence, the tender heart became stone, and the lamblike disposition gave way to one of tiger-like fierceness.[1]

This passage is remarkable because of its unusual description of what Douglass called the "dehumanizing" effects of slavery. According to Douglass, the victims of those effects are not black slaves alone but also whites whose "superior" position in the slavery context corrupts their humanity.

It is easy to understand why Douglass would think it important to emphasize the negative consequences of slavery for whites as well as for blacks. His *Narrative,* first published by the Anti-Slavery Office during the height of the mid-nineteenth-century abolitionist movement, was really an extension of his oratorical work for the Massachusetts Anti-Slavery Society. Because many northern whites had never witnessed the realities of slavery firsthand, the public addresses by ex-slaves were a necessary feature of abolitionist organizing. It was through these oral narratives that audiences were educated about the horrors of life under the slave system.

Frequently, after making numerous appearances before the public, the slave orators eventually committed their stories to print. There were two primary reasons for this development. One was that the written narrative provided the opportunity for authors to present details of their lives that could not be developed in the more restrictive form of the public address. The relation of these details often proved to be very important since the ex-slaves' ability to give specific, verifiable facts regarding their bondage helped defend them from charges by proslavery forces that they had fabricated their stories. The other reason that ex-slaves turned to the printed word as a means of presenting their life narratives is that they could reach a wider audience through books and pamphlets than through public address.

Frederick Douglass's *Narrative* has long been recognized as the prime example of the published account of the life of a male slave.[2] Douglass had the ability not only to describe the details of his life with great vividness but also to present his experiences as an individual in such a way as to relate them to the effects of slavery on the larger population. This last factor—a key part of the general abolitionist strategy—explains the emphasis Douglass places on slavery's dehumanizing effects on whites. Since the success of the abolitionist movement depended on winning to the cause large numbers of whites, whose numbers and political power were superior to blacks', it was crucial to demonstrate how whites, as well as blacks, were affected by the slave culture.

This anthology strives to achieve the same type of effect that Douglass's *Narrative* did. It aims to demonstrate how prejudicial social attitudes are oppressive to the target group and harmful to those who are not immediate objects of negative sentiment. The parallels between the struggles of blacks and the struggles of lesbians, gay males, and bisexuals have often been recognized within the community of sexual minorities, and the community's struggle for liberation has often been modeled on the fight for racial justice as well as on the feminist struggle. It can be very useful and empowering to recognize the links and parallels between blacks' social position and that of lesbians, gay males, and bisexuals. At the same time, it is very important to acknowledge the differences between the struggles for racial justice and sexual freedom if the two movements are to be useful to each other. (It is also important to remember that any division we draw between the lesbian, gay, and bisexual communities and the African-American community is always artificial, to a large extent, since there are many people who identify both as African-American and as lesbian, gay, or bisexual.) In order to identify some of the crucial differences between blacks' experience of oppression and that experienced by lesbians, gays, and bisexuals, we first have to recognize the different ways that antiblack racism itself is manifested today in comparison with the slave era that Douglass describes.

Slavery was a very clear, concrete manifestation of the racial prejudices that have characterized U.S. society throughout its history. Not only was it an extremely brutal institution, physically and psychically detrimental to its victims, but its brutal qualities were quite evident to anyone who believed in the humanity of people of African descent and who bothered to determine what life was like for those held in bondage. Thus, while it was in place, slavery was the clear target of those in the society who fought against racial injustice. The most insightful and eloquent of the abolitionists were able to argue, as Frederick Douglass did, that slavery was detrimental to whites as well as to blacks and thereby to win increased support for the antislavery cause. If we think about it carefully, though, we will see that the strength of this argument depended on certain facts about slavery that are not necessarily true of all forms of oppression, racial or otherwise.

In the situation with his Baltimore mistress that Douglass describes in his *Narrative,* the dehumanization that Sophia Auld undergoes is a result of the direct control that she has over the slave's every action. Douglass explicitly refers to "the fatal poison of irresponsible power" as the cause of his mistress's moral descent. We know, of course, that, in the society that Douglass describes, *all* whites, slaveowners or not, northern or southern, held power over blacks socially and politically. In the context of slavery, though, the power relationship was made vividly clear because the slave and the master, to a large extent, shared a domestic environment. Because the black slave and the white master lived in close physical proximity to one another, the power that the white held over the black was made evident in countless ways. The most striking of these, of course, was the corporal punishment that was often meted out to slaves for various "offenses" committed against the master. There were other instances, though, in which whites' power became clear; in Douglass's case, it was manifested in his mistress's refusal to allow him to learn to read. In any case, it is clear that, in the slave relationship, the white slaveowner had complete control over what the slave did with his or her person.

The abolition of slavery, while it did not signal an end to racial prejudice, did alter to a large degree the means by which whites exercised control over blacks in southern society.[3] The transitional period in the nature of this control was embodied in the Reconstruction, which lasted from the close of the Civil War in 1865 through 1877, when the last Union troops were withdrawn from southern soil. During Reconstruction, the states of the Southern Confederacy were subject to control by the federal government, which oversaw the modification of those states' (racist) social and legal institutions as preparation for their full readmission to the Union. Through these modifications, blacks were accorded voting rights, formed political organizations, held office in southern state legislatures, and made other significant social and political strides, although these things were by no means easy to achieve. With the Compromise of 1877, the balance tipped again in favor of racist sentiment, as Republican presidential candidate Rutherford B. Hayes negotiated to win the electoral votes of three key states by promising the withdrawal of Union troops from the Confederate states and the consequent "reconciliation" of North and South. This withdrawal effectively restored political autonomy to whites in the South and ensured that the region could establish its own racial policies largely without interference from the government. Slavery was not reinstituted, but many restrictions on blacks' social and economic activity were enacted, with the infamous system of "Jim Crow" laws being solidified during this period. The era was also characterized by a dramatic increase of activity by the Ku Klux Klan and other white supremacist groups that had begun operating as underground organizations during Reconstruction; the violent retaliation that such groups enacted against blacks who appeared in any way to challenge the dominance of the white population is well known.[4]

The violence of the KKK must be recognized, though, as fundamentally different from the control exercised by whites over black slaves: slavery was systemic and legally sanctioned, while the Klan operated outside the law (although often with the tacit approval of the pertinent law enforcement officials). Legally speaking, the means for controlling blacks had shifted from the explicit physical dominance of their persons by individual whites to the restriction of their social, political, and economic activity. The new forms of control, while clearly resulting in consequences that were physically detrimental to large numbers of black people, were not themselves as *directly* physical as the means of control that were common during the slave era had been. This general development, toward less and less directly physical restrictions on blacks' personal freedom, has largely characterized the history of African-Americans from the time of slavery through the present day.

Black people's struggle for civil rights has largely fit itself to this continual development in the nature of racist oppression. The doctrine of "separate but equal," which characterized racial politics in the United States throughout the early twentieth century, was, by the 1950s, subjected to attack by civil rights organizers, who worked both through the legal system and through direct, nonviolent action to address legally sanctioned discrepancies in the treatment of blacks and whites around the country. Restrictions on blacks' freedom were now enforced not so much by individual white citizens, as in the context of slavery, as by a more generalized legal mechanism that supported the suppression of African-American liberty. It was, nonetheless, still relatively easy to identify the objects of black protest: the laws that mandated the inferior status of blacks in all aspects of national life. The objective of civil rights activists through the 1950s and early 1960s was to eliminate these laws from the books, and thus to rectify the compromised legal position that blacks faced in most states.

As the Jim Crow laws and other legal restrictions on blacks' activities began to erode under the pressure of civil rights activism, a new awareness developed among many members of the black community (including Martin Luther King, Jr., who was developing an increasingly radical critique of U.S. society when he was assassinated) that the problems blacks faced were rooted deep in the very ideologies on which the nation was founded. Consequently, the mere passage of civil rights legislation would not be enough to redress the country's racial problems. Even if blacks were to accept the principles generally taken to reflect the "American way," it was clear that they would not be able to take an active part in the further shaping of that ideology without gaining access to a power structure that has historically been dominated by white males. In other words, since the late 1960s, blacks and other racial minorities have been thoroughly educated as to the limits of legislative activism. The strides that civil rights legislation represents (and these advances are themselves always tenuous and subject to revision by a conservative Congress, president, or Supreme Court) are limited to the arenas where legal sanction has an effect. These gains cannot work a great deal of change in the relatively private bastions of national power—in particular, corporate industry and the interrelated social contexts of prep schools, elite universities, and associated clubs in which networks of industry leadership are negotiated. The fabric and operation of these social contexts (and of the many other, less obviously powerful but more pervasive social contexts that constitute the "mainstream" of U.S. life) are governed not so much by official legislation as by personal attitudes—attitudes that themselves underlie many of the racist restrictions characteristic of U.S. legislative history.

This fact explains, to a large degree, the cliché that is well rehearsed among black civil rights activists—that the fight against racism has, paradoxically, grown more difficult rather than less so over the past thirty years. After all, attitudes are much more difficult to change than laws are, and the progress that has been made in the legislative arena has actually made it clear that, fundamentally, what we are fighting against are attitudes. It is in this fact—which we always know on some gut level but which nonetheless has to be demonstrated again and again—that antiracism struggles most closely correspond with the antihomophobia work performed by lesbians, bisexuals, and gay men.

It is probably true that, in the United States at least, the systematic oppression of gays, lesbians, and bisexuals has always been less physicalized than that of blacks. I do not mean to suggest that gay people have not suffered grave physical consequences because of their gayness. Many, if not most of us, have—either through individual acts of "queer bashing" or institutionally, through imprisonment or incarceration in mental hospitals, for instance. These acts of physical violence or restraint have not, however, been *systematic;* they have not been applied across the board to all gays, lesbians, and bisexuals. Indeed, it may well be that the only reason they have not been is that not all gays, lesbians, and bisexuals are easily identifiable as such; by contrast, most, although by no means all, black people are visibly identifiable as being of African descent. Because gay, lesbian, or bisexual identity is of a different nature than African-American identity, the forms of oppression faced by people because they are gay, lesbian, or bisexual will be different from those faced by people because they are black.

This does not mean that people working against homophobia cannot learn from people working against racism, or vice versa. What it means is that we must not lose sight of the specific natures of the different struggles, even while we recognize their similarities and interrelatedness. It also means that we can learn as much from the differences between the antiracism work and antihomophobia work as we can from the similarities between them. This is particularly true, I think, when it comes to considering the effects of the two prejudices on people who are members of neither a sexual minority nor a racial minority. In order to explain exactly what I mean, let me return to Frederick Douglass to examine his argument regarding the detrimental effects of slavery on whites.

Douglass's point was that slavery had a *dehumanizing* effect on those whites who held slaves (and, by extension, on those who might not have held slaves but who, by action or inaction, supported the institution of slavery). The brilliance of Douglass's assessment lies in the fact that it recognizes as the primary effect of slavery on whites the very attribute that white racism ascribed to blacks; that is, Douglass's analysis reverses the conventional racist perception that identifies blacks as less than human and whites as superior to them. If we characterize racist oppression as an attempt by the dominant group to prove its superiority over the dominated group, then we can see the ironic power of Douglass's analysis since he shows us that, by exercising unjust power, the dominant group actually demonstrates its moral inferiority. Thus, what white racists try to identify as traits that are external to themselves—in this case, brutal, inhuman qualities—are actually shown to exist within their own personalities.[5]

Homophobic activity—violent or otherwise—operates according to a similar, but almost inverse, logic. If it is true (and I think it is) that homophobia derives, in part, from heterosexuals' fear and anxiety about their own sexuality—fear about the homosexual desire that might exist within their own psyches—then homophobic activity represents the homophobe's impulse to *externalize* those homosexual tendencies, to emphasize to the world that "these other people are 'sick,' but I'm not, and I'm proving it to you by demonstrating my hostility toward them." (The acquisition of homophobia is a complex and multifaceted process; this is merely one aspect.) If we understand part of the nature of homophobic sentiment in this way, then we will understand, as well, that homophobic activity—although clearly most detrimental, on all levels, to gays, lesbians, and bisexuals themselves—actually represents the homophobe's self-hatred, his hostility toward something that lies within himself. (I use the masculine pronoun here because I take young males to represent the most dangerously homophobic element in our society.) The results of this self-hatred, although more subtle than the results of queer bashing on the victim, are nonetheless evident in the ways many heterosexuals repress healthy parts of their personalities because they associate them with homosexuality. This sort of repression is dealt with elsewhere in this book, so I will not go into the issue here. What is worth noting is the similar messages about the dominant groups' sense of itself that are inherent in racism and homophobia. Racism, by representing hostility toward some external group that is perceived as different from and inferior to the majority, actually renders the hostile party morally inferior to the victim of the hostility. Homophobia has the same result, except that it partially originates with the homophobe's negative feelings about something inside his own psyche, which he tries to externalize through homophobic activity.

It is probably easier to see this similarity between the "backfire" effects of racism and homophobia now, in the late twentieth century, than it ever was before. The reason has to do with changes in the nature of racist activity since the end of the slavery era. As legally sanctioned control over blacks' personal freedoms has been eroded, the roots of that immoral control in prejudicial attitudes have become increasingly clear. As a consequence, we have become better able to discern the sociological similarities between racism and homophobia, whose roots in moral attitudes have always been relatively evident since *homosexuality* became a character definition in the late nineteenth century. At this historical juncture, the constraints on blacks' freedoms and on those of gays, lesbians, and bisexuals, while not by any means identical, are more comparable than ever. In a great many locales, explicit discriminatory activity toward members of either group is legally barred, but tacitly sanctioned repression of both blacks and gays continues nonetheless. If we understand the similarities and the subtle differences between the two different types of oppression (and this essay represents only a very tentative first step toward such an understanding), then we can make significant strides in combatting both injustices and thus move our society that much closer toward full democratic freedom.

NOTES

1. *Narrative of the Life of Frederick Douglass, an American Slave, Written by Himself* (1845). (See excerpt in this book, p. 56.)
2. The effects of gender difference made the experiences of black women in slavery distinct from those of black men; Douglass's narrative cannot therefore be considered as representing the life of the female slave. One of the best examples of the female slave's narrative is Harriet A. Jacobs's *Incidents in the Life of a Slave Girl* ([1861], ed. Jean Fagan Yellin [Cambridge, Mass.: Harvard University Press, 1987]).
3. It is worth stating explicitly that antiblack racism has never been a purely southern institution in the United States. The South does, however, offer the clearest examples of the blatant control that characterizes the relation of white to black in the nineteenth century. As my discussion moves chronologically into the twentieth century, the differences between North and South will largely fall away.
4. This history is usefully summarized in Howard Zinn, *A People's History of the United States* (New York: Harper & Row, 1980) 167–205.
5. For further elaboration on this idea, see Joel Kovel, *White Racism* (New York: Columbia University Press, 1984).

Genocidal Ideology: Trauma and Cure

ROBERT J. LIFTON WITH ERIC MARKUSEN

Genocide, or its potential, can only be understood as occurring within a particular historical context. . . . Isaiah Berlin sees nationalism as emerging from a "wound to group consciousness" and as including "a new vision of life" which helps to heal that wound. The Nazis have taught us that a nation's potential for genocide depends greatly upon how it defines its collective trauma and upon the kind of ideological response brought forth as relief and cure.

The Nazi Biomedical Vision: Racial Therapy

> We more than deserved this defeat [of the First World War].
> It is only the greatest outward symptom of decay among
> quite a series of internal ones.
>
> —Adolf Hitler

Prior to embracing Hitler, the German people felt themselves to be in the grip of an intolerable affliction. The ending of the First World War involved much more than military defeat. It was associated with a sense of national humiliation, economic chaos from catastrophic inflation, and near civil war. Loss on the battlefield was trauma enough to a nation that had prided itself on its military; but the trauma entered into still deeper social and psychological layers of dislocation and demoralization. For individual Germans, the world fell apart. They experienced a sense of personal disintegration and despair about their individual and collective future.

The general atmosphere of the time, political and otherwise, was described by one historian as "oppressive with doom, almost eschatological." For in 1918, the Germans had become survivors of killing and dying on an unprecedented scale, and of the death of resplendent national and social visions, of meaning itself. The First World War, entered into with extraordinary enthusiasm, had been seen as the means of overcoming the deep confusions or and "cultural despair" accompanying German historical struggles with modernization and unification from the mid-nineteenth century. The war had been a miserable failure, and the Versailles Treaty, with its requirement of reparations and assumptions of German guilt alone for the war, came to symbolize, and serve as an exaggerated focus for, the entire spectrum of national humiliation.

Germany's defeat in the First World War was in this sense an additional "wound" to an existing nationalism whose intensity belied its vulnerability. The result was a fierce new assertion of nationalism, drawing upon and contributing to some of the most dangerous ideological currents, political and racial, of its time. Crucial to these ideological responses was the meaning given to the wound—the collective survivor formulation of what had occurred. That formulation came to include victimization from without (Germany was suffering because of unfair treatment by the other Western nations at Versailles) but more powerfully from within (the legend of the "stab in the back" by political and racial enemies, especially Jews) in ways that resulted in profound internal decay (as Hitler expressed in the epigraph . . .). Cure, then, required extensive purification in order to achieve regeneration of nation and self—or, one might say, of national and racial self.

Collective trauma seeks resolution and cure, and the key to that process is ideological. The healing ideology must, above all, promise new collective energy or life power—a vision of collective revitalization. Hitler's national success was undoubtedly related to his claim of a deeper "diagnosis" of Germany's affliction. That diagnosis, while put forward as political doctrine, claimed ultimate *biological* truth. Hitler wrote in *Mein Kampf,* in the mid-1920s, "Anyone who wants to cure this era, which is inwardly sick and rotten, must first of all summon up the courage to make clear the causes of this disease." Those causes were biological and, specifically, racial: The Aryan race, the only race that was "culture-creating," had permitted itself to be rendered weak and its survival endangered by the one "culture-destroying race," the Jews. The agent of "racial pollution" and "racial tuberculosis," "the Jew" was a form of "bacteria" or "parasite" which brought about the "infection" and become "a maggot in a rotting corpse." This medical imagery was no mere colorful metaphor: it was a social theory of collective decay, a social diagnosis containing a clear direction of treatment. As early as 1920, Hitler had made clear that the only solution for the Aryan malady was "the removal of the Jews from the midst of our people." The vision, then, was not just biological but biomedical.

The sole purpose of the Nazi state Hitler then projected was to bring about this racial cure: "The state [is] only a means to an end, and as its end it considers the preservation of the racial existence of man." The state, that is, was merely a vehicle for the "mission of the German people on earth," which was that of "assembling and preserving the most valuable stocks of basic racial elements in this [Aryan] people . . . [and] . . . raising them to a dominant position." The state was an extension of race, subsumed to a biological mission of propagating "those Aryan elements" that would bring about "the beauty and the dignity of a higher humanity." This focus alone, Hitler believed, could be the means of transforming racial demise into new racial vitality: "From a dead mechanism which only lays claim to existence for its own sake, there must be formed a living organism with the exclusive aim of serving a higher idea."

Nazi racial thought and policy were wildly visionary and romanticized on the one hand, and narrowly technocratic and scientistic on the other. These two seemingly contradictory patterns were, in fact, inseparable. Consider two comments by Nazi doctors. A leading medical administrator for the regime reported that he had joined the Nazi party the day after hearing a speech by Rudolf Hess in which the deputy party leader had declared, "National Socialism is nothing but applied biology." And a still more malignant comment was made by a Nazi doctor in Auschwitz when asked by a prisoner physician how he could reconcile the smoking crematoria they viewed in the distance with his Hippocratic oath: "Of course I am a doctor and I want to preserve life. And out of respect for human life, I would remove a gangrenous appendix from a diseased body." Both of these statements are visionary in the extreme: the one, a claim to have discovered the means to reduce all political and historical process to biological principles; the other, invoking a higher therapeutic purpose to justify the mass murder of Jews. What the Nazis called "scientific racism" or "racial hygiene" was in actuality a mystical and lethal approach to biology in particular and to science in general.

We can speak, then, of the biomedical ideology as "totalistic"— as containing an all-or-none set of assumptions which are equally absolute in their claim to truth and in their rejection of alternative claims. Parallel to the psychological principle of totalism is what the Nazis themselves called their "political principle of totalitarianism," according to which any differing political ideas were to be "ruthlessly dealt with, as the symptom of an illness which threatens the healthy unity of the indivisible national organism." That monitoring of the environment for potential opposition in order to suppress it is an expression of *milieu control,* always fundamental to ideological totalism.

Also characteristic of a totalistic environment is the kind of *sacred science* we have been discussing. While ideas of race had been of scientific interest from the time of the eighteenth century, it was the emergence of physical anthropology during the late nineteenth and early twentieth centuries that gave rise to claims of "scientific racism." Within that tradition, not only physical but also psychological and moral characteristics could be attributed specifically to race. Developing principles in genetics and biology in general also entered the constellation. Particularly important was the emergence of *eugenics,* a term coined by the eccentric English scientist Francis Galton, who had in mind a science for improving human stock by giving "the more suitable races or strains of blood a better chance of prevailing speedily over the less suitable." Eugenics had enormous appeal for a wide variety of thinkers and nonthinkers in Europe and the United States but, despite its evolutionary claims and later reference to genetic laws, has never had genuine scientific standing. These haphazard racial ideas took on special passion when they became associated with the idea of nation, when "racism and nationalism began to fuse." And "the fear which haunted racial thought after the mid-nineteenth century was that of degeneration."

Thus, Fritz Lenz, a leading German physician-geneticist who was later to become a prominent Nazi biomedical ideologue, prefigured some of Nazi racial thought and had direct influence on Adolf Hitler. As early as 1917, Lenz was writing about the duty of the state and the individual to "serve the race," and expressed fear that without a radical eugenics project, "our race is doomed to extinction." The Nazis were to claim that theirs was a *scientific* resolution of the problem, and that "the final solution of the Jewish question"—the murder of every Jew they could lay their hands on—was part of their "applied biology." For the Nazis brought to their biology emotions resembling those of millenarian movements of the Middle Ages whose ideological sources tended to derive mainly from the Book of Revelation and, to a lesser extent, from Old Testament sources such as the Book of Daniel. Like these movements, the Nazis sought purification and cleansing of their version of evil, but for them the biologically demonic source of evil was the Jews. The Nordic race, because of the influence of that evil, had become "biologically fallen," in need of redemption. This biological dimension of millenarian mysticism contributed strongly to Nazi totalism: Jews were absolutely and unredeemably evil; and the Nordic race, through its representative, the Nazi movement, was the source of all virtue.

That biological and millenarian polarization contributed directly to the ultimate feature of totalism—the *dispensing of existence.* When good and evil are absolute and clear, and particularly when they can be readily identified in biological terms, it is a relatively easy step to decide that biological evil should perish and only biological good survive. That ideological dichotomy pervaded the institutions and policies of Nazi Germany in ways that went beyond the beliefs of any individual. Nazi doctors in Auschwitz, for instance, varied greatly in their ideological convictions; but belief in that dichotomy made it psychologically easier for them to take part in the killing.

To embrace this ideology and work from it could be a heady experience for biologists and doctors. The medical administrator mentioned earlier told how, between 1934 and 1939, he made hundreds of speeches to colleagues as well as general audiences presenting the Nazi biomedical vision as a fundamental truth about humankind, and advocating a Nazi version of "biological socialism"; he emphasized that dealing with the Jews had nothing to do with old-fashioned anti-Semitism but only with "the aim of self-fulfillment, *völkisch* self-fulfillment." It was, he declared, "a beautiful time for me." He was referring to nothing short of a "high state," an experience of transcendence, afforded those living out this visionary biological claim. Those high states could be experienced by others in the movement who had little to do with biology as such. The central ideological principle, the promise of revitalization, offered individual people surges of immediate vitality and a sustained state of the shared immortality of the movement. It was, at bottom, a biological promise.

The ideology exerted its power over those who believed only bits and pieces of it. Among Nazi doctors, for instance, even partial beliefs, or "ideological fragments," contributed greatly to their participation in the projects of the regime. The typical Nazi doctor was not a fanatical ideologue but a conservative or reactionary nationalist drawn to the movement by its promise of collective revitalization; could laugh at the more extreme claims of Nazi racial theory while being attracted to the general biological emphasis and to certain principles of "scientific racism"; had fuzzy convictions about superior features of the Germanic or Nordic race and was worried about "racial mixing"; considered himself a "rational" rather than a fanatical anti-Semite; pointed critically to the number and prominence of Jewish doctors, especially in large German cities, and associated them with socialized medical insurance schemes which he detested; had not marched in the streets with the Nazis but was willing to offer them obedience and service in exchange for high social, economic, and military standing; and brought to the enterprise a certain opportunistic careerism and corruptibility.

A kind of apocalyptic biology led, perhaps inevitably, to a vision and practice of killing to heal. The Nazi cure was as literal as it was murderous and consisted of ridding the world of "life unworthy of life" by means of five identifiable steps: coercive sterilization, the killing of "impaired" children, the killing of "impaired" adults (these latter two steps erroneously called "euthanasia"), the selection and killing of "impaired" inmates of concentration camps, and finally the mass killings of Jews in the extermination camps themselves. The two "euthanasia" programs, though initiated by the regime, were conducted within medical jurisdiction and can therefore be described as "direct medical killing." This first Nazi genocide of more than 100,000 people was directed mostly at German non-Jews who had been given psychiatric diagnoses. The mass murder of Jews in extermination camps could also have a medical aura, notably in Auschwitz, and can therefore be described as "medicalized killing." While many divergent forces contributed to the sequence, these steps were consistent with one another. They were all expressions of biological purification, of destroying "bad" genes and "bad" racial elements in order to revitalize the Nordic race and the world at large. Had the Nazis named their institutions according to their ideological concepts, a "euthanasia" institution might well have been referred to as a "Center for Therapeutic Genetic Killing," while Auschwitz would have been called a "Center for Therapeutic Racial Killing."

Much of the cure was either coordinated or carried out by the élite SS corps (the letters stand for *Schutzstaffel* which literally means "protection" or "guard detachment"), initiated by Hitler as his bodyguard, the protector of his personal security, which was in turn equated with the security of the Nazi state. Heinrich Himmler built the SS into an all-encompassing police, intelligence, and military network that had elements of both a state within a state and a vast religious order. The mystical dimension was essential, since the SS was itself to epitomize the ultimate racial mission. Its members themselves were to have pure Aryan family trees in order to carry out a sacred function, which was "to ensure the eternal existence of the Germanic people of Germany." The SS was meant to be not just a vanguard but an ideological essence, a realization, in what it did and what it was, of the Nazi vision of murderous purification.

Killing as a project took on the quality of a religious ordeal, as expressed by Himmler in his infamous speech at Posen in October 1943:

Most of you must know what it means to see a hundred corpses lie side by side, or five hundred, or a thousand. To have stuck this out and—excepting in cases of human weakness—to have kept our integrity, this is what has made us hard. In our history, this is an unwritten and never-to-be-written page of glory.

One must, that is, make sacrifices—or, as some SS officers put it, "overcome" oneself—for the sake of the higher therapeutic purpose. One has taken one's place in an ideological narrative within which the murderers are virtuous, the victims evil, and the killing necessary.

Man Is Endowed with a Strong Aggressive Nature

SIGMUND FREUD

Translated and adapted by D. G. Luttinger

Man is not simply a gentle being who desires to be loved, and who at most defends himself if attacked; he is, rather, a creature among whose instinctual traits is to be found a potent share of aggressive nature. As a result, his neighbor is for him not only a potential soul mate or sexual object, but someone who as well tempts his need for aggression, a person to be exploited for labor without compensatory reward, a being to be sexually used without consent, a person to rob of his possessions, to be humiliated, to inflict pain upon, to torture and even kill. Who, in the face of all experience of life and history, would have the bravery to dispute this assertion? Generally, man's cruelty and aggression toward man waits for a provocation, or puts itself at the service of some purpose whose goal might also have been reached by milder measures. In circumstances favorable to it, when the mental counter-force or conscience is out of action, aggression manifests itself spontaneously and reveals man as a bestial savage to whom consideration towards his own kind is something alien. Anyone who calls to mind the atrocities committed during the racial migrations and invasions of the Huns, or the people known as "Mongols" under Jenqhiz Khan and Tamerlane, or at the capture of Jerusalem by

the pious Crusaders, or, indeed, the horrors of the recent World War
—anyone who remembers these occurrences will have to bow with
humility before the veracity of this view.

The existence of this inclination to aggression, which is detected
in ourselves and justly assumed to be present in others, is a factor
which disturbs our relations with our neighbor and which forces civilization into such a high energy expenditure in war and preparations
for war. As a consequence of this primary mutual hostility of human
beings, civilized society is perpetually threatened with disintegration.
The interest of common labor would not hold it together; instinctual
passions are stronger than reasonable interests. Civilization has to use
its utmost efforts to set limits upon man's aggressive instincts and to
hold its manifestations of them in check by physical reaction-forma-
tions. The use of methods, therefore, intended to incite people into
identifications and aim-inhibited relationships of love, and thus the
restriction upon sexual life, and thus, also, the ideal commandment to
love one's neighbor as oneself—a commandment found in most systems of spirituality or religion exactly because it runs so strongly
counter to the original aggressive nature of man. Despite every effort
of such civilizing endeavors, human society has not yet achieved much
civilization. It hopes to prevent the crudest excess of brutality, by itself
assuming the right to use violence against criminals, but the law is not
able to lay hold of the more cautious and refined manifestations of
human aggressiveness. When we learn how much difficulty and pain
has been added to our lives by ill-will, the time comes when each one
of us has to give up as illusory expectations those hopes, which in our
youths, we pinned upon our fellow humans.

Still, it would be unfair to reproach civilization with trying to
eliminate strife and competition from human activity. These things are
undoubtedly indispensable.* But opposition is not necessarily enmity;
it is merely misused and made an occasion for enmity.

The communists believe that they have found the path to deliverance from all societal evils. According to them, man is wholly good
and is well-disposed to his neighbor, but the institution of private
property has corrupted his nature. The ownership of private wealth
gives the individual power, and with that power temptation to abuse
his neighbor, while the man who is excluded from possession is bound

[* *See Appendix: The Seville Statement on Violence.*]

to rebel in hostility against his oppressor. If private property were abolished, all wealth made common to all, and everyone allowed to share in the enjoyment of it, ill-will and hostility would disappear among men. Since everyone's needs would be satisfied, no one would have any reason to regard another as his enemy; all would willingly undertake the necessary labors. I've no concern with any economic criticism of the communist system; I can't inquire into whether the abolition of private property is expedient or advantageous. I'm able, however, to recognize that the psychological premises on which the system is based are an untenable illusion. In abolishing private property we deprive the human love of aggression of one of its instruments, and certainly a very important one, though not its most important; but we have in no way altered the differences in power and influence, say in bureaucracies, which are misused by aggressiveness. We have altered nothing in the nature of aggression itself, however. Aggressiveness was not created by property. It reigned almost without limit in primitive societies of every kind, and when property was scanty. . . .

Slaves were sold out of Africa by their own kind, as well as stolen by invaders, just as wars took place between tribes of peoples of the same race of all kinds everywhere, and various sects of religious zealots, of the same supposed race or nationality have murdered or sold one another out in the name of their god, or murdered each other in a dispute over the nature of their god.

Aggression shows itself in the nursery, almost before property has given up its primal, anal form; it forms the basis of every relation of affection and love among people . . . as we must have an enemy to have a "we," against that "enemy." We create a "They"—an enemy outside our family, tribe, or group—in order that we might bond together in kinship and camaraderie, and even love, against that enemy. And, onto that enemy we project all the evils and failings that we feel capable of ourselves. We project our hateful aggression onto that enemy and accuse him of what we know we are capable of, aggression and hatred. . . . Thereby we feel that we ourselves are rid of our vices, as they live instead in the other, the "they" onto whom we have projected them. In any case, since all men are capable of aggression, and history has proven this, we need hardly project onto another what is already present in all of us, a nature full of forceful aggressive tendencies. But, by psychologically projecting this nature onto another, we have the illusion that our aggression toward that other is therefore justified. Only by recognizing this need for enemies in ourselves and acknowledging it may we ever hope to overcome it, to outwit our need for an enemy, or need to project evil onto another, different from ourselves. We must be careful to note that, often, what we hate most in others, in "the enemy," is what we hate most in ourselves. Often, what we dislike most about our enemies gives us a clue to our own feelings of inadequacy, our own sense of failure at being less than ideally human and succeeding fully.

Baby Villon

PHILIP LEVINE

He tells me in Bangkok he's robbed
Because he's white; in London because he's black;
In Barcelona, Jew; in Paris, Arab:
Everywhere and at all times, and he fights back.

He holds up seven thick little fingers
To show me he's rated seventh in the world,
And there's no passion in his voice, no anger
In the flat brown eyes flecked with blood.

He asks me to tell all I can remember
Of my father, his uncle; he talks of the war
In North Africa and what came after,
The loss of his father, the loss of his brother,

The windows of the bakery smashed and the fresh bread
Dusted with glass, the warm smell of rye
So strong he ate till his mouth filled with blood.
"Here they live, here they live and not die,"

And he points down at his black head ridged
With black kinks of hair. He touches my hair,
Tells me I should never disparage
The stiff bristles that guard the head of the fighter.

Sadly his fingers wander over my face,
And he says how fair I am, how smooth.

We stand to end this first and last visit.
Stiff, 116 pounds, five feet two,

No bigger than a girl, he holds my shoulders,
Kisses my lips, his eyes still open,
My imaginary brother, my cousin,
Myself made otherwise by all his pain.

Our Need for Enemies

DOROTHY ROWE

D o you have enemies? If so, who are they?
Many people, certainly many of the people who would read this book, would say that they had no enemies. They feel that being aggressive and having enemies is quite wrong. They themselves are friendly with everyone and totally unaggressive.

Many more people, certainly the kind of people who would *not* read this book, would say that they did have enemies. These enemies could be Communists or Capitalists, Arabs or Jews, Protestants or Catholics, Sikhs or Hindus, blacks or whites and so on. They would say that they themselves were not aggressive, but their enemies were aggressive and dangerous too, and so they have to defend themselves against their enemies.

A few people would say that they felt quite secure so at the moment they have no enemies and feel quite unaggressive. However they know that that could change. If someone should threaten their lives or the lives of their loved one, if they were unfairly dismissed from their jobs, or were cheated out of what was rightly theirs, or if someone near to them was treacherous and disloyal and betrayed their trust, then they would become aggressive and, seeing the person who had harmed them as an enemy, would seek to defend themselves. In such a situation, they would say, 'you know who your friends are.'

The first group of people are nice, kind, well-meaning people who are fooling themselves. We can no more give up aggression than we can give up breathing, and I know this only too well, when at the end of every lecture where I have talked about how enemies are necessary, these people advance upon me menacingly, demanding, 'How dare you say I'm aggressive?'

The second group, the largest group, are those people who have never questioned the way they were brought up and the way their society is organized. All their lives they have felt much pain and the anger of a life frustrated, and they relieve their pain and anger, and so survive, by taking their bad feelings out on the people they have been taught to see as their enemies. Without such enemies their pain and anger would be unendurable.

The third group are the people who have actually confronted the perennial problem that we need our anger and aggression to survive in a dangerous world, to carry our lives forward and to be creative. They have seen that we can express our aggression in a multitude of ways, from the firmness of saying, 'I find your behavior unacceptable' to the violence of killing. They know that it is vitally important to learn how to distinguish those people who are actually intending to harm us from those who are simply the unwitting bearers of our aggressive fantasies. They know that the enemies in our heads are a greater danger to us than our enemies in reality.

The enemies in our heads are not mere random fantasies, derived from our watching of television violence. They are an essential part of the necessary process whereby we learned to live and work with others.

To understand this we need to understand the basic nature of how we function as human beings.

How We Perceive and Know

When we look about us in our ordinary lives, we see a world which looks solid and real. In fact, the world looks like that because we are a certain size and possess sense organs which function in a certain way. If we were much smaller or much bigger, or if we could borrow, say, a fly's eyes or a dog's ears, we would perceive the world in a totally different way. We would have no difficulty then understanding that while there is probably some kind of real reality, some constantly shifting, changing something, we can never know what it is. All we can ever know are the structures we create in order to live within something we can never know.

The structures we create are what we see, hear, touch, smell, feel, think and speak. Whether we see a world full of colour depends on whether we have the necessary equipment in our eyes: how we perceive and evaluate the world we live in depends on which language we have learned to speak.

If you speak or have ever tried to learn a second language, you will know that different languages are not just different sets of labels stuck on to the objects in one reality. Languages are different attempts at dividing up an amorphous changing something-or-other to create a structure which the speakers of that language call reality. It is language which creates reality, not reality which creates language.

So, what we call reality is, in fact, a set of structures which we have created.

The creation of such structures can begin in only one way.

The nature of our sense organs is such that we can perceive only when we can identify some contrast or differential. If we lived in a world of perpetual light with no shadows, we would not have a concept of light. To know light there must be dark. If we lived in a world where nothing ever died, we would not know that we were alive. To know life there must be death. If we lived in a world where everything was perfect, we would not know perfection. To know perfection there must be imperfection. If we lived in a world where everyone was unfailingly kind and friendly, we would not know friendship. To know friends there must be enemies.

Thus we define the group we belong to in terms of those who are excluded from our group.

These are the basic conditions by which we perceive and know. (If you would like to read further on this see the first three chapters of my book *Choosing, Not Losing*.)

If every moment of our lives we were consciously aware that what we were seeing and acting on were mere structures that we had created, we would be unable to act. We have to put from our consciousness this knowledge and act as if the world was the way we see it, solid and real. Whenever something happens to remind us the reality is not what we think it is, we feel fear, and to survive and overcome the fear we feel anger and to carry our anger and to hammer our structures back into place and to insist that reality is what we say it is, we feel aggression. Without aggression we are lost.

However, while anger and aggression are essential to maintain us as individuals, they create great problems for us when we try to fulfil one of our basic needs and that is other people.

Being a Member of a Group

We cannot live alone. Babies that are fed and kept warm but are never held in the enclosing circle of another person's arms go grey and die. Adults put in solitary confinement for an indefinite period go mad. So babies cry to be picked up and hostages, in the way that we will eat anything when we are starving, make friends with their captors.

We need other people in order to survive, but it is other people who threaten and try to destroy our structures. Trees don't tell us we have got our structures wrong. Other people do that, and they always will, because each of us creates our own individual world of meaning and no two worlds are the same.

Thus, to maintain the structure which we call 'myself and the way I see things' we have to be aggressive. Sometimes we are aggressive in a purely defensive way, saying, 'I'll see it my way and you see it yours,' and other times we defend our structures by trying to get other people to relinquish their structures and accept ours. We can do this by persuasion or by threat. Power is essentially the ability to get other people to accept your definition of reality.

As developmental psychologists have been showing over the last few years, we are born with the ability to distinguish human faces and voices from all other shapes and noises and in the first days of life to identify our mother's face and voice from all other faces and voices.

When we are born we know that we need other people, and so we love the person who mothers us. We want to please her and, later, those people we have learned to call 'my family.' We discover that, much as our family loves us, we are not good enough. If we want to be accepted into the family group we have to give up being ourselves.

Babies are born greedy, angry, spontaneous and selfish. If they were not they would not survive. A baby who is not greedy will not suck. A baby who is not angry cannot react to clear an obstruction to his breathing. A baby who cannot respond spontaneously to the pressures in his body cannot relieve these pressures by urinating, defecating and vomiting. A baby who is not selfish will not cry in protest when he feels in some way endangered.

Within weeks of our birth our family begins teaching us that our characteristics of greed, anger, spontaneity and selfishness are unacceptable. If we want to become a member of the family group we have to give up such characteristics.

We are taught that we cannot expect to be fed when we wish. We have to eat when and what our family decrees. We are taught that anger is wicked: some of us are taught that no one in our family ever gets angry, while others are taught that adults can get angry with children, but not children with adults. We are taught to see spontaneity as dirtiness and irresponsibility, and so we become clean and responsible. We are taught that it is wrong to be concerned with our own needs. We must always consider other people's interests before our own, especially the needs of our parents and members of our family.

We learn all this in the first five years of our life and we are taught it in ways which involve threats of abandonment, physical pain and humiliation. If we do not learn it, or if we protest, we are told that we are 'spoilt' and need 'a damn good hiding.' (Adults who, as children, learned to conform envy those children and adolescents who refuse to conform, and such envy is murderous.)

Some of you reading this will be remembering a few of the painful events of your childhood and saying, 'Yes, this is so.' Others of you will be saying, 'My childhood was not like that. My parents were wonderful,' and thus obeying the rule which Alice Miller calls 'Thou shalt not be aware.' You must forget what your parents did to you. Thus in adult life, whenever you say something critical about your parents you immediately feel guilty and say, 'But really my parents are wonderful. They would do anything for me.'

The reason we as children agree to follow the rule 'Thou shalt not be aware' is that we want our parents to be perfect. A few people reading this will be saying to themselves, 'My parents weren't wonderful. They didn't care about me at all, and I hate them.' Such people, like the ones who claim their parents were wonderful, are still clinging to the desire to have the security of parents who are perfect. They are not prepared to accept the insecurity of having parents who are simply human.

In the process whereby we, as children, are taught to conform to the rules of our family (and thus the rules of our family's race, religion, nationality, class, and sexes) we are taught that the unacceptable characteristics we have are the characteristics of those people who are excluded from our family and from the groups to which our family belongs. As a child I was taught that these despicable characteristics were possessed by the children of Happy Valley (people unemployed in the Depression of the 1930s lived in shacks in Happy Valley in New-castle, Australia), by the Aborigines, Catholics, Chinese and, during the war, the Germans, Italians and Japanese. You might like to make a similar list from your childhood.

In our childhood such enemies of the group to which we belong help us to survive as persons. When the pain our parents and teachers inflict on us threatens to overwhelm us and wipe us out, annihilate us as a person, we can defend ourselves by, in fantasy, taking those characteristics for which we are being punished and projecting them on to our group's enemies. We say to ourselves, 'I am not dirty and irresponsible, like those blacks,' and, 'We are not aggressive like those Russians (or militarists and politicians).'

Thus, to survive as persons and members of a group we create our enemies in the head.

Since all children in all cultures are socialized in the same way, all children grow up with enemies in their head. Hence the enemies in our heads can also be our enemies in reality. Distinguishing the enemies in our heads from the enemies who are really threatening us can be difficult.

The people who find this task relatively easy are people who grew up in families which did not insist on conformity to rigid standards of goodness, who inflicted little pain on the children and who accepted the children *as themselves*. Thus these children could grow up accepting their own anger, aggressiveness, greed and envy.

But there are not many such families. More frequently the people who can distinguish the two kinds of enemy and react appropriately are those who have undertaken the painful task of reviewing their childhood, coming to terms with it and accepting that we are all simply human.

The Need for Scapegoats

ROBERT COLES

We know, through theory, through the reflection of important thinkers, about our various psychological drives; about the way social and political forces connect with our everyday lives, including our dreams and fantasies. But by no means do we have enough knowledge of how individuals (and their leaders) manage in the face of the actual conflicts, the racial and religious and national confrontations, the wars that grab our attention on the evening news.

A Pakistani in Ulster

I have in mind, for example, Northern Ireland, where I have been working in recent years. A terrible religious war, of sorts, has plagued that sector of Europe, off and on, for generations. Catholics and Protestants, one is told again and again, are locked into an impasse that seems unbreakable. The more that historians or social scientists have studied the situation, the less encouraging they have been with respect to answers or solutions. Yet here is what a Pakistani man, a soldier in the British Army, stationed in Ulster, told my young son and me in 1979: "These people hate each other; you are right. But they would become brothers overnight if 500 or 1,000 Pakistanis, like me, came to settle in Belfast—brothers under the skin!"

Merely an anecdotal remark, a soldier's grim and wry sense of things. But, in fact, that young man had done his own kind of psychological and sociological research. He had heard the meanness and nastiness of Irish Catholics and Irish Protestants give way, in his case, to a fear or two about "Pakis," and he had conjectured, as did Freud in Group Psychology and the Analysis of the Ego, that people can indeed change, and dramatically, given a new set of social or racial circumstances. We crave scapegoats, targets to absorb our self-doubts, our feelings of worthlessness and hopelessness. The Pakistani soldier knew this: What Protestants and Catholics have been doing for centuries to one another could, in a moment, turn into a racial rather than a religious confrontation. He also knew an oft-repeated truth: "I guess you could bring the whole earth together—no more war!—if there were another planet, and there were people on it, and they were a threat to us, and we looked upon them as our enemies."

To be hopeful, this soldier recognized, at least, that there are possibilities for a larger sense of loyalty and affiliation than seem to exist now; that the nation-state, or skin color, are not the only symbolic rallying grounds for human beings as they try to define who they are and what they believe to be important. I have heard similar observation in South Africa, where a racial deadlock seems all too evidently a permanent aspect of life—and where a violent war seems never too remote a likelihood. A black child from Soweto kept asking me why white people "don't find other people to hate, and leave us [blacks] alone." A colored child from Capetown kept asking why white people "only see us as darker than themselves, but forget that we're lighter than the Zulus." A white child from Pretoria wondered why the Japanese are considered "white" by the South African government, but not the Chinese. The white child's father observed that such a designation for Japanese visitors was merely "honorary"—a response to obvious commercial imperatives, given Japan's extremely strong economic situation. But the child was undaunted: "If we can do it with the Japanese, we can do it with everyone, and then the country will be even richer than it'll be doing business with Japan, because we won't have a war coming, so we'll save a lot of money that way."

How Children Learn

Such a mix of innocence, practicality, and intelligent compassion—in a child whose parents are tough Afrikaners, all too committed to the principles of apartheid. We need to know more about the manner in which children like that one learn their moral and political values— the manner in which nationally sanctioned ideologies become each individual's articles of personal faith. We also need to know about the inconsistencies in the various nationalist slogans and political ideologies that mesmerize so many millions of this earth's people. I have for

years heard American children say, in one breath, how kind and generous we must all be with one another, as Christ urged, and as their
Sunday school teachers urge, and, in the next breath, talk about the
importance of winning at all costs; and if others lose, "then that's the
way it is." Similarly in Ulster, or worse because Christ, of all people, is
used as a justification for paramilitary wars.

One wonders whether there might not be a positive means by
which solidarity can be achieved without a new outcast group.

A Possible Answer

I will never forget an interview I did in 1963 with a member of the Ku
Klux Klan. A desperate, hateful man poured out his frustrations and
bitterness, his lifelong resentments and failures. His language was full
of obscenities and self-revealing (and self-debasing) cries for struggle
and social upheaval—as if, then, he would have his much-wanted (and
needed) second chance to show himself able to make something of
himself in the world. He was urging, really, a war—a war of all against
all. He was mad, I thought. Yet he was also an ordinary American
workingman, having a fairly hard time making a living, and with lots
of sickness in his family and little money to meet the growing stack of
bills on his kitchen table. I told him, in a moment of exasperation, that
he seemed to be arguing the desirability of one more world war; and
that I doubted that human life on this planet would survive such an
outcome. He looked at me sharply and long; I girded myself for still
additional irrationalities, banalities, indecencies. Instead, this: "There's
a side of everyone that's mean as can be. There's another side that's
good, like my 7-year-old daughter can be, most of the time. What
makes the difference is how you live. If you've got a lousy life, the
meanness wins. If you've got things pretty good, you have a better
chance of being nice to others. The same goes with countries. When a
country is in bad shape, its people turn sour, and vice versa. We'll
always have wars, where you have a lot of people not having their next
meal to take for granted. If the people with lots gave to the people
with little, there might be less trouble between countries."

A beginning, that, in thinking about wars. A beginning agenda
for psychologists, as well—to try to comprehend how such sentiments,

often present and unrecognized in even the most truculent of people, might become harnessed to a given nation's, a given continent's, a given world's social policies.

Lampshades of Human Skin

DANIELA GIOSEFFI

I was born in 1941.
The sky was falling. The chairs of state
were arranging themselves in "isms" of death.
I learned to speak by fingering an apple,
rolling its crimson shine around in baby fingers,
because my mother's Slavic smile seemed to
give it onto the table of my highchair
in that Newark kitchen of new wintry mornings,
bright leaves at frosty windows just met
for the first time: autumn sunlight, warm hands. "God bless Mommy!
God bless Daddy! God bless spaghetti!"
I chortled up to the big people
around my bedtime crib. When they laughed
I learned I had a pen for a tongue
that could please them.

Meantime, the bombs were falling,
the blitz began blitzing, Jewish, Polish flesh
sizzled
in Hitler's ovens, lampshades of human skin,
gold fillings pulled from dead mouths remade into wedding rings.
Are you wearing one?
Has your gold ring come from a mother's mouth opened
forever in mortified howl filled with poison gas
in the stifling chamber where she bled
menstrual blood down her thighs bereft of clothes,
crushing her child to her crowded breasts.
"Empathy" is my favorite word.
My peasant mother—war orphaned,

my lame Italian immigrant father,
"greenhorn guinea" they called him. "Guinea gimp!"
they shouted as he sold newspapers
for the state "Education of the Poet"
he gave to me, raising me in the ghetto of Newark
to speak good English
where the worst that happened then was when
a boy named Herby chased me, cornering me down the alley
and kissed me, sticking his tongue in my mouth,
choking me with mysterious sex
as the other kids laughed:
"Herby French-kissed Daniela!" A grand joke
of the neighborhood. Nothing much else happened
until I was abused by a Klansman
in a dark jail cell one midnight,
Sheriff of Montgomery County,
the only law for miles around Selma where
I integrated Deep South television
as a journalist announcing Freedom Rides and Sit-ins,
not out of bravery,
but idealistic naiveté.

Somewhere in between then and then,
I met a book full of rotting corpses,
photos of mutilated bodies on battlefields
or in concentration camps,
dead faces distorted by screams,
dying hearts impaled on bayonets,
and all my orgasms, ever since,
have been screams of letting go of horrors
—guilty gaping skulls
full of gold filled teeth.

I'm a "Jersey girl" who grew up, half Polish war orphan,
part Jew, half Italian immigrant
daughter of a lame "guinea gimp," who was a poet dying
of the word *"empathy"* he carried on his back
and taught me Shakespeare's English.
He said I was too pretty for my own good
and read me Yeats's poem to his daughter,

but now I'm fifty, menopausal, insomniac,
and don't care much about looks. My greatest moment
of joy came in near death—not when I was jailed
by the Klansman Sheriff,
but when I gave birth to my daughter who came
by emergency Caesarean,
bright with hope, lovely girl,
do you feel the ambulance siren of guilt,
grieving in your near death birth, the rebirth of your mother
and your moment of almost not being new life
greeting me in your eyes, my eyes
peering back at me, questioning,
after the fever subdued.

Here's your crimson apple of being, daughter,
amidst new wars and books always repeating themselves
like autumn where death turns to beauty in dying leaves
singing their windy sighs
into the lies of hypocritical histories
of hand on reborn hand by hand murdered and bleached to bones
or held warm or cold at fifty I can't sleep
well anymore. I grow fat eating love, I remember thrills
of my childhood autumns when the maples sang with sparrows
outside fall windows and the kitchen was warm as apples
turned crimson in pale hands—color of blood simply
being before I found the book of corpses
from ovens, battlefields,
the ring of gold that broke in divorce
from your father whom I still love
and mourn. Now, I take you, daughter,
to the woods to meet the scarlet maples,
feed the wild deer, crush
the leaves and acorns with your steps,

dance in the moonlight,
your mother is no orphan,
like hers was, your father is not lame
like mine was,
but the Earth, Our Mother,
and all Her creatures swirl in clouds of gas garbage greed

the language of oppression:
"nigger, pollack, guinea, mick, spick,
kike, jap, kraut, cunt, prick."

The White House of Washington confronts its manufactured
  Butcher
of Baghdad and *"sand niggers"*
are decried on Wall Street where
the banks collapse in graft
and a tenuous thread of life secretes onto the page thickens
my eyes become someone else's. Are they yours? Daughter?
I collect a book on ethnocentricism, chemical,
biological, nuclear
warfare and hate
the rich nuclear and oil barons who are your enemy.
We cannot live without enemies, Freud said,
These oil, nuclear, chemical, and germ warfare
profiteers hold us all hostage,
you, me,
and them,
to the screams of skulls
with their forever gold
teeth, lampshades of human skin,
their ears are ours
filled with a siren of guilt
from the history book
of corpses, daughter,
poet. It talks to autumn.
It says: *"Empathize!"*
Because we all die
to live and eat and see
and hold our crimson apple.

It's beauty makes us sing.

Our Earth Is a Vulnerable Abused Place

MAURICE F. STRONG

O ur Earth is a vulnerable, abused place. Its opulent forests are rapaciously felled, its rivers and oceans polluted, its already degraded soils worked lifeless, its delicate envelope of atmosphere—the very basis for life on this planet—is contaminated. In bending nature to our implacable will, we are also destroying her. Our material progress is achieved at the cost of passing on a wasteland to our grandchildren. As this turbulent century closes, we must alter radically our ways of life, patterns of consumption, systems of values, even the manner in which we organize our societies, if we are to ensure survival of the Earth, and ourselves.

As we reawaken our consciousness that humankind and the rest of nature are inseparably linked, we will need to look to the world's more than 250 million indigenous peoples. They are the guardians of the extensive and fragile ecosystems that are vital to the wellbeing of the planet. Indigenous peoples have evolved over many centuries a judicious balance between their needs and those of nature. The notion of sustainability, now recognized as the framework for our future development, is an integral part of most indigenous cultures.

In the last decades, indigenous peoples have suffered from the consequences of some of the most destructive aspects of our development. They have been separated from their traditional lands, and ways of life, deprived of their means of livelihood, and forced to fit into societies in which they feel like aliens. They have protested and resisted. Their call is for control over their own lives, the space to live and the freedom to live in their own ways. And it is a call not merely to save their own territories, but the Earth itself.

While no-one would suggest that the remainder of the more than 5 billion people on our planet would live at the level of indigenous societies, it is equally clear that we cannot pursue our present course of development. Nor can we rely on technology to provide an easy answer. What modern civilization has gained in knowledge, it has perhaps lost in sagacity. The indigenous peoples of the world retain our collective evolutionary experience and insights which have slipped our grasp. Yet these hold critical lessons for our future. Indigenous peoples are thus indispensible partners as we try to make a successful transition to a more secure and sustainable future on our precious planet.

From Earth in the Balance

AL GORE

Few communities want to serve as a dumping ground for toxic waste; studies have noted the disproportionate number of landfills and hazardous waste facilities in poor and minority areas. For example, a major study, *Toxic Wastes and Race in the United States,* by the United Church of Christ, came to the following conclusion:

> *Race proved to be the most significant among variables tested in association with the location of commercial hazardous waste facilities. This represented a consistent national pattern. Communities with the greatest number of commercial hazardous waste facilities had the highest composition of racial and ethnic residents. In communities with two or more facilities or one of the nation's five largest landfills, the average minority percentage of the population was more than three times that of communities without facilities (38% vs. 12%).*

It's practically an American tradition: waste has long been dumped on the cheapest, least desirable land in areas surrounded by less fortunate citizens. But the volume of hazardous waste being generated is now so enormous that it is being transported all over the country by haulers who are taking it wherever they can. A few years ago, some were actually dumping it on the roads themselves, opening a faucet underneath the truck and letting the waste slowly drain out as they crossed the countryside. In other cases, hazardous waste was being turned over to unethical haulers controlled by organized crime who dumped the waste on the side of the road in rural areas or into rivers in the middle of the night. . . . As the dramatic environmental problems in Eastern Europe show, freedom is a necessary condition for an effective stewardship of the environment. Here in the United States, a hugely disproportionate number of the worst hazardous waste sites are in poor and minority communities that have relatively little political power because of race or poverty or both. Indeed, almost wherever people at the grass-roots level are deprived of a voice in the decisions that affect their lives, they and the environment suffer. I have therefore come to believe that an essential prerequisite for saving the environment is the spread of democratic government to more nations of the world.

But as we attempt to make other governments more accountable to their citizens, we need to pay close attention to the problems that currently inhibit the proper functioning of our democracy—and remedy them. By strengthening our own political system, we will empower new environmental stewards in areas where they are needed the most.

This task is crucial. Because if our basic method of making group decisions is not working properly, it is both an important explanation for why we have plunged headlong down a blind alley and an obstacle to coping with the problems that have resulted. Success in changing our destructive relationship to the global environment will depend on our ability to develop a keener understanding of how to make self-government respond to the environmental concerns shared by millions more people around the world each year. In fact, the agendas of the environmental movement and the democracy movement must become intertwined. The future of human civilization depends on our stewardship of the environment and—just as urgently—our stewardship of freedom.

The powerful forces working against stewardship are the same in both cases: greed, self-involvement, and a focus on short-term exploitation at the expense of the long-term health of the system itself. The current weakness of our political system reflects an emphasis on expediency and a failure to nurture our capacity for self-determination. We have not paid adequate attention to the serious problems undermining the accountability of government and the confidence citizens have in it . . .

When the lack of accountability is due to corruption, the damage to democracy is especially severe. And in many countries, corruption is one of the principal causes of environmental destruction. To take only one of literally thousands of examples, concessions to clear-cut the rain forest of Sarawak, in East Malaysia, were sold personally by the minister of environment for Sarawak. Even though he was officially responsible for protecting the integrity of [the rain forest].

. . . Consider Cancer Alley in the Lower Mississippi River Valley between Baton Rouge and New Orleans, where more than a quarter of America's chemicals are produced and where some of the highest cancer rates in the nation are found. Pat Bryant, an African-American political activist who got his start in the early 1980s by organizing public housing tenants in St. Charles Parish, shifted his attention to the constant respiratory and eye problems of the children who lived near the Union Carbide and Monsanto complexes. In Bryant's view—a view shared by many others—Cancer Alley was made possible by ethnic discrimination and political powerlessness.

I met Bryant in Atlanta at the Southern Environmental Assembly, a gathering of mostly white people. As he said later, "A lot of the environmentalists were middle class. We all speak English, but what we say doesn't always mean the same thing. We must put aside foolish customs that divide us and work together, at least for the sake of our children." True to this vision, Bryant organized a coalition of environmental and labor groups to create the Louisiana Toxics Project, which contributed to the passage of the state's first air quality law in 1989.

But the coalition wasn't finished, and Bryant's view of the problem extended beyond Cancer Alley. The following year, during the Senate's consideration of the Clean Air Act, Bryant and one of the national groups linked with his project brought a glaring loophole to my attention; it would have allowed companies emitting toxic air pollutants (the most deadly class of air pollution) to avoid the tougher emissions standards by buying up neighborhoods downwind of their facilities and creating what environmentalists call "dead zones," large areas devoid of people and inevitably bordering poor neighborhoods, whose property values would drop. Of course, whenever the wind shifted, the toxic pollutants that were supposed to fall in the dead zone would fall somewhere else—most often on impoverished black families. The national coalition was instrumental in passing the amendment to close the loophole.

Bryant's perspective is especially important because of continuing fears on the part of some activists who work with the poor and oppressed that the environmental movement will divert attention from their priorities. As Bryant puts it, "The environment is the number-one problem in this country. As an African American, my hope and aspiration to be free are greatly dimmed by the prospect of environmental destruction. If we're going to make great strides on this problem, we're going to have to build African American-European American coalitions." . . .

Most, though not all, of the generation that wrote the Constitution were partially blind when it came to the inalienable rights of the African Americans held as slaves. They felt themselves separate from people of a different color, so they failed to understand that the rights they so passionately defended for themselves and all others to whom they felt connected by "common destiny" were rights held in common by all. Similarly, most were blind when it came to the right of women to vote. But this blindness did not prevent subsequent generations from developing a fuller understanding of the truths embodied in the Constitution, even if they were not fully visible to those who first had the courage to use them as the foundation stones for democratic government.

Today, most—though not all—are partially blind when it comes to our connection with the natural world. The philosophy of life we have inherited, which tells us we are separate from the earth, obscures our understanding of our common destiny and renders us vulnerable to an ecological catastrophe, just as our forebears' assumption that they were morally and spiritually connected to their slaves led to the catastrophe of the Civil War. What we need now is an expanded understanding of what these freedoms involve and how they can be extended once more.

The largest promise of the democratic idea is that, given the right to govern themselves, free men and women will prove to be the best stewards of their own destiny. It is a promise that has been redeemed against the challenge of every competing idea.

Today, most of the world is looking the other way, pretending not to notice industrial civilization's terrible onslaught against the natural world. But alarms are now being sounded all over the world in the same familiar tones of courage and conscience. Standing bravely against this new juggernaut, a new kind of resistance fighter has appeared: men and women who have recognized the brutal nature of the force now grinding away at the forests and oceans, the atmosphere and fresh water, the wind and the rain, and the rich diversity of life itself.

As individuals, today's resistance fighters often share the character traits psychologists found in those from World War II. Whether these new fighters live in Africa, Asia, Latin America, or environmentally stressed areas of the industrial world, they are in most cases ordinary people with a deeply embedded sense of right and wrong—usually imparted by a strong and caring parent during their upbringing—and a stubborn refusal to bend their principles even when the opposing force appears invincible and even deadly.

. . . The indigenous peoples, including the Penan, the Kenyah, the Kayan, the Kelabit, and the Lun Bawang, Iban, finally took matters into their own hands after erosion had so damaged their lands that their water was unfit for drinking. Those who relied on the rapidly disappearing forest for their survival became especially desperate. Although these resistance fighters had little chance against the powerful forces arrayed against them, their courage inspired international protests that are still continuing.

One of the Sarawak peoples, the Penan, sent a delegation to the United States with the help of an environmental group, the Friends of the Earth. They walked into my office one winter day, looking a little like visitors from another millennium, their straw headgear and wooden bracelets the only remnants of the culture they left behind, wearing borrowed sweaters as protection against the unaccustomed cold. Using a translator who had painstakingly learned their language, the Penans described how the logging companies had set up floodlights to continue their destruction of the forest all through the night as well as the day. Like the shell-shocked inhabitants of a city under siege, they described how not even the monsoon rains slowed the chain saws and logging machinery that were destroying the ancestral home of their people. Before they left, they gave me the following statement, translated into halting English:

Almost all the forest reserve of the Penan are gone. The river water has become more silted especially during the rainy season like at present. Many of the village people fall sick. The children often get stomach ache. Food is also not enough. We have to walk to far places to look for food. If we are lucky, after one or two days only can we find food . . . medicines are also difficult to find. When we set up blockades from June to October 1987 the situation became a little better. The river water was beginning to be clear. Forest destruction stopped temporarily . . . many police and soldiers come with helicopters and weapons.

We say that the problems of the Penan make the Penan people set up blockades. Penans want the land and forest of their ancestors. The police and soldiers reply that there are now new laws. If we do not open our blockades, we will be caught and sent to prison. We Penans do not want to fight with force. We do not want families and village people getting hurt. When the police and soldiers opened the blockades, we did not resist. When we seek the help of the police they do not come. When the company asks, the police come and stay near our village for a long time. Why is the new law so harsh? We want laws that help us. But the new law is most disappointing. We are not being killed by weapons, but when our lands are taken, it is the same as killing us.

These are the front lines of the war against nature now raging throughout the world. These words from the Penans are hauntingly similar to the pleas of the Ethiopians invaded by Mussolini's forces in 1935 and the calls for help from Hungary when Soviet tanks rolled through its streets in 1956. The weak and powerless are the early victims, but the relentless and insatiable drive to exploit and plunder the earth will soon awaken the conscience of others who are only now beginning to interpret the alarms and muffled cries for help. In the famous words of Pastor Martin Niemoller, about how the Nazis were able to take over an entire society: "In Germany the Nazis came first for the Communists, and I didn't speak up because I wasn't a Communist. Then they came for the Jews, and I didn't speak up because I wasn't a Jew. Then they came for the trade unionists, and I didn't speak up because I wasn't a trade unionist. Then they came for the Catholics, and I didn't speak up because I was a Protestant. Then they came for me, and by that time there was no one left to speak for me."

Amazon Rain Forest:
Missing the People for the Trees

SUSANNA HECHT AND ALEXANDER COCKBURN

The First World tends to see the Amazon in terms of trees rather than people. Although tribe after tribe of Indians has been exterminated through the decades, and hundreds of rural organizers harassed and murdered across the region, such crimes have scarcely been a preoccupation of the North American media.

There was of course one recent substantial exception to this pattern. The rubber tapper leader Chico Mendes was gunned down outside his house in Xapuri on December 22 of last year and the story of his assassination went around the world. His was probably the best publicized murder in the history of the Amazon. But the way in which it was reported told only part of the story.

Mendes has been described over and over again as an environmentalist, locked in conflict with ranchers and land speculators but still apparently secluded from class conflict or politics. His struggle was seen in terms of trees and not justice.

But Mendes was one of the founding members of the Workers Party—now Brazil's mass based party of the left—and had been active also in CONTAG, a network of rural base communities organized by the Catholic Church. He was concerned about trees, but saw the fundamental issue as one of property.

The "extractive reserves" conceived by him and his fellow rubber tappers, constituted a far-reaching challenge to traditional property relations in the Amazon, and elsewhere in Brazil, since they put land into collective ownership based on usufruct rights and cooperative marketing of forest products. They removed land from the domain of the speculator.

It might be naive to expect North American reporters from the corporate mainstream to set Mendes in context, but his canonization as some kind of St. Francis of the Forest renders journalists blind to the realities of the region's bloody conflicts. The Uniao Democratica Rural, or UDR, which organized Mendes' murder, is a group of land owners whose outlook is simple: any encroachment on the rights of property is communism; in the necessary crusade to defend the rights of property (i.e., very often their own thefts) the state is either incapable or compromised; ergo, the landowner and the rancher are obliged to take the law into their own hands.

Some of the more conspicuous victims of this white terror were commemorated at the Easter meeting of the Forest Peoples' Alliance in Rio Branco, in the state of Acre, earlier this year. Under the heading, "UDR nao e siglo, e morte" ("UDR is no acronym, it's death"), a dozen names were painted on a sheet. They included Wilson Pinheiro, the much beloved predecessor of Mendes as leader of the rubber workers, murdered by UDR goons in 1980; Jesus Mathias, popular organizer, murdered in 1983; and many others.

Mendes was killed in the far western reaches of the Amazon. The international media were at least there to cover his murder, however limited the terms in which they described it. But throughout the Amazon, people fall regularly as they try to defend their ways of life and bits of land. Not only labor organizers die; so do women, children, anyone else who gets on the wrong side of superior force.

Scores of journalists have roamed through Mendes' village of Xapuri in search of his story, but almost never, amid the dispatches sent north, appears the fact that the entire directorate of the Rubber Tappers Council, members of its elected slates and popular organizers, are under threat of death.

The Catholic Church keeps the rudimentary statistics on human rights violations and conflicts in rural areas. It also characterizes the kinds of conflicts that take place: whether these revolve around the struggle for land, or are workplace conflicts or political murders. In addition, the statistics note monthly incidents of torture or threats. The overall picture is one of savage and continuous pressure by landlords, backed up by violence and ignored by the state. This is the "normalcy" that is almost never described to North Americans. In fact Brazil's status in the imagination of North American news organizations is curious. In the category of travelogue and feature story it has mostly been displayed as the home of Carnival, of psychedelic religious cults like *santo dame,* of soccer and of beach life.

But it is also the Third World country most indebted to First World banks and thus incurs an obligatory usage by North American journalists discussing economically frail countries with the capacity to menace the stability of North American banks. Here the approach is one of truly astounding uniformity: the need of the beleaguered economy to be opened to "market forces," to increase its exports, to cut back on public services and other wasteful expenditures by the state.

There are stories about Brazilian slums, but never about the class structure that permits capital flight which has now risen to about $12 billion a year. Nor does the press discuss the private and state elites that probably recycle to North American and European bank accounts more than 75 percent of all the aid sent down. Yet the destiny of this money, and the strategies imposed on Brazil go to the heart of human rights in that country.

The story of Mendes' murder would probably never have been relayed to North America had it not been for the role of forest destruction in the "greenhouse effect" that has now, and not for disinterested reasons, largely replaced starvation in Africa as a topic for First World concern. But what the North American media cannot deal with in any consistent way is the fact that the future of the Amazon rainforest—which editors perceive rightly to be a concern for many of their customers—will be fought out on political terrain in the idiom of socialist priorities: common ownership of assets, collective forms of marketing and credit.

No mainstream North American journalists discuss the Amazon, or any other part of the world, in such terms. They don't see the fight for human rights in such a perspective, but Chico Mendes certainly did. Here's a message he scribbled out on a piece of scrap paper three months before he was murdered:

"Attention youth of the future: 6th of September of the year 2120 Anniversary for first centenary of the World Socialist Revolution, that unified all the people of the planet. Not just an ideal, and not just a thought of socialist unity. . . . Occurrences that I really will never see, but which I have the pleasure of having dreamed."

From the Garden of Eden

STANLEY BARKAN

I. AS YET UNBORN

Oh to be Adam
again
with all his ribs
yearning for a woman
as yet unborn,
mouth free
of the taste of apples,
mindless of
nakedness and shame
in the garden
of gentle creatures
waiting for a name.

II. FIRST BIRTH

Covered with leaves
she rises out of the earth—
she first,
not Adam.
How much more likely
(more provable),
he from her pit
than she from his rib.
It was a man
who wrote the myth.

From "Planetary Feminism: The Politics of the 21st Century"

ROBIN MORGAN

Because virtually all existing countries are structured by patri- ... archal mentality, the standard for being human is being male —and female human beings *per se* become "other," and invisible. This permits governments and international bodies to discuss "the world's problems"—war, poverty, refugees, hunger, disease, illiteracy, over-population, ecological imbalance, the abuse or exploitation of children and the elderly, etc.—without noticing that those who suffer most from "the world's problems" are *women,* who, in addition, are not consulted about possible solutions.

"While women represent half the global population and one-third of the labor force, they receive only one-tenth of the world income and own less than one percent of world property. They also are responsible for two-thirds of all working hours," said former UN Secretary General Kurt Waldheim in his "Report to the UN Commission on the Status of Women."[1] This was a diplomatic understatement of the situation.

Two out of three of the world's illiterates are now women, and while the general illiteracy rate is falling, the female illiteracy rate is rising. One third of all families in the world are headed by women. In the developing countries, almost half of all single women over age fifteen are mothers. Only one third of the world's women have any access to contraceptive information or devices, and more than one half have no access to trained help during pregnancy and childbirth. Women in the developing world are responsible for more than 50 percent of all food production (on the African continent women do 60 to 80 percent of all agricultural work, 50 percent of all animal husbandry, and 100 percent of all food processing). In industrialized countries, women still are paid only one half to three quarters of what men earn at the same jobs, still are ghettoized into lower-paying "female-intensive" job categories, and still are the last hired and the first fired; in Europe and North America, women constitute over 40 percent of the paid labor force, *in addition* to contributing more than 40 percent of the Gross Domestic Product in *un*paid labor in the home. As of 1982, 30 million people were unemployed in the industrialized countries and 800 million people in the Third World were living in absolute poverty; most of those affected are migrant workers and their families, youth, the disabled, and the aged—and the majority of all those categories are women. Approximately 500 million people suffer from hunger and malnutrition; the most seriously affected are children under age five and women. Twenty million persons die annually of hunger-related causes and one billion endure chronic undernourishment and other poverty deprivations; the majority are women and children.[2] And this is only part of the picture.

Not only are females most of the poor, the starving, and the illiterate, but women and children constitute more than 90 percent of all refugee populations. Women outlive men in most cultures and therefore *are* the elderly of the world, as well as being the primary caretakers of the elderly. The abuse of children is a women's problem because women must bear responsibility for children in virtually all cultures, and also because it is mostly female children who are abused —nutritionally, educationally, sexually, psychologically, etc. Since women face such physical changes as menarche, menstruation, pregnancy, childbearing, lactation, and menopause—in addition to the general health problems we share with men—the crisis in world health is a crisis of women. Toxic pesticides and herbicides, chemical warfare, leakage from nuclear wastes, acid rain, and other such deadly pollutants usually take their first toll as a rise in cancers of the female reproductive system, and in miscarriages, stillbirths, and congenital deformities. Furthermore, it is women's work which must compensate for the destruction of ecological balance, the cash benefits of which accrue to various Big Brothers: deforestation (for lumber sales as export or for construction materials) results in a lowering of the water table, which in turn causes parched grasslands and erosion of topsoil; women, as the world's principal water haulers and fuel gatherers, must walk farther to find water, to find fodder for animals, to find cooking-fire fuel.[3] This land loss, combined with the careless application of advanced technology (whether appropriate to a region or not), has created a major worldwide trend: rural migration to the cities. That, in turn, has a doubly devastating effect on women. Either they remain behind trying to support their children on unworkable land while men go to urban centers in search of jobs, or they also migrate—only to find that they are considered less educable and less employable than men, their survival options being mainly domestic servitude (the job category of two out of five women in Latin America), factory work (mostly for multinational corporations at less than $2 US per day), or prostitution (which is growing rapidly in the urban centers of developing countries). Since women everywhere bear the "double job" burden of housework in addition to outside work, we are most gravely affected by the acknowledged world crisis in housing—and not only in less developed countries. In Britain, the Netherlands, and the United States, women were the founders of spontaneous squatters' movements; in Hungary, the problem is so severe that women have been pressuring to have lack of housing declared as a ground for abortion; in Portugal, Mexico, and the USSR, women have been articulating the connections between the housing crisis, overcrowding, and a rise in the incidence of wife battery and child sexual abuse.

But the overlooked—and most important—factor in the power of women as a world political force is the magnitude of suffering combined with the magnitude of women: *women constitute not an oppressed minority, but a majority—of almost all national populations, and of the entire human species.* As that species approaches critical mass and the capacity to eradicate all life on the planet, more than ever before in recorded history, that majority of humanity now is mobilizing. The goal not only is to change drastically our own powerless status worldwide, but to redefine all existing societal structures and modes of existence. . . .

A growing awareness of the vast resources of womanpower is becoming evident in a proliferation of plans of action, resolutions, legislative reforms, and other blueprints for change being put forward by national governments, international congresses and agencies, and multinational corporations. Women have served or are serving as heads of states and governments in more nations than ever before, including Belize, Bolivia, Dominica, Iceland, India, Israel, Norway, Portugal, Sri Lanka, the United Kingdom, and Yugoslavia. Yet these women still must function within systems devised and controlled by men and imbued with androcentric values. What resonates with even greater potential is what "ordinary" women all over the globe are beginning to whisper, say, and shout, to ourselves and one another, *autonomously*—and what we are proceeding to *do*, in our own countries and across their borders.

The quality of feminist political philosophy (in all its myriad forms) makes possible a totally new way of viewing international affairs, one less concerned with diplomatic postures and abstractions, but focused instead on concrete, *unifying* realities of priority importance to the survival and betterment of living beings. For example, the historical, cross-cultural opposition women express to war and our healthy skepticism of certain technological advances (by which most men seem overly impressed at first and disillusioned at last) are only two instances of shared attitudes among women which seem basic to a common world view. Nor is there anything mystical or biologically deterministic about this commonality. It is the result of a *common condition* which, despite variations in degree, is experienced by all human beings who are born female.

The Inside Agitator

No matter where she was born, no matter where she turns, a stereotype awaits her. She is a hot Latin or a cold WASP, a wholesome Dutch matron, a docile Asian or a Dragon Lady, a spoiled American, a seductive Scheherazade, a hip-swaying Pacific Island hula maiden, a Caribbean matriarch, a merry Irish colleen, a promiscuous Scandinavian, a noble-savage Native Indian, a hero-worker mother. Is it any wonder that so many articles in this book, from countries as distant as Afghanistan and Hungary, Chile and both Germanies, Pakistan and Cuba, again and again have as refrains the images of fragmentation, . alienation, fractured profiles, silence, nonexistence, being "women of smoke" or, in the words of New Zealand's Ngahuia Te Awekotuku and Marilyn Waring, "foreigners in one's own land"?

But stereotypes become ineffectual unless constantly enforced. This necessitates the patriarchy's vast and varied set of rules that define not only a woman's physical appearance but her physical reality itself, from her forced enclosure in *purdah* to her forced exposure in beauty contests and pornography, from female genital mutilation to cosmetic plastic surgery, from facial scarification to carcinogenic hair dye, from the veil to the dictates of fashion. Both the Indian and the Nepalese Contributors to *Sisterhood Is Global* speak of fighting the concept of a woman's "uncleanness," her "untouchability"—and so do the Contributors from Ghana, Iran, Israel, Italy, New Zealand, and Saudi Arabia.

Still, a forced physical reality, however hideous, is not sufficient. For the power holders to be secure, it is necessary to constrain women's minds as well as our bodies. Organized religion, custom, tradition, and all the abstract patriarchal "isms" (nationalism, capitalism, communism, socialism, patriotism, etc.) are called into play, doubtless in the hope that women will not notice just *who* has dogmatized the religions, corrupted the customs, defined the traditions, and created, perpetuated, and profited by the various other "isms." The most pernicious of all patriarchal tactics to keep women a divided and subhuman world caste is the lie that "feminism is an 'outside' or alien phenomenon, not needed or desired by 'our' [local] women."[4]

This argument is wondrously chameleonic. In many Third World countries, feminists are warned that the "imported thought" of feminism is a neocolonialist plot. In Western industrialized countries, on the other hand, feminists frequently are regarded as being radical agents of communism. In the USSR and some other Eastern European nations, feminists are attacked as bourgeois agents of imperialism. (Truly, it is quite amazing how the male Right and the male Left can forge such a literal Big Brotherhood in response to the threat posed by women merely insisting on being recognized as part of humanity.) . . .

The strongest argument to the "feminists as outside agitators" attack is the simple truth: *an indigenous feminism has been present in every culture in the world and in every period of history since the suppression of women began.* Indeed, that has emerged as the predominant theme of *Sisterhood Is Global.* It will be difficult, I think, for anyone to finish this book and ever again believe that feminism is a geographically narrow, imported, or even for that matter recent, phenomenon, anywhere.

We know that history is written by the conquerors, with the consequent process of distortion or outright erasure of facts. As "herstory," or women's history, begins to be recovered by feminist historians and scholars, a wholly different past reappears—a past in which women never were "content with their lot." Feminists in each nation have begun to learn about their own feminist lineage, their own foremothers. . . .

How many of us know that Gandhi's nonviolent resistance tactics were acknowledged by him to have been copied from the nineteenth-century Indian women's movement? Or that it was a woman's action which inspired the contemporary Solidarity free-trade-union movement in Poland? Or that the contemporary Women's Party in Iceland, the Feminist Party in Canada, and the Feminist Party in Spain are making crucial statements about women placing no more trust in male political parties? For that matter, how many of us know of the existence, as early as 1918, of the Argentinian National Feminist Party, or, in 1946, of the Chilean Women's Party? How many of us know the names, much less the accomplishments, of such hidden heroines as Gualberta Beccari who, in 1866, at age eighteen, founded the Italian feminist journal *Donna;* or María Jesús Alvarada Rivera, who forged a militant Peruvian feminist movement in 1900, and endured imprisonment and exile; or Me Katilili, the seventy-year-old woman who organized the Giriama uprising against the British in Kenya in 1911? Why are the triumphs of such women warriors as Yaa Asantewaa of the Ashanti people of Ghana, or of the Thai leader Thao Thepsatri, not familiar to us, and often not even to women in their own countries? What pride might women everywhere feel in learning about the waves of female rebellion in China's long history—how it was a woman, the young astronomer Wang Zhenyi (1768–97), who discovered the law of lunar eclipses; how Hong Xuanjiao led forty armies of 2,500 women each, fighting for women's rights during the 1851 Taiping Rebellion; how Jiu Jin, the nineteenth-century feminist, poet, teacher, and revolutionary, dressed in men's clothing for freedom of movement, founded a girls' school, and was arrested and executed in 1908 because she refused to compromise her beliefs? What inspiration might all women draw from claiming as a foremother Raden Ajeng Kartini of Indonesia, who was forced to leave school by religious constraints at age twelve, educated herself, spoke out against polygyny, forced marriage, and colonial oppression, founded the modern Indonesian women's rights movement, started a girls' school which had an enrollment of 120 students by 1904—all before she died in childbirth at age twenty-five?

These women comprise our shared heritage, a heritage we can each affirm with emphatic pride across all male-devised borders. They are joined by the thousands of other women whose struggles illumine these pages: the first woman doctor in a country, the first woman lawyer, the first woman notary, the first woman journalist, the first woman to run for public office. Stop for a moment and imagine the hours of work, the nights of despair, the years of endured ridicule and rejection, the personal cost, the exhaustion, the stubborn vision, of just one such life.

Perhaps it becomes easier to understand why the imposition of stereotypes and the enforced silence are necessary to Big Brother. Perhaps it also becomes easier to strip off the masks, to break the silence, to examine the pervasiveness of those institutions which have buried our past and which daily bury our present.

Biological Materialism

To many feminist theorists, the patriarchal control of women's bodies as the means of reproduction is the crux of the dilemma, along with the embittering irony that this invaluable contribution of childbearing still is not regarded as such, because it is "biologically natural"—ergo unpaid, ergo not valued. Yet women do, as Savané of Senegal writes, "reproduce and maintain the work force itself," and Lidia Falcón of Spain delineates how her countrywomen virtually and consciously rebuilt the decimated Spanish population after World War II.

But the desire of mankind [sic] to define and control women's reproductive freedom is an old one. Modern history is replete with examples of governments "giving" women the right to contraceptive use and abortion access when male authority felt the nation had an overpopulation problem, then abolishing that right when male authority felt the population was dropping too low or for other political reasons "in the national interest." The point, of course, is that this is *the right of an individual woman* herself, *not a gift to be bestowed or taken back.* But until women are a major force in the political and scientific circles of the world, genuinely safe, humane, and free reproductive options will not become a priority. The United Nations Fund for Population Activities reports, "Currently, only about twenty developing countries have the capability to carry on biomedical research in family planning, and about ten more are developing these resources. A five-to-ten-year buildup is necessary for a single institution to achieve self-reliance, depending on the initial level of expertise and facilities and the national commitment and level of investment."[5]

In the meantime, women everywhere suffer from the *absence* of contraceptive information and devices and the suppression of traditional women's knowledge of them, or from the *presence* of unsafe means of preventing conception. Sterilization programs, sometimes carried out at the command of authoritarian governments or under neocolonial pressure, have for the most part focused on women, despite the fact that vasectomy for men is a simpler, quicker, and infinitely less dangerous operation than is tubal ligation or hysterectomy for women. Another highly questionable solution was proposed on July 16, 1982, when *World Health,* the magazine of the UN World Health Organization, carried a report on a recent WHO meeting which had concluded that Depo-Provera (DMPA), the controversial injectable contraceptive, was "an acceptable method of fertility regulation." Despite this drug's having been the target of feminist protests in numerous countries (based on research showing it to be dangerous to the hormonal system and possibly carcinogenic), representatives from drug-regulatory agencies of India, Mexico, Sweden, Thailand, the United Kingdom, and the United States—*as well as representatives of the pharmaceutical industries from those countries*—found that it "shows no additional and possibly fewer adverse effects than those found with other hormonal methods of contraception." The meeting added, "however, as DMPA has been used for a relatively short period of time, little can be said about its potential long-term effects."[6]

Meanwhile, and despite much head-shaking in international development circles over "the population issue," a semi-conscious conspiracy of Church, State, and ignorance persists in viewing "population problems" as separate from "women's problems." Population programs which at first referred to women as "targets" now have come at least as far as the terminology "acceptors"—which still connotes passivity.[7] And women everywhere continue to suffer—being forced to bear unwanted children, being kept from having wanted children, and having to bear children in desperate circumstances:

Thirty to fifty percent of all "maternal" deaths in Latin America are due to improperly performed illegal abortions or to complications following abortion attempts.

Fifty percent of all women in India gain no weight during the third trimester of pregnancy, owing to malnourishment. Every ten minutes in 1980, an Indian woman died of a septic abortion.

More than half of all live births in Venezuela are out of wedlock. Illegal abortion is the leading cause of female deaths in Caracas.

The average Soviet woman has between twelve and fourteen abortions during her lifetime, because contraceptives, although legal, are extremely difficult to obtain.

In Peru, 10 to 15 percent of all women in prison were convicted for having had illegal abortions; 60 percent of the women in one Lima prison were there for having had or performed illegal abortions.

Eighty percent of pregnant and nursing rural women in Java have anemia.

Everywhere, throughout history, an individual woman's right to reproductive freedom has been used as a political pawn. In Nazi Germany, one of Hitler's first acts on coming to power was the outlawing of contraceptive advertising and the closing of birth-control clinics; abortion became tantamount to an act of sabotage against the State. Comparably, an ultra-Right and Christian fundamentalist minority in the United States today is attempting to legislate severe restrictions on contraceptive access and to re-criminalize abortion. Reproductive freedom always is a first target of conservative, racist, and ethnocentric forces: in the USSR, it is more difficult for a "white" Russian woman to obtain contraceptives or an abortion than for a woman in one of the ethnic republics, because the government is concerned about the darker-skinned and Asiatic population's outnumbering whites; comparably, in the US, birth-control policy has at times resulted in Afro-American, Native American, and Hispanic-American women being sterilized without their informed consent. In the international arena, the same racial and ethnic bigotries are writ large in population strategies foisted by Northern countries on Southern ones, by the "developed world" on the "developing." This of course provokes racial, nationalistic, and cultural resistance against foreign interference—but the dialogue, however antagonistic, is carried on between male governments, and the women themselves are rarely consulted, if ever.

The presence of organized patriarchal religion in all this cannot be overemphasized. It shows itself in the Arab world wherever Islamic fundamentalism surfaces, in "traditionalist" Hindu practice, in the orthodox Hebrew lobby in Israel, and across the Latin world through the influence of the Roman Catholic Church. The ethical contradictions created are bizarre. For example, in Ecuador and Mexico, abortion is virtually illegal, but infanticide committed for reasons of "family honor" within the first eight days of life, or if the child is unregistered, gains a more lenient sentence or no punishment at all. Latin America today hosts a number of self-styled revolutionary regimes which have a strong pronatalist attitude; the Roman Catholic Church has been supportive of such social revolutions and, as more than one of the Latin American Contributors notes, the Left therefore doesn't wish to alienate such a powerful ally over the question of reproduction. Thus, in Nicaragua, abortion still is illegal unless there is proven danger to the woman's life—and that proof must be ruled upon by a minimum of three doctors, *with* the consent of the woman's spouse or guardian. In the Irelands, too, this issue is central to the women's movement. . . .

The centrality of *a woman's right to choose* whether or not or how and when to bear a child is incontrovertible—and is inextricable from every other issue facing women. Because we are viewed as "reproducers" we are exploited in the labor force as secondary "producers" (even where we are primary ones). Because paternity (e.g., "ownership of issue") becomes such an obsession, our virginity assumes vital importance, clitoridectomy and infibulation persist as literal chastity belts of human flesh, "honor murders" of women are condoned. Because older women are past child bearing age, we are discarded as useless (whatever the contrary rhetoric) in most societies: Japan, Denmark, and the United States are only three of the countries where older women's feminist activism is emerging strongly.

The tragedy within the tragedy is that because we are regarded primarily as reproductive beings rather than full human beings, we are viewed in a (male-defined) sexual context, with the consequent epidemic of rape, sexual harassment, forced prostitution, and sexual traffick in women, with transacted marriage, institutionalized family structures, and the denial of individual women's own sexual expression.

The heavy fabric suffocating women is woven so tightly from so many strands that it is impossible to examine one without encountering those intertwined with it. . . .

The theory that marriage[8] has functioned as an instrument of patriarchal possession of women has been promulgated by feminists for centuries. Women in industrialized nations have confronted this reality in many ways: laws which stipulate that "the husband and wife are one, and that one is the husband," and which deny married women our own names, property rights, credit ratings, autonomous business dealings, and child custody, and the "offstage" suffering of battery and other family violence, marital rape, sexual frustration and betrayal, personality subsumation, etc. Yet just how profoundly antagonistic this institution is to women's selfhood becomes clear only in an international, historical context.

Marriage is used to reinforce class, racial, religious, and ethnic differences, casting women literally as an exchange of "property" to strengthen group bonds (despite scientific evidence that the evolutionary gene pool of the species is enriched by exogamy). In almost all cultures, marriage (with its attendant duties of nonsalaried housewifery and child-raising) is regarded as the goal of a woman's entire life, whether such a regard is validated by local legal systems or (infrequently) challenged by them. This results in the definition of a woman as a (solely) reproductive being, which in turn restricts both her sexual and her reproductive freedom. It results in women being excluded from employment, or exploited by employers as "auxiliary income earners" and free "family laborers," and channeled into part-time, seasonal, and marginal jobs, always low in payment and prestige. It limits a woman's scope of physical and intellectual movement to the private sphere, minimizing her as a political force and eradicating her as an historical presence. It constrains her educational opportunities, since the focus of her training is on serving a husband-to-be and his family, on household skills, and on motherhood. It affects her entire life span, from childhood to old age:

Child marriage, although opposed by law in many countries, still persists: in Nepal, as of 1971, 13.36 percent of all females age 10–14 (and 2.33 percent of all females age 6–9) already were married.

The suicide rate of elderly women in Japan is higher than in any other country, because, according to the Japanese Contributor Keiko Higuchi, of the way in which society isolates widows and regards them as useless.

In the rural Punjab, the custom of a woman being given in marriage to the husband of her deceased elder sister still is observed.

In parts of China, Mexico, and Italy, kidnapping of brides (or "bridenapping") remains a tradition.

Polygyny, child marriage, forced marriage, and the right of a husband to "chastise" a wife physically are affirmed by fundamentalist interpretations of Islamic, Hindu, and various customary laws.

The concept of Patria Potestad, omnipresent in the laws of Latin American countries (with the strong support of the Roman Catholic Church), defines a husband as the supreme authority over his wife and family—in terms of choice of domicile, financial and property matters, decisions about the children's education, the wife's right to travel or go to school or seek a job outside the home, and child custody.

In the Eastern European socialist countries, legislation ensures a married woman's right to work, yet other legislation (restricting contraceptive or abortion access, rewarding large families, emphasizing and giving special benefits to homemakers and mothers) ironically manages to refocus women on the home and to perpetuate their position as second-class citizens in the labor force.

Is it then any wonder that women's-rights activists have been working for laws against wife battery and marital rape—both in the United States[9] and in all the republics of the Soviet Union?[10] Is it any surprise that indigenous feminist agitation against polygyny has been going on for decades in Indonesia, Sri Lanka, and Egypt? Is it so shocking that there were Anti-Marriage Sisterhoods in nineteenth-century China, whose members pledged to commit suicide rather than marry? Is it not natural that Argentinian, Brazilian, and other Latin American feminists have attacked Patria Potestad laws, that a Southern Italian woman who had been "bridenapped" defied tradition and went to court to accuse the man of a criminal act? . . .

It is not then difficult to understand why the basic human right to be free of an oppressive situation is so opposed by male Church and male State, or why for most women all over the world a taken-for-granted right in some countries still is regarded as radical or unattainably miraculous: the right to divorce.

Double Standards of Divorce

. . . A woman's right to divorce was the single most controversial issue in the Chinese Revolution. It still is a basic right to be won in many countries where strictly interpreted Islamic jurisprudence or Roman Catholic dogma underlies or influences secular law, and in Israel, where conservative Rabbinical Courts control the issues of marriage, family, and divorce. A man's right to divorce has been a given in most societies—usually along with a woman's *lack* of rights to *contest* his decision. *Talaq,* or divorce by verbal renunciation, is solely a male right in parts of the Arab world and among Islamic communities in some other countries—a right sometimes opposed but largely affirmed in the secular laws of the relevant nations, and an issue which is the focus of much Islamic feminist activism. In countries where equal divorce laws do exist, the recriminations against the woman are still severe: economic difficulties, nonpayment of child support, family disapproval, social stigma, and sometimes automatic loss of child custody.

Nor is it only a cross-cultural sin against heaven and earth for a woman to leave a painful marriage situation. It is a sin, revealingly enough, against *property*.

Dowry—The Price of a Life (and Death)

Few institutions expose the "woman is property" concept so tragically as dowry. Whether in the form of payment in money or goods from the groom's family to the bride's (in effect, a purchase of the woman) or from the bride's family to that of the groom (to enhance her marriageability and ostensibly to provide her with property of her own), the bridewealth is almost never controlled by the woman herself. Masquerading as a gesture of respect or even love for the woman, this practice in fact binds her all the more to a situation she may not have chosen and may wish to leave. (Return of the dowry is one of the most frequent reasons families on either side oppose divorce.) The practice is as old as the Incans and was abolished by law in Greece as late as 1983. It still exists in most parts of the world, and is required by custom and even by statute in some countries. Furthermore, even where legislation prohibiting it has been laboriously passed, loopholes are found to get around the law, or the practice manifests itself in ingenious new ways.

. . . Despite repeated anti-dowry legislation in India (most recently passed in 1961) the transaction remains widespread, is growing in commercial intensity, and has reached proportions of such violence as to necessitate denunciations from the Prime Minister and new and stronger (proposed) legislation. The 1975 Report from the Indian Commission on the Status of Women declared dowry to be one of the gravest problems affecting women in the entire country. Yet in the year 1980–81, there were still 394 cases of brides burned to death reported by the police in Delhi alone; Indian women's groups claim that nationwide the police register only one out of 100 cases of dowry murder and attempted dowry murder that come to their attention, and that for each of these cases six go unreported. The practice frequently becomes a form of extortion, with the husband and his family harassing, beating, or torturing a bride to extract more money from her family. In extreme cases, she is murdered (so that the husband may marry again and receive more dowry); most dowry murders are made to look accidental (e.g., dousing the woman with kerosene, setting her afire, and claiming it was a cooking accident) or are made to appear acts of suicide. Massive anti-dowry demonstrations have been a major focus of Indian feminist activism in recent years; *Manushi,* the Indian feminist journal which publishes both in Hindi and in English, has courageously focused its coverage on dowry-murder cases and has initiated a crusade of pledges not to give or accept dowry.[11]

Only by such indigenous women's activism will practices like these—whether so dramatically posed as in India or subtly preserved through "trousseau" commercialism and symbolic "giving the bride away" in the West—be eradicated, and with that eradication come the end of transacted love, and of women's marital servitude.

The War Against Female Sexuality

The brutal or subtle suppression of female sexuality is sometimes said to be a concern only of "bourgeois" or "spoiled" women in industrialized nations, since such women allegedly need not have economic issues as a priority. (It is never assumed that men in developing countries are unconcerned with sexuality just because they are, along with their sisters, faced with life-and-death economic issues, nor is it ever assumed that men in industrialized nations who are so concerned with *their* sexuality are merely "bourgeois" or "spoiled.") . . .

Whatever the individual choice of sexuality, however, the subject itself is of deep concern to women everywhere. There is a poverty of sexual freedom women suffer just as hideously as a poverty of economics or of education. Possibly this is because wherever genuine pleasure, affection, and the energy of erotic delight begin to flower, the State and its linear structures are in danger of exposure as being ridiculous at best and tyrannical at worst.[12]

The True "Workers of the World"

It is appalling that such questions as "Should women work?" and even "Do women work?" still are asked seriously in the twentieth century. In fact, it can be said that women do everything . . . but control nothing. . . . As Kathleen Newland wrote, "Of 70 developing countries surveyed by the Organization for Economic Cooperation and Development in 1973, only six counted the value of carrying water to its point of use in the GNP's. And only two assigned any economic value to housewives' services."[13] Or, as the Sri Lankan Contributor notes, a "women as 26 percent of the labor force" statistic in her country was overturned by a 1973 labor-force survey which for the first time included housewives as a component, precipitously raising the figure to 44.9 percent.

Women's "GNP invisibility" becomes all the more absurd in light of the fact that women comprise almost the totality of the world's food producers[14] and are responsible for most of the world's hand-portage of water and fuel. . . . As "unpaid family workers," women appear fitfully on national labor charts, although in many parts of Asia and Africa women are *the* agricultural workers on small farms; as one New Zealand farm wife phrased it, "I would assure the Government that if women entirely pulled out of farming, agriculture would suffer to an almost collapsed state in a very short time."[15]

Women comprise a large portion of tourist-industry workers, and in some countries women *are* that industry, where packaged sex-tourism is promoted (see below).

In most nations, handicrafts are largely or solely the products of female labor—mostly created as piece-work done at home for (extremely low) wage pay, with no benefits or pensions. . . .

"Free-zone activities" and "free-zone industry," using primarily unskilled female labor, particularly exploit women by suddenly expanding the female labor market and just as suddenly abandoning it, a phenomenon described by Sonia Cuales, from the Dutch-speaking Caribbean, and by Goonatilake from Sri Lanka; the latter also makes a basic feminist connection, noticing how the colonizer adapts the way in which he has treated his own countrywomen as a model for the way he treats the women of the country he is colonizing: "Women and children were employed as a source of cheap industrial labor in nine-teenth-century Britain, and this method of exploitation was intro-duced into the Sri Lankan tea estates."

Carmen Lugo of Mexico is one of the many Third World Con-tributors who describe how Big Brother's multinational corporations rely on the sweatshop labor of women, certainly exploiting the indige-nous male population as well, but at least training the men in some technological methods and in many cases promoting men (but never women) to middle-management or even higher positions.

The manipulation of women workers as a temporary labor force is notorious. In agrarian economies, women form the bulk of mi-grant-labor populations and seasonal workers; in industrialized coun-tries, the bulk of part-time workers. Even where women form a large percentage of the employed labor force, as in such highly developed nations as Japan or the Netherlands, we are still auxiliary, marginal, or part-time workers. This in turn means that women all over the world are deprived of full work benefits and are *de facto* discriminated against in pension plans, which almost always are based on the amount of cumulative lifetime salary earned and hours worked. It also means that women's chances of promotion are reduced or eradicated, effectively keeping us out of decision-making positions which might change pol-icy.

This vicious circle is worn as a halo around Big Brother's head: his excuse for women's part-time worker ghettoization is his solicitous concern over women's family role and responsibilities—yet those re-sponsibilities aren't counted as "work."

Patriarchal solutions to the double-job burden have been delete-rious, and at times insultingly trivial, to women. For example, special stipends or time off to reward employed women who are mothers may appear supportive, but actually can serve to keep women in the home, *unless* the same benefit is extended to male parents. The availability of part-time positions to employed mothers can compartmentalize them as such, unless, again, these jobs are available to men, *along with* educa-tion of public consciousness to ensure equal male participation in parenting and in housework. "Protective" labor legislation can militate against women being hired or promoted in many industries, *unless* that protection is extended to men in an equal way. All these supposed benefits to women can be (and have been) turned against us, and this will continue until the entire context is reevaluated and women have real decision-making power about new modes of organization and implementation.

The truth is that the interest of a patriarchal State isn't served in finding genuine solutions to the double-job burden. A marginal female labor force is a highly convenient asset: cheap, always available, easily and callously disposed of. Nawal El Saadawi, of Egypt . . . , writes perceptively about the conspiratorial fashion in which, as the economy declines and jobs become scarcer, cries of "women should be back in the home" increase from religious fundamentalists, but with tacit State support. Titkow of Poland depicts a parallel situation. Comparably, the "Rosie the Riveter" syndrome was noted in the United States during the 1940's: when women were needed by industry because men were away at war, government propaganda lauded the patriotic woman who worked pluckily in the factory; when the men returned, the propaganda changed, implying that the employed woman was unwomanly, indifferent to her family's needs, cold, and "un-American."

But where are the trade unions in all this? And what about the New International Economic Order? What about "development" and high technology?

Sadly, most trade unions have proven ineffectual and even indifferent to the dilemmas of women workers, despite the vital part women have played in organizing unions in those countries where they exist. . . . Male trade-union leadership has been accused of "selling out" women constituents, whether from a calculated sense of brotherhood with male workers, male management, and male government, or from a more benign ignorance about the status and real problems of women workers.

The majority of employed women work in jobs not even covered by trade unions—jobs on which, nonetheless, entire economies depend: in agriculture, secretarial/clerical work, homemaking, or domestic service. This last category is hardly ever covered by insurance benefits (Ecuador, Mexico, Nicaragua, and Portugal are among the rare exceptions), and even when legislation does exist to grant domestic servants coverage, there is precious little implementation of the law to ensure it.

In the developed nations, this good-legislation-poor-implementation problem is epidemic. Even in Sweden, which can be justifiably proud of progressive legislation on women's rights, job discrimination persists (and with it the accompanying discrimination of lower pensions, etc.). Rita Liljeström demonstrates how men have entered women's (paid) jobs in greater numbers than the reverse—the result being that women are deprived of work in a previously "female-intensive" labor category but still are unable to break the gender barrier in more rewarded employment areas. Thus, even in those countries which have passed equal-pay-for-equal-work legislation, the law may have little meaning since job categorization remains in overt or covert force. For precisely this reason, the women's movements in Australia, Canada, and the United States, among others, have begun to push for the concept of "equal pay for *comparable* work" or "equal pay for work of equal *value*"—which expands the issue into hitherto uncovered areas.

If industrialized nations have such a poor record in equalizing wealth and opportunity within their own borders (whatever their political ideology), it doesn't augur well for the New International Economic Order—or, rather, it implies that the alleged redistribution and equalizing of wealth between countries will in fact take place between *men* of different countries, out of the reach of the respective women involved, in a brothers'-business-as-usual fashion. (This is neatly described by Rayna Green of the US as European men making treaties with those unauthorized to make them, e.g., what happened to the Native Americans.) . . .

But what of "economic development"? What good—or harm—does it do when these basic connections aren't made in the minds of those who define it? Improving educational opportunities can worsen inequality if only the boys are educated. Technological advances can mean a setback if, for example, tractors shorten the working hours of men who do the plowing but lengthen the working hours of women who do the weeding. "Modernization" can mean merely more advanced feudalism for women if it disenfranchises matrilineal or matrifocal peoples, or introduces agrobusiness (and trains only men in new farming techniques) in a country where women traditionally have been the landowners, farmers, and marketers. Where is the "progress" if, as in Indonesia, rice-hulling machines cut women's income by more than $55 million and reduced half-time employment by more than 8.3 months for 1 million women, while income for men in the new mills increased by $5 million? In that same country, imports and mechanization have forced 90 percent of women weavers out of work; batik-making also has been mechanized—with men who operate the machinery earning *400–500 percent more than women* in the labor-intensive jobs. . . .

"Integrating" women into development—the new cure-all—still utterly misses the point, since women then are caught up in a pre-devised plan which still does not address our specific needs. . . .

Most ideas of "development" and "modernization" also are among the major culprits in what could be termed the "citification of the planet"—the massive rural-to-urban migration taking place all over the world. . . . The Caribbean, Ecuador, Kenya, Pakistan, Peru, Senegal, and Thailand are among those who refer to this phenomenon as affecting the lives of women—women who migrate *or* women who remain behind. Olivia Muchena of Zimbabwe writes about the social-emotional schizophrenia forced on a woman who must function as a capable head of household while her man is far away working in the city for long periods, and who then is expected to become a traditionally subordinate wife during his rare visits. There is also *cross-national* migration: developed countries importing women from less developed countries as cheap labor, with a resultant clash of cultures. . . .

At the 1980 UNITAR Seminar in Oslo on Creative Women in Changing Societies, women urged the creation of an International Commission for Alternative Development with Women, since "many development models are no longer valid, for, by omitting the female component, they not only continue to minimize the female input into production and consumption (both social and economic), but also perpetuate the exploitation, low status, and nonrecognition of women." The need for such a basic *attitudinal* change is underscored by Aisha Almana of Saudi Arabia, who explores how, even in such a wealthy and rapidly developing country as hers, women are left isolated unless the connections are made and the consciousness itself is transformed.[16]

Meanwhile, the invisible woman continues her visible work. But she has begun to fight back, whether in the manner of market-women's demonstrations in Thailand or of the Belgian flight attendant who sued Sabena Airlines over sex discrimination, lost her case in the

Belgian courts, and then successfully appealed it as a discrimination case to the European Common Market Court of Justice.

To fight back in solidarity, however, as a real political force, requires that women transcend the patriarchal barriers of class and race, and furthermore transcend even the *solutions* the Big Brothers propose to problems they themselves created. . . .

"Women," we are told, "really have nothing in common with one another, given class, race, caste, and comparable barriers." . . .

Nor is class the only categorization invented by patriarchy to divide and conquer. As the Peruvian Contributor puts it, "class oppression often masks other oppressions." *Clanism, tribalism* and *racism* both, *the caste system, religious bigotry,* the *rural peasant–urbanite split, ethnic categorization,* and the waves of *discrimination visited on Native Indian peoples*—all such compartmentalizations of human beings cause additional suffering among women—women within the various oppressed groups and women trying to build bridges between such groups.

It is moving to hear the impassioned desire for solidarity . . . the vibrant understanding between organizers from the Greek Women's Union and women olive-growers; the determination in the voice of an old woman who has lived her entire life by an oasis in the Libyan desert:

> *I have been married for thirty years and always been an obedient wife. But when my husband and son prohibited my daughters from joining the [educational] center I became very angry and threatened to leave home. I insisted very hard that all my four daughters should be educated, and thank God I won. If I were still young, I myself would have joined the center. Educated women are more respected . . . Their husbands will not divorce them, and will no longer treat them like they treat their animals on the farm. . . .*

The anger of rural women, Native Indian women, nomad or peasant or village women—the unheard of the earth—is a feminist anger, which might surprise some readers who ethnocentrically may have thought such women untouched by feminism. *Feminism has been invented, and is continually reinvented, precisely by such women.*

It is electrifying to encounter the audacity of that feminist vision unalloyed, a radical perspective which insists on simultaneous and profound change, on freedom for all with no one waiting "until after" some promised moment, an uncompromising demand for true revolution.

NOTES

1. Statistics from Development Issue Paper No. 12, UNDP.
2. Statistics from the World Conference of the United Nations Decade for Women (Copenhagen, 1980), from the Oxford Committee for Famine Relief, and from the 1982 UN *Report on the World Situation.* The 1982 UN *Report* also noted that military research and development expenditures, estimated at $35 billion for 1980, surpassed all public funds spent on research and development in the fields of energy, health, pollution control, and agriculture *combined,* and amounted to at least six times the total research-and-development expenditures of all developing countries.
3. In 1872, 14 percent of all potentially arable land was desert; in 1952, 33 percent; by 1982, almost 66 percent was dry and barren. The United Nations estimates that there will be half as much farm land per person by the year 2000 as there is now, given the rates of population growth and agricultural land loss.
4. This is hardly a new tactic. It has been used by colonists about native populations, by slaveholders in the early American South, by management about workers trying to unionize, etc. Discontent and rebellion among the oppressed, according to those in power, is always the work of "outside agitators."
5. United Nations Development Programme, UNFPA, Report of the Executive Director, DP/1983/21, Apr. 12, 1983.
6. Press Release, UN Department of Public Information, New York (H/2647), July 16, 1982.
7. See "Women, Population, and International Development in Latin America: Persistent Legacies and New Perceptions for the 1980's," by Ieda Siqueira Wiarda and Judith F. Helzner, Program in Latin American Studies Occasional Paper Series 13, International Area Studies Programs, University of Massachusetts at Amherst, 1981.
8. I am speaking here of marriage *as an institution,* in its legalistic, religious-fundamentalist, and sexual-fundamentalist terms, not of marriage as a freely chosen and affirmed commitment between two persons (of either sex) living as sexual lovers in an emotional bond and sharing of resources.
9. As of 1983, only 10 states had enacted specific legislation against wife beating, although most other states had provisions for civil actions, protection orders, etc.; husbands could be fully prosecuted for marital rape in only 19 of the 50 states, and the severity of sentence varied from state to state.
10. There are no laws specifying the illegality of wife battery or marital rape in the USSR.
11. A few samples of *Manushi*'s coverage of hundreds of attempted and committed dowry-murder cases include the following:
    "On March 9, 1981, police entered the house of Kanta Porwal's in-laws in

Udaipur and found her chained on the roof, starving and on the verge of collapse. . . . Her in-laws say that she was mad and prone to violence. In fact, Kanta is a scholarship holder, but after marriage she was being harassed, tortured, and driven to madness because she had not brought enough dowry. Her four-month-old son was snatched away from her, her husband . . . sent her back to her parents many times in the last few years. Finally her in-laws tried to starve her to death by keeping her chained on the roof in the scorching sun for over two months. . . . A women's group called Udaipur Mahila Samiti is giving support to Kanta and other women like her. The police have registered a case of attempt to murder and wrongful confinement."

"Eight-year-old Savithri of Ootakalu village in Pathikonda taluk, Kurnool district of Andhra Pradesh, was married to Karuva Rayappa of Peravalli village. . . . Rayappa, his father . . . and others of the household used to abuse and beat her everyday, demanding Rs. 3000 dowry which had been promised to them. Savithri endured this cruelty for seven years. Now she is fifteen. Six months ago, her in-laws sent her to her parents' house, ordering her to come back with the money, but Savithri decided not to return . . . because she could not suffer any more. Infuriated, Savithri's husband . . . went to her village and with the help of some toughs, dragged her out of the house, overcoming her resistance. . . . They put iron rings on her feet, tied her up, put her in a bullock cart and took her back to Peravalli. Savithri says she was then locked up without food or water and not even allowed to visit the toilet. On April 8, she was forced to do the housework, with her legs still chained. On the same day, Savithri's mother . . . met a local lawyer who filed a petition with the . . . magistrate of Pathikonda, . . . [who] appointed an enquiry commission and issued a search warrant. When Savithri was finally released, she was found to be still wearing the iron rings."

"On September 5, Veena had returned to her in-laws' house, . . . having spent four days attending a wedding at her parents' house in Jullundur. A few hours later she was dead. . . . Ever since she got married, she was being harassed by her in-laws to get more things from her parents. Her life became more miserable when she gave birth to a daughter, a year ago. She was taunted with having brought a 'burden' into the family, beaten and made to work like a housemaid. . . . On September 5, at 9 P.M., the neighbors saw fire in the kitchen and ran out to help, but found the door locked. Veena's father-in-law came out and said she had committed suicide by burning herself. The neighbors suspected foul play and played a crucial role in bringing the culprits to book. . . . [Veena's] in-laws were trying hurriedly to get her body cremated, but the neighbors physically prevented them, and kept vigil round the house until the police came. The neighbors also formed an action committee, raised funds and engaged a lawyer to fight the case. It is alleged that the in-laws heavily bribed the police. . . ."

12. Orwell's Big Brother knew this well: "It was not merely that the sex instinct created a world of its own which was outside the Party's control and which therefore had to be destroyed if possible. What was more important was that sexual privation induced hysteria [*sic*], which was desirable because it could be transformed into war fever and leader worship." Orwell's totalitarian State also foresaw the alliance between the repressors of genuine eroticism and the purveyors of sexual degradation, a truly perverted alliance we see today in the West between right-wing legislators and a huge pornographic industry: "Pornosec, the subsection of the Fiction Department which turned out cheap pornography for distri-

bution among the proles . . . to be bought furtively by proletarian youths under the impression that they were buying something illegal."

13. Worldwatch Paper 37, "Women, Men, and the Division of Labor," by Kathleen Newland, Worldwatch Institute, Washington, D.C., 1980.

14. See "Women and Food: Feminist Perspectives," by Marilyn J. Waring, M.P., a paper presented at the University of New South Wales, Feb. 25, 1982.

15. Quoted in "Women in Agriculture: A Survey of Rural Women in New Zealand," in *Straight Furrow* (Newspaper of the Federated Farmers of New Zealand), Sept. 1981.

16. The "integration of women into development" syndrome is compounded, of course, when the issues of science and high technology are engaged: "In approximately 40 percent of developing countries, women comprise fewer than five percent of the trained human resources for science and technology." (From the Implementation of the Vienna Program of Action on Science and Technology for Development, UN General Assembly A/CN.11/38, May 3, 1983.)

My Country Is the World

VIRGINIA WOOLF

Therefore if you insist upon fighting to protect me, or "our" country, let it be understood, soberly and rationally between us, that you are fighting to gratify a sex instinct which I cannot share; to procure benefits which I have not shared and probably will not share; but not to gratify my instincts, or to protect either myself or my country. "For," the outsider will say, "in fact, as a woman, I have no country. As a woman I want no country. As a woman my country is the whole world." And if, when reason has said its say, still some obstinate emotion remains, some love of England dropped into a child's ears by the cawing of rooks in an elm tree, by the splash of waves on a beach, or by English voices murmuring nursery rhymes, this drop of pure, if irrational, emotion she will make serve her to give to England first what she desires of peace and freedom for the whole world.

Ain't I a Woman

SOJOURNER TRUTH

The man over there says women need to be helped into carriages and lifted over ditches, and to have the best places everywhere. Nobody ever helps me into carriages or over puddles, or gives me the best place—and ain't I a woman? . . . I could work as much and eat as much as a man—when I could get it—and bear the lash as well. And ain't I a woman? I have born thirteen children, and seen most of 'em sold into slavery, and when I cried out with my mother's grief, none but Jesus heard me—and ain't I a woman?

"Ethnically Cleansed" or Cleaning Women

LUCIA MARIA PERILLO

In 1989, I was one of forty Americans on a tour bus headed south from Dubrovnik. "We have six republics, five nations, four languages, three religions, and two alphabets," said our guide as we entered the republic of Montenegro, where the mountains proved true to their name and loomed up cloud-capped and brooding, "but there is only one Yugoslavia." She was reciting the national tour company's favorite slogan in the years before the country's breakup. The slogan, like the tour company, aimed to prove the success of Marshal Tito's experiment in socialism, ethnic tolerance, and forged national identity.

Our guide was from Zagreb, presumably a Croatian, though to know this didn't seem important then. She was an attractive young woman educated in San Francisco; her English was flawless and her manner urbane. She explained to us that Montenegro was renowned for its handsome men, who were tall and dark and had piercing blue eyes. But alas, she sighed, they were notoriously lazy. And to illustrate, our guide told us this joke:

A woman goes into the police station and announces she has just been raped. She knows her assailant is a Montenegrin. "How can you be certain?" the policeman asks, and the woman answers that her assailant was tall and dark and blue-eyed. "But that's not proof," the policeman says. "Well, he must have been from Montenegro," the woman insists. "I had to do all the work!"

Though we tried to muster the requisite laughter, most of us on the bus were drop-jawed, having just heard a de facto government emissary tell what in our country would be the equivalent of a Polack Joke. And not only was this an example of boneheaded ethnic stereotyping: her joke also carried the tacit condonation of sexual assault.

Now, three years later, my tour guide's story seems like a template for the violence that is being waged across the former Yugoslavia, violence in which women function as living doubles to the real landscape, as terrain over which ethnic wars are battled. We read that in a prison camp in the Bosnian town of Tesanj, Croatian and Muslim women are detained so they can be raped and forced to bear Serbian young. "Now you will have Serbian babies the rest of your lives!" is reported to be their captors' worst taunt. Serbian women and children are also detained, by Croatian militiamen who favor Nazi salutes—as though seized by a bout of collective amnesia regarding the 1.7 million Yugoslavians who died in a war that would save the country from fascism (though the irony of Yugoslavia's WWII casualties is that most Yugoslavians were killed not by Germans and Italians, but by one another's hands.)

We Americans understand about hating what we are not. What is unfathomable to us is how people who have interbred for centuries—people who look so much alike—could have suddenly turned on each other. In the months before war broke out, the Croatian community in my town tried to rally the émigré *esprit de corps* by forming a club they named "Only Croatia." Its leader was an exiled Croatian journalist, a fervent anti-Communist who at the club's first meeting gave a lecture in which he pinned the blame on Serbia for atrocities committed during Tito's reign. Afterwards, I cornered him to point out that Tito was himself Croatian. "Okay, that's true," the journalist admitted. "But you know, the greatest traitors come from within."

For my own relatives, Yugoslavian ethnicity was like a ball of mercury that fractured whenever it was touched. My grandmother's family, who came from the island Unije on Croatia's north coast, insisted they were Austrian (the Austrian empire encompassed Croatia until after WWI). When my grandmother immigrated to New York with her family and found there a Croatian man to marry, her choice of husband made her an outcast. He was too dark, the family said. (In fact, he was fair-skinned, from another island only 150 miles down the coast.) He was a Bolshevik, they said. (He had come to America to escape having to serve in the Austrian navy during WWI.) My grandmother's father would not speak to her for years and admitted no interest in her children. *Dear Father,* reads one of my grandmother's letters, dated February 1916: *I would like to have your blessing and forgiveness for getting married against your will and without your consent. I have had nothing but hard luck since my little son was born, that I imagine that because I haven't your forgiveness, this has all happened.* The letter was returned to my grandmother, its delivery refused.

We expect such encounters with prejudice to be instructive when we find ourselves on their receiving end. What is sad about my grandmother's story is how she replayed it herself when it came her daughter's turn to marry. My aunt had met a man from Dubrovnik—or so he claimed, though his dark hair (like my grandfather's) and dark skin (not like my grandfather's) made the family suspect of his being in truth from Bosnia. "That Turk," my grandmother exclaimed disparagingly, though in the end the marriage proceeded. In fact my grandmother and the Turk spent the next twenty years baiting each other across the Bronx street where their apartments looked out on each other.

Belief in the virtue of "ethnic cleansing" requires a conviction that one's own identity is monolithic, so that everything "other" can be easily identified and routed out. In the case of a country like Yugoslavia, whose history is so labyrinthine that it's unlikely an average citizen can give an accurate and complete retelling, attempts to construct monolithic identities invariably require fudging. So Tito becomes a Serbian. The past is obliterated. This was brought home to me when I visited the island of Hvar to search for the graves of my grandfather's ancestors. I couldn't find any stones dated before the turn of the century, and it wasn't until I walked behind the maintenance shed that I found the reason. A back hoe was parked there, and the old tombstones, which had been dug up, were piled in a heap.

"Ethnic cleansing" also requires (in addition to the geographic removal of impure elements) a societal effort to control the sexual lives of women, who will produce each succeeding generation. So it's not surprising that the warfare of "ethnic cleansing" includes not only bullets and bombings, but also the rape and imprisonment of civilian women. Of course it doesn't necessarily take war to spur ethnic factionalism; war is perhaps just an artifact of economic hardship. Here in the United States, declining standards of living have made cultural identity the most divisive issue of our time, as factions grapple for slices of the capitalist pie. And simultaneously, we have witnessed what amounts to a grassroots movement aimed at taking control of women's bodies (manifest in abortion restrictions, birth control suppression, and the recent attempts to segregate employment and housing on the basis of sexual orientation). It's no coincidence that the sort of rap music that advocates racial violence also advocates brutalizing women. Likewise, at the other end of an artificial racial spectrum, "Murphy Brown" becomes a white man's code words for women who are breeding—and here the adverb is key—*uncontrollably*.

The Aryan Nation has a plan to stave off future ethnic unrest in the United States: Aryans take the Northwest, Hispanics take the Southwest, Blacks take the Southeast, Jews take the Northeast, and the government mandates the immigration of citizens to their appropriate new homes. The similarity of this "solution" to what is happening in Yugoslavia is unsettling. Though Croats and Slovenes exult in their freedom, many Yugoslavian-Americans (particularly those of mixed-regional descent) mourn not only Yugoslavia's division but also the violence that this division perpetuates, as borders are disputed and Serbs and Croats continue to kill Moslems for control of Bosnia-Herzegovina.

The reluctance of other nations to intervene in Yugoslavia's violent disassembly no doubt stems from an unspoken, Lamarckian belief that the millennia of warfare between Balkan peoples (their *bloodline,* as we say) has made them an incurably hostile race. Charles Simic, an American poet born in Belgrade, has translated a group of Serbian oral poems, centuries old, that were known as "women's songs." Among them is the song of the shepherd Radoye, asleep in a meadow and resisting his sister's attempts to rouse him. "Get up, crazy Radoye," she says. "Your sheep have wandered off." Though I am no Lamarckian, in Radoye's answer I hear something about the ancient and heartbreaking complicity of women in the wars (and the so-called jokes) of men:

Let them, sister, let them.
The witches have feasted on me,
Mother carved my heart out,
Our aunt held the torch for her.

Sky Woman and Her Sisters

PAULA GUNN ALLEN of the
Laguna/Lakota Nation

Not until recently have American Indian women chosen to define themselves politically as Indian women—a category that retains their basic racial and cultural identity but distinguishes women as a separate political force in a tribal, racial, and cultural context. This self-redefinition among Indian women who intend that their former stature be restored has resulted from several political factors. The status of tribal women has seriously declined over the centuries of white dominance, as they have been all but voiceless in tribal decision-making bodies since reconstitution of the tribes through colonial fiat and U.S. law. But, as writer Stan Steiner observes in *The New Indians,* the breakdown of women's status in tribal communities led to their migration in large numbers into the cities, where they regained the self-sufficiency and positions of influence they had held in earlier centuries. He writes, "Election of tribal women to the leadership of these urban Indian centers has been a phenomenon in modern Indian life." Women function as council members and tribal chairs for at least one fourth of the federally recognized tribes. In February 1981, the Albuquerque *Journal* reported that 67 American Indian tribes had women heads of state.

The coming of the white man created chaos in all the old systems, the success of which depended on complementary institutions and organized relationships among all sectors of their world. The significance of each part was seen as necessary to the balanced and harmonious functioning of the whole, and both private and public aspects of life were viewed as valuable and necessary components of society. The private ("inside") was shared by all, though certain rites and knowledge were shared only by clan members or by initiates into ritual societies, some of which were gender-specific and some of which were not. Most were male-dominated or female-dominated with helping roles assigned to members of the opposite gender. One category of inside societies was exclusive to "berdaches"—males only —and "berdaches"—females only. (The term "berdaches" is applied —or rather misapplied—to both lesbian women and gay males. It is originally an Arabic word meaning sex-slave boy, or a male child used sexually by adult males. As such it has no relevance to American Indian men or women.) All categories of ritual societies function in present-day American Indian communities, though the exclusively male societies are best recorded in ethnographic literature.

The "outside" was characterized by various social institutions, all of which had bearing on the external welfare of the group: hunting, gathering, building, ditch cleaning, horticulture, seasonal and permanent moves, intertribal relationships, law and policy decisions affecting the whole, crafts, and child-rearing. These were most directly affected by white government policies; the inside institutions were most affected by Christianization. Destruction of the institutions rested on the overthrow or subversion of the gynocratic nature of the tribal system.

Consider, for example, John Adair's remark about the Cherokee, as reported by Carolyn Foreman (*Indian Women Chiefs,* Zenger Publishing): "[The Cherokee] had been for a considerable while under petticoat government and they were just emerging, like all of the Iroquoian Indians, from the matriarchal period." Adair's idea of "petticoat government" included the power of the Women's Council of the Cherokee. The head of the council was the Beloved Woman of the Nation, "whose voice was considered that of the Great Spirit, speaking through her." The Iroquoian peoples, including the Hurons and the Susquehanna, set the penalty for killing a woman at double that for killing a man.

The Iroquois story is currently one of the best chronicles of the overthrow of the gynocracy. Material about the status of women in North American groups such as the Montagnais-Naskapi, Keres, Navajo, Crow, Hopi, Pomo, Yurok, Kiowa, and Natchez, and in South American groups such as the Bari and Mapuche, to name just a few, is lacking. Any original documentation that exists is buried under the flood of published material written from the colonizer's patriarchal perspective. Male dominance may have characterized a number of tribes, but it was by no means as universal (or even as preponderant) as colonialist propaganda has led us to believe.

The Seneca prophet Handsome Lake did not appreciate "petti-coat government" any more than did John Adair. When his code became the standard for Iroquoian practice in the early nineteenth century, power shifted from the hands of the "meddling old women," as he characterized them, to men. Under the old laws, the Iroquois were a mother-centered, mother-right people whose political organization was based on the central authority of the Matrons, the Mothers of the Longhouses (clans). Handsome Lake advocated that young women cleave to their husbands rather than to their mothers and abandon the clanmother-controlled longhouse in favor of a patriarchal, nuclear family arrangement. Until Handsome Lake's time, the sachems were chosen from certain families by the Matrons of their clans and were subject to impeachment by the Matrons should they prove inadequate or derelict in carrying out their duties as envisioned by the Matrons and set forth in the Law of the Great Peace of the Iroquois Confederacy. By provision in the Law, the women were to be considered the progenitors of the nation, owning the land and the soil.

At the end of the Revolutionary War, the Europeans declared the Iroquois living on the U.S. side of the United States—Canadian border defeated. Pressed from all sides, their fields burned and salted, the traditional power of the Matrons under assault from missionaries who flocked to Iroquois country to "civilize" them, the Iroquois became a captive people. Into this chaos stepped Handsome Lake, who encouraged the shift from woman-centered to patriarchal society.

The Iroquois were not the only nation to fall under patriarchalization. No tribe escaped that fate, though some western groups retained their gynecentric egalitarianism until well into the latter half of the twentieth century. Among the hundreds of tribes forced into patriarchal modes, the experiences of the Montagnais-Naskapi, the Mid-Atlantic Coastal Algonkians, and the Bari of Colombia, among others, round out the hemisphere-wide picture.

Among the Narragansett of the area now identified as Rhode Island was a woman chief, one of the six sachems of that tribe. Her name was Magnus, and when the Narragansett were invaded by Major Talcot and defeated in battle, the Sunksquaw Magnus was executed along with 90 others. Her fate was a result of her position; in contrast, the wife and child of the sachem known as King Philip among the colonizers were sold into slavery in the West Indies. (Like the Anglo-Saxon "forbidden" word "cunt," "squaw" is now mostly used as an insult to women; it means "queen" or "lady." Under patriarchal dominance, the proudest names come to be seen as degrading epithets, which the conquered and conqueror alike are forbidden to use without the risk of sounding racist.)

This sunksquaw, or hereditary female head of state, was one of scores in the Mid-Atlantic region. One researcher, Robert Grumet, identifies a number of women chiefs who held office during the seventeenth and eighteenth centuries. Grumet details the nonauthoritarian character of the Mid-Atlantic Coastal Algonkians and describes their political system, which included inheritance of rank by the eldest child through the maternal line.

The first sunksquaw Grumet mentions was noted in John Smith's journal as "Queene of Appamatuck." She was present during the council that decided on his death—a decision that Pocahontas, daughter of one of the sachems, overturned. The Wampanoag Confederacy's loss of control over the Chesapeake Bay area did not cause an end to the rule of sunksquaws or of the empress: George Fox, founder of the Quakers, recorded that "the old Empress [of Accomack] . . . sat in council" when he visited in March 1673. In 1705, Robert Beverley mentioned two towns governed by queens: Pungoteque and Nanduye. Pungoteque, he said, was a small Nation, and he listed Nanduye as "a seat of the Empress." While Nanduye was a small settlement of "not above 20 families," the old Empress had "all the Nations of this shore under Tribute."

From before 1620 until her death in 1667, a squaw-sachem known as the "Massachusetts Queen" by the Virginia colonizers governed the Massachusetts Confederacy. The Pocasset sunksquaw Weetamoo was King Philip's ally and "served as a war chief commanding over 300 warriors" during his war with the British. Queen Weetamoo was given the white woman Mary Rowlandson, who wrote descriptions of the sunksquaw in her captivity narrative. Awashonks, another queen in the Mid-Atlantic region, was squaw-sachem of the Sakonnet; she reigned in the latter part of the seventeenth century. After fighting against the British during King Philip's War, she was forced to surrender. Because she then convinced her warriors to fight *with* the British, she was able to save them from enslavement in the West Indies.

The last sunksquaw Grumet mentions was named Mamanuchqua. An Esopus and one of the five sachems of the Esopus Confederacy, Mamanuchqua is said to be only one name that she used. The others include Mamareoktwe, Mamaroch, and Mamaprocht, unless they were the names of other Esopus sunksquaws. Grumet wisely comments: "Ethnohistorians have traditionally assigned male gender to native figures in the documentary record unless otherwise identified. They have also tended to not identify native individuals as leaders unless so identified in the specific source. This policy . . . has successfully masked the identities of a substantial number of Coastal Algonkian leaders of both sexes."

It also falsifies the record of people who are not able to set it straight; it reinforces patriarchal socialization among all Americans, who are thus led to believe that there have never been any alternative structures; it masks the genocide attendant on the falsification of evidence, as it masks the gynocidal motive behind the genocide.

Politics played an even greater role in the destruction of the Cherokee gynocracy, in a region that included parts of Georgia and North Carolina. Cherokee women had the power to decide the fate of captives, decisions that were made by vote of the Women's Council and relayed to the district at large by the War Woman or Pretty Woman. The decisions had to be made by female clan heads because a captive who was to live would be adopted into one of the families whose affairs were directed by the clanmothers. The clanmothers also had the right to wage war, and the stories about Amazon warriors were not so farfetched considering how many Indian women were famous warriors and powerful voices in the councils. The Women's Council, as distinguished from the district, village, or confederacy councils, may have had the deciding voice on what males would serve on the councils, as its northern sisters had. Certainly the Women's Council was influential in tribal decisions, and its spokeswomen served as War Women and as Peace Women. Their other powers included the right to speak in men's council, the right to inclusion in public policy decisions, the right to choose whom and whether to marry, the right to bear arms, and the right to choose their extramarital occupations.

During the colonization of the Cherokee, the British worked

hard to lessen the women's power. They took Cherokee men to England and educated them in English ways. By the time the Removal
Act was under consideration by Congress in the early 1800s, many of
these British-educated men wielded considerable power over the nation's policies. In the ensuing struggle, women endured rape and murder, but they had no voice in the future direction of the Cherokee
Nation. The Cherokee were by this time highly stratified, and many
were Christianized. The male leadership bought and sold not only
black men and women but also men and women of neighboring
tribes; the women of the leadership class retreated to Bible classes,
sewing circles, and petticoats that rivaled those worn by their white
sisters.

In an effort to stave off removal, the Cherokee in the early 1800s,
under the leadership of men, drafted a constitution that disenfranchised women and blacks. It was modeled after the Constitution of
the United States, whose favor they were attempting to curry.

The Cherokee, like their northern cousins, were entirely represented by men in the white courts, in the U.S. Congress, and in
lobbying white officials. The last Beloved Woman, Nancy Ward, resigned her office in 1817, sending her cane and her vote on important
questions to the Cherokee Council. In spite of their frantic attempts to
prevent their removal to Indian Territory by aping the white man in
patriarchal particulars, the Cherokee were removed, as were the other
tribes of the region and those living north and west of them, whom
the Cherokee thought of as "uncivilized."

The cases cited above might be explained as a general conquest
over male Indian systems that happened to have some powerful
women functioning within them, rather than as a deliberate attempt to
wipe out female leadership. But the case of the Montagnais women
clarifies an otherwise obscure issue. The Montagnais-Naskapi of the
St. Lawrence Valley were contacted early in the fifteenth century by
fur traders and explorers, and later fell under the sway of Jesuit mis-
sionizing. The good fathers had to loosen the hold of Montagnais
women on tribal policies and convince men and women that a
woman's proper place was under the authority of her husband and a
man's proper place under the authority of the priests. In pursuit of this
end, the priests had to undermine the status of the women, who,
according to one of Father Paul Le Jeune's reports, had "great power.

. . . A man may promise you something and if he does not keep his promise, he thinks he is sufficiently excused when he tells you that his wife did not wish him to do it."

Undaunted, Le Jeune composed a plan which, he was certain, would turn the Montagnais into proper, civilized people. He figured that the first requirement was the establishment of permanent settlements and the placement of officially constituted authority in the hands of one person. More ominously, he believed that the institution of punishment was essential. He was most distressed that the "savages" thought physical abuse a terrible crime. He commented on this aberration in a number of reports, emphasizing that its cure rested in the abduction or seduction of the children to Jesuit-run schools located a good distance from their homes. Last, Le Jeune wished to implement a new social system whereby the Montagnais would live within the European family structure with its twin patriarchal institutions of male authority and female fidelity. These would be enforced by the simple expediency of forbidding divorce.

Le Jeune had his work cut out for him: working with people who, in his own words, could not "endure in the least those who seem desirous of assuming superiority over the others; they place all virtue in a certain gentleness," who ". . . imagine that they ought by right of birth, to enjoy the liberty of wild ass colts, rendering no homage to anyone whomsoever, except when they like."

The wily Le Jeune did succeed in some measure. While the Montagnais retained their love of gentleness and nurturing, they became rather more male-centered than not. Shamans were male, leaders were male, and matrilocality had become patrilocality. With the rate of assimilation increasing and with the national political and economic situation of Indians in Canada— which is different in details but identical in intent and disastrous effect to that of Indians in the United States —the Montagnais will likely be fully patriarchal before the turn of the next century.

Montagnais men who would not subscribe to the Jesuit program (and there were many) were not given authority. Under patriarchy men are given power only if they use it in ways congruent with the authoritarian, punitive model. The records attest, in contrast, that gynecentric systems distribute power evenly among men, women, and berdaches as well as among all age groups. Economic distribution follows a similar pattern; reciprocal exchange of goods and services among individuals and between groups is ensured because women are in charge at all points along the distribution network.

Effecting the social transformation from egalitarian, gynecentric systems to hierarchical, patriarchal systems requires meeting four objectives. The first is accomplished when the primacy of female as creator is replaced by male-gendered creators (generally generic, as the Great Spirit concept overtakes the multiplicitous tribal designation of deity). This objective has largely been met across North America. The Hopi goddess Spider Woman has become Maseo or Tawa, referred to in the masculine, and the Zuni goddess is on her way to malehood. Changing Woman of the Navajo has contenders for her position, while the Keres Thought Woman trembles on the brink of displacement by her sister-goddess-cum-god Utset. Among the Cherokee, the goddess of the river foam is replaced by Thunder in many tales, and the Iroquois divinity Sky Woman now gets her ideas and powers from her dead father or her monstrous grandson.

The second objective is achieved when tribal governing institutions and philosophies are destroyed. The conqueror has demanded that the tribes that wish federal recognition and protection institute "democracy," in which powerful officials are elected by majority vote. Until recently, these powerful officials were inevitably male and were elected mainly by nontraditionals, the traditionals being, until recently, unwilling to participate in a form of governance imposed on them by right of conquest. Democracy by coercion is hardly democracy.

The third objective is accomplished when the people are pushed off their lands, deprived of their economic livelihood, and forced to curtail or end pursuits on which their ritual system, philosophy, and subsistence depend. Now dependent on white institutions for survival, tribal systems can ill afford gynocracy when patriarchy requires male dominance. Not that submission to white laws and customs results in economic prosperity; the unemployment rates on most reservations is about 50 to 60 percent, and the situation for urban Indians who are undereducated (as many are) is almost as bad.

The fourth objective requires that the clan structure be replaced, in fact if not theory, by the nuclear family. Women clan heads are replaced by elected male officials and the psychic net that is formed and maintained by the nature of nonauthoritarian gynecentricity, grounded in respect for diversity of gods and people, is thoroughly rent. Decimation of populations through starvation, disease, and disruption of all social, spiritual, and economic structures along with abduction and brainwashing of the young serve in meeting this goal.

Along the way, each of these parts of the overall program of degynocraticization is subject to image control and information control. Recasting archaic tribal versions of tribal history, customs, institutions, and the oral tradition increases the likelihood that the patriarchal revisionist versions of tribal life, skewed or simply made up by patriarchal non-Indians and patriarchalized Indians, will be incorporated into the spiritual and popular traditions of the tribes. This is reinforced by the loss of rituals, medicine societies, and entire clans, through assimilation and a dying off of tribal members familiar with the elder rituals and practices. Consequently, Indian control of the image-making and information-distributing process is crucial, and the contemporary prose and poetry of American Indian writers, particularly woman-centered writers, is a major part of Indian resistance to cultural and spiritual genocide.

ABC OF CULTURE

So the angel of death whistles Mozart
(As we knew he would)
Bicycling amid the smoke of Auschwitz,
The Jews of Auschwitz,
In the great museum of Western Art.

—HARVEY SHAPIRO

One of the most common themes of literature through the ages has been
that of the prejudiced person or that of the person or persons prejudiced
against. World Literature is replete with such examples supporting what
must be called a most disturbing premise: no culture holds a monopoly on
prejudice. Given the proper time and the right conditions, prejudice will
reappear like the plague—if by chance it has remained dormant for a time.

—CHARLES R. LARSON,
20 Tales of Oppression and Liberation

PART TWO

Cultural Destruction and Cultural Affirmation

Käthe Kollwitz, *The Volunteers*, Kl.178.
Courtesy Galerie St. Etienne, New York.

Colonization, Education, Language,
History, Folk Art, Religion, Literary
Art, Tradition, Media Stereotyping
and Media Control, Cultural Collapse,
Cultural Reaffirmation, Pride or
Prejudice, Ethnocentrism, Fascist
Bigotry, Democracy, and Tolerance

Language

BEI DAO

Translated by Bonnie S. McDougall

many languages
fly around the world
producing sparks when they collide
sometimes of hate
sometimes of love

reason's mansion
collapses without a sound
baskets woven of thoughts
as flimsy as bamboo splints
are filled with blind toadstools

the beasts on the cliff
run past, trampling the flowers
a dandelion grows secretly
in a certain corner
the wind has carried away its seeds

many languages
fly around the world
the production of languages
can neither increase nor decrease
mankind's silent suffering

From The Language of Oppression

HAIG A. BOSMAJIAN

Sticks and stones may break my bones, but words can never hurt me." To accept this adage as valid is sheer folly. "What's in a name? that which we call a rose by any other name would smell as sweet." The answer to Juliet's question is "Plenty!" and to her own response to the question we can only say that this is by no means invariably true. The importance, significance, and ramifications of naming and defining people cannot be over-emphasized. From *Genesis* and beyond, to the present time, the power which comes from naming and defining people has had positive as well as negative effects on entire populations.

The magic of words and names has always been an integral part of both "primitive" and "civilized" societies. As Margaret Schlauch has observed, "from time immemorial men have thought there is some mysterious essential connection between a thing and the spoken name for it. You could use the name of your enemy, not only to designate him either passionately or dispassionately, but also to exercise a baleful influence."[1]

Biblical passages abound in which names and naming are endowed with great power; from the very outset, in *Genesis,* naming and defining are attributed a significant potency: "And out of the ground the Lord God formed every beast of the field and every fowl of the air; and brought them unto Adam to see what he would call them: and whatsoever Adam called every living creature, that was the name thereof."[2] Amidst the admonitions in *Leviticus* against theft, lying, and fraud is the warning: "And ye shall not swear my name falsely, neither shalt thou profane the name of thy God: I am the Lord."[3] So important is the name that it must not be blasphemed; those who curse and blaspheme shall be stoned "and he that blasphemeth the name of the Lord, he shall surely be put to death, and all the congregation shall certainly stone him."[4] So important is the name that the denial of it is considered a form of punishment: "But ye are they that foresake the Lord, that forget my holy mountain. . . . Therefore will I number you to the sword, and ye shall all bow down to the slaughter: because when I called, ye did not answer; when I spake, ye did not hear. . . . Therefore thus saith the Lord God, behold, my servants shall eat, but ye shall be hungry. . . . And ye shall leave your name for a curse unto my chosen: for the Lord God shall slay thee, and call his servants by another name."[5]

To be unnamed is to be unknown, to have no identity. William Saroyan has observed that "the word nameless, especially in poetry and in much prose, signifies an alien, unknown, and almost unwelcome condition, as when, for instance, a writer speaks of 'a nameless sorrow.' " "Human beings," continues Saroyan, "are for the fact of being named at all, however meaninglessly, lifted out of an area of mystery, doubt, or undesirability into an area in which belonging to everybody else is taken for granted, so that one of the first questions asked by new people, two-year-olds even, whether they are speaking to other new people or to people who have been around for a great many years, is 'What is your name?' "[6]

To receive a name is to be elevated to the status of a human being; without a name one's identity is questionable. In stressing the importance of a name and the significance of having none, Joyce Hertzler has said that "among both primitives and moderns, an individual has no definition, no validity for himself, without a name. His name is his badge of individuality, the means whereby he identifies himself and enters upon a truly subjective existence. My own name, for example, stands for me, a person. Divesting me of it reduces me to a meaningless, even pathological, nonentity."[7]

In his book *What Is in a Name?* Farhang Zabeeth reminds us that "the Roman slaves originally were without names. Only after being sold they took their master's praenomen in the genitive case followed by the suffix—'por' (boy), e.g., 'Marcipor,' which indicates that some men, so long as they were regarded by others as cattle, did not need a name. However, as soon as they became servants some designation was called forth."[8] To this day one of the forms of punishment meted out to wrongdoers who are imprisoned is to take away their names and to give them numbers. In an increasingly computerized age people are becoming mere numbers—credit card numbers, insurance numbers, bank account numbers, student numbers, et cetera. Identification of human beings by numbers is a negation of their humanity and their existence.

Philologist Max Muller has pointed out that "if we examine the most ancient word for 'name,' we find it is *naman* in Sanskrit, *nomen* in Latin, *namo* in Gothic. This *naman* stands for gnaman and is derived from the root, *gna,* to know, and meant originally that by which we know a thing."[9] In the course of the evolution of human society, R. P. Masani tells us, the early need for names "appears to have been felt almost simultaneously with the origin of speech . . . personality and the rights and obligations connected with it would not exist without the name."[10] In his classic work *The Golden Bough* James Frazer devotes several pages to tabooed names and words in ancient societies, taboos reflecting the power and magic people saw in names and words. Frazer notes, for example, that "the North American Indian regards his name, not as a mere label, but as a distinct part of his personality, just as much as are his eyes or his teeth, and believes that injury will result as surely from the malicious handling of his name as from a wound inflicted on any part of his physical organism."[11]

A name can be used as a curse. A name can be blasphemed. Name-calling is so serious a matter that statutes and court decisions prohibit "fighting words" to be uttered. In 1942 the United States Supreme Court upheld the conviction of a person who had addressed a police officer as "a God damned racketeer" and "a damned Fascist." (*Chaplinsky v. New Hampshire,* 315 U.S. 568). Such name-calling, such epithets, said the Court, are not protected speech. So important is one's "good name" that the law prohibits libel.

History abounds with instances in which the mere utterance of a name was prohibited. In ancient Greece, according to Frazer, "the names of the priests and other high officials who had to do with the performance of the Eleusinian mysteries might not be uttered in their lifetime. To pronounce them was a legal offense."[12] Jorgen Ruud reports in *Taboo: A Study of Malagasy Customs and Beliefs* that among the Antandroy people the father has absolute authority in his household and that "children are forbidden to mention the name of their father. They must call him father, daddy. . . . The children may not mention his house or the parts of his body by their ordinary names, but must use other terms, i.e., euphemisms."[13]

It was Iago who said in *Othello:*

Who steals my purse steals trash; 'tis something nothing;
'Twas mine, 'tis his, and has been slave to thousands;
But he that filches from me my good name

Robs me of that which not enriches him
And makes me poor indeed.

Alice, in Lewis Carroll's *Through the Looking Glass,* had trepidations about entering the woods where things were nameless: "This must be the wood," she said thoughtfully to herself, "where things have no names. I wonder what'll become of *my* name when I go in? I shouldn't like to lose it at all—because they'd have to give me another, and it would almost certain to be an ugly one."

A Nazi decree of August 17, 1938 stipulated that "Jews may receive only those first names which are listed in the directives of the Ministry of the Interior concerning the use of first names." Further, the decree provided: "If Jews should bear first names other than those permitted . . . they must . . . . adopt an additional name. For males, that name shall be Israel, for females Sara." Another Nazi decree forbade Jews in Germany "to show themselves in public without a Jew's star. . . . [consisting] of a six-pointed star of yellow cloth with black borders, equivalent in size to the palm of the hand. The inscription is to read 'JEW' in black letters. It is to be sewn to the left breast of the garment, and to be worn visibly."

The power which comes from names and naming is related directly to the power to define others—individuals, races, sexes, ethnic groups. Our identities, who and what we are, how others see us, are greatly affected by the names we are called and the words with which we are labelled. The names, labels, and phrases employed to "identify" a people may in the end determine their survival. The word "define" comes from the Latin *definire,* meaning to limit. Through definition we restrict, we set boundaries, we name.

"When I use a word," said Humpty Dumpty in *Through the Looking Glass,* "it means just what I choose it to mean—neither more nor less." "The question is," said Alice, "whether you can make words mean so many different things." "The question is," said Humpty Dumpty, "which is to be master—that's all."

During his days as a civil rights-black power activist, Stokely Carmichael accurately asserted: "It [definition] is very, very important because I believe that people who can define are masters."[14] Self-determination must include self-definition, the ability and right to name oneself; the master-subject relationship is based partly on the master's power to name and define the subject.

While names, words and language can be and are used to inspire us, to motivate us to humane acts, to liberate us, they can also be used to dehumanize human beings and to "justify" their suppression and even their extermination. It is not a great step from the coercive suppression of dissent to the extermination of dissenters (as the United States Supreme Court declared in its 1943 compulsory flag salute opinion in *West Virginia State Board of Education v. Barnette*); nor is it a large step from defining a people as non-human or sub-human to their subjugation or annihilation. One of the first acts of an oppressor is to redefine the "enemy" so they will be looked upon as creatures warranting separation, suppression, and even eradication.

The Nazis redefined Jews as "bacilli," "parasites," "disease," "demon," and "plague." In his essay "The Hollow Miracle," George Steiner informs us that the Germans "who poured quicklime down the openings of the sewers in Warsaw to kill the living and stifle the stink of the dead wrote about it. They spoke of having to 'liquidate vermin'. . . . Gradually, words lost their original meaning and acquired nightmarish definitions. *Jude, Pole, Russe* came to mean two-legged lice, putrid vermin which good Aryans must squash, as a [Nazi] Party manual said, 'like roaches on a dirty wall.' 'Final solution,' *endgültige Lösung,* came to signify the death of six million human beings in gas ovens."[15]

The language of white racism has for centuries been used to "keep the nigger in his place." Our sexist language has allowed men to define who and what a woman is and must be. Labels like "traitors," "saboteurs," "queers," and "obscene degenerates" were applied indiscriminately to students who protested the war in Vietnam or denounced injustices in the United States. Are such people to be listened to? Consulted? Argued with? Obviously not! One does not listen to, much less talk to, traitors and outlaws, sensualists and queers. One only punishes them or, as Spiro Agnew suggested in one of his 1970 speeches, there are some dissenters who should be separated "from our society with no more regret than we should feel over discarding rotten apples."[16]

What does it mean to separate people? When the Japanese-Americans were rounded up in 1942 and sent off to "relocation camps" they were "separated." The Jews in Nazi Germany were "separated." The Indians of the United States, the occupants of the New World before Columbus "discovered" it, have been systematically "separated." As "chattels" and slaves, the blacks in the United States were "separated"; legally a black person was a piece of property, although human enough to be counted as three-fifths of a person in computing the number of people represented by white legislators.

How is the forcible isolation of human beings from society at large justified? To make the separation process more palatable to the populace, what must the oppressor first do? How does he make the populace accept the separation of the "creatures," or, if not accept it, at least not protest it? Consideration of such questions is not an academic exercise without practical implications. There is a close nexus between language and self-perception, self-awareness, self-identity, and self-esteem. Just as our thoughts affect our language, so does our language affect our thoughts and eventually our actions and behavior. As Edward Sapir has observed, we are all "at the mercy of the particular language which has become the medium of expression" in our society. The "real world," he points out, "is to a large extent unconsciously built up on the language habits of the group. . . . We see and hear and otherwise experience very largely as we do because the language habits of our community predispose certain choices of interpretation."[17]

George Orwell has written in his famous essay "Politics and the English Language": "A man may take to drink because he feels himself to be a failure, and then fail all the more completely because he drinks. It is rather the same thing that is happening to the English language. It becomes ugly and inaccurate because our thoughts are foolish, but the slovenliness of our language makes it easier for us to have foolish thoughts."[18] Orwell maintains that "the decadence in our language is probably curable" and that "silly words and expressions have often disappeared, not through any evolutionary process but owing to the conscious action of a minority."[19] Wilma Scott Heide, speaking as president of the National Organization for Women several years ago, indicated that feminists were undertaking this conscious action: "In any social movement, when changes are effected, the language sooner or later reflects the change. Our approach is different. Instead of passively noting the change, we are changing language patterns to actively effect the changes, a significant part of which is the conceptual tool of thought, our language."[20]

This then is our task—to identify the decadence in our language, the inhumane uses of language, the "silly words and expressions" which have been used to justify the unjustifiable, to make palatable the unpalatable, to make reasonable the unreasonable, to make decent the indecent. Hitler's "Final Solution" appeared reasonable once the Jews were successfully labelled by the Nazis as sub-humans, as "parasites," "vermin," and "bacilli." The segregation and suppression of blacks in the United States was justified once they were considered "chattels" and "inferiors." The subjugation of the "American Indians" was defensible since they were defined as "barbarians" and "savages." As Peter Farb has said, "cannibalism, torture, scalping, mutilation, adultery, incest, sodomy, rape, filth, drunkenness—such a catalogue of accusations against a people is an indication not so much of their depravity as that their land is up for grabs."[21] As long as adult women are "chicks," "girls," "dolls," "babes," and "ladies," their status in society will remain "inferior"; they will go on being treated as subjects in the subject-master relationship as long as the language of the law places them into the same class as children, minors, and the insane.

It is my hope that an examination of the language of oppression will result in a conscious effort by the reader to help cure this decadence in our language, especially that language which leads to dehumanization of the human being. One way for us to curtail the use of the language of oppression is for those who find themselves being defined into subjugation to rebel against such linguistic suppression. It isn't strange that those persons who insist on defining themselves, who insist on this elemental privilege of self-naming, self-definition, and self-identity encounter vigorous resistance. Predictably, the resistance usually comes from the oppressor or would-be oppressor and is a result of the fact that he or she does not want to relinquish the power which comes from the ability to define others. . . .

Once one has identified the language of oppression and determined that it is instrumental in subjugating individuals and groups, that the power of the word has been and is used to justify the inhumanities and atrocities of the past and present, then it becomes necessary to consider appropriate remedies. We can no longer afford simply to stand by and say "Oh, they're only words." " 'A mere matter of words,' we say contemptuously," Aldous Huxley asserted, "forgetting that words have power to mould men's thinking, to canalize their feeling, to direct their willing and acting. Conduct and character are largely determined by the nature of the words we currently use to discuss ourselves and the world around us."[22]

The implications of all this is that if we can minimize the use of the language of oppression we can reduce the degradation and subjugation of human beings. If the nature of our language is oppressive and deceptive then our character and conduct will be different from that which would ensue from humane and honest use of language.

One option to control the distorted, deceptive, and dehumanizing language is to prohibit by law the utterance of such speech. We already have statutes and court decisions prohibiting "fighting words," "obscene" and libelous language. On various occasions the courts have determined that such types of speech can be harmful to either individuals or society and hence do not warrant First Amendment protection.

In 1940 the Supreme Court said in *Cantwell v. Connecticut* that "resort to epithets or personal abuse is not in any proper sense communication of information or opinion safeguarded by the Constitution, and its punishment as a criminal act would raise no question under that instrument."[23]

Two years later the Court elaborated in *Chaplinsky v. New Hampshire* the kinds of speech which could be prohibited: "There are certain well-defined and narrowly limited classes of speech, the prevention and punishment of which have never been thought to raise any constitutional problem. These included the lewd and obscene, the profane, the libelous, and the insulting or 'fighting words' . . . which by their very utterance inflict injury or tend to incite to an immediate breach of the peace. It has been well observed that such utterances are no essential part of any exposition of ideas, and are of such slight social value as a step to truth that any benefit that may be derived from them is clearly outweighed by the social interest in order and morality."[24]

The effects of language which denegrates and dehumanizes a group of people is no less damaging than the effects of "obscene" or libelous speech.

Attempts have been made through group libel laws to control the use of language which exposes citizens of any race, color, creed or religion "to contempt, derision, or obloquy." An Illinois statute which was upheld by the Supreme Court in 1952 (the statute was repealed in 1961) read: "It shall be unlawful for any person, firm or corporation to manufacture, sell or offer for sale, advertise or publish, present or exhibit in any public place in this state any lithograph, moving picture, play, drama, or sketch, which publication or exhibition portrays depravity, immorality, unchastity or lack of virtue of a class of citizens of any race, color, creed, or religion which said publication or exhibit exposes to contempt, derision, or obloquy or which produces breach of the peace or riots."

In *Beauharnais v. Illinois* the Supreme Court found against Beauharnais who had been convicted of unlawfully exhibiting "in public places lithographs, which publications portray depravity, criminality, unchastity or lack of virtue of citizens of Negro race and color and which exposes [*sic*] citizens of Illinois of the Negro race and color to contempt, derision, or obloquy. . . . The lithograph complained of was a leaflet setting forth a petition calling on the Mayor and City Council of Chicago 'to halt the further encroachment, harassment and invasion of white people, their property, neighborhood and persons, by the Negro. . . .' Below was a call for 'One million self respecting white people in Chicago to unity. . . .' with the statement added that 'if persuasion and the need to prevent the white race from becoming mongrelized by the Negro will not unite us, then the aggressions . . . rapes, robberies, knives, guns and marijuana of the Negro, surely will.' "[25]

In reviewing the history of racial conflicts and violence in Illinois, the Court stated that "in many of these outbreaks utterances of the character here in question, so the Illinois legislature could conclude, played a significant part."[26] Justice Frankfurter, speaking for the majority, concluded that "in the face of this history and its frequent obligato of extreme racial and religious propaganda, we would deny experience to say that the Illinois legislature was without reason in seeking ways to curb false or malicious defamation of racial and religious groups, made in public places and by means calculated to have a powerful emotional impact on those to whom it was presented."[27]

Four Justices dissented, including Hugo Black who warned: "This Act sets up a system of state censorship which is at war with the kind of free government envisioned by those who forced adoption of our Bill of Rights. The motives behind the state law may have been to do good. But the same can be said about most laws making opinions punishable as crimes. History indicates that urges to do good have led to the burning of books and even to the burning of 'witches.' "[28]

Justice Douglas also dissented, expressing some of the same concerns of Black and then warning of legislative encroachment on First Amendment rights:

"Today a white man stands convicted for protesting in unseemly language against our decisions invalidating restrictive covenants. Tomorrow a Negro will be hailed before a court for denouncing lynch law in heated terms. Farm laborers in the West who compete with field hands drifting up from Mexico; whites who feel the pressure of orientals; a minority which finds employment going to members of the dominant religious group—all of these are caught in the mesh of today's decision. Debate and argument even in the courtroom are not always calm and dispassionate. Emotions sway speakers and audiences alike. Intemperate speech is a distinctive characteristic of man. Hot heads blow off and release destructive energy in the process. They shout and rave, exaggerating weaknesses, magnifying error, viewing with alarm. So it has been from the beginning; and so it will be throughout time. The Framers of the Constitution knew human nature as well as we do. They too had lived in dangerous days; they too knew the suffocating influence of orthodoxy and standardized thought. They weighed the compulsions for restrained speech and thought against the abuses of liberty. They chose liberty. That should be our choice today no matter how distasteful to us the pamphlet of Beauharnais may be. It is true that this is only one decision which may later be distinguished or confined to narrow limits. But it represents a philosophy at war with the First Amendment—a constitutional interpretation which puts free speech under legislative thumb. It reflects an influence moving ever deeper into our society. It is notice to the legislatures that they have the power to control unpopular blocs. It is a warning to every minority that when the Constitution guarantees free speech it does not mean what it says."[29]

The effects of *Beauharnais* were minimal at best. James C. Brown and Carl L. Stern, referring to *Beauharnais* in their article dealing with group libel, wrote in 1964: "The hope that this long awaited legal ruling stirred in the hearts of defamation victims was vain. The decision produced no new similar legislation, nor has it produced increased litigation. In total effect, *Beauharnais* exists in a vacuum."[30]

In 1970 Professor Thomas I. Emerson of the Yale Law School observed that "little remains of the doctrinal structure of *Beauharnais.*"[31] It is his view that "our experience indicates that group libel laws are not the answer. In those States where they appear upon the statute books, they have rarely been used. The Illinois statute had, prior to *Beauharnais,* been before the courts only twice in the thirty years of its existence. Yet one cannot doubt that there had been countless violations."[32]

Group libel prohibitions would not only be difficult to square with our First Amendment rights, but would be almost impossible to define and circumscribe. Some of our significant and influential literature includes passages and language which deprecate or "defame" races, sexes, religious and ethnic groups. Shall *Mein Kampf* be banned from our bookstores and libraries? Shall the film *Birth of a Nation* be censored or possibly destroyed? Shall the dramatic production of *The Merchant of Venice* be prohibited? Civil libertarian John de J. Pemberton, Jr. concludes his questioning article "Can the Law Provide a Remedy for Race Defamation in the United States?" with the answer: "Despite the enormous risks inherent in uninhibited speech about racial, ethnic and religious groups, the risks in suppressing such speech are ultimately much greater."[33] The solution to the problem of the language of oppression does not lie in the legislatures or the courts.[34]

Hence, given the fact that we will always have with us power-seekers and tyrants, some petty and others extremely dangerous, who will use deceptive and inhumane language to gain and sustain power, and given that legal prohibitions are noxious to and futile in a free society, we have to turn to other means for minimizing the uses and effects of denegrating verbal assaults.

There is considerable truth and applicability here to Anselm Bellegarrigue's observation that "in the end there are no tyrants, only slaves."[35] An oppressed group, or a group in the process of being subjugated, has some power to free itself from injustice and tyrannical rule. Those who find themselves being defined into an "inferior" status have the option to resist the efforts of others to gain linguistic superiority over them. This usually is not an easy task since the oppressor will not voluntarily relinquish the power that comes from the ability to define others. But as Orwell has indicated . . . decadent language has been controlled by concerted efforts of minorities. The efforts by blacks in the 1960s to define themselves was one important strike against their white oppressors. Women during the 1970s have become freer human beings as a result of their concerted efforts to eradicate oppressive language used for so long to justify their second-class status.

Linguistic assaults often are used by persons who show no visible evil intent. While their motivations may not be to deprecate, the effects of what they say are damaging. Efforts must be made to make such people conscious that their speech is degrading to other human beings.

More difficult to reach are those who take the "What difference does it make?" attitude. They do not recognize that the negative labels we attach to people and groups have effects on their identities and perhaps their survival. Those with this attitude scoff at the need to stop calling women "chicks," "babes," "ladies," and "girls." These people see nothing wrong with labels like "colored folks," "boy," and "nigger." They cannot understand why "American Indians" resent being portrayed as savages, heathens, and barbarians. To simply point out the oppressive nature of their language to these individuals is not enough; they must be persuaded that such language is dangerous and has far-reaching implications involving inconsiderate treatment of fellow human beings.

These two groups—those who will discard their suppressive language if it is identified for them and those who will alter the language if persuaded of the viciousness of such speech—constitute a large part of the population. Their power to influence still others cannot be minimized, especially if their occupations place them in positions where they can institute a variety of sanctions on the uses of the language of oppression. Publishers, personnel managers, judges, teachers, students, librarians, educational administrators, and television producers should discourage the use of defamatory and dehumanizing language.

In 1971 the National Council of Teachers of English passed several resolutions regarding the need to define and isolate the language of distortion and oppression. One of the resolutions pointed to the need to detect "dishonest and inhumane uses of language and literature by advertisers." Another resolution urged teachers "to study the relation of language to public policy, to keep track of, publicize, and combat semantic distortion by public officials, candidates for office, political commentators, and all those who transmit through the media."[36]

In 1972 the Council established a Committee on Public Double-speak which was charged "(1) to create a series of concrete classroom exercises (lesson plans, discussion outlines) which would focus students' attention on irresponsible uses of language; and (2) to alert the profession generally to the forces that in the committee's judgment are misusing language: government and its military, industry and its advertisers, educators, you and me."[37]

Leading publishing houses are now consciously trying to keep sexist and racist language out of their textbooks. The *New York Times* reported on September 12, 1974 that "a new, nonsexist era is dawning at McGraw-Hill, one of the world's largest publishing houses. In a sweeping assault on 'sexist assumptions,' the company will try to eliminate male-female stereotypes from its nonfiction publications—textbooks, reference works, trade journals, children's books and educational materials—to provide 'fair, accurate and balanced treatment of both sexes.' "[38]

The McGraw-Hill guidelines "prescribes highly specific changes in the description and characterization of women, and in the depiction of sexual roles. A list of forbidden phrases includes 'the fair sex,' 'the better half,' and 'the girls or the little women,' and lists such forms as 'suffragette,' 'usherette' and 'aviatrix.' 'Co-ed' should be changed to 'student' and 'sweet young thing' to 'young woman,' the guidelines say."[39]

In 1974 Lippincott's educational publishing division decided to revise its basic series of reading textbooks with the intent to minimize the sexual and racial biases in school curriculum materials. Lippincott editor Lozelle J. DeLuz conceded that several stories in the series have included ethnic slurs about the American Indian and have made him "seem less civilized than the white man."[40]

Educators like Lillian Rosen at Public School 183 in New York City began in 1974 to consciously eradicate from classroom study the negative and dehumanizing stereotyping of Indians.[41]

Officials in governmental agencies can take a lesson from Casper Weinberger, Secretary of Health, Education and Welfare, who in May 1974 ordered "that all references to the sex of workers be deleted from employee rating forms. One form by which the 139,000 department employees are rated annually by their supervisors contains repeated references to 'he,' 'his,' or 'himself' while making no references to females."[42]

To those who take the position that efforts to change the images and status of human beings by altering language is self-defeating and perhaps futile, McGraw-Hill Associate Editor Timothy Yohn answers:

"The reality that concerns us lies in the perceptions of the small children and young people who are ultimate recipients of the material in many of our publications—their perceptions and the values these instill. From a very early age, children in this society are conditioned to accept the role models arbitrarily assigned on the basis of gender. In our opinion, this fact operates to prevent members of both sexes, but particularly women, from realizing the full potential of their talents and their humanity. One aim of the guidelines, but not the only one, is to alert our authors and editors to the role of language in this inhibitory mechanism. An examination of our publications showed sexism to be widespread and deeply embedded in language."[43]

Such efforts will inevitably have positive effects on individuals who are persuaded that there is a viciousness in using the language of oppression. There are, however, some people who derive a psychological lift from using language which degrades others.

Little is achieved with this group by pointing out their use of verbal insults and inhumane language or the tragic effects of such speech. Their status in life is too interwoven and dependent on designating others as inferior; their failures in life and their anxieties demand scapegoats. Because of their insecurity, some men cannot give up the put-downs "chick," "broad," or "girl." Some whites cannot linguistically treat blacks as equals; these whites psychologically need to express their resentments and suspicions for ego gratification. Hitler filled the disillusioned, anxiety-ridden Germans with a sense of superiority by creating the Jew as "vermin" and "pestilence."

The empty lives of so many people unfortunately need to be supported with a sense of superiority which cannot be achieved through their accomplishments; hence the turn to verbal deprecation of others. The malaise of these people is an invitation to the agitator who can identify for them their imagined sources of trouble: the "mongrelizing Negroes," the "Jewish plague," the "barbaric drunken Indians." Having dehumanized these "enemies," the agitator then proceeds to suggest that all will be well if these sub-humans or non-humans are segregated or even eradicated.[44]

Supreme Court Justice Tom Clark, speaking of the language of group defamation, declared in 1964 that "we cannot expect the judicial process to control such utterances. Heads get too hot and evil too rampant. The *final* control must await the elimination of the three I's of this evil: Intolerance, Ignorance, and Ignobility. They *can* be destroyed. They are not the inevitable results of increased social intercourse. They are not inherited—they are acquired. They cannot be legislated or decreed into the hearts and minds of men. It is for us—in the words of George Washington—'To bigotry, give no sanction.' "[45]

If "Intolerance, Ignorance, and Ignobility" are acquired then their destruction can partially be achieved by the eradication of the language of oppression since "the three I's" are not only reflected in our language but are aggravated by the learned language of deception and dehumanization. For those who wish to help achieve and live in a more linguistically humane world it is within their power to give no sanction to the language of bigotry.

NOTES

1. Margaret Schlauch, *The Gift of Language* (New York: Dover, 1955), p. 13.
2. *Genesis* 2:19.
3. *Leviticus* 19:12.
4. *Leviticus* 25:16.
5. *Isaiah* 65:11–12.
6. William Saroyan, "Random Notes on the Names of People," *Names,* 1 (December 1953), p. 239.
7. Joyce Hertzler, *The Sociology of Language* (New York: Random House, 1965), p. 271.
8. Farhang Zabeeth, *What Is In a Name?* (The Hague: Martinus Nijhoff, 1968), p. 66.
9. Cited in Elsdom Smith, *Treasury of Name Lore* (New York: Harper and Row, 1967), p. vii.
10. R. P. Masani, *Folk Culture Reflected in Names* (Bombay: Popular Prakashan, 1966), p. 6.
11. James Frazer, *The Golden Bough* (New York: Macmillan, 1951), p. 284.
12. *Ibid.,* p. 302.
13. Jorgen Ruud, *Taboo: A Study of Malagasy Customs and Beliefs* (Oslo: Oslo University Press, 1960), p. 15.
14. Stokely Carmichael, speech delivered in Seattle, Washington, April 19, 1967.
15. George Steiner, *Language and Silence* (New York: Antheneum, 1970), p. 100.
16. *New York Times,* October 21, 1969, p. 25.
17. Cited in John Carroll (ed.), *Language, Thought and Reality: Selected Writings of Benjamin Lee Whorf* (Cambridge, MA: The MIT Press, 1956), p. 134.
18. George Orwell, "Politics and the English Language," in *The Borzoi Reader,* C. Muscatine and M. Griffith, eds., 2nd ed. (New York: Alfred A. Knopf, 1971), p. 88.
19. *Ibid.*

20. Wilma Scott Heide, "Feminism: The Sina Qua Non for a Just Society," *Vital Speeches*, 38 (1972), p. 402.

21. Peter Farb, "Indian Corn," *The New York Review*, 17 (December 16, 1971), p. 36.

22. Aldous Huxley, *Words and Their Meanings* (Los Angeles: The Ward Ritchie Press, 1940), p. 9.

23. *Cantwell v. Connecticut*, 310 U.S. 296, 310, 311 (1940).

24. *Chaplinsky v. New Hampshire*, 315 U.S. 568, 571 (1942).

25. *Beauharnais v. Illinois*, 343 U.S. 250, 252 (1952).

26. *Ibid.*, p. 259.

27. *Ibid.*, p. 261.

28. *Ibid.*, p. 274.

29. *Ibid.*, pp. 286–87.

30. James C. Brown and Carl L. Stern, "Group Defamation in the U.S.A.," *Cleveland-Marshall Law Review*, 13 (January 1964), p. 19.

31. Thomas I. Emerson, *The System of Freedom of Expression* (New York: Random House, 1970), p. 396.

32. *Ibid.*, p. 399.

33. John de J. Pemberton, Jr., "Can the Law Provide a Remedy for Race Defamation in the United States?" *New York Law Forum*, 14 (Spring 1968), p. 48.

34. However, see David Fryer, "Group Defamation in England"; Manfred Zuleeg, "Group Defamation in West Germany"; Jean Peytel, "Group Defamation in France"; W. H. Bijleveld, "Group Defamation in the Netherlands" in *Cleveland-Marshall Law Review*, 13 (January 1964), pp. 33–94 for discussions of how group defamation laws have and are applied in other countries. See also Horace Kallen, " 'Group Libel' and Equal Liberty"; Anthony Dickey, "English Law and Race Defamation"; John de J. Pemberton, Jr., "Can the Law Provide a Remedy for Race Defamation in the United States?" Nathan Lerner, "International Definitions of Incitement to Racial Hatred," *New York Law Forum*, 14 (Spring 1968), pp. 1–59.

35. Cited in Mulford Q. Sibley (ed.), *The Quiet Battle* (Chicago: Quadrangle Books, 1963), p. 96.

36. "On Dishonest and Inhumane Uses of Language," and "On the Relation of Language to Public Policy," *College English*, 33 (April 1972), p. 828.

37. *Public Doublespeak Newsletter*, Spring 1974, p. 1.

38. Grace Glueck, "McGraw Hill Bars Sexism in Nonfiction," *New York Times*, September 12, 1974, p. 46.

39. *Ibid.*

40. Carole Martin, "Textbooks Are Due for Change," *Seattle Post-Intelligencer*, February 20, 1974, p. B7.

41. Richard Flaste, "American Indians: Still a Stereotype to Many Children," *New York Times*, September 27, 1974, p. 46.

42. *New York Times,* May 8, 1974.

43. Timothy Yohn, "Sexism in Everyday Language," *Washington Post*, October 9, 1974.

44. See Leo Lowenthal and Norbert Guterman, *Prophets of Deceit* (Palo Alto, CA: Pacific Books, 1970).

45. Tom Clark, "The Problem of Group Defamation," *Cleveland-Marshall Law Review*, 13 (January 1964), p. 3.

Teotihuacán*

CAROLE STONE

Cortes marched from Vera Cruz,
bringing horses and guns.
The Aztecs welcomed him, Quetzalcoatl,
the fair-haired god, risen from the flames.

Near the Pemex oil fields,
stone temples climb into the sky.
I ascend the steep narrow stairs
into thin polluted air

and rest in the shade of a pillar,
fleeing from the same sun that fed
on Aztec hearts and fired
Spanish armor, sacks of gold.

In this highest light,
the blood of old supplications
blazes up,
a language full of killing.

"If Black English Ain't a Language, Then Tell Me What Is?"

JAMES BALDWIN

The argument concerning the use, or the status, or the reality, of black English is rooted in American history and has absolutely nothing to do with the question the argument supposes itself to be posing. The argument has nothing to do with language itself but with

---

* Teotihuacán (Nahuatl meaning: "Where men become gods") is one of the most important and largest cities of pre-Columbian central Mexico, located thirty-three miles north of Mexico City. It contains the pyramids of the sun and the moon.

the role of language. Language, incontestably, reveals the speaker. Language, also, far more dubiously, is meant to define the other—and, in this case, the other is refusing to be defined by a language that has never been able to recognize him.

People evolve a language in order to describe and thus control their circumstances or in order not to be submerged by a situation that they cannot articulate. (And if they cannot articulate it, they are submerged.) A Frenchman living in Paris speaks a subtly and crucially different language from that of the man living in Marseilles; neither sounds very much like a man living in Quebec; and they would all have great difficulty in apprehending what the man from Guadeloupe, or Martinique, is saying, to say nothing of the man from Senegal—although the "common" language of all these areas is French. But each has paid, and is paying, a different price for this "common" language, in which, as it turns out, they are not saying, and cannot be saying, the same things: They each have very different realities to articulate, or control.

What joins all languages, and all men, is the necessity to confront life, in order, not inconceivably, to outwit death: The price for this is the acceptance, and achievement, of one's temporal identity. So that, for example, though it is not taught in the schools (and this has the potential of becoming a political issue) the south of France still clings to its ancient and musical Provençal, which resists being described as a "dialect." And much of the tension in the Basque countries, and in Wales, is due to the Basque and Welsh determination not to allow their languages to be destroyed. This determination also feeds the flames in Ireland for among the many indignities the Irish have been forced to undergo at English hands is the English contempt for their language.

It goes without saying, then, that language is also a political instrument, means, and proof of power. It is the most vivid and crucial key to identity: It reveals the private identity, and connects one with, or divorces one from, the larger, public, or communal identity. There have been, and are, times and places, when to speak a certain language could be dangerous, even fatal. Or, one may speak the same language, but in such a way that one's antecedents are revealed, or (one hopes) hidden. This is true in France, and is absolutely true in England: The range (and reign) of accents on that damp little island make England coherent for the English and totally incomprehensible for everyone else. To open your mouth in England is (if I may use black English) to "put your business in the street." You have confessed your parents, your youth, your school, your salary, your self-esteem, and, alas, your future.

Now, I do not know what white Americans would sound like if there had never been any black people in the United States, but they would not sound the way they sound. *Jazz,* for example, is a very specific sexual term, as in *jazz me, baby,* but white people purified it into the Jazz Age. *Sock it to me,* which means, roughly, the same thing, has been adopted by Nathaniel Hawthorne's descendants with no qualms or hesitations at all, along with *let it all hang out* and *right on! Beat to his socks,* which was once the black's most total and despairing image of poverty, was transformed into a thing called the Beat Generation, which phenomenon was, largely, composed of *uptight,* middle-class white people, imitating poverty, trying to *get down,* to get *with it,* doing their *thing,* doing their despairing best to be *funky,* which we, the blacks, never dreamed of doing—we were funky, baby, like *funk* was going out of style.

Now, no one can eat his cake, and have it, too, and it is late in the day to attempt to penalize black people for having created a language that permits the nation its only glimpse of reality, a language without which the nation would be even more *whipped* than it is.

I say that the present skirmish is rooted in American history, and it is. Black English is the creation of the black diaspora. Blacks came to the United States chained to each other, but from different tribes. Neither could speak the other's language. If two black people, at that bitter hour of the world's history, had been able to speak to each other, the institution of chattel slavery could never have lasted as long as it did. Subsequently, the slave was given, under the eye, and the gun, of his master, Congo Square, and the Bible—or, in other words, and under those conditions, the slave began the formation of the black church, and it is within this unprecedented tabernacle that black English began to be formed. This was not, merely, as in the European example, the adoption of a foreign tongue, but an alchemy that transformed ancient elements into a new language: *A language comes into existence by means of brutal necessity, and the rules of the language are dictated by what the language must convey.*

There was a moment, in time, and in this place, when my brother, or my mother, or my father, or my sister, had to convey to me, for example, the danger in which I was standing from the white man standing just behind me, and to convey this with a speed and in a language, that the white man could not possibly understand, and that, indeed, he cannot understand, until today. He cannot afford to understand it. This understanding would reveal to him too much about himself and smash that mirror before which he has been frozen for so long.

Now, if this passion, this skill, this (to quote Toni Morrison) "sheer intelligence," this incredible music, the mighty achievement of having brought a people utterly unknown to, or despised by "history" —to have brought this people to their present, troubled, troubling, and unassailable and unanswerable place—if this absolutely unprecedented journey does not indicate that black English is a language, I am curious to know what definition of languages is to be trusted.

A people at the center of the western world, and in the midst of so hostile a population, has not endured and transcended by means of what is patronizingly called a "dialect." We, the blacks, are in trouble, certainly, but we are not inarticulate because we are not compelled to defend a morality that we know to be a lie.

The brutal truth is that the bulk of the white people in America never had any interest in educating black people, except as this could serve white purposes. It is not the black child's language that is despised. It is his experience. A child cannot be taught by anyone who despises him, and a child cannot afford to be fooled. A child cannot be taught by anyone whose demand, essentially, is that the child repudiate his experience, and all that gives him sustenance, and enter a limbo in which he will no longer be black, and in which he knows that he can never become white. Black people have lost too many black children that way.

And, after all, finally, in a country with standards so untrustworthy, a country that makes heroes of so many criminal mediocrities, a country unable to face why so many of the nonwhite are in prison, or on the needle, or standing, futureless, in the streets—it may very well be that both the child, and his elder, have concluded that they have nothing whatever to learn from the people of a country that has managed to learn so little.

From The Gaia Atlas of First Peoples: *"Cultural Collapse"*

JULIAN BURGER

"As we approach the 21st century (as the White man reckons time), we Indians are desperately seeking ways to maintain our tribal identities and ways to survive as distinct cultural entities."

—REUBEN SNAKE,
Winnebago Indian

"Next to shooting indigenous peoples, the surest way to kill us is to separate us from our part of the Earth. Once separated, we will either perish in body or our minds and spirits will be altered so that we end up mimicking foreign ways, adopt foreign languages, accept foreign thoughts. . . . Over time, we lose our identity and . . . eventually die or are crippled as we are stuffed under the name of 'assimilation' into another society."

—HAYDEN BURGESS,
World Council of Indigenous Peoples

"An Indian without land is a dead Indian and an ethnic community without a language is a dying community."

—RODOLFO STAVENHAGEN

"Without my language I couldn't possibly understand my culture and its values. I was denied what is essentially a basic human right—access to myself. Now we've got to change that."

—CATHY DEWES, *Maori teacher*

"We do not wish to destroy your religion, or take it from you. We only want to enjoy our own."

—RED JACKET, *Iroquois*

"I remember my mother very well. She used to sit there smoking a pipe, sewing and chatting to us about a variety of things in our own language. My father would wake me early in the morning and we would go fishing. I used to wade into the water up to my waist to scoop up the salmon he would catch. Then we would go home and teach the younger ones how to clean the fish. Then my father would sing and dance."

—SUSIE BEAR, *1988*

"How can you respect yourself if you don't know who you are? I have taught my children the only way I know which was the way my mother taught me and I have lived it to the best of my ability. The quality of future life depends on how we demonstrate our beliefs to our children."

—MARIE WILSON, *elder of the Gitksan Nation*

"When an Aboriginal man or woman cannot walk into a hotel or a shop or anywhere without getting stared at, without getting called, 'black bastards, coons, heathens, savages, lazy, shiftless, stupid, dirty, filthy niggers'—this is violence."

—*Gwalwa Daraniki Association*

"only the white . . . think that their race has the key to cultural development, or that we, only by intermarrying with them, can improve our quality as human beings. This way of thinking is a totally outrageous offence to the dignity of our people."

—Council of *Amaut'as,* Bolivia

"The land is the physical and spiritual core that binds communities together. When indigenous peoples lose their land, they lose their language, their complex social and political systems, and their knowledge. At a deeper level traditions are eroded with their sacred beliefs. Although some may integrate and recover meaning to their lives, the removal of first peoples from their land can be likened to genocide in slow motion."

—JULIAN BURGER

From The Gaia Atlas of First Peoples: *"Missionary Childhood"*

SHARON VENNE of the Cree Nation

> *. . . loss of identity is accelerated by loss of language. Indigenous languages are rarely, if ever, given legal recognition and in many cases are banned in schools. Less than five per cent of Maori school children now speak their own language. In Canada, Cree children in the past forbidden to speak their own language at school developed psychological and learning problems. Language is a means of transmitting oral knowledge of myths, history, cultural tradition, and the natural world. By separating young children from their parents the destructive process of assimilation has been accelerated. In Indonesia the government has declared it will remove tribal children from their homes "to keep them from settling into their parents' lifestyle."*
>
> —Julian Burger, *The Gaia Atlas of First Peoples*

The other children were taken into the residential school at 5 and 6 years. I was lucky, I went at 9. And my grandmother raised me in the traditional way, so I had a strong sense of identity. I only spoke Cree, not a word of English.

In the school we were not allowed to speak our own language or practise our religion. Nor were we allowed to talk to our own relatives, especially the boys. The ceremonies we have at the age of puberty which celebrate the change from childhood to adulthood were denied us. It was as if we were not human beings. We are a very affectionate people; we walk arm in arm and so on. These gestures were completely forbidden. They did their best to make you lose your self-esteem, your sense of being Indian.

When we did not obey the rules we were hit and pushed and shouted at. This was a shock because in our community we do not raise our voice at children or hit them. And to punish us they would cut our hair because they know it would bring shame for a long time. So we were afraid even to speak our language.

Under the treaties, schools had been set up on reserves, but the missionaries complained that we kept up our old ways, spoke our own language, practised our religion. So in 1886 the government established residential schools a long way from the reserves to make sure we were assimilated. For the next 80 years all Indian children from the age of 6 to 16 were taken from their families and brought up in these institutions run by the Churches. In 1969 the system was ended but the nightmare goes on. Even today, when I see a nun I freeze inside. The legacy is with us still. We are dealing with the problems today; people who have lost direction, had their culture denigrated. Of the group of girls in my grade at the residential school, only I am still alive. I am 38 years old.

African Language Writing

PHYLLIS BISCHOF

African language writing, first seen in the work of missionaries who tried to reach potential converts in their own languages, has become controversial for a number of reasons. The missionaries were right in their judgment of how to reach people, of course, for even today, most African people do not speak Western languages. When African writers have written in Western languages, no matter how seditiously, African governments have not for the most part interfered with them. But we do see a marked difference when these same writers write the same words in an African tongue.

Kenya's Ngugi wa Thiongo was arrested and jailed only at the moment he abandoned English and began to write in his mother tongue, Gikuyu. Imprisoned for a year because of his play *Ngaahika Ndeenda* (*I Will Marry When I Want*) and later denied a return to teaching at the University of Nairobi, Ngugi was subsequently driven into exile without his family, where he has remained for the past six to seven years. He spoke recently at U.C. Berkeley on the subject of writing in African languages, which he continues to support eloquently at great personal cost.

You may wonder just what sort of explosive rhetoric qualified Ngugi for the harsh censorship he has received: Hence, I quote briefly from the text of his play:

All: The trumpet of the poor has been blown.

Let's unite and organize.
Organization is our club.
Organization is our sword.
Organization is our gun.
Organization is our shield.
Organization is our way.
Organization is our strength.
The trumpet of the masses has been blown . . .

African language publishing is controversial, however, for reasons other than its potential to reach the masses, approximately 65 percent of whom are still illiterate, and very few of whom speak Western languages. It is also controversial because it tends to be uneconomical. Africa is a marvelously rich linguistic area. Out of 3,000 major world languages, Africa accounts for well over 1,200, with about 600 transcribed. S. I. A. Kotei writes in *Publishing in Africa in the Seventies* that "Nigeria alone accounts for 200, Ghana 30, and Sierra Leone, with a population of only 2 million, has 18, not of course counting dialects. The complexity of African language phonology and grammar is yet another hindrance to publishing. One expert claims to have recognized 57 different tense forms in Yoruba alone." Yoruba's multiplicity of tense forms has not, however, prevented a flourishing in the publication of Yoruba books and pamphlets on every conceivable subject.

The abundance of African languages means that for all but the largest populations (such as Nigeria's Yoruba, and Swahili speakers in East Africa), African language publication print runs will inevitably be smaller than ever, financing harder to acquire, and a reading audience abroad will necessarily be forgone, at least until translations appear.

Writing in the African languages does appear to be on the increase, and as desktop publishing reaches the African scene, smaller press runs may permit an easier publication of works directed toward smaller reading populations. The third edition of *African Books in Print* states: "Over 4,000 titles, or some 23 percent of all records in this edition are in 102 African languages, including more than 1,000 titles of African literatures. However, there are weaknesses in several language areas, such as Amharic, or especially for southern African languages. The most represented languages are Kiswahili, Yoruba, Hausa, Igbo, Zulu, Twi, Malagasy, Shona and Ndebele."

If a writer chooses to write in a Western language, this has usually meant that writing is done in a second language, not the one in which a person dreams and sings. This means a potential loss of literary power and persuasiveness, and the intimate connection with the culture the writer seeks to express may be lost.

From "Breaking the Silence: Strategic Imperatives for Preserving Culture"

ROBERT VISCUSI

> *Until yesterday I was among folks who understood me. This morning I seemed to have awakened in a land where my language meant little more to the native (as far as meaning was concerned) than the pitiful noises of a dumb animal. Where was I to go? What was I to do? Here was the promised land. The elevated rattled by and did not answer. The automobiles and trolley sped by, heedless of me.*
> —Bartolomeo Vanzetti

The language spoken by poor and regional populations in . . . Italy has been the instrument of their suppression for hundreds of years. [This is so for all minority populations who have their own language colonized by a majority's tongue.] This history of suppression has two phases. In the first phase, the rich learned standard literary Tuscan in school, erecting a wall of shibboleth that excluded everyone else from serious discursive power. That practice prevailed for centuries, but in the present it has been supplanted by the new method of forcing everyone to speak the standard dialect. The modern policy gives to native speakers of regional languages indisputable access to a measure of central power, but it exacts as a price most of their own local linguistic self-possession. Though these approaches work differently, both have the effect of weakening the authority of discourse anywhere except in the centers—here local and standard may be seen to coalesce, as in the formula *lingua toscana in bocca romana*. To these Italian deprivations has in the United States been added the cataclysm suffered by Italian migrants and their offspring when entering the order of English, a language with its own walls of shibboleth— walls that have required, for most families, two or three generations even to approach, much less surmount. Then, one would need to follow as well the effects of Italian Fascism upon the freedom of speech in Italian America, and the devastating impact of the war upon such prestige as the speaking of Italian may still have possessed in the United States. What has been the effect of all these deprivations but silence? And what is such silence but degradation? The contemporary Sicilian poet Ignazio Buttita writes

Un popolu,	A nation
diventa poviru e servu,	turns poor and servile
quannu ci arrobbanu a lingua	when they steal its language
addutata di patri:	handed down by its fathers;
è persu pi sempri.	it is lost forever.

Forever is a strong word. While we are entitled to hope that it will turn out to have been too strong for the future that awaits us, such an outcome is scarcely certain. For it is plain that Italian America much resembles a nation whose language has been stolen from it. We are all proud of our famous crooners and divas and actors and actresses, no doubt, but we do not look to them for the power of utterance. Characteristically, they are the instruments of other people's words. Likewise, no number of brilliant artists, architects, designers, business executives, dancers, musicians, composers, or cinematographers can break the silence with which we are afflicted. When we look for discursive power, we find a prospect relieved by very few figures indeed. It is good to report that we are not totally speechless. The governor of the State of New York has made genuine contributions to the language of American politics. The literary theorist Frank Lentricchia has developed powerful methods for using criticism as form of social action. But these and a handful of others one might name do not constitute a thriving tradition of discursive power. And this is what we require. . . .

What is discursive power? It is the capacity for authoritative speech. Persons who possess it are able to use language to deal with their personal, social, and political problems. Persons who lack discursive power are often reduced to servile responses—to violence or to dumbshow—when confronted with serious personal, social, or political problems. None of these is a satisfactory way to deal with a complex or threatening situation. . . .

Discursive power, on the contrary, allows its possessors to grapple directly with the problems that confront them.

While we can simply define this power as the capacity for authoritative speech, we must immediately problematize the definition by pointing to the complex structure of this power. We can do this readily enough by saying that discursive power requires or subsumes three distinct, though overlapping, possessions: these are a *language*, a *narrative*, and a *dialectics*.

Italian America must be bilingual. This is basic. While it is true that the achievement of linguistic competency in English has exercised the energies of two and even four generations in many families, it is also true that a nation which loses its language is itself lost. The language of Italian America is not English. Neither is it Italian, but an interlingual diglossic speech that passes freely between these two. The widespread attainment of bilingualism may appear an unrealistic goal. *Unrealistic*, in this as in many cases, is merely another word for *difficult*. . . .

Italian Americans often still recognize some lost strength in the lost language they mildly invoke. However, such desire as most people feel has not often enough resulted in an understanding that for Italian America bilingualism is a strategic imperative.

Why *imperative*? Italian names can only be read in Italian. In English they became other names. Italian contemporaries can only be spoken with in Italian, or at best in diglot. Without Italian interlocutors, we are disconnected from not only our roots but our branches as well.

"But English is good enough for us," some people say. If they are content to be identified as Italian Americans but to have no way to respond to Italian American problems *as* Italian Americans, then English *is* good enough for them. If their dialect for social problems can be the taxonomic monologue of the social sciences, then they must rest comfortable in the categories assigned to them by this monologue. But if they wish to escape this objectification, then they need to be able to speak with their own tongues. And those tongues are, by history itself, decreed to be forked. To be Italian Americans we must speak the diglot.

Perhaps the most powerful reason, if not the most convincing, to regard Italian as an imperative is the motive of pleasure. . . .

There is an enormous satisfaction, analogous to what we derive from the light of the sun, that comes from speaking the language in which one's own name is a word. . . .

The history of a people, considered in the fullest sense, is a narrative of its collective purpose. Clearly, given such a definition, the history of a people is always and everywhere impossible. Collective purpose, since it does not exist except as an abstraction, is incapable of full representation. However, fullness is not required for authority. What is required is articulation. To articulate a collective purpose *is* possible. To articulate such a purpose as narrative is history.

There is also the vast increase in assurance that belongs to a people that can read both sides of the page in its own history. Imagine a Jewish people in which hardly anyone could read Aramaic or Hebrew. But that is hard to imagine, because the Jewish people has been extremely attentive to the role of its own languages in sustaining its authority as a people, even under the worst possible historical conditions. Only that assurance and that authority enable a people to confront the contradictions in its own situation. . . .

Dialectics. Without contraries [there] is no progression. But Italian America has cultivated that monotone cheerfulness which experienced observers always know for the clearest sign of uncertainty and stasis. Such fears, I should add, have not always ruled the forum. In the first four or even five decades of this century, when Italian America was still predominantly bilingual, it still possessed a lively tradition of dialectic, of internal critique. It had not forgotten the social inequities that had driven its people out of Italy. It still could hear the debates of class and culture that were continuing to emerge from the powerful struggles taking place there. One may reflect that two of the most effective oppositional voices in that period in the United States belonged to Italian Americans—the anarchist editor Carlo Tresca and the American Labor Party's one vote in the House of Representatives, the member from Italian Harlem Vito Marcantonio. That each of these has recently been the subject of a biography by a scholar not of Italian descent is not only a compliment to their historical importance for the United States but also a suggestion that Sal La Gumina, who in the early 1970s published serious studies of Marcantonio, has not had all the honor he might deserve from younger generations of Italian American scholars. We can never study carefully enough the oppositional clarities of Marcantonio or Di Donato, Giovanitti or Tresca. But it is fair to say that the dialectical tradition in Italian America that produced these clarities has been muted in recent years.

The Old Italians Dying

LAWRENCE FERLINGHETTI

For years the old Italians have been dying
all over America
For years the old Italians in faded felt hats
have been sunning themselves and dying
You have seen them on the benches
in the park in Washington Square
the old Italians in their black high button shoes
the old men in their old felt fedoras
                    with stained hatbands
have been dying and dying
                    day by day
You have seen them
every day in Washington Square San Francisco
the slow bell
tolls in the morning
in the Church of Peter & Paul
in the marzipan church on the plaza
toward ten in the morning the slow bell tolls
in the towers of Peter & Paul
and the old men who are still alive
sit sunning themselves in a row
on the wood benches in the park
and watch the processions in and out
funerals in the morning
weddings in the afternoon

slow bell in the morning Fast bell at noon
In one door out the other
the old men sit there in their hats
and watch the coming & going
You have seen them
the ones who feed the pigeons
                    cutting the stale bread
                          with their thumbs & penknives
the ones with old pocketwatches
the old ones with gnarled hands
                          and wild eyebrows
the ones with the baggy pants
                          with both belt & suspenders
the grappa drinkers with teeth like corn
the Piemontesi the Genovesi the Siciliani
                    smelling of garlic & pepperoni
the ones who loved Mussolini
the old fascists
the ones who loved Garibaldi
the old anarchists reading *L'Umanita Nova*
the ones who loved Sacco & Vanzetti
They are almost all gone now
They are sitting and waiting their turn
and sunning themselves in front of the church
over the doors of which is inscribed
a phrase which would seem to be unfinished
from Dante's *Paradiso*
about the glory of the One
                    who moves everything . . .
The old men are waiting
for it to be finished
for their glorious sentence on earth
                    to be finished
the slow bell tolls & tolls
the pigeons strut about
not even thinking of flying
the air too heavy with heavy tolling
The black hired hearses draw up
the black limousines with black windowshades

shielding the widows
the widows with the long black veils
who will outlive them all
You have seen them
madre di terra, madre di mare
The widows climb out of the limousines
The family mourners step out in stiff suits
The widows walk so slowly
up the steps of the cathedral
fishnet veils drawn down
leaning hard on darkcloth arms
Their faces do not fall apart
They are merely drawn apart
They are still the matriarchs
outliving everyone
the old dagos dying out
in Little Italys all over America
the old dead dagos
hauled out in the morning sun
that does not mourn for anyone
One by one Year by year
they are carried out
The bell
never stops tolling
The old Italians with lapstrake faces
are hauled out of the hearses
by the paid pallbearers
in mafioso mourning coats & dark glasses
The old dead men are hauled out
in their black coffins like small skiffs
They enter the true church
for the first time in many years
in these carved black boats
           ready to be ferried over
The priests scurry about
          as if to cast off the lines
The other old men
            still alive on the benches
watch it all with their hats on

You have seen them sitting there
waiting for the bocci ball to stop rolling
waiting for the bell
                    to stop tolling & tolling
for the slow bell
               to be finished tolling
telling the unfinished *Paradiso* story
as seen in an unfinished phrase
             on the face of a church
as seen in a fisherman's face
in a black boat without sails
making his final haul

English Revisited

CAROLYNE WRIGHT

On certain streets in the "tourist areas" of downtown Calcutta, the foreign visitor is apt to be waylaid by a pack of street children, all clamoring for her attention—and rupees—by waving, plucking at her arm, chattering at her in a Babel of languages, with English predominating: "Hello Madame! Guide, Madame? See nice temples? Very beautiful! Rickshaw, Madame?" Inevitably, there will be the tiny but determined beggar girl, who will latch onto the visitor and shadow her steps, one grimy hand cupped in dogged supplication. She will chant in a low, almost mechanical monotone, "No mama, no papa, please Madame baksheesh dao, no mama no papa baksheesh dao . . ." and trot alongside until the foreigner pushes her away or escapes around the corner.

If the startled visitor decides to ignore these urchins, they will try a few other greetings "from p'hornen": "Français, Madame? Bonjour!" or "Guten Tag!" "Buenos dias!" If the visitors don't appear to be of European origin, the children don't give up. I've seen the more venturesome of them vowing to groups of camera-laden Far Easterners, making their pitches in pidgin Japanese! If they meet with nothing but refusals, these young hustlers fall to jabbering among themselves in their own tongue (usually Hindi or Bengali), and scamper off to await other likely prey.

At the other end of Calcutta's socio-economic spectrum is the English-medium educated Bengali writer-housewife, who teaches English in one of the many good colleges for upper-middle-class students —not because she needs the money (her husband has a big position in a major company), but because it provides a mildly stimulating, and constructive, alternative to the household routine, a social life of her own. It is this sort of woman I've watched carrying on three or four running conversations in as many languages at once. As I've sat in amazement, mid-morning teacup poised in my hand, I've listened to my hostess argue on the phone, in a stream of heated Bengali, about the distribution for her latest novel; then cover the receiver with her hand and stage-whisper, "How is your tea?" and "Do take some of the sandesh, it's not too sweet." Hanging up the phone, she would shout up to the Hyderabadi servant, and when he appeared at the door, tell him in Urdu what he should buy at the market for our lunch.

These scenarios from two extremes of Calcutta life share one common element: a multilingualism essential to the survival of the individual and the smooth functioning of the social dynamic. In classrooms and offices as well it is necessary to master at least two languages besides one's own. University students may speak Assamese, Oriya, Marathi, or Telegu at home; in class, their professor lecture to them in English, the language in which most of their textbooks are also written. In the sciences it is especially crucial to have a command of English, since most research materials are written in (or translated to) that language, there are no funds for the translation of these materials to regional languages, and most science graduates seek advanced degrees, and jobs, in the West. English is vital, in other words, for the successful functioning of what Indians who stay at home lament as the "brain drain."

In government offices, documents are printed in Hindi with English underneath; only occasionally do regional language versions of the same forms exist. Clerks and bureaucrats must be reasonably fluent in both of these languages, because they must deal with so many people from other states or from abroad. Even to watch TV in Indian one needs three languages: to follow the Hindi films and sit-coms, the American movies, the educational and cultural program in the local language.

The Delhi-based central government, attempting to govern a chaotic collection of states with some sixteen standard regional languages and untold hundreds of dialects, would like to impose Hindi as the official medium of government and inter-regional communication. It is, after all, the language with the largest number of native speakers; it also happens to be the first language of the Nehru-Gandhi family, as well as the North Indian states which surround the federal district of New Delhi. All Indian children who attend school do, in fact, study Hindi for several years; whether they like it or not, it does help them deal with taxi drivers, policemen, and odd-job men (in Calcutta, most of these are Hindi-speaking economic refugees from the feudal state of Bihar), and they can understand the Hindi movies better on TV.

But non-Hindi speakers (who outnumber native Hindi speakers by about two to one) resent the unfair advantage Hindi speakers have in any official discourse; many of them who can afford it send their children to English-medium schools. Those who can't afford it place their children in regional language-medium schools, especially in Eastern India and the Dravidian South. English continues to be the second language of choice in these regions; many speakers of Dravidian-based tongues (Kannada, Tamil, Telegu, Malayalam) refuse to learn Hindi, one descendant of the tongue spoken by Aryan conquerors who overran their idyllic, vegetarian, pre-Vedic subcontinent some 5,000 years ago. Better, the modern reasoning goes, for both to be speaking a language not native to either of them. So, ironically, though memories of the Raj still rankle and the British are still blamed for many of the country's ills, the language of this most recent and resented conqueror remains viable, and offers a curiously neutral alternative in the ongoing controversy over the universal second language.

In light of all this multilingual debate, with English as the biggest chunk of industrial quartz in the linguistic crown, the initiatives to adopt English as the official language of the U.S. look rather silly. As if it were in any danger of being supplanted. But perhaps a few instructive parallels with India can be drawn. Both countries are large, with diverse populations and ethnic groups. Both are self-involved, concerned more with domestic than foreign issues; in both, a degree of xenophobia exists, both between different linguistic and ethnic communities in the country, and toward the world beyond national boundaries. But in India, the differences between ethnic and linguistic groups are more pronounced and of longer standing. Each community has been evolving in its own villages and region for thousands of years; mobility between communities, intermarriage, and movement up the social scale are still relatively minimal, particularly in rural areas and among the poor. There is little likelihood, even with the advent of television, that ancient customs will soon be abandoned, or that Indians could be persuaded to speak one language nationwide, even to agree on one universal second language.

Not so in the U.S. The dominant white culture has assumed that most members of ethnic groups would assimilate by the second generation into a tradition-free "melting pot," casting off their old lives and languages. Old customs were to be forgotten, or at most preserved as a memento of "roots." Even American English is spoken with ever more standardized accents in the wake of "broadcast standard." Since the U.S. after World War II emerged as the leading global power, and English became the primary language of diplomacy and trade, many Americans have believed that everyone wanted to learn it, partake of the so-called American way of life, come to this country and become Americans themselves. If anyone wanted to speak with us, the reasoning has been, they could do so in our language: an attitude not much different from that of the British in their days of Empire and Raj. Sputnik, the Peace Corps, and the economic ascendancy of Japan aside, many Americans have not often felt any practical need, as in India or Europe, to learn other languages, or much aesthetic interest in coming to understand the cultures embodied in them.

It is ironic, and appropriate, that waves of economic and political refugees from Southeast Asia and Latin America, coupled with an influx of Japanese companies and their management staff, at a time of resurgence of ethnic pride and interest among many Americans, that the English-only movement would gain strength. These more recent immigrants have often preferred to form their own communities and maintain their languages and customs, while taking advantage of job and betterment opportunities that brought them here. They are not so different from the Hindi-speaking landless peasants of Bihar and the Muslim Bangladeshi peasants who flock to Bengali-speaking, Hindu Calcutta, to pull rickshaws, drive taxis, sweep floors and haul trash, and return to their own settlements on sidewalks or in the bustees at night, grateful to have paying work in a big city, a water pump at the end of the brick-paved lane, the promise from the Municipal Corporation of electricity in ten years or so, if they vote to keep the CP in power: in short, a far better life, for all its discomforts, than they had back in the feudal estates.

The employees of foreign corporations newly entrenched in America are not so different from the Marwaris, entrepreneurial Rajasthanis who enrich themselves from business ventures—factories, shops, construction firms—that provide needed jobs in a Calcutta overcrowded with jobseekers from Bihar, Bangladesh, and elsewhere. The Marwaris use their wealth to build great mansions in the Calcutta suburbs, endow hospitals and research institutions and Jain temples. Both groups of foreigners are resented and deplored by Bengalis, who pride themselves on being intellectuals with little business sense and no desire to do hard physical labor, who complain about outsiders taking over their city, but in the same breath will say that someone's got to do that work. Unlike foreign-language minorities in the U.S., the Marwaris and the pavement dwellers are not expected—or encouraged—to assimilate. Like the Hakka Chinese who run tanneries and restaurants in Tangra on the outskirts of Calcutta, whose ancestors came five generations ago as coolie laborers, but who have never been granted Indian citizenship, and who must pay bribes every year to renew their resident alien permits even though every single one of them was born in Calcutta, neither the Marwaris nor the economic refugees will ever be accepted as Calcuttans.

The U.S. is not so xenophobic (with some notable extremist exceptions), and official policy has encouraged assimilation. For large numbers of immigrants to settle in this country, take advantage of its opportunities, but prefer to remain in their own communities and traditions, not abandoning their own cultures for the cult of the melting pot, is an affront to the America: Love It Or Leave It types. That Hispanics, the largest and fastest-growing foreign-language minority, could establish their own enclaves where they can live complete lives—transacting business, partaking of entertainment, and electing legislative representatives—without learning English, offends and threatens those who regard the American Dream as a religion demanding the immigrant's complete inner conversion in the crucible of citizenship. English-only advocates may be forgetting that their own ancestors were once newcomers to the Land of Opportunity, and may have lived in ethnic communities, speaking the Old Country language and leaving it to their American-born children to complete the assimilation process. Time will tell whether or not this same process will occur with more recent immigrants.

After living in polyglot India, I find it hard to be moved by the concerns of official-English proponents, or to see any threat to the primacy of English in this country or in the international market. Given the disinterest most of the 220 million or so English-speaking Americans have in learning other languages (is this one reason they are so offended by non-English-speaking immigrants' seeming reluctance with respect to English?), it is highly unlikely that any other language could "take over." If current economic and immigration trends continue, of course, bilingual programs in schools may also encompass a few years of Spanish or Japanese for English-speaking students; a few years at least of Spanish should probably be required now. Americans would benefit from greater openness to other cultures on those cultures' own terms—and in their own languages—and we might relearn some of the old immigrant virtues of resilience and adaptability that helped so many of our newly arrived ancestors achieve success in the past.

We may never see such a direct connection between our acquisition of a second language and our own advancement as do Indian schoolchildren preparing for graduate study, and possible careers, abroad; or as do Indian streetchildren looking forward to their next meal after a successful hustle of foreign tourists; or even as do the majority of the foreign-language-speaking immigrants to our own country. But if we can accept the reality of other languages and cultural diversity within our borders, and even try to understand some of this diversity ourselves, we may make it easier for recent immigrants to come out of their ethnic shells, neither abandoning their own cultures nor clinging to them as a defense against the hostility of the English-speaking world around them. English-only initiatives seem to point toward greater rigidity in our national life, a sign perhaps that our culture has passed its prime and feels vulnerable to threats from without. Attempts to suppress cultural differences by legislating language uniformity could backfire, though, as they have in India, in its various violent separatist movements. Let us hope that most Americans continue to view cultural diversity within America with interest, and that government policies can reflect a similarly positive attitude.

From Make-Believe Media: *"Make-Believe History"*

MICHAEL PARENTI

Imperialism has never recognized the humanity of its victims. By treating the colonized as subhuman, the colonizers can more easily justify exterminating them. John Wayne summed it up in one of his horse operas, *The Searchers* (1956): "There's humans and then there's Comanches." In World War II films, Japanese soldiers, played by Chinese-American actors, were portrayed as pitiless, sadistic demons. Hence, killing them posed no great moral problems. As the sergeant in *Guadalcanal Diary* (1943) explains: "Besides, they're not people." . . .

Americans are among the most ignorant people in the world when it comes to history. Opinion surveys have shown that large percentages of them do not know the difference between World War I and World War II. Many believe that Germany and the Soviet Union were allies in the latter conflict. As already noted, relatively few ever heard of the multinational invasion of Soviet Russia in which the United States was a participant. Many never heard of Hiroshima and have no idea that the United States dropped an atomic bomb on that city. Many could not tell you what issues were involved in the Vietnam war or other armed conflicts in which the United States has participated. Nor could they say much about the history of aggression perpetrated against Native Americans and the slavery inflicted upon Africans in America. The centuries of imperialism imposed on Asia, Africa, and Latin America by the European and North American powers are, for the most part, nonevents in the collective American psyche. Not many Americans could put together two intelligent sentences about the histories of Mexico, Canada, Puerto Rico, or Cuba —to name the United States closest neighbors. Most would not have the foggiest idea about what was at stake in the French Revolution, the Russian Revolution, the Spanish Civil War, or the Chinese Revolution.

Americans themselves are not totally to blame for this. They are taught almost nothing of these things in primary and secondary school nor even at the university level. And what they are taught is usually devoid of the urgent political economic realities that allow both past and present to inform each other, making history meaningful to us. Nor do U.S. political leaders, news pundits, and other opinion makers find much reason to place current developments in an historical context, especially one that might raise troublesome questions about the existing social order. Popular ignorance is not without its functions. Those at the top prefer that people know little about history's potentially troublesome lessons (except those parts of history that have been specially packaged with superpatriotic, system-supporting messages).

As noted earlier, when portrayed in movies and television dramas, history is usually stood on its head or reduced to personal heroics. In this regard, the make-believe media reinforce the kind of history taught in the schools, mouthed by political leaders, and recorded by the news media. One can present almost any subject in the U.S. news and entertainment media: sex and scandal, deviancy and depravity, and sometimes even racial oppression and gender discrimination. What cannot be touched is the taboo subject of *class,* specifically the importance of class power and class struggle. . . .

Even the class realities of earlier precapitalist eras are not considered a fit entertainment subject. The ancient world, for instance, as represented in the costume epics produced in such abundance by television and Hollywood, is viewed almost exclusively from its upper reaches, a perspective so rarified as to be devoid of class conflict, in fact, devoid of main characters from any class but the aristocracy and military. Such is the case with the television mini-series "I Claudius" and other less well-done productions. In movies like *Quo Vadis?* (1951, 1985) and *Caligula* (1980), the decadence of the imperial court and the violence of the Roman arena are presented in a sensationalistic manner but not the cruel class realities of Roman society, not the exploitation and impoverishment of the Roman people, and not the pillage and bloodletting perpetrated across the Mediterranean by Roman imperialism, all of which greatly advantaged the landed aristocracy.

Except for the occasional appearance of slaves who wait upon the lead characters, make-believe media offer hardly a hint that Rome was a place of terrible class injustices, heroic rebellions, and horrific repressions. An exception here is *Spartacus* (1960), produced by Edward Lewis, which tells of a famous uprising and puts Hollywood on record as being against slavery—at least of the ancient Roman variety.

When the common victims of Rome's rule do appear in the

make-believe media, they usually turn out to be pagans or Jews who convert to Christianity after a stressful bout in a Roman dungeon or arena. During the anticommunist heyday of the 1950s, as already noted, producers like Cecil B. deMille consciously played up the allegorical link thrown into the squalor and disorder that comes when slavery is abolished. The Southern gentlemen of the former slavocracy are obligated to use vigilante violence to deal with ruffian ex-slaves and low-life Whites.

In the absence of anything better, *Gone with the Wind* has been, for several generations of Americans (thanks to movie and television reruns and videos), the most vivid and reliable image of what the antebellum South must have been like, an image only partly blurred by the more recent television series "Roots," which did portray some of the brutality of slavery.

Even more notorious is D. W. Griffith's silent era *Birth of a Nation* (1915), which paints a frightening picture of the Reconstruction period, complete with corrupt and villainous Black legislators, arrogant mulattoes who treat old Confederates with bruising insolence, and leering Black soldiers who lust after White women. Only the night-riding Ku Klux Klan is able to rectify matters. *Birth of a Nation* helped promote the revival of the Klan outside the South. The movie's message was received so seriously that schoolchildren throughout the country were taken to see it in order to learn "history." It was rereleased in 1921, 1922, and 1930 and continues to be featured in film series as a "classic" and in university film courses as a "landmark production" of early cinematography. . . .

In the early years of the movie industry, the images of African-Americans were unrestrainedly racist—as reflected in such silent films as *The Wooing and Wedding of a Coon* (1904), *For Massa's Sake* (1911), *Coon Town Suffragettes* (1914), and *The Nigger* (1915). Whether he was called Sambo or Rastus, whether played by Blacks or black-faced Whites, the cinematic African-American male was usually a simpleminded buffoon, quick to laugh, irresponsible, lazy, fearful, and rhythmic. His female counterpart was good-natured, motherly yet sometimes sassy, able to work but complaining about it, and employed as a cook, seamstress, or servant. One Black actor, Lincoln Perry, so encapsulated the shuffling, childish slouch that the character he played, "Steppin' Fetchit," actually became his Hollywood stage name.

From the 1920s through World War II, grotesque black-faced

caricatures with huge red lips and bulging eyes appeared as cannibals and dancing darkies in animated cartoons. They adorned pancake mix packages and tobacco advertisements. Of 100 motion pictures made during this period that had Black themes or characters "of more than passing significance," the great majority were classified as anti-Black, according to one study. . . .

How have Italian-Americans been represented in the media? In ways not unlike other ethnic groups:

The Invisible Man. To use the title of Ralph Ellison's book about Blacks, for a long time the Italian, like every other ethnic, was invisible, nonexistent. Be it radio, movies, television dramas, popular literature, or the Dick-and-Jane readers of grade school, the world was inhabited by middle- and upper-middle-class WASPs, creamy-faced suburban youngsters with executive-looking fathers and trim American-beauty mothers, visions of Anglo-Protestant affluence and gentility.

Minor Stock Characters. In the early days of movies and radio when Italians did make an appearance in the Anglo American world, it was usually as minor stock characters: the cheerful waiter, the talkative barber, the simple pushcart vendor, human scenery on the urban landscape with no lives of their own—or certainly no lives deemed worthy of narrative treatment. As unassimilated oddities, Italians were treated no differently than other ethnic stand-ins, such as the Irish cleaning lady, the Jewish shopkeeper, and the Black domestic.

The Grateful Immigrant. One of the stock characters of the late 1940s and early 1950s became a featured personality in a radio series and subsequently a television series called *Life with Luigi*. Played by an Irish-American actor, J. Carroll Naish, Luigi was the cloyingly sweet immigrant who spent his time gratefully exclaiming, "Mama mia, I'm-a love-a deese a bootifull-a country, Amerrreeca!" Naish's understanding of an Italian immigrant's looks, accent, and mannerisms, painfully reminiscent of Chico Marx (another caricature), bore little resemblance to the real thing. Luigi was a creature conjured up by the make-believe media as a confirmation of the goodness of the existing American social order. In Luigi and characters like him, we had evidence that the immigrant was not a victim but a joyful, appreciative beneficiary of his adopted country.

The Mafia Gangster. In the fearful imagination of nativistic America, crime was always associated with the big city and the swarthy foreigner. In the 1930s and 1940s, the Italian mobster had to share the Hollywood screen with his Irish and Jewish counterparts. In later years, with television series like "The Untouchables" and movies like *The Godfather,* the Italian was fashioned into the archetypal gangster, so that eventually the association of Italian-Americans with crime was instantaneous and international. One can travel throughout Europe and most other lands where Hollywood films are shown and encounter the stereotype. While in Lisbon during the revolutionary ferment of 1975, I talked to a Portuguese army lieutenant who, upon discovering I was Italian-American, commented gleefully "Ah, mafioso!" A half-hour later, the exact same response was accorded me by a Portuguese army captain. The lieutenant had right-wing sympathies and the captain was leftist—which demonstrates how Hollywood can cut its swath across the ideological spectrum.

With the help of the media, a few thousand hoodlums in the organized rackets who are of Italian origin, representing a tiny fraction of the Italian-American population, became representative of an entire ethnic group. In one of his stand-up feature films, the comedian Richard Pryor joked: "Not all Italians are in the Mafia. They just all *work* for the Mafia." The Mafia association became one of those respectable forms of bigotry.

There have been Irish, Jewish, Black, Latino, Italian, and even Anglo-Protestant mobsters in our history. None of these hoodlums is representative of the larger ethnic formations from which they happened to originate. Needless to say, none of the movies dealing with such characters has ever provided an authentic rendition of the rich cultural heritages and working-class histories of these groups. . . .

The make-believe media are predominantly White media. Of the sixty or seventy major performers in the new TV shows each season, relatively few are African-American. It took the television industry over four decades before it could get around to featuring African-American talk-show hosts such as Oprah Winfrey and Arsenio Hall. For other people of color, the situation has been at least as bad. As of the late 1970s, Asian-Americans, Native American Indians, and Latinos (that is, all persons of Spanish-speaking origin, including Chicanos and Puerto Ricans) together constituted less than 3 percent of the characters in teleplays and sitcoms. Nor has the situation improved markedly since then. . . .

Finally, it must be noted that the media deny the seriousness of the ethnic experience and thereby evade the larger, more taboo question of class struggle. The ethnics' attention is directed toward irrelevant caricatures of themselves that serve as objects of either emulation or insult or both. The ethnics—of whom the Italians are only a more obvious example—are told what to think of themselves by the make-believe media. Controversies about ethnic "identity," group "dignity," and "assimilation" continue endlessly. Ignored by the make-believe media are the pressing problems of working-class ethnics: the demoralizing hardships of underemployment, layoffs, low wages, high taxes, job-connected disabilities, and staggering living costs.

Having their identities suppressed or falsified is but one manifestation of a larger violation that ethnics are made to suffer. What has been stolen from many of them is their labor, their health, their communities, and their ability to live with a sufficient measure of ease and security. So the ethnics are distracted from their own struggle and their own experience by the daily psychological muggings of Hollywood and television, by fabricated images of the world and of themselves. The medium is the message, and the media are the Mafia.

The Colonisation of Our Pacific Islands

CHAILANG PALACIOS

Micronesia was colonised by the Spanish in the fifteenth century. When the Spanish soldiers came, so did the missionaries. Hand in hand. They landed in Guam and spread out over the Marianas, then all over Micronesia. The missionaries together with the soldiers began to Christianise our ancestors. They were very scared and ran away—they hadn't seen a white person before. It was hard for us to embrace Christianity. The Spanish missionaries were blessing all the soldiers while the soldiers were cutting my ancestors into half, killing our men, raping our women.

When they arrived we were about 40,000. And we ended up just 4,000 because they killed everyone that didn't want to embrace Christianity, which was the Catholic faith. So the Spanish stayed over 100 years. They came to do good work. And they did it very well, because today we are 97% Catholic.

Another nation came, which is the Germans. Both the Spanish

and the Germans came for their economic purposes. The Germans again, the same story—killing our men, raping our women. They took our land. The Germans brought their own missionaries, who tried to teach us the Protestant religion. And this started making us, the indigenous group, fight amongst ourselves over who was more Protestant and who was more Catholic. That is always the way: when white nations come to conquer us, to colonize us, they divide us. And it is still happening. But the Germans didn't stay very long. They took off.

And then there is this nation just like an octopus. The octopus that goes very slowly, very slowly, and suddenly it gets you. That is like the Japanese. They came and were exactly the same. They want us to join their religion, Buddhism. They liked our islands so much they stayed. They took our land for sugar plantations, for pineapple plantations. They again made my ancestors their slaves, together with the Korean and Okinawa people, paying them five cents for the whole day.

Then the Japanese and the USA sat down planning to have war. We, the Micronesian people, were the victims of that war—World War II. We suffered all over the Marianas. It was heavily damaged because it was a big military place for the Japanese. So, once again, my ancestors suffered.

After stripping them of their culture, their language, their land, the Japanese forced my ancestors up into the mountains. They made us dig a hole just in case the Americans and the Japanese fought. We would be safe in the hole. But it didn't happen like that. It was Sunday morning when the war came. Everyone was far away from their holes, visiting grandparents, relatives, friends. All of a sudden—bombs from the sky and the ocean. The people were crushed fifty to one hundred in one hole because there was no way they could get back to their own place to hide. There was no water for those people. It was so hot, so dark, bombs all over. A lot of people died. Children died because their mothers' breasts dried up. No food.

You have heard it, and I have heard it too, from the older generation: "Oh, we are so grateful that the Americans won the war. They saved us from the communists, from Russia." Yet right after the war the Americans came, like the early missionaries, in the name of God, saying, "We are here to Christianize you, to help you love one another, be in peace." We still have the Bible while the missionaries and their white governments have all the land. . . .

For some years we were "off limits." No one could come in and no one could go out unless you were CIA or military American. The whole reason for that is that the U.S. had planned to take over mainland China. So all these nationalist Chinese were in my islands learning how to fight. In time of peace children would be crying at night: there was big bombing and it could be heard all over the island. And the house started to shake. The only thing I remember is my parents saying, "Pray that there will be no more war." So next day I said, "Why do you pray and say 'No more war'?" And she just held me and said, "Oh, my daughter, I feel so sorry for your generation because probably I will not see the next war. But the next war will be so terrible that you won't need to hide." I think I was only 11 or 12 years old. I looked at her and I didn't understand. Naturally my mother died. She was not an educated woman, but with her terrible memories of World War II she just *connected*. "You won't need to hide." Those were her words. I never forget them.

Trumpets from the Island of Their Eviction

MARTIN ESPADA

At the bar two blocks away,
immigrants with Spanish mouths
hear trumpets
from the islands of their eviction.
The music swarms into the barrio
of a refugee's imagination,
along with predatory squad cars
and bullying handcuffs.

Their eviction:
like Mrs. Alfaro, evicted
when she trapped ten mice,
sealed them in plastic sandwich bags
and gifted them to the landlord;
like Daniel, the boy stockaded
in the back of retarded classrooms
for having no English

to comfort third-grade teachers;
like my father thirty-five years ago,
brown skin darker than the Air Force uniform
that could not save him, seven days county-jailed
for refusing the back of a Mississippi bus;
like the nameless Florida jíbaro
the grocery stores would not feed
in spite of the dollars he showed,
who returned with a machete,
collected cans from shelves
and forced the money
into the clerk's reluctant staring hand.

We are the ones identified by case number,
summons in the wrong language,
judgment without stay of execution.
Mrs. Alfaro has thirty days
to bundle the confusion of five children
down claustrophobic stairs
and away from the apartment.

And at the bar two blocks away,
immigrants with Spanish mouths
hear trumpets
from the islands of their eviction.
The sound scares away devils
like tropical fish
darting between the corals.

White Earth Land Struggle: Omissions and Stereotypes

WINONA LA DUKE of the Chippewa Nation

When the Mississippi band of Ojibway (Anishinabeg) negotiated the 1867 treaty with the federal government, they negotiated for good lands. Perhaps that was the problem: today only 6% of the

White Earth reservation is held commonly by Indians. Mainstream US media have not paid much attention to the struggle of the Anishinabeg to reclaim their land.

Federal, state and county governments currently hold almost a third of the White Earth reservation—some 240,000 acres in Minnesota grabbed over 50 years from Indian people. Most religious denominations seem to have summer camps there, as do the Boy Scouts. And a lot of urban dwellers have summer homes on the 47 lakes within the reservation. Finally, there are second and third-generation farmers, who occupy about a third of the land.

Indian settlements are squeezed in between the relatively vast non-Indian holdings. As a part of its "war on poverty," the US Department of Housing and Urban Development built pink, blue, red, lime-green and other uncharacteristically bright homes, giving a suburban look to reservation villages like Pine Point, White Earth and Naytauwaush, where many Anishinabeg live. These villages are also home to 75% unemployment rates, high school attrition, and a myriad of conditions stemming from chronic poverty, which a recent White Earth study indicates is getting worse with each generation.

The impact of white land ownership and economic control is obvious to many people in White Earth. So, too, is the need to regain control over the reservation land and rebuild their community. White Earth residents see this as an essential prerequisite for protecting their human rights and the security of future Indian generations.

Native American land rights are human rights, but the US media consistently sidestep this fact. Coverage of White Earth is indicative of coverage of Native land struggles generally, trivialized and replete with racist undertones. Major print and broadcast media have perpetuated old stereotypes, reviving a dangerous American frontier myth: that Indians are oppressing white people and that in the end, the Indian will die again. Such distortions were evident in a *New York Times Sunday Magazine* article by Louise Erdrich and Michael Dorris, and in a novel, *Red Earth, White Earth,* by Will Weaver, that was subsequently presented as a TV movie on CBS.

In the *Times Magazine* piece (9-4-88), Erdrich and Dorris, both Native writers, bent over backwards to present the views of the non-Indians on the reservation. Jane Reish, a virulent opponent of Indian treaty rights, appears almost pious when she tells the authors, "I never look at my neighbors and say you are the cause of my problems."

Similarly the Jirava family—third-generation farmers—become the classic pioneers of the American dream. The *Times* illustrated their words with a photo of young Stephanie Jirava draped in an American flag. . . .

This type of media presentation conveys a frightening message: that hardworking, flag-waving Americans are threatened by Indians claiming their land rights and, through legislation or the gun, the flag-wavers will emerge victorious. Consider that a Wisconsin bumper sticker reads, "Save a Deer/Shoot an Indian," and that until recently one could get a license to shoot an Indian in Brazil.

The denial of human rights to Indians is a disgrace. US media have perpetuated the Manifest Destiny myth far too long, and they should put a stop to it.

Reporting "Terrorism": The Experience of Northern Ireland

BRIAN HAMILTON-TWEEDALE

The experience of reporting a violent political conflict on its own doorstep has profoundly challenged the liberal values of the British media, and in doing so has undermined the legitimacy of its claim to perform a vital role in the democratic process. In theory, where governments and communities are in conflict, but not in a state of war, newspapers and television should perform their duties independently from the executive, the legislature and the judiciary, defending each against the excesses of the other and upholding, in the process, the public interest. In practice, where Northern Ireland is concerned, the British media have become committed to a perspective of the conflict which, since the early 1970s, has increasingly equated the interests of the public with those of the state. In the process a strategy for reporting events in the North has evolved which, though falling short of direct censorship, effectively denies the public the information and analysis it requires to arrive at a meaningful understanding of the conflict, and makes it difficult for it to engage in an informed debate as to how it can be best resolved.

The conflict in Northern Ireland is, above all else, a political conflict and one with deep historical and social roots. Yet in so far as it has featured as an issue in the British media, the story has been predominantly one of violence. In his analysis of news during two periods in 1974 and 1975 (each of which contained a major election campaign in an effort to maximize the level of political reporting) Philip Elliott found that violence and law enforcement stories accounted for 72 percent of the coverage accorded to the North by national television, 58 percent of the coverage in the quality press, and 65 percent in the popular press. In all only a third of the stories dealt with politics and other matters. Elliot contrasted this approach with that of the Irish media which not only carried more stories (a ratio of about 5 to 1) but were also much more concerned with the political dimension.[1]

British media coverage of events in the North has not only focused on violence at the expense of politics, it has also tended to present violence in a de-contextualized form with little if any attempt being made to go beyond the immediate details and human tragedy of reported incidents, or to place them within a broader and more analytical framework. However, while this style of reporting may make for graphic and at times moving detail, it excludes much of what could give some sense or meaning to the violence and thereby renders it less, rather than more, explicable: the result is a continual procession of violent episodes differentiated only by the scale and location of the violence and the personal characteristics of those involved.

According to statistics published by the *Irish Times,* 2304 people had been killed in Northern Ireland up to June 1983 as a direct consequence of the conflict. The figures showed that republican paramilitaries had been responsible for 1264 of these deaths, loyalist paramilitaries for 613, the army and police for 264, while a further 163 were 'non-classified'. Further statistics showed that of the civilian victims 775 were Catholic, 495 were Protestant, and a further 29 were not natives of the North.[2]

The complex pattern of state, anti-state, and intercommunal violence suggested by these statistics has been largely obscured by newspapers and television which have tended to be preoccupied with the violence of those who oppose rather than those who represent authority. Critics have noted a strong tendency within the British media to cast the army and police in a positive light; to minimize and at times ignore their involvement in violence even when it clearly breaches democratic and legal standards and, when army and police violence is reported, to treat it in an uncritical and sympathetic manner.[3] An editorial carried by *The Star* following the controversial shooting by the SAS of three unarmed IRA members in Gibraltar is illustrative of the general attitude of many papers towards violence emanating from 'official' sources. Under the headline 'Their just deserts', the paper informed its readers that:

> *There will be howls of protest from Irish Republicans over the killing of three terrorists in Gibraltar.*
>
> *They will say the victims were unarmed. That their suspect car did not contain explosives.*
>
> *SHED NO TEARS.*
>
> *This was not the cold blooded killing of three innocents. It was the destruction of a bomb gang who planned to massacre hundreds of people.*
>
> *That they FAILED is down to the vigilance of our security forces and the efficiency of the SAS.*
>
> *Three evil monsters have got what they deserve.*
>
> *(8.3.88)*

However, while journalists have been quick to condemn 'unofficial' violence, they have generally refrained from exploring on the public's behalf the complex factors which give rise to it. Instead the tendency within British journalism has been to present the violence of Northern Ireland as being the product of 'psychopaths', 'terrorists', and other such terms of convenience. A point clearly illustrated by the coverage accorded to the Enniskillen bombing in November 1987 which was widely interpreted as being the work of 'evil men' (*Daily Mirror*), 'Maniacs' (*The Star*), 'terrorist Godfathers' (*Today*), 'cowardly bigots' (*Sun*) and 'men whose infatuation with blood transcends their dopey belief in a federal, socialist, united Ireland' (*Daily Express*). Needless to say, the repetitive use of such labels serves only to obscure and mystify, rather than clarify and explain, the social and political factors which may underpin the violence. In doing so they feed off, and in the process reinforce, a view of the violence as being largely inexplicable.

British journalists have not only been preoccupied with 'terrorism' as opposed to other forms and sources of violence, but even within this narrowly defined category they have been selective and sometimes tendentious. As has been noted above, loyalist groups have been responsible for as many as 600 of the 2304 deaths recorded up to June 1983, and almost all of their victims have been civilians. Yet despite this the British media has tended to present 'terrorist' violence as if it were the sole preserve of the IRA and other republican groups. So much so that the casual observer of British media coverage could be forgiven for arriving at the conclusion that the IRA are almost exclusively to blame for the violence in Northern Ireland. Philip Elliot, for example, notes that while IRA violence has dominated the headlines the involvement of loyalists in acts of violence has been played down to such an extent that 'protestant extremists have themselves complained about the lack of attention paid to their efforts'.[4] During the period examined by Elliott the death toll in the North was sixteen Catholics, six Protestants, one member of the security forces, and one other. Yet despite the fact that Catholics were the main victims, the media blamed most of the violence on the IRA or some other republican group.

The publicity so often accorded to 'terrorist' violence contrasts sharply with the attention paid to the views of the various paramilitary groups, which over the years have been studiously ignored. Television interviews with representatives of republican groups in particular have been extremely rare, and as the recent outcry over the *Real Lives* programme 'At the Edge of the Union' clearly demonstrated, have provoked instant outrage from politicians and the press. Liz Curtis, for example, can trace only four occasions when the BBC has transmitted interviews with people speaking on behalf of the IRA or INLA, and four such occasions featuring only the IRA on ITV.[5] The record of the British press, which has consistently criticized such interviews as providing a propaganda platform for the enemies of the state, has scarcely been any better.

All sides to the Irish conflict have recognized the importance of propaganda, and all sides have been equal in their efforts to get their point of view across to the public. Their chances of succeeding, however, have been far from equal: the speed and efficiency of the information services operated by the army and the police; the pressure on journalists to seed out official accounts; the fact that official sources carry with them the authority of the state, and the generally held view that the word of the 'terrorists' cannot be trusted, have all tipped the scales heavily in favour of the authorities. As the journalist Simon Hoggart has commented: 'When the British press prints an account of an incident as if it were established fact, and it is clear that the reporter himself was not on the spot, it is a 99 percent certainty that it is the army's version which is being given.'[6] Thus while the 'terrorists' have scored the occasional propaganda victory, the advantage remains firmly with the army and the police.

The problem in Northern Ireland, however, is that on occasions official sources have proved to be as unreliable as the 'terrorists' are so often assumed to be. Since the early 1970s evidence has continued to accumulate that the army, and more recently the police, have deliberately exploited their strategic position as a news source to manipulate and mislead journalists; usually to implicate the IRA in violence committed by loyalists, often to cover up their own involvement in illegal or questionable activities, and frequently to discredit their political opponents.[7] Despite this evidence, however, British journalists, increasingly starved of resources, are more reliant upon and less critical of these sources today than at any other time in the past.

Since the early 1970s as the violence has tailed off, British media interest in Northern Ireland has diminished, and is now only temporarily revived when something spectacular like the Enniskillen bombing occurs. Reading a British paper in 1988, and a popular newspaper in particular, it is often difficult to remember that there is still a conflict taking place in the North. The problem with this pattern of reporting is that it contributes to an image of 'normalcy' which is belied by the reality of the political situation in the North.

NOTES

1. Elliott, Philip. 'Reporting Northern Ireland: a study of news in Britain, Ulster and the Irish Republic'. In *Ethnicity and the Media*. Paris: UNESCO, 1977.
2. *The Irish Times,* 4 November 1983.
3. Curtis, Liz. *Ireland: the propaganda war.* London: Pluto Press, 1984.
4. Elliott, Philip. Op. cit., 1977.
5. Curtis, Liz. Op. cit., 1984. Chapter 7.
6. Hoggart, Simon. 'The army PR men of Northern Ireland'. *New Society,* 11 October 1973.
7. See Curtis, op. cit., 1984.

In addition to the above see also:

Kirkaldy, John. 'Northern Ireland and Fleet Street'. In Yonha Alexander (ed.), *Terrorism in Ireland*. London: Croom Helm, 1983.
Schlesinger, Philip. *Putting Reality Together*. London: Constable, 1978.
Schlesinger, Philip, Graham Murdock and Philip Elliott. *Televising Terrorism*. London: Comedia, 1983.

Name in Print!

LANGSTON HUGHES

"Just look at the front pages of the newspapers," said Simple, spreading his nightly copy of the *Daily News* out on the bar. "There is never hardly any colored names anywhere. Most headlines is all about white folks."

"That is not true today," I said. "Many headlines are about Negroes, Chinese, Indians, and other colored folks like ourselves."

"Most on the inside pages," said Simple, blowing foam from his beer. "But I am talking about front-page news. The only time colored folks is front-page news is when there's been a race riot or a lynching or a boycott and a whole lot of us have been butchered up or arrested. Then they announce it."

"You," I said, "have a race phobia. You see prejudice where there is none, and Jim Crow where it doesn't exist. How can you be constructive front-page news if you don't *make* front-page news?"

"How can I make front-page news in a white paper if I am not white?" asked Simple. "Or else I have to be Ralph Bunche or Eartha Kitt. That is why I am glad we have got colored papers like the *Afro, Defender, Courier,* and *Sepia,* so I can be news, too."

"I presume that when you say 'I' you mean the racial I—Negroes. You are not talking about yourself."

"Of course I am not talking about myself," said Simple, draining his glass. "I have never been nowhere near news except when I was in the Harlem Riots. Then the papers did not mention me by name. They just said 'mob.' I were a part of the mob. When the Mayor's Committee report come out, they said I were 'frustrated.' Which is true, I were. It is very hard for a Negro like me to get his name in the news, the reason being that white folks do not let us nowhere near news in the first place. For example, take all these graft investigations that's been going on in Brooklyn and New York every other week, unions and docks, cops and bookies, and million-dollar handouts. Do you read about any Negroes being mixed up in them, getting even a hundred dollars of them millions, or being called up before the grand jury? You do not. White folks are just rolling in graft! But where are the Negroes? Nowhere near the news. Irish names, Italian names, Jewish names, all kinds of names in the headlines every time Judge Liebowitz opens his mouth. Do you read any colored names? The grand jury don't even bother to investigate Harlem. There has never been a million dollars' worth of graft in Harlem in all the years since the Indians sold Manhattan for a handful of beads. Indians and Negroes don't get nowhere near graft, neither into much news. Find me some Negro news in tonight's *News*."

"I would hardly wish to get into the papers if I had to make news by way of graft," I said. "There is nothing about graft of which any race can be proud."

"Our race could do right well with some of that big money, though," said Simple, signaling the barman for another beer. "But it does not have to be graft, in unions or out. I am just using that as an example. Take anything else on the front pages. Take flying saucers in the sky. Everybody but a Negro has seen one. If a Negro did see a flying saucer, I bet the papers wouldn't report it. They probably don't even let flying saucers fly over Harlem, just to keep Negroes from seeing them. This morning in the subway I read where Carl Krubelewski had seen a flying saucer, also Ralph Curio saw one. And way up in Massachusetts a while back, Henry Armpriester seen one. Have you ever read about Roosevelt Johnson or Ralph Butler or Carl Jenkins or anybody that sounded like a Negro seeing one? I did not. Has a flying saucer ever passed over Lenox Avenue? Nary one! Not even Daddy Grace has glimpsed one, neither Mother Horne, nor Adam Powell. Negroes can't get on the front page no kind of way. We can't even see a flying saucer."

"It would probably scare the wits out of you, if you did see one," I said, "so you might not live to read your name in the papers."

"I could read my name from the other world then," said Simple, "and be just as proud. Me, Jesse B. Semple—my name in print for once—killed by looking at a flying saucer."

say french

D. H. MELHEM

say french:
who knows what lebanese is?
or syrian? (serbian? siberian?)
protectorate is close to
protector

of course there's your culture
a tradition of teachers and doctors
an elegant descent
from phoenicians

but
immigration officials
and neighbors
employers
perplexed by exotics
non-anglo saxon
non-westeuropean-nontoxic
attest
the best are
types here
longer

the immigration official
said to me,
syrian?
what's
that?

(and sallow
with a menacing
guttural tongue)

your teacher accused
arabic spoken
at home:
"you have an accent"

though fearing strangers
and the foreign school
I went
showed myself
clean   educated
stopped her

still she detested
your rivalling
the girl on her lap
whose braids she caressed
before the class

people don't mean
to be mean
nevertheless
better say
french

Beyond Belief: The Press and the Holocaust

DEBORAH E. LIPSTADT

There is a widely held belief that until Allied soldiers liberated the German concentration camps, the West had little idea of the enormity of the Holocaust. But an examination of US newspapers during the war years tells a very different story. The facts were there, but published in such a tentative way as to minimize the impact on US readers.

In the Spring of 1942, US correspondents who had been stranded in Germany were exchanged for Axis nationals held in the United States. The reporters returned with details of the mass murder of Polish and Russian Jews. In the *New York Times* (5-18-42), UP's Glenn Stadler described what had happened to Jews in Latvia, Estonia and Lithuania as an "open hunt." Joseph Grigg, also of UP, wrote in the *New York Journal American* (6-1-42): "Thousands lie in . . . mass graves they were forced to dig before the firing squads as SS troops cut them down. . . . In Latvia . . . responsible Nazi sources admitted

56,000 men, women and children were killed. . . . The slaughter went on for days. . . . The entire Jewish population of many towns and villages was driven into the country, forced to dig graves and then machine gunned. . . . The slaughter in Poland was horrible with 80,000 killed . . . one German rifleman boasted . . . that he had killed thirty-seven in one night picking them off as a hunter does rabbits."

Grigg observed that correspondents who had lived in Germany had no doubt that Hitler "and his agents have done everything to make [Hitler's] prophecy" of Jewish destruction "come true."

This was not the first news of the Final Solution to reach the West. Deportations, massacres and mass graves had been reported since the Germans had invaded Russia in June 1941. An AP dispatch (8-8-41) spoke of "an orgy of murder and rape in Lvov." The *New York Journal American* (11-13-41) reported "25,000 Jews killed in Odessa." The *New York Times* (10-6-41) told of the machine gunning of "masses of Jews deported from Hungary to Galicia." The *New York Herald Tribune* (12-5-41) described the Jews' fate as "nothing less than systematic extermination." The Hearst papers (12-1-41) accused Germany of the "extermination of an ancient and cultured race."

June 1942 brought more ominous news. The Jewish Bund in Warsaw and the Polish government in exile confirmed that Germany had embarked on a systematic program to kill European Jewry. They listed the cities where the Jewish population had disappeared and reported on the use of "gas chamber" vehicles in which 90 people were killed at a time, a thousand people a day. The report documented Germany's intention to "annihilate all the Jews in Europe."

But the way the US press handled these reports left many people doubting their veracity. The *Seattle Times* (6-26-42) buried the news in a page-30 article which, though it spoke of "the systematic extermination of the Jewish population," ran under the very small headline, "700,000 Jews Reported Slain." The *New York Times* (6-27-42) ran an 18-line story at the end of a series of other articles, including one about the death of 800 in reprisal for the murder of Nazi leader Reinhard Heydrich; it mentioned gas chambers, but was silent about a systematic slaughter program.

A 13-line, page-3 article in the *Los Angeles Times* (6-30-42) simply stated that the British section of the World Jewish Congress estimated "that more than one million Jews have been killed or died as the result of ill treatment." It carried the headline: "Nazi's Kill Million Jews, Says Survey." The *Chicago Tribune* (6-30-42) buried its 11-line story on the bottom of page 6. Five days later a summary of the Jewish Bund report appeared in the *New York Times* (7-2-42) on page 6; in addition to listing death tolls as high as 35,000 it noted that 25,000 had been taken from Lublin and "nothing has been heard from them since."

The press treatment of this news can be explained in part by a headline over the *New York Journal American*'s front page, 8-line article (6-29-42): "Jews list their dead at million." This was a Jewish story, worthy of reporting, but not of complete trust since Jews were interested parties. Throughout the war, news released by Nazi perpetrators was treated with greater credulity than that released by their victims.

Subsequent stories, including those authenticated by the Allies, were handled with remarkable restraint. Rarely on page one, they were usually buried deep inside the paper. In July 1942, a month after the Polish announcement that "deportation" meant death for Jews, the *Chicago Tribune* (7-26-42) reported that the Nazis would shortly begin deporting all Dutch Jews between the ages of 18 and 40; this story ran on page 9.

That same month the Poles detailed the execution of 200,000 Jews and a quarter million Poles. The *New York World Telegram* story (7-27-42), which omitted mention of Jews, was on page 22 next to an article about a doctor who hypnotized himself into making a parachute jump. In December 1942, after the Allies confirmed the news of a systematic killing program, the *Chicago Tribune* (12-20-42) ran a story with a headline saying that Poland had become a "Jewish abattoir" on page 18 next to a marriage announcement. In other leading dailies, stories about atrocities were to be found on weather, obituary and comic pages.

This pattern did not change even when the news became more detailed. The *New York Times* (2-18-44) devoted 32 lines on page 7 to a UP report that Holland's 180,000 Jews had been "completely wiped out." This article ran beneath a longer humorous story about how the King of England had awakened a sleeping American sergeant.

There were notable exceptions, including the *New Republic, PM, The Nation, Commonweal,* the *New York Post* and even the Hearst papers, which exhorted US citizens to "Remember . . . THIS IS NOT A JEWISH PROBLEM. It is a HUMAN PROBLEM"

(9-4-43). Anne O'Hare McCormack, writing in the *New York Times* (3-3-43), called on Christians to do "the utmost to rescue Jews remaining in Europe," for the "Jew was a symbol of what this war is all about."

Given the treatment of this news, it is not surprising that many Americans were skeptical. In the final weeks of the war, a *Washington Post* correspondent accompanying the Allied forces in Europe observed, "where atrocities are concerned, most American fighting men have to be shown to believe." (4-16-45). Even Americans who believed so underestimated the number of Jews killed that it was clear they had no conception of the magnitude of the tragedy or that it was a systematic plan.

The US media no longer doubt that millions can be massacred systematically. During World War Two it was beyond belief, today it is boring. We have become inured to human horror. This, too, is a legacy of the Holocaust.

Invisible Victims

MARTIN A. LEE AND GLORIA CHANNON

Most mainstream human rights organizations place a de facto priority on questions of physical integrity and violations of political and civil rights. Social and economic rights are addressed only insofar as they have a direct bearing on the political and civil issues; labor organizing, for example, is a form of free association, and restraints on culture often involve restraints on conscience and expression. The emphasis on civil-political rights reinforces the dominant US media tendency to define human rights far more narrowly than the UN Universal Declaration. Social, economic and cultural rights are treated as distinctly lesser categories of rights, if at all, in the US media.

Human rights groups and the media both focus largely on abuses wherein the state is directly involved as an active agent of repression. "But what happens," asks Felice Gaer, director of the New York–based International League for Human Rights, "when the government is a passive accomplice in structural or cultural abuses, rather than an active agent?"

Gaer cites abuses specific to women, which are often deeply entangled in cultural and religious practices, but not attributable directly to government action. Abuses of women fall largely within the social and economic spheres.

Consider, for example, a widespread practice such as genital mutilation of women, a subject almost never mentioned in the mass media. (One suspects more attention would be given if male genitals were being systematically mutilated.) Clitoridectomies, arguably a form of torture, cause life-long pain and life-threatening infections in an estimated 84 million women in Africa and Asia. But this violation of physical integrity isn't treated as a human rights issue by mainstream human rights groups and the media, in part because governments may not be explicitly involved in perpetrating these acts.

The same logic applies to bride-burnings and various forms of trafficking in women. Prostitution, like that servicing Subic Bay and Clark Air Force Base in the Philippines—or the "sex tourist" trade in Thailand—could not go on without implicit government sanction.

The widespread sterilization of Puerto Rican and Native American women is largely ignored by the press, even though US government agencies have been involved in promoting such abuses. Other violations committed in the name of population control have received scant media attention.

An editorial in the *New York Times* (4-19-89) strongly criticized the Chinese government for its policy of mandatory abortions. On the other side of the natal coin, Romania has undertaken "an aggressive and intrusive campaign to promote population growth," according to the US State Department (*Country Reports,* 1988). Under the Romanian government's forced natalization program, "abortions and all forms of birth control are illegal. Pregnancy tests and physical examinations continue to be required of female workers . . . to insure that pregnancies are . . . carried to term." Such practices also constitute a violation of human rights, but US journalists, usually quick to condemn Communist abuses, have said little about this.

Then there are human rights abuses committed against people because of their sexual orientation. Even in countries closely scrutinized by the US media, abuses against gays and lesbians have rarely been cited as human rights issues. In Iran, for example, people have been executed for engaging in homosexual relations. In some countries, lesbians and gay men have been incarcerated in camps or mental institutions. Amnesty International is reevaluating its policy of not categorizing as prisoners of conscience those imprisoned for their sexual orientation. The Information Secretariat of the International Lesbian and Gay Association, based in Stockholm, acts as a global monitor for human rights abuses against gays and lesbians.

Another "omission by definition" applies to human rights violations committed not by governments but by multinational corporations, which often wield more power than states, or other transnational actors like the International Monetary Fund (IMF), whose policies cause untold misery for millions of people in the developing world. . . . Human rights do not figure prominently in international business coverage, except when activists force issues such as divestment from South Africa or the Nestle's infant formula boycott into public consciousness.

Meanwhile the "debt bomb" is ticking. Third World governments, under pressure from the IMF and World Bank, impose callous policies that exacerbate hardship and discontent, resulting in food riots or rebellions which are invariably quelled by state repression. The debt problem is unquestionably a human rights issue, with direct relevance to political and civil rights.

The suppression of labor unions is severe in countries like Chile, which gears its economy to attracting foreign investment, and South Korea, which keeps a tight lid on workers' rights in an effort to promote rapid economic growth. Thus the circle of abused socio-economic and civil-political rights remains unbroken.

Encouraged by mainstream human rights groups, media coverage of human rights focuses mainly on government abuse of individuals. But one doesn't have to be a political dissident to be a victim of human rights abuse. Poor people around the world are victimized as a class. "Poverty leads millions of Asian kids into slavery," read a recent *Miami Herald* headline (7-16-89). And women are victimized on the basis of gender; consequently they own only one tenth of the world's property, and many are denied property rights and access to credit and education—facts not emphasized on the business pages.

Indigenous peoples, victimized on the basis of race, language and culture, are in some ways the most invisible of all. Many are waging a protracted struggle against genocide and ecological catastrophe wrought by the engines of unchecked state and corporate power.

"We cannot separate individual rights from collective rights, because both are needed for there to be social justice," Argentine Nobel

Peace Laureate Adolfo Perez Esquivel told *Extra!* "Social rights cannot be sacrificed in the name of individual liberties or free corporate enterprise. Nor can we accept the denial of individual liberties in the name of social equality."

An Ocean Away, a World Apart: The Same Old Hatreds

ANDREI CODRESCU

I am drinking a mug of beer at an outdoor cafe in the town of my birth, Sibiu, Transylvania, Romania. Seated at a table on my left, two young country teachers argue politics in Hungarian. An elderly German gent with a feathered Tirolean hat on his head tells the Romanian waiter to bring him another. All around us, the mountains glisten under a cloudless blue sky. You could be in a vacation paradise, but you are not. You are in an infinitely complicated part of the world, used mercilessly by a cruel and ongoing history.

Home is a sore subject with me right now. I was born in the beautiful medieval town of Sibiu just after World War II. The Russians were coming, and Sibiu—a mostly German town also known as Hermannstadt—was in a panic. Many of our neighbors were fleeing. Others were burying family heirlooms in the walls of the tunnels that honeycomb Sibiu, layers and layers of tunnels used as escape routes over long centuries during which somebody scary was always coming: the Turks, the Wallachians, the Magyars, the Germans. Others yet, like my mother, resorted to subtler means of protection. She named me Andrei, a Russian name, guessing quite rightly that a pretty young mom with a Russian-named baby had nothing to fear. She was right. The Soviet officers fell over each other trying to dance with mom.

I called Sibiu home for 18 years. I liked it very much, and was only rarely made to feel uneasy because I was Jewish. Jews had always been more or less at home in Transylvania, which had been part of the Austro-Hungarian Empire until 1916. After the Communists came to power on the turrets of Soviet tanks in 1946, the year of my birth, being Jewish did not make much of a difference in a country where everybody was becoming more poor and miserable every day. But perhaps I was only too young to notice anti-semitism which, according to my relatives, never really went away.

By 1965, when Nicolae Ceauşescu succeeded Gheorghiu-Dej as first secretary of the Romanian Communist Party, Romania's once-abundant resources had dwindled to almost nothing. Jews and Germans were two of the few commodities left that were still convertible to hard currency. The business of selling people got seriously under way: Germans to West Germany, and Jews to Israel, at $10,000 a head. My mother and I applied for our exit visas in 1964. They were granted in 1965. I had no interest whatsoever in going to Israel because the rock 'n' roll I was beginning to appreciate had its source in America. I was going to where the beat came from. I figure that the rock 'n' roll industry, especially the Beatles, the Rolling Stones and Bob Dylan, owe Israel $10,000 for seducing me.

Thus began a succession of new homes: Rome, Paris, Detroit, New York, San Francisco, Monte Rio, Baltimore, Baton Rouge, New Orleans. It's possible I've forgotten one or two places. I liked all these places, my temporary homes, but I made a provisory philosophy regarding them, just in case I lost them, which I inevitably did. Man's destiny, according to my philosophy, is to be away from home, in perpetual exile. Being born is being expelled from the only true home human beings will ever know. God is the only native because He never left the womb.

And then came the Romanian Revolution of December 1989! I returned on the first train allowed back—the Budapest-Istanbul Orient Express—and was moved to tears by the spectacle of a euphoric nation that had shaken off the loathsome tyranny of the Ceauşescus, the world's bloodiest Communist dynasty. Romanian flags with the socialist emblem cut out of the middle fluttered over the snow of the border. Young soldiers raised their fingers in the victory salute. In Bucharest, gutted buildings were still smoking in the Square of the Republic. At the television station throngs of sleepless people celebrated the birth of a free nation. I was carried along by the joy of return—after 25 years—to my native country, and to my hometown. I had never thought that the day would finally come when such a return would be possible. My exile, I thought, was over. You *can* go home again.

I returned to New Orleans ecstatic after spending 10 days in revolutionary Romania. In the next few months, while the world was still watching that corner of the world, strange things began to happen. The miracle of the revolution began to evaporate little by little as seemingly unrelated revelations appeared in the media. In an hour-long special from Bucharest, Ted Koppel reported on *Nightline* what were the first doubts as to the authenticity of the "revolution." A reported massacre of children on the steps of the Timişoara Cathedral, seen by the whole world via Romanian television, appeared to be a fabrication. The extraordinary number of victims, reported at 60,000, was revised by the ruling National Salvation Front to less than 1,000. The provisional government, led by Ion Iliescu, was suspiciously full of high-ranking Ceauşescu functionaries. Worst of all, the dreaded "Securitate"—the secret police—which reportedly had been mounting fierce resistance to the "people's army," appeared to have vanished immediately after the events. The hasty execution of the Ceauşescus, though welcomed by most people, left many doubts. Had the Ceauşescus been killed so that they wouldn't talk? The National Salvation Front, which had promised to dissolve after calling for April elections, constituted itself into a political party instead and took credit for the revolution. The early days of Free Romanian Television, when the leaders of the Front had appeared, seemingly out of nowhere, were paying off. Most people believed that the Front had been spontaneously formed in the heat of battle against the tyrant.

In retrospect, the TV appearances as well as the legal changes quickly enacted after December had been carefully planned. It now appears that the December Revolution in Romania was a coup d'etat planned in great detail at the highest levels of the party, army and Securitate. It appears also that the people killed in Timişoara, Bucharest, Sibiu and Cluj were killed solely to induce mass hysteria and to give the illusion that a popular uprising was in progress. Power had passed from the Ceauşescus into the hands of their henchmen, who remained solidly in place.

But in fact, a popular uprising did take place, a fact that surprised the leaders of the coup. A genuine revolution occurred as a result of the sudden disruption. Students, workers and young army officers took the opportunity to demand genuine democracy, a free press and an end to the Communist Party bureaucracy. This was a development both unexpected and unwelcome—and ultimately intolerable—to the clique in power. On June 14, 1990, President Ion Iliescu called on the "miners" to clear University Square in Bucharest of the thousands of protesters demanding an end to Communism. These so-called miners —who were in fact army recruits with secret-police training—brutally beat students, but also passers-by, including women and children. Armed with lists of dissidents, and led by Securitate officers, they destroyed opposition parties' headquarters, vandalized the Architecture School of the University of Bucharest and then, in an orgy of destruction, fanned out into the Gypsy neighborhoods and savagely attacked anyone who crossed their path. The world saw these events on television, and, suddenly, all the sympathy and goodwill acquired by Romania during the days of December vanished.

Was I going to lose my just-regained home once more? In July, two weeks after the bloody suppression of dissent, I returned to Romania to see things with my own eyes.

I came expecting a city at war. But Bucharest was no Beirut. If anything, it was narcotically peaceful, in a deep-green midsummer way. People strolled lazily in the warm evening. The cinemas were doing brisk business. Two theaters, one specializing in musical comedy, the other in satire, had their doors wide open. On one of their posters, a wit had added the name of Romania's prime minister, Petre Roman, to those of the actors. In Cișmigiu Gardens lovers on benches were wrapped obliviously about one another. On other benches, ladies and gents of a certain age were murmuring and nodding in the twilight, their gestures unhurried. Children were playing soccer on the grass. A dog lying lazily on a traveled street barely got up when a Romanian Dacia barreled past him.

Around University Square, where not long ago the coal-smeared "miners" attacked protesters with lead pipes and rubber batons, the Gypsies were doing a lively business selling the latest papers, some of them like *Românul* (*The Romanian*) literally born that day, others, like *Sărutul* (*The Kiss*), Romania's first erotic publication, inconceivable six months ago. The pictures in *The Kiss* were so fuzzy the nudes looked like distant inkblots from outer space. There were, in fact, elements of exuberant silliness and touching humor to the mushrooming free press of Romania. But the chief opposition newspaper, *România Liberă* was not easy to find: A vendor pulled it from under his box when I handed him twice the cover price.

These nearly idyllic scenes soon vanished when I approached the people. Anger lay beneath the calm. Not far from the raucous vendors, by a fountain in University Square, a crowd argued politics. All about them were reminders of the June violence, mostly on the graffiti-scarred walls. I read: ILIESCU = CEAUȘESCU, FREE MARIAN MUNTEANU—the student leader beaten and arrested in June—, ILIESCU THE NIGHTSTICK, THERE IS NO DEMOCRACY WITHOUT PLURALISM, DOWN WITH THE DICTATOR-SHIP.

There were no demonstrators now, and the police presence seemed minimal. But on street corners, and leaning casually against buildings, familiar shadowy figures watched everything with hawk eyes. Gypsies had appointed themselves keepers of the candles still lit at the sites commemorating the dead of December. Last winter, when I first came here, they burned dramatically in the ice-covered snow. Now they seemed makeshift, like campfires, blackening the university walls. I stepped carefully over streamlets of infernal black goo from the candles of the dead, guarding my pockets. The unsightly barbecue pit smoldering in the heart of the capital felt like an omen of things to come.

I could not forget that this was the place only recently torn by the terrible February earthquake, and ripped apart by violence. The façade of every building was pockmarked by bullets from first to last floors. Only weeks ago these sidewalks flowed with blood. The wounds were still open.

"The government is lying!" a man told me. "We are sick, everyone in it is sick. . . . If we don't get the truth we are all going to die. . . . You Americans . . ."—he poked me accusingly in the chest—"you have no sense. . . . We need help. . . . You do not punish a sick person, you help them. . . . But now you stand smugly by, refusing us. . . ." Another man joined in: "This country is being sold piecemeal by Gypsy speculators, torn apart by Hungarians, ruled by Jews. . . . The government is bankrupt!" he shouted.

Here they were again, those old hatreds.

. . .

The trees, so peaceful-looking only yesterday, now seemed rather sad and underwatered. Those lovers sitting on benches under them had probably had little to eat since yesterday. If they were to make the mistake of marrying and trying to live on something more than love, they'd be hopelessly navigating Bucharest's empty "food complexes," after long workdays, in search of something other than rusty cans of congealed fat and sausages that are better left unpictured.

There was a market next to the store where tomatoes and peaches at extravagant prices lay unattended under swarms of flies. It wasn't a great start for free enterprise. Starved for fresh fruit, I bought a kilo of peaches, which I carried in my shirt because paper bags were non-existent. I bit greedily into one, juice running down my shirt. The old people on benches eyed me hungrily but politely, looking at me from a great distance, as if I were still an ocean apart. And I was—an ocean of worthless local money obtained from a few dollars, a rich émigré trailing pricey peach juice behind me like gold dust.

I couldn't wait to leave Bucharest for Sibiu and the mountains of Transylvania. I left on the morning of July 4, not without thinking nostalgically of the great big parties back home in New Orleans. As I caught myself saying "back home" I began to wonder. Where was home? This was once my home, but no more.

As I drove out of the city, the majestic Carpathian Mountains began unfolding their deep-green forests. The road climbed into crags and peaks. Nestled between them were clean villages with pretty peasant houses with carved wooden porches. Women sat weaving on benches, children played in streams. We waited for hay-laden carts to pass. Perched atop them were old peasants who lifted their lambskin caps in greeting. We waited for a flock of sheep to pass. The shepherd, followed by a shaggy dog, lifted his walking stick to salute me. At the well of one village, young girls dressed in embroidered blouses gossiped while drawing water. Time had stood still here. But no sooner had I allowed myself to sink into the pleasant dream of Arcadia than the sky took on an ochre tinge sprinkled with wisps of black smoke. Without warning, the landscape changed from glad verdure to earth stripped bare, enveloped in clouds of coal dust. We were near the town of Tîrgu-Jiu. As we approached, the raw ugliness of stripped land gave way to equally ugly cement cubes inhabited by industrial workers.

Walking about in grimy clothes, or standing with a mug of beer at outdoor cafes, they all had a dour, bitter expression on their faces.

Happily, this too disappeared when I drove into my hometown of Sibiu, which had changed little in the past 25 years. The cobblestone streets twisted up to Gothic towers; shady plazas with statues of forgotten horsemen slumbered in the late afternoon sun. Sibiu has miraculously escaped the demolition mania of the dictator who envisioned the entire country covered with beehives of cement cubicles. Some attribute this to the benevolent dictatorship of Nicu Ceauşescu, the ex-dictator's son, who had quite a bit of sympathy here.

My old high-school friend Ion told me that Sibiu had not suffered deprivation as badly as Bucharest. He himself seemed to have done well. As we sat reminiscing, sipping wine at an outdoor cafe, an acquaintance of Ion's, a city slicker smoking a Kent—a sure sign of black-market know-how—approached us. When he heard me speak, he said, "You talk just like the kikes who are coming back." His use of "kike" was casual. "And your mother," I asked him, "was she Hitler's dentist?" He was offended.

Here it was—in my old home, my childhood paradise—once more—that hateful ethnic hatred.

My friend apologized for the rudeness of his acquaintance, but when I broached the subject of prejudice it proved impossible to talk reasonably to my Romanian Transylvanian friend about his Hungarian neighbors. "They didn't tell you," he said, leaning conspiratorially into my ear, "that the Hungarians played football with the head of a Romanian priest and that they paraded an impaled Romanian child through villages. . . ." When I asked for proof, he just shook his head, disbelieving my disbelief.

For the next few days, I wandered the melancholic streets of my ancient burg. I saw, occasionally, a quick glimpse of the child I once was, rounding a corner. As I listened to the voices of my friends, as well as to the voices in my head, I saw little reason to hope. Communism had torn up people's souls. There were hatred, resentment and despair everywhere I looked. "We've got to do something about the Hungarians, the Gypsies and the others," a member of the nationalist *Vatra Românească* (Romanian Hearth) told me, in what had by now become a familiar refrain. Nonetheless, this "others" chilled the Jewish blood in my veins to a temperature, alas, only too familiar throughout history. The jump from nationalist hatred to multiculturalism is a jump from prehistory into the postmodern. It's too big a leap for people steeped for decades in the acrid juices of suspicion and discontent.

The days of my brief stay passed dreamlike. Soon it was time to return to Bucharest for the flight back, to my other "home," to my true home, when all is said and done. I would have liked to be able to draw some conclusions from the long days and sleepless nights spent talking, talking, talking. Romania was a country of voices, long-suppressed voices, speculating, debating, shouting, wondering. I closed my eyes and listened to them, unsure of where they were headed.

The morning of my scheduled departure, I had a beer at the Intercontinental Hotel in Bucharest. This ugly looming monster of cement and corruption where all the news reporters stay is the only place to get cold beer in Bucharest. In the lobby, varied human fauna were conducting all sorts of shady business. I felt as if the entire slime of this country were sloshing against the police-beige walls. I spotted liver-colored vampires of both sexes standing ready to spread infection under the ghastly neon. I watched the money-changers, now paying 120 lei to the dollar. A good monthly salary is 2,500 lei or 21 American dollars. I saw people dealing anything foreign, from disposable lighters to condoms. Was this the beginning of the famous change to the market economy touted by everyone from government ministers to street-corner philosophers? If so, there was little to sing about.

Everyone I had talked to wanted to leave. Paradoxically, now that it was possible to have some freedom, the only freedom anyone wanted was to get out.

At Otopeni International Airport, I clutched my ticket tightly, happy to be leaving. I experienced, in an attenuated form, the same mixture of intoxicated elation and fear that I experienced when I first left Romania in that faraway year 1965, sure that I would never return.

I was brought suddenly to my senses by the barking of the immigration officer. *"Where is your exit form?"* I didn't know. "I don't have it," I told her. She glanced at my visa: *"Journalist?"* Her voice dripped with contempt. "Yes," I said, "you have something against journalists?" *"Codrescu?"* she said, with the same hatred. I saw myself suddenly in her eyes: a journalist out to bad-mouth her country, and an émigré. How she wished for the old days! *"I am an immigration officer!"*

she shouted. *"I can ask you to the next room!"* I could imagine the next room well: a small green chamber with rusty flakes of blood all over it. But she refrained, and I was glad.

This would be the end of the story if life were as neat as stories. But no sooner had I gotten out of the clutches of the Romanian police apparatus than I discovered my flight would be delayed until the next day. Used to the endemic paranoia of Romanians, I immediately assumed that a crisis was at hand.

Going once more through the routine of retrieving luggage and getting a taxi back to Bucharest, I saw little to look forward to.

I was wrong.

Massed by thousands in University Square, students from all the universities in the capital were marching toward the Justice Ministry.

They were demanding the release of their imprisoned leader, Marian Munteanu. FREE MARIAN MUNTEANU! The students carried flowers; their slogans echoed throughout Bucharest. "DORMIȚI UȘOR, DORMIȚI UȘOR, AȚI ALES UN DICTA-TOR!" ("SLEEP WELL, SLEEP WELL, YOU'VE ELECTED A DICTATOR!") they sang. "JOS COMUNISMUL!" ("DOWN WITH COMMUNISM!")

I joined the demonstration, not as a reporter or as a supporter, but as a body, feeling at once that there was hope yet. As the crowd rounded the corner to Opera Square to listen to Mihai Gheorghiu, the vice president of the Student League, speak, I knew who was going to save this country. Time, with all its old hatreds, had stood still in Romania. But a revolution did take place in December, and then in June. It was a revolution of the young against the prejudices of the older generation, which includes, sad to say, many of my old friends. This revolution is going on still. Whoever let the tiger out of its cage is in no position to put it back.

My last glimpse of Romania was from the airplane. A Carpathian peak with a bit of snow on it stood stubbornly against the hot summer sky.

Brought Up on Right-Wing Anthologies

AMIRI BARAKA, interviewed by Bertrand Mathieu

First of all, when I said this morning that most of us were . . . literary types or "intellectuals" brought up on right-wing anthologies, I meant that we go to these colleges and we study the poets proposed by official society. We learn literature from the perspective of officialdom. We study Ezra Pound, who was a fascist, who talked bad about Blacks, Jews, and others. We study this and we're told it's great poetry. No matter that Pound is talking bad about us or putting us down, this must be great. The book *says* it's great! Eliot is a royalist talking about bringing back the King, the Church, but we suck it all up and use it as a measure of all we call literature, when the actual revolutionary tradition in literature in the U. S. A. is either given to us confused, mixed up, or *not at all!* We begin with Henry James, T. S. Eliot, Ezra Pound, John Crowe Ransom and so forth and so on. We are given all those folks as Great Literature. But in terms of us understanding, let's say, Mark Twain, Melville, Jack London, Dreiser, Richard Wright, Langston Hughes, W. E. B. Du Bois—*another old* tradition, the *revolutionary* tradition in American literature which goes at least as far back as Tom Paine—that is given to us so confused that we don't understand it, we don't see them as writers who are part of a tradition. We don't see that there is a revolutionary tradition in American writing *as well* as a counter-revolutionary one.

When I came to New York, I looked up Allen Ginsberg, who is actually a scholar on a truly impressive scale—in terms of Western poetry I haven't met anybody recently who knows as much about poetry as Allen Ginsberg, a marvelous Blake scholar. Now what Allen was trying to do was to find alternatives to the well-made American poem that Eberhart and John Crowe Ransom were producing. He had begun to study alternative forms, not only Walt Whitman and the American speech tone but William Carlos Williams and the American idiom. The actual sound of America. What *is* the sound of America? What do things *sound* like in America? America is not England. What do things *sound* like here in America? What does it sound like when you *sing* in American? What does an American poem sound like? But then Ginsberg started doing all sorts of take-offs on Whitman. He saw

Whitman as a true alternative because of Whitman's Populist tradition, which is actually trying to *identify* with the masses of the people in the U. S. A.—that long, cadenced, heroic line of Whitman's—the heroic *singing* line. And then of course the fact that Whitman was a non-conformist and a homosexual—and so was Allen Ginsberg. So that tied that up even tighter. But primarily the kind of non-conformist, heroic-line, Populist elements in Whitman. It was Ginsberg who first turned me on to all that and actually started me reading Whitman. Who was the other writer you asked about?

. . . Melville, yeah. See, the thing about Melville, again, was that in traditional Academe—the official Academy—Henry James was always talked about as The Writer, the Great American Novelist. When actually in terms of America, in terms of the great bursting-out tradition of *America*—the New Found Land—you have to go to Melville. It's Melville who takes the American experience of whaling and turns it into some kind of profound, eighty-five-levels-of-ambiguity Existential novel! That's *Melville* who does that! It's Melville who writes *Benito Cereno,* who writes *Pierre.* It's *Melville* who puts us in touch with that crucial kind of American experience. So it was a question again of the Tradition, what tradition are you coming from? Melville was important to us because it was our revolutionary American tradition that he associated himself with from the start. He grabbed those basic, troubling, distinctive American dilemmas and tried to make literature out of them. And like W. C. Williams, he tried to seize the difficult problems of American *speech* as well. And he didn't shirk the big problem of race. You can see how that makes him doubly important. Like, if you're Black, then after you get to the question of how to deal with America, you have to deal with the Black thing. But, see, the point is, according to the Academy you're not even American, you're *English!* Because they're still trying to take you into their English works. *English Lit. Limited!* They don't even want to admit that the war in 1776 was fought and that the Colonies freed themselves. Over at Yale, they're not even sure of *that* to this day! (Laughter)

. . . Yeah, well what's wrong with *American* art? So what I saw was young poets fighting to be *American,* to say that we in America have an experience, we're not in Europe, we're in the United States. And that there is a *particular* experience here. And so as that began to dawn on me, I realized that that means that I too had an even *more particular* experience because I'm an Afro-American. That is a very *particular* experience. It doesn't separate you from the others necessarily, but it is a particularity that must be expressed. Just as the American experience as such doesn't make all of us separate from the rest of the human race, off in the clouds. But it is a *particular* experience. And to try and gloss over that and hold up European or English models to us—which a lot of the Academy still does—is detrimental to literature.

From "Literary Hegemonies"*

HELEN BAROLINI

The dominant culture, working under its own rules and . . . models, within a tight network of insiders—editors, agents, reviewers, critics—is not eager to recognize and include in its lists that which does not reflect its own style, taste, and sense of what is worthwhile. . . .

Literature is not only in the great and practiced writer. It is also in the new voices which add to the store of human experience; in the voices which, by enriching and extending the national literary achievement, become of permanent value.

Ethnic writing was not given entry to the cultural mainstream of the American literary world but existed, at best, in some backwater of folklore and curiosities [until very recently.] . . .

In a country this size, comprised of such rich and varied strains, there should be room for all facets of literary expression and familiarity with them. But that is not the case. There are hierarchies and hegemonies which, consciously or unconsciously, promote and decide what is literature and what is not. The facts of literary life are elementary: it is not simply publication, but what comes both before and after that counts.

. . . Books which are not reviewed are buried.

And that is exactly what happens to the overwhelming majority of books which are published without special advocacy: if they are not signaled for attention by powerful names, they die.

---

* A section of the Introduction to *The Dream Book: the Writings of Italian-American Women*.

Harvey Shapiro, former editor of *The New York Times Book Review,* and also a panelist at [a] symposium, revealed a dismaying statistic: *The Times,* which does more reviewing than any other publication in the country, can mention only about 8 percent of all books published in a given year. Even so, between the daily edition and the Sunday book review section, it manages to give double reviews to some books (all too predictable) while the vast number are not reviewed at all. Too bad, says Shapiro, but that's how it is.

Books that are not reviewed are not picked up elsewhere along the tightly linked chain of literary life. Literary achievement is gauged by appearance in required reading lists, literature course outlines, textbooks, anthologies, critical appraisal, book reviews, and bibliographies. . . .

When I was in school, American literature was identified regionally—the New Englanders, the Southern school, the expatriates, Western Expansion. Jules Chametzky, a scholar of cultural pluralism as reflected in American literature, has written about literary regionalism. It became, toward the end of the nineteenth century, "a strategy for ignoring or minimizing social issues of great significance. These issues concerned race and class and the new money-power; an upheaval in American ethnic composition; far-reaching challenges to older American social assumptions and mores. Such matter called for serious literary treatment; but such matter deeply explored could upset notions of unified national culture."[1] Local color and regional literature could be accepted by the dominant public and leading editors, but only insofar as they reinforced notions of a basically homogenous rather than a conflicted nation and culture.

Katherine Newman, a scholar and critic, has proposed discarding many of the old theories of American literature "since they were fitted to a specific body of literature: that of the Anglo-American seaboard culture." Taking a wider view of the whole oeuvre, other characteristics can be discerned, and she sees one characteristic of American literature (particularly relevant from the ethnic perspective) as eccentricity, in its exact meaning of being off-center, asymmetrical, irregular, uneven. . . .

For that is another characteristic of American literature that Newman cites as deriving from the pressure of pluralism: "It is *choice-making,* value-seeking, repudiating the superficialities of our society. . . . The greatest American theme is *not* the fulfillment of 'the American dream' of material success, but rather the selection of a cultural mode which will satisfy the spiritual and emotional needs of the individual. The chief preoccupation of our writers is *the necessity* of choice."[2] . . .

Literary history is falsified if it doesn't record all voices and give access to these voices by publishing, keeping in print, and making part of study courses those writers who aren't only the prominent ones of the dominant tradition. As Newman says, the critical function is to examine works on their own aesthetic terms, to relate them to the entire corpus of American literature, and to overcome the internalized stereotypes and cultural myths that have caused critical myopia. . . .

Publishers say they cannot afford to be crusaders. But Black writer Zora Neale Hurston replied that she refused to be humbled by second place in a contest she never designed, and she identified what comes out of safe, marketable publishing as candidates for the American Museum of Unnatural History, i.e., a weird collection of stereotypes—nondimensional figures that can be taken in at a glance, as, the expressionless American Indian, the shuffling Negro, the inarticulate Italian, etc. . . .

NOTES

1. Jules Chametzky, "Our Decentralized Literature," a paper presented at John F. Kennedy-Institut fur Amerikastudien, Heidelberg, June 4, 1971, and published in *Proceedings*.
2. Katherine Newman, "An Ethnic Literary Scholar Views American Literature," *Melus*, Spring 1980, p. 6.

Orange: Hiring

HARRIET ZINNES

Those lips. Very red, and behind them the teeth, irregular, and not a full set. Why not a full set? He doesn't ask, but he looks at her. Straight at her face. Her yellow face. Her hair bound, but a few strands hover near her face, that yellow face. She is not oriental. No, not oriental. She is a wispy young thing, comes from Alaska. How did she get to the States, he asks. Romona looks at him, frightened. How do I know how she got here. Aren't you pleased that she is here, simply here.

Why should I be pleased? She's hardly the kind of young woman who will be useful to me. How can she be useful to me? Does she look strong? Is she able to talk? She certainly doesn't understand English. What will I do with her?

Ramona does not know. How do I know, she asks. I thought you were looking for someone from Alaska. I called the agency, and here she is. Isn't that fulfilling an assignment? Why don't you think I am doing things right? Why do you make me frightened? Didn't I find you an Alaskan woman?

But look at her, Dwight said, just look at her. What can she do? Can she type? No, she doesn't even know the language. Look at her, can she sweep the floor, she is so little, so wispy, so weak. Can she go shopping for me? Can she run errands? Can she answer the phone? Answer me, Ramona, what do you think? Can she do any of these things?

How do I know? All I know is that you wanted a woman from Alaska, I called the agency, and right away, quick, they sent you a young woman from Alaska. What more do you want? You must find out her capabilities. Maybe she has some talent you can use. Find out. Aren't you going to find out?

Dwight sat down. Pulled the Alaskan woman down next to him. It did not require any strength. Like a feather she seemed to fall falteringly right on the bench next to him. What is your name, he asked. Do you have a name?

She shook her head. No, she said in good English. I do not have a name.

Why don't you have a name, Dwight asked.

Because. Simply because, she said. Maybe because I have no father, no mother. I was raised by Americans. They were living in a, yes, I think it was a school. The man was a teacher. The woman passed out the papers, erased the board, and smiled. She always smiled. I smiled too and that is why I was able to learn English. Would you like me to recite a poem, an American poem? Do you want me to do that? Here is the poem. It is by a strange American woman. Her name was Emily. Maybe her full name was Emily Dickinson. I like the poem. Will you hear it?

For Christ's sake, I don't want to hear any poems. I need a typist, not a reciter of poems. Can you type? Ramona seems to think you can do nothing, say nothing, be absolutely useless. Can you type?

Yes, I can type. The smiling American woman taught me to type. I can type. But she refused to teach me how to use a computer. I can't use a computer. Do you want me to learn the computer or is it enough to type for you?

Yes, it is enough for you to type for me. We'll begin work tomorrow then. Where are you going to live?

Live? I'll be living with you. She said that if you wanted me to and if you thought I must I could eat and sleep with you. In your bed.

At this, Ramona came up close to the woman. She raised her hand and slapped her, twice, with her right hand.

The young woman said nothing, didn't even touch her face. She looked at Dwight, who, stunned, at first was silent. Then he turned angrily to Ramona. "You fool. What did you do? Are you crazy? This woman doesn't understand a thing. What does she know about the bed? Don't you see she's out of it, completely out of it. What does she know? Oh yes, she knows Emily Dickinson. Emily Dickinson, who knew nothing about the bed, you crazy woman."

Ramona began to cry. The Alaskan went over to her, gently put her arms around her, and rocked her to and fro. Ramona did not stop crying nor did she remove the Alaskan woman's arms.

Now what am I going to do with two crazy women, Dwight groaned.

Ramona stopped crying. The Alaskan walked away. Dwight said, all right, you two. We'll make an arrangement. First of all, we've got to name this woman. What shall we call her, Ramona. You name her.

Ramona wiped her tears away with her right hand. She smiled. Let's call her Orange.

Orange? OK, we'll call her Orange. Do you like the name, little woman, he asked.

Yes, I like the name. Orange smiled. Suddenly Ramona laughed. Dwight laughed.

And now let me recite the poem, Orange said. Let me recite the poem.

I started early, took my dog,
And visited the sea;

The mermaids in the basement
Came out to look at me,

And frigates in the upper floor
Extended hempen hands,
Presuming me to be a mouse
Aground, upon the sands.

But no man moved me till the tide
Went past my simple shoe,
And past my apron and my belt,
And past my bodice too,

And made as he would eat me up
As wholly as a dew
Upon a dandelion's sleeve—
And then I started too.

And he—he followed close behind;
I felt his silver heel
Upon my ankle,—then my shoes
Would overflow with pearl.

Until we met the solid town,
No man he seemed to know;
And bowing with a mighty look
At me, the sea withdrew.

Strangers in the Village

DAVID MURA

Recently, in *The Village Voice*, a number of articles were devoted to the issue of race in America. Perhaps the most striking article, "Black Women, White Kids: A Tale of Two Worlds," was about Black women in New York City who take care of upper-middle-class and upper-class white children. Merely by describing the situation of these Black women and recording their words, the article pointed out how race and class affects these women's lives: "As the nanny sits in the park watching a tow-haired child play, her own kids are coming home from school; they will do their homework alone and make dinner."

None of the white people who employed these nannies seemed at all cognizant of the contradictions of this description. Instead the whites seemed to view the Black nannies as a natural facet of their lives, an expected privilege. Yet, on another less-conscious level, the whites appeared to have misgivings that they could not express. One of the nannies, named Bertha, talked about how she objected to the tone of voice her employer, Barbra, used: "You wait a minute here, Barbra. I'm not a child," Bertha would tell Barbra, "I can talk to you any way I want. This is a free country, it's not a commie country." Every time Bertha and Barbra have an argument, Barbra buys Bertha presents: "She bought me shoes, a beautiful blouse, a Mother's Day present . . . she's a very generous person. She's got a good heart." But Bertha doesn't really like the presents. "It always made me feel guilty. To tell you the truth about it, I never had too many people give me presents, so it just made me feel bad.

"Another reason we don't get along," Bertha continues, "is she is always trying to figure me out. See, I'm a very complicated person. I'm a very moody person . . . I'm independent. I figure I can deal with it myself. And we would sit there, I could just feel her eyes on me, and I'd have to get up and leave the room . . . She just wants you to be satisfied with her all the time . . . She wants me to tell her I love you. I just can't."

The author of the article says that sometimes Barbra seems to want love and sometimes she seems to want forgiveness. "But perhaps for most white people, a black person's affection can never mean more than an act of absolution for historical and collective guilt, an affection desired not because of how one feels about that particular person but because that person is black."

As a middle-class third generation Japanese-American, I read this article with mixed feelings. On one level, I have much more in common with Bertha's employer, Barbra, than I do with Bertha. Although at one time Japanese-Americans worked in jobs similar to Bertha's and were part of the lower class, by my generation this was not the case. I grew up in the suburbs of Chicago, went to college and graduate school, married a pediatrician who is three-quarters WASP and one-quarter Jewish. Although I will most likely assume a large portion of our child care when we have children, my wife and I will probably use some form of outside child care. Most likely, we would not employ a Black nanny, even if we lived in New York City, but I could not help feeling a sense of guilt and shame when I read the article. I could understand Barbra's wish to use acts of kindness to overlook inequalities of class and race; her desire to equate winning the affections of a Black servant with the absolution of historical and collective guilt. I would not, in the end, act like Barbra, but I do recognize her feelings.

At the same time, I also recognize and identify with the anger Bertha feels toward her white employer. In part, Bertha's anger is a recognition of how profoundly race has affected her and Barbra's lives, and also that Barbra does not truly understand this fact. Although generalizations like this can sometimes be misused—more about this later—American culture defines white middle-class culture as the norm. As a result, Blacks and other colored minorities, must generally know two cultures to survive—the culture of middle-class whites and their own minority culture. Middle-class whites need only to know one culture. For them, knowledge of a minority culture is a seeming —and I use the word "seeming" here purposely—luxury; they can survive without it.

On a smaller scale than Bertha I have experienced the inability of members of the white majority to understand how race has affected my life, to come to terms with the differences between us. Sometimes I can bridge this gap, but never completely; more often, a gulf appears between me and white friends that has previously been unacknowledged. I point out to them that the images I grew up with in the media were all white, that the books I read in school—from Dick and Jane onwards—were about whites and later, about European civilization. I point out to them the way beauty is defined in our culture and how, under such definitions, slanted eyes, flat noses, and round faces just don't make it. And as I talk, I often sense their confusion, the limits of their understanding of the world. They become angry, defensive. "We all have experiences others can't relate to," they reply and equate the issue of race with prejudice against women or Italians or rich people. Such generalizations can sometimes be used to express sympathy with victims of prejudice, but as used by many whites, it generally attempts to shut down racial anger by denying the distinct causes of that anger, thereby rendering it meaningless. Another form of this tactic is the reply, "I think of you just as a white person," or, a bit less chauvinistically, "I think of you as an individual." While, at one time in my life, I would have taken this for a compliment, my reply now is, "I don't want to be a white person. Why can't I be who I am? Why can't you think of me as a Japanese-American *and* as an individual?"

I'd like to leave these questions a moment and, because I'm a writer, take up these themes in terms of literature. In my talks with whites about race, I very quickly find myself referring to history. As many have pointed out, America has never come to terms with two fundamental historical events: the enslavement of Blacks by whites and the taking of this continent by Europeans from the Native Americans and the accompanying policies of genocide. A third historical event that America hasn't come to terms with—and yet is closer to doing so than with the other two—is the internment of Japanese-Americans during World War II. Although some maintain that the camps were caused simply by wartime hysteria, the determining factors were racism and a desire for the property owned by the Japanese-Americans. Recently, in *War without Mercy,* John Dower has demonstrated how the war in the Pacific, on both sides, took on racist overtones and used racist propaganda that were absent in the war in Europe. In wartime propaganda, while the Nazis were somehow kept separate from the rest of the German race, the Japanese, as a race, were characterized as lice and vermin. This racist propaganda was both caused by and intensified a phenomenon that led to the internment camps: A large number of white Americans were unable to distinguish between the Japanese as the enemy and Japanese-Americans.

Knowing the history behind the camps, knowing that during the internment the lives of many Japanese-Americans, particularly the Issei (first generation), were permanently disrupted; knowing the internment caused the loss of millions of dollars of property, I, as a Japanese-American, feel a kinship to both Blacks and Native Americans that I do not feel with white Americans. It is a kinship that comes from our histories as victims of injustice. Of course, our histories are more than simply being victims, and we must recognize that these histories are also separate and distinct, but there is a certain power and solace in this kinship.

This kinship is reinforced by our current position as minorities in a white-dominated culture. For instance, when Blacks or Native Americans or Chicanos complain about their image in the media, it is a complaint I easily understand. I myself have written a number of pieces about this subject, analyses of the stereotypes in such films as *Rambo* or *Year of the Dragon*. Recently, I read a play by a Sansei playwright, Philip Kan Gotanda, *Yankee Dawg You Die,* and I was struck by the similarities between this play about two Japanese-American actors and Robert Townsend's *Hollywood Shuffle,* a film about a Black actor trying to make it in Hollywood.

In both works, the actors must struggle with the battle between economics and integrity, between finding no parts or playing in roles that stereotype their minority. In *Hollywood Shuffle,* we see the hero, clearly a middle-class Black, trying and failing to portray a pimp in his bathroom mirror. Later in the film, there is a mock Black acting school where Black actors learn to talk in jive, to move like a pimp, to play runaway slaves, to shuffle their feet. In *Yankee Dawg You Die,* a young third-generation Japanese-American actor, Bradley, is fired at one point because he will not mix up his r's and l's when playing a waiter. Throughout the play, he keeps chastizing an older Japanese-American actor for selling out, for playing stereotyped "coolie" and "dirty Jap" parts. Essentially, what Bradley is accusing Vincent of being is a Tom:

> *The Business. You keep talking about the business. The industry. Hollywood. What's Hollywood? Cutting up your face to look more white? So my nose is a little flat. Fine! Flat is beautiful. So I don't have a double fold in my eye-lid. Great! No one in my entire racial family has had it in the last 10,000 years.*
>
> *My old girlfriend used to put scotch tape on her eyelids to get the double folds so she could look more "cau-ca-sian." My new girlfriend—she doesn't mess around, she got surgery. Where does it stop? "I never turned down a role." Where does it begin? Vincent? Where does it begin? All that self hate. You and your Charlie Chop Suey roles.*

Vincent tells Bradley that he knows nothing about the difficulties he, Vincent, went through: "You want to know the truth? I'm glad I did it . . . in some small way it is a victory. Yes, a victory. At least an oriental was on the screen acting, being seen. We existed!" At this point, the scene slides into a father and son mode, where the father-figure, Vincent, tells Bradley that he should appreciate what those who went before him have done; it's easy now for Bradley to spout the rhetoric of Asian-American consciousness, but in the past, such rhetoric was unthinkable. (Earlier in the play, when Vincent says, "I do not really notice, or quite frankly care, if someone is oriental or caucasian . . ." Bradley makes a certain connection between Asian-American rights and other liberation movements. "It's Asian, not oriental," he says. "Asian, oriental. Black, negro. Woman, girl. Gay, homosexual.")

But Bradley then gets on a soapbox and makes a cogent point, though a bit baldly, and I can easily imagine a young Black actor making a similar argument to an old Black actor who has done Stepin Fetchit roles:

> *You seem to think that every time you do one of those demeaning roles, all that is lost is your dignity . . . Don't you realize that every time you do a portrayal like that millions of people in their homes, in movie theatres across the country will see it. Be influenced by it. Believe it. Every time you do any old stereotypic role just to pay the bills, you kill the right of some Asian-American child to be treated as a human being. To walk through the school yard and not be called a "chinaman gook" by some taunting kids who just saw the last Rambo film.*

By the end of the play, though, it's clear Bradley's been beaten down. After scrambling through failed audition after audition, wanting to make it in the business, he cries when he fails to get a role as a butler because he doesn't know kung fu. He also reveals he has recently had his nose fixed, á la Michael Jackson.

What do the similarities I've been pointing out mean for an Asian-American writer? Recently, there have been a spate of books, such as Allan Bloom's *The Closing of the American Mind,* which call for a return to the classics and a notion of a core-cultural tradition; these critiques bemoan the relativism and "nihilism" of the sixties and the multicultural movements which, in the name of "tolerance," have supposedly left our culture in a shambles. Unfortunately, such critics never really question the political and historical bases of cultural response. If they did, they would understand why, contrary to Allan Bloom, other minority writers represent a valuable resource for Asian-American writers and vice versa: our themes and difficulties are similar; we learn from each other things we cannot receive from a Saul Bellow or John Updike or even Rousseau or Plato.

It is not just the work of Asian-American writers like Gotanda that sustain me. I know a key point in my life was when I discovered the work of Frantz Fanon, particularly his book, *Black Skin, White Masks*. My experience with that work and others like it shows why multiculturalism, for a member of a racial minority, is not simply tolerance, but an essential key to survival.

In his work, Fanon, a Black psychologist, provides a cogent analysis of how a majority can oppress a minority through culture: it makes the victim or servant identify with the ruler and, in so doing, causes the victim to direct whatever anger he/she feels at the situation towards himself/herself in the form of self-hatred.

> *In the Antilles . . . in the magazines, the Wolf, the Devil, the Evil Spirit, the Bad Man, the Savage are always symbolized by Negroes or Indians; since there is always identification with the victor, the little Negro, quite as easily as the little white boy, becomes an explorer, an adventurer, a missionary "who faces the danger of being eaten by the wicked Negroes" . . . The black school boy . . . who in his lessons is forever talking about "our ancestors, the Gauls," identifies himself with the explorer, the bringer of civilization, the white man who carries truth to the savages—an all-white truth . . . the young Negro . . . invests the hero, who is white, with all his own aggression—at that age closely linked to sacrificial dedication, a sacrificial dedication permeated with sadism.*

This passage can be taken as another version of Bradley's speech to Vincent on the effects of stereotypes on an Asian-American child.

Fanon was incredibly aware of how the economic, social, and political relations of power create and warp an individual's psychic identity. He was quick to point out that psychic sickness does not always find its source in the neuroses of an individual or that individual's family, but in the greater sickness of a society. In such cases, for the individual to become healthy, he or she must recognize that society is sick, and that the ideas he or she has received from that society are part of that sickness.

In short, what Fanon recognized and taught me was the liberating power of anger.

After reading Fanon and the Black French poet from Martinique, Aime Cesaire, I wrote a number of poems in which I chose to ally myself with people of color, anti-colonialist movements, and a non-Eurocentric consciousness. When writing these poems, I was aware of how such poems can often become vehicles for slogans and cheap rhetoric; still I tried to discover a language with a denseness which would prevent such reduction, increase thought, and turn words like "gook" and "nigger" against their original meaning, bending and realigning the slang of racism. Here is the ending of one of those poems:

> . . . *and we were all good niggers, good gooks and japs, good spics and rice eaters saying mem sab, sahib, bwana, boss-san, señor, father, heartthrob oh honored and most unceasing, oh devisor and provider of our own obsequious, ubiquitous ugliness, which stares at you baboon-like, banana-like, dwarf-like, tortoise-like, dirt-like, slant-eyed, kink-haired, ashen and pansied and brutally unredeemable, we are whirling about you, tartars of the air all the urinating, tarantula grasping, ant multiplying, succubused, hothouse hoards yes, it us, it us, we, we knockee, yes, sir, massa, boss-san, we tearee down your door!*

I was scared at first by the anger of this poem, but I also saw it as an answer, an antidote to the depression I had been feeling, a depression brought on by a lack of self-worth and by my dropping out of English graduate school. As my therapist had told me, depression is the repression of anger and grief. In my diary I wrote about the unlocking of this repression:

> *In the first stages of such a process, one can enter a position where the destruction of one stereotype creates merely a new stereotype, and where the need to point out injustice overwhelms and leaves the writing with a baldness that seems both naive and sentimental. Still, the task must be faced, and what I am now trying to do in both my writing and my life is to replace self-hatred and self-negation with anger and grief over my lost selves, over the ways my cultural heritage has been denied to me, over the ways that people in*

*America would assume either that I am not American or, con-
versely, that I am just like them; over the ways my education and
the values of European culture have denied that other cultures exist.
I know more about Europe at the time when my grandfather came
to America than I know about Meiji Japan. I know Shakespeare
and Donne, Sophocles and Homer better than I know Zeami,
Bashō or Lady Murasaki. This is not to say I regret what I know,
but I do regret what I don't know. And the argument that the
culture of America is derived from Europe will not wipe away this
regret.*

I am convinced if I had not read Fanon, if I had not reached these
insights, and gone on to explore beyond white European culture, I
would have died as a writer and died spiritually and physically as a
person. I would have ended up denying who I am and my place in
history. Thus, I think that to deny a people a right to determine their
own cultural tradition is a type of genocide.

Of course, arguing for multiculturalism is not the same thing as
saying that, as a minority writer, I don't need to read the works of
European culture. It's not a case of either/or. As Carlos Fuentes remarked, "We [Latin Americans] have to know the cultures of the West
even better than a Frenchman or an Englishman, and at the same time
we have to know our own cultures. This sometimes means going back
to the Indian cultures, whereas the Europeans feel they don't have to
know our cultures at all. We have to know Quetzalcoatl and Descartes.
They think Descartes is enough." I think Fuentes would agree with
Jesse Jackson that there was something wrong with those students who
greeted his appearance at Stanford with the chant, "Hey hey, ho ho/
Western culture's got to go." As Jackson pointed out, Western culture
was their culture. It is difficult to strike an appropriate balance.

In the same issue of the *Village Voice* that the article about the
Black nannies appeared, Stanley Crouch wrote a perceptive, challenging critique of James Baldwin. Crouch argues that at the beginning of
Baldwin's career, Baldwin was able to maneuver his way through subtleties of the Black writer's position. As an example of this, Crouch
cites Baldwin's distinction between sociology and literature in evaluat-
ing the work of Richard Wright; Baldwin argues that despite the good

intentions of protest novels, they cannot succeed if they are "badly written and wildly improbable." Still Crouch maintains that very early Baldwin's vision began to blur, and cites this passage from the essay, "Stranger in the Village," a depiction of Baldwin's visit to a Swiss town and his sense of alienation from its people:

> *These people cannot be, from the point of view of power, strangers anywhere in the world; they have made the modern world, in effect, even if they do not know it. The most illiterate among them is related, in a way that I am not, to Dante, Shakespeare, Michaelangelo, Aeschylus, da Vinci, Rembrandt, and Racine; the cathedral at Chartres says something to them that it cannot say to me, as indeed would New York's Empire State Building, should anyone here ever see it. Out of their hymns and dances come Beethoven and Bach. Go back a few centuries and they are in their full glory—but I am in Africa, watching the conquerors arrive.*

Crouch charges Baldwin with slipping into a simplistic dualistic thinking, with letting his rage create a we-they attitude which denies the complexity of the race situation:

> *Such thinking led to the problem we still face in which too many so-called nonwhite people looked upon "the West" as some catchall in which every European or person of European descent is somehow part of a structure bent solely on excluding or intimidating the Baldwins of the world. Were Roland Hayes, Marian Anderson, Leontyne Price, Jessye Norman, or Kiri Te Kanawa to have taken such a position, they would have locked themselves out of a world of music that originated neither among Afro-Americans nor Maoris. Further, his ahistorical ignorance is remarkable, and perhaps willful.*

If Baldwin's position is that Afro-Americans cannot learn, or enjoy or perform European culture, or that European culture is worthless to an Afro-American, that is nonsense. But that is not Baldwin's position. He is simply arguing that his relationship to that culture is different from a white European; he views that culture through the experience of a Black American, and if he is to be faulted, it is because he does not give a detailed enough explanation of how his experience as a Black American informs his experience of European culture. But none of this—including the success of opera stars like Jessye Norman —negates the fact that, in America and Europe, European culture has political—that is, ideological—effects and one effect is to reinforce the political power of those of European descent and to promote a view of whites as superior to coloreds. (It is not the only effect of that culture, but again, neither Baldwin nor I am arguing that it is.)

Crouch goes on to argue that "breaking through the mask of collective whiteness—collective guilt—that Baldwin imposes would demand recognition of the fact that, as history and national chauvinism prove, Europe is not a one-celled organism." I will say more about collective guilt a bit later, but it is interesting to note that Crouch refuses the concept of collectivity when it comes to guilt, yet at the same time charges that Baldwin refuses to entertain the possibility of "the international wonder of human heritage." Guilt can never be held collectively, but culture, specifically European culture, can be universal.

Yet, at the same time Crouch argues the non-exclusivity of European culture, he chastizes Baldwin for taking the themes of Third-World writers and adapting them to the context of America: "the denial by Europeans of non-Western cultural complexity—or parity; the social function of the inferiority complex colonialism threw over the native like a net; the alignment of Christianity and cruelty under colonialism, and the idea that world views were at odds, European versus the 'spirit of Bandung,' or the West in the ring with the Third World." How sharp the boundaries of culture should be is a difficult question; it may seem that both Crouch and Baldwin want things both ways: they just disagree on which cultures can attain universality, European culture or that of the Third World. To sort out the specifics of each of their cases requires us to connect attitudes towards culture with feelings about race, specifically the rage of Blacks and other colored minorities in America.

As I've already argued with my own reading of Frantz Fanon, I do think it is illuminating and useful to use Third-World problems in looking at the race issue in America. Still, I also agree with Crouch that there are fundamental differences between the position of Blacks in America and that of colonials in the Third World. To forget these differences in a desire to be at one with all oppressed peoples is both false and dangerous. And I recognize that when borrowing or learning from the language of Third-World peoples and American Blacks, Japanese-Americans, like myself, must still recognize fundamental differences between our position and that of other people of color, whether here or in the Third World.

Part of the danger is that if we ignore the specifics of the situation of our own minority group, in essence we both deny who we are and our own complexity. We also run the risk of using our victimhood as a mask for sainthood, of letting whatever sins the white race has committed against us become a permanent absolution for us, an excuse to forgo moral and psychological introspection. Crouch argues somewhat convincingly that this is exactly the trap that Baldwin fell into and cites as evidence Baldwin's remark that "Rage can only with difficulty, and never entirely, be brought under the domination of the intelligence and is therefore not susceptible to any arguments whatever." According to Crouch, Baldwin, as his career progressed, sold out to rage, despair, self-righteousness, and a will to scandalize:

> In America . . . fat-mouthing Negroes . . . chose to sneer at the heroic optimism of the Civil Rights Movement; they developed their own radical chic and spoke of Malcolm X as being beyond compromise, of his unwillingness to cooperate with the white man, and of his ideas of being too radical for assimilation. Baldwin was sucked into this world of intellectual airlessness. By The Fire Next Time, Baldwin is so happy to see white policemen made uncomfortable by Muslim rallies, and so willing to embrace almost anything that disturbs whites in general, that he starts competing with the apocalyptic tone of the Nation of Islam.

In focusing on Baldwin's inability to transform or let go his rage, I feel Crouch finally hits upon something. I also feel a shudder of self-recognition. Yet the condition Crouch pictures here is a bit more complex than he admits. Certainly, a convincing argument can be made that King's appeal to a higher yet common morality was and will be more effective than Malcolm X's in changing the hearts and minds of whites in America, yet in his very approach to the problem, Crouch seems to put the burden for change upon the Black minority rather than on the white majority. There is something intellectually and morally dishonest about this. For whether one judges King's philosophy or Malcolm X's as correct depends in part on a reading of the hearts and minds of white Americans. If those hearts and minds are fiercely unchanging, then Malcolm X's might seem the more logical stance. Either way, it is a judgment call and it involves a great deal of uncertainty, especially since that judgment involves actions in the future. Yet nowhere in his argument does Crouch concede this.

Shaw called hatred the coward's revenge for ever having been intimidated, says Crouch, and Crouch sees this hatred as the basis of Baldwin's attitude towards whites and towards European culture. I find something skewed in Crouch's use of Shaw's quip here. Given the history of race in America, equating a Black man's sense of intimidation solely with cowardice seems a simplification; couldn't that intimidation in many cases be an acknowledgment of reality? Admittedly, there is in Baldwin that self-righteousness, that rage not quite under control. I know myself how easy it is to give in to it. But Crouch's approach to the dialectics of rage seem to me entirely unrealistic. In my poem, "Song For Artaud, Fanon, Cesaire, Uncle Tom, Tonto and Mr. Moto," I recognize a certain demagogic tone, a triumphant and self-righteous bitterness and rage. And yet, I also recognize that my rage needed to be released, that it had been held back in my own psyche for too many years, held back within my family, and held back within my race in America. That rage was liberating for me, just as it is for any oppressed people. As should be obvious to anyone, those who are oppressed cannot change their situation, cannot own themselves, unless they finally own their rage at their condition and those who have caused it. Crouch seems to have wanted Baldwin to overcome or stand above this rage, but there is a certain wishful thinking in this. One does not overcome or stand above this rage: one first goes through it, and then leaves it behind.

The problem is that this process is both long and complicated and neither Crouch nor Baldwin quite understands what it entails: one must learn first how liberating anger feels, then how intoxicating, then how damaging, and in each of these stages, the reason for these feelings must be admitted and accurately described. It may be argued that Baldwin accomplished the first of these tasks—the liberation that comes from rage—and that he alluded or hinted at the second—the intoxication that comes from rage—and even at times alluded or hinted at the third, but for the most, because he never accurately described how intoxicating the rage he felt was, he could never see how damaging it was.

For it is intoxicating after years of feeling inferior, after years of hating oneself, it is so comforting to use this rage not just to feel equal to the oppressor, but superior, and not just superior, but simply blameless and blessed, one of the prophetic and holy ones. It is what one imagines a god feels like, and in this state one does feel like a god of history, a fate; one knows that history is on one's side, because one is helping to break open, to recreate history. And how much better it is to feel like a god after years of worshipping the oppressor as one.

But once one can clearly describe all this, one realizes that such a stance represents a new form of hubris, an intoxicating blindness: human beings are not gods, are not superior to other human beings. Human beings are fallible, cannot foresee the future, cannot demand or receive freely the worship of others. In aligning one's rage with a sense of superiority, one fails to recognize how this rage is actually fueled by a sense of inferiority: one's own version of history and views on equality need, on some level, the approval, the assent, the defeat of the oppressor. The wish for superiority is simply the reverse side of feeling inferior, not its cure. It focuses all the victim's problems on the other, the oppressor. Yet until it is recognized how one has contributed to this victimhood, the chains are still there, inside, are part of the psyche. Conversely, liberation occurs only when one is sure enough of oneself, feels good enough, to admit fault, admit their portion of blame.

Given the difficulty of this process, it's not wonder so many stumble in the process or stop midway through. And it is made much more difficult if the oppressor is especially recalcitrant, is implacable towards change. When this happens, fresh wound after fresh wound is inflicted, causing bundle after bundle of rage: bitterness then becomes too tempting; too much energy is required to heal. To his credit, Crouch shows some understanding of this fact in relationship to Baldwin: "Perhaps it is understandable that Baldwin could not resist the contemptuous pose of militance that gave focus to all of his anger for being the homely duckling, who never became a swan, the writer who would perhaps never have been read by so many Black people otherwise, and the homosexual who lived abroad most of his adult life in order to enjoy his preferences."

In the end, though, Crouch never comes to terms with the sources of Baldwin's rage. One reason for this is Crouch's belief that "collective whiteness—and *collective guilt*" were merely a mask, a simplification for Baldwin.

. . .

Part of Crouch's problem is that he distorts Baldwin's position. On the one hand, it is a simplification to pretend that collective whiteness and collective guilt are the *only* ways to view the race situation in America. But it is not a simplification to say that collective whiteness and collective white guilt *do exist.* The superior economic and political power of whites as compared to colored minorities in this country is a fact, and on some level, every white in this country benefits from that power. Of course, this does not mean that every white has more economic and political power than every member of the colored minorities. But it is not just this inequality of power that makes collective white guilt a fact; it is the way that power was acquired and the way its sources have been kept hidden from the consciousness of both whites and colored minorities that makes this term applicable.

Here I return to the fundamental historical events I mentioned earlier in this essay: the enslavement of Blacks, the taking of Native American land and the genocidal policies that accomplished it. One can think of other related historical events: the internment camps, the Asian-Exclusion act, the condition of the Asian workers building the American railroads, the conditions of migrant farm workers and illegal aliens. The list could go on and on. But that is to point out the obvious. What is not so obvious is how the laws of property in our society have served to make permanent what was stolen in the past. Those who bought my grandparents' property for a song still benefit from that property today; there has been no compensation, just as there has been no compensation to Blacks for the institution of slavery or to Native Americans for the taking of a continent and the destruction of their peoples and culture. And as long as there is no movement toward a just compensation, the collective guilt will remain.

And yet I also recognize that a just compensation is not possible. The wrongs are too great, run too far back in history, and human beings are fallible and forgetful. Justice demands too high a price.

Therefore we must settle for less, for a compromise. The concept of white collective guilt reminds us of this compromise, that there has been and probably will always be a less than even settling of the debt. However whites protest that they want equality and justice, they are, in the end, not willing to pay the price. And when those they have wronged call for the price, the reaction of whites is almost always one of anger and resentment.

Now, in this situation, the whites have two choices. When they accept the concept of collective guilt, they admit that they feel unjustifiable anger and resentment at any measure that threatens any part of their privileged position, much less any of the measures that approach just compensation. When whites don't admit collective guilt, they try to blame racial troubles on those who ask for a just settlement and remain baffled at the anger and resentment of the colored minorities.

Whether in the area of culture or in economic relations, these choices remain. In the realm of culture in America, white European culture has held the floor for centuries; just as with any one-sided conversation, a balance can only be achieved if the speaker who has dominated speaks less and listens more. That is what conservative cultural critics are unwilling to do; for them there is no such thing as collective guilt, much less the obligation such guilt bestows. It is not just that the colored minorities in America need to create and receive their own cultural images, nor that, for these minorities, the culture of the Third World and its struggles against white-dominated cultures provides insights into race in America that cannot be found in European literature. This much ought to seem obvious. But there is more: only when whites in America begin to listen to the voices of the colored minorities and the Third World will they come to understand not just those voices but also themselves and their world. Reality is not simply knowing who we think we are, but also what others think of us. And only with this knowledge will whites ever understand what needs to be done to make things equal.

The situation in the *Voice* article on nannies is no different: without admitting the concept of collective guilt, the white middle-class Barbra remains unable to comprehend her nanny Bertha, unable to understand what this Black woman feels. Ultimately, Barbra does not want to admit that the only way she is going to feel comfortable with Bertha is if they meet as equals; that society must be changed so that Barbra and her children will not enjoy certain privileges they have taken as rights. In short, Barbra and other whites will have to give up power; that is what it means to make things equal. At the same time she must admit that no matter how much she works for change, how much society changes, there will never, on this earth, be a just settling of accounts. That is the burden she has to take up; she may think it will destroy her, but it will not. And, ultimately, this process would not only help Bertha to meet and know Barbra as an equal, but for Barbra to understand and accept who she is, to know herself.

Modern Secrets: "Last Night I Dreamt in Chinese . . ."

SHIRLEY GEOK-LIN LIM

Last night I dreamt in Chinese.
Eating Yankee shredded wheat,
I told it in English terms
To a friend who spoke
In monosyllables,
All of which I understood:
The dream shrunk
To its fiction.
I knew its end
Many years ago.
The sallow child
Eating from a rice-bowl
Hides in the cupboard
With the tea-leaves and china.

What Means Switch

GISH JEN

There we are, nice Chinese family—father, mother, two born-here girls. Where should we live next? My parents slide the question back and forth like a cup of ginseng neither one wants to drink. Until finally it comes to them, what they really want is a milkshake (chocolate) and to go with it a house in Scarsdale. What else? The broker tries to hint: the neighborhood, she says. Moneyed. Many delis. Meaning rich and Jewish. But someone has sent my parents a list of the top ten schools nationwide (based on the opinion of selected educators and others) and so *many-deli* or not we nestle into a Dutch colonial on the Bronx River Parkway. The road's windy where we are, very charming; drivers miss their turns, plough up our flowerbeds, then want to use our telephone. "Of course," my mom tells them, like it's no big deal, we can replant. We're the type to adjust. You know—the lady drivers weep, my mom gets out the Kleenex for them. We're a bit down the hill from the private plane set, in other words. Only in our dreams do our jacket zippers jam, what with all the lift tickets we have stapled to them, Killington on top of Sugarbush on top of Stowe, and we don't even know where the Virgin Islands are— although certain of us do know that virgins are like priests and nuns, which there were a lot more of in Yonkers, where we just moved from, than there are here.

This is my first understanding of class. In our old neighborhood everybody knew everything about virgins and nonvirgins, not to say the technicalities of staying in-between. Or almost everybody, I should say; in Yonkers I was the laugh-along type. Here I'm an expert.

"You mean the man . . . ?" Pig-tailed Barbara Gugelstein spits a mouthful of Coke back into her can. "That is *so* gross!"

Pretty soon I'm getting popular for a new girl, the only problem is Danielle Meyers, who wears blue mascara and has gone steady with two boys. "How do *you* know," she starts to ask, proceeding to edify us all with how she French-kissed one boyfriend and just regular kissed another. ("Because, you know, he had braces.") We hear about his rubber bands, how once one popped right into her mouth. I begin to realize I need to find somebody to kiss too. But how?

Luckily, I just about then happen to tell Barbara Gugelstein I know karate. I don't know why I tell her this. My sister Callie's the liar in the family; ask anybody. I'm the one who doesn't see why we should have to hold our heads up. But for some reason I tell Barbara Gugelstein I can make my hands like steel by thinking hard. "I'm not supposed to tell anyone," I say.

The way she backs away, blinking, I could be the burning bush.

"I can't do bricks," I say—a bit of expectation management. "But I can do your arm if you want." I set my hand in chop position.

"Uhh, it's okay," she says. "I know you can, I saw it on TV last night."

That's when I recall that I too saw it on TV last night—in fact, at her house. I rush on to tell her I know how to get pregnant with tea.

"With *tea?*"

"That's how they do it in China."

She agrees that China is an ancient and great civilization that ought to be known for more than spaghetti and gunpowder. I tell her I know Chinese. *"Be-yeh fa-foon,"* I say. *"Shee-veh. Ji nu."* Meaning, "Stop acting crazy. Rice gruel. Soy sauce." She's impressed. At lunch the next day, Danielle Meyers and Amy Weinstein and Barbara's crush, Andy Kaplan, are all impressed too. Scarsdale is a liberal town, not like Yonkers, where the Whitman Road Gang used to throw crabapple mash at my sister Callie and me and tell us it would make our eyes stick shut. Here we're like permanent exchange students. In another ten years, there'll be so many Orientals we'll turn into Asians; a Japanese grocery will buy out that one deli too many. But for now, the mid-sixties, what with civil rights on TV, we're not so much accepted as embraced. Especially by the Jewish part of town—which, it turns out, is not all of town at all. That's just an idea people have, Callie says, and lots of them could take us or leave us same as the Christians, who are nice too; I shouldn't generalize. So let me not generalize except to say that pretty soon I've been to so many bar and bas mitzvahs, I can almost say myself whether the kid chants like an angel or like a train conductor, maybe they could use him on the commuter line. At seder I know to forget the bricks, get a good pile of that mortar. Also I know what is schmaltz. I know that I am a goy. This is not why people like me, though. People like me because I do not need to use deodorant, as I demonstrate in the locker room before and after gym. Also, I can explain to them, for example, what is tofu (*der-voo*, we say at home). Their mothers invite me to taste-test their Chinese cooking.

"Very authentic." I try to be reassuring. After all, they're nice people, I like them. "De-lish." I have seconds. On the question of what we eat, though, I have to admit, "Well, no, it's different than that." I have thirds. "What my mom makes is home style, it's not in the cookbooks."

Not in the cookbooks! Everyone's jealous. Meanwhile, the big deal at home is when we have turkey pot pie. My sister Callie's the one introduced them—Mrs. Wilder's, they come in this green-and-brown box—and when we have them, we both get suddenly interested in helping out in the kitchen. You know, we stand in front of the oven and help them bake. Twenty-five minutes. She and I have a deal, though, to keep it secret from school, as everybody else thinks they're gross. We think they're a big improvement over authentic Chinese home cooking. Ox-tail soup—now that's gross. Stir-fried beef with tomatoes. One day I say, "You know, Ma, I have never seen a stir-fried tomato in any Chinese restaurant we have ever been in, ever."

"In China," she says, real lofty, "we consider tomatoes are a delicacy."

"Ma," I say. "Tomatoes are *Italian.*"

"No respect for elders." She wags her finger at me, but I can tell it's just to try and shame me into believing her. "I'm tell you, tomatoes *invented* in China."

"*Ma.*"

"Is true. Like noodles. Invented in China."

"That's not what they said in *school.*"

"In *China,*" my mother counters, "we also eat tomatoes un-cooked, like apple. And in summertime we slice them, and put some sugar on top."

"Are you sure?"

My mom says of course she's sure, and in the end I give in, even though she once told me that China was such a long time ago, a lot of things she can hardly remember. She said sometimes she has trouble remembering her characters, that sometimes she'll be writing a letter, just writing along, and all of a sudden she won't be sure if she should put four dots or three.

"So what do you do then?"

"Oh, I just make a little sloppy."

"You mean you *fudge?*"

She laughed then, but another time, when she was showing me how to write my name, and I said, just kidding, "Are you sure that's the right number of dots now?" she was hurt.

"I mean, of course you know," I said. "I mean, *oy.*"

Meanwhile, what *I* know is that in the eighth grade, what people want to hear does not include how Chinese people eat sliced tomatoes with sugar on top. For a gross fact, it just isn't gross enough. On the other hand, the fact that somewhere in China somebody eats or has eaten or once ate living monkey brains—now that's conversation.

"They have these special tables," I say, "kind of like a giant collar. With a hole in the middle, for the monkey's neck. They put the monkey in the collar, and then they cut off the top of its head."

"Whadda they use for cutting?"

I think. "Scalpels."

"*Scalpels?*" says Andy Kaplan.

"Kaplan, don't be dense," Barbara Gugelstein says. "The Chinese *invented* scalpels."

Once a friend said to me, You know, everybody is valued for something. She explained how some people resented being valued for their looks; others resented being valued for their money. Wasn't it still better to be beautiful and rich than ugly and poor, though? You should be just glad, she said, that you have something people value. It's like having a special talent, like being good at ice-skating, or opera-singing. She said, You could probably make a career out of it.

Here's the irony: I am.

Anyway. I am ad-libbing my way through eighth grade, as I've described. Until one bloomy spring day, I come in late to homeroom, and to my chagrin discover there's a new kid in class.

Chinese.

So what should I do, pretend to have to go to the girls' room, like Barbara Gugelstein the day Andy Kaplan took his ID back? I sit down; I am so cool I remind myself of Paul Newman. First thing I realize, though, is that no one looking at me is thinking of Paul Newman. The notes fly:

"*I* think he's cute."

"Who?" I write back. (I am still at an age, understand, when I believe a person can be saved by aplomb.)

"I don't think he talks English too good. Writes it either."

"Who?"

"They might have to put him behind a grade, so don't worry."

"He has a crush on you already, you could tell as soon as you walked in, he turned kind of orangish."

I hope I'm not turning orangish as I deal with my mail, I could use a secretary. The second round starts:

"What do you mean who? Don't be weird. Didn't you *see* him??? Straight back over your right shoulder!!!!"

I have to look; what else can I do? I think of certain tips I learned in Girl Scouts about poise. I cross my ankles. I hold a pen in my hand. I sit up as though I have a crown on my head. I swivel my head slowly, repeating to myself, *I* could be Miss America.

"Miss Mona Chang."

Horror raises its hoary head.

"Notes, please."

Mrs. Mandeville's policy is to read all notes aloud.

I try to consider what Miss America would do, and see myself, back straight, knees together, crying. Some inspiration. Cool Hand Luke, on the other hand, would, quick, eat the evidence. And why not? I should yawn as I stand up, and boom, the notes are gone. All that's left is to explain that it's an old Chinese reflex.

I shuffle up to the front of the room.

"One minute please," Mrs. Mandeville says.

I wait, noticing how large and plastic her mouth is.

She unfolds a piece of paper.

And I, Miss Mona Chang, who got almost straight A's her whole life except in math and conduct, am about to start crying in front of everyone.

I am delivered out of hot Egypt by the bell. General pandemonium. Mrs. Mandeville still has her hand clamped on my shoulder, though. And the next thing I know, I'm holding the new boy's schedule. He's standing next to me like a big blank piece of paper. "This is Sherman," Mrs. Mandeville says.

"Hello," I say.

"Non how a," I say.

I'm glad Barbara Gugelstein isn't there to see my Chinese in action.

"Ji nu," I say. *"Shee veh."*

Later I find out that his mother asked if there were any other Orientals in our grade. She had him put in my class on purpose. For now, though, he looks at me as though I'm much stranger than anything else he's seen so far. Is this because he understands I'm saying "soy sauce rice gruel" to him or because he doesn't?

"Sher-man," he says finally.

I look at his schedule card. Sherman Matsumoto. What kind of name is that for a nice Chinese boy?

(Later on, people ask me how I can tell Chinese from Japanese. I shrug. You just kind of know, I say. *Oy!*)

Sherman's got the sort of looks I think of as pretty-boy. Monsignor-black hair (not monk brown like mine), bouncy. Crayola eyebrows, one with a round bald spot in the middle of it, like a golf hole. I don't know how anybody can think of him as orangish; his skin looks white to me, with pink triangles hanging down the front of his cheeks like flags. Kind of delicate-looking, but the only truly uncool thing about him is that his spiral notebook has a picture of a kitty cat on it. A big white fluffy one, with a blue ribbon above each perky little ear. I get much opportunity to view this, as all the poor kid understands about life in junior high school is that he should follow me everywhere. It's embarrassing. On the other hand, he's obviously even more miserable than I am, so I try not to say anything. Give him a chance to adjust. We communicate by sign language, and by drawing pictures, which he's better at than I am; he puts in every last detail, even if it takes forever. I try to be patient.

A week of this. Finally I enlighten him. "You should get a new notebook."

His cheeks turn a shade of pink you mostly only see in hyacinths.

"Notebook." I point to his. I show him mine, which is psychedelic, with big purple and yellow stick-on flowers. I try to explain he should have one like this, only without the flowers. He nods enigmatically, and the next day brings me a notebook just like his, except that this cat sports pink bows instead of blue.

"Pret-ty," he says. "You."

He speaks English! I'm dumbfounded. Has he spoken it all this time? I consider: Pretty. You. What does that mean? Plus actually, he's said *plit-ty,* much as my parents would; I'm assuming he means pretty, but maybe he means pity. Pity. You.

"Jeez," I say finally.

"You are wel-come," he says.

I decorate the back of the notebook with stick-on flowers, and hold it so that these show when I walk through the halls. In class I mostly keep my book open. After all, the kid's so new; I think I really ought to have a heart. And for a livelong day nobody notices.

Then Barbara Gugelstein sidles up. "Matching notebooks, huh?"

I'm speechless.

"First comes love, then comes marriage, and then come chappies in a baby carriage."

"Barbara!"

"Get it?" she says. "Chinese Japs."

"Bar-*bra,*" I say to get even.

"Just make sure he doesn't give you any *tea,*" she says.

Are Sherman and I in love? Three days later, I hazard that we are. My thinking proceeds this way: I think he's cute, and I think he thinks I'm cute. On the other hand, we don't kiss and we don't exactly have fantastic conversations. Our talks *are* getting better, though. We started out, "This is a book." "Book." "This is a chair." "Chair." Advancing to, "What is this?" "This is a book." Now, for fun, he tests me.

"What is this?" he says.

"This is a book," I say, as if I'm the one who has to learn how to talk.

He claps. "Good!"

Meanwhile, people ask me all about him, I could be his press agent.

"No, he doesn't eat raw fish."

"No, his father wasn't a kamikaze pilot."

"No, he can't do karate."

"Are you sure?" somebody asks.

. . .

Indeed he doesn't know karate, but judo he does. I am hurt I'm not the one to find this out; the guys know from gym class. They line up to be flipped, he flips them all onto the floor, and after that he doesn't eat lunch at the girls' table with me anymore. I'm more or less glad. Meaning, when he was there, I never knew what to say. Now that he's gone, though, I seem to be stuck at the "This is a chair" level of conversation. Ancient Chinese eating habits have lost their cachet; all I get are more and more questions about me and Sherman. "I dunno," I'm saying all the time. *Are* we going out? We do stuff, it's true. For example, I take him to the department stores, explain to him who shops in Alexander's, who shops in Saks. I tell him my family's the type that shops in Alexander's. He says he's sorry. In Saks he gets lost; either that, or else I'm the lost one. (It's true I find him calmly waiting at the front door, hands behind his back, like a guard.) I take him to the candy store. I take him to the bagel store. Sherman is crazy about bagels. I explain to him that Lender's is gross, he should get his bagels from the bagel store. He says thank you.

"Are you going steady?" people want to know.

How can we go steady when he doesn't have an ID bracelet? On the other hand, he brings me more presents than I think any girl's ever gotten before. Oranges. Flowers. A little bag of bagels. But what do they mean? Do they mean thank you, I enjoyed our trip; do they mean I like you; do they mean I decided I liked the Lender's better even if they are gross, you can have these? Sometimes I think he's acting on his mother's instructions. Also I know at least a couple of the presents were supposed to go to our teachers. He told me that once and turned red. I figured it still might mean something that he didn't throw them out.

More and more now, we joke. Like, instead of "I'm thinking," he always says, "I'm sinking," which we both think is so funny that all either one of us has to do is pretend to be drowning and the other one cracks up. And he tells me things—for example, that there are electric lights everywhere in Tokyo now.

"You mean you didn't have them before?"

"Everywhere now!" He's amazed too. "Since Olympics!"

"Olympics?"

"1960," he says proudly, and as proof, hums for me the Olympic theme song. "You know?"

"Sure," I say, and hum with him happily. We could be a picture on a UNICEF poster. The only problem is that I don't really understand what the Olympics have to do with the modernization of Japan, any more than I get this other story he tells me, about that hole in his left eyebrow, which is from some time his father accidentally hit him with a lit cigarette. When Sherman was a baby. His father was drunk, having been out carousing; his mother was very mad but didn't say anything, just cleaned the whole house. Then his father was so ashamed he bowed to ask her forgiveness.

"Your mother cleaned the house?"

Sherman nods solemnly.

"And your father *bowed?*" I find this more astounding than anything I ever thought to make up. "That is so weird," I tell him.

"Weird," he agrees. "This I no forget, forever. *Father* bow to *mother!*"

We shake our heads.

As for the things he asks me, they're not topics I ever discussed before. Do I like it here? Of course I like it here, I was born here, I say. Am I Jewish? Jewish! I laugh. *Oy!* Am I American? "Sure I'm American," I say. "Everybody who's born here is American, and also some people who convert from what they were before. You could become American." But he says no, he could never. "Sure you could," I say. "You only have to learn some rules and speeches."

"But I Japanese," he says.

"You could become American anyway," I say. "Like I *could* become Jewish, if I wanted to. I'd just have to switch, that's all."

"But you Catholic," he says.

I think maybe he doesn't get what means switch.

I introduce him to Mrs. Wilder's turkey pot pies. "Gross?" he asks. I say they are, but we like them anyway. "Don't tell anybody." He promises. We bake them, eat them. While we're eating, he's drawing me pictures.

"This American," he says, and he draws something that looks like John Wayne. "This Jewish," he says, and draws something that looks like the Wicked Witch of the West, only male.

"I don't think so," I say.

He's undeterred. "This Japanese," he says, and draws a fair rendition of himself. "This Chinese," he says, and draws what looks to be another fair rendition of himself.

"How can you tell them apart?"

"This way," he says, and he puts the picture of the Chinese so that it is looking at the pictures of the American and the Jew. The Japanese faces the wall. Then he draws another picture, of a Japanese flag, so that the Japanese has that to contemplate. "Chinese lost in department store," he says. "Japanese know how go." For fun, he then takes the Japanese flag and fastens it to the refrigerator door with magnets. "In school, in ceremony, we this way," he explains, and bows to the picture.

When my mother comes in, her face is so red that with the white wall behind her she looks a bit like the Japanese flag herself. Yet I get the feeling I better not say so. First she doesn't move. Then she snatches the flag off the refrigerator, so fast the magnets go flying. Two of them land on the stove. She crumples up the paper. She hisses at Sherman, *"This is the U. S. of A., do you hear me!"*

Sherman hears her.

"You call your mother right now, tell her come pick you up."

He understands perfectly. *I,* on the other hand, am stymied. How can two people who don't really speak English understand each other better than I can understand them? "But Ma," I say.

"Don't *Ma* me," she says.

Later on she explains that World War II was in China, too. "Hitler," I say. "Nazis. Volkswagens." I know the Japanese were on the wrong side, because they bombed Pearl Harbor. My mother explains about before that. The Napkin Massacre. *"Nan-*king," she corrects me.

"Are you sure?" I say. "In school, they said the war was about putting the Jews in ovens."

"Also about ovens."

"About both?"

"Both."

"That's not what they said in school."

"Just forget about school."

Forget about school? "I thought we moved here for the schools."

"We moved here," she says, "for your education."

Sometimes I have no idea what she's talking about.

"I like Sherman," I say after a while.

"He's nice boy," she agrees.

Meaning what? I would ask, except that my dad's just come home, which means it's time to start talking about whether we should build a brick wall across the front of the lawn. Recently a car made it almost into our livingroom, which was so scary, the driver fainted and an ambulance had to come. "We should have discussion," my dad said after that. And so for about a week, every night we do.

"Are you just friends, or more than just friends?" Barbara Gugelstein is giving me the cross-ex.

"Maybe," I say.

"Come on," she says, "I told you *everything* about me and Andy."

I actually *am* trying to tell Barbara everything about Sherman, but everything turns out to be nothing. Meaning, I can't locate the conversation in what I have to say. Sherman and I go places, we talk, one time my mother threw him out of the house because of World War II.

"I think we're just friends," I say.

"You think or you're sure?"

Now that I do less of the talking at lunch, I notice more what other people talk about—cheerleading, who likes who, this place in White Plains to get earrings. On none of these topics am I an expert. Of course, I'm still friends with Barbara Gugelstein, but I notice Danielle Meyers has spun away to other groups.

Barbara's analysis goes this way: To be popular, you have to have big boobs, a note from your mother that lets you use her Lord & Taylor credit card, and a boyfriend. On the other hand, what's so wrong with being unpopular? "We'll get them in the end," she says. It's what her dad tells her. "Like they'll turn out too dumb to do their own investing, and then they'll get killed in fees and then they'll have to move to towns where the schools stink. And my dad should know," she winds up. "He's a broker."

"I guess," I say.

But the next thing I know, I have a true crush on Sherman Matsumoto. *Mis*ter Judo, the guys call him now, with real respect; and the more they call him that, the more I don't care that he carries a notebook with a cat on it.

I sigh. "Sherman."

"I thought you were just friends," says Barbara Gugelstein.

"We were," I say mysteriously. This, I've noticed, is how Danielle Meyers talks; everything's secret, she only lets out so much, it's like she didn't grow up with everybody telling her she had to share.

And here's the funny thing: The more I intimate that Sherman and I are more than just friends, the more it seems we actually are. It's the old imagination giving reality a nudge. When I start to blush, he starts to blush; we reach a point where we can hardly talk at all.

"Well, there's first base with tongue, and first base without," I tell Barbara Gugelstein.

In fact, Sherman and I have brushed shoulders, which was equivalent to first base I was sure, maybe even second. I felt as though I'd turned into one huge shoulder; that's all I was, one huge shoulder. We not only didn't talk, we didn't breathe. But how can I tell Barbara Gugelstein that? So instead I say, "Well there's second base and second base."

Danielle Meyers is my friend again. She says, "I know exactly what you mean," just to make Barbara Gugelstein feel bad.

"Like *what* do I mean?" I say.

Danielle Meyers can't answer.

"You know what I think?" I tell Barbara the next day. "I think Danielle's giving us a line."

Barbara pulls thoughtfully on one of her pigtails.

If Sherman Matsumoto is never going to give me an ID to wear, he should at least get up the nerve to hold my hand. I don't think he sees this. I think of the story he told me about his parents, and in a synaptic firestorm realize we don't see the same things at all.

So one day, when we happen to brush shoulders again, I don't move away. He doesn't move away either. There we are. Like a pair of bleachers, pushed together but not quite matched up. After a while, I have to breathe, I can't help it. I breathe in such a way that our elbows start to touch too. We are in a crowd, waiting for a bus. I crane my neck to look at the sign that says where the bus is going; now our wrists are touching. Then it happens: He links his pinky around mine.

Is that holding hands? Later, in bed, I wonder all night. One finger, and not even the biggest one.

. . .

Sherman is leaving in a month. Already! I think, well, I suppose he will leave and we'll never even kiss. I guess that's all right. Just when I've resigned myself to it, though, we hold hands all five fingers. Once when we are at the bagel shop, then again in my parents' kitchen. Then, when we are at the playground, he kisses the back of my hand.

He does it again not too long after that, in White Plains.

I invest in a bottle of mouthwash.

Instead of moving on, though, he kisses the back of my hand again. And again. I try raising my hand, hoping he'll make the jump from my hand to my cheek. It's like trying to wheedle an inchworm out the window. You know, *This way, this way.*

All over the world, people have their own cultures. That's what we learned in social studies.

If we never kiss, I'm not going to take it personally.

It is the end of the school year. We've had parties. We've turned in our textbooks. Hooray! Outside the asphalt already steams if you spit on it. Sherman isn't leaving for another couple of days, though, and he comes to visit every morning, staying until the afternoon, when Callie comes home from her big-deal job as a bank teller. We drink Kool-Aid in the backyard and hold hands until they are sweaty and make smacking noises coming apart. He tells me how busy his parents are, getting ready for the move. His mother, particularly, is very tired. Mostly we are mournful.

The very last day we hold hands and do not let go. Our palms fill up with water like a blister. We do not care. We talk more than usual. How much airmail is to Japan, that kind of thing. Then suddenly he asks, will I marry him?

I'm only thirteen.

But when old? Sixteen?

If you come back to get me.

I come. Or you can come to Japan, be Japanese.

How can I be Japanese?

Like you become American. Switch.

He kisses me on the cheek, again and again and again.

His mother calls to say she's coming to get him. I cry. I tell him how I've saved every present he's ever given me—the ruler, the pencils, the bags from the bagels, all the flower petals. I even have the orange peels from the oranges.

All?

I put them in a jar.

I'd show him, except that we're not allowed to go upstairs to my room. Anyway, something about the orange peels seems to choke him up too. *Mis*ter Judo, but I've gotten him in a soft spot. We are going together to the bathroom to get some toilet paper to wipe our eyes when poor tired Mrs. Matsumoto, driving a shiny new station wagon, skids up onto our lawn.

"Very sorry!"

We race outside.

"Very sorry!"

Mrs. Matsumoto is so short that about all we can see of her is a green cotton sunhat, with a big brim. It's tied on. The brim is trembling.

I hope my mom's not going to start yelling about World War II.

"Is all right, no trouble," she says, materializing on the steps behind me and Sherman. She's propped the screen door wide open; when I turn I see she's waving. "No trouble, no trouble!"

"No trouble, no trouble!" I echo, twirling a few times with relief.

Mrs. Matsumoto keeps apologizing; my mom keeps insisting she shouldn't feel bad, it was only some grass and a small tree. Crossing the lawn, she insists Mrs. Matsumoto get out of the car, even though it means trampling some lilies-of-the-valley. She insists that Mrs. Matsumoto come in for a cup of tea. Then she will not talk about anything unless Mrs. Matsumoto sits down, and unless she lets my mom prepare her a small snack. The coming in and the tea and the sitting down are settled pretty quickly, but they negotiate ferociously over the small snack, which Mrs. Matsumoto will not eat unless she can call Mr. Matsumoto. She makes the mistake of linking Mr. Matsumoto with a reparation of some sort, which my mom will not hear of.

"Please!"

"No no no no."

Back and forth it goes: "No no no no." "No no no no." "No no no no." What kind of conversation is that? I look at Sherman, who shrugs. Finally Mr. Matsumoto calls on his own, wondering where his wife is. He comes over in a taxi. He's a heavy-browed businessman, friendly but brisk—not at all a type you could imagine bowing to a lady with a taste for tie-on sunhats. My mom invites him in as if it's an idea she just this moment thought of. And would he maybe have some tea and a small snack?

Sherman and I sneak back outside for another farewell, by the side of the house, behind the forsythia bushes. We hold hands. He kisses me on the cheek again, and then—just when I think he's finally going to kiss me on the lips—he kisses me on the neck.

Is this first base?

He does it more. Up and down, up and down. First it tickles, and then it doesn't. He has his eyes closed. I close my eyes too. He's hugging me. Up and down. Then down.

He's at my collarbone.

Still at my collarbone. Now his hand's on my ribs. So much for first base. More ribs. The idea of second base would probably make me nervous if he weren't on his way back to Japan and if I really thought we were going to get there. As it is, though, I'm not in much danger of wrecking my life on the shoals of passion; his unmoving hand feels more like a growth than a boyfriend. He has his whole face pressed to my neck skin so I can't tell his mouth from his nose. I think he may be licking me.

From indoors, a burst of adult laughter. My eyelids flutter. I start to try and wiggle such that his hand will maybe budge upward.

Do I mean for my top blouse button to come accidentally undone?

He clenches his jaw, and when he opens his eyes, they're fixed on that button like it's a gnat that's been bothering him for far too long. He mutters in Japanese. If later in life he were to describe this as a pivotal moment in his youth, I would not be surprised. Holding the material as far from my body as possible, he buttons the button. Somehow we've landed up too close to the bushes.

What to tell Barbara Gugelstein? She says, "Tell me what were his last words. He must have said something last."

"I don't want to talk about it."

"Maybe he said, Good-bye?" she suggests. "Sayonara?" She means well.

"I don't want to talk about it."

"Aw, come on, I told you everything about . . ."

I say, "Because it's private, excuse me."

She stops, squints at me as though at a far-off face she's trying to make out. Then she nods and very lightly places her hand on my forearm.

The forsythia seemed to be stabbing us in the eyes. Sherman said, more or less, *You will need to study how to switch.*

And I said, *I think you should switch. The way you do everything is weird.*

And he said, *You just want to tell everything to your friends. You just want to have boyfriend to become popular.*

Then he flipped me. Two swift moves, and I went sprawling through the air, a flailing confusion of soft human parts such as had no idea where the ground was.

It is the fall, and I am in high school, and still he hasn't written, so finally I write him.

I still have all your gifts, I write. *I don't talk so much as I used to. Although I am not exactly a mouse either. I don't care about being popular anymore. I swear. Are you happy to be back in Japan? I know I ruined everything. I was just trying to be entertaining. I miss you with all my heart, and hope I didn't ruin everything.*

He writes back, *You will never be Japanese.*

I throw all the orange peels out that day. Some of them, it turns out, were moldy anyway. I tell my mother I want to move to China-town.

"Chinatown!" she says.

I don't know why I suggested it.

"What's the matter?" she says. "Still boy-crazy? That Sherman?"

"No."

"Too much homework?"

I don't answer.

"Forget about school."

Later she tells me if I don't like school, I don't have to go every day. Some days I can stay home.

"Stay home?" In Yonkers, Callie and I used to stay home all the time, but that was because the schools there were *waste of time*.

"No good for a girl be too smart anyway."

For a long time I think about Sherman. But after a while I don't think about him so much as I just keep seeing myself flipped onto the ground, lying there shocked as the Matsumotos get ready to leave. My head has hit a rock; my brain aches as though it's been shoved to some new place in my skull. Otherwise I am okay. I see the forsythia, all those whippy branches, and can't believe how many leaves there are on a bush—every one green and perky and durably itself. And past them, real sky. I try to remember about why the sky's blue, even though this one's gone the kind of indescribable gray you associate with the insides of old shoes. I smell grass. Probably I have grass stains all over my back. I hear my mother calling through the back door, "Mon-a! Everyone leaving now," and "Not coming to say good-bye?" I hear Mr. and Mrs. Matsumoto bowing as they leave—or at least I hear the embarrassment in my mother's voice as they bow. I hear their car start. I hear Mrs. Matsumoto directing Mr. Matsumoto how to back off the lawn so as not to rip any more of it up. I feel the back of my head for blood—just a little. I hear their chug-chug grow fainter and fainter, until it has faded into the whuzz-whuzz of all the other cars. I hear my mom singing, *"Mon-a! Mon-a!"* until my dad comes home. Doors open and shut. I see myself standing up, brushing myself off so I'll have less explaining to do if she comes out to look for me. Grass stains—just like I thought. I see myself walking around the house, going over to have a look at our churned-up yard. It looks pretty sad, two big brown tracks, right through the irises and the lilies-of-the-valley, and that was a new dogwood we'd just planted. Lying there like that. I hear myself thinking about my father, having to go dig it up all over again. Adjusting. I think how we probably ought to put up that brick wall. And sure enough, when I go inside, no one's thinking about me, or that little bit of blood at the back of my head, or the grass stains. That's what they're talking about—that wall. Again. My mom doesn't think it'll do any good, but my dad thinks we should give it a try. Should we or shouldn't we? How high? How thick? What will the neighbors say? I plop myself down on a hard chair. And all I can think is, we are the complete only family that has to worry about this. If I could, I'd switch everything to be different. But since I can't, I might as well sit here at the table for a while, discussing what I know how to discuss. I nod and listen to the rest.

The Souls of Black Folks

W. E. B. DU BOIS

The Nation has not yet found peace from its sins; the freedman has not yet found in freedom his promised land. Whatever of good may have come in these years of change, the shadow of a deep disappointment rests upon the Negro people. . . .

But alas! while sociologists gleefully count his bastards and his prostitutes, the very soul of the toiling, sweating black man is darkened by the shadow of a vast despair. Men call the shadow prejudice, and learnedly explain it as the natural defence of culture against barbarism, learning against ignorance, purity against crime, the "higher" against the "lower" races. To which the Negro cries Amen! and swears that to so much of this strange prejudice as is founded on just homage to civilization, culture, righteousness, and progress, he humbly bows and meekly does obeisance. But before that nameless prejudice that leaps beyond all this he stands helpless, dismayed, and well-nigh speechless; before that personal disrespect and mockery, the ridicule and systematic humiliation, the distortion of fact and wanton license of fancy, the cynical ignoring of the better and the boisterous welcoming of the worse, the all-pervading desire to inculcate disdain for everything black, from Toussaint to the devil,—before this there rises a sickening despair that would disarm and discourage any nation save that black host to whom "discouragement" is an unwritten word.

But the facing of so vast a prejudice could not but bring the inevitable self-questioning, self-disparagement, and lowering of ideals which ever accompany repression and breed in an atmosphere of contempt and hate. Whisperings and portents came borne upon the four winds: Lo! we are diseased and dying, cried the dark hosts; we cannot write, our voting is vain; what need of education, since we must always cook and serve? And the Nation echoed and enforced this self-criticism, saying: Be content to be servants, and nothing more; what need of higher culture for half-men? Away with the black man's ballot, by force or fraud,—and behold the suicide of a race! Nevertheless, out of the evil came something of good,—the more careful adjustment of education to real life, the clearer perception of the Negroes' social responsibilities, and the sobering realization of the meaning of progress.

So dawned the time of *Sturm und Drang:* storm and stress today rocks our little boat on the mad waters of the world-sea; there is within and without the sound of conflict, the burning of body and rending of soul; inspiration strives with doubt, and faith with vain questionings. The bright ideals of the past,—physical freedom, political power, the training of brains and the training of hands,—all these in turn have waxed and waned, until even the last grows dim and overcast. Are they all wrong,—all false? No, not that, but each alone was over-simple and incomplete,—the dreams of a credulous race-childhood, or the foul imaginings of the other world which does not know and does not want to know our power. To be really true, all these ideals must be melted and welded into one. The training of the schools we need to-day more than ever,—the training of deft hands, quick eyes and ears, and above all the broader, deeper, higher culture of gifted minds and pure hearts. The power of the ballot we need in sheer self-defence,—else what shall save us from a second slavery? Freedom, too, the long-sought, we still seek,—the freedom of life and limb, the freedom to work and think, the freedom to love and aspire. Work, culture, liberty,—all these we need, not singly but together, not successively but together, each growing and aiding each, and all striving toward that vaster ideal that swims before the Negro people, the ideal of human brotherhood, gained through the unifying ideal of Race; the ideal of fostering and developing the traits and talents of the Negro, not in opposition to or contempt for other races, but rather in large conformity to the greater ideals of the American Republic, in order that some day on American soil two world-races may give each to each those characteristics both so sadly lack. We the darker ones come even now not altogether empty-handed: there are to-day no truer exponents of the pure human spirit of the Declaration of Independence than the American Negroes; there is no true American music but the wild sweet melodies of the Negro slave; the American fairy tales and folklore are Indian and African; and, all in all, we black men seem the sole oasis of simple faith and reverence in a dusty desert of dollars and smartness.

[1903]

Blacks with a Capital B

GWENDOLYN BROOKS,
interviewed by D. H. Melhem

GB: . . . Do Blacks realize that they now have—since they got rid of the term "Negro"—NO capitalizations for their *essence?* Publishers refuse to capitalize Blacks. The Johnson Publishing Company of Chicago *does* capitalize Blacks, etc., but insists on capitalizing whites, etc., also. Whites *have* their capitalization: Caucasians. The Caucasians. A Caucasian. The Caucasian. "They spoke of Caucasian matters." Incidentally, the Johnson Publishing Company is Black.

We all happily, even though guiltily, capitalize Native American —which adulteration seems to me an insult to what we used to call "Indians"! I don't know *what* they should be called, but "Native American" suggests that until Amerigo Vespucci emerged, the "Indians" were as nothing. That is: they began to breathe and have being when whites came over to Bless them (and immediately to pollute them).

DH: "African American" has been proposed as a substitute name for Blacks. What is your opinion?

GB: The current motion to make the phrase "African American" an official identification is cold and excluding. What of our Family Members in Ghana?—in Tanzania?—in Kenya?—in Nigeria? —in South Africa?—in Brazil? Why are we pushing *them* out of our consideration?

The capitalized names *Black* and *Blacks* were appointed to compromise an open, wide-stretching, unifying, empowering umbrella.

Some Blacks announce: "That name *Black* does not describe *all* of us." Does the name "white" describe all of the people claiming its services? Those skins are yellow and rose and cocoa and cream and pink and gray and scarlet, and rust and purple and taupe and tan. Ecru. *But* that word "white," to those who wear it, is sacrosanct, is to be guarded, cherished.

Recently, one of our Black Spokesmen listened, with careful respect, to a passionate, sly, strategic white query: "Do you see a day coming when we can forget about EVERYTHING ELSE and just all be 'Americans'?" "Softly" answered our Black Spokesman: "We are *all* aiming toward that day, making progress toward that day—when we can *all* be Americans *merely.*"

MEANING? Meaning we are to remember nothing. Meaning we are to renounce *or* forget our culture, our history, all the richness that is our heritage. Our new and final hero is to be Don John *Trump*.

I share *Family*hood with Blacks wherever they may be. I am a *Black*. And I capitalize my name.

Critical Thinking: Racism and Education in the U.S. "Third World"

SHARON SPENCER

Note: *Within the context of this essay "critical thinking" will be understood to mean "common sense: sound practical judgment that is independent of specialized knowledge, training, or the like: normal native intelligence."* The Random House College Dictionary, *1968*

Unless they live in California, Texas, or in the urban Northeast, North Americans are unlikely to be aware that the population is gradually shifting to an anticipated majority of "people of color." The causes of this shift are immigration (both legal and illegal) and the high birth rate, primarily of people of South and Central American origins. For example, according to a 1988 Census Bureau report, since 1980 the Latino population of the United States has increased five times faster than that of any other group, reaching an estimated 19.4 million. California counts the highest per state Latino population—6.6 million. (*Los Angeles Times Magazine,* February 19, 1989). The November/

December issue of *Change: The Magazine of Higher Learning* reports that "According to the Immigration and Naturalization Service, 1.75 million East, Southeast, and South Asian immigrants were admitted legally to the U.S., with Asians now constituting the largest group of legal immigrants annually." To cite a home-grown example of population change, I taught a Freshman Composition course in the summer of 1989; of twenty-five students, three were first-generation European immigrants; two were Latinos (a relatively small number for M.S.C. [Montclair State College]); two were African-Americans; and six were Asian (three from Vietnam, three from India).

Fully aware of the enormous cultural differences among, for example, Asians or Latinos, we must give deep thought to the ways in which U.S. life might be affected in the future by this gradual shift. At best, the new immigrants will be welcomed by the descendants of the former immigrants from Europe, who have inherited a consciousness of their ancestors' struggle in the "new" world. The new immigrants will benefit from equal opportunities to find safe work at fair pay and comfortable housing as well as educational programs that will meet their diverse needs. This in itself is an immense problem; the new immigrants have widely varied skills and needs; indeed, this is the major focus of the *Change* issue subtitled "Asian and Pacific Americans: Behind the Myths." East Indians and West Indians generally have remarkably good English language skills, often higher than those of their U.S.-born peers, while people from China, the Philippines, Vietnam, Korea, and various Central and South American countries often need intensive language training before they can participate in society even marginally.

I would like to believe, even to hope, that the newcomers will be welcomed and invited to participate fully in our society. But this belief is very difficult to sustain, especially considering shrinking U.S. economic achievements and prospects and the new wave of racist-inflamed violence that is so ugly a feature of contemporary life.

Although I grew up in a small midwestern community and went to high school in Denver, I have been a resident of Manhattan and northern New Jersey since I was sixteen and came to New York to attend college. My experience in the Northeast suggests a much grimmer, even a tragic future, a racially and, of course, economically bifurcated society that may have many of the features of present-day South Africa. In this grim social possibility, the numerical majority of "people of color," not only the new immigrants but also many African-Americans and Puerto Ricans, will work at unskilled jobs to support an increasingly small number of multinational corporations whose managers will be persons of European origins.

A particularly brutal aspect of this dreaded possibility is that there will be fierce competitive in-fighting among "people of color" (encouraged by those in power to ensure the continuance of their own privileges); the new groups will resist solidarity with the Native Americans, the African-Americans, and the Puerto Ricans, who, in turn, will resent advances made by the newly arrived, mostly Latinos and Asians. As we have already seen in Miami, there may be continued strife between underemployed African-Americans and more affluent and politically powerful Cuban-Americans. This strife will, of course, serve the interests of the governing class, who will isolate their homes in communities far away from the urban ghettos where crime may rage at an even more accelerated rate than at present, stimulated by the deadly combination of poverty and the availability of never-ending supplies of murderous drugs.

What does all this have to do with critical thinking? A great deal. To illustrate I need to resort to a self-congratulatory reminiscence. When I was seven or eight years old and still living in a predominantly rural community, a friend of the same age quoted her father as having said that "All Jews are . . ." Even though I had no awareness of what a Jew was, I knew that what she had said could not be true. I argued with her. I was convinced that her father's assertion could not be true because all of any group of people could not accurately be described as anything at all (except human). I rejected the generalization as impossible. When I got home I told my parents what had happened, and they provided me with the knowledge to support my opposition to my friend's parroted defamation of Jews.

Let's look at the relation between critical thinking and racism pragmatically. Even if it were not the right thing to do to treat other people as we wish to be treated—an axiom of European existentialism, though couched in much more sophisticated language—there is a very sound practical reason to do so. People who are unjustly treated eventually become very angry; the longer they are unfairly treated, the angrier they become. Although for a long time they may express their rage against members of their own group, eventually they begin to direct it at the perpetrators of the injustice they have experienced. If it is organized, this rage can lead to revolution; if it is not organized, it can lead to anarchy, and if it is exacerbated by extensive drug trafficking, it can lead to random violence. At present the society we live in is vainly trying to deal with this cycle of injustice and consequent rage by building more jails in which to lock the angry people. The Afrikaner rulers of the indigenous peoples of South Africa let their captive population work for them, and then carefully contain them in an attempt to repress the anticipated violence.

To push my argument a little bit further, I'd like to suggest that there is a crucial, but often overlooked link between being the victims of a crime and the process of critical thinking. How many victims of street crimes—rapes and muggings, for example—see a connection between the injustice they have been subjected to and the injustice experienced by the perpetrator(s) of the crime? There are victims, and there are victims of victims. Although I myself have been the victim of numerous petty crimes (the most frightening was being mugged at knife-point), I did not examine the connection between being violated and society's larger racism until I entered into a detailed discussion with a friend, who was the victim of an especially brutal cross-racial crime.

She was living in Boston in a supposedly "good" (i.e., "safe") neighborhood. On the day after Thanksgiving in the afternoon she opened her door to an expected friend and found it forced open by the butt of a gun. Three men then forced their way into her apartment. At first—it seemed—they had intended only to rob her, but after a discussion they decided to assault her sexually as well. My friend endured five hours of verbal and sexual abuse.

During this time she begged her attackers to kill her. After the assailants left, she wriggled out of the ropes they had tied her in and called the police. Eventually, the men were apprehended, tried, and given three consecutive life sentences.

What is remarkable about the victim of this horrendous crime is her understanding that she was as much a victim of racism as the men who robbed and tortured her mercilessly. Once she recovered from the trauma of having been so severely violated, my friend changed her professional goals. She entered law school with the intent of becoming a Public Defender.

Racism manifests a tragic lack of critical thinking. Racism is irrational; it is based on mass projections of despised and supposedly shameful attributes by one group of people onto another. Racism can be automatically reversed; it is grounded in nothing more quantifiable than clustered projections. Racism causes enmity and produces enemies. Besides displaying a lack of critical thinking, racism displays a lack of human empathy. A lack of humanism. A lack of humanity.

As teachers—and learners—we are in a unique position to combat the projections that underlie racism. Especially if we work in a humanities discipline, we enjoy a platform and a space of time that gives us the opportunity to challenge students to search their educational books and other materials as well as their life experiences for the common elements of humanity, for the ties that bind and blend, without losing awareness of the culturally specific differences that give groups of people the original identities that enhance their shared human identity.

A good place to begin is by encouraging students to think of the "world" globally. As recently as 1983 when I was searching publishers' catalogs for a possible anthology to be used as a text in our two new World Literature courses, I found that no such collection was available. I located several anthologies with "world" in the title, but in every case "world" meant the Western world (typically beginning either with the Bible as literature or with the "Golden Age" of Greece, the fifth century "B.C."). Thinking of the world globally means recognizing that for most of the world's people the designation "B.C." to denote historical time is offensive, or perhaps merely irrelevant, the inherited historical designation of conquerors. Thinking of the world globally means developing the parallel awareness that "America" denotes an area vastly larger than the United States. A marvelous example of how the word "America" changes, depending on who is using it lies in the following accolade on a poster portraying the Virgin of Guadalupe, the Patron Saint of Mexico. She is called the "Queen of Mexico, the Empress of America." Thinking of the world globally means challenging ourselves to develop an awareness of how we are perceived by others.

This is why the two World Literature courses that are a sophomore-level General Education Requirement at M.S.C. are based on thematically related literary works drawn from a wide variety of the world's literatures. One is subtitled "The Coming of Age Theme" (indicating any transition in the life cycle) and the other "Voices of Tradition and Challenge." Instructors are free to choose any works they wish, providing there are a substantial number of non-Western texts. (Yes, it is true. The term "non-Western" is objectionable; it describes something by what it is not—by "otherness." Simone de Beauvoir long ago demonstrated how men have used "otherness" [wo-man] to denigrate women, and more recently Edward Said has used the same argument to show Western projections incongruously clustered and thrust upon Easterners [Orientalism].)

As the person who coordinated the development of the two World Literature courses, I wish to share the two most basic problems connected to their successful presentation and implementation. The first is the difficulty of identifying faculty members who can transcend their feelings of insecurity about teaching isolated literary works from a national literature when they have had no extensive training in the history of that literature. ("How can I teach a Japanese novel? I don't know anything at all about Japanese literature!") Without critical thinking, Western-oriented instructors may use terms like "Renaissance" or "Enlightenment" to describe the literatures of, for example, Malaysia or Turkey. Recently, a visiting lecturer who was hired to evaluate a faculty development program in non-Western literature inadvertently aroused the participants' laughter: after hearing a detailed presentation of a twentieth-century Japanese novel (*The Waiting Years* by Fumiko Enchi), he commented with absolute assurance: "Obviously, it's a pastoral elegy!"

Such blunders are caused by unexamined habits and by failing to review and revise language. They are caused by a lack of critical thinking. Even when multicultural courses and programs are supported by faculty development projects, there will be some faculty members who will remain convinced that—as the late Doors lead singer Jim Morrison wryly put it—"The West is the best."

A more profound problem with the implementation of the two World Literature courses is the way that students may resist emotionally processing the new materials. I stress the word "emotionally," because even the most resistant students can intellectually master the works; they can do well on exams and papers, but this does not mean that they have gained an understanding of the relativity of their assumptions about other people and their cultures, nor that they have attained an enhanced awareness of what it means to be human in a world of superficial differences. To state the issue bluntly: how readily will students of European origins enter into an emotional identification with a fictional character who is African, Asian, or Native American? Unless this emotional identification takes place, the student will not truly experience a given literary work in a profound and complete way.

Certain responses of students in a recent World Literature course ("Voices of Tradition and Challenge") will illustrate this problem. Because of events occurring in the Americas and in Mexico, I felt the urgency of students understanding something about these areas. My reading list was slanted to include a number of Caribbean works; one was V. S. Naipaul's *Miguel Street,* a collection of stories and sketches describing his early life in a poor section of Port of Spain, Trinidad. I began the course with a Xeroxed excerpt, "The Autobiography of Miguel Duran," an Urban Marginal (from Cali, Colombia). I also showed the film *El Norte,* which depicts the urgent journey of a Guatemalan brother and sister to California by way of Mexico. Other works included the films *The World of Apu* and *Hiroshima, Mon Amour,* collections of stories from Africa and Japan, and Khushwant Singh's novel about the partitioning of India, *Train to Pakistan.*

On the first day of class I reviewed the list of films and books with the class and explained—I thought—that the purpose of the course was to introduce students to literary materials depicting cultures other than their own so that they could make essential comparisons with the intent of attaining a deeper understanding both of themselves and others. Of twenty-five students five were assertively challenging at the start. Typical questions were: "What is the point of this course?" "What is this course about?" "Why do we have to read all these books about Caribbean people?"

In spite of what I thought were clear explanations, these questions persisted. One totally unwilling student withdrew. Three others had to be quieted, one rather sharply. Finally, I asked, "Is there still a need for me to explain the purpose of this course?"

I was delighted. I was rescued by an intelligent student, who called out: "Not again!" There was laughter, and we could move on to the assigned reading.

Nevertheless, one student remained possessed of incorrigible prejudices. One night she complained about the large number of "foreigners" teaching in the business department. "After all, we have all those foreigners in the business department!"

She said this in spite of the fact that the class constituency included a Jamaican, a Trinidadian, three identifiable and one "passing" Latino, and three African-Americans. Not one of the students challenged her. My response was tart; I commented that at least we knew what her opinion was, and moved the discussion back to the text.

At the end of the semester perhaps as many as five students remained as thoroughly saturated with a sense of their own racial and cultural superiority as when the class started. Others, who were silent, were probably also unaffected. However, one woman who had an "Anglo" name took me aside to tell me that her native language was Spanish, though she no longer spoke it. After seeing *El Norte,* five or six students told me that their attitudes toward undocumented immigrants had become much more favorable because they had gained an understanding of the conditions that might drive people to cross national boundaries furtively, risking their lives to do so. Most students attained a basic understanding of Hinduism from the student panel that responded to *The World of Apu,* as well as a historical framework for the conflicts among Hindus, Moslems, and Sikhs that are so frequently described by media.

In 1983 when M.S.C. initiated the World Literature courses we were unique in making such a course a G.E.R. requirement. I am sure that by now many more colleges have introduced similar courses. And it is my intense hope that we will continue to develop courses and programs in multicultural studies that will meet the needs of a student body that will increasingly reflect the population of the world.

The possibility of a society based on de facto apartheid is a potential tragedy that we must avoid not only by welcoming the newcomers but also by cultivating the generosity to share our declining riches with them in a just manner. Who would willingly make an enemy when it is so much more intelligent to acquire a friend?

To think critically is to examine one's prejudices, to explore one's unconscious assumptions, to look directly at the connections between racism and crime, and to relinquish the arrogance of racial and cultural superiority that has reduced the concept of the world to a small number of embattled whites. A world of difference is—fundamentally—a world of sameness, and it is filled with a diversity of riches.

Justice Denied in Massachusetts*

EDNA ST. VINCENT MILLAY

Let us abandon then our gardens and go home
And sit in the sitting-room.
Shall the larkspur blossom or the corn grow under this cloud?
Sour to the fruitful seed
Is the cold earth under this cloud,
Fostering quack and weed, we have marched upon but cannot
    conquer;
We have bent the blades of our hoes against the stalks of them.

Let us go home, and sit in the sitting-room.
Not in our day
Shall the cloud go over and the sun rise as before,
Beneficent upon us
Out of the glittering hay,
And the warm winds be blown inward from the sea
Moving the blades of corn
With a peaceful sound.
Forlorn, forlorn,
Stands the blue hay-rack by the empty mow.
And the petals drop to the ground,
Leaving the tree unfruited.
The sun that warmed our stooping backs and withered the weed
    uprooted—
We shall not feel it again.
We shall die in darkness, and be buried in the rain.

What from the splendid dead
We have inherited—
Furrows sweet to the grain, and the weed subdued—

* This poem was written in 1927 on the occasion of the execution of Sacco and Vanzetti, immigrant labor organizers, by the bigoted Judge Thayer of Massachusetts, who was known to have called them "dirty dagoes." Millay, as a poet of some celebrity at the time, along with several other well-known American writers marched against the unfair trial and execution. Many labor organizers among immigrant populations were poorly treated, or red-baited, throughout North American history since early colonial times.

See now the slug and the mildew plunder.
Evil does overwhelm
The larkspur and the corn;
We have seen them go under.

Let us sit here, sit still,
Here in the sitting-room until we die;
At the step of Death on the walk, rise and go;
Leaving to our children's children this beautiful doorway,
And this elm,
And a blighted earth to till
With a broken hoe.

Immigrant Education: From the Transcripts of the Sacco and Vanzetti Trial

NICOLO SACCO

A:* . . . When I was in Italy, a boy, I was a Republican, so I always thinking Republican has more chance to manage education, develop, to build some day his family, to raise the child and education, if you could. But that was my opinion; so when I came to this country I saw there was not what I was thinking before, but there was all the difference, because I been working in Italy not so hard as I been work in this country. I could live free there just as well. Work in the same condition but not so hard, about seven or eight hours a day, better food. I mean genuine. Of course, over here is good food, because it is bigger country, to any those who got money to spend, not for the working and laboring class, and in Italy is more opportunity to laborer to eat vegetable, more fresh, and I came in this country. When I been started work here very hard and been work thirteen years, hard worker, I could not been afford much a family the way I did have the idea before. I could not put any money in the bank; I could no push my boy some to go to school and other things. I teach over here men who is with me. The free idea gives any man a chance to profess his own idea, not the supreme idea, not to give any person, not to be like

* A = Sacco; Q = Prosecutor.

Spain in position, yes, about twenty centuries ago, but to give a chance to print and education, literature, free speech, that I see it was all wrong. I could see the best men, intelligent, education, they been arrested and sent to prison and died in prison for years and years without getting them out, and Debs, one of the great men in his country, he is in prison, still away in prison, because he is a Socialist. He wanted the laboring class to have better conditions and better living, more education, give a push his son if he could have a chance some day, but they put him in prison. Why? Because the capitalist class, they know, they are against that, because the capitalist class, they don't want our child to go to high school or college or Harvard College. There would be no chance, there would not be no,—they don't want the working class educationed; they want the working class to be a low all the times, be underfoot, and not to be up with the head. So, sometimes, you see, the Rockefellers, Morgans, they give fifty,—I mean they give five hundred thousand dollars to Harvard College, they give a million dollars for another school. Everyday say, "Well, D. Rockefeller is a great man, the best man in the country." I want to ask him who is going to Harvard College? What benefit the working class they will get by those million dollars they give by Rockefeller, D. Rockefellers. They won't get, the poor class, they won't have no chance to go to Harvard College because men who is getting $21 a week or $30 a week, I don't care if he gets $80 a week, if he gets a family of five children he can't live and send his child and go to Harvard College if he wants to eat everything nature will give him. If he wants to eat like a cow, and that is the best thing but I want men to live like men. I like men to get everything that nature will give best, because they belong,—we are not the friend of any other place, but we are belong to nations. So that is why my idea has been changed. So that is why I love people who labor and work and see better conditions every day develop, makes no more war. We no want fight by the gun, and we don't want to destroy young men. The mother been suffering for building the young man. Some day need a little more bread, so when the time the mother get some bread or profit out of that boy, the Rockefellers, Morgans, and some of the peoples, high class, they send to war. Why? What is war? The war is not shoots like Abraham Lincoln's and Abe Jefferson, to fight for the free country, for the better education to give chance to any other peoples, not the white people but the black and the others, because they believe and know they are mens like the rest, but they are war for the great millionaire. No war for the civilization of men. They are war for business, million dollars come on the side. What right we have to kill each other? I been work for the Irish. I have been working with the German fellow, with the French, many other peoples. I love them people just as I could love my wife, and my people for that did receive me. Why should I go kill them men? What he done to me? He never done anything, so I don't believe in no war. I want to destroy those guns. All I can say, the Government put the literature, give us educations. I remember in Italy, a long time ago, about sixty years ago, I should say, yes, about sixty years ago, the Government they could not control very much those two,—devilment went on, and robbery, so one of the government in the cabinet he says, "If you want to destroy those devilments, if you want to take off all those criminals, you ought to give a chance to Socialist literature, education of people, emancipation. That is why I destroy governments, boys." That is why my idea I love Socialists. That is why I like people who want education and living, building, who is good, just as much as they could. That is all.

Q: And that is why you love the United States of America?
A: Yes.

Q: She is back more than twenty centuries like Spain, is she?
A: At the time of the war they do it. . . .

Q: Do you remember speaking of educational advantages before the recess?
A: Yes, sir.

Q: Do you remember speaking of Harvard University?
A: Yes, sir.

Q: Do you remember saying that you could not get an education there unless you had money? I do not mean you used those exact words. I do not contend you did, but, in substance, didn't you say that?
A: They have to use money in the rule of the Government.

Q: No. You don't understand. Did you hear it, perhaps?
A: I can't understand.

Q: I will raise my voice a little bit. Did you say in substance you could not send your boy to Harvard?
A: Yes.

Q: Unless you had money. Did you say that?
A: Of course.

Public School No. 18: Paterson, New Jersey

MARIA MAZZIOTTI-GILLAN

Miss Wilson's eyes, opaque
as blue glass, fix on me:
"We must speak English.
We're in America now."
I want to say, "I am American,"
but the evidence is stacked against me.

My mother scrubs my scalp raw, wraps
my shining hair in white rags
to make it curl; Miss Wilson
drags me to the window, checks my hair
for lice. My face wants to hide.

At home, my words smooth in my mouth,
I chatter and am proud. In school,
I am silent; I grope for the right English
words, fear the Italian word will sprout
from my mouth like a rose.

I fear the progression of teachers
in their sprigged dresses,
their Anglo-Saxon faces.

Without words, they tell me
to be ashamed.
I am.
I deny that booted country
even from myself,
want to be still
and untouchable
as these women
who teach me to hate myself.

Years later, in a white
Kansas City house,
the psychology professor tells me

I remind him of the Mafia leader
on the cover of *Time* magazine.
My anger spits
venomous from my mouth:

I am proud of my mother,
dressed all in black,
proud of my father
with his broken tongue,
proud of the laughter
and noise of our house.

Remember me, ladies,
the silent one?
I have found my voice
and my rage will blow
your house down.

The Wife's Story

BHARATI MUKHERJEE

Imre says forget it, but I'm going to write David Mamet. So Patels
are hard to sell real estate to. You buy them a beer, whisper Glen-
garry Glen Ross, and they smell swamp instead of sun and surf. They
work hard, eat cheap, live ten to a room, stash their savings under
futons in Queens, and before you know it they own half of Hoboken.
You say, where's the sweet gullibility that made this nation great?

Polish jokes, Patel jokes: that's not why I want to write Mamet.
Seen their women?

Everybody laughs. Imre laughs. The dozing fat man with the
Barnes & Noble sack between his legs, the woman next to him, the
usher, everybody. The theater isn't so dark that they can't see me. In
my red silk sari I'm conspicuous. Plump, gold paisleys sparkle on my
chest.

The actor is just warming up. *Seen their women?* He plays a salesman, he's had a bad day and now he's in a Chinese restaurant trying to

loosen up. His face is pink. His wool-blend slacks are creased at the crotch. We bought our tickets at half-price, we're sitting in the front row, but at the edge, and we see things we shouldn't be seeing. At least I do, or think I do. Spittle, actors goosing each other, little winks, streaks of makeup.

Maybe they're improvising dialogue too. Maybe Mamet's provided them with insult kits, Thursdays for Chinese, Wednesdays for Hispanics, today for Indians. Maybe they get together before curtain time, see an Indian woman settling in the front row off to the side, and say to each other: "Hey, forget Friday. Let's get *her* today. See if she cries. See if she walks out." Maybe, like the salesmen they play, they have a little bet on.

Maybe I shouldn't feel betrayed.

Their women, he goes again. *They look like they've just been fucked by a dead cat.*

The fat man hoots so hard he nudges my elbow off our shared armrest.

"Imre. I'm going home." But Imre's hunched so far forward he doesn't hear. English isn't his best language. A refugee from Budapest, he has to listen hard. "I didn't pay eighteen dollars to be insulted."

I don't hate Mamet. It's the tyranny of the American dream that scares me. First, you don't exist. Then you're invisible. Then you're funny. Then you're disgusting. Insult, my American friends will tell me, is a kind of acceptance. No instant dignity here. A play like this, back home, would cause riots. Communal, racist, and antisocial. The actors wouldn't make it off stage. This play, and all these awful feelings, would be safely locked up.

I long, at times, for clear-cut answers. Offer me instant dignity, today, and I'll take it.

"What?" Imre moves toward me without taking his eyes off the actor. "Come again?"

Tears come. I want to stand, scream, make an awful scene. I long for ugly, nasty rage.

The actor is ranting, flinging spittle. *Give me a chance. I'm not finished, I can get back on the board. I tell that asshole, give me a real lead. And what does that asshole give me? Patels. Nothing but Patels.*

This time Imre works an arm around my shoulders. "Panna, what is Patel? Why are you taking it all so personally?"

I shrink from his touch, but I don't walk out. Expensive girls' schools in Lausanne and Bombay have trained me to behave well. My manners are exquisite, my feelings are delicate, my gestures refined, my moods undetectable. They have seen me through riots, uprootings, separation, my son's death.

"I'm not taking it personally."

The fat man looks at us. The woman looks too, and shushes.

I stare back at the two of them. Then I stare, mean and cool, at the man's elbow. Under the bright blue polyester Hawaiian shirt sleeve, the elbow looks soft and runny. "Excuse me," I say. My voice has the effortless meanness of well-bred displaced Third World women, though my rhetoric has been learned elsewhere. "You're exploiting my space."

Startled, the man snatches his arm away from me. He cradles it against his breast. By the time he's ready with comebacks, I've turned my back on him. I've probably ruined the first act for him. I know I've ruined it for Imre.

It's not my fault; it's the *situation*. Old colonies wear down. Patels —the new pioneers—have to be suspicious. Idi Amin's lesson is permanent. AT&T wires move good advice from continent to continent. Keep all assets liquid. Get into 7-Elevens, get out of condos and motels. I know how both sides feel, that's the trouble. The Patel sniffing out scams, the sad salesmen on the stage: postcolonialism has made me their referee. It's hate I long for; simple, brutish, partisan hate.

After the show Imre and I make our way toward Broadway. Sometimes he holds my hand; it doesn't mean anything more than that crazies and drunks are crouched in doorways. Imre's been here over two years, but he's stayed very old-world, very courtly, openly protective of women. I met him in a seminar on special ed. last semester. His wife is a nurse somewhere in the Hungarian countryside. There are two sons, and miles of petitions for their emigration. My husband manages a mill two hundred miles north of Bombay. There are no children.

"You make things tough on yourself," Imre says. He assumed Patel was a Jewish name or maybe Hispanic; everything makes equal sense to him. He found the play tasteless, he worried about the effect of vulgar language on my sensitive ears. "You have to let go a bit." And as though to show me how to let go, he breaks away from me, bounds ahead with his head ducked tight, then dances on amazingly jerky legs. He's a Magyar, he often tells me, and deep down, he's an

Asian too. I catch glimpses of it, knife-blade Attila cheekbones, despite the blondish hair. In his faded jeans and leather jacket, he's a rock video star. I watch MTV for hours in the apartment when Charity's working the evening shift at Macy's. I listen to WPLJ on Charity's earphones. Why should I be ashamed? Television in India is so up-lifting.

Imre stops as suddenly as he'd started. People walk around us. The summer sidewalk is full of theatergoers in seersucker suits; Imre's year-round jacket is out of place. European. Cops in twos and threes huddle, lightly tap their thighs with night sticks and smile at me with benevolence. I want to wink at them, get us all in trouble, tell them the crazy dancing man is from the Warsaw Pact. I'm too shy to break into dance on Broadway. So I hug Imre instead.

The hug takes him by surprise. He wants me to let go, but he doesn't really expect me to let go. He staggers, though I weigh no more than 104 pounds, and with him, I pitch forward slightly. Then he catches me, and we walk arm in arm to the bus stop. My husband would never dance or hug a woman on Broadway. Nor would my brothers. They aren't stuffy people, but they went to Anglican board-ing schools and they have a well-developed sense of what's silly.

"Imre." I squeeze his big, rough hand. "I'm sorry I ruined the evening for you."

"You did nothing of the kind." He sounds tired. "Let's not wait for the bus. Let's splurge and take a cab instead."

Imre always has unexpected funds. The Network, he calls it, Class of '56.

In the back of the cab, without even trying, I feel light, almost free. Memories of Indian destitutes mix with the hordes of New York street people, and they float free, like astronauts, inside my head. I've made it. I'm making something of my life. I've left home, my hus-band, to get a Ph.D. in special ed. I have a multiple-entry visa and a small scholarship for two years. After that, we'll see. My mother was beaten by her mother-in-law, my grandmother, when she'd registered for French lessons at the Alliance Française. My grandmother, the eldest daughter of a rich zamindar, was illiterate.

Imre and the cabdriver talk away in Russian. I keep my eyes closed. That way I can feel the floaters better. I'll write Mamet to-night. I feel strong, reckless. Maybe I'll write Steven Spielberg too; tell him that Indians don't eat monkey brains.

We've made it. Patels must have made it. Mamet, Spielberg: they're not condescending to us. Maybe they're a little bit afraid.

Charity Chin, my roommate, is sitting on the floor drinking Chablis out of a plastic wineglass. She is five foot six, three inches taller than me, but weighs a kilo and a half less than I do. She is a "hands" model. Orientals are supposed to have a monopoly in the hands-modelling business, she says. She had her eyes fixed eight or nine months ago and out of gratitude sleeps with her plastic surgeon every third Wednesday.

"Oh, good," Charity says. "I'm glad you're back early. I need to talk."

She's been writing checks. MCI, Con Ed, Bonwit Teller. Envelopes, already stamped and sealed, form a pyramid between her shapely, knee-socked legs. The checkbook's cover is brown plastic, grained to look like cowhide. Each time Charity flips back the cover, white geese fly over sky-colored checks. She makes good money, but she's extravagant. The difference adds up to this shared, rent-controlled Chelsea one-bedroom.

"All right. Talk."

When I first moved in, she was seeing an analyst. Now she sees a nutritionist.

"Eric called. From Oregon."

"What did he want?"

"He wants me to pay half the rent on his loft for last spring. He asked me to move back, remember? He *begged* me."

Eric is Charity's estranged husband.

"What does your nutritionist say?" Eric now wears a red jumpsuit and tills the soil in Rajneeshpuram.

"You think Phil's a creep too, don't you? What else can he be when creeps are all I attract?"

Phil is a flutist with thinning hair. He's very touchy on the subject of *flautists* versus *flutists*. He's touchy on every subject, from music to books to foods to clothes. He teaches at a small college upstate, and Charity bought a used blue Datsun ("Nissan," Phil insists) last month so she could spend weekends with him. She returns every Sunday night, exhausted and exasperated. Phil and I don't have much to say to each other—he's the only musician I know; the men in my family are lawyers, engineers, or in business—but I like him. Around me, he loosens up. When he visits, he bakes us loaves of pumpernickel bread. He waxes our kitchen floor. Like many men in this country, he seems to me a displaced child, or even a woman, looking for something that passed him by, or for something that he can never have. If he thinks I'm not looking, he sneaks his hands under Charity's sweater, but there isn't too much there. Here, she's a model with high ambitions. In India, she'd be a flat-chested old maid.

I'm shy in front of the lovers. A darkness comes over me when I see them horsing around.

"It isn't the money," Charity says. Oh? I think. "He says he still loves me. Then he turns around and asks me for five hundred."

What's so strange about that, I want to ask. She still loves Eric, and Eric, red jump suit and all, is smart enough to know it. Love is a commodity, hoarded like any other. Mamet knows. But I say, "I'm not the person to ask about love." Charity knows that mine was a traditional Hindu marriage. My parents, with the help of a marriage broker, who was my mother's cousin, picked out a groom. All I had to do was get to know his taste in food.

It'll be a long evening, I'm afraid. Charity likes to confess. I unpleat my silk sari—it no longer looks too showy—wrap it in muslin cloth and put it away in a dresser drawer. Saris are hard to have laundered in Manhattan, though there's a good man in Jackson Heights. My next step will be to brew us a pot of chrysanthemum tea. It's a very special tea from the mainland. Charity's uncle gave it to us. I like him. He's a humpbacked, awkward, terrified man. He runs a gift store on Mott Street, and though he doesn't speak much English, he seems to have done well. Once upon a time he worked for the railways in Chengdu, Szechwan Province, and during the Wuchang Uprising, he was shot at. When I'm down, when I'm lonely for my husband, when I think of our son, or when I need to be held, I think of Charity's uncle. If I hadn't left home, I'd never have heard of the Wuchang Uprising. I've broadened my horizons.

Very late that night my husband calls me from Ahmadabad, a town of textile mills north of Bombay. My husband is a vice president at Lakshmi Cotton Mills. Lakshmi is the goddess of wealth, but LCM (Priv.), Ltd., is doing poorly. Lockouts, strikes, rock-throwings.

My husband lives on digitalis, which he calls the food for our *yuga* of discontent.

"We had a bad mishap at the mill today." Then he says nothing for seconds.

The operator comes on. "Do you have the right party, sir? We're trying to reach Mrs. Butt."

"Bhatt," I insist. *"B* for Bombay, *H* for Haryana, *A* for Ahmadabad, double *T* for Tamil Nadu." It's a litany. "This is she."

"One of our lorries was firebombed today. Resulting in three deaths. The driver, old Karamchand, and his two children."

I know how my husband's eyes look this minute, how the eye rims sag and the yellow corneas shine and bulge with pain. He is not an emotional man—the Ahmadabad Institute of Management has trained him to cut losses, to look on the bright side of economic catastrophes—but tonight he's feeling low. I try to remember a driver named Karamchand, but can't. That part of my life is over, the way *trucks* have replaced *lorries* in my vocabulary, the way Charity Chin and her lurid love life have replaced inherited notions of marital duty. Tomorrow he'll come out of it. Soon he'll be eating again. He'll sleep like a baby. He's been trained to believe in turnovers. Every morning he rubs his scalp with cantharidine oil so his hair will grow back again.

"It could be your car next." Affection, love. Who can tell the difference in a traditional marriage in which a wife still doesn't call her husband by his first name?

"No. They know I'm a flunky, just like them. Well paid, maybe. No need for undue anxiety, please."

Then his voice breaks. He says he needs me, he misses me, he wants me to come to him damp from my evening shower, smelling of sandalwood soap, my braid decorated with jasmines.

"I need you too."

"Not to worry, please," he says. "I am coming in a fortnight's time. I have already made arrangements."

Outside my window, fire trucks whine, up Eighth Avenue. I wonder if he can hear them, what he thinks of a life like mine, led amid disorder.

"I am thinking it'll be like a honeymoon. More or less."

When I was in college, waiting to be married, I imagined honeymoons were only for the more fashionable girls, the girls who came from slightly racy families, smoked Sobranies in the dorm lavatories and put up posters of Kabir Bedi, who was supposed to have made it as a big star in the West. My husband wants us to go to Niagara. I'm not to worry about foreign exchange. He's arranged for extra dollars through the Gujarati Network, with a cousin in San Jose. And he's bought four hundred more on the black market. "Tell me you need me. Panna, please tell me again."

I change out of the cotton pants and shirt I've been wearing all day and put on a sari to meet my husband at JFK. I don't forget the jewelry; the marriage necklace of *mangalsutra,* gold drop earrings, heavy gold bangles. I don't wear them every day. In this borough of vice and greed, who knows when, or whom, desire will overwhelm.

My husband spots me in the crowd and waves. He has lost weight, and changed his glasses. The arm, uplifted in a cheery wave, is bony, frail, almost opalescent.

In the Carey Coach, we hold hands. He strokes my fingers one by one. "How come you aren't wearing my mother's ring?"

"Because muggers know about Indian women," I say. They know with us it's 24-karat. His mother's ring is showy, in ghastly taste anywhere but India: a blood-red Burma ruby set in a gold frame of floral sprays. My mother-in-law got her guru to bless the ring before I left for the States.

He looks disconcerted. He's used to a different role. He's the knowing, suspicious one in the family. He seems to be sulking, and finally he comes out with it. "You've said nothing about my new glasses." I compliment him on the glasses, how chic and Western-executive they make him look. But I can't help the other things, necessities until he learns the ropes. I handle the money, buy the tickets. I don't know if this makes me unhappy.

Charity drives her Nissan upstate, so for two weeks we are to have the apartment to ourselves. This is more privacy than we ever had in India. No parents, no servants, to keep us modest. We play at housekeeping. Imre has lent us a hibachi, and I grill saffron chicken breasts. My husband marvels at the size of the Perdue hens. "They're big like peacocks, no? These Americans, they're really something!" He tries out pizzas, burgers, McNuggets. He chews. He explores. He judges. He loves it all, fears nothing, feels at home in the summer odors, the clutter of Manhattan streets. Since he thinks that the American palate is bland, he carries a bottle of red peppers in his pocket. I wheel a shopping cart down the aisles of the neighborhood Grand Union, and he follows, swiftly, greedily. He picks up hair rinses and high-protein diet powders. There's so much I already take for granted.

One night, Imre stops by. He wants us to go with him to a movie. In his work shirt and red leather tie, he looks arty or strung out. It's only been a week, but I feel as though I am really seeing him for the first time. The yellow hair worn very short at the sides, the wide, narrow lips. He's a good-looking man, but self-conscious, almost arrogant. He's picked the movie we should see. He always tells me what to see, what to read. He buys the *Voice*. He's a natural avant-gardist. For tonight he's chosen *Numéro Deux*.

"Is it a musical?" my husband asks. The Radio City Music Hall is on his list of sights to see. He's read up on the history of the Rockettes. He doesn't catch Imre's sympathetic wink.

Guilt, shame, loyalty. I long to be ungracious, not ingratiate myself with both men.

That night my husband calculates in rupees the money we've wasted on Godard. "That refugee fellow, Nagy, must have a screw loose in his head. I paid very steep price for dollars on the black market."

Some afternoons we go shopping. Back home we hated shopping, but now it is a lovers' project. My husband's shopping list startles me. I feel I am just getting to know him. Maybe, like Imre, freed from the dignities of old-world culture, he too could get drunk and squirt Cheez Whiz on a guest. I watch him dart into stores in his gleaming leather shoes. Jockey shorts on sale in outdoor bins on Broadway entrance him. White tube socks with different bands of color delight him. He looks for microcassettes, for anything small and electronic and smuggle-able. He needs a garment bag. He calls it a "wardrobe," and I have to translate.

"All of New York is having sales, no?"

My heart speeds watching him this happy. It's the third week in August, almost the end of summer, and the city smells ripe, it cannot bear more heat, more money, more energy.

"This is so smashing! The prices are so excellent!" Recklessly, my prudent husband signs away traveller's checks. How he intends to smuggle it all back I don't dare ask. With a microwave, he calculates, we could get rid of our cook.

This has to be love, I think. Charity, Eric, Phil: they may be experts on sex. My husband doesn't chase me around the sofa, but he pushes me down on Charity's battered cushions, and the man who has never entered the kitchen of our Ahmadabad house now comes toward me with a dish tub of steamy water to massage away the pavement heat.

Ten days into his vacation my husband checks out brochures for sightseeing tours. Shortline, Grayline, Crossroads: his new vinyl briefcase is full of schedules and pamphlets. While I make pancakes out of a mix, he comparison-shops. Tour number one costs $10.95 and will give us the World Trade Center, Chinatown, and the United Nations. Tour number three would take us both uptown *and* downtown for $14.95, but my husband is absolutely sure he doesn't want to see Harlem. We settle for tour number four: Downtown and the Dame. It's offered by a new tour company with a small, dirty office at Eighth and Forty-eighth.

The sidewalk outside the office is colorful with tourists. My husband sends me in to buy the tickets because he has come to feel Americans don't understand his accent.

The dark man, Lebanese probably, behind the counter comes on too friendly. "Come on, doll, make my day!" He won't say which tour is his. "Number four? Honey, no! Look, you've wrecked me! Say you'll change your mind." He takes two twenties and gives back change. He holds the tickets, forcing me to pull. He leans closer. "I'm off after lunch."

My husband must have been watching me from the sidewalk. "What was the chap saying?" he demands. "I told you not to wear pants. He thinks you are Puerto Rican. He thinks he can treat you with disrespect."

The bus is crowded and we have to sit across the aisle from each other. The tour guide begins his patter on Forty-sixth. He looks like an actor, his hair bleached and blow-dried. Up close he must look middle-aged, but from where I sit his skin is smooth and his cheeks faintly red.

"Welcome to the Big Apple, folks." The guide uses a microphone. "Big Apple. That's what we native Manhattan degenerates call our city. Today we have guests from fifteen foreign countries and six states from this U.S. of A. That makes the Tourist Bureau real happy. And let me assure you that while we may be the richest city in the richest country in the world, it's okay to tip your charming and talented attendant." He laughs. Then he swings his hip out into the aisle and sings a song.

"And it's mighty fancy on old Delancey Street, you know. . . ."

My husband looks irritable. The guide is, as expected, a good singer. "The bloody man should be giving us histories of buildings we are passing, no?" I pat his hand, the mood passes. He cranes his neck. Our window seats have both gone to Japanese. It's the tour of his life. Next to this, the quick business trips to Manchester and Glasgow pale.

"And tell me what street compares to Mott Street, in July. . . ."

The guide wants applause. He manages a derisive laugh from the Americans up front. He's working the aisles now. "I coulda been somebody, right? I coulda been a star!" Two or three of us smile, those of us who recognize the parody. He catches my smile. The sun is on his harsh, bleached hair. "Right, your highness? Look, we gotta maharani with us! Couldn't I have been a star?"

"Right!" I say, my voice coming out a squeal. I've been trained to adapt; what else can I say?

We drive through traffic past landmark office buildings and churches. The guide flips his hands. "Art deco," he keeps saying. I hear him confide to one of the Americans: "Beats me. I went to a cheap guide's school." My husband wants to know more about this Art Deco, but the guide sings another song.

"We made a foolish choice," my husband grumbles. "We are sitting in the bus only. We're not going into famous buildings." He scrutinizes the pamphlets in his jacket pocket. I think, at least it's air-conditioned in here. I could sit here in the cool shadows of the city forever.

Only five of us appear to have opted for the "Downtown and the Dame" tour. The others will ride back uptown past the United Nations after we've been dropped off at the pier for the ferry to the Statue of Liberty.

An elderly European pulls a camera out of his wife's designer tote bag. He takes pictures of the boats in the harbor, the Japanese in kimonos eating popcorn, scavenging pigeons, me. Then, pushing his wife ahead of him, he climbs back on the bus and waves to us. For a second I feel terribly lost. I wish we were on the bus going back to the apartment. I know I'll not be able to describe any of this to Charity, or to Imre. I'm too proud to admit I went on a guided tour.

The view of the city from the Circle Line ferry is seductive, unreal. The skyline wavers out of reach, but never quite vanishes. The summer sun pushes through fluffy clouds and dapples the glass of office towers. My husband looks thrilled, even more than he had on the shopping trips down Broadway. Tourists and dreamers, we have spent our life's savings to see this skyline, this statue.

"Quick, take a picture of me!" my husband yells as he moves toward a gap of railings. A Japanese matron has given up her position in order to change film. "Before the Twin Towers disappear!"

I focus, I wait for a large Oriental family to walk out of my range. My husband holds his pose tight against the railing. He wants to look relaxed, an international businessman at home in all the financial markets.

A bearded man slides across the bench toward me. "Like this," he says and helps me get my husband in focus. "You want me to take the photo for you?" His name, he says, is Goran. He is Goran from Yugoslavia, as though that were enough for tracking him down. Imre from Hungary. Panna from India. He pulls the old Leica out of my hand, signaling the Orientals to beat it, and clicks away. "I'm a photographer," he says. He could have been a camera thief. That's what my husband would have assumed. Somehow, I trusted. "Get you a beer?" he asks.

"I don't. Drink, I mean. Thank you very much." I say those last words very loud, for everyone's benefit. The odd bottles of Soave with Imre don't count.

"Too bad." Goran gives back the camera.

"Take one more!" my husband shouts from the railing. "Just to be sure!"

The island itself disappoints. The Lady has brutal scaffolding holding her in. The museum is closed. The snack bar is dirty and expensive. My husband reads out the prices to me. He orders two french fries and two Cokes. We sit at picnic tables and wait for the ferry to take us back.

"What was that hippie chap saying?"

As if I could say. A day-care center has brought its kids, at least forty of them, to the island for the day. The kids, all wearing name tags, run around us. I can't help noticing how many are Indian. Even a Patel, probably a Bhatt if I looked hard enough. They toss hamburger bits at pigeons. They kick styrofoam cups. The pigeons are slow, greedy, persistent. I have to shoo one off the table top. I don't think my husband thinks about our son.

"What hippie?"

"The one on the boat. With the beard and the hair."

My husband doesn't look at me. He shakes out his paper napkin and tries to protect his french fries from pigeon feathers.

"Oh, him. He said he was from Dubrovnik." It isn't true, but I don't want trouble.

"What did he say about Dubrovnik?"

I know enough about Dubrovnik to get by. Imre's told me about it. And about Mostar and Zagreb. In Mostar white Muslims sing the call to prayer. I would like to see that before I die: white Muslims. Whole peoples have moved before me; they've adapted. The night Imre told me about Mostar was also the night I saw my first snow in Manhattan. We'd walked down to Chelsea from Columbia. We'd walked and talked and I hadn't felt tired at all.

"You're too innocent," my husband says. He reaches for my hand. "Panna," he cries with pain in his voice, and I am brought back from perfect, floating memories of snow, "I've come to take you back. I have seen how men watch you."

"What?"

"Come back, now. I have tickets. We have all the things we will ever need. I can't live without you."

A little girl with wiry braids kicks a bottle cap at his shoes. The pigeons wheel and scuttle around us. My husband covers his fries with spread-out fingers. "No kicking," he tells the girl. Her name, Beulah, is printed in green ink on a heart-shaped name tag. He forces a smile, and Beulah smiles back. Then she starts to flap her arms. She flaps, she hops. The pigeons go crazy for fries and scraps.

"Special ed. course is two years," I remind him. "I can't go back."

My husband picks up our trays and throws them into the garbage before I can stop him. He's carried disposability a little too far. "We've been taken," he says, moving toward the dock, though the ferry will not arrive for another twenty minutes. "The ferry costs only two dollars round-trip per person. We should have chosen tour number one for $10.95 instead of tour number four for $14.95."

With my Lebanese friend, I think. "But this way we don't have to worry about cabs. The bus will pick us up at the pier and take us back to midtown. Then we can walk home."

"New York is full of cheats and whatnot. Just like Bombay." He is not accusing me of infidelity. I feel dread all the same.

That night, after we've gone to bed, the phone rings. My husband listens, then hands the phone to me. "What is this woman saying?" He turns on the pink Macy's lamp by the bed. "I am not understanding these Negro people's accents."

The operator repeats the message. It's a cable from one of the directors of Lakshmi Cotton Mills. "Massive violent labor confrontation anticipated. Stop. Return posthaste. Stop. Cable flight details. Signed Kantilal Shah."

"It's not your factory," I say. "You're supposed to be on vacation."

"So, you are worrying about me? Yes? You reject my heartfelt wishes but you worry about me?" He pulls me close, slips the straps of my nightdress off my shoulder. "Wait a minute."

I wait, unclothed, for my husband to come back to me. The water is running in the bathroom. In the ten days he has been here he has learned American rites: deodorants, fragrances. Tomorrow morning he'll call Air India; tomorrow evening he'll be on his way back to Bombay. Tonight I should make up to him for my years away, the gutted trucks, the degree I'll never use in India. I want to pretend with him that nothing has changed.

In the mirror that hangs on the bathroom door, I watch my naked body turn, the breasts, the thighs glow. The body's beauty amazes. I stand here shameless, in ways he has never seen me. I am free, afloat, watching somebody else.

Multiculturalism: E Pluribus Plures

DIANE RAVITCH

Questions of race, ethnicity, and religion have been a perennial source of conflict in American education. The schools have often attracted the zealous attention of those who wish to influence the future, as well as those who wish to change the way we view the past. In our history, the schools have been not only an institution in which to teach young people skills and knowledge, but an arena where interest groups fight to preserve their values, or to revise the judgments of history, or to bring about fundamental social change. In the nineteenth century, Protestants and Catholics battled over which version of the Bible should be used in school, or whether the Bible should be used at all. In recent decades, bitter racial disputes—provoked by policies of racial segregation and discrimination—have generated turmoil in the streets and in the schools. The secularization of the schools during the past century has prompted attacks on the curricula and textbooks and library books by fundamentalist Christians, who object to whatever challenges their faith-based views of history, literature, and science.

Given the diversity of American society, it has been impossible to insulate the schools from pressures that result from differences and tensions among groups. When people differ about basic values, sooner or later those disagreements turn up in battles about how schools are organized or what the schools should teach. Sometimes these battles remove a terrible injustice, like racial segregation. Sometimes, however, interest groups politicize the curriculum and attempt to impose their views on teachers, school officials, and textbook publishers. Across the country, even now, interest groups are pressuring local school boards to remove myths and fables and other imaginative literature from children's readers and to inject the teaching of creationism in biology. When groups cross the line into extremism, advancing their own agenda without regard to reason or to others, they threaten public education itself, making it difficult to teach any issues honestly and making the entire curriculum vulnerable to political campaigns.

For many years, the public schools attempted to neutralize controversies over race, religion, and ethnicity by ignoring them. Educators believed, or hoped, that the schools could remain outside politics; this was, of course, a vain hope since the schools were pursuing policies based on race, religion, and ethnicity. Nonetheless, such divisive questions were usually excluded from the curriculum. The textbooks minimized problems among groups and taught a sanitized version of history. Race, religion, and ethnicity were presented as minor elements in the American saga; slavery was treated as an episode, immigration as a sidebar, and women were largely absent. The textbooks concentrated on presidents, wars, national politics, and issues of state. An occasional "great black" or "great woman" received mention, but the main narrative paid little attention to minority groups and women.

With the ethnic revival of the 1960s, this approach to the teaching of history came under fire, because the history of national leaders —virtually all of whom were white, Anglo-Saxon, and male—ignored the place in American history of those who were none of the above. The traditional history of elites had been complemented by an assimilationist view of American society, which presumed that everyone in the American melting pot would eventually lose or abandon those ethnic characteristics that distinguished them from mainstream Americans. The ethnic revival demonstrated that many groups did not want to be assimilated or melted. Ethnic studies programs popped up on campuses to teach not only that "black is beautiful," but also that every other variety of ethnicity is "beautiful" as well; everyone who had "roots" began to look for them so that they too could recover that ancestral part of themselves that had not been homogenized.

As ethnicity became an accepted subject for study in the late 1960s, textbooks were assailed for their failure to portray blacks accurately; within a few years, the textbooks in wide use were carefully screened to eliminate bias against minority groups and women. At the same time, new scholarship about the history of women, blacks, and various ethnic minorities found its way into the textbooks. At first, the multicultural content was awkwardly incorporated as little boxes on the side of the main narrative. Then some of the new social historians (like Stephan Thernstrom, Mary Beth Norton, Gary Nash, Winthrop Jordan, and Leon Litwack) themselves wrote textbooks, and the main narrative itself began to reflect a broadened historical understanding of race, ethnicity, and class in the American past. Consequently, today's history textbooks routinely incorporate the experiences of women, blacks, American Indians, and various immigrant groups.

Although most high school textbooks are deeply unsatisfactory (they still largely neglect religion, they are too long, too encyclopedic, too superficial, and lacking in narrative flow), they are far more sensitive to pluralism than their predecessors. For example, the latest edition of Todd and Curti's *Triumph of the American Nation,* the most popular high school history text, has significantly increased its coverage of blacks in America, including profiles of Phillis Wheatley, the poet; James Armistead, a revolutionary war spy for Lafayette; Benjamin Banneker, a self-taught scientist and mathematician; Hiram Revels, the first black to serve in the Congress; and Ida B. Wells-Barnett, a tireless crusader against lynching and racism. Even better as a textbook treatment is Jordan and Litwack's *The United States,* which skillfully synthesizes the historical experiences of blacks, Indians, immigrants, women, and other groups into the mainstream of American social and political history. The latest generation of textbooks bluntly acknowledges the racism of the past, describing the struggle for equality by racial minorities while identifying individuals who achieved success as political leaders, doctors, lawyers, scholars, entrepreneurs, teachers, and scientists.

As a result of the political and social changes of recent decades, cultural pluralism is now generally recognized as an organizing principle of this society. In contrast to the idea of the melting pot, which promised to erase ethnic and group differences, children now learn that variety is the spice of life. They learn that America has provided a haven for many different groups and has allowed them to maintain their cultural heritage or to assimilate, or—as is often the case—to do both; the choice is theirs, not the state's. They learn that cultural pluralism is one of the norms of a free society; that differences among groups are a national resource rather than a problem to be solved. Indeed, the unique feature of the United States is that its common culture has been formed by the interaction of its subsidiary cultures. It is a culture that has been influenced over time by immigrants, American Indians, Africans (slave and free) and by their descendants. American music, art, literature, language, food, clothing, sports, holidays, and customs all show the effects of the commingling of diverse cultures in one nation. Paradoxical though it may seem, the United States has a common culture that is multicultural.

Our schools and our institutions of higher learning have in recent years begun to embrace what Catherine R. Stimpson of Rutgers University has called "cultural democracy," a recognition that we must listen to a "diversity of voices" in order to understand our culture, past and present. This understanding of the pluralistic nature of American culture has taken a long time to forge. It is based on sound scholarship and has led to major revisions in what children are taught and what they read in school. The new history is—indeed, must be—a warts-and-all history; it demands an unflinching examination of racism and discrimination in our history. Making these changes is difficult, raises tempers, and ignites controversies, but gives a more interesting and accurate account of American history. Accomplishing these changes is valuable, because there is also a useful lesson for the rest of the world in America's relatively successful experience as a pluralistic society. Throughout human history, the clash of different cultures, races, ethnic groups, and religious has often been the cause of bitter hatred, civil conflict, and international war. The ethnic tensions that now are tearing apart Lebanon, Sri Lanka, Kashmir, and various republics of the Soviet Union remind us of the costs of unfettered group rivalry. Thus, it is a matter of more than domestic importance that we closely examine and try to understand that part of our national history in which different groups competed, fought, suffered, but ultimately learned to live together in relative peace and even achieved a sense of common nationhood.

Alas, these painstaking efforts to expand the understanding of American culture into a richer and more varied tapestry have taken a new turn, and not for the better. Almost any idea, carried to its extreme, can be made pernicious, and this is what is happening now to multiculturalism. Today, pluralistic multiculturalism must contend with a new, particularistic multiculturalism. The pluralists seek a richer common culture; the particularists insist that no common culture is possible or desirable. The new particularism is entering the curriculum in a number of school systems across the country. Advocates of particularism propose an ethnocentric curriculum to raise the self-esteem and academic achievement of children from racial and ethnic minority backgrounds. Without any evidence, they claim that children from minority backgrounds will do well in school *only* if they are immersed in a positive, prideful version of their ancestral culture. If children are of, for example, Fredonian ancestry, they must hear that Fredonians were important in mathematics, science, history, and literature. If they learn about great Fredonians and if their studies use

Fredonian examples and Fredonian concepts, they will do well in school. If they do not, they will have low self-esteem and will do badly.

At first glance, this appears akin to the celebratory activities associated with Black History Month or Women's History Month, when schoolchildren learn about the achievements of blacks and women. But the point of those celebrations is to demonstrate that neither race nor gender is an obstacle to high achievement. They teach all children that everyone, regardless of their race, religion, gender, ethnicity, or family origin, can achieve self-fulfillment, honor, and dignity in society if they aim high and work hard.

By contrast, the particularistic version of multiculturalism is unabashedly filiopietistic and deterministic. It teaches children that their identity is determined by their "cultural genes." That something in their blood or their race memory or their cultural DNA defines who they are and what they may achieve. That the culture in which they live is not their own culture, even though they were born here. That American culture is "Eurocentric," and therefore hostile to anyone whose ancestors are not European. Perhaps the most invidious implication of particularism is that racial and ethnic minorities are not and should not try to be part of American culture; it implies that American culture belongs only to those who are white and European; it implies that those who are neither white nor European are alienated from American culture by virtue of their race or ethnicity; it implies that the only culture they do belong to or can ever belong to is the culture of their ancestors, even if their families have lived in this country for generations.

The war on so-called Eurocentrism is intended to foster self-esteem among those who are not of European descent. But how, in fact, is self-esteem developed? How is the sense of one's own possibilities, one's potential choices, developed? Certainly, the school curriculum plays a relatively small role as compared to the influence of family, community, mass media, and society. But to the extent that curriculum influences what children think of themselves, it should encourage children of all racial and ethnic groups to believe that they are part of this society and that they should develop their talents and minds to the fullest. It is enormously inspiring, for example, to learn about men and women from diverse backgrounds who overcame poverty, discrimination, physical handicaps, and other obstacles to achieve success in a variety of fields. Behind every such biography of accomplishment is a story of heroism, perseverance, and self-discipline. Learning these stories will encourage a healthy spirit of pluralism, of mutual respect, and of self-respect among children of different backgrounds. The children of American society today will live their lives in a racially and culturally diverse nation, and their education should prepare them to do so.

The pluralist approach to multiculturalism promotes a broader interpretation of the common American culture and seeks due recognition for the ways that the nation's many racial, ethnic, and cultural groups have transformed the national culture. The pluralists say, in effect, "American culture belongs to us, all of us; the U.S. is us, and we remake it in every generation." But particularists have no interest in extending or revising American culture; indeed, they deny that a common culture exists. Particularists reject any accommodation among groups, any interactions that blur the distinct lines between them. The brand of history that they espouse is one in which everyone is either a descendant of victims or oppressors. By doing so, ancient hatreds are fanned and recreated in each new generation. Particularism has its intellectual roots in the ideology of ethnic separatism and in the black nationalist movement. In the particularist analysis, the nation has five cultures: African American, Asian American, European American, Latino/Hispanic, and Native American. The huge cultural, historical, religious, and linguistic differences within these categories are ignored, as is the considerable intermarriage among these groups, as are the linkages (like gender, class, sexual orientation, and religion) that cut across these five groups. No serious scholar would claim that all Europeans and white Americans are part of the same culture, or that all Asians are part of the same culture, or that all people of Latin-American descent are of the same culture, or that all people of African descent are of the same culture. Any categorization this broad is essentially meaningless and useless.

Several districts—including Detroit, Atlanta, and Washington, D.C.—are developing an Afrocentric curriculum. *Afrocentricity* has been described in a book of the same name by Molefi Kete Asante of Temple University. The Afrocentric curriculum puts Africa at the center of the student's universe. African Americans must "move away from an [*sic*] Eurocentric framework" because "it is difficult to create freely when you use someone else's motifs, styles, images, and perspectives." Because they are not Africans, "white teachers cannot in-

spire in our children the visions necessary for them to overcome limitations." Asante recommends that African Americans choose an
African name (as he did), reject European dress, embrace African religion (not Islam or Christianity) and love "their own" culture. He
scorns the idea of universality as a form of Eurocentric arrogance. The
Eurocentrist, he says, thinks of Beethoven or Bach as classical, but the
Afrocentrist thinks of Ellington or Coltrane as classical; the Eurocentrist lauds Shakespeare or Twain, while the Afrocentrist prefers Baraka,
Shange, or Abiola. Asante is critical of black artists like Arthur Mitch-
ell and Alvin Ailey who ignore Afrocentricity. Likewise, he speaks
contemptuously of a group of black university students who spurned
the Afrocentrism of the local Black Student Union and formed an
organization called Inter-race: "Such madness is the direct consequence of self-hatred, obligatory attitudes, false assumptions about society, and stupidity."

The conflict between pluralism and particularism turns on the
issue of universalism. Professor Asante warns his readers against the
lure of universalism: "Do not be captured by a sense of universality
given to you by the Eurocentric viewpoint; such a viewpoint is contradictory to your own ultimate reality." He insists that there is no
alternative to Eurocentrism, Afrocentrism, and other ethnocentrisms.
In contrast, the pluralist says, with the Roman playwright Terence, "I
am a man: nothing human is alien to me." A contemporary Terence
would say "I am a person" or might be a woman, but the point
remains the same: You don't have to be black to love Zora Neale
Hurston's fiction or Langston Hughes's poetry or Duke Ellington's
music. In a pluralist curriculum, we expect children to learn a broad
and humane culture, to learn about the ideas and art and animating
spirit of many cultures. We expect that children, whatever their color,
will be inspired by the courage of people like Helen Keller, Vaclav
Havel, Harriet Tubman, and Feng Lizhe. We expect that their response to literature will be determined by the ideas and images it
evokes, not by the skin color of the writer. But particularists insist that
children can learn only from the experiences of people from the same
race.

Particularism is a bad idea whose time has come. It is also a
fashion spreading like wildfire through the education system, actively
promoted by organizations and individuals with a political and professional interest in strengthening ethnic power bases in the university, in

the education profession, and in society itself. One can scarcely pick up an educational journal without learning about a school district that is converting to an ethnocentric curriculum in an attempt to give "self-esteem" to children from racial minorities. A state-funded project in a Sacramento high school is teaching young black males to think like Africans and to develop the "African Mind Model Technique," in order to free themselves of the racism of American culture. A popular black rap singer, KRS-One, complained in an op-ed article in the *New York Times* that the schools should be teaching blacks about their cultural heritage, instead of trying to make everyone Americans. "It's like trying to teach a dog to be a cat," he wrote. KRS-One railed about having to learn about Thomas Jefferson and the Civil War, which had nothing to do (he said) with black history.

Pluralism can easily be transformed into particularism, as may be seen in the potential uses in the classroom of the Mayan contribution to mathematics. The Mayan example was popularized in a movie called *Stand and Deliver,* about a charismatic Bolivian-born mathematics teacher in Los Angeles who inspired his students (who are Hispanic) to learn calculus. He told them that their ancestors invented the concept of zero; but that wasn't all he did. He used imagination to put across mathematical concepts. He required them to do homework and to go to school on Saturdays and during the Christmas holidays, so that they might pass the Advanced Placement mathematics examination for college entry. The teacher's reference to the Mayans' mathematical genius was a valid instructional device: It was an attention-getter and would have interested even students who were not Hispanic. But the Mayan example would have had little effect without the teacher's insistence that the class study hard for a difficult examination.

Ethnic educators have seized upon the Mayan contribution to mathematics as the key to simultaneously boosting the ethnic pride of Hispanic children and attacking Eurocentrism. One proposal claims that Mexican-American children will be attracted to science and mathematics if they study Mayan mathematics, the Mayan calendar, and Mayan astronomy. Children in primary grades are to be taught that the Mayans were first to discover the zero and that Europeans learned it long afterwards from the Arabs, who had learned it in India. This will help them see that Europeans were latecomers in the discovery of great ideas. Botany is to be learned by study of the agricultural techniques of the Aztecs, a subject of somewhat limited relevance to children in urban areas. Furthermore, "ethnobotanical" classifications of plants are to be substituted for the Eurocentric Linnaean system. At first glance, it may seem curious that Hispanic children are deemed to have no cultural affinity with Spain; but to acknowledge the cultural tie would confuse the ideological assault on Eurocentrism.

This proposal suggests some questions: Is there any evidence that the teaching of "culturally relevant" science and mathematics will draw Mexican-American children to the study of these subjects? Will Mexican-American children lose interest or self-esteem if they discover that their ancestors were Aztecs or Spaniards, rather than Mayans? Are children who learn in this way prepared to study the science and mathematics that are taught in American colleges and universities and that are needed for advanced study in these fields? Are they even prepared to study the science and mathematics taught in *Mexican* universities? If the class is half Mexican-American and half something else, will only the Mexican-American children study in a Mayan and Aztec mode or will all the children? But shouldn't all children study what is culturally relevant for them? How will we train teachers who have command of so many different systems of mathematics and science?

The efficacy of particularist proposals seems to be less important to their sponsors than their value as ideological weapons with which to criticize existing disciplines for their alleged Eurocentric bias. In a recent article titled "The Ethnocentric Basis of Social Science Knowledge Production" in the *Review of Research in Education,* John Stanfield of Yale University argues that neither social science nor science are objective studies, that both instead are "Euro-American" knowledge systems which reproduce "hegemonic racial domination." The claim that science and reason are somehow superior to magic and witchcraft, he writes, is the product of Euro-American ethnocentrism. According to Stanfield, current fears about the misuse of science (for instance, "the nuclear arms race, global pollution") and "the power-plays of Third World nations (the Arab oil boycott and the American-Iranian hostage crisis) have made Western people more aware of nonscientific cognitive styles. These last events are beginning to demonstrate politically that which has begun to be understood in intellectual circles: namely, that modes of social knowledge such as theology, science, and magic are different, not inferior or superior. They represent different ways of perceiving, defining, and organizing knowledge of life experiences." One wonders: If Professor Stanfield broke his leg, would he go to a theologian, a doctor, or a magician?

Every field of study, it seems, has been tainted by Eurocentrism, which was defined by a professor at Manchester University, George Ghevarughese Joseph, in *Race and Class* in 1987, as "intellectual racism." Professor Joseph argues that the history of science and technology—and in particular, of mathematics—in non-European societies was distorted by racist Europeans who wanted to establish the dominance of European forms of knowledge. The racists, he writes, traditionally traced mathematics to the Greeks, then claimed that it reached its full development in Europe. These are simply Eurocentric myths to sustain an "imperialist/racist ideology," says Professor Joseph, since mathematics was found in Egypt, Babylonia, Mesopotamia, and India long before the Greeks were supposed to have developed it. Professor Joseph points out too that Arab scientists should be credited with major discoveries traditionally attributed to William Harvey, Isaac Newton, Charles Darwin, and Sir Francis Bacon. But he is not concerned only to argue historical issues; his purpose is to bring all of these different mathematical traditions into the school classroom so that children might study, for example, "traditional African designs, Indian *rangoli* patterns and Islamic art" and "the language and counting systems found across the world."

This interesting proposal to teach ethnomathematics comes at a time when American mathematics educators are trying to overhaul present practices, because of the poor performance of American children on national and international assessments. Mathematics educators are attempting to change the teaching of their subject so that children can see its uses in everyday life. There would seem to be an incipient conflict between those who want to introduce real-life applications of mathematics and those who want to teach the mathematical systems used by ancient cultures. I suspect that most mathematics teachers would enjoy doing a bit of both, if there were time or student interest. But any widespread movement to replace modern mathematics with ancient ethnic mathematics runs the risk of disaster in a field that is struggling to update existing curricula. If, as seems likely, ancient mathematics is taught mainly to minority children, the gap between them and middle-class white children is apt to grow. It is worth noting that children in Korea, who score highest in mathematics on international assessments, do not study ancient Korean mathematics.

Particularism is akin to cultural Lysenkoism, for it takes as its premise the spurious notion that cultural traits are inherited. It implies a dubious, dangerous form of cultural predestination. Children are taught that if their ancestors could do it, so could they. But what happens if a child is from a cultural group that made no significant contribution to science or mathematics? Does this mean that children from that background must find a culturally appropriate field in which to strive? How does a teacher find the right cultural buttons for children of mixed heritage? And how in the world will teachers use this technique when the children in their classes are drawn from many different cultures, as is usually the case? By the time that every culture gets its due, there may be no time left to teach the subject itself. This explosion of filiopietism (which, we should remember, comes from adults, not from students) is reminiscent of the period some years ago when the Russians claimed that they had invented everything first; as we now know, this nationalistic braggadocio did little for their self-esteem and nothing for their economic development. We might reflect, too, on how little social prestige has been accorded in this country to immigrants from Greece and Italy, even though the achievements of their ancestors were at the heart of the classical curriculum.

Filiopietism and ethnic boosterism lead to all sorts of odd practices. In New York State, for example, the curriculum guide for eleventh grade American history lists three "foundations" for the United States Constitution, as follows:

A. Foundations
  1. 17th and 18th century Enlightenment thought
  2. Haudenosaunee political system
     a. Influence upon colonial leadership and European intellectuals (Locke, Montesquieu, Voltaire, Rousseau)
     b. Impact on Albany Plan of Union, Articles of Confederation, and U.S. Constitution
  3. Colonial experience

Those who are unfamiliar with the Haudenosaunee political system might wonder what it is, particularly since educational authorities in New York State rank it as equal in importance to the European Enlightenment and suggest that it strongly influenced not only colonial leaders but the leading intellectuals of Europe. The Haudenosaunee political system was the Iroquois confederation of five (later six) Indian tribes in upper New York State, which conducted war and civil affairs through a council of chiefs, each with one vote. In 1754, Benjamin Franklin proposed a colonial union at a conference in Albany; his plan, said to be inspired by the Iroquois Confederation, was rejected by the other colonies. Today, Indian activists believe that the Iroquois Confederation was the model for the American Constitution, and the New York State Department of Education has decided that they are right. That no other state sees fit to give the American Indians equal billing with the European Enlightenment may be owing to the fact that the Indians in New York State (numbering less than forty thousand) have been more politically effective than elsewhere or that other states have not yet learned about this method of reducing "Eurocentrism" in their American history classes.

Particularism can easily be carried to extremes. Students of Fredonian descent must hear that their ancestors were seminal in the development of all human civilization and that without the Fredonian contribution, we would all be living in caves or trees, bereft of art, technology, and culture. To explain why Fredonians today are in modest circumstances, given their historic eminence, children are taught that somewhere, long ago, another culture stole the Fredonians' achievements, palmed them off as their own, and then oppressed the Fredonians.

I first encountered this argument almost twenty years ago, when I was a graduate student. I shared a small office with a young professor, and I listened as she patiently explained to a student why she had given him a D on a term paper. In his paper, he argued that the Arabs had stolen mathematics from the Nubians in the desert long ago (I forget in which century this theft allegedly occurred). She tried to explain to him about the necessity of historical evidence. He was unconvinced, since he believed that he had uncovered a great truth that was beyond proof. The part I couldn't understand was how anyone could lose knowledge by sharing it. After all, cultures are constantly influencing one another, exchanging ideas and art and technology, and the exchange usually is enriching, not depleting.

Today, there are a number of books and articles advancing controversial theories about the origins of civilization. An important work, *The African Origin of Civilization: Myth or Reality,* by Senegalese scholar Cheikh Anta Diop, argues that ancient Egypt was a black civilization, that all races are descended from the black race, and that the achievements of "western" civilization originated in Egypt. The views of Diop and other Africanists have been condensed into an everyman's paperback titled *What They Never Told You in History Class* by Indus Khamit Kush. This latter book claims that Moses, Jesus, Buddha, Mohammed, and Vishnu were Africans; that the first Indians, Chinese, Hebrews, Greeks, Romans, Britains, and Americans were Africans; and that the first mathematicians, scientists, astronomers, and physicians were Africans. A debate currently raging among some classicists is whether the Greeks "stole" the philosophy, art, and religion of the ancient Egyptians and whether the ancient Egyptians were black Africans. George G. M. James's *Stolen Legacy* insists that the Greeks "stole the Legacy of the African Continent and called it their own." James argues that the civilization of Greece, the vaunted foundation of European culture, owed everything it knew and did to its African predecessors. Thus, the roots of western civilization lie not in Greece and Rome, but in Egypt and, ultimately, in black Africa.

Similar speculation was fueled by the publication in 1987 of Martin Bernal's *Black Athena: The Afroasiatic Roots of Classical Civilization,* Volume 1, *The Fabrication of Ancient Greece,* 1785–1985, although the controversy predates Bernal's book. In a fascinating foray into the politics of knowledge, Bernal attributes the preference of Western European scholars for Greece over Egypt as the fount of knowledge to nearly two centuries of racism and "Europocentrism," but he is uncertain about the color of the ancient Egyptians. However, a review of Bernal's book last year in the *Village Voice* began, "What color were the ancient Egyptians? Blacker than Mubarak, baby." The same article claimed that white racist archeologists chiseled the noses off ancient Egyptian statues so that future generations would not see the typically African facial characteristics. The debate reached the pages of the *Biblical Archeology Review* last year in an article titled "Were the Ancient Egyptians Black or White?" The author, classicist Frank J. Yurco, argues that some Egyptian rulers were black, others were not, and that "the ancient Egyptians did not think in these terms." The issue, wrote Yurco, "is a chimera, cultural baggage from our own society that can only be imposed artificially on ancient Egyptian society."

Most educationists are not even aware of the debate about whether the ancient Egyptians were black or white, but they are very sensitive to charges that the schools' curricula are Eurocentric, and they are eager to rid the schools of the taint of Eurocentrism. It is hardly surprising that America's schools would recognize strong cultural ties with Europe since our nation's political, religious, educational, and economic institutions were created chiefly by people of European descent, our government was shaped by European ideas, and nearly 80 percent of the people who live here are of European descent. The particularists treat all of this history as a racist bias toward Europe, rather than as the matter-of-fact consequences of European immigration. Even so, American education is not centered on Europe. American education, if it is centered on anything, is centered on itself. It is "Americentric." Most American students today have never studied any world history; they know very little about Europe, and even less about the rest of the world. Their minds are rooted solidly in the here and now. When the Berlin Wall was opened in the fall of 1989, journalists discovered that most American teenagers had no idea what it was, nor why its opening was such a big deal. Nonetheless, Eurocentrism provides a better target than Americentrism.

In school districts where most children are black and Hispanic, there has been a growing tendency to embrace particularism rather than pluralism. Many of the children in these districts perform poorly in academic classes and leave school without graduating. They would fare better in school if they had well-educated and well-paid teachers, small classes, good materials, encouragement at home and school, summer academic programs, protection from the drugs and crime that ravage their neighborhoods, and higher expectations of satisfying careers upon graduation. These are expensive and time-consuming remedies that must also engage the larger society beyond the school. The lure of particularism is that it offers a less complicated anodyne, one in which the children's academic deficiencies may be addressed—or set aside—by inflating their racial pride. The danger of this remedy is that it will detract attention from the real needs of schools and the real interests of children, while simultaneously arousing distorted race pride in children of all races, increasing racial antagonism and producing fresh recruits for white and black racist groups.

The particularist critique gained a major forum in New York in 1989, with the release of a report called "A Curriculum of Inclusion," produced by a task force created by the State Commissioner of Education, Thomas Sobol. In 1987, soon after his appointment, Sobol appointed a Task Force on Minorities to review the state's curriculum for instances of bias. He did this not because there had been complaints about bias in the curriculum, but because—as a newly appointed state commissioner whose previous job had been to superintend the public schools of a wealthy suburb, Scarsdale—he wanted to demonstrate his sensitivity to minority concerns. The Sobol task force was composed of representatives of African American, Hispanic, Asian American, and American Indian groups.

The task force engaged four consultants, one from each of the aforementioned racial or ethnic minorities, to review nearly one hundred teachers' guides prepared by the state. These guides define the state's curriculum, usually as a list of facts and concepts to be taught, along with model activities. The primary focus of the consultants, not surprisingly, was the history and social studies curriculum. As it happened, the history curriculum had been extensively revised in 1987 to make it multicultural, in both American and world history. In the 1987 revision the time given to Western Europe was reduced to one-quarter of one year, as part of a two-year global studies sequence in which equal time was allotted to seven major world regions, including Africa and Latin America.

As a result of the 1987 revisions in American and world history, New York State had one of the most advanced multicultural history-social studies curricula in the country. Dozens of social studies teachers and consultants had participated, and the final draft was reviewed by such historians as Eric Foner of Columbia University, the late Hazel Hertzberg of Teachers College, Columbia University, and Christopher Lasch of the University of Rochester. The curriculum was overloaded with facts, almost to the point of numbing students with details and trivia, but it was not insensitive to ethnicity in American history or unduly devoted to European history.

But the Sobol task force decided that this curriculum was biased and Eurocentric. The first sentence of the task force report summarizes its major thesis: "African Americans, Asian Americans, Puerto Ricans/Latinos, and Native Americans have all been the victims of an intellectual and educational oppression that has characterized the culture and institutions of the United States and the European American world for centuries."

The task force report was remarkable in that it vigorously denounced bias without identifying a single instance of bias in the curricular guides under review. Instead, the consultants employed harsh, sometimes inflammatory, rhetoric to treat every difference of opinion or interpretation as an example of racial bias. The African-American consultant, for example, excoriates the curriculum for its "White Anglo-Saxon (WASP) value system and norms," its "deep-seated pathologies of racial hatred" and its "white nationalism"; he decries as bias the fact that children study Egypt as part of the Middle East instead of as part of Africa. Perhaps Egypt should be studied as part of the African unit (geographically, it is located on the African continent); but placing it in one region rather than the other is not what most people think of as racism or bias. The "Latino" consultant criticizes the use of the term "Spanish-American War" instead of "Spanish-Cuban-American War." The Native American consultant complains that tribal languages are classified as "foreign languages."

The report is consistently Europhobic. It repeatedly expresses negative judgments on "European Americans" and on everything Western and European. All people with a white skin are referred to as "Anglo-Saxons" and "WASPs." Europe, says the report, is uniquely responsible for producing aggressive individuals who "were ready to 'discover, invade and conquer' foreign land because of greed, racism and national egoism." All white people are held collectively guilty for the historical crimes of slavery and racism. There is no mention of the "Anglo-Saxons" who opposed slavery and racism. Nor does the report acknowledge that some whites have been victims of discrimination and oppression. The African American consultant writes of the Constitution, "There is something vulgar and revolting in glorifying a process that heaped undeserved rewards on a segment of the population while oppressing the majority."

The New York task force proposal is not merely about the reconstruction of what is taught. It goes a step further to suggest that the history curriculum may be used to ensure that "children from Native American, Puerto Rican/Latino, Asian American, and African American cultures will have higher self-esteem and self-respect, while children from European cultures will have a less arrogant perspective of being part of the group that has 'done it all.' "

In February 1990, Commissioner Sobol asked the New York Board of Regents to endorse a sweeping revision of the history curriculum to make it more multicultural. His recommendations were couched in measured tones, not in the angry rhetoric of his task force.

The board supported his request unanimously. It remains to be seen whether New York pursues the particularist path marked out by the Commissioner's advisory group or finds its way to the concept of pluralism within a democratic tradition.

The rising tide of particularism encourages the politicization of all curricula in the schools. If education bureaucrats bend to the political and ideological winds, as is their wont, we can anticipate a generation of struggle over the content of the curriculum in mathematics, science, literature, and history. Demands for "culturally relevant" studies, for ethnostudies of all kinds, will open the classroom to unending battles over whose version is taught, who gets credit for what, and which ethno-interpretation is appropriate. Only recently have districts begun to resist the demands of fundamentalist groups to censor textbooks and library books (and some have not yet begun to do so).

The spread of particularism throws into question the very idea of American public education. Public schools exist to teach children the general skills and knowledge that they need to succeed in American society, and the specific skills and knowledge that they need in order to function as American citizens. They receive public support because they have a public function. Historically, the public schools were known as "common schools" because they were schools for all, even if the children of all the people did not attend them. Over the years, the courts have found that it was unconstitutional to teach religion in the common schools, or to separate children on the basis of their race in the common schools. In their curriculum, their hiring practices, and their general philosophy, the public schools must not discriminate against or give preference to any racial or ethnic group. Yet they are permitted to accommodate cultural diversity by, for example, serving food that is culturally appropriate or providing library collections that emphasize the interests of the local community. However, they should not be expected to teach children to view the world through an ethnocentric perspective that rejects or ignores the common culture. For generations, those groups that wanted to inculcate their religion or their ethnic heritage have instituted private schools—after school, on weekends, or on a full-time basis. There, children learn with others of the same group—Greeks, Poles, Germans, Japanese, Chinese, Jews, Lutherans, Catholics, and so on—and are taught by people from the same group. Valuable as this exclusive experience has been for those who choose it, this has not been the role of public education. One of the primary purposes of public education has been to create a national community, a definition of citizenship and culture that is both expansive and *inclusive*.

The curriculum in public schools must be based on whatever knowledge and practices have been determined to be best by professionals—experienced teachers and scholars—who are competent to make these judgments. Professional societies must be prepared to defend the integrity of their disciplines. When called upon, they should establish review committees to examine disputes over curriculum and to render judgment, in order to help school officials fend off improper political pressure. Where genuine controversies exist, they should be taught and debated in the classroom. Was Egypt a black civilization? Why not raise the question, read the arguments of the different sides in the debate, show slides of Egyptian pharoahs and queens, read books about life in ancient Egypt, invite guest scholars from the local university, and visit museums with Egyptian collections? If scholars disagree, students should know it. One great advantage of this approach is that students will see that history is a lively study, that textbooks are fallible, that historians disagree, that the writing of history is influenced by the historian's politics and ideology, that history is written by people who make choices among alternative facts and interpretations, and that history changes as new facts are uncovered and new interpretations win adherents. They will also learn that cultures and civilizations constantly interact, exchange ideas, and influence one another, and that the idea of racial or ethnic purity is a myth. Another advantage is that students might once again study ancient history, which has all but disappeared from the curricula of American schools. (California recently introduced a required sixth grade course in ancient civilizations, but ancient history is otherwise *terra incognita* in American education.)

The multicultural controversy may do wonders for the study of history, which has been neglected for years in American schools. At this time, only half of our high school graduates ever study any world history. Any serious attempt to broaden students' knowledge of Africa, Europe, Asia, and Latin America will require at least two, and possibly three years of world history (a requirement thus far only in California). American history, too, will need more time than the one-year high-school survey course. Those of us who have insisted for years on the importance of history in the curriculum may not be ready to assent to its redemptive power, but hope that our new allies will ultimately join a constructive dialogue that strengthens the place of history in the schools.

As cultural controversies arise, educators must adhere to the principle of "E Pluribus Unum." That is, they must maintain a balance between the demands of the one—the nation of which we are common citizens—and the many—the varied histories of the American people. It is not necessary to denigrate either the one or the many. Pluralism is a positive value, but it is also important that we preserve a sense of an American community—a society and a culture to which we all belong. If there is no overall community with an agreed-upon vision of liberty and justice, if all we have is a collection of racial and ethnic cultures, lacking any common bonds, then we have no means to mobilize public opinion on behalf of people who are not members of our particular group. We have, for example, no reason to support public education. If there is no larger community, then each group will want to teach its own children in its own way, and public education ceases to exist.

History should not be confused with filiopietism. History gives no grounds for race pride. No race has a monopoly on virtue. If anything, a study of history should inspire humility, rather than pride. People of every racial group have committed terrible crimes, often against others of the same group. Whether one looks at the history of Europe or Africa or Latin America or Asia, every continent offers examples of inhumanity. Slavery has existed in civilizations around the world for centuries. Examples of genocide can be found around the world, throughout history, from ancient times right through to our own day. Governments and cultures, sometimes by edict, sometimes simply following tradition, have practiced not only slavery, but human sacrifice, infanticide, cliterodectomy, and mass murder. If we teach children this, they might recognize how absurd both racial hatred and racial chauvinism are.

What must be preserved in the study of history is the spirit of inquiry, the readiness to open new questions and to pursue new understandings. History, at its best, is a search for truth. The best way to portray this search is through debate and controversy, rather than through imposition of fixed beliefs and immutable facts. Perhaps the most dangerous aspect of school history is its tendency to become

Official History, a sanctified version of the Truth taught by the state to captive audiences and embedded in beautiful mass-market textbooks as holy writ. When Official History is written by committees responding to political pressures, rather than by scholars synthesizing the best available research, then the errors of the past are replaced by the politically fashionable errors of the present. It may be difficult to teach children that history is both important and uncertain, and that even the best historians never have all the pieces of the jigsaw puzzle, but it is necessary to do so. If state education departments permit the revision of their history courses and textbooks to become an exercise in power politics, then the entire process of state-level curriculum-making becomes suspect, as does public education itself.

The question of self-esteem is extraordinarily complex, and it goes well beyond the content of the curriculum. Most of what we call self-esteem is formed in the home and in a variety of life experiences, not only in school. Nonetheless, it has been important for blacks—and for other racial groups—to learn about the history of slavery and of the civil rights movement; it has been important for blacks to know that their ancestors actively resisted enslavement and actively pursued equality; and it has been important for blacks and others to learn about black men and women who fought courageously against racism and who provide models of courage, persistence, and intellect. These are instances where the content of the curriculum reflects sound scholarship, and at the same time probably lessens racial prejudice and provides inspiration for those who are descendants of slaves. But knowing about the travails and triumphs of one's forebears does not necessarily translate into either self-esteem or personal accomplishment. For most children, self-esteem—the self-confidence that grows out of having reached a goal—comes not from hearing about the monuments of their ancestors but as a consequence of what they are able to do and accomplish through their own efforts.

As I reflected on these issues, I recalled reading an interview a few years ago with a talented black runner. She said that her model is Mikhail Baryshnikov. She admires him because he is a magnificent athlete. He is not black; he is not female; he is not American-born; he is not even a runner. But he inspires her because of the way he trained and used his body. When I read this, I thought how narrow-minded it is to believe that people can be inspired *only* by those who are exactly like them in race and ethnicity.

A human being is part of the whole, called by us the universe. A part limited in time and space. He experiences himself, his thoughts and feelings, as something separate from the rest, a kind of optical delusion of his consciousness. This delusion is a kind of prison for us, restricting us to our personal desires and to affection for a few persons nearest to us. Our task must be to free ourselves from this prison by widening our circle of compassion to embrace all living creatures.

—ALBERT EINSTEIN, *Beyond War*, 1944

Coming to the end
of autumn, now I wonder what
my neighbor does.

—MATSUO BASHO, 1694

PART THREE

Beyond Culture and Prejudice, Toward Pride and Tolerance

Käthe Kollwitz, *The Joy of Motherhood*, Kl.244.
Courtesy Galerie St. Etienne, New York.

Problems and Solutions for
Interculturalism and Understanding,
Cross-Cultural and Intercultural
Communication, Nonviolent Activism
Toward True Democracy, Ecological
Sanity, and Planetary Citizenship

Proxemics in a Cross-Cultural Context: Japan and the Arab World

EDWARD T. HALL

Proxemic patterns play a role in man comparable to display behavior among lower life forms; that is, they simultaneously consolidate the group and isolate it from others by on the one hand reinforcing intragroup identity and on the other making intergroup communication more difficult. Even though man may be physiologically and genetically one species, the proxemic patterns of the Americans and the Japanese often strike one as being as disparate as the territorial display patterns of the American grouse and the Australian bowerbirds. . . .

Japan

In old Japan, space and social organization were interrelated. The Tokugawa shoguns arranged the daimyo, or nobles, in concentric zones around the capital, Ado (Tokyo). Proximity to the core reflected closeness of relationship and loyalty to the shogun; the most loyal formed an inner protective ring. On the other side of the island, across the mountains and to the north and south, were those who were less trusted or whose loyalty was in question. The concept of the center that can be approached from any direction is a well-developed theme in Japanese culture. This entire plan is characteristically Japanese and those who know them will recognize it as a manifestation of a paradigm that functions in virtually all areas of Japanese life.

As noted earlier, the Japanese name intersections rather than the streets leading into them. In fact, each separate corner of the intersection has a different identification. The route itself from point *A* to point *B* seems almost whimsical to the Westerner and is not stressed as it is with us. Not being in the habit of using fixed routes, the Japanese zero in on their destination when they travel across Tokyo. Taxicab drivers have to ask local directions at police booths, not just because streets are not named but because houses are numbered in the order in which they were built. Neighbors often do not know each other and so cannot give directions. In order to cope with this aspect of Japanese space, the American occupation forces after V-J Day named a few main thoroughfares in Tokyo, putting up street signs in English (Avenues A, B, and C). The Japanese waited politely until the end of the occupation to take the signs down. By then, however, the Japanese were trapped by a foreign cultural innovation. They discovered that it is actually helpful to be able to designate a route that connects two points. It will be interesting to see how persistent this change in Japanese culture will be.

It is possible to see the Japanese pattern that emphasizes centers not only in a variety of other spatial arrangements but, as I hope to demonstrate, even in their conversations. The Japanese fireplace (*hibachi*) and its location carries with it an emotional tone that is as strong, if not stronger, than our concept of the hearth. As an old priest once explained, "To really know the Japanese you have to have spent some cold winter evenings snuggled together around the *hibachi*. Everybody sits together. A common quilt covers not only the *hibachi* but everyone's lap as well. In this way the heat is held in. It's when your hands touch and you feel the warmth of their bodies and everyone feels together—that's when you get to know the Japanese. That is the real Japan!" In psychological terms there is positive reinforcement toward the center of the room and negative reinforcement toward the edges (which is where the cold comes from in the winter). Is it any wonder then that the Japanese have been known to say that our rooms look bare (because the centers are bare).

Another side of the center-edge contrast has to do with how and under what circumstances one moves and what is considered to be fixed-feature and what semifixed-feature space. To us the walls of a house are fixed. In Japan they are semifixed. The walls are movable and rooms are multipurpose. In the Japanese country inns (the *ryokan*), the guest discovers that things come to him while the scene shifts. He sits in the middle of the room on the *tatami* (mat) while sliding panels are opened or closed. Depending on the time of day, the room can include all outdoors or it can be shrunk in stages until all that remains is a boudoir. A wall slides back and a meal is brought in. When the meal is over and it is time to sleep, bedding is unrolled in the same spot in which eating, cooking, thinking, and socializing took place. In the morning, when the room is again opened to all outdoors, bright rays of sunshine or the subtle pine scent of the mountain mists penetrates intimate space and sweeps it refreshingly clean.

A fine example of the differences in the perceptual world of the East and the West is the Japanese film *Woman in the Dunes*. The sensual involvement of the Japanese was never more clearly illustrated than in this film. Viewing it one has the feeling of being inside the skin of the screen subjects. At times it is impossible to identify what part of the body one is looking at. The lens of the camera travels slowly, examining every detail of the body. The landscape of the skin is enlarged; its texture is seen as topography, at least by Western eyes. Goose pimples are large enough to be examined individually while grains of sand become like rough quartz pebbles. The experience is not unlike that of looking at the pulsing life of a fish embryo under a microscope.

One of the terms most frequently used by Americans to describe the Japanese *modus operandi* is the word "indirection." An American banker who had spent years in Japan and made the minimum possible accommodation told me that what he found most frustrating and difficult was their indirection. "An old-style Japanese," he complained, "can drive a man crazy faster than anything I know. They talk around and around and around a point and never do get to it." What he did not realize, of course, was that American insistence on "coming to the point" quickly is just as frustrating to the Japanese, who do not understand why we have to be so "logical" all the time.

Young Jesuit missionaries working in Japan have great difficulty at first, for their training works against them. The syllogism on which they depend to make their points clashes with some of the most basic patterns of Japanese life. Their dilemma is: to be true to their training and fail, or to depart from it and succeed. The most successful Jesuit missionary in Japan at the time of my 1957 visit violated group norms when he espoused local custom. After a brief syllogistic introduction he would switch and talk around the point and dwell at length on what wonderful *feelings* (important to the Japanese) one had if one was a Catholic. What interested me was that even though his Catholic brothers knew what he was doing and could observe his success, the hold of their own culture was sufficiently strong so that few could bring themselves to follow his example and violate their own mores.

HOW CROWDED IS CROWDED?

To the Westerner of a non-contact group, "crowding" is a word with distasteful connotations. The Japanese I have known prefer crowding, at least in certain situations. They feel it is congenial to sleep close together on the floor, which they refer to as "Japanese style" as contrasted with "American style." It is not surprising, therefore, to discover that according to Donald Keene, author of *Living Japan,* there is no Japanese word for privacy. Yet one cannot say that the concept of privacy does not exist among the Japanese but only that it is very different from the Western conception. While a Japanese may not want to be alone and doesn't mind having people milling around him, he has strong feelings against sharing a wall of his house or apartment with others. He considers his house and the *zone immediately surrounding it* as one structure. This free area, this sliver of space, is considered to be as much a part of the house as the roof. Traditionally, it contains a garden even though tiny, which gives the householder direct contact with nature.

THE JAPANESE CONCEPT OF SPACE INCLUDING THE *MA*

Differences between the West and Japan are not limited to moving around the point *vs.* coming to the point, or the stressing of lines as contrasted with intersections. The entire experience of space in the most essential respects is different from that of Western culture. When Westerners think and talk about space, they mean the distance between objects. In the West, we are taught to perceive and to react to the arrangements of objects and to think of space as "empty." The meaning of this becomes clear only when it is contrasted with the Japanese, who are trained to give *meaning* to spaces—to perceive the shape and arrangement of spaces; for this they have a word, *ma*. The *ma*, or interval, is a basic building block in all Japanese spatial experience. It is functional not only in flower arrangements but apparently is a hidden consideration in the layout of all other spaces. Japanese skill in the handling and arrangement of the *ma* is extraordinary and produces admiration and occasionally even awe in Europeans. Skill in handling spaces is epitomized in the fifteenth century Zen monastery garden of Ryoanji outside the old capital of Kyoto. The garden itself comes as a surprise. Walking through the darkened, paneled main building one rounds a bend and is suddenly in the presence of a powerful creative force—fifteen rocks rising from a sea of crushed gravel. Viewing Ryoanji is an emotional experience. One is overcome by the order, serenity, and the discipline of extreme simplicity. Man and nature are somehow transformed and can be viewed as in harmony. There is also a philosophical message regarding man's relation to nature. The grouping is such that no matter where one sits to contemplate the scene, one of the rocks that make up the garden is always hidden (perhaps another clue to the Japanese mind). They believe that memory and imagination should always participate in perceptions.

Part of the Japanese skill in creating gardens stems from the fact that in the perception of space the Japanese employ vision and all the other senses as well. Olfaction, shifts in temperature, humidity, light, shade, and color are worked together in such a way as to enhance the use of the whole body as a sensing organ. In contrast to the single point perspective of Renaissance and Baroque painters, the Japanese garden is designed to be enjoyed from many points of view. The designer makes the garden visitor stop here and there, perhaps to find his footing on a stone in the middle of a pool so that he looks up at precisely the right moment to catch a glimpse of unsuspected vista. *The study of Japanese spaces illustrates their habit of leading the individual to a spot where he can discover something for himself.*

The Arab patterns which are described below have nothing to do with "leading" people anywhere. In the Arab world one is expected to connect widely separated points on his own, and very quickly too. For this reason the reader has to shift gears mentally when considering the Arabs.

The Arab World

In spite of over two thousand years of contact, Westerners and Arabs still do not understand each other. Proxemic research reveals some insights into this difficulty. Americans in the Middle East are immediately struck by two conflicting sensations. In public they are compressed and overwhelmed by smells, crowding, and high noise levels; in Arab homes Americans are apt to rattle around, feeling exposed and often somewhat inadequate because of too much space! (The Arab houses and apartments of the middle and upper classes which Americans stationed abroad commonly occupy are much larger than the dwellings such Americans usually inhabit.) Both the high sensory stimulation which is experienced in public places and the basic insecurity which comes from being in a dwelling that is too large provide Americans with an introduction to the sensory world of the Arab.

BEHAVIOR IN PUBLIC

Pushing and shoving in public places is characteristic of Middle Eastern culture. Yet it is not entirely what Americans think it is (being pushy and rude) but stems from a different set of assumptions concerning not only the relations between people but how one experiences the body as well. Paradoxically, Arabs consider northern Europeans and Americans pushy, too. This was very puzzling to me when I started investigating these two views. How could Americans who stand aside and avoid touching be considered pushy? I used to ask Arabs to explain this paradox. None of my subjects was able to tell me specifically what particulars of American behavior were responsible, yet they all agreed that the impression was widespread among Arabs. After repeated unsuccessful attempts to gain insight into the cognitive world of the Arab on this particular point, I filed it away as a question that only time would answer. When the answer came, it was because of a seemingly inconsequential annoyance.

While waiting for a friend in a Washington, D.C., hotel lobby and wanting to be both visible and alone, I had seated myself in a solitary chair outside the normal stream of traffic. In such a setting most Americans follow a rule, which is all the more binding because we seldom think about it, that can be stated as follows: as soon as a person stops or is seated in a public place, there balloons around him a small sphere of privacy which is considered inviolate. The size of the sphere varies with the degree of crowding, the age, sex, and the importance of the person, as well as the general surroundings. Anyone who enters this zone and stays there is intruding. In fact, a stranger who intrudes, even for a specific purpose, acknowledges the fact that he has intruded by beginning his request with "Pardon me, but can you tell me . . . ?"

To continue, as I waited in the deserted lobby, a stranger walked up to where I was sitting and stood close enough so that not only could I easily touch him but I could even hear him breathing. In addition, the dark mass of his body filled the peripheral field of vision on my left side. If the lobby had been crowded with people, I would have understood his behavior, but in an empty lobby his presence made me exceedingly uncomfortable. Feeling annoyed by this intrusion, I moved my body in such a way as to communicate annoyance. Strangely enough, instead of moving away, my actions seemed only to encourage him, because he moved even closer. In spite of the temptation to escape the annoyance, I put aside thoughts of abandoning my post, thinking, "To hell with it. Why should I move? I was here first and I'm not going to let this fellow drive me out even if he is a boor." Fortunately, a group of people soon arrived whom my tormentor immediately joined. Their mannerisms explained his behavior, for I knew from both speech and gestures that they were Arabs. I had not been able to make this crucial identification by looking at my subject when he was alone because he wasn't talking and he was wearing American clothes.

In describing the scene later to an Arab colleague, two contrasting patterns emerged. My concept and my feelings about my own circle of privacy in a "public" place immediately struck my Arab friend as strange and puzzling. He said, "After all, it's a public place, isn't it?" Pursuing this line of inquiry, I found that in Arab thought I had no rights whatsoever by virtue of occupying a given spot; neither my place nor my body was inviolate! For the Arab, there is no such thing as an intrusion in public. Public means public. With this insight, a great range of Arab behavior that had been puzzling, annoying, and sometimes even frightening began to make sense. I learned, for example, that if *A* is standing on a street corner and *B* wants his spot, *B* is within his rights if he does what he can to make *A* uncomfortable enough to move. In Beirut only the hardy sit in the last row in a movie theater, because there are usually standees who want seats and who push and shove and make such a nuisance that most people give up and leave. Seen in this light, the Arab who "intruded" on my space in the hotel lobby had apparently selected it for the very reason I had: it was a good place to watch two doors and the elevator. My show of annoyance, instead of driving him away, had only encouraged him. He thought he was about to get me to move.

Another silent source of friction between Americans and Arabs is in an area that Americans treat very informally—the manners and rights of the road. In general, in the United States we tend to defer to the vehicle that is bigger, more powerful, faster, and heavily laden. While a pedestrian walking along a road may feel annoyed he will not think it unusual to step aside for a fast-moving automobile. He knows that because he is moving he does not have the right to the space around him that he has when he is standing still (as I was in the hotel lobby). It appears that the reverse is true with the Arabs who apparently *take on rights to space as they move*. For someone else to move into a space an Arab is also moving into is a violation of his rights. It is infuriating to an Arab to have someone else cut in front of him on the highway. It is the American's cavalier treatment of moving space that makes the Arab call him aggressive and pushy.

CONCEPTS OF PRIVACY

The experience described above and many others suggested to me that Arabs might actually have a wholly contrasting set of assumptions concerning the body and the rights associated with it. Certainly the Arab tendency to shove and push each other in public and to feel and pinch women in public conveyances would not be tolerated by Westerners. It appeared to me that they must not have any concept of a private zone outside the body. This proved to be precisely the case.

In the Western world, the person is synonymous with an individual inside a skin. And in northern Europe generally, the skin and even the clothes may be inviolate. You need permission to touch either if you are a stranger. This rule applies in some parts of France, where the mere touching of another person during an argument used to be legally defined as assault. For the Arab the location of the person in relation to the body is quite different. The person exists somewhere down inside the body. The ego is not completely hidden, however, because it can be reached very easily with an insult. It is protected from touch but not from words. The dissociation of the body and the ego may explain why the public amputation of a thief's hand is tolerated as standard punishment in Saudi Arabia. It also sheds light on why an Arab employer living in a modern apartment can provide his servant with a room that is a boxlike cubicle approximately 5 by 10 by 4 feet in size that is not only hung from the ceiling to conserve floor space but has an opening so that the servant can be spied on.

As one might suspect, deep orientations toward the self such as the one just described are also reflected in the language. This was brought to my attention one afternoon when an Arab colleague who is the author of an Arab-English dictionary arrived in my office and threw himself into a chair in a state of obvious exhaustion. When I asked him what had been going on, he said: "I have spent the entire afternoon trying to find the Arab equivalent of the English word 'rape.' There is no such word in Arabic. All my sources, both written and spoken, can come up with no more than an approximation, such as 'He took her against her will.' There is nothing in Arabic approaching your meaning as it is expressed in that one word."

Differing concepts of the placement of the ego in relation to the body are not easily grasped. Once an idea like this is accepted, however, it is possible to understand many other facets of Arab life that would otherwise be difficult to explain. One of these is the high population density of Arab cities like Cairo, Beirut, and Damascus. According to the animal studies described in the earlier chapters, the Arabs should be living in a perpetual behavioral sink. While it is probable that Arabs are suffering from population pressures, it is also just as possible that continued pressure from the desert has resulted in a cultural adaptation to high density which takes the form described above. Tucking the ego down inside the body shell not only would permit higher population densities but would explain why it is that Arab communications are stepped up as much as they are when compared to northern European communication patterns. Not only is the sheer noise level much higher, but the piercing look of the eyes, the touch of the hands, and the mutual bathing in the warm moist breath during conversation represent stepped-up sensory inputs to a level which many Europeans find unbearably intense.

The Arab dream is for lots of space in the home, which unfortunately many Arabs cannot afford. Yet when he has space, it is very different from what one finds in most American homes. Arab spaces inside their upper middle-class homes are tremendous by our standards. They avoid partitions because Arabs *do not like to be alone*. The form of the home is such as to hold the family together inside a single protective shell, because Arabs are deeply involved with each other. Their personalities are intermingled and take nourishment from each other like the roots and soil. If one is not with people and actively involved in some way, one is deprived of life. An old Arab saying reflects this value: "Paradise without people should not be entered because it is Hell." Therefore, Arabs in the United States often feel socially and sensorially deprived and long to be back where there is human warmth and contact.

Since there is no physical privacy as we know it in the Arab family, not even a word for privacy, one could expect that the Arabs might use some other means to be alone. Their way to be alone is to stop talking. Like the English, an Arab who shuts himself off in this way is not indicating that anything is wrong or that he is withdrawing, only that he wants to be alone with his own thoughts or does not want to be intruded upon. One subject said that her father would come and go for days at a time without saying a word, and no one in the family thought anything of it. Yet for this very reason, an Arab exchange student visiting a Kansas farm failed to pick up the cue that his American hosts were mad at him when they gave him the "silent treatment." He only discovered something was wrong when they took him to town and tried forcibly to put him on a bus to Washington, D.C., the headquarters of the exchange program responsible for his presence in the U.S.

ARAB PERSONAL DISTANCES

Like everyone else in the world, Arabs are unable to formulate specific rules for their informal behavior patterns. In fact, they often deny that there are any rules, and they are made anxious by suggestions that such is the case. Therefore, in order to determine how the Arab sets distances, I investigated the use of each sense separately. Gradually, definite and distinctive behavioral patterns began to emerge.

Olfaction occupies a prominent place in the Arab life. Not only is it one of the distance-setting mechanisms, but it is a vital part of a complex system of behavior. Arabs consistently breathe on people when they talk. However, this habit is more than a matter of different manners. To the Arab good smells are pleasing and a way of being involved with each other. To smell one's friend is not only nice but desirable, for to deny him your breath is to act ashamed. Americans, on the other hand, trained as they are not to breathe in people's faces, automatically communicate shame in trying to be polite. Who would expect that when our highest diplomats are putting on their best manners they are also communicating shame? Yet this is what occurs constantly, because diplomacy is not only "eyeball to eyeball" but breath to breath.

By stressing olfaction, Arabs do not try to eliminate all the body's odors, only to enhance them and use them in building human relationships. Nor are they self-conscious about telling others when they don't like the way they smell. A man leaving his house in the morning may be told by his uncle, "Habib, your stomach is sour and your breath doesn't smell too good. Better not talk too close to people today." Smell is even considered in the choice of a mate. When couples are being matched for marriage, the man's go-between will sometimes ask to smell the girl, who may be turned down if she doesn't "smell nice." Arabs recognize that smell and disposition may be linked.

In a word, the olfactory boundary performs two roles in Arab life. It enfolds those who want to relate and separates those who don't. The Arab finds it essential to stay inside the olfactory zone as a means of keeping tab on changes in emotion. What is more, he may feel crowded as soon as he smells something unpleasant. While not much is known about "olfactory crowding," this may prove to be as significant as any other variable in the crowding complex because it is tied directly to the body chemistry and hence to the state of health and emotions. (The reader will remember that it was olfaction in the Bruce effect that suppressed pregnancies in mice.) It is not surprising, therefore, that the olfactory boundary constitutes for the Arabs an informal distance-setting mechanism in contrast to the visual mechanisms of the Westerner.

FACING AND NOT FACING

One of my earliest discoveries in the field of intercultural communication was that the position of the bodies of people in conversation varies with the culture. Even so, it used to puzzle me that a special Arab friend seemed unable to walk and talk at the same time. After years in the United States, he could not bring himself to stroll along, facing forward while talking. Our progress would be arrested while he edged ahead, cutting slightly in front of me and turning sideways so we could see each other. Once in this position, he would stop. His behavior was explained when I learned that for the Arabs to view the other person peripherally is regarded as impolite, and to sit or stand back-to-back is considered very rude. You must be involved when interacting with Arabs who are friends.

One mistaken American notion is that Arabs conduct all conversations at close distances. This is not the case at all. On social occasions, they may sit on opposite sides of the room and talk across the room to each other. They are, however, apt to take offense when Americans use what are to them ambiguous distances, such as the four- to seven-foot social-consultative distance. They frequently complain that Americans are cold or aloof or "don't care." This was what an elderly Arab diplomat in an American hospital thought when the American nurses used "professional" distance. He had the feeling that he was being ignored, that they might not take good care of him. Another Arab subject remarked, referring to American behavior, "What's the matter? Do I smell bad? Or are they afraid of me?"

Arabs who interact with Americans report experiencing a certain flatness traceable in part to a very different use of the eyes in private and in public as well as between friends and strangers. Even though it is rude for a guest to walk around the Arab home eying things, Arabs look at each other in ways which seem hostile or challenging to the American. One Arab informant said that he was in constant hot water with Americans because of the way he looked at them without the slightest intention of offending. In fact, he had on several occasions barely avoided fights with American men who apparently thought their masculinity was being challenged because of the way he was looking at them. As noted earlier, Arabs look each other in the eye when talking with an intensity that makes most Americans highly uncomfortable.

INVOLVEMENT

As the reader must gather by now, Arabs are involved with each other on many different levels simultaneously. Privacy in a public place is foreign to them. Business transactions in the bazaar, for example, are not just between buyer and seller, but are participated in by everyone. Anyone who is standing around may join in. If a grownup sees a boy breaking a window, he must stop him even if he doesn't know him. Involvement and participation are expressed in other ways as well. If two men are fighting, the crowd must intervene. On the political level, *to fail to intervene* when trouble is brewing is to take sides, which is what our State Department always seems to be doing. Given the fact that few people in the world today are even remotely aware of the cultural mold that forms their thoughts, it is normal for Arabs to view *our* behavior as though it stemmed from *their* own hidden set of assumptions.

FEELINGS ABOUT ENCLOSED SPACES

In the course of my interviews with Arabs the term "tomb" kept cropping up in conjunction with enclosed space. In a word, Arabs don't mind being crowded by people but hate to be hemmed in by walls. They show a much greater overt sensitivity to architectural crowding than we do. Enclosed space must meet at least three requirements that I know of if it is to satisfy the Arabs: there must be plenty of unobstructed space in which to move around (possibly as much as a thousand square feet); very high ceilings—so high in fact that they do not normally impinge on the visual field; and, in addition, there must be an unobstructed view. It was spaces such as these in which the Americans referred to earlier felt so uncomfortable. One sees the Arab's need for a view expressed in many ways, even negatively, for to cut off a neighbor's view is one of the most effective ways of spiting him. In Beirut one can see what is known locally as the "spite house." It is nothing more than a thick, four-story wall, built at the end of a long fight between neighbors, on a narrow strip of land for the express purpose of denying a view of the Mediterranean to any house built on the land behind. According to one of my informants, there is also a house on a small plot of land between Beirut and Damascus which is completely surrounded by a neighbor's wall built high enough to cut off the view from all windows!

BOUNDARIES

Proxemic patterns tell us other things about Arab culture. For example, the whole concept of the boundary as an abstraction is almost impossible to pin down. In one sense, there are no boundaries.

"Edges" of towns, yes, but permanent boundaries out in the country (hidden lines), no. In the course of my work with Arab subjects I had a difficult time translating our concept of a boundary into terms which could be equated with theirs. In order to clarify the distinctions between the two very different definitions, I thought it might be helpful to pinpoint acts which constituted trespass. To date, I have been unable to discover anything even remotely resembling our own legal concept of trespass.

Arab behavior in regard to their own real estate is apparently an extension of, and therefore consistent with, their approach to the body. My subjects simply failed to respond whenever trespass was mentioned. They didn't seem to understand what I meant by this term. This may be explained by the fact that they organize relationships with each other according to closed social systems rather than spatially. For thousands of years Moslems, Marinites, Druses, and Jews have lived in their own villages, each with strong kin affiliations. Their hierarchy of loyalties is: first to one's self, then to kinsman, townsman, or tribesman, co-religionist and/or countryman. Anyone not in these categories is a stranger. Strangers and enemies are very closely linked, if not synonymous, in Arab thought. Trespass in this context is a matter of who you are, rather than a piece of land or a space with a boundary that can be denied to anyone and everyone, friend and foe alike.

In summary, proxemic patterns differ. By examining them it is possible to reveal hidden cultural frames that determine the structure of a given people's perceptual world. Perceiving the world differently leads to differential definitions of what constitutes crowded living, different interpersonal relations, and a different approach to both local and international politics. There are in addition wide discrepancies in the degree to which culture structures involvement, which means that planners should begin to think in terms of different kinds of cities, cities which are consistent with the proxemic patterns of the peoples who live in them.

Against Stereotyping: The Native Irishman

A CONVERTED SAXON (ANONYMOUS)

Before I came across the sea
   To this delightful place,
I thought the native Irish were
   A funny sort of race;

I thought they bore shillelagh-sprigs,
   And that they always said:
"Och hone, acushla, tare-an-ouns,"
   "Begorra," and "bedad!"

I thought they sported crownless hats
   With dhudeens in the rim;
I thought they wore long trailing coats
   And knickerbockers trim;
I thought they went about the place
   As tight as they could get;
And that they always had a fight
   With every one they met.

I thought their noses all turned up
   Just like a crooked pin;
I thought their mouths six inches wide
   And always on the grin;
I thought their heads were made of stuff
   As hard as any nails;
I half suspected that they were
   Possessed of little tails.

But when I came unto the land
   Of which I heard so much,
I found that the inhabitants
   Were not entirely such;
I found their features were not all
   Exactly like baboons';
I found that some wore billycocks,
   And some had pantaloons.

I found their teeth were quite as small
    As Europeans' are,
And that their ears, in point of size,
    Were not pecul-iar.
I even saw a face or two
    Which might be handsome called;
And by their very largest feet
    I was not much appalled.

I found them sober, now and then;
    And even in the street,
It seems they do not have a fight
    With every boy they meet.
I even found some honest men
    Among the very poor;
And I have heard some sentences
    Which did not end with "shure."

It seems that praties in their skins
    Are not their only food,
And that they have a house or two
    Which is not built of mud.
In fact, they're not all brutes or fools,
    And I suspect that when
They rule themselves they'll be as good,
    Almost, as Englishmen!

The Leaders of the Crowd

W. B. YEATS

They must to keep their certainty accuse
All that are different of a base intent;
Pull down established honour; hawk for news
Whatever their loose fantasy invent
And murmur it with bated breath, as though
The abounding gutter had been Helicon
Or calumny a song. How can they know

Truth flourishes where the student's lamp has shone,
And there alone, that have no solitude?
So the crowd come they care not what may come.
They have loud music, hope every day renewed
And heartier loves; that lamp is from the tomb.

America: The Multinational Society

ISHMAEL REED

> At the annual Lower East Side Jewish Festival yesterday, a Chinese woman ate a pizza slice in front of Ty Thuan Duc's Vietnamese grocery store. Beside her a Spanish-speaking family patronized a cart with two signs: "Italian Ices" and "Kosher by Rabbi Alper." And after the pastrami ran out, everybody ate knishes.
> —New York Times, *23 June 1983*

On the day before Memorial Day, 1983, a poet called me to describe a city he had just visited. He said that one section included mosques, built by the Islamic people who dwelled there. Attending his reading, he said, were large numbers of Hispanic people, forty thousand of whom lived in the same city. He was not talking about a fabled city located in some mysterious region of the world. The city he'd visited was Detroit.

A few months before, as I was leaving Houston, Texas, I heard it announced on the radio that Texas's largest minority was Mexican-American, and though a foundation recently issued a report critical of bilingual education, the taped voice used to guide the passengers on the air trams connecting terminals in Dallas Airport is in both Spanish and English. If the trend continues, a day will come when it will be difficult to travel through some sections of the country without hearing commands in both English and Spanish; after all, for some western states, Spanish was the first written language and the Spanish style lives on in the western way of life.

Shortly after my Texas trip, I sat in an auditorium located on the campus of the University of Wisconsin at Milwaukee as a Yale professor—whose original work on the influence of African cultures upon those of the Americas has led to his ostracism from some monocultural intellectual circles—walked up and down the aisle, like an old-time southern evangelist, dancing and drumming the top of the lectern, illustrating his points before some serious Afro-American intellectuals and artists who cheered and applauded his performance and his mastery of information. The professor was "white." After his lecture, he joined a group of Milwaukeeans in a conversation. All of the participants spoke Yoruban, though only the professor had ever traveled to Africa.

One of the artists told me that his paintings, which included African and Afro-American mythological symbols and imagery, were hanging in the local McDonald's restaurant. The next day I went to McDonald's and snapped pictures of smiling youngsters eating hamburgers below paintings that could grace the walls of any of the country's leading museums. The manager of the local McDonald's said, "I don't know what you boys are doing, but I like it," as he commissioned the local painters to exhibit in his restaurant.

Such blurring of cultural styles occurs in everyday life in the United States to a greater extent than anyone can imagine and is probably more prevalent than the sensational conflict between people of different backgrounds that is played up and often encouraged by the media. The result is what the Yale professor, Robert Thompson, referred to as a cultural bouillabaisse, yet members of the nation's present educational and cultural Elect still cling to the notion that the United States belongs to some vaguely defined entity they refer to as "Western civilization," by which they mean, presumably, a civilization created by the people of Europe, as if Europe can be viewed in monolithic terms. Is Beethoven's Ninth Symphony, which includes Turkish marches, a part of Western civilization, or the late nineteenth- and twentieth-century French paintings, whose creators were influenced by Japanese art? And what of the cubists, through whom the influence of African art changed modern painting, or the surrealists, who were so impressed with the art of the Pacific Northwest Indians that, in their map of North America, Alaska dwarfs the lower forty-eight in size?

Are the Russians, who are often criticized for their adoption of "Western" ways by Tsarist dissidents in exile, members of Western civilization? And what of the millions of Europeans who have black

African and Asian ancestry, black Africans having occupied several countries for hundreds of years? Are these "Europeans" members of Western civilization, or the Hungarians, who originated across the Urals in a place called Greater Hungary, or the Irish, who came from the Iberian Peninsula?

Even the notion that North America is part of Western civilization because our "system of government" is derived from Europe is being challenged by Native American historians who say that the founding fathers, Benjamin Franklin especially, were actually influenced by the system of government that had been adopted by the Iroquois hundreds of years prior to the arrival of large numbers of Europeans.

Western civilization, then, becomes another confusing category like Third World, or Judeo-Christian culture, as man attempts to impose his small-screen view of political and cultural reality upon a complex world. Our most publicized novelist recently said that Western civilization was the greatest achievement of mankind, an attitude that flourishes on the street level as scribbles in public restrooms: "White Power," "Niggers and Spics Suck," or "Hitler was a prophet," the latter being the most telling, for wasn't Adolf Hitler the archetypal monoculturalist who, in his pigheaded arrogance, believed that one way and one blood was so pure that it had to be protected from alien strains at all costs? Where did such an attitude, which has caused so much misery and depression in our national life, which has tainted even our noblest achievements, begin? An attitude that caused the incarceration of Japanese-American citizens during World War II, the persecution of Chicanos and Chinese-Americans, the near-extermination of the Indians, and the murder and lynchings of thousands of Afro-Americans.

Virtuous, hardworking, pious, even though they occasionally would wander off after some fancy clothes, or rendezvous in the woods with the town prostitute, the Puritans are idealized in our schoolbooks as "a hardy band" of no-nonsense patriarchs whose discipline razed the forest and brought order to the New World (a term that annoys Native American historians). Industrious, responsible, it was their "Yankee ingenuity" and practicality that created the work ethic. They were simple folk who produced a number of good poets, and they set the tone for the American writing style, of lean and spare lines, long before Hemingway. They worshiped in churches whose colors blended in with the New England snow, churches with simple structures and ornate lecterns.

The Puritans were a daring lot, but they had a mean streak. They hated the theater and banned Christmas. They punished people in a cruel and inhuman manner. They killed children who disobeyed their parents. When they came in contact with those whom they considered heathens or aliens, they behaved in such a bizarre and irrational manner that this chapter in the American history comes down to us as a late-movie horror film. They exterminated the Indians, who taught them how to survive in a world unknown to them, and their encounter with the calypso culture of Barbados resulted in what the tourist guide in Salem's Witches' House refers to as the Witchcraft Hysteria.

The Puritan legacy of hard work and meticulous accounting led to the establishment of a great industrial society; it is no wonder that the American industrial revolution began in Lowell, Massachusetts, but there was the other side, the strange and paranoid attitudes toward those different from the Elect.

The cultural attitudes of that early Elect continue to be voiced in everyday life in the United States: the president of a distinguished university, writing a letter to the *Times,* belittling the study of African civilizations; the television network that promoted its show on the Vatican art with the boast that this art represented "the finest achievements of the human spirit." A modern up-tempo state of complex rhythms that depends upon contacts with an international community can no longer behave as if it dwelled in a "Zion Wilderness" surrounded by beasts and pagans.

When I heard a schoolteacher warn the other night about the invasion of the American educational system by foreign curriculums, I wanted to yell at the television set, "Lady, they're already here." It has already begun because the world is here. The world has been arriving at these shores for at least ten thousand years from Europe, Africa, and Asia. In the late nineteenth and early twentieth centuries, large numbers of Europeans arrived, adding their cultures to those of the European, African, and Asian settlers who were already here, and recently millions have been entering the country from South America and the Caribbean, making Yale Professor Bob Thompson's bouillabaisse richer and thicker.

One of our most visionary politicians said that he envisioned a time when the United States could become the brain of the world, by which he meant the repository of all of the latest advanced information systems. I thought of that remark when an enterprising poet friend of mine called to say that he had just sold a poem to a computer magazine and that the editors were delighted to get it because they didn't carry fiction or poetry. Is that the kind of world we desire? A humdrum homogeneous world of all brains and no heart, no fiction, no poetry; a world of robots with human attendants bereft of imagination, of culture? Or does North America deserve a more exciting destiny? To become a place where the cultures of the world crisscross. This is possible because the United States is unique in the world: The world is here.

The Law of Love and Nonviolent Action

LEO TOLSTOY

In our time the continuation of life on bases which are outlived and already sharply opposed to all men's consciousness of truth has become impossible, and that is why, whether we wish it or not, we must in the arrangement of our life establish the law of love in the place of violence. But how in effect is the life of men to be established on a basis of love, excluding violence? No one can answer this question, and moreover, such an answer is not necessary for anyone either. The law of love is not the law of the social arrangements of this or that people or government which can be furthered when you foresee or rather imagine that you foresee those conditions, under which the wished for change may be accomplished. The law of love, that will be the law of life of each separate individual, is in place of that law of life of the whole of mankind and that is why it would be senseless to imagine that it is possible to know and to wish to know the ultimate end of one's own life and still more of the life of all mankind.

The fact that we do not know and cannot even represent to ourselves how will be the life of men, believing in the law of love just as people now believe in the inevitability of violence, shows only that when we follow the law of love, we truly live, doing that which each ought to do for himself what as well he ought to do for the life of all mankind. We know that following the law of love we do that which we ought for ourselves, because only when we follow this law do we receive the greatest wellbeing. We know also that, following this law, we do that too which we ought [and] for the whole of mankind, because the wellbeing of mankind is in unity, and nothing can of its own nature so closely and joyfully unite men as that very law of love which gives the highest wellbeing to each separate man.

That is all that I wished to say.

Believing with my whole soul that we are living on the eve of a world-wide great revolution in the life of men and that every effort for the swiftest destruction of that which cannot be destroyed and the swiftest realisation of that which cannot not be realised, every effort, however weak, assists the coming of this revolution, I could not, living in all probability the last days of my life, not attempt to convey to other men this, my belief.

Yes, we stand on the threshold of a quite new joyful life and entry into this life depends only on our freeing ourselves from the superstition, tormenting us ever more and more, of the inevitability of violence for the common life of men and on acknowledging that eternal principle of love, which has already lived a long time in the consciousness of men and must inevitably replace the principle of violence, outlived and already long unnecessary and only ruinous for men.

From Science and Liberty

ALDOUS HUXLEY

The pen and the voice are at least as mighty as the sword; for . . . the sword is wielded in obedience to the spoken or the written word. Progressive technology has strengthened the powers that be by providing them not only with bigger and better instruments of coercion, but also with instruments of persuasion incomparably superior to those at the disposal of earlier rulers. . . . In countries where the press is said to be free, newspapers are subsidized primarily by advertisers, and to a lesser extent by political parties, financial or professional groups. In countries where the press is not free, newspapers are subsidized by the central government. The man who pays the piper always calls the tune. In capitalist democracies the popular press supports its advertisers by inculcating the benefits of centralized industry and finance, coupled with as much centralized government as will enable these institutions to function at a profit. In totalitarian states all newspapers preach the virtues of governmental omnipotence, one-party politics and state control of everything. In both cases progressive technology has strengthened the hands of the local bosses by providing them with the means of persuading the many that concentration of political and economic power is for the general benefit. . . .

Undesirable propaganda will not cease until the persons who pay for propaganda either change their minds, or are replaced by other persons willing to pay for something else. Meanwhile there is no remedy for the evil except personal self-denial. . . .

In the course of the past two or three generations science and technology have equipped the political bosses who control the various national states with unprecedentedly efficient instruments of coercion. . . . Today, if the central executive wishes to act oppressively, it finds an almost miraculously efficient machine of coercion standing ready to be set in motion. Thanks to the genius and co-operative industry of highly trained physicists, chemists, metallurgists and mechanical inventors, tyrants are able to dragoon larger numbers of people more effectively, and strategists can kill and destroy more indiscriminately and at greater distances, than ever before. On many fronts nature has been conquered; but, as Tolstoy foresaw, man and his liberties have sustained a succession of defeats.

Overwhelming scientific and technological superiority cannot be resisted on their own plane. . . . After a century of scientific and technological progress no weapons available to the masses of the people can compete with those in the arsenals controlled by the ruling minority. Consequently, if any resistance is to be offered by the many to the few, it must be offered in a field in which technological superiority does not count. In countries where democratic institutions exist and the executive is prepared to abide by the rules of the democratic game, the many can protect themselves against the ruling few by using their right to vote, to strike, to organize pressure groups, to petition the legislature, to hold meetings and conduct press campaigns in favor of reform. But where there are no democratic institutions, or where a hitherto democratic government declines any longer to abide by the rules of the game, a majority which feels itself oppressed may be driven to resort to direct action. But since science and technology, in conquering nature have thereby enormously increased the military and police power of the ruling few, this direct action cannot hope for a successful outcome, if it is violent; for in any armed conflict, the side which has the tanks, planes and flame-throwers cannot fail to defeat the side which is armed at the very best only with small arms and hand grenades.

Is there any way out of the unfavorable political situation in which, thanks to applied science, the masses now find themselves? So far only one hopeful issue has been discovered. In South Africa and, later, in India, Gandhi and his followers were confronted by an oppressive government armed with overwhelming military might. Gandhi, who is not only an idealist and a man of principle, but also an intensely practical politician, attempted to cope with this seemingly desperate situation by organizing a non-violent form of direct action, which he called *satyagraha*. . . .

It is often argued that *satyagraha* cannot work against an organization, whose leaders are prepared to exploit their military superiority without qualm or scruple. And of course this may very well be the case. No more than any other form of political action, violent or otherwise, can *satyagraha* guarantee success. But even though, against an entirely ruthless and fanatical opponent, non-co-operation and what Thoreau called "civil disobedience," coupled with a disciplined willingness to accept and even to court sacrificial suffering, may prove unavailing, the resulting situation could not be, materially, any worse than it would have been if the intolerable oppression had been passively accepted or else resisted unavailingly by force; while, psychologically and morally, it would in all probability be very much better— better for those participating in the *satyagraha,* and better in the eyes of spectators and of those who merely heard of the achievement at second hand. . . .

Satyagraha

MAHATMA GANDHI

At the time of writing, I never think of what I have said before. My aim is not to be consistent with my previous statements on a given question, but to be consistent with truth, as it may present itself to me at a given moment. The result has been that I have grown from truth to truth; I have saved my memory an undue strain; and what is more, whenever I have been obliged to compare my writing even of fifty years ago with the latest, I have discovered no inconsistency between the two. But friends who observe inconsistency, will do well to take the meaning that my latest writing may yield, unless they prefer the old. But before making the choice, they should try to see if there is not an underlying and abiding consistency between the two seeming inconsistencies. . . .

How has the undoubted military valour of Poland served her against the superior forces of Germany and Russia? Would Poland unarmed have fared any worse if it had met the challenge of these combined forces with the resolution to face death without retaliation? Would the invading forces have taken a heavier toll from an infinitely more valorous Poland? It is highly probable that their essential nature would have made them desist from a wholesale slaughter of the innocent. . . .

. . . I have no choice as to the means. It must always be purely nonviolent, whether I am closeted with members of the Working Committee or with the Viceroy. . . . But assuming that God had endowed me with full powers, which He never does, I would at once ask the Englishmen to lay down arms, free all their vassals, take pride in being called "little Englanders" and defy all the totalitarians of the world to do their worst. . . . I would further invite the Indians to cooperate with Englishmen in this Godly martyrdom. . . . It will be an indissoluble partnership drawn up in letters of the blood of their own bodies, not of their so-called enemies. But I have no such general power. Nonviolence is a plant of slow growth. It grows imperceptibly, but surely. And even at the risk of being misunderstood, I must act in obedience to "the still small voice." . . .

. . . My nonviolence does recognise different species of violence, defensive and offensive. It is true that, in the long run, the difference is obliterated, but the initial merit persists. A nonviolent person is bound, when the occasion arises, to say which side is just. Thus I wished success to the Abyssinians, the Spaniards, the Czechs, the Chinese and the Poles, although, in each case, I wished that they could have offered nonviolent resistance. . . .

If a man fights with his sword singlehanded against a horde of dacoits, armed to the teeth, I should say he is fighting almost nonviolently. Have I not said to our women that if, in defense of their honour, they used their nails and teeth and even dagger, I should regard their conduct nonviolent? She does not know the distinction between *himsa* and *ahimsa*. She acts spontaneously. Supposing a mouse, in fighting a cat, tried to resist the cat with his sharp beak, would you call that mouse violent? In the same way, for the Poles to stand violently against the German hordes, vastly superior in number and military equipment and strength, was almost nonviolence. I should not mind repeating that statement over and over again. You must give its full value to the word "almost."

—Statement given in 1940

"I Am Against Fanatics"

A DIALOG BETWEEN ELIE WIESEL AND MERLE HOFFMAN

The first time I heard it was in Detroit in 1982. The words shot out at me like bullets, creating an immediate mental image that could not be shared. I had just finished responding to Jerry Falwell on national television. He had asked me how I would feel "meeting my maker with the blood of thousands of babies on my hands" when the TV host turned to the audience for comments. The woman who rose was obviously distraught, her voice shaking. She relayed her own experience with abortion. The guilt still with her, the doctor's coldness, how "they" would not let her see her child—and then, extending her hand and pointing an accusing finger at me, she said "You—you are nothing but a Hitler to me."

Throughout the years, as the frustration, intensity and rhetoric of the antichoice movement has grown, there has been an ever-increasing tendency to liken abortion to the Holocaust. Individual women making private moral decisions are compared to the wholesale slaughter of the Jews during the Second World War. Recently, an abortion clinic in Westchester was labelled "Auschwitz on the Hudson," while anti-abortion protestors use Nazi insignias to make their points in front of clinics across the country. Pseudoscientific books have been written detailing Nazi experiments in concentration camps and their supposed similarities to procedures in abortion clinics, while the specter of Hitler's death camps abounds in terminology like "Abortoriums" and "Child Killing Centers."

These analogies are reinforced by radical, right-wing Christian ideology which preaches that "money-hungry Jews" are behind the abortion industry. Many times patients have been accosted outside Choices by the faithful screaming—"They're after blood money." If the patient happens to be African-American she is told, "You are desecrating the legacy of Dr. Martin Luther King."

The power of this rhetoric, backed by the hierarchy of the Catholic Church which gives financial and spiritual succor to participants in Operation Rescue and other radical antiabortion groups, results in clinic bombers stating that they plant bombs in clinics on Christmas to "Give a present to Jesus on His birthday."

This past June, the newly-seated Archbishop of Brooklyn and Queens presented his antiabortion strategy in front of CHOICES at 7:30 a.m. on a Saturday morning. Telling the press that his intention was not violence but the desire to pray for all the souls of the "murdered unborn," he and 1000 parishioners rhythmically recited the Hail Mary for two hours as surprised and distressed patients were escorted into the clinic through a gauntlet of religious supplicants!

Responding to my request for a meeting, Bishop Daily stated there was nothing to meet about—"children were being killed." When a reporter asked about my charges that his "Vigil" was harassment and psychological abuse of women, Bishop Daily replied "I feel badly about that—but think about what happened—someone got killed there." (*Long Island Catholic*, 6/13/90).

"Someone got killed there?" Lives in struggle, economic deprivation, abuse, anxiety, despair, power, autonomy, love, survival—women's lives—these were the words that meant abortion to me—not "Someone got killed." But when you live in difficult places, you don't close your mind; you listen and you try to understand. Try to understand all the different questions and all the conflicting answers.

It was with these and other questions that I went to meet Elie Wiesel. The day was unusually warm for November. I felt that the strangeness of the weather was somehow symbolic—as if for this special encounter things should not be in their usual places.

I first met Elie Wiesel, as most of the world does, through his writing. As part of my studies in graduate school, I explored the nature of "endings." As I was sifting through hundreds of graduation speeches, one stopped me, moved me so profoundly that I was amazed. I don't remember a word of it now. I only remember that, from that moment in time, Elie Wiesel was important to me.

I learned that at the age of 14 he was wrenched from his studious Hasidic life in Sighet in the Carpathian Mountains and deported to Auschwitz for extermination simply because he was a Jew. That his first night in the camps, his mother and sister were gassed; later he watched his father bludgeoned to death, studied the Talmud from memory with another inmate and, after liberation, almost died from food poisoning, yet still managed to survive. For 10 years he lived in Paris, worked, studied, starved and kept silent. But his need for expression—to tell the tale of the Camps, the horrors, the brutality, the unbelievable evil, and his burning desire to help prevent its re-occurrence while insuring that the world would not forget the victims—drove him to write.

And it was to his writings that I turned while following his public and political activities. His appearance at the White House asking President Reagan to cancel his trip to Bittburg, because "his place was with the victims;" his testimony at the Klaus Barbie trial; and his lecture upon receiving the Nobel Prize for Peace in 1986 when he stated "The lesson, the only lesson I have learned from my experiences is twofold; first that there are no plausible answers to what we have endured. There are no theological answers, there are no psychological answers, there are no literary answers, there are no religious answers. The only conceivable answer is a moral answer. Second, that just as despair can be given to me only by another human being, hope too can be given to me only by another human being."

So I immersed myself in his writing, reading almost all of his 30 books in the past year. I was continually moved, enthralled and transported by his novels and analytic work which all spoke of his inner journey, his continual search for meaning and God in a world filled with evil and despair. His constant commitment to the *moral* dimension in life; to the "moral answer."

In a recent book, *Journey of Faith,* Wiesel and John Cardinal O'Connor engage in dialogue. O'Connor said that he agreed with Mother Theresa when she stated during her Nobel Prize ceremony that the "Greatest enemy to world peace is abortion," and that "We have created a mentality of violence—massive, manipulated, propagandized movements that have brought about more than a million-and-a-half unborn deaths every year."

Reproductive freedom, women's lives, legal abortion are now not "merely killing," but a threat to world peace? Eve is not only to be blamed for the first fall, but for the likely nuclear one as well. Elie Wiesel didn't agree. The violence he was concerned about was the violence of the abortion debate itself. After reading that he had to think more about it and was "Not saying whether he was for or against," I decided that I had to meet with him and discuss it.

It seemed to me that he is a person unlike any other, and yet he shares the fate of millions—and he also is a person of many more questions than answers.

So it was with many conflicting, excited emotions that I got off the elevator on the 26th floor of his New York apartment building. When I turned left, the first thing I saw was an open door revealing a room with shelves and shelves of books. In front of that open door was a small, smiling, intense man. I took his hand, met his eyes and asked my first question.

You have said that you are uncomfortable with the violence of the abortion debate, but when John Cardinal O'Connor first came to New York he held a press conference in which he stated that legal abortion was the "Second Holocaust." How do you feel about abortion being likened to the genocidal slaughter of the Jews?

I am uncomfortable with the language of this debate. I resent the violence of the language—the words that they use like Holocaust—no it is not a Holocaust. It is blasphemy to reduce a tragedy of such monumental proportions to this human tragedy, and abortion is a human tragedy. What should be done is to give back the human proportion to the abortion issue, and when we see it as such we may be able to have much more understanding for the woman who chooses it.

Women who choose abortion are consistently labelled killers, and I personally have been compared to Hitler and called a great murderer.

A woman who feels she cannot go on, and with pain and despair she decides that she has to give up her child, is this woman a killer? Really—really. But look, you cannot let these words hurt you. You have to be strong not to pay any attention because those who do that —call you a Hitler and relate it to the Holocaust—prove that they do not know what the Holocaust was.

You speak and write a great deal about silence. The silence of God during The Event. The silence of the Pope, of the church as they were slaughtering children. When I read what you wrote about them taking live children and throwing them in the fire—that an act of "mercy" by an SS guard was to bash their heads against a rock so that they lost consciousness before—this image will haunt me forever. So I wonder if it is at all possible that the church is so vehemently against abortion at this historical moment as a response to the indictment of their silence during the Holocaust.

I don't like to speak for the church. There are people who will speak for them. But that the church, the hierarchy of the church was silent—yes. There were exceptions of course, there were some good courageous priests. John XXIII spoke out. Of course there were others who saved Jews and/or resisted Nazism.

But not enough.

The church in Rome at that time, the leaders, the Princes of the Church did not speak out. I am convinced if the Pope and the hierarchy had said "save the Jews," many priests in many villages would have done so.

In your conversation with Philippe de-Saint-Cheron [a French journalist] in the recent book Evil & Exile *you stated that in the Talmud it is written that it is better not to be born than to be born. It is more comfortable not to live. Can we relate this to abortion?*

Actually, I was quoting a type of humor in the Talmud. There were two schools of thought among those who had nothing better to do for two-and-one-half years than to argue about whether or not it is better to be born or not to be born. The question is not whether to live or not to live, but whether or not to be born.

Because once you are born, you must live, and according to the Talmud, if you live you must study.

But this is not a question at all of whether or not to have children. The first law, the first commandment in the Bible is to have children.

When abortion was debated in 1977 in the Knesset in Israel, the antiabortionists articulated the feeling that abortion was annihilating the Jewish people, that there were no "unwanted" Jewish children and that how can we after the Holocaust, slaughter Jewish children in the womb?

Fanatics are all the same. These are fanatics. I am against fanatics everywhere. I don't understand these words: Abortionist, antiabortionist. Those who give women the right of choice—he or she [sic] is an abortionist? What kind of articulation is that?

There is a feeling that women who choose abortions are not active moral agents. That women's reproductive capacities and women's lives are secondary to political ideology or religious morality.

I don't like generalizations. Some people feel that they need abortion. For them this is their morality. Other people say that for moral reasons they are against abortion. I don't like simplistic definitions.

But you have said that you feel abortion is a tragedy. Why?

For me the tragedy is for the mother, and there is a father involved also. I don't think that much about the child. I haven't thought about the child. I have to think it through. I cannot believe that there is a mother who does it lightheartedly. I simply cannot believe it. For the mother, it's difficult, very difficult, it must be. Therefore, once you accept that it is difficult, then it requires more thinking, more soul-searching. As for the child and the question of when is a child a child, this is a different subject which has to be dealt with but for the moment we are dealing with the mother; if she comes to the conclusion that she cannot have this child for whatever reason, then it is a tragedy.

Perhaps one of the greatest tragedies is that the majority of women make the decision of abortion for economic reasons, out of a struggle for survival, and a desire not to bring another child into the world without adequate means of support.

Exactly. We must improve the economic situation of the world, but at the same time, I tell you I understand—I must understand—it is my duty to understand those who are against abortion. I don't like the shouting, I don't like the cursing, I don't like the idea of saying anyone who is for abortion is a Hitler or that abortion is a Holocaust. I am very troubled by this. But their pain, too, must be taken into account.

In a sense I would be uncomfortable if people had no ethical dilemmas about abortion. It is a very profound issue.

Of course they should have. And I understand why there is a debate, but I don't want this debate to become so hostile. It is "war." I tell you I am getting letters all the time asking me to speak up against the "Holocaust of abortion." A debate doesn't bother me if it is civilized and humanizing, but just mention the word abortion and flames start to fly.

But there are possible areas of common ground. It would seem that the prevention of unwanted pregnancies would be an issue for both sides to join on, yet many antichoice people, particularly the Catholic Church, are violently against any type of "artificial" birth control.

Perhaps there should be a high level conference, but a quiet one, without publicity, without shouting.

Why don't you convene it? The leaders of the antichoice movement have refused to meet with us. Neither Cardinal O'Connor nor Bishop Daily will even respond to requests. You held an international conference on hatred recently—was anything learned?

I think so because of the people I invited [Elena Bonner, Nelson Mandela]. My conferences are civilized. There is never a heated or violent word.

Unfortunately, this issue is very heated and has become very violent quite beyond words. Clinics have been firebombed and attacked and women patients are constantly accosted and harassed.

Exactly. I would really like to plead for more comprehension on both sides and stop using certain words.

Recently, to cap the "Year of the Child," there was a children's summit held at the UN where an International Bill of Rights of the Child was drafted and presented for all the countries of the world to sign. President Bush refused to sign it because it did not have an antiabortion platform and called for the abolition of the death penalty for anyone under 18 years of age. Your reaction?

I am crazy about children—any children, especially Jewish children. When I see a child who is hungry I do whatever I can to help because I have seen too many Jewish children perish. As a result I feel outrage and pain when a child suffers. One of my main motivations for my work is to work for children. All children. And therefore, when I read about this children's summit, on the one hand I said to myself— my God, the world has changed. When I was a child, Jewish children were handed over to the killers. There were no summits, no Presidents, no Prime Ministers to save them. There were times when we could have saved Jewish children for money. There was no money. For a few visas—there were no visas. Nobody cared. Today people do care. There has been a change and I think that's good, but reading about the plight of children today I wish I could do more.

You have written that the very concept of love—that the word itself may fade and disappear. What is your definition of love and what do you think is its highest form of expression?

There is no real definition of love, for once you define it it disappears. The act of trying to define it diminishes it. It is a mystery, but it is a kind of identification with another person where that other person is as important as yourself and that person's life as important as yours. It means that I would exchange my life for hers. Does it mean sacrifice? Not at all. It means offering. Love is that. Every gesture becomes an offering.

You have also written that "The thing I learned about man in the camps is that evil, like good, is infinite and that the two are combined in man," and also that "one man with a machine gun can kill a thousand sages." So if each one of us holds good and evil within us, aren't we all as individuals responsible for saving or destroying the world?

Absolutely. The purpose inherent in literature and education are human relations and the possibility of imparting the responsibility for one another. Evil is in all of us. No one is perfect—no one is a saint. It is for each of us to fight that evil within. The choice presents itself to us every day. If I sit here with you it is my choice, whether it is the evil part within me (which I hope is small) that faces you, or the good part that faces you. It is also your responsibility to bring out the good part. It is a kind of symphony where all these relationships play their parts, the violins . . . the cellos . . .

But who is conducting?
Ah, that is the question, that is the question.

If God's divinity is expressed through humanity and ultimately through love, and, as you have said many times, "Everything died in Auschwitz," how can we expect love to save us?
My favorite words are "and yet." Everything died in Auschwitz and yet—yes there are reasons for me to despair, and yet—yes there are reasons for me not to believe in God and yet, and yet . . .

Che Guevera has written that "The true revolutionary is motivated by great feelings of love." Do you believe it is possible for political systems to address social inequities? Can politics answer questions of equality and justice?
I am not a politician. I have never been involved in politics. I don't know much about it.

But you are an activist.
I try to act *on* politicians. I believe in the moral dimension of everything, literature, education, philosophy, whatever it is. Without it we are lost. Politics without moral dimensions are cheap, corrupt procedures. We need the moral dimension to prevent that.

There is a continual debate in this country, particularly acute in the abortion issue, about the separation of church and state. There are people who believe that you cannot bring your religion (which many people view as morality) into the political arena.
I am not speaking about religion. I am speaking about morality. I believe when religion becomes politics that is a disaster, and when

politics becomes a religion it is also a disaster. We should separate both.

You have never called for hate, love or vengeance as a response to the Holocaust but faith—and then you have written that the only punishment commensurate with the Holocaust is the destruction of the world. Aren't we coming close to that now with the events in the Middle East?

I am afraid of that but I believe once we realize how dangerous this is we could prevent it. But yes, there is no punishment for such a crime. The only punishment is that the whole world should be destroyed. I don't want it to be destroyed. I don't want any human being to be destroyed; that is why we must always remember the crime.

You have always said that we can never truly understand the Holocaust and then there are those who say that if we can truly understand it we must forgive it. But if we can never understand it how can we ever hope to prevent it from happening again?

We must always tell the story.

In your novel Twilight, *Adam asks God to reconsider His creation. To take it back. He says that if the world were not created, "countless souls would escape the curse of being born only to die . . . trees will not be felled by men . . . animals will not be slaughtered" . . . etc., etc. What do you think is the real purpose for us being on this planet?*

I wish I knew. There are all kinds of answers. But I have been thinking about this question seriously. In the beginning, why did God create the world? What did He need it for? Philosophy, theology offer their own reasons, but there are no answers and once you don't have an answer you must ask the question—what is the meaning of *my* life —why am *I* here. You had better have an answer for that. You are here because you have to fight certain battles and I have mine. I want to enlarge the understanding of humanity. But we better know why we are here—we have no right to say we don't know.

You have often said that "He or she who did not live through The Event will never know it and that he or she who did live through The Event can never reveal it." Do you think this paradox was in any way operative in the suicides of Primo Levi and Bruno Bettelheim?

I like paradoxes.

I know. You are a person who likes questions more than answers.

Bruno Bettelheim, I don't know. I never met him. Primo Levi—yes, perhaps. Many writers who have written about the Holocaust have committed suicide. More than musicians and painters.

Why do you think this is?

Perhaps it is this paradox. A writer must reveal—that is what he [sic] does—communicate, and he or she can't communicate their experience. It is beyond their ability. I knew Primo Levi. We were together in the camps and later I felt that indeed he might commit suicide one day.

What is your attitude about the current struggle to feminize Judaism—the recent actions at the Kotel—the attempt to bring women into positions of spiritual authority?

I don't want to give apologia. I dislike easy answers. I would like to see a conclave of great Halachic and Rabbinic scholars and authorities to think about it. It may take two years—so what? We are dealing with centuries. I would like to see that because it could be a way to show what is wrong and there are things that *are* wrong. According to Rabbinic law in Talmudic times (centuries ago) women could not serve as witnesses. What kind of injustice is this? A woman is a human being, isn't she?

And they also are not allowed to be heard singing.

Ah, but this is something else. We give them too much power. That means that if I hear a woman's voice I am supposed to be sexually aroused. So what—so what?

You give us power on the one hand and then try to take it away on the other.

(laughing) We don't take it away, we try to convince you not to use it. But so what, if a woman is beautiful. I like women to be beautiful. Still, I think something has to be done about the role of women, but I would like it to come from the Orthodox community. Let them take up the subject and decide how much we should do. How far we should go.

What is your position on the reunification of Germany?

I am against it and was one of the few to say so publicly. It was done in haste and with a total insensitivity to those who survived the war. And the money involved. They bought Russia, they bought Eastern Germany. I don't trust Kohl. After all, he is the man of Bittburg, and what was Bittburg? Bittburg had only one purpose—to whitewash the SS. But he wanted to rationalize it and show that many of these SS were just good soldiers—good soldiers? They were termed a criminal group in the Nuremberg Trials; Kohl wanted to whitewash them and "normalize," sanitize their actions. A unified Germany in the hands of Kohl bothers me.

You have been severely criticized for not condemning Israel about the intifada. What is your current position on the Palestinian situation?

I have been criticized for many things . . . Yes, I refuse to systematically condemn Israel.

For anything?

There are certain red lines that I will not cross. If I had known at the time that Israel was involved in torturing I would have spoken out, but it was too late. When I found out, a commission had already been formed and justice prevailed, but I don't feel I have the right to apply public pressure on Israel.

But you have the moral authority.

But what if I am wrong?

Can't you afford to be wrong?

Yes, but only if I pay the price. What if I am wrong and *they* pay the price? What if I apply such pressure on a decision and that decision may bring disaster or at least tragedy to Israel? Do I have the right to do this? It is their children who will pay the price, not mine. I do go to Israel and speak to the leaders—there I can say what I feel. But here, especially here, I have no right to speak out publicly. As for the intifada, I have said on television and in an op-ed piece in the *New York Times* that I understand the young Palestinians. How did it start? It started in December 1987 when there was a high level meeting, a kind of summit meeting in Amman. The last item on the agenda was the Palestinian issue. The Palestinians were non-persons. There is nothing worse than that and that is why I said I understood the young Palestinians. They refused to be non-persons; then the violence started and they began throwing stones. Violence is a language. When there is no other language you use violence. But then I turned to them and pleaded, why don't you use words. Before, no one was listening—now the whole world will listen to you. I did speak to Palestinians but I am offended when I see Jewish intellectuals who all of a sudden remember their Jewishness only to use that Jewishness to attack Israel. These are men and women who have never done anything for Israel—all of a sudden they remember they are Jews.

What is your reaction to the assassination of Meir Kahane?

I didn't like Kahane. He was a man of hate and a racist. I was embarrassed by a man of such a reputation and I refused to engage him in debate. He is a Jew. I am a Jew. Something is wrong.

Do you mean to say a Jew cannot hate? Who should a Jew be in the world today?

A Jew should not hate. A Jew should be a human being. No Jew should be a racist. At the same time I am outraged by the violence that killed him. Those who assassinated him and those who hired the assassin. I am harsher on them than on Kahane, because they were the criminals, the murderers.

To what do you attribute the increasing rise of anti-Semitism in both Europe and the U.S.?

There will always be anti-Semitism—always.

Why?

There are all kinds of answers. We are the world's conscience—envy, jealousy—all of them are true but still . . . there is something else. It is a complicated issue. It would take hours, days to analyze it here.

You said your teacher of mysticism taught you to love madmen. Explain.

I love madmen—mystical madmen—not those who destroy but those who create.

You say that "In the beginning I thought I could change man. Now I know that I cannot. If I still shout and scream it is to prevent man from changing me." Has man changed you?

People ask me so often if receiving the Noble Prize has changed me. Ten Noble Prizes would not change me—but it *has* changed my schedule.

Nationalism Is Always Oppressive

AMIRI BARAKA, interviewed by D. H. Melhem

DH: . . . In terms of your current position, your article in the *Village Voice*, "Confessions of a Former Anti-Semite"—

AB: —which is not my title.

DH: Oh, it wasn't? What was your title?

AB: My title was "A Personal View of Anti-Semitism." That's our friend [David] Schneiderman, who was the editor. That's his idea of something that would sell papers. Which apparently it did.

DH: Okay. Well, in that article, you equate Zionism with white racism as "reactionary." Would you now add Black Nationalism to that list?

AB: Well, I say this. To me, all nationalism, finally, taken to any extreme, has got to be oppressive to the people who are not in that nationality. You understand what I mean? If it's taken to the extreme, any nationalism has got to be exclusive and has got to say, "Us, yes; you, no." I mean, that's the nature of nationalism. But you have to make a distinction between, say, people who are oppressed as a nationality, who are fighting national liberation struggles. I think in terms of Zionism, the difference is this: that previous to the Second World War, Jews generally were not interested in Zionism, what Chaim Weizmann and, you know, the other dude put forward. Generally it was like some right-wing intellectuals, some right-wing nationalist intellectuals. Once the British got hold of that, the Balfour Declaration, in which then it's made a part of British foreign policy to settle Jews in a Palestinian homeland, you know, obviously to look over the oil interests—that changes into an instrument of imperialist policy. Now, a certain sector of the Jewish population becomes interested in Zionism as a result of the Holocaust, for obvious reasons, for obvious reasons. Once you knock off seven million people, then, if there's somebody saying, "Look, you got to get out of here, that's the reason, you got to get out of here," then that's going to become attractive.

But I do not believe that Zionism is the general ideology of Jews in the world. I think the great contributions that Jews have made in the world have been much more advanced than a narrow nationalism, and I think obviously what [Menachem] Begin and Company are doing now, it just isolates the State of Israel from the world. I think more and more people will come to see, and especially Jews, that the State of Israel and Jews are two separate entities. And I think that it's a great cover story for somebody who may jump on Israel, for you to say you're attacking Jews generally, and you have to shut up. But I don't think that's going to work. It's very interesting, for instance, to see a lot of Palestinian Jews, now, the kind of lines that have come out recently in some of these organizations. It's an incredible thing, but I think of course in New York, when you've got a stronghold of world Zionist organization, it's very hard for you to say things like that without people beating you to death as being anti-Jewish, which has been my fate. Even that article I wrote, which was an attempt to set the record straight, you know, was hacked up so unmercifully. It made you wonder just what they wanted to present. I mean, at the end it seemed like they wanted to present you as an anti-Semite, even though I volunteered to write the article.

DH: You're talking about the editing of that article?

AB: Oh, yes, yes, oh yes. You see, what I did—

DH: The "Confession," with Jewish people I've spoken to, was not received as any kind of apology.

AB: Oh, no. Well, the thing on Zionism, the minute you jump on Zionism, you're going to get it back, no matter what you say. You see, what was removed, to me, was critical, because I did a whole history of anti-Semitism. Essentially, it's an ideological justification for fundamentally economic and political oppression. Anti-Semitism rises, you know, in the struggle between the Greeks and Jews in the Middle East, and the Romans and the Jews, and basically then in the Middle Ages as an attempt to keep economic superiority. Economic attack is what it justifies: "These people are Christ-killers. Let's take their money." You know, it's like the Japanese you've put in a concentration camp: "These people are our enemies; let's get their truck farms.

Let's get their truck farms; these people are our enemies." You know what I mean. There's always an ideological justification for some economic and political shenanigans. That's what it essentially is. No matter that you might have some people down the road who really believe it, like you might have some Klansmen walking around who really believe such and such a thing is true, when actually, what's happening is you've got some landowners who are not going to let Black people, for instance, have democracy down there because it means they're not going to control that land. They're not going to control the U.S. Senate or the colonies anymore. You always have people who walk around, who believe stuff on one level; but you also have the people who are putting that out, who are gaining from that. That's the real significance of that. . . .

Meeting in Jerusalem

MONA ELAINE ADILMAN

On the mountainside an Arab waits.
He is old. He cannot breathe,
lungs weakened from DDT dust.
His lips are atrophied like purple grapes
in a drought. Only the eyes are luminous,
piercing the mist, searching . . . searching.

On the rugged trail a tousled donkey
climbs, stumbles, falls back, fragile
hoofs clinging with goat-like precision
to the precipice. The animal carries
cylinders of oxygen strapped to her flanks.
A young Israeli Jew holds the reins.

Higher, higher, the agile donkey climbs
until she stands beside a hut of clay.
The young Jew hands the oxygen tanks
to the Arab. They embrace. History rides
on the stooped shoulders of a donkey,
and the world breathes free again.

A Forgiving Land; Postwar Vietnam

LADY BORTON

Hands up, American!" Second Treasure said in Vietnamese. She poked my ribs. "You're under arrest!"

I lifted my sandals over my head. In the moonlight, the tiger cactuses along the rice paddy loomed like phantoms with prickly limbs.

"Forward!" Second Treasure said, in a teasing voice.

She was leading me into Ban Long, a village of 4,000 people in the Mekong delta southwest of Ho Chi Minh City. Throughout the war, Ban Long had been a Vietcong base. American B-52's had bombed the village, turning houses into craters, families into corpses. Agent Orange had stripped the earth of green.

Now, 15 years after the war, foliage obscured the moon. Milk trees hung heavy with fruit. Frogs chortled. Frangipani flowers like tiny trumpets broadcast their insistent perfume.

Amazing, I thought: The earth has forgiven us.

During the war, I'd worked in Vietnam with the Quakers as a health administrator. Ten years later, in 1980, I lived in Malaysia's largest refugee camp for Boat People who'd fled Vietnam. Now, I wanted to know Vietnamese who had chosen to stay.

"We'll stop at my father's," Second Treasure said. She pointed to a wooden house in a grove of breadfruit trees. I balked. Between me and the house stood a creek with a "monkey bridge"—a single palm trunk. Muddy footprints greased the palm's bark.

"Dead already," I muttered in Vietnamese.

Second Treasure stepped onto the bridge. Her face was open, like a lotus at midday. She reached for my hand. In the darkness, braced by this former Vietcong woman, I edged across.

This trip, earlier this year, was my fourth visit to Ban Long since the war. I remained the only foreign writer whom the Vietnamese allowed to live with peasants in the countryside. I was watched by the curious villagers. Unbearably so. I was the circus come to town.

"A giant!" the kids announced. Wherever I went, they stepped on my heels, petted my arms. "She's furry like a monkey!" "Look," they whispered, surprised that hair could be curly, "it's like dead vines."

"The giant is timid, like a toddler," they said whenever I teetered across a bridge.

These children had never seen an American. Even teen-agers couldn't remember the war. In contrast, during his 80 years, Second Treasure's father had known only 15 years of peace.

I called Second Treasure's father Senior Uncle, the same title the Vietnamese had given Ho Chi Minh. Uncle was a tiny man with huge hands. He could swing among the waterapple trees, gathering the dimpled fruit as nimbly as his grandsons. His mind was equally keen. Yet with me Uncle repeated himself, as if to make up for the years he had missed knowing me.

"Child," Uncle said each evening as we rinsed our bowls in the creek, "always save rice for tomorrow. Who knows? Tomorrow you may have nothing to eat. Never drink from the creek. Drink from the rain-water crock under the eaves. . . ."

"Father. . . ."

Second Treasure worried I might find Uncle boring. She hovered, tending me as if I belonged to an endangered species.

During the war, Second Treasure had commanded 100 Vietcong guerrillas. She would load her canoe with weapons, concealing the contraband with leaves. Then she'd slip along sluices and creeks. When helicopters appeared, she'd jump overboard.

"Always keep two holes above water," she said, touching her nostrils.

"We were rats," her father said. "We lived underground, in tunnels. Slept by day, prowled at night. Our feet knew the way. But we were different from rats." He chuckled. "We were smarter."

During the war, Uncle had organized Ban Long's literacy campaign. To his lifetime treasures—a Confucian primer, a book on Lenin, a volume of Ho Chi Minh's poetry—he now added the photo book of America my father had sent with me. Uncle showed the photographs to every neighbor who visited.

"Do you have a water buffalo?" one woman asked me.

"Do you eat watermelon?" a second said.

"Do you fish in a bomb crater?" Fifth Brother asked.

"You don't grow rice?" his mother, Third Sister, exclaimed.

She'd lost three sons during the war. Toothless, she mashed her betel nut in an American shell casing. "Then how do you eat?"

One day, Third Sister laughed so hard she couldn't finish her betel nut. Eight women had come to visit. Middle-aged, they looked like a bridal party posing for a silver anniversary photo. All wore overblouses in varying hues and the traditional loose, black trousers. They asked about American bridal dress.

"What?" Third Sister said at my description. "No trousers?" The women rollicked at this immodest thought.

As with everything else, the villagers watched me harvest. Second Treasure, standing among them, chuckled as I stepped off the paddy dike.

"Please!" said an old woman bent like a walking cane, "don't take your pretty white legs into the paddy muck."

I sank to midcalf in mud. I slogged toward the row of women harvesting. The mud sucked me off balance.

"Did she drink rice wine?" the old woman asked.

The harvesters cut the tall rice with sickles. They set the grasses aside on the stubble. They cut and set, cut and set, moving together in a long line, as if choreographed. Sickle in hand, I joined them.

"Hold the grass farther down," Second Treasure yelled.

I slid my left hand down.

"No! Five plants at once."

I sliced the grass.

"No, no, farther up."

I set the grasses aside.

"Lay the stems even!"

I felt like a dancing bear. I'd had days of this. I was tired of Second Treasure telling me when to wash my feet, how many bowls of rice to eat, when to shake out my grass mat. I stood up, sickle in hand, fuming.

"Didn't Uncle Ho say, 'Eat with the people, live with them, work with them?' "

"Yes."

"When did Uncle say, 'Stand on the dike, give orders'?"

Second Treasure looked dismayed. Her face wilted.

I was horrified. I'd been insensitive. Rude. "Forgive me," I said in Vietnamese.

"Hello?" Second Treasure said in English. To get me to smile, she tried all the phrases I'd taught her. "O.K.? Thank you?" Then she herded the watchers down the paddy dike, her laughter reaching back across the mud and stubble.

My last evening, the harvesters came to visit. They brought milk fruit, waterapples, breadfruit and dried tamarind. "Please," they said, "take these gifts to the women in America."

After they left, Uncle approached me. In his palms he cradled a tiny photograph. He pressed it into my hands. "This is the only picture of me young. Give it to your father. Tell him to come live with me in Ban Long. I'll take care of him in his old age."

It's even more amazing, I thought: the people have forgiven us.

Later that evening, Second Treasure and I swung together in the hammock. She worried about her teen-age son, who ran with a fast crowd in town. She couldn't keep him in bicycle brakes. She worried about her father alone in the countryside. Recently he'd fallen from a tree.

"Older Sister," I asked when the conversation lulled, "are you a Communist?"

Her fingers fluttered, No

"Uncle?"

"No, no! Father fought the French rulers 30 years before he heard of Communists."

Second Treasure nodded toward her father's house under the breadfruit trees. The fragrance of ripe fruit tinged the air. In the distance, an owl called out, *"cu cu,"* sounding its Vietnamese name.

"Don't you understand, Little Sister?" Second Treasure said. "This is all we wanted."

To Hannah Vo-Dinh, a Young Poet of Vietnam

FRAN CASTAN

Almost-round face, yellow-brown eyes,
Close-cropped hair so very like his crew-cut,
Intelligent, mysterious images, words

Of just the right weight, Hannah,
Hannah Vo-Dinh, you could be his daughter.

Now that I am older, not the young
Widow of 27 he left behind,
I am less jealous; I do wish he had made love
To a lovely woman, someone perhaps
Like your own mother. Hannah, Hannah Vo-Dinh,
How I wish you were his daughter.

I am always half in one world,
Half in another, ever since
My return from the Far East in 1966,
Carrying our year-old child on my left hip
And a baggage ticket like a hot coal,
A hot coal in my right hand,
Ever since I dropped that burning coal
At the baggage claim in New York,
And got his coffin. His coffin.
His coffin in the baggage
Compartment of the plane.
He, himself, no longer human,
Baggage, Hannah, baggage!

A neighbor tried to comfort me,
"If I could get my hands on the Gook
Who killed your husband, I'd break his neck,
I would, with my own two hands."

I felt so unprotected when he said that,
So alone with his hate, his failure
To recognize us as a single species.
O, Hannah, Hannah Vo-Dinh,
How I wish, how I wish, you were
Just a few years older, then you would be
A tangible presence, a living possibility
Of my best fantasy: As *you,* Daughter,
In *your* shoes, he still walks.
O, Hannah, Hannah Vo-Dinh, I will not rest
In this or any other life
Until the Vietnamese names

Rise on the giant V in Washington,
Until they are formed
In the same stone of honor as the American names,
As you are formed, dear
Lotus, of a single, human moment of transcendence.

From The Gaia Atlas of First Peoples: *"A Global Voice"*

JULIAN BURGER

> *"We are on the one hand the most oppressed people on the globe. On the other hand, we are the hope for the future of people on the planet. The peoples that surround us now are beginning to experience in the 20th century that there are limitations to the kinds of economic organization that define their societies."*
> —John Mohawk, Haudenosaunee writer

> *"We must go beyond the arrogance of human rights. We must go beyond the ignorance of civil rights. We must step into the reality of natural rights because all the natural world has a right to existence. We are only a small part of it. There can be no trade off."*
> —John Trudell at the Survival Gathering, 1980

Indigenous peoples are one of the world's most persistent voices of conscience, alerting humankind to the dangers of environmental destruction. And as the world searches for alternative strategies to deal with global problems, it is turning more and more to indigenous peoples. Much of their respect for nature, their methods of resource management, social organization, values, and culture are finding echoes in the writing of scientists, philosophers, politicians, and thinkers.

In the face of an increasingly unsustainable world economy, ever-faster rates of productivity, consumption, and change, respect is growing for ways of life attuned to the constraints of natural environments. Ranged on the frontline of the ecological crisis, indigenous peoples have been forced to defend their culture, lands, and way of life. They have developed new strategies to protect the environment, to manage declining resources, and to advance the cause of peace. With financial support the Kuna Indians of Panama have established and fully manage a forest park and botanical reserve on their territory. The Inuit have initiated an Arctic Conservation Programme. Indigenous women in the USA have formed a network that campaigns creatively for social change. Pacific islanders—and particularly women—are working for a nuclear-free Pacific. All are fighting to ensure a future for their own children and in so doing are working for all humankind.

Diplomacy and Directness: Kayapo Halt the Altamira Dam

"We don't need your electricity. Electricity won't give us food. . . . We need our forests to hunt and gather in. We don't want your dam. Everything you tell us is a lie."
—Kayapo woman to Brazilian official at Altamira meeting

Brazil aims to quadruple its electricity supply in the next 25 years to meet the needs of mining companies and cities. Plans to build 136 dams, 68 of them on indigenous land, were opposed by the indigenous population. But the Kayapo Indians began a well-planned publicity programme to rally opinion and halt the building of five local dams.

The dam-building programme could inundate up to 250,000 sq km (97,000 sq miles) and displace 500,000 people. It is not only a potential human disaster but could also be working against the long-term economic and environmental interests of Brazil.

In 1988 a group of Kayapo Indians launched an extraordinary campaign to halt the construction of the Barbaquara and Kararao dams, which threatened their territory at Altamira on the Xingu River. Their leaders visited the headquarters of the World Bank to request the withdrawal of a US$500 million loan. They met US senators, toured European capitals, talked to members of parliament, and explained their concerns to environmentalists and human rights groups. Then, in February 1989, at the site of the proposed dam, the

Indians convened an international meeting. The fate of the Altamira dam had become international news.

In March, following the pressure, the World Bank announced that it would no longer fund the dam. Instead it is ready to support improvements in electricity transmission and distribution. The result is more than just a victory for the Kayapo. It has challenged the economic strategy of the Brazilian government.

From "Speech to the U.S. Congress"

NELSON MANDELA

It is a fact of the human condition that each shall, like a me-
. . . teor, a mere brief passing moment in time and space, flit across the human stage and pass out of existence. Even the golden lads and lasses, as much as the chimney sweepers, come, and tomorrow are no more. After them all, they leave the people, enduring, multiplying, permanent, except to the extent that the same humanity might abuse its own genius to immolate life itself.

And we have come to Washington in the District of Columbia, and into these hallowed Chambers of the U.S. Congress, not as pretenders to greatness, but as a particle of a people whom we know to be noble and heroic—enduring, multiplying, permanent, rejoicing in the expectation and knowledge that their humanity will be reaffirmed and enlarged by open and unfettered communion with the nations of the world.

We have come here to tell you, and through you, your own people, who are equally noble and heroic, of the troubles and trials, the fond hopes and aspirations, of the people from whom we originate. . . .

. . . Our people demand democracy. Our country, which continues to bleed and suffer pain, needs democracy. It cries out for the situation where the law will decree that the freedom to speak of freedom constitutes the very essence of legality and the very thing that makes for the legitimacy of the constitutional order.

It thirsts for the situation where those who are entitled by law to carry arms, as the forces of national security and law and order, will not turn their weapons against the citizens simply because the citizens assert that equality, liberty and the pursuit of happiness are fundamental human rights which are not only inalienable but must, if necessary, be defended with the weapons of war.

We fight for and visualize a future in which all shall, without regard to race, color, creed or sex, have the right to vote and to be voted into all elective organs of state. We are engaged in struggle to ensure that the rights of every individual are guaranteed and protected, through a democratic constitution, the rule of law, an entrenched bill of rights, which should be enforced by an independent judiciary, as well as a multi-party political system. What we have said concerning the political arrangements we seek for our country is seriously meant. It is an outcome for which many of us went to prison, for which many have died in police cells, on the gallows, in our towns and villages and in the countries of southern Africa. Indeed, we have even had our political representatives killed in countries as far away from South Africa as France.

Unhappily, our people continue to die to this day, victims of armed agents of the state who are still determined to turn their guns against the very idea of a nonracial democracy. . . .

To deny any person their human rights is to challenge their very humanity. To impose on them a wretched life of hunger and deprivation is to dehumanize them. But such has been the terrible fate of all black persons in our country under the system of apartheid. The extent of the deprivation of millions of people has to be seen to be believed. The injury is made that more intolerable by the opulence of our white compatriots and the deliberate distortion of the economy to feed that opulence.

We believe that the fact of the Apartheid structure of the South African economy and the enormous and pressing needs of the people, make it inevitable that the democratic government will intervene in this economy, acting through the elected parliament. We have put the matter to the business community of our country that the need for a public sector is one of the elements in a many-sided strategy of economic development and restructuring that has to be considered by us all, including the private sector.

We must also make the point, very firmly, that the political settlement and democracy itself cannot survive unless the material needs of the people—their bread-and-butter issues—are addressed as part of the process of change and as a matter of urgency. It should never be that the anger of the poor should be the finger of accusation pointed at all of us because we failed to respond to the cries of the people for food, for shelter, for the dignity of the individual. . . .

. . . One of the benefits that should accrue to both our peoples and to the rest of the world should surely be that this complex South African society, which has known nothing but racism for three centuries, should be transformed into an oasis of good race relations, where the black shall to the white be sister and brother, a fellow South African, an equal human being, both citizens of the world.

To destroy racism in the world, we, together, must expunge Apartheid racism in South Africa. Justice and liberty must be our tool, prosperity and happiness our weapon.

On the initiative of the ANC, the process toward the conclusion of a peaceful settlement has started. According to a logic dictated by our situation, we are engaged in an effort which includes the removal of obstacles to negotiations. This will be followed by a negotiated determination of the mechanism which will draw up the new constitution.

This should lead to the formation of this constitution-making institution, and therefore the elaboration and adoption of a democratic constitution. Elections would then be held on the basis of this constitution, and, for the first time South Africa would have a body of lawmakers which would, like yourselves, be mandated by the whole people. . . .

We must contend still with the reality that South Africa is a country in the grip of the Apartheid crime against humanity. The consequences of this continue to be felt, not only within our borders, but throughout southern Africa, which continues to harvest the bitter fruits of conflict and war, especially in Mozambique and Angola. Peace will not come to our country and region until the Apartheid system is ended. . . .

We could not have made an acquaintance through literature with human giants such as George Washington, Abraham Lincoln and Thomas Jefferson, and not been moved to act as they were moved to act. We could not have heard of and admired John Brown, Sojourner Truth, Frederick Douglass, W.E.B. DuBois, Marcus Garvey, Martin Luther King, Jr. and others—we could not have heard of these and not be moved to act as they were moved to act. We could not have known of your Declaration of Independence and not elected to join in the struggle to guarantee the people life, liberty and the pursuit of happiness. . . .

. . . You have given us the power to join hands with all people of conscience to fight for the victory of democracy and human rights throughout the world. . . .

. . . The day may not be far when we will borrow the words of Thomas Jefferson and speak of the will of the South African nation. In the exercise of that will, by this united nation of black and white people, it must surely be that there will be born a country on the southern tip of Africa which you will be proud to call a friend and an ally, because of its contribution to the universal striving towards liberty, human rights, prosperity and peace among the peoples.

Let that day come now. Let us keep our arms locked together so that we form a solid phalanx against racism, to ensure that that day comes now. By our common actions, let us ensure that justice triumphs without delay. When that has come to pass, then shall we all be entitled to acknowledge the salute when others say of us, "blessed are the peacemakers."

"Yes, Mandela"

DENNIS BRUTUS

Yes, Mandela, some of us
we admit embarrassedly
wept to see you step free
so erectly, so elegantly
shrug off the prisoned years
a blanket cobwebbed of pain and grime:

behind, the island's sea sand,
harsh, white and treacherous
ahead, jagged rocks and crannies
bladed crevices of racism and deceit

in the salt island air
you swung your hammer grimly stoic

facing the dim path of interminable years,
now, vision blurred with tears
we see you step out to our salutes
bearing our burden of hopes and fears
and impress your radiance
on the gray morning air.

Breaking the Chains

BISHOP DESMOND TUTU

Sometimes you get the notion that people try to inject the notion into your heart that what you do is insignificant; it cannot make a difference. Let me disabuse you of that notion. When people see a colossal problem, they wonder whether they could do anything to make a difference. They need to keep remembering what they are told about how you eat an elephant—one piece at a time. What you do, where you are, counts and makes a difference, if only to those who have their noses rubbed daily in the dust, to know that the world cares.

I stand here appealing to people of conscience. Help us. Please help us. Our country is burning. Our children are dying. An 11-year-old was kept in jail for five months in solitary confinement because he had thrown a stone in protest against being treated as less than what God intended for him. It is a country that some have said is a last bastion of Cain's community.

If people are concerned for the fate of white South Africans, the best way of ensuring that white South Africans survive is to be part of the process of dismantling apartheid.

I speak with a heavy heart. I love that country and its people passionately and I do not like to see it destroyed. I speak on behalf of people among the white community, which has some tremendous people, who by right ought to be saying, "We cannot oppose a system that provides us with such substantial privileges," and yet they are not. However, South African whites are not demons. They are ordinary people, many of them scared people.

The best way of ensuring they survive is to be part of a process that will ensure the destruction of this monster that dehumanizes both the victim and the perpetrator and perhaps, dehumanizes the perpetrator even more.

Still I Rise

MAYA ANGELOU

You may write me down in history
With your bitter, twisted lies,
You may trod me in the very dirt
But still, like dust, I'll rise.

Does my sassiness upset you?
Why are you beset with gloom?
'Cause I walk like I've got oil wells
Pumping in my living room.

Just like moons and like suns,
With the certainty of tides,
Just like hopes springing high,
Still I'll rise.

Did you want to see me broken?
Bowed head and lowered eyes?
Shoulders falling down like teardrops,
Weakened by my soulful cries.

Does my haughtiness offend you?
Don't you take it awful hard
'Cause I laugh like I've got gold mines
Diggin' in my own back yard.

You may shoot me with your words,
You may cut me with your eyes,
You may kill me with your hatefulness,
But still, like air, I'll rise.

Does my sexiness upset you?
Does it come as a surprise
That I dance like I've got diamonds
At the meeting of my thighs?

Out of the huts of history's shame
I rise
Up from a past that's rooted in pain
I rise
I'm a black ocean, leaping and wide,
Welling and swelling I bear in the tide.

Leaving behind nights of terror and fear
I rise
Into a daybreak that's wondrously clear
I rise
Bringing the gifts that my ancestors gave,
I am the dream and the hope of the slave.
I rise
I rise
I rise.

From "On Loving Your Enemies" and "Declarations of Independence"

MARTIN LUTHER KING, JR.

On Loving Your Enemies*

. . . Let us be practical and ask the question, *How do we love our enemies?*

First, we must develop and maintain the capacity to forgive. He who is devoid of the power to forgive is devoid of the power to love. It

---

* This sermon was delivered at the Dexter Avenue Baptist Church in Montgomery, Alabama, at Christmas, 1957. Martin Luther King wrote it while in jail for committing nonviolent civil disobedience during the Montgomery bus boycott.

is impossible even to begin the act of loving one's enemies without the prior acceptance of the necessity, over and over again, of forgiving those who inflict evil and injury upon us. It is also necessary to realize that the forgiving act must always be initiated by the person who has been wronged, the victim of some great hurt, the recipient of some tortuous injustice, the absorber of some terrible act of oppression. The wrongdoer may request forgiveness. He may come to himself, and, like the prodigal son, move up some dusty road, his heart palpitating with the desire for forgiveness. But only the injured neighbor, the loving father back home, can really pour out the warm waters of forgiveness.

Forgiveness does not mean ignoring what has been done or putting a false label on an evil act. It means, rather, that the evil act no longer remains as a barrier to the relationship. Forgiveness is a catalyst creating the atmosphere necessary for a fresh start and a new beginning. It is the lifting of a burden or the canceling of a debt. The words "I will forgive you, but I'll never forget what you've done" never explain the real nature of forgiveness. Certainly one can never forget, if that means erasing it totally from his mind. But when we forgive, we forget in the sense that the evil deed is no longer a mental block impeding a new relationship. Likewise, we can never say, "I will forgive you, but I won't have anything further to do with you." Forgiveness means reconciliation, a coming together again. Without this, no man can love his enemies. The degree to which we are able to forgive determines the degree to which we are able to love our enemies.

Second, we must recognize that the evil deed of the enemy-neighbor, the thing that hurts, never quite expresses all that he is. An element of goodness may be found even in our worst enemy. Each of us is something of a schizophrenic personality, tragically divided against ourselves. A persistent civil war rages within all of our lives. Something within us causes us to lament with Ovid, the Latin poet, "I see and approve the better things, but follow worse," or to agree with Plato that human personality is like a charioteer having two headstrong horses, each wanting to go in a different direction, or to repeat with the Apostle Paul, "The good that I would I do not: but the evil which I would not, that I do."

This simply means that there is some good in the worst of us and some evil in the best of us. When we discover this, we are less prone to hate our enemies. When we look beneath the surface, beneath the impulsive evil deed, we see within our enemy-neighbor a measure of goodness and know that the viciousness and evilness of his acts are not quite representative of all that he is. We see him in a new light. We recognize that his hate grows out of fear, pride, ignorance, prejudice, and misunderstanding, but in spite of this, we know God's image is ineffably etched in his being. Then we love our enemies by realizing that they are not totally bad and that they are not beyond the reach of God's redemptive love.

Third, we must not seek to defeat or humiliate the enemy but to win his friendship and understanding. At times we are able to humiliate our worst enemy. Inevitably, his weak moments come and we are able to thrust in his side the spear of defeat. But this we must not do. Every word and deed must contribute to an understanding with the enemy and release those vast reservoirs of goodwill which have been blocked by impenetrable walls of hate.

The meaning of love is not to be confused with some sentimental outpouring. Love is something much deeper than emotional bosh. Perhaps the Greek language can clear our confusion at this point. In the Greek New Testament are three words for love. The word *eros* is a sort of aesthetic or romantic love. In the Platonic dialogues *eros* is a yearning of the soul for the realm of the divine. The second word is *philia,* a reciprocal love and the intimate affection and friendship between friends. We love those whom we like, and we love because we are loved. The third word is *agape,* understanding and creative, redemptive goodwill for all men. An overflowing love which seeks nothing in return, *agape* is the love of God operating in the human heart. At this level, we love men not because we like them, nor because their ways appeal to us, nor even because they possess some type of divine spark; we love every man because God loves him. At this level, we love the person who does an evil deed, although we hate the deed that he does.

Now we can see what Jesus meant when he said, "Love your enemies." We should be happy that he did not say, "Like your enemies." It is almost impossible to like some people. "Like" is a sentimental and affectionate word. How can we be affectionate toward a person whose avowed aim is to crush our very being and place innumerable stumbling blocks in our path? How can we like a person who is threatening our children and bombing our homes? This is impossible. But Jesus recognized that *love* is greater than *like*. When Jesus bids us to love our enemies, he is speaking neither of *eros* nor *philia;* he is speaking of *agape,* understanding and creative, redemptive goodwill for all men. Only by following this way and responding with this type of love are we able to be children of our Father who is in heaven.

Let us move now from the practical *how* to the theoretical *why: Why should we love our enemies?* The first reason is fairly obvious. Returning hate for hate multiplies hate, adding deeper darkness to a night already devoid of stars. Darkness cannot drive out darkness; only light can do that. Hate cannot drive out hate; only love can do that. Hate multiplies hate, violence multiplies violence, and toughness multiplies toughness in a descending spiral of destruction. So when Jesus says "Love your enemies," he is setting forth a profound and ultimately inescapable admonition. Have we not come to such an impasse in the modern world that we must love our enemies—or else? The chain reaction of evil—hate begetting hate, wars producing more wars— must be broken, or we shall be plunged into the dark abyss of annihilation. . . .

*Declarations of Independence**

. . . There is at the outset a very obvious and almost facile connection between the war in Vietnam and the struggle I, and others, have been waging in America. A few years ago there was a shining moment in that struggle. It seemed as if there was a real promise of hope for the poor—both black and white—through the Poverty Program. Then came the build-up in Vietnam, and I watched the program broken and eviscerated as if it were some idle political plaything of a society gone mad on war, and I knew that America would never invest the necessary funds or energies in rehabilitation of its poor so long as Vietnam continued to draw men and skills and money like some demonic, destructive suction tube. So I was increasingly compelled to see the war as an enemy of the poor and to attack it as such.

Perhaps the more tragic recognition of reality took place when it became clear to me that the war was doing far more than devastating the hopes of the poor at home. It was sending their sons and their

* Martin Luther King, Jr., gave this address at Riverside Church, New York City, Tuesday, April 4, 1967.

brothers and their husbands to fight and to die in extraordinarily high proportions relative to the rest of the population. We were taking the young black men who had been crippled by our society and sending them 8000 miles away to guarantee liberties in Southeast Asia which they had not found in Southwest Georgia and East Harlem. So we have been repeatedly faced with the cruel irony of watching Negro and white boys on TV screens as they kill and die together for a nation that has been unable to set them together in the same schools. So we watch them in brutal solidarity burning the huts of a poor village, but we realize that they would never live on the same block in Detroit. I could not be silent in the face of such cruel manipulation of the poor . . . in the ghettos of the North over the last three years—especially the last three summers. As I have walked among the desperate, rejected and angry young men, I have told them that Molotov cocktails and rifles would not solve their problems. I have tried to offer them my deepest compassion while maintaining my conviction that social change comes most meaningfully through nonviolent action. But, they asked, what about Vietnam? They asked if our own nation wasn't using massive doses of violence to solve its problems, to bring about the changes it wanted. Their questions hit home, and I knew that I could never again raise my voice against the violence of the oppressed in the ghettos without having first spoken clearly to the greatest pur veyor of violence in the world today—my own government.

For those who ask the question, "Aren't you a Civil Rights leader?" and thereby mean to exclude me from the movement for peace, I have this further answer. In 1957 when a group of us formed the Southern Christian Leadership Conference we chose as our motto: "To save the soul of America." We were convinced that we could not limit our vision to certain rights for black people, but instead affirmed the conviction that America would never be free or saved from itself unless the descendants of its slaves were loosed from the shackles they still wear.

Now, it should be incandescently clear that no one who has any concern for the integrity and life of America today can ignore the present war. If America's soul becomes totally poisoned, part of the autopsy must read "Vietnam." It can never be saved so long as it destroys the deepest hopes of men the world over. . . .

And as I ponder the madness of Vietnam, my mind goes constantly to the people of that peninsula. I speak now not of the soldiers of each side, not of the junta in Saigon, but simply of the people who have been living under the curse of war for almost three continuous decades. I think of them, too, because it is clear to me that there will be no meaningful solution there until some attempt is made to know them and their broken cries. . . .

They must see Americans as strange liberators. The Vietnamese proclaimed their own independence in 1945 after a combined French and Japanese occupation. . . .

. . . For nine years following 1945 we denied the people of Vietnam the right of independence. For nine years we vigorously supported the French in their abortive effort to re-colonize Vietnam.

. . . Now they languish under our bombs and consider us—not their fellow Vietnamese—the real enemy. They move sadly and apathetically as we herd them off the land of their fathers into concentration camps where minimal social needs are rarely met. They know they must move or be destroyed by our bombs. So they go.

They watch as we poison their water, as we kill a million acres of their crops. They must weep as the bulldozers destroy their precious trees. They wander into the hospitals, with at least 20 casualties from American firepower for each Viet Cong-inflicted injury. So far we may have killed a million of them—mostly children. . . .

In 1957 a sensitive American official overseas said that it seemed to him that our nation was on the wrong side of a world revolution. During the past ten years we have seen emerge a pattern of suppression which now has justified the presence of U.S. military "advisors" in Venezuela. The need to maintain social stability for our investments accounts for the counterrevolutionary action of American forces in Guatemala. It tells why American helicopters are being used against guerrillas in Colombia and why American napalm and green beret forces have already been active against rebels in Peru. With such activity in mind, the words of John F. Kennedy come back to haunt us. Five years ago he said, "Those who make peaceful revolution impossible will make violent revolution inevitable."

Increasingly, by choice or by accident, this is the role our nation has taken—by refusing to give up the privileges and the pleasures that come from the immense profits of overseas investment.

I am convinced that if we are to get on the right side of the world revolution, we as a nation must undergo a radical revolution of values.

When machines and computers, profit and property rights are considered more important than people, the giant triplets of racism, materialism, and militarism are incapable of being conquered. . . .

A true revolution of values will soon cause us to question the fairness and justice of many of our past and present policies. True compassion is more than flinging a coin to a beggar; it is not haphazard and superficial. It comes to see that an edifice which produces beggars needs restructuring. A true revolution of values will soon look uneasily on the glaring contrast of poverty and wealth. With righteous indignation, it will look across the seas and see individual capitalists of the West investing huge sums of money in Asia, Africa, and South America, only to take the profits out with no concern for the social betterment of the countries, and say: "This is not just." It will look at our alliance with the landed gentry of Latin America and say: "This is not just." The Western arrogance of feeling that it has everything to teach others and nothing to learn from them is not just. A true revolution of values will lay hands on the world order and say of war: "This way of settling differences is not just." This business of burning human beings with napalm, of filling our nation's homes with orphans and widows, or injecting poisonous drugs of hate into the veins of people normally humane, of sending men home from dark and bloody battlefields physically handicapped and psychologically deranged, cannot be reconciled with wisdom, justice, and love. A nation that continues year after year to spend more money on military defense than on programs of social uplift is approaching spiritual death. . . .

These are revolutionary times. All over the globe men are revolting against old systems of exploitation and oppression, and out of the wombs of a frail world, new systems of justice and equality are being born. The shirtless and barefoot people of the land are rising up as never before. "The people who sat in darkness have seen a great light." We in the West must support these revolutions. It is a sad fact that, because of comfort, complacency, a morbid fear of communism, and our proneness to adjust to injustice, the Western nations that initiated so much of the revolutionary spirit of the modern world have now become the arch anti-revolutionaries. This has driven many to feel that only Marxism has the revolutionary spirit. Therefore, communism is a judgment against our failure to make democracy real and follow through on the revolutions that we initiated. Our only hope today lies in our ability to recapture the revolutionary spirit and go out into a sometimes hostile world declaring eternal hostility to poverty, racism, and militarism. . . .

Now let us begin. Now let us re-dedicate ourselves to the long and bitter—but beautiful—struggle for a new world. . . .

Caria

YANNIS RITSOS

Translated by Edmund Keeley

The ancients and their gods seem more logical, more human.
Apart from their many accomplishments and frequent miracles,
     they dispense
wisdom and compassion. For example, when Staphylus's daughter
absentmindedly let the new wine flow out—the whole year's
     production—
and in despair, as well as in fear of her father, threw herself
into the sea from the high rocks of Castabos
and was followed by her two sisters, Apollo, moved by her act,
gathered her up and carried her in his arms as far as Caria,
where she was worshipped as a goddess, patron of ailing and
     feeble women
in their tribulation and during difficult deliveries.
                                        Now all
     that strikes us as a lie.
Each of us says about the next man: "So what if he drowns?"
     But who knows,
maybe even now an invisible god might gather them up and
     carry them
to another Caria, while we here on this shore, we—
shortsighted, harassed, and much preoccupied—cannot see it at all,
can't even imagine it—by no means can imagine it.
                                        Leros, March 19, 1968

From "Fourth of July Speech to a White Audience, 1852"

FREDERICK DOUGLASS

The rich inheritance of justice, liberty, prosperity and independence, bequeathed by your fathers, is shared by you, not by me. The sunlight that brought light and healing to you, has brought stripes and death to me. This Fourth of July is yours, not mine. You may rejoice, I must mourn. . . .

Let me give you a word of the philosophy of reforms. The whole history of the progress of human liberty shows that all concessions yet made to her august claims have been born of struggle. . . . If there is no struggle there is no progress. Those who profess to favor freedom and yet deprecate agitation, are men who want crops without plowing up the ground. They want rain without thunder and lightning. They want the ocean without the awful roar of its many waters. The struggle may be a moral one; or it may be a physical one; or it may be both moral and physical, but it must be a struggle. Power concedes nothing without a demand. It never did and it never will.*

---

* "A hundred years after the Civil War, Frederick Douglass's statement was still true. Blacks were being beaten, murdered, abused, humiliated and segregated from the cradle to the grave and the regular organs of democratic representative government were silent collaborators. . . . The Fourteenth Amendment, born in 1868 of the Civil War struggles declared 'equal protection of the laws.' But this was soon dead—interpreted into nothingness by the Supreme Court, unenforced by presidents for a century. Even the most liberal of presidents, Franklin D. Roosevelt, would not ask Congress to pass a law making lynching a crime. Roosevelt, through World War II, maintained racial segregation in the armed forces and was only induced to set up a commission on fair employment for blacks when black union leader A. Philip Randolph threatened a march on Washington. President Harry Truman ended segregation in the armed forces only after he was faced with the prospect—again it was by the determined A. Philip Randolph—of black resistance to the draft."

—Howard Zinn, from *Declarations of Independence*, p. 240

From "A Bench by the Side of the Road"

TONI MORRISON

There is no place you or I can go, to think about or not think about, to summon the presences of, or recollect the absences of slaves; nothing that reminds us of the ones who made the journey and of those who did not make it. There is no suitable memorial or plaque or wreath or wall or park or skyscraper lobby. There's no 300-foot tower. There's no small bench by the road. There is not even a tree scored, an initial that I can visit or you can visit in Charleston or Savannah or New York or Providence or, better still, on the banks of the Mississippi.

But somebody told me that there's a gentleman in Washington who makes his living by taking busloads of people around to see the monuments of the city. He has complained because there is never anything there about black people that he can show. And he's black. I can't explain to you why I think it's important but I really do. . . . I think it would refresh. Not only that, not only for black people. It could suggest the moral clarity among white people when they were at their best, when they risked something, when they didn't have to risk and could have chosen to be silent; there's no monument for that either.

I don't have any model in mind, or any person, or even any art form. I just have the hunger for a permanent place. It doesn't have to be a huge, monumental face cut into a mountain. It can be small, some place where you can go put your feet up. It can be a tree. It doesn't have to be a statue of liberty.

There's Been a Misunderstanding About the Sixties

LERONE BENNETT, JR.

There's been this misunderstanding of the sixties. Media people have been bashing them as a matter of course: "People protested when they had nothing else to do." Actually, it was one of the great decades of the century. Everybody thought the promised land was around the next turning. It wasn't. We should learn from that.

Thanks to the sixties, we have a new climate of race relations in the country. Black mayors in our largest cities. Corporate executives. On the other hand, we have Depression levels of unemployment, the collapse of the public school system, and the epidemic of hard drugs. Everything appears to have changed, yet nothing has changed. Black people are still on the bottom.

In a way, we're back to the first Reconstruction period. One hundred years ago, we had these great civil-rights laws. They were stronger than those passed in the 1960s and 1970s. We had a black governor in Louisiana. We had a black majority in the South Carolina legislature. We had Senators from Mississippi. *We had it made a hundred years ago.* The Supreme Court and a conservative movement reversed it as they're trying to do today.

People are disillusioned. They don't think it will ever work. I don't believe that. I'm committed to the historical view that this is a struggle. You win a few, you lose a few. If you can't hold what you won, you go back and organize again. Nobody gave black people anything in this country. Nobody's gonna give them anything, not even the time of day, if we don't organize.

We hear people say, "We tried integration and it failed." That isn't so. Integration has never been tried in this country. It has not even been defined. What is integration? If you put two, three blacks in an all-white institution, it's not integrated. It requires a complete change in the way you think as an institution. Real integration involves a change in values.

When blacks came out of slavery, hundreds of thousands of black soldiers and laborers were the key in the transformation. Those were crucial moments in the summers of 1865, 1866, 1867. Black people roamed all over Georgia and South Carolina with major demands: education and land. Forty acres and a mule. It was inconceivable to them that the federal government would free them and not give them the wherewithal to make their freedom real. It was a betrayal of the Emancipation.

What Martin Luther King realized a hundred years later is that we did not provide the twentieth-century equivalent of forty acres and a mule. We needed the vote, but we also needed the economic foundation. The revolution of the sixties provided us with one, but not the other.

Blaming the victim has become fashionable these days. They are lazy, should get out and work, lift themselves up by their bootstraps. We're not very history-minded in this country. After the first Reconstruction period, after the votes were taken away from us, after we were pushed out of the city halls and legislatures, the same phenomenon emerged in the 1890s. Booker T. Washington was saying what black conservatives are saying today. A period of this kind always produces the black intellectual who says we ought to stop protesting, stop marching, and pick ourselves up by our bootstraps.

Frederick Douglass and all the great black leaders kept the two things together: protest and organize as well as strive for excellence and self-determination. You don't eliminate one part of the equation and expect it to work. King said it. A. Philip Randolph said it. Frederick Douglass said it: "Power concedes nothing without a demand. It never did and it never will."

There's an anger, there's a bitterness, an overwhelming disillusionment. You see idle men standing on streetcorners. You see broken families. You see young people destroyed by dope, an epidemic of which brings murderously high rates of violence. Rap music is the expression of anguish of black America, which faces its greatest crisis since slavery time. So there's a numbness, a dead end.

A whole new environment has been created for young people by the electronic media. You have a never-never land of new gadgetry, of new rhythms, new desires, new dreams, and the sense of "I want it now." All day long on TV, they see people who have three square meals a day, gleaming appliances, and swimming pools. "Here I am cooped up in this one-room place with roaches and rats. Who decided

I had to live this way and the people on television can live that way? Who decided that the South Side had to live this way and the North Side that way?"

You get young black kids killing each other over NFL jackets and tennis shoes. For society to create situations where people need these means of expression is a crime.

It's not that we haven't black leadership. It's that we've not had anywhere in America white leadership comparable to that produced in the black community. People are shocked when I say it. Yet what we need now is a white Martin Luther King to tell poor white people there's no way in the world they can save themselves unless we save all poor people, including blacks. This is the moment.

The massive attack on the sixties takes the form of antiaffirmative action. They're against quotas, they say. For three hundred years in this country, there's been a 99.9 percent quota of white males in all the institutions: the church, the university, the corporate world. There is no way you can begin to create a level playing field without affirmative action. In the late sixties, after the death of King, there was a great Puritan confession. Universities, banks, corporations were confessing: "We've done wrong, we must make amends. Find us some blacks and we'll put them in management programs." It lasted two, three years. Then people started dragging their feet, and now we're where we are today.

During that period, I sat on a number of boards with people who said, "We want to do it right. We're for fair employment, but our middle managers won't do it." Everybody was looking for a super-Negro to hire. I've said to them: "People are the same everywhere. You've got some brilliant ones and some dull ones. Don't look for a black Einstein. Put him in the middle where you put all other middle people."

I still have hope. Know why? Given the way blacks are forced to live in this society, the miracle is that so many still stand and love and teach and earn degrees. The miracle is not that so many black families are broken, but that so many are still together. That so many black fathers are still at home. That so many black women are still raising good children.

If you go to the Robert Taylor Homes and see the indescribable conditions, the miracle is that college students come out of these places. What sociologists visiting these dreadful projects miss is that thousands of black boys and girls somehow manage to survive. It is the incredible toughness in people that gives me hope.

My hope is based on the incredible story of African-Americans in this country. We survived the slave trade. We survived slavery. We survived segregation. We survived shacks, blood, cotton, roaches, and rats. History says we can and will survive if we do what our spiritual tells us: Keep your hand on the plow, hold on.

W. E. B. Du Bois died at ninety-six. He'd lived through the first Reconstruction, its betrayal, World War I and the betrayal of its truce, through the New Deal and World War II. He was tried in court and humiliated. Yet, in his final death statement, he expressed hope.

Do you know what happened the day he died?

They launched the March on Washington. August 26, 1963.

For Medgar Evers

DAVID IGNATOW

They're afraid of me
because I remind them of the ground.
The harder they step on me
the closer I am pressed to earth,
and hard, hard they step,
growing more frightened
and vicious.

Will I live?
They will lie in the earth
buried in me
and above them a tree will grow
for shade.

Coalitions of Indigenous Peoples: Will the White Man Understand?

JULIAN BURGER AND PAULINHO PAIAKAN,
Kayapo Chief

Indigenous peoples are now looking beyond their own individual struggles. They have defined a shared agenda and are pursuing their common goals in unison. At the same time, their demands are reaching an increasingly sympathetic audience among all those concerned for the future.

The survival of first peoples rests on a radical change in political and economic conditions. Demands for self-determination and land are a direct challenge to the authority of governments, and can translate into local political conflict. International support is therefore crucial.

Since the 1960s a wave of pro-indigenous organizations has emerged to join well-established bodies, such as the Anti-Slavery Society. Survival International in the UK, the Copenhagen-based International Work Group for Indigenous Affairs, Cultural Survival in the USA, Gesellschaft für bedrohte Völker in Germany, the Dutch Workgroup for Indigenous Peoples, the Swiss group Incomindios and other smaller groups are actively campaigning, publishing and raising funds for indigenous peoples. Human rights organizations, such as Amnesty International, are also increasingly concerned with indigenous rights.

On a broader level, the aims of human rights organizations, environmental organizations, religious groups, development NGOs, scientists, and political parties are converging with those of first peoples. And together they now form a global network for human survival working to promote human rights and a healthy environment.

> *"Until recently we didn't have much reason to think that the white man would ever understand, in fact want to understand, the Indians, our ways of thinking and living . . . It is true, though, that recently we have seen groups of Indians and white people working together and organizing in order to try and change the way people think."*
>
> —Paulinho Paiakan, Kayapo chief

Predictions about the future are rarely more than guesswork—we are continuously surprised by the turn of events. However, many now agree that our survival depends on more sustainable management of the Earth's resources, and greater international co-operation. At the same time, there is a growing desire to control affairs on a more human scale—to move away from hierarchies and centralization, and to rethink how we organize politically.

The experiences and values of indigenous peoples may well take on a special significance. Their struggle for self-determination is part of a larger struggle for freedom; their beliefs about nature offer insights into how the whole environment should be protected; their social organizations may throw into question our own fragmented communities.

Too often we think we are powerless to change events, or even to protest. Yet we need a common humanitarian culture, and those who suffer most need the support of those who are free to speak out. . . .

> *"It seems to us that from the earliest times, man's natural state was to be free as our grandfathers told us and we believe that freedom is inherent to life. We recognize this principle as the key to peace, respect for one another and the understanding of the natural law that prevails over all the universe and adherence to this law is the only salvation of our future on the planet, Mother Earth."*
> —Oren Lyons, Onondaga

What Treaty That the Whites Have Kept Has the Red Man Broken?

SITTING BULL, Chief of the Sioux Nation

What treaty that the whites have kept has the red man broken? Not one. What treaty that the whites ever made with us red men have they kept? Not one. When I was a boy the Sioux owned the world. The sun rose and set in their lands. They sent 10,000 horsemen to battle. Where are the warriors today? Who slew them? Where are our lands? Who owns them?

What white man can say I ever stole his lands or a penny of his money? Yet they say I am a thief. What white woman, however lonely, was ever when a captive insulted by me? Yet they say I am a bad Indian. What white man has ever seen me drunk? Who has ever come to me hungry and gone unfed? Who has ever seen me beat my wives or abuse my children? What law have I broken? Is it wrong for me to love my own? Is it wicked in me because my skin is red; because I am a Sioux; because I was born where my fathers lived; because I would die for my people and my country?

From Man's Most Dangerous Myth: The Fallacy of Race

ASHLEY MONTAGU

"Ethnic Group" and "Race"

In the First Unesco Statement on Race, paragraph 6 reads as follows: "National, religious, geographic, linguistic and cultural groups do not necessarily coincide with racial groups; and the cultural traits of such groups have no demonstrated genetic connection with racial traits. Because serious errors of this kind are habitually committed when the term 'race' is used in popular parlance, it would be better when speaking of human races to drop the term 'race' altogether and speak of *ethnic groups*."

The principal objection of the term "race" with reference to man is that it takes for granted as solved problems which are far from being so, and tends to close the mind to problems to which it should always remain open. If, with ritual fidelity, one goes on repeating long enough that "the Nordics" are a race or that "the Armenoids" are, or that "the Jews" are, or that races may be determined by their blood group gene frequencies, we shall have already determined what a "race" is. Since there are today quite a number of physical anthropologists who question the validity of the term "race" when applied to man, and some biologists who question its value when applied to some non-human groups of animals,[1] the following discussion will not appear as revolutionary as it once did.

In 1936 Huxley and Haddon repudiated the term "race" in favor of "ethnic group,"[2] and somewhat later Calman recommended that the term "variety" should be avoided altogether and suggested that "Other terms such as 'geographical race,' 'form,' 'phase,' and so forth, may be useful in particular instances but are better not used until some measure of agreement is reached as to their precise meaning."[3] Kalmus writes: "A very important term which was originally used in systematics is 'race.' Nowadays, however, its use is avoided as far as possible in genetics."[4] In a more recent work Kalmus writes, "It is customary to discuss the local varieties of humanity in terms of 'race.' However, it is unnecessary to use this greatly debased word, since it is easy to describe populations without it."[5] G. S. Carter, in his book on *Animal Evolution,* writes that the terms " 'race,' 'variety,' and 'form' are used so loosely and in so many senses that it is advisable to avoid using them as infraspecific categories."[6] Professor Ernst Hanhart denies that there are any "true races" in man,[7] and Professor L. S. Penrose, in a review of Dunn and Dobzhansky's little book *Heredity, Race and Society,* writes that he is unable to "see the necessity for the rather apologetic retention of the obsolete term 'race,' when what is meant is simply a given population differentiated by some social, geographical or genetic character, or . . . merely by a gene frequency peculiarity. The use of the almost mystical concept of race makes the presentation of the facts about the geographical and linguistic groups . . . unnecessarily complicated."[8] Dr. J. P. Garlick, reviewing two books on "race," writes, "The use of 'race' as a taxonomic unit for man seems out-of-date, if not irrational."[9] Finally, Professor P. A. Parsons writes, "There are good arguments for abandoning the term race, as it is clearly arbitrary, undefinable, and without biological meaning. The term, population, although suffering from many of the same difficulties, at least has a lesser emotional content."[10]

In spite of these strictures many biologists will continue to use the term, and if they can use it in an adequately defined manner so that their meaning can be clearly understood by other scientists, erroneous though that usage may be, it will be all the more easy for the critic to direct attention to the sources of the error. It cannot be too frequently emphasized that definitions are not to be achieved at the beginning of an inquiry but only at the end of one. Such inquiries have not yet been completed to the satisfaction of most scientists who have paid considered attention to the subject of "race." The term, therefore, at best is at the present time not really allowable on any score in man. One may or may not be of the opinion that the term "race" ought to be dropped altogether from the vocabulary, because it is so prematurely defined and confusing and because biologists and other scientists are frequently guilty of using it incorrectly, and that therefore it would be better if they did not lend the aura of their authority to the use of so confusing a word. The term "subspecies" has been used as the equivalent of the term "race," but this suffers from the same disadvantages, and has been as misused as its equivalent.[11] The term "race" is so embarrassed by confused and mystical meanings, and has so many blots upon its escutcheon, that a discouragement of its use would constitute an encouragement to clearer thinking.

In opposition to this view a number of objections have been expressed. One doesn't change anything by changing names. It's an artful dodge. A subterfuge. Why not meet the problem head-on? If, in popular usage, the term "race" has been befogged and befouled, why not cleanse it of the smog and foulness and restore it to its pristine condition? Re-education should be attempted by establishing the true meaning of "race," not by denying its existence. The "race" problem is not merely a matter of faulty semantics. One cannot combat racism by enclosing the word in quotes. It is not the word that requires changing but people's ideas about it. It is a common failing to argue from the abuse of an idea to its total exclusion. And so on.

It was Francis Bacon who remarked that truth grows more readily out of error than it does out of confusion. The time may come when it may be possible for most men to use the term "race" in a legitimate scientific sense, with clarity and with reason. But that time is not yet. It does not appear to be generally realized that while stone walls do not a prison make, scientific terms are capable of doing so. Until people are soundly educated to understand the muddlement of ideas which is represented by such terms as "race" they will continue to believe in absurdities. And as Voltaire so acutely remarked, "As long as people believe in absurdities they will continue to commit atrocities." Words are what men breathe into them. Men have a strong tendency to use words and phrases which cloak the unknown in the undefined or undefinable. As Housman put it, "calling in ambiguity of language to promote confusion of thought."[12] Sooner or later most words tend to decay into imprecision, and the word "race" represents a conspicuous example of such a degeneration. The race problem is certainly not a matter of faulty semantics, but the faulty semantics implicit in the common conception of "race" certainly contributes to the exacerbation of that problem.

The layman's conception of "race" is so confused and emotionally muddled that any attempt to modify it would seem to be met by the greatest obstacle of all, the term "race" itself. This is another reason why the attempt to retain the term "race" in popular parlance must fail. The term is a trigger word; utter it and a whole series of emotionally conditioned responses follow. The phrase "ethnic group" suffers from no such defect. If we are to clarify the minds of those who think in terms of "race" we must cease using the word primarily because in the layman's mind the term defines conditions which do not in fact exist. There is no such thing as the kind of "race" in which the layman believes. If we are to re-educate him in a sound conception of the meaning of that population or somatological or genetic group which we prefer to designate by the general and noncommittal phrase *ethnic group,* then it would seem far more reasonable to convey to him the temporariness of the situation with a general rather than with a particular term. This is particularly desirable when it is sought to remove a prevailing erroneous conception and substitute one that clarifies without solidifying. Professor Henry Sigerist has well said that "it is never sound to continue the use of terminology with which the minds of millions of people have been poisoned even when the old terms are given new meanings."[13] And Professor George Gaylord Simpson has written, "A word for which everyone has a different definition, usually unstated, ceases to serve the function of communication and its use results in futile arguments about nothing. There is also a sort of Gresham's Law for words; redefine them as we will, their worst or most extreme meaning is almost certain to remain current and to tend to drive out the meaning we might prefer."[14] Bertrand Russell has suggested that for words that have strong emotional overtones we should substitute in our arguments the letters of the alphabet.

The biologist who has been largely concerned with the study of animal populations will be likely to take an oversimplified view of the problems here involved and to dismiss such attempts at re-education of the layman as unsatisfactory. By substituting one term for another, he will say, one solves nothing. It is quite as possible to feel "ethnic group prejudice" as it is to feel "race prejudice." Perhaps. But this kind of comment indicates that the real point has been missed. The phrase "ethnic group" is *not* a substitute for the term "race." The grounds upon which it is suggested constitute a fundamental difference in viewpoint which significantly differentiates what the phrase stands for from what the term stands for. It is not a question of changing names, and there is no question of resorting to devices or artful dodges—the imputation would be silly. If what the phrase "ethnic group" means is clearly understood and accepted, "ethnic group prejudice" would hardly require to be taken seriously. There have been some who have felt that the use of the phrase "ethnic group" was an avoidance of the main issue. On the other hand, most students of human nature would take the view that such a usage constitutes a more realistic and more promising approach to the problem of lay thinking on this subject than the method of attempting to put new meaning into the old bottle of "race." I agree with Korzybski that "because of the great semantic influence of the structure of language on the masses of mankind, leading, as it does, through lack of better understanding and *evaluation to speculation on terms,* it seems advisable to abandon completely terms which imply to the *many* the suggested elementalism, although these terms are used in a proper nonelementalistic way by the few."[15]

The ground on which the phrase "ethnic group" is principally suggested is that it is easier to re-educate people by introducing a new conception with a new distinctive term, particularly, I repeat, when it is desired to remove a prevailing erroneous conception and introduce a new and more correct one. Those who do not understand that the greatest obstacle to the process of re-education would be the retention of the old term "race," a term which enshrines the errors it is desired to remove, do not understand the deep implicit meanings which this word has inescapably come to possess for so many of its users. The question may, then, be asked: Will the phrase "ethnic group" be sufficient to cause such persons to alter their ideas? The answer is for some "No," for others, "It will help"; and for still others, "Yes." No one should be so naive as to suppose that by this means alone one is going to solve the "race" problem! The suggestions here made are calculated to help; they can do no more at best. Each time one uses the term "race" most individuals believe they understand what is meant, when in fact the chances are that what they understand by the term is largely false. "Race" is something so familiar that in speaking of it one takes one's private meaning completely for granted and one never thinks to question it. On the other hand, when one uses the phrase "ethnic group" wherever "race" would have been used, the question is generally asked: "What do you mean by 'ethnic group'?" And that at once affords the opportunity to discuss the facts and explain their meaning as well as the falsities of the prevailing conception of "race." This, it seems to me, is one of the greatest educational advantages of the phrase "ethnic group" over the term "race." Another advantage of the phrase is that it leaves all question of definition open, it refers specifically to human populations which are believed to exhibit a certain degree, amount, or frequency of undetermined physical likenesses or homogeneity. An ethnic group has already been described as one of a number of populations, which populations together comprise the species *Homo sapiens,* and which individually maintain their differences, physical and cultural, by means of isolating mechanisms such as geographic and social barriers. These differences vary as the power of the geographic and social barriers varies. Where these barriers are of high power, such ethnic groups will tend to remain distinct from each other geographically or ecologically.

English and English write as follows, "Ethnic group is an intentionally vague or general term used to avoid some of the difficulties of *race.* The ethnic group may be a nation, a people (such as the Jews), a language group (the Dakota Indians), a sociologically defined so-called race (the American Negro), or a group bound together in a coherent cultural entity by a religion (the Amish)."[16] To which one may add that the group may be characterized by a certain unity of genetic or physical traits.

Yet another advantage of the phrase "ethnic group" is that it avoids the reductionist or "nothing but" fallacy, that is to say, the notion that men are nothing but the resultant of their biological heredity, that they are what they are because of their genes. The phrase "ethnic group" is calculated to provide the necessary corrective to this erroneous viewpoint by eliminating the question-begging emphases of the biologistic bias on purely physical factors and differences, and demanding that the question of definition be left open until the necessary scientific research and answers are available. The emphasis is shifted to the fact that man is a uniquely cultural creature as well as a physical organism, and that under the influence of human culture the plasticity of man, both mentally and physically, is greatly increased—indeed, to such an extent as to lead anthropologists to the creation of races upon the basis of physical traits which were subsequently discovered to be due to cultural factors, as, for example, the head forms of the so-called Armenoid and Dinaric "races."

Here, too, reply may be made to those who may object that the phrase "ethnic group" is too reminiscent of the cultural. But this is precisely why the phrase is so well found. The Greek word *ethnos* originally meant a number of people living together, and subsequently came to be used in the sense of a tribe, group, nation, or people. In modern times the term "ethnic" has occasionally been used to refer to a group identified by ties both of race and of nationality. This is pretty much what the phrase "ethnic group" ought to be taken to mean in the sense given in our description of an "ethnic group."

If it be said that what the student of man's variety is interested in is the way in which human groups came to be what they are, and that for this reason it is the biological fact and mechanisms in which he must be chiefly interested, the answer must be made that anyone who believes this must be disabused of his belief as quickly as possible. For it must be emphasized again that man is not merely a physical organism but a *human* being who as a member of a cultural group has been greatly influenced by his culture. Human populations have had a remarkable assortment of marriage or breeding regulations, for instance, varying standards of sexual selection, different kinds of social barriers, mobility, and similar variables, all of which have probably played an appreciable part in the evolution of ethnic differences. These are the very kinds of factors which are most neglected by those who come to the study of man with a biologistic bias. It would for such students of man, especially those who come in from the nonhuman biological fields, as well as for the layman, be a great advantage to be required to look at the problem of human variety from the viewpoint of the "ethnic group" rather than from that of "race." Where man is concerned the biologist, like the layman, needs to add a cultural dimension to his horizons. This is what the phrase "ethnic group" will help him to do.

The conception of an "ethnic group" is quite different from that which is associated with the term "race." The phrase "ethnic group" represents a different way of looking at populations, an open, non-question-begging way, a tentative, noncommittal, experimental way, based on the new understanding which the sciences of genetics and anthropology have made possible. A term is discontinued, retired, but another is not merely substituted for it; rather a new conception of human populations is introduced replacing the old one, which is now dropped, and a term or phrase suitable to this new conception is suggested. The old conception is *not* retained and a new name given to it, but a new conception is introduced under its own name. That is a very different thing from a mere change in names. It is important to be quite clear upon this point, for the *new conception* embraced in the phrase "ethnic group" renders the possibility of the development of "ethnic group prejudice" quite impossible, for as soon as the nature of this conception is understood it cancels the possibility of any such development. It is a noncontaminating neutral concept.

Perhaps the greatest advantage of the phrase "ethnic group" is that it is noncommittal and somewhat flexible. It may be applied to any group concerning which physical and cultural traits are so identified that it is given a certain distinctiveness which appears to separate it from other groups. The phrase may also be used as embracing the definition of race in the biological sense, and particularly groups which are less clearly defined, which may or may not be races and hence should not be called races in the absence of the necessary scientific demonstration. All that we say when we use the phrase "ethnic group" is that here is a group of people who physically, and perhaps in other additional ways, may be regarded as a more or less distinct group. Until we know what it really is, and until we understand thoroughly what we are talking about with respect to this and all other groups, let us call such groups "ethnic groups." In other words, the concept of "ethnic group" implies a question mark, *not* a period. It implies that many questions remain to be asked, and that many answers will have to be given before we can say precisely what any particular ethnic group represents.

To conclude and summarize: The advantages of the phrase "ethnic group" are: first, while emphasizing the fact that one is dealing with a distinguishable group, this noncommittal phrase leaves the whole question of the precise status of the group on physical and other grounds open for further discussion and research; second, it recognizes the fact that it is a group which has been subject to the action of cultural influences; and third, it eliminates all obfuscating emotional implications.

As for the suggested dropping or the restricted or suspended use of the term "race," there are many parallels for this in science. Possibly the most striking one in recent times is the dropping of the term "instinct" by psychologists for similar reasons to those which make the term "race" undesirable.[17] Similarly, in anthropology the term "savage" has been completely dropped, while the term "primitive" as referring to living peoples is largely being abandoned in favor of the term "nonliterate" for much the same reason, namely, the inaccuracy of the earlier terms, and hence their unsuitability. In biology the term "unit character," as erroneously referring to single genes as determining single characters or traits, has been forever banished from the scientific vocabulary. Retardative concepts like "phlogiston" of eighteenth-century chemistry have been dropped never to be readopted. It may be that the terms "instinct" and "race" may someday be shown to have more than a merely verbal validity of common usage, but this is very unlikely, and it would be more in accordance with the scientific spirit to declare a moratorium on the use of the term "race."

The phrase "ethnic group" serves as a challenge to thought and as a stimulus to rethink the foundations of one's beliefs. It encourages the passage from ignorant certainty to thoughtful uncertainty. For the layman, as for others, the term "race" closes the door on his understanding; the phrase "ethnic group" opens it.

NOTES

1. Montagu (ed.), *The Concept of Race;* Livingstone, "On the Non-Existence of Human Races," in Montagu (ed.), *The Concept of Race,* pp. 46–60; Hiernaux, "Adaptation and Race," *Advancement of Science* (1967), 658–62.
2. Huxley and Haddon, *We Europeans,* pp. 82–83.
3. Calman, *The Classification of Animals,* p. 14.
4. Kalmus, *Genetics,* p. 45.
5. Kalmus, *Variation and Heredity,* p. 30.
6. Carter, *Animal Evolution,* p. 163.
7. Hanhart, "Infectious Diseases," in A. Sorsby (ed.), *Clinical Genetics,* p. 545.
8. Penrose, in *Annals of Eugenics,* XVII (1952), 252–53.
9. Garlick, in *Annals of Human Genetics,* XXV (1961), 169–70.
10. Parsons, "Genetic Determination of Behavior (Mice and Men)," in Ehrman, Omenn, and Caspari (eds.), *Genetics, Environment, and Behavior,* p. 94.
11. Hall, "Zoological Subspecies of Man at the Peace Table," *Journal of Mammalogy,* XXVII (1946), 358–64.
12. Housman, *The Name and Nature of Poetry,* p. 31.

13. Sigerist, *A History of Medicine*, p. 101.
14. Simpson, *The Major Features of Evolution*, p. 268.
15. Korzybski, *Science and Sanity*, p. 31.
16. English and English, *A Comprehensive Dictionary of Psychological and Psychoanalytical Terms*, p. 189.
17. See Bernard, *Instinct: A Study in Social Psychology*.

The Term "Miscegenation"

The term "miscegenation" provides a remarkable exhibit in the natural history of nonsense. The term today is used in a pejorative sense as referring to "race mixture." The prefix "mis" (from the Latin *miscere*, "mix") has probably contributed its share to the misunderstanding of the nature of "race" mixture. Words that begin with the prefix "mis" suggest a "mistake," "misuse," "mislead," and similar erroneous ideas implying wrong conduct.

The word "miscegenation" was invented as a hoax, and published in an anonymous pamphlet at New York in 1864, with the title *Miscegenation: The Theory of the Blending of the Races, Applied to the White Man and Negro*. The pamphlet was almost certainly the joint product of two members of the New York *World* staff, David Goodman Croly,[1] an editor, and George Wakeman, one of the reporters. The purpose of the authors was to raise the "race" issue in aggravated form in the 1864 presidential campaign by attributing to the abolitionist Republicans and the Republican party the views set forth in *Miscegenation*. The pamphlet was intended to commit the Republican leaders to "the conclusions to which they are brought by their own principles," without any hope of success but in the expectation that their folly would be made all the more clear to them in granting the Negro the franchise. The brief introduction sets the tone of the whole pamphlet.

"The word is spoken at last. It is Miscegenation—the blending of the various races of men—the practical recognition of all the children of the common father. While the sublime inspirations of Christianity have taught this doctrine, Christians so-called have ignored it in denying social equality to the colored man; while democracy is founded upon the idea that all men are equal, democrats have shrunk from the logic of their own creed, and refused to fraternize with the people of all nations; while science has demonstrated that the intermarriage of diverse races is indispensable to a progressive humanity, its votaries, in this country at least, have never had the courage to apply that rule to the relations of the white and colored races. But Christianity, democracy, and science are stronger than the timidity, prejudice, and pride of short-sighted men; and they teach that a people, to become great, must become composite. This involves what is vulgarly known as amalgamation, and those who dread that name, and the thought and fact it implies, are warned against reading these pages."

The word "miscegenation" is defined by the authors as follows: "*Miscegenation*—from the Latin *Miscere,* to mix, and *Genus,* race, is used to denote the abstract idea of the mixture of two or more races."

Thus, the word "miscegenation" was invented by the satirists to replace the vulgar term "amalgamation," as not being sufficiently elevated or distinguished.[2] Indeed, the word does carry with it a sort of authoritative aura, implying, however, a certain lack of respectability,[3] and even responsibility. The extent of the prejudice inherent in and engendered by this word may be gathered from the fact that *Webster's New International Dictionary* illustrates the use of the word by the example of "one who is guilty of miscegenation."

The word should be replaced by ordinary English words such as "intermixture," "mixture," "admixture," and "intermarriage."

NOTES

1. Croly's son Herbert was the author of *The Promise of American Life,* 1909, the classic statement of the progressive movement in America. Herbert was also the founder of *The New Republic.*
2. The pamphlet is the subject of an excellent little book, Bloch, *Miscegenation, Melaleukation, and Mr. Lincoln's Dog.*
3. This is well illustrated by a remark made by former President Harry S. Truman. When asked whether he thought "racial" intermarriages would become widespread in the United States, he answered, "I hope not. I don't believe in it. What's that word about four feet long? Miscegenation?" New York *Times,* 12 September, 1963.

From Leaves of Grass: "*I Sing the Body Electric*"

WALT WHITMAN

. . .

The man's body is sacred and the woman's body is sacred,
No matter who it is, it is sacred—is it the meanest one in the
    laborers' gang?
Is it one of the dull-faced immigrants just landed on the wharf?
Each belongs here or anywhere just as much as the well-off, just as
    much as you,
Each has his or her place in the procession.

(All is a procession,
The universe is a procession with measured and perfect motion.)

Do you know so much yourself that you call the meanest ignorant?
Do you suppose you have a right to a good sight, and he or she has
    no right to a sight?
Do you think matter has cohered together from its diffuse float, and
    the soil is on the surface, and water runs and vegetation sprouts,
For you only, and not for him and her?

7

A man's body at auction,
(For before the war I often go to the slave-mart and watch the sale,)
I help the auctioneer, the sloven does not half know his business.

Gentlemen look on this wonder,
Whatever the bids of the bidders they cannot be high enough for it,
For it the globe lay preparing quintillions of years without one
    animal or plant,
For it the revolving cycles truly and steadily roll'd.

In this head the all-baffling brain,
In it and below it the makings of heroes.

Examine these limbs, red, black, or white, they are cunning in
  tendon and nerve,
They shall be stript that you may see them.

Exquisite senses, life-lit eyes, pluck, volition,
Flakes of breast-muscle, pliant backbone and neck, flesh not flabby,
  good-sized arms and legs,
And wonders within there yet.

Within there runs blood,
The same old blood! the same red-running blood!
There swells and jets a heart, there all passions, desires, reachings,
  aspirations,
(Do you think they are not there because they are not express'd in
  parlors and lecture-rooms?)

This is not only one man, this the father of those who shall be
  fathers in their turns,
In him the start of populous states and rich republics,
Of him countless immortal lives with countless embodiments and
  enjoyments.

How do you know who shall come from the offspring of his
  offspring through the centuries?
(Who might you find you have come from yourself, if you could
  trace back through the centuries?)

8

A woman's body at auction,
She too is not only herself, she is the teeming mother of mothers,
She is the bearer of them that shall grow and be mates to the
  mothers.

Have you ever loved the body of a woman?
Have you ever loved the body of a man?
Do you not see that these are exactly the same to all in all nations
  and times all over the earth?

If any thing is sacred the human body is sacred,
And the glory and sweet of a man is the token of manhood
  untainted,

And in man or woman a clean, strong, firm-fibred body, is more
beautiful than the most beautiful face.

Have you seen the fool that corrupted his own live body? or the
fool that corrupted her own live body?
For they do not conceal themselves, and cannot conceal themselves.

9

O my body! I dare not desert the likes of you in other men and
women, nor the likes of the parts of you,
I believe the likes of you are to stand or fall with the likes of the
soul, (and that they are the soul,)
I believe the likes of you shall stand or fall with my poems, and that
they are my poems,
Man's, woman's, child's, youth's, wife's, husband's, mother's,
father's, young man's, young woman's poems,
Head, neck, hair, ears, drop and tympan of the ears,
Eyes, eye-fringes, iris of the eye, eyebrows, and the waking or
sleeping of the lids,
Mouth, tongue, lips, teeth, roof of the mouth, jaws, and the jaw-
hinges,
Nose, nostrils of the nose, and the partition,
Cheeks, temples, forehead, chin, throat, back of the neck, neck-
slue,
Strong shoulders, manly beard, scapula, hind-shoulders, and the
ample side-round of the chest,
Upper-arm, armpit, elbow-socket, lower-arm, arm-sinews, arm-
bones,
Wrist and wrist-joints, hand, palm, knuckles, thumb, forefinger,
finger-joints, finger-nails,
Broad breast-front, curling hair of the breast, breast-bone, breast-
side,
Ribs, belly, backbone, joints of the backbone,
Hips, hip-sockets, hip-strength, inward and outward round, man-
balls, man-root,
Strong set of thighs, well carrying the trunk above,
Leg-fibres, knee, knee-pan, upper-leg, under-leg,
Ankles, instep, foot-ball, toes, toe-joints, the heel;

All attitudes, all the shapeliness, all the belongings of my or your
  body or of any one's body, male or female,
The lung-sponges, the stomach-sac, the bowels sweet and clean,
The brain in its folds inside the skull-frame,
Sympathies, heart-valves, palate-valves, sexuality, maternity,
Womanhood and all that is a woman, and the man that comes from
  woman,
The womb, the teats, nipples, breast-milk, tears, laughter, weeping,
  love-looks, love-perturbations and risings,
The voice, articulation, language, whispering, shouting aloud,
Food, drink, pulse, digestion, sweat, sleep, walking, swimming,
Poise on the hips, leaping, reclining, embracing, arm-curving and
  tightening,
The continual changes of the flex of the mouth, and around the
  eyes,
The skin, the sunburnt shade, freckles, hair,
The curious sympathy one feels when feeling with the hand the
  naked meat of the body,
The circling rivers the breath, and breathing it in and out,
The beauty of the waist, and thence of the hips, and thence
  downward toward the knees,
The thin red jellies within you or within me, the bones and the
  marrow in the bones,
The exquisite realization of health;
O I say these are not the parts and poems of the body only, but of
  the soul,
O I say now these are the soul!

From "Democracy": A Public Speech

BARBARA JORDAN

. . . We believe that the government which represents the authority of all the people, not just one interest group, but
all the people, has an obligation to actively, underscore actively, seek
to remove those obstacles which would block individual achievement

. . . obstacles emanating from race, sex, economic condition. The government must seek to remove them.

. . . We are a people in a quandary about the present. We are a people in search of our future. We are a people in search of a national community.

We are a people trying not only to solve the problems of the present: unemployment, inflation . . . but we are attempting on a larger scale to fulfill the promise of America. We are attempting to fulfill our national purpose; to create and sustain a society in which all of us are equal.

Throughout our history, when people have looked for new ways to solve their problems, and to uphold the principles of this nation, many times they have turned to political parties. They have often turned to the Democratic Party.

What is it, what is it about the Democratic Party that makes it the instrument that people use when they search for ways to shape their future? Well I believe the answer to that question lies in our concept of governing. Our concept of governing is derived from our view of people. It is a concept deeply rooted in a set of beliefs firmly etched in the national conscience, of all of us. . . . Well I am going to close my speech by quoting a Republican President and I ask you that as you listen to these words of Abraham Lincoln, relate them to the concept of a national community in which every last one of us participates: "As I would not be a slave, so I would not be a master. This expresses my idea of Democracy. Whatever differs from this, to the extent of the difference is no Democracy."

True Democracy Demands Moral Conviction

VACLÁV HAVEL

Translated and adapted by Daniela Gioseffi with Sophia Buzevska

Individual freedom, equality, the universality of civil rights (including the right to property ownership), the rule of law, a democratic political system, local self-government, the separation of parliamentary, executive, and judiciary powers, the revival of civil society, all flow from the idea of human rights, and all of them are the fulfillment of that ideal.

Human rights are universal and indivisible. Human freedom is not separate from these: if it's denied to anyone anywhere, it is therefore denied, indirectly, to all. This is why we can't remain silent in the countenance of evil or violence; silence merely encourages evil and violence. . . . Respect for the universality of human and civil rights, their inalienability and indivisibility, is perforce possible only when it's understood—at least in the philosophical or existential sense—that one is "responsible for the whole world" and that one must behave in the manner in which all ought to behave, even if not all do. . . .

As ridiculously quixotic as it may seem these days, one thing feels certain to me: that it's my responsibility to stress over and over again, the moral origin of all genuine politics, to stress the significance of moral values and standards in all areas of social life, including economics, and to explain that if we don't try, within ourselves, to discover or recreate or cultivate what I call "higher responsibility," things will come out very badly indeed. . . . The authoritarian regime imposed a certain order—if "order" is the correct word for it—upon the vices of evil and violence (and in doing so "legitimized" them, in a governmental sense). Such order has now been broken to bits, but a new order that seeks to merely limit rather than exploit such vices, an order based on freely accepted responsibility to and for all of society, has not yet been built—nor could it have been, for such an order develops slowly over the years and must be consistently cultivated.

We are witness to a bizarre state of affairs: society has freed itself; it's true, but in some ways it behaves worse than when confined in chains. Criminality has grown rapidly, and the usual sewage that in times of historical reversal always wells up from the deeper regions of the collective id has overflowed into the mass media, especially the gutter press. But there's other, more serious and treacherous symptoms: hatred among nationalities, xenophobia, racism; even signs of Fascism; political pandering; an unrestrained, brutish struggle for specific selfish-interests; unadulterated ambition; fanatical desires of every conceivable kind; new and unprecedented forms of thievery; the rise of various organized crime syndicates; and a prevailing dearth of tolerance, compassion, taste, moderation, patient reasoning. There's a new attraction to ideologies, too—as if communism, as perverted from the

Marxist social ideal into monstrous totalitarianism, had left behind it a huge, disturbing void—yet to be filled at any price.

Genuine politics—politics worthy of the name, and the only politics I'm willing to devote myself to—is simply a matter of service to those who have put one in service through the democratic process: serving the community, and serving those who will come after us. Its deepest roots are moral because it's human responsibility, expressed through action, to and for the whole, a responsibility that's what it is —a "higher, finer" responsibility. . . .

The Riot of Colors

TESS ONWUEME

For seasons, I've been counting . . .
Counting, counting, and shifting; shifting and counting cards
To play Black as hit number in the rainbow—
The more games I win,
The more I'm played out . . .
My cord cut as string
To spread black and brown colors in the rainbow—
Knowing all else but me . . . finding all else but me
—Missing . . . missing . . . always, always . . .
Turned around and around and around
Shifted out of the game
Shifted out of fame
—Missing and missing—and made to lie
In limbo . . .

As colors advance in the rainbow,
images of me crawl. Backwards, crawl . . . crawl, cry, backwards—
Crawl, black wards, crawl black! Cry back!
Crow! Black raven beauty! Crow Black Crow!
Cry back your beauty, your glowing black beauty!
Croon . . . croon-croon! As colors advance in the rainbow.
Reflected behind clouds, the graceful black crow
streaks across the sky. The zebra crosses my face!

Leaving me a riot of colors, the rainbow in me
To spread the color Black, and not hang it by the neck!

Where is the sure spot in winds for me to spread the color,
black? History? Who talks about history and reads it?
I am the story, HERstory! I am the history of herstory!
You care to know me? Come . . . feast all senses on these fingers.
Screaming from the relish of tatoos by sweet licking and twisting
Without prejudice my waist around the west!
You care to know me? Come! I'm too much color dyed in winds,
    broken,
scattering races and scattered in the race among faces rioting.
I am too much color, so much! My cord is strong, though cut again
and again, defying the wind. I am the beautiful Black woman of
    Africa!
I stand amidst the rainbow riot of color, trees, zebras, earth, crows,
    sky!
Red sunset, yellow faces, black faces, white faces, red faces, flowers
    of every
hue! I am the perception of color which is contrast! Black makes
    white possible.
White makes black possible. I stand amidst the color, the riot of
    color the glory
of color. I am. I am the beautiful Black woman of Africa. My cord
    is strong.
Defying wind . . . I AM!

Children Are Color-Blind

GENNY LIM

I never painted myself yellow
the way I colored the sun when I was five.
The way I colored whitefolks with the "flesh" crayola.
Yellow pages adults thumbed through for restaurants,
taxis, airlines, plumbers . . .
The color of summer squash, corn, eggyolk, innocence and tapioca.

My children knew before they were taught.
They envisioned rainbows emblazoned over alleyways;
Clouds floating over hilltops like a freedom shroud.
With hands clasped, time dragged them along and they followed.

Wind-flushed cheeks persimmon,
eyes dilated like dark pearls staring out the backseat windows,
they speed through childhood like greyhounds
into the knot of night, hills fanning out,
an ocean ending at an underpass,
a horizon blunted by lorries, skyscrapers,
vision blurring at the brink of poverty.

Dani, my three-year-old, recites the alphabet from
billboards flashing by like pages of a cartoon flipbook,
where above, carpetbaggers patrol the freeways like
Olympic gods hustling their hi-tech neon gospel,
looking down from the fast lane,
dropping Kool dreams, booze dreams, fancy car dreams,
fast foods dreams, sex dreams and no-tomorrow dreams
like eight balls into your easy psychic pocket.

"Only girls with black hair, black eyes can join!"
My eight-year-old was chided at school for excluding a blonde
from her circle. "Only girls with black hair, black eyes
can join!" taunted the little Asian girls, black hair,
black eyes flashing, mirroring, mimicking what they heard
as the message of the medium, the message of the world-at-large:
   "Apartheid, segregation, self-determination!
   Segregation, apartheid, revolution!"
Like a contrapuntal hymn, like a curse that refrains in
a melody trapped.

Sometimes at night I touch the children when they're sleeping
and the coolness of my fingers sends shivers through them that
is a foreshadowing, a guilt imparted.

Dani doesn't paint herself yellow
the way I colored the sun.
The way she dances in its light as I watch from the shadow.
No, she says green is her favorite color.
"It's the color of life!"

From "Poem of the End": "Poets of Truth"

MARINA TSVETAYEVA

Translated and adapted by Daniela Gioseffi
with Sophia Buzevska

Thick as a horse's mane,
rain in our eyes. Hills ahead.
We've passed the outskirts.
Now we're far from town. . . .

Rain insanely tears at us.
We stand and part from each other.
In three months, we hope for
a few moments of sharing.

Outside! Comprehend? We're nationless!
That means we've passed the walls within.
Life's a place where it's forbidden
to live. Like the Hebrew quarter.

Isn't it more worthy to
become an eternal Jew?
Anyone not a viper
suffers the same pogrom.

Life's for converts only
Judases of all faiths.
Let's live on segregated, leprous islands,
or in hell, anywhere, only not

in a compromised life nurturing traitors,
among those who are sheep to butchers!
This passport which gives me the
right to live—I stamp. Under my feet.

Destroy as vengeance for the star
of David. For heaps of corpses,

and their executioners (Toothsome!) saying,
"after all, the Jews didn't want to live."

Ghetto of the resolute! Beyond this
ditch, no mercy abounds
in this most Christian of worlds,
all poets of truth are Jews!

Worldwide and *Awake*

FAZIL HÜSNÜ DAĞLARCA

Translated by Talât Sait Halman

Worldwide

Here or in India or in Africa
All things resemble each other.
Here or in India or in Africa
We feel the same love for grains.
Before death we tremble together.

Whatever tongue he may speak,
His eyes will utter the meaning.
Whatever tongue he may speak,
I hear the same winds
That he is gleaning.

We humans have fallen apart.
Boundaries of land split our mirth.
We humans have fallen apart.
Yet birds are brothers in the sky,
And wolves on the earth.

Awake

That we are sisters, that we are brothers
At the breasts of fire and air and mothers
Boy or girl, in an idiot's dream,
How does it escape us all
As the rivers roll?

That we are sisters, that we are brothers
As wheat grows green,
Lonelier than animals,
How is it we don't know, for heaven's sake,
The trees whisper it till daybreak?

That we are sisters, that we are brothers
The same star is Fate to us and to others
Since the first darkness of the earth,
It escapes us all, why,
Though we keep staring at the sky?

Appendix: Selected Human Rights Declarations and Statements on Race

The Seville Statement on Violence

UNESCO INTERNATIONAL SCHOLARS

Believing that it is our responsibility to address from our particular disciplines the most dangerous and destructive activities of our species, violence and war; recognizing that science is a human cultural product which cannot be definitive or all-encompassing; and gratefully acknowledging the support of the authorities of Seville and representatives of the Spanish UNESCO; we, the undersigned scholars from around the world and from relevant sciences, have met and arrived at the following Statement on Violence. In it, we challenge a number of alleged biological findings that have been used, even by some in our disciplines, to justify violence and war. Because the alleged findings have contributed to an atmosphere of pessimism in our time, we submit that the open, considered rejection of these misstatements can contribute significantly to the International Year of Peace.

Misuse of scientific theories and data to justify violence and war is not new but has been made since the advent of modern science. For example, the theory of evolution has been used to justify not only war, but also genocide, colonialism, and suppression of the weak.

We state our position in the form of five propositions. We are aware that there are many other issues about violence and war that could be fruitfully addressed from the standpoint of our disciplines, but we restrict ourselves here to what we consider a most important first step.

IT IS SCIENTIFICALLY INCORRECT to say that we have inherited a tendency to make war from our animal ancestors. Although fighting occurs widely throughout animal species, only a few cases of destructive intra-species fighting between organized groups have ever been reported among naturally living species, and none of these involve the use of tools designed to be weapons. Normal predatory feeding upon other species cannot be equated with intra-species violence. Warfare is a peculiarly human phenomenon and does not occur in other animals.

The fact that warfare has changed so radically over time indicates that it is a product of culture. Its biological connection is primarily through language which makes possible the coordination of groups, the transmission of technology, and the use of tools. War is biologically possible, but it is not inevitable, as evidenced by its variation in occurrence and nature over time and space. There are cultures which have not engaged in war for centuries, and there are cultures which have engaged in war frequently at some times and not at others.

IT IS SCIENTIFICALLY INCORRECT to say that war or any violent behavior is genetically programed into our human nature. While genes are involved at all levels of nervous system function, they provide a developmental potential that can be actualized only in conjunction with the ecological and social environment. While individuals vary in their predispositions to be affected by their experience, it is the interaction between their genetic endowment and conditions of nurturance that determines their personalities. Except for rare pathologies, the genes do not produce individuals necessarily predisposed to violence. Neither do they determine the opposite. While genes are co-involved in establishing our behavioral capacities, they do not by themselves specify the outcome.

IT IS SCIENTIFICALLY INCORRECT to say that in the course of human evolution there has been a selection for aggressive behavior more than for other kinds of behavior. In all well-studied species, status within the group is achieved by the ability to cooperate and to fulfill social functions relevant to the structure of that group. 'Dominance' involves social bondings and affiliations; it is not simply a matter of the possession and use of superior physical power, although it does involve aggressive behaviors. Where genetic selection for aggressive behavior has been artificially instituted in animals, it has rapidly succeeded in producing hyper-aggressive individuals; this indicates that aggression was not maximally selected under natural conditions. When such experimentally-created hyper-aggressive animals are present in a social group, they either disrupt its social structure or are driven out. Violence is neither in our evolutionary legacy nor in our genes.

IT IS SCIENTIFICALLY INCORRECT to say that humans have a 'violent brain.' While we do have the neural apparatus to act violently, it is not automatically activated by internal or external stimuli. Like higher primates and unlike other animals, our higher neural processes filter such stimuli before they can be acted upon. How we act is shaped by how we have been conditioned and socialized. There is nothing in our neurophysiology that compels us to react violently.

IT IS SCIENTIFICALLY INCORRECT to say that war is caused by 'instinct' or any single motivation. The emergence of modern warfare has been a journey from the primacy of emotional and motivational factors, sometimes called 'instincts,' to the primacy of cognitive factors. Modern war involves institutional use of personal characteristics such as obedience, suggestibility, and idealism, social skills such as language, and rational considerations such as cost-calculation, planning, and information processing. The technology of modern war has exaggerated traits associated with violence both in the training of actual combatants and in the preparation of support for war in the general population. As a result of this exaggeration, such traits are often mistaken to be the causes rather than the consequences of the process.

We conclude that biology does not condemn humanity to war, and that humanity can be freed from the bondage of biological pessimism and empowered with confidence to undertake the transformative tasks needed in this International Year of Peace and in the years to come. Although these tasks are mainly institutional and collective, they also rest upon the consciousness of individual participants for whom pessimism and optimism are crucial factors. Just as 'wars begin in the minds of men,' peace also begins in our minds. The same species who invented war is capable of inventing peace. The responsibility lies with each of us.

Seville, May 16, 1986

David Adams, Psychology, Wesleyan University, Middletown, CT, USA

S. A. Barnett, Ethology, The Australian National University, Canberra, Australia

N. P. Bechtereva, Neurophysiology, Institute for Experimental Medicine of Academy of Medical Sciences of USSR, Leningrad, USSR

Bonnie Frank Carter, Psychology, Albert Einstein Medical Center, Philadelphia, PA, USA

José M. Rodríguez Delgado, Neurophysiology, Centro de Estudios Neurobiológicos, Madrid, Spain

José Luis Díaz, Ethology, Instituto Mexicano de Psiquiatría, Mexico D.F., Mexico

Andrzej Eliasz, Individual Differences Psychology, Polish Academy of Sciences, Warsaw, Poland

Santiago Genovés, Biological Anthropology, Instituto de Estudios Antropolóqicos, Mexico D.F., Mexico

Benson E. Ginsburg, Behavior Genetics, University of Connecticut, Storrs, CT, USA

Jo Groebel, Social Psychology, Erziehungswissenschaftliche Hochschule, Landau, Federal Republic of Germany

Samir-Kumar Ghosh, Sociology, Indian Institute of Human Sciences, Calcutta, India

Robert Hinde, Animal Behavior, Cambridge University, UK

Richard E. Leakey, Physical Anthropology, National Museums of Kenya, Nairobi, Kenya

Taha H. Malasi, Psychiatry, Kuwait University, Kuwait

J. Martin Ramírez, Psychobiology, Universidad de Sevilla, Spain

Federico Mayor Zaragoza, Biochemistry, Universidad Autónoma, Madrid, Spain

Diana L. Mendoza, Ethology, Universidad de Sevilla, Spain

Ashis Nandy, Political Psychology, Center for the Study of Developing Societies, Delhi, India

John Paul Scott, Animal Behavior, Bowling Green State University, Bowling Green, OH, USA

Riitta Wahlström, Psychology, University of Jyväskylä, Finland

Two Statements on Race

UNESCO INTERNATIONAL SCHOLARS

*III. Proposals on the Biological Aspects of Race

MOSCOW, August 1964

The undersigned, assembled by UNESCO in order to give their views on the biological aspects of the race question and in particular to formulate the biological part for a statement foreseen for 1966 and intended to bring up to date and to complete the declaration on the nature of race and racial differences signed in 1951, have unanimously agreed on the following:

1. All men living today belong to a single species, *Homo sapiens,* and are derived from a common stock. There are differences of opinion regarding how and when different human groups diverged from this common stock.

2. Biological differences between human beings are due to differences in hereditary constitution and to the influence of the environment on this genetic potential. In most cases, those differences are due to the interaction of these two sets of factors.

3. There is great genetic diversity within all human populations. Pure races—in the sense of genetically homogeneous populations—do not exist in the human species.

4. There are obvious physical differences between populations living in different geographical areas of the world, in their average appearance. Many of these differences have a genetic component.

Most often the latter consist in differences in the frequency of the same hereditary characters.

5. Different classifications of mankind into major stocks, and of those into more restricted categories (races, which are groups of populations, or single populations) have been proposed on the basis of hereditary physical traits. Nearly all classifications recognize at least three major stocks.

* The Third Statement on Race by UNESCO Scholars. The first two statements are discussed and summarized in the Introduction to this book.

Since the pattern of geographic variation of the characteristics used in racial classification is a complex one, and since this pattern does not present any major discontinuity, these classifications, whatever they are, cannot claim to classify mankind into clearcut categories; moreover, on account of the complexities of human history, it is difficult to determine the place of certain groups within these racial classifications, in particular that of certain intermediate populations.

Many anthropologists, while stressing the importance of human variation, believe that the scientific interest of these classifications is limited, and even that they carry the risk of inviting abusive generalizations.

Differences between individuals within a race or within a population are often greater than the average differences between races or populations.

Some of the variable distinctive traits which are generally chosen as criteria to characterize a race are either independently inherited or show only varying degrees of association between them within each population. Therefore, the combination of these traits in most individuals does not correspond to the typological racial characterization.

6. In man as well as in animals, the genetic composition of each population is subject to the modifying influence of diverse factors: natural selection, tending towards adaptation to the environment, fortuitous mutations which lead to modifications of the molecules of deoxyribonucleic acid which determine heredity, or random modifications in the frequency of qualitative hereditary characters, to an extent dependent on the patterns of mating and the size of populations.

Certain physical characters have a universal biological value for the survival of the human species, irrespective of the environment. The differences on which racial classifications are based do not affect these characters, and therefore, it is not possible from the biological point of view to speak in any way whatsoever of a general inferiority or superiority of this or that race.

7. Human evolution presents attributes of capital importance which are specific to the species.

The human species which is now spread over the whole world, has a past rich in migrations, in territorial expansions and contractions.

As a consequence, general adaptability to the most diverse environments is in man more pronounced than his adaptation to specific environments.

For long millenniums progress made by man, in any field, seems to have been increasingly, if not exclusively, based on culture and the transmission of cultural achievements and not on the transmission of genetic endowment. This implies a modification in the role of natural selection in man today.

On account of the mobility of human populations and of social factors, mating between members of different human groups which tend to mitigate the differentiations acquired, has played a much more important role in human history than in that of animals. The history of any human population or of any human race, is rich in instances of hybridization and those tend to become more and more numerous.

For man, the obstacles to interbreeding are geographical as well as social and cultural.

8. At all times, the hereditary characteristics of the human populations are in dynamic equilibrium as a result of this interbreeding and of the differentiation mechanisms which were mentioned before. As entities defined by sets of distinctive traits, human races are at any time in a process of emergence and dissolution.

Human races in general present a far less clearcut characterization than many animal races and they cannot be compared at all to races of domestic animals, these being the result of heightened selection for special purposes.

9. It has never been proved that interbreeding has biological disadvantages for mankind as a whole.

On the contrary, it contributes to the maintenance of biological ties between human groups and thus to the unity of the species in its diversity.

The biological consequences of a marriage depend only on the individual genetic make-up of the couple and not on their race.

Therefore, no biological justification exists for prohibiting intermarriage between persons of different races, or for advising against it on racial grounds.

10. Man since his origin has at his disposal ever more efficient cultural means of nongenetic adaptation.

11. Those cultural factors which break social and geographic bar-

riers, enlarge the size of the breeding populations and so act upon their genetic structure by diminishing the random fluctuations (genetic drift).

12. As a rule, the major stocks extend over vast territories encompassing many diverse populations which differ in language, economy, culture, etc.

There is no national, religious, geographic, linguistic, or cultural group which constitutes a race *ipso facto;* the concept of race is purely biological.

However, human beings who speak the same language and share the same culture have a tendency to intermarry, and often there is as a result a certain degree of coincidence between physical traits on the one hand, and linguistic and cultural traits on the other. But there is no known causal nexus between these and therefore it is not justifiable to attribute cultural characteristics to the influence of the genetic inheritance.

13. Most racial classifications of mankind do not include mental traits or attributes as a taxonomic criterion.

Heredity may have an influence in the variability shown by individuals within a given population in their responses to the psychological tests currently applied.

However, no difference has ever been detected convincingly in the hereditary endowments of human groups in regard to what is measured by these tests. On the other hand, ample evidence attests to the influence of physical, cultural and social environment on differences in response to these tests.

The study of this question is hampered by the very great difficulty of determining what part heredity plays in the average differences observed in so-called tests of over-all intelligence between populations of different cultures.

The genetic capacity for intellectual development, like certain major anatomical traits peculiar to the species, is one of the biological traits essential for its survival in any natural or social environment.

The peoples of the world today appear to possess equal biological potentialities for attaining any civilizational level. Differences in the achievements of different peoples must be attributed solely to their cultural history.

Certain psychological traits are at times attributed to particular peoples. Whether or not such assertions are valid, we do not find any basis for ascribing such traits to hereditary factors, until proof to the contrary is given.

Neither in the field of hereditary potentialities concerning the overall intelligence and the capacity for cultural development, nor in that of physical traits, is there any justification for the concept of 'inferior' and 'superior' races.

The biological data given above stand in open contradiction to the tenets of racism. Racist theories can in no way pretend to have any scientific foundation and the anthropologists should endeavour to prevent the results of their researches from being used in such a biased way that they would serve non-scientific ends.

Moscow, 18 August 1964.

Professor Nigel Barnicot, Department of Anthropology, University College, London

Professor Jean Benoist, Director, Department of Anthropology, University of Montreal, Montreal

Professor Tadeusz Bielicki, Institute of Anthropology, Polish Academy of Sciences, Wroclaw

Dr. A. E. Boyo, Head, Federal Malaria Research Institute, Department of Pathology and Haematology, Lagos University Medical School, Lagos

Professor V. V. Bunak, Institute of Ethnography, Moscow

Professor Carleton S. Coon, Curator, The University Museum, University of Pennsylvania, Philadelphia, Pa. (United States)

Professor G. F. Debetz, Institute of Ethnography, Moscow

Mrs. Adelaide G. de Diaz Ungria, Curator, Museum of Natural Sciences, Caracas

Professor Santiago Genoves, Institute of Historical Research, Faculty of Sciences, University of Mexico, Mexico

Professor Robert Gessain, Director, Centre of Anthropological Research, Musée de l'Homme, Paris

Professor Jean Hiernaux (Scientific Director of the meeting), Laboratory of Anthropology, Faculty of Sciences,

University of Paris, Institute of Sociology, Free University of Brussels

Dr. Yaya Kane, Director, Senegal National Centre of Blood Transfusion, Dakar

Professor Ramakhrishna Mukherjee, Head, Sociological Research Unit, Indian Statistical Institute, Calcutta

Professor Bernard Rensch, Zoological Institute, Westfälische Wilhelms-Universität, Münster (Federal Republic of Germany)

Professor Y. Y. Roguinski, Institute of Ethnography, Moscow

Professor Francisco M. Salzano, Institute of Natural Sciences, Pôrto Alegre, Rio Grande do Sul (Brazil)

Professor Alf Sommerfelt, Rector, Oslo University, Oslo

Professor James N. Spuhler, Department of Anthropology, University of Michigan, Ann Arbor, Mich. (United States)

Professor Hisashi Suzuki, Department of Anthropology, Faculty of Science, University of Tokyo, Tokyo

Professor J. A. Valsik, Department of Anthropology and Genetics, J. A. Komensky University, Bratislava (Czechoslovakia)

Dr. Joseph S. Weiner, London School of Hygiene and Tropical Medicine, University of London, London

Professor V. P. Yakimov, Moscow State University, Institute of Anthropology, Moscow

*IV. Statement on Race and Racial Prejudice

PARIS, September 1967

1. "All men are born free and equal both in dignity and in rights." This universally proclaimed democratic principle stands in jeopardy wherever political, economic, social and cultural inequalities affect human group relations. A particularly striking obstacle to the recognition

---

* The Fourth Statement on Race by UNESCO Scholars. See Introduction, pp. xiii–xv for summary and discussion of I and II.

of equal dignity for all is racism. Racism continues to haunt the world. As a major social phenomenon it requires the attention of all students of the sciences of man.

2. Racism stultifies the development of those who suffer from it, perverts those who apply it, divides nations within themselves, aggravates international conflict and threatens world peace.

3. Conference of experts meeting in Paris in September 1967, agreed that racist doctrines lack any scientific basis whatsoever. It reaffirmed the propositions adopted by the international meeting held in Moscow in 1964 which was called to re-examine the biological aspects of the statements on race and racial differences issued in 1950 and 1951. In particular, it draws attention to the following points:

(a) All men living today belong to the same species and descend from the same stock.

(b) The division of the human species into "races" is partly conventional and partly arbitrary and does not imply any hierarchy whatsoever. Many anthropologists stress the importance of human variation, but believe that "racial" divisions have limited scientific interest and may even carry the risk of inviting abusive generalization.

(c) Current biological knowledge does not permit us to impute cultural achievements to differences in genetic potential. Differences in the achievements of different peoples should be attributed solely to their cultural history. The peoples of the world today appear to possess equal biological potentialities for attaining any level of civilization.

Racism grossly falsifies the knowledge of human biology.

4. The human problems arising from so-called "race" relations are social in origin rather than biological. A basic problem is racism, namely, antisocial beliefs and acts which are based on the fallacy that discriminatory intergroup relations are justifiable on biological grounds.

5. Groups commonly evaluate their characteristics in comparison with others. Racism falsely claims that there is a scientific basis for arranging groups hierarchically in terms of psychological and cultural characteristics that are immutable and innate. In this way it seeks to

make existing differences appear inviolable as a means of permanently maintaining current relations between groups.

6. Faced with the exposure of the falsity of its biological doctrines, racism finds ever new stratagems for justifying the inequality of groups. It points to the fact that groups do not intermarry, a fact which follows, in part, from the divisions created by racism. It uses this fact to argue the thesis that this absence of intermarriage derives from differences of a biological order. Whenever it fails in its attempts to prove that the source of group differences lies in the biological field, it falls back upon justifications in terms of divine purpose, cultural differences, disparity of educational standards or some other doctrine which would serve to mask its continued racist beliefs. Thus, many of the problems which racism presents in the world today do not arise merely from its open manifestations, but from the activities of those who discriminate on racial grounds but are unwilling to acknowledge it.

7. Racism has historical roots. It has not been a universal phenomenon. Many contemporary societies and cultures show little trace of it. It was not evident for long periods in world history. Many forms of racism have arisen out of the conditions of conquest, out of the justification of Negro slavery and its aftermath of racial inequality in the West, and out of the colonial relationship. Among other examples is that of antisemitism, which has played a particular role in history, with Jews being the chosen scapegoat to take the blame for problems and crises met by many societies.

8. The anti-colonial revolution of the twentieth century has opened up new possibilities for eliminating the scourge of racism. In some formerly dependent countries, people formerly classified as inferior have for the first time obtained full political rights. Moreover, the participation of formerly dependent nations in international organizations in terms of equality has done much to undermine racism.

9. There are, however, some instances in certain societies in which groups, victims of racialistic practices, have themselves applied doctrines with racist implications in their struggle for freedom. Such an attitude is a secondary phenomenon, a reaction stemming from men's search for an identity which prior racist theory and racialistic practices denied them. None the less, the new forms of racist ideology, resulting from this prior exploitation, have no justification in

biology. They are a product of a political struggle and have no scientific foundation.

10. In order to undermine racism it is not sufficient that biologists should expose its fallacies. It is also necessary that psychologists and sociologists should demonstrate its causes. The social structure is always an important factor. However, within the same social structure, there may be great individual variation in racialistic behaviour, associated with the personality of the individuals and their personal circumstances.

11. The committee of experts agreed on the following conclusions about the social causes of race prejudice:

(a) Social and economic causes of racial prejudice are particularly observed in settler societies wherein are found conditions of great disparity of power and property, in certain urban areas where there have emerged ghettoes in which individuals are deprived of equal access to employment, housing, political participation, education, and the administration of justice, and in many societies where social and economic tasks which are deemed to be contrary to the ethics or beneath the dignity of its members are assigned to a group of different origins who are derided, blamed, and punished for taking on these tasks.

(b) Individuals with certain personality troubles may be particularly inclined to adopt and manifest racial prejudices. Small groups, associations, and social movements of a certain kind sometimes preserve and transmit racial prejudices. The foundations of the prejudices lie, however, in the economic and social system of a society.

(c) Racism tends to be cumulative. Discrimination deprives a group of equal treatment and presents that group as a problem. The group then tends to be blamed for its own condition, leading to further elaboration of facist theory.

12. The major techniques for coping with racism involve changing those social situations which give rise to prejudice, preventing the prejudiced from acting in accordance with their beliefs, and combating the false beliefs themselves.

13. It is recognized that the basically important changes in the social structure that may lead to the elimination of racial prejudice may require decisions of a political nature. It is also recognized, however, that certain agencies of enlightenment, such as education and other means of social and economic advancement, mass media, and law can be immediately and effectively mobilized for the elimination of racial prejudice.

14. The school and other instruments for social and economic progress can be one of the most effective agents for the achievement of broadened understanding and the fulfilment of the potentialities of man. They can equally much be used for the perpetuation of discrimination and inequality. It is therefore essential that the resources for education and for social and economic action of all nations be employed in two ways:

(a) The schools should ensure that their curricula contain scientific understandings about race and human unity, and that invidious distinctions about peoples are not made in texts and classrooms.

(b) (i) Because the skills to be gained in formal and vocational education become increasingly important with the processes of technological development, the resources of the schools and other resources should be fully available to all parts of the population with neither restriction nor discrimination;

(ii) Furthermore, in cases where, for historical reasons, certain groups have a lower average education and economic standing, it is the responsibility of the society to take corrective measures. These measures should ensure, so far as possible, that the limitations of poor environments are not passed on to the children.

In view of the importance of teachers in any educational pro-Teachers should be made conscious of the degree to which they reflect the prejudices which may be current in their society. They should be encouraged to avoid these prejudices.

15. Governmental units and other organizations concerned

should give special attention to improving the housing situations and work opportunities available to victims of racism. This will not only counteract the effects of racism, but in itself can be a positive way of modifying racist attitudes and behaviour.

16. The media of mass communication are increasingly important in promoting knowledge and understanding, but their exact potentiality is not fully known. Continuing research into the social utilization of the media is needed in order to assess their influence in relation to formation of attitudes and behavioural patterns in the field of race prejudice and race discrimination. Because the mass media reach vast numbers of people at different educational and social levels, their role in encouraging or combating race prejudice can be crucial. Those who work in these media should maintain a positive approach to the promotion of understanding between groups and populations. Representation of peoples in stereotypes and holding them up to ridicule should be avoided. Attachment to news reports of racial designations which are not germane to the accounts should also be avoided.

17. Law is among the most important means of ensuring equality between individuals and one of the most effective means of fighting racism.

The Universal Declaration of Human Rights of 10 December 1948 and the related international agreements and conventions which have taken effect subsequently can contribute effectively, on both the national and international level, to the fight against any injustice of racist origin.

National legislation is a means of effectively outlawing racist propaganda and acts based upon racial discrimination. Moreover, the policy expressed in such legislation must bind not only the courts and judges charged with its enforcement, but also all agencies of government of whatever level or whatever character.

It is not claimed that legislation can immediately eliminate prejudice. Nevertheless, by being a means of protecting the victims of acts based upon prejudice, and by setting a moral example backed by the dignity of the courts, it can, in the long run, even change attitudes.

18. Ethnic groups which represent the object of some form of discrimination are sometimes accepted and tolerated by dominating groups at the cost of their having to abandon completely their cultural identity. It should be stressed that the effort of these ethnic groups to preserve their cultural values should be encouraged. They will thus be

better able to contribute to the enrichment of the total culture of humanity.

19. Racial prejudice and discrimination in the world today arise from historical and social phenomena and falsely claim the sanction of science. It is, therefore, the responsibility of all biological and social scientists, philosophers, and others working in related disciplines, to ensure that the results of their research are not misused by those who wish to propagate racial prejudice and encourage discrimination.

This statement was prepared by a committee of experts on race and racial prejudice which met at Unesco House, Paris, from 18 to 26 September 1967. The following experts took part in the committee's work:

Professor Muddathir Abdel Rahim, University of Khartoum (Sudan)

Professor Georges Balandier, Université de Paris (France)

Professor Celio de Oliveira Borja, University of Guanabara (Brazil)

Professor Lloyd Braithwaite, University of the West Indies (Jamaica)

Professor Leonard Broom, University of Texas (United States)

Professor G. F. Debetz, Institute of Ethnography, Moscow (U.S.S.R.)

Professor J. Djordjevic, University of Belgrade (Yugoslavia)

Dean Clarence Clyde Ferguson, Howard University (United States)

Dr. Dharam P. Ghai, University College (Kenya)

Professor Louis Guttman, Hebrew University (Israel)

Professor Jean Hiernaux, Université Libre de Bruxelles (Belgium)

Professor A. Kloskowska, University of Lodz (Poland)

Judge Kéba M'Baye, President of the Supreme Court (Senegal)

Professor John Rex, University of Durham (United Kingdom)

Professor Mariano R. Solveira, University of Havana (Cuba)

Professor Hisashi Suzuki, University of Tokyo (Japan)

Dr. Romila Thapar, University of Delhi (India)

Professor C. H. Waddington, University of Edinburgh (United Kingdom)

*Women's Pentagon Action** Unity Statement

COLLECTIVELY WRITTEN, APRIL 1982

For two years we have gathered at the Pentagon because we fear for our lives. We still fear for the life of this planet, our Earth, and the life of the children who are our human future.

We are women who come in most part from the northeastern region of our United States. We are city women who know the wreckage and fear of city streets; we are country women who grieve the loss of the small farm and have lived on the poisoned earth. We are young and older, we are married, single, lesbian. We live in different kinds of households, in groups, families, alone; some are single parents.

We work at a variety of jobs. We are students-teachers-factory workers-office workers-lawyers-farmers-doctors-builders-waitresses-weavers - poets - engineers - homeworkers - electricians - artists - blacksmiths. We are all daughters and sisters.

We came to mourn and rage and defy the Pentagon because It Is the workplace of the imperial power which threatens us all. Every day while we work, study, love, the colonels and generals who are planning our annihilation walk calmly in and out the doors of its five sides. They have accumulated over 30,000 nuclear bombs at the rate of three to six bombs every day.

They are determined to produce the billion-dollar MX missile. They are creating a technology called Stealth—the invisible, unperceivable arsenal. They have revived the cruel old killer, nerve gas. They have proclaimed Directive 59 which asks for "small nuclear wars, prolonged but limited." The Soviet Union works hard to keep up with United States initiatives. We can destroy each other's cities, towns, schools, children many times over. The United States has sent "advisors," money and arms to El Salvador and Guatamala to enable those juntas to massacre their own people.

The very same men, the same legislative committees that offer trillions of dollars to the Pentagon have brutally cut day care, children's lunches, battered women's shelters. The same men have concocted the Family Protection Act which will mandate the strictly pa-

---

* See note p. 685, Grace Paley, Sybil Claiborne, Vera Williams, WRL, et. al.

triarchal family and thrust federal authority into the lives we live in our own homes. They are preventing the passage of ERA's simple statement and supporting the Human Life Amendment which will deprive all women of choice and many women of life itself.

In this environment of contempt and violence, racism, woman-hating and the old European habit of Jew-hatred—called anti-semitism —all find their old roots and grow.

We are in the hands of men whose power and wealth have separated them from the reality of daily life and from the imagination. We are right to be afraid.

At the same time our cities are in ruins, bankrupt; they suffer the devastation of war. Hospitals are closed, our schools deprived of books and teachers. Our Black and Latino youth are without decent work. They will be forced, drafted to become the cannon fodder for the very power that oppresses them. Whatever help the poor receive is cut or withdrawn to feed the Pentagon which needs about $500,000,000 a day for its murderous health. It extracted $157 billion dollars last year from our own tax money, $1800 from a family of four.

With this wealth our scientists have been corrupted; over 40% work in government and corporate laboratories that refine the methods for destroying or deforming life.

The lands of the Native American people have been turned to radioactive rubble in order to enlarge the nuclear warehouse. The uranium of South Africa, necessary to the nuclear enterprise, enriches the white minority and encourages the vicious system of racist oppression and war.

The President has just decided to produce the neutron bomb, which kills people but leaves property (buildings like this one) intact.

There is fear among the people, and that fear, created by the industrial militarists is used as an excuse to accelerate the arms race. "We will protect you . . ." they say, but we have never been so endangered, so close to the end of human time.

We women are gathering because life on the precipice is intolerable.

We want to know what anger in these men, what fear which can only be satisfied by destruction, what coldness of heart and ambition drives their days.

We want to know because we do not want that dominance which is exploitative and murderous in international relations, and so dangerous to women and children at home—we do not want that sickness transferred by the violent society through the fathers to the sons.

What is it that we women need for our ordinary lives, that we want for ourselves and also for our sisters in new nations and old colonies who suffer the white man's exploitation and too often the oppression of their own countrymen?

We want enough good food, decent housing, communities with clean air and water, good care for our children while we work. We want work that is useful to a sensible society. There is a modest technology to minimize drudgery and restore joy to labor. We are determined to use skills and knowledge from which we have been excluded —like plumbing or engineering or physics or composing. We intend to form women's groups or unions that will demand safe workplaces, free of sexual harassment, equal pay for work of comparable value. We respect the work women have done in caring for the young, their own and others, in maintaining a physical and spiritual shelter against the greedy and militaristic society. In our old age we expect our experience, our skills, to be honored and used.

We want health care which respects and understands our bodies. Physically challenged sisters must have access to gatherings, actions, happy events, work.

We want an education for children which tells the true story of our women's lives, which describes the earth as our home to be cherished, to be fed as well as harvested.

We want to be free from violence in our streets and in our houses. One in every three of us will be raped in her lifetime. The pervasive social power of the masculine ideal and the greed of the pornographer have come together to steal our freedom, so that whole neighborhoods and the life of the evening and night have been taken from us. For too many women the dark country road and the city alley have concealed the rapist. We want the night returned, the light of the moon, special in the cycle of our female lives, the stars and the gaiety of the city streets.

We want the right to have or not to have children—we do not want gangs of politicians and medical men to say we must be sterilized for the country's good. We know that this technique is the racist's method for controlling populations. Nor do we want to be prevented from having an abortion when we need one. We think this freedom should be available to poor women as it always has been to the rich. We want to be free to love whomever we choose. We will live with women or with men or we will live alone. We will not allow the oppression of lesbians. One sex or one sexual preference must not dominate another.

We do not want to be drafted into the army. We do not want our young brothers drafted. We want *them* equal with *us*.

We want to see the pathology of racism ended in our time. It has been the imperial arrogance of white male power that has separated us from the suffering and wisdom of our sisters in Asia, Africa, South America and in our own country.

To some women racism has offered privilege and convenience. These women often fail to see that they themselves have lived under the unnatural authority and violence of men in governement, at work, at home. Privilege does not increase knowledge or spirit or understanding. There can be no peace while one race dominates another, one people, one nation, one sex despises another.

We must not forget that tens of thousands of American women live much of their lives in cages, away from family, lovers, all the growing-years of their children. Most of them were born at the intersection of oppressions: people of color, female, poor. Women on the outside have been taught to fear those sisters. We refuse that separation. We need each other's knowledge and anger in our common struggle against the builders of jails and bombs.

We want the uranium left in the earth and the earth given back to the people who tilled it. We want a system of energy which is renewable, which does not take resources out of the earth without returning them. We want those systems to belong to the people and their communities, not to the giant corporations which invariably turn knowledge into weaponry. We want the sham of Atoms for Peace ended, all nuclear plants decommissioned and the construction of new plants stopped. That is another war against the people and the child to be born in fifty years.

We want an end to the arms race. No more bombs. No more amazing inventions for death.

We understand all is connectedness. The earth nourishes us as we with our bodies will eventually feed it. Through us, our mothers connected the human past to the human future. We know the life and work of animals and plants in seeding, reseeding and in fact simply inhabiting this planet. Their exploitation and the organized destruction of never to be seen again species threatens and sorrows us.

With that sense, that ecological right, we oppose the financial connections between the Pentagon and the multinational corporations and banks that the Pentagon serves.

Those connections are made of gold and oil.

We are made of blood and bone, we are made of the sweet and finite resource, water.

We will not allow these violent games to continue. If we are here in our stubborn thousands today, we will certainly return in the hundreds of thousands in the months and years to come.

We know there is a healthy sensible loving way to live and we intend to live that way in our neighborhoods and our farms in these United States, and among our sisters and brothers in all the countries of the world.

Disabled People's Bill of Rights*

AMERICAN COALITION OF CITIZENS WITH DISABILITIES

Preamble

We believe that all people should enjoy certain rights. Because people with disabilities have consistently been denied the right to fully participate in society as free and equal members, it is important to state and affirm these rights. All people should be able to enjoy these rights, regardless of race, creed, color, sex, religion, or disability.

1. The right to live independent, active, and full lives.
2. The right to the equipment, assistance, and support services necessary for full productivity, provided in a way that promotes dignity and independence.

* Reprinted by permission of the American Coalition of Citizens with Disabilities, 1200 15th Street, N.W., Washington, D.C. 20005.

3. The right to an adequate income or wage, substantial enough to provide food, clothing, shelter, and other necessities of life.

4. The right to accessible, integrated, convenient, and affordable housing.

5. The right to quality physical and mental health care.

6. The right to training and employment without prejudice or stereotype.

7. The right to accessible transportation and freedom of movement.

8. The right to bear or adopt and raise children and have a family.

9. The right to a free and appropriate public education.

10. The right to participate in and benefit from entertainment and recreation.

11. The right of equal access to and use of all businesses, facilities, and activities in the community.

12. The right to communicate freely with all fellow citizens and those who provide services.

13. The right to a barrier free environment.

14. The right to legal representation and to full protection of all legal rights.

15. The right to determine one's own future and make one's own life choices.

16. The right of full access to all voting processes.

The United Nations Universal Declaration of Human Rights

Whereas recognition of the inherent dignity and of the equal and inalienable rights of all members of the human family is the foundation of freedom, justice and peace in the world,

Whereas disregard and contempt for human rights have resulted in barbarous acts which have outraged the conscience of mankind, and the advent of a world in which human beings shall enjoy freedom of speech and belief and freedom from fear and want has been proclaimed as the highest aspiration of the common people,

Whereas it is essential, if man is not to be compelled to have recourse, as a last resort, to rebellion against tyranny and oppression, that human rights should be protected by the rule of law,

Whereas it is essential to promote the development of friendly relations between nations,

Whereas the peoples of the United Nations have in the Charter reaffirmed their faith in fundamental human rights, in the dignity and worth of the human person and in the equal rights of men and women and have determined to promote social progress and better standards of life in larger freedom,

Whereas Member States have pledged themselves to achieve, in co-operation with the United Nations, the promotion of universal respect for and observance of human rights and fundamental freedoms,

Whereas a common understanding of these rights and freedoms is of the greatest importance for the full realization of this pledge,

Now, therefore, the General Assembly:

Proclaims this Universal Declaration of Human Rights as a common standard of achievement for all peoples and all nations, to the end that every individual and every organ of society, keeping this Declaration constantly in mind, shall strive by teaching and education to promote respect for these rights and freedoms and by progressive measures, national and international, to secure their universal and effective recognition and observance, both among the peoples of Member States themselves and among the peoples of territories under their jurisdiction.

Article 1: All human beings are born free and equal in dignity and rights. They are endowed with reason and conscience and should act towards one another in a spirit of brotherhood.

Article 2: Everyone is entitled to all the rights and freedoms set forth in this Declaration, without distinction of any kind, such as race, color, sex, language, religion, political or other opinion, national and social origin, property, birth or other status.

Furthermore, no distinction shall be made on the basis of the political, jurisdictional or international status of the country or territory to which a person belongs, whether it be independent, trust, non-self-governing or under any other limitation of sovereignty.

Article 3: Everyone has the right to life, liberty and security of person.

Article 4: No one shall be held in slavery or servitude; slavery and the slave trade shall be prohibited in all their forms.

Article 5: No one shall be subjected to torture or to cruel, inhuman or degrading treatment or punishment.

Article 6: Everyone has the right to recognition everywhere as a person before the law.

Article 7: All are equal before the law and are entitled without any discrimination to equal protection of the law. All are entitled to equal protection against any discrimination in violation of this Declaration and against any incitement to such discrimination.

Article 8: Everyone has the right to an effective remedy by the competent national tribunals for acts violating the fundamental rights granted him by the constitution or by law.

Article 9: No one shall be subjected to arbitrary arrest, detention or exile.

Article 10: Everyone is entitled in full equality to a fair and public hearing by an independent and impartial tribunal, in the determination of his rights and obligations and of any criminal charge against him.

Article 11: Everyone charged with a penal offence has the right to be presumed innocent until proved guilty according to law in a public trial at which he has had all the guarantees necessary for his defence. No one shall be held guilty of any penal offence on account of any act or omission which did not constitute a penal offence, under national or international law, at the time when it was committed. Nor shall a heavier penalty be imposed than the one that was applicable at the time the penal offence was committed.

Article 12: No one shall be subjected to arbitrary interference with his privacy, family, home or correspondence, nor to attacks upon his honors and reputation. Everyone has the right to the protection of the law against such interference or attacks.

Article 13: Everyone has the right to freedom of movement and residence within the borders of each State. Everyone has the right to leave any country, including his own, and to return to his country.

Article 14: Everyone has the right to seek and enjoy in other countries asylum from persecution. This right may not be invoked in the case of prosecutions genuinely arising from non-political crimes or from acts contrary to the purposes and principles of the United Nations.

Article 15: Everyone has the right to a nationality. No one shall be arbitrarily deprived of his nationality nor denied the right to change his nationality.

Article 16: Men and women of full age, without any limitation due to race, nationality or religion, have the right to marry and to found a family. They are entitled to equal rights as to marriage, during marriage and at its dissolution. Marriage shall be entered into only with the free and full consent of the intending spouses. The family is the natural and fundamental group unit of society and is entitled to protection by society and the State.

Article 17: Everyone has the right to own property alone as well as in association with others. No one shall be arbitrarily deprived of his property.

Article 18: Everyone has the right to freedom of thought, conscience and religion; this right includes freedom to change his religion or belief, either alone or in community with others and in public or private, to manifest his religion or belief in teaching, practice, worship and observance.

Article 19: Everyone has the right to freedom of opinion and expression; this right includes freedom to hold opinions without interference and to seek, receive and impart information and ideas through any media and regardless of frontiers.

Article 20: Everyone has the right to freedom of peaceful assembly and association. No one may be compelled to belong to an association.

Article 21: Everyone has the right to take part in the government of his country, directly or through freely chosen representatives. Everyone has the right to equal access to public service in his country. The will of the people shall be the basis of the authority of government; this will shall be expressed in periodic and genuine elections which shall be by universal and equal suffrage and shall be held by secret vote or by equivalent free voting procedures.

Article 22: Everyone, as a member of society, has the right to social security and is entitled to realization, through national effort and international co-operation and in accordance with the organization and resources of each State, of the economic, social and cultural rights indispensable for his dignity and the free development of his personality.

Article 23: Everyone has the right to work, to free choice of employment, to just and favorable conditions of work and to protection against unemployment. Everyone, without any discrimination, has the right to equal pay for equal work. Everyone who works has the right to just and favorable remuneration ensuring for himself and his family an existence worthy of human dignity, and supplemented, if necessary, by other means of social protection. Everyone has the right to form and to join trade unions for the protection of his interests.

Article 24: Everyone has the right to rest and leisure, including reasonable limitation of working hours and periodic holidays with pay.

Article 25: Everyone has the right to a standard of living adequate for the health and well-being of himself and of his family, including food, clothing, housing and medical care and necessary social services, and the right to security in the event of unemployment, sickness, disability, widowhood, old age or other lack of livelihood in circumstances beyond his control. Motherhood and childhood are entitled to special care and assistance. All children, whether born in or out of wedlock, shall enjoy the same social protection.

Article 26: Everyone has the right to education. Education shall be free, at least in the elementary and fundamental stages. Elementary education shall be compulsory. Technical and professional education shall be made generally available and higher education shall be equally accessible to all on the basis of merit. Education shall be directed to the full development of the human personality and to the strengthening of respect for human rights and fundamental freedoms. It shall promote understanding, tolerance and friendship among all nations, racial or religious groups, and shall further the activities of the United Nations for the maintenance of peace. Parents have a prior right to choose the kind of education that shall be given to their children.

Article 27: Everyone has the right freely to participate in the cultural life of the community, to enjoy the arts and to share in scientific advancement and its benefits. Everyone has the right to the protection of the moral and material interests resulting from any scientific, literary or artistic production of which he is the author.

Article 28: Everyone is entitled to a social and international order in which the rights and freedoms set forth in this Declaration can be fully realized.

Article 29: Everyone has duties to the community in which alone the free and full development of his personality is possible. In the exercise of his rights and freedoms, everyone shall be subject only to such limitations as are determined by law solely for the purpose of securing due recognition and respect for the rights and freedoms of others and of meeting the just requirements of morality, public order and the general welfare in a democratic society. These rights and freedoms may in no case be exercised contrary to the purposes and principles of the United Nations.

Article 30: Nothing in this Declaration may be interpreted as implying for any State, group or person any right to engage in any activity or to perform any act aimed at the destruction of any of the rights and freedoms set forth herein.

Bibliographical Biographies of Contributors

MONA ELAINE ADILMAN (1924–1991), born in Montreal, Canada, was an internationally published poet, activist, dedicated ecologist, and composer of musical comedies. A pioneer in the fight to preserve vanishing open lands and an early crusader against harmful pesticides, she taught Literature and Ecology at Concordia University. A lifelong advocate of human and animal rights, she edited an anthology of international poetry by prisoners of conscience, *Spirits of the Age* (1989). Her books include *Cult of Concrete* and *Candles in the Dark,* her latest work.

PAULA GUNN ALLEN has published five books of poems and a novel, as well as the nonfiction *Spider Woman's Granddaughters* and *Grandmothers of the Light* (Beacon Press, Boston). She is a leading Native American feminist author and spokesperson for her people. The selection printed here was originally excerpted from *The Sacred Hoop: Recovering the Feminine in American Indian Tradition* (Beacon Press, 1986, 1992). All of her books are recommended reading, as is her novel *The Woman Who Owned the Shadows.* She is a foremost Native American literary critic.

MAYA ANGELOU (b. 1928), American author, performer, and Black activist, was born in St. Louis, Missouri. After her parents' divorce, she and her brother lived with their grandmother in Stamps, Arkansas. Overcoming abuse as a child, she survived her painful history, and that spirit of transcendence gives profundity to her work. In her teens she moved to California and began a multifaceted career in what she calls a "roller coaster life." In the 1920s she toured Europe and Africa in Gershwin's *Porgy and Bess* as a dancer. During that tour, she found her rich and moving natural voice by singing Black spirituals while the rest of the company trained on European opera. Part of the "Black soul" cultural movement in the United States, she joined the famed Harlem Writers Guild while she earned her living singing in nightclubs and performing in Jean Genet's *The Blacks.* In the 1960s during her involvement in the civil rights movement, she met Malcolm X, among many Black activists, and then spent several years in Ghana as editor of *African Review.* Her multivolume autobiography, beginning with *I Know Why the Caged Bird Sings* (1970), was an enormous success, full of triumph over adversity, humor, and folk wisdom. She has published several collections of verse, including *Still I Rise* (1987), which contains the poem selected here. She has served, in recent years, as the Reynolds Professor of American Studies at Wake Forest University, Winston-Salem, North Carolina. She attracted great attention for her participation in the Clinton inaugural in January 1993, the first poet since Robert Frost (and the only other) to participate in the inauguration of a U.S. president. She was a contributor to this editor's last compendium, *Women on War*. Though Angelou campaigns against censorship, she stands for a meaningful rather than a decadent or elite form of art, from, to, of, and by the people, all the people. She believes that a nation without poetry becomes "brutish," a conviction shared by this anthologist—herein mixing poetry, fiction, and nonfiction for a balance of *pathos, ethos,* and *logos*.

WILLIAM APES (1798–1836?), known only by his white name, was a mixed-blood, part Pequod Indian descended from King Philip (Metacomet, son of Massasoit) of the Pequod Nation, New England's coastal tribe. He lived during the period when Pilgrims and Puritans poured into the New World and demanded more land of indigenous peoples. He observed the history of continuing strife, a legacy of the long Pequod Wars, begun in 1637, when the colonists set fire to the Pequod stronghold and massacred its inhabitants over a land dispute resulting in the death of a white trader. European styles of land ownership were alien to formerly friendly and welcoming native tribes of New England who saw their lands as merely leased to all by the benevolence of the Great Spirit. The concept of land ownership brought to the New World by white Europeans caused rebellion among the natives, who depended upon sustenance from the land. The half-breed William Apes was ordained a Methodist preacher in 1829, as an example of Christianity's mission in the New World. In 1836, having been established in his parish at the Odeon on Federal Street in Boston, he delivered a stirring eulogy on King Philip, the famed warrior chief of the Pequod. The eulogy revealed that William Apes was a preacher/activist for his people, as Martin Luther King, Jr., would be more than a century later. Soon after his rousing oratory, Apes disappeared mysteriously, probably murdered by white extremists. Apes was the author of the first published Native American biography, *The Complete Writings of William Apes, a Pequod* (edited by Barry O. Connell, 1992). Apes's work foreshadowed other illustrious Native American biographies of the nineteenth century such as *The Travels of Kah-ge-ga-gah-bowh* (1847) and *Sarah Winnemucca Hopkin's Life among the Piutes* (1883). Such narratives in turn heralded the current renaissance of Native American literature. (Also see MAURICE KENNY, JOSEPH BRUCHAC, and PAULA GUNN ALLEN.)

PHILIP APPLEMAN (b. 1926) was graduated from high school in his home state of Indiana and went immediately into the U.S. Army Air Corps during World

War II and later into the merchant marine. His war experiences have influenced his view and inspired his antiwar themes. Having taken a Ph.D. at Northwestern University, he returned to his native state to teach, culminating his teaching career as Distinguished Professor of English at Indiana University. He has published six volumes of poetry, the latest of which are *Darwin's Ark* (Indiana University Press, 1984) and *Let There Be Light* (HarperCollins, 1991), both with poems on prejudice, the latter containing the selection reprinted here. He has also published three novels and several works of nonfiction, including the widely used Norton Critical Edition of *Darwin*. He lives on Long Island with his wife, the playwright Marjorie Appleman.

JAMES BALDWIN (1924–1987), internationally known and celebrated Black American author, was born and brought up in a particularly impoverished area of New York's Harlem—the primary location of the modern African American cultural renaissance. After many odd jobs, he moved to Europe, where he lived as an expatriate writer, mainly in Paris, from 1948 to 1957. He returned to the states to participate in the civil rights movement, lending his eloquent voice against racism's injustices. His novels, essays, and plays, which contain many autobiographical elements of his experience of injustice and prejudice, are all relevant to the understanding of xenophobia: *Go Tell It on the Mountain* (1954), *Giovanni's Room* (1957), *Another Country* (1963), *Tell Me How Long the Train's Been Gone* (1968), *Just above My Head* (1979), *Notes of a Native Son* (1955), *The Fire Next Time* (1963), *The Amen Corner* (1955), *Blues for Mr. Charlie* (1964), and *The Women at the Well* (1972). All are recommended reading. He died in the south of France, disillusioned with the slow progress of the civil rights movement and its meager accomplishments, but ever forward-thinking and hopeful of true change.

AMIRI BARAKA (b. 1934), formerly known as LeRoi Jones, is a successful civil rights organizer as well as an educator and prominent writer. His first book, *Preface to a Twenty Volume Suicide Note* (1961), brought him national attention. His poetry and fiction won him a John Hay Whitney fellowship in 1961. In a few years he was instrumental in creating an uncompromising radical Black literary movement. His highly charged, original poetry brought him attention from the avant-garde. In 1964 he received an Obie Award for his drama *Dutchman* and in 1966 a prize for *The Slave* at the First World Festival of Drama in Dakar, Senegal. In 1969 he published *Four Black Revolutionary Plays* and in 1967, *Baptism and the Toilet*. His anthology *Black Fire: An Anthology of Afro-American Writing* (1968), edited with Larry Neal, was among the seminal works of the contemporary Black Power and Black Is Beautiful movements in literature. A prolific critic of Black literature and music, as well as a gifted sociopolitical commentator controversial, like Malcolm X, for his new Black nationalism, Amiri Baraka offers an astute and timely analysis of racism.

STANLEY BARKAN (b. 1936), born in Brooklyn, is editor and publisher of the *Cross-Cultural Review Series of World Literature and Art in Sound, Print, and Motion*. He codirected the Reading Series at the United Nations and was the recipient of the 1991 NYC Poetry Teacher of the Year Award. His latest book is *Bubbes and Bubbemeises* (Lincoln Springs Press, 1993), from which the poem printed here comes. He lives in Merrick, New York, with his two children and wife, Bebe Barkan, an artist and educator who illustrates and designs for his extensive and internationally celebrated Cross-Cultural Series. The Barkans are worldwide pioneers of the multicultural movement in literature and have produced more than seventy-five titles of bilingual literary art for an international audience.

HELEN BAROLINI (b. c. 1940) was born and raised in Syracuse and graduated magna cum laude from Syracuse University. She lived for many years in Italy with her three daughters and her husband, the Italian author Antonio Barolini. Her books include intercultural novels: *Umbertina* and *Love in the Middle Ages*. She edited the ground-breaking anthology of Italian American women writers *The Dream Book* and brought out *Festa: Recipes and Recollections of Italian Holidays* and *Aldus and His Dream Book*. Her forthcoming essay collection is titled *A Circular Journey*. Her stories and essays have appeared in many literary reviews and collections, with a citation in *Best American Essays, 1991*. She's had an NEA award, a 1986 American Book Award and a Susan Koppelman Award for the best anthology in the feminist study of American culture.

MATSUO BASHO (1644–1694), of samurai warrior blood, was born at a time when Japan was stable and at peace and the warrior class was devoting itself to the arts, particularly poetry, a popular genre of the day. At age eight he became the page of a nobleman's son, Sengin, young lord of a castle in Iga, in the south of Japan. From Sengin and his master, Kigin, Basho became schooled in the art of poetry as it was then practiced—a succinct and subtle form known as *haiku*. Basho invented his own style at Kyoto and became known for his work in Tokyo, where he followed Kigin after the death of his young lord. He converted to Zen Buddhism in 1681 and thereafter produced the most powerful works of his career, as a teacher of compassion and tolerance. Among his works are *Sarashina Journey* and *Narrow Roads in Oku*. His works are premier classics of Japanese culture.

LERONE BENNETT, JR. (b. 1928) is known as the "resident historian" of the Johnson Publishing Company, which publishes *Ebony, Jet,* and *Ebony, Jr.* Born in Clarksdale, Mississippi, and educated in the public schools of Jackson, he became student editor of the newspaper at Morehouse College in Atlanta and, in 1960, senior editor of *Ebony.* The author of many books, he received the Literature Award from the American Academy of Arts and Science in 1978. In 1969 he published a revised and enlarged edition of *Before the Mayflower: A History of Black America,* documenting the arrival of Africans in the United States preceding the arrival of European colonists. One of his most renowned works is *Wade in the Water: Great Moments in Black History* (1979). In 1982 he published his fifth revised and enlarged edition of this popular Black history. He is also a nationally known lecturer on the subject— and on all issues of racism. The selection printed here is from Studs Terkel's *Race* (Norton and Anchor, New York, 1992). Bennet's works are particularly useful reading.

PHYLLIS BISCHOF, an eminent bibliophile fully schooled in the subject of which she writes, prefers to state simply that she is a librarian of the African and African American collections at the University of California at Berkeley.

CHIEF ANDREW J. BLACKBIRD (c. 1840–?) of the Ottawa Nation wrote his indictment of the British conquerers' heinous crimes in 1887. The Ottawas and the Ojibways or Chippewas held the Great Lakes region and were the most formidable enemies of the British who were competing with the French for control of the land. The Pequods, Naticks, and Narragansetts, who had welcomed the Pilgrims to Plymouth, had been nearly exterminated by ruthless war crimes perpetrated by xenophobic Puritans and other British settlers. Several historians say that the British resorted to germ warfare to assassinate native tribes in large numbers. Nearly two thousand Ottawa people and nearby native tribes died from an epidemic of smallpox. Germ warfare, a growing concern in our technological times—especially since its hugely expanded research during the Reagan and Bush years—was not a new idea even in the eighteenth century. General Jeffrey Amherst had recommended use of smallpox to his soldiers: "You will be well advised to infect the Indians with sheets upon which small pox patients have been lying or by any other means which may serve to exterminate this accursed race. I should be very glad if your plan of hunting them down with dogs were to prove practicable," Amherst wrote.

BLACK HAWK (1767–1838) was a famed Sauk warrior, commended for dignity and bravery and mercy toward his enemies, who by the time he was thirty-five had triumphed over many warriors of the Osage and Cherokee—for there was war and ethnocentrism *between* native tribes before and after Europeans began to colonize North America. Black Hawk came to fame in 1832 when compelled to fight U.S. troops in northern Illinois in a war which involved the twenty-three-year-old Abe Lincoln, captain of a company of volunteers. The odds were too great against Black Hawk. The government in Washington had suddenly sent many more troops to the frontier, and Black Hawk's braves were pushed up into Wisconsin, onto a small island in the Bad Axe River where the aged brave fought his last battle. Black Hawk never knew that his Winnebago guides had treacherously betrayed him and were bought by the white enemy. Just as Black slave traders sold Black slaves to Europeans—making slave trading possible on a larger scale than it might have been (see JAN ROGOZIŃKI's "The World of the Slaves")—so many Native American tribes were set against each other by "divide and conquer" tactics, a timeless technique of the conquerers which depends on prejudice and treachery between or among the vanquished natives. (See the Introduction to this book.) Black Hawk surrendered rather than have his remaining braves massacred. He was delivered in bondage to Washington where he told President Jackson he had taken up the tomahawk only under duress from his people to avenge monumental injuries which could no longer be tolerated by them as rightful inhabitants of the land. He dictated the passage included here in 1833 to Brigadier General H. Atkinson in his last attempt at diplomacy for the sake of his now greatly outnumbered tribe.

ELENA (YELENA) BONNER (b. 1923), a Soviet civil rights activist, was born in Moscow. Following the arrest of her parents in Stalin's purge of 1937, and after the execution of her father and the jailing of her mother, she was taken to Leningrad by her grandmother. Her eyes were seriously injured when she served as a lieutenant in the army during World War II. After the war she married and worked as a physician, separating from her husband in 1965, when she joined the Communist party of the Soviet Union. She became disaffected and disillusioned—like so many—upon the Soviet invasion of Czechoslovakia in 1968 and moved toward a dissident position. She then married the famed Soviet dissident Andrei Sakharov in 1971 and resigned from the Communist party shortly after. For fourteen years she and Sakharov inspired the Soviet dissident movement, much as Nelson and Winnie Mandela of South Africa became an active worldwide symbol of resistance. In 1980, Sakharov was banished to silence or "internal exile" in Gorky. Bonner met the same fate in 1984, but after hunger strikes like GANDHI's, a technique often used as well by Irish resistance fighters, she was given the chance to travel to Italy for special eye treatments. The couple was finally released from Gorky in 1986 under Gorbachev's *glasnost* policy. Sakharov died in 1989, but Bonner remains a prominent campaigner for democracy. She is author of the memoir *Alone Together* (Knopf, New York, 1986). The excerpt printed here is from a longer piece translated from the Russian by Antonina W. Bouis.

LADY BORTON first went to Vietnam more than twenty years ago on assignment with The American Friends Service Committee during the war. Because of her healing work and successful cross-cultural communication, she became the only foreigner whom the Vietnamese trusted to live and work with a family in a village. She is the author of *Sensing the Enemy: An American Woman Among the Boat People of Vietnam* (Dial/Doubleday, 1984) and *After Sorrow: An American Among the Vietnamese* (Viking Penguin, 1994). She has written "Hers" columns in the *New York Times* and is a weekly op-ed columnist for the *Akron Beacon Journal* as well as a regular commentator for National Public Radio's "Sunday Weekend Edition." For many years she lived on a farm in Appalachian Ohio, driving a school bus for children and adults with mental retardation and developmental disabilities. She now lives in Philadelphia with the Quaker Friends Service Committee. Her books are an excellent focus for intercultural understanding and do much to break down stereotypical attitudes toward Asians.

HAIG A. BOSMAJIAN (b. 1928) is a professor in the Department of Speech and Communication at the University of Washington. His principal areas of scholarship and interest are dissent, the First Amendment freedoms of the U.S. Constitution, and rhetoric and language. He received the George Orwell Award from the National Council of Teachers of English in 1983 for his book *The Language of Oppression,* excerpted here. In 1991 he was the recipient of the Western Speech Communication Association's Bicentennial of the Bill of Rights Award. His most recent publications include the five-volume First Amendment in the Classroom Series (Neal-Schuman, Publishers) and *Metaphor and Reason in Judicial Opinions* (Southern Illinois University Press). This essay on the semantics of prejudice, though written before the enactment of recent "verbal" assault legislation against biased crimes in various U.S. states, is extremely vital today.

GWENDOLYN BROOKS (b. 1917) was born in Topeka, Kansas, and is a poet, novelist and educator who taught poetry at Columbia College and Northeastern Illinois College, Chicago. She was the first Black woman to win the Pulitzer Prize for Poetry (1950) and has served as a consultant in poetry to the Library of Congress (1985–86). She is a member of the Illinois Arts Council, Poet Laureate of Illinois, and the recipient of a Lifetime Achievement Award from the National Endowment for the Arts as well as a winner of a Creative Writing Award from the American Academy of Arts and Letters, plus numerous other awards. Her many books include *Annie Allen* (1949), *The Bean*

Eaters (1960), *Selected Poems* (1963), *Primer for Blacks* (1980), *The Near-Johan-nesburg Boy* (1986), *Blacks* (1987), and *Children Coming Home* (1991). The Gwendolyn Brooks Chair in Black Literature and Creative Writing was established in her honor at Chicago State University in 1990.

JOSEPH BRUCHAC (b. 1942) is a storyteller and poet of the Abenaki Nation and English and Slovak ancestry. He lives in the Adirondack foothills of New York State and has published fourteen collections of poetry and six collections of traditional Abenaki and Iroquois tales and been the featured performer at the National Storytelling Festival in Jonesboro, Tennessee and other festivals throughout the world. His work appears in more than five hundred magazines and anthologies, including *National Geographic*. Esteemed for his leadership in the revival of Native Americana, he's held fellowships from the NEA and the Rockefeller Foundation and won a Cherokee Nation Prose Award. His traditional tales from the Abenaki and the Iroquois include *The Faithful Hunter* and *Return of the Sun* and, with Michael Caduto, he has authored environmental stories for children: *Keepers of the Earth* and *Keepers of the Animals*. Four audiocassette tapes of this storytelling have been released, including *Gluskabe Stories,* which won a 1990 Parent's Choice Award, and *The Boy Who Lived with the Bears* (1991). His anthology *Survival This Way: Interviews with American Indian Poets,* among many he's authored, is particularly recommended reading. He has been storyteller-in-residence at the Onondaga Indian School and the Akwesasne Mohawk School and frequently represents the Abenaki Nation of Vermont as their storyteller, "Sozap." A graduate of Cornell University, with an M.A. in Creative Writing from Syracuse University and a Ph.D. in Comparative Literature from Union Graduate School, he also taught in Ghana, West Africa.

DENNIS BRUTUS, born in Zimbabwe, is a widely known South African poet and human rights activist who lives in exile in the United States after residing in Algiers, China, and elsewhere following his liberation from prison in 1966. Educated in South Africa, he became a schoolmaster there and was imprisoned, shot, and banned for using his writing and teaching as a tool against Apartheid. He has campaigned throughout the world against apartheid and was instrumental in having South Africa excluded from the Olympic Games. Winner of the first Paul Robeson Award for Artistic Excellence, Political Consciousness, and Integrity, he has taught at Northwestern University, Swarthmore College, and the University of Pittsburgh; he currently teaches African Studies at the University of Colorado at Boulder. He has published many volumes of poetry, among them *Airs and Tributes* (Whirlwind Press, 1989, African Network, Box 5366, Evanston, IL 60204). His first book, *Sirens, Knuckles, Boots* (1962), was published in Nigeria. Other books are *Letters to Martha and Other Poems from a South African Prison* (1968), *Stubborn Hope* (1979), and *Salutes and Censures* (1989). He received the LANGSTON HUGHES Award in 1987. See also *The Heinemann Book of African Poetry in English,* selected by Adewale Naja-Pearce, Heinemann International, Portsmouth, NH 03801.

JULIAN BURGER, PH.D., author of *The Gaia Atlas of First Peoples, with Campaigning Groups of Native Peoples Worldwide* (Anchor, New York, 1991), is a consultant with the United Nations Center for Human Rights. (See Appendix.) He was formerly deputy director of the Independent Commission for International Humanitarian Issues in Geneva and director of research at the venerable Anti-Slavery Society of London. His atlas, subtitled *A Future for the Indigenous World,* was first published by Gaia Books, London. He has been involved as a pioneer activist in the United Nations Working Group on Indigenous Peoples and has written innumerable books and articles on the plight of indigenous peoples worldwide. Like AL GORE, he demonstrates that the salvation of our environment and biological diversity worldwide depend greatly on our respecting the rights of local peoples everywhere, who are often the best protectors of the land, air, and water in their domains. (Also see WINONA LA DUKE.)

FRAN CASTAN (b. 1938) born in Brooklyn, New York, was living in Hong Kong with her baby daughter when her husband, Sam Castan, *Look* magazine's Asian bureau chief, was killed covering the war in Vietnam in 1966. In 1990 at a poetry conference, she met Hannah Vo-Dinh, whose beautiful Asian American name inspired the poem in this collection. Castan worked as a teacher, filmmaker, magazine writer, and editor before becoming a poet at age forty. Her poems have appeared in many magazines and anthologies and have won several prizes, including the Lucille Medwick Award from the Poetry Society of America.

GLORIA (MARCHISIO) CHANNON (b. 1923), born in Sussex County, New Jersey, became a journalist after twenty-six years of devoted teaching in New York City schools. She wrote the book *Homework: Running an Open Class Room in Harlem* (1972) and is senior editor of *Propaganda Review,* San Francisco Media Alliance.

ALEXANDER COCKBURN (b. 1941), born in Argway, Scotland, is a journalist, author, and political commentator well known for his progressive views, expressed with candor and wit in his column "Beat the Devil" in *The Nation.* He has earned a reputation for his outspoken criticism and opinions on biased and ethnocentric conservatism in the U.S. media and the inadequacy of U.S. press coverage of the Middle East and Central America. He has written for

The Wall Street Journal, the *Village Voice, The Atlantic, Harper's,* the *New York Review of Books,* and FAIR's *Extra.* His books include *Idle Passion: Chess and the Dance of Death* (1974) and, with James Ridgeway, *Smoke: Another Jimmy Carter Adventure* (Times Books, 1978). For the same publishers, he has edited *Political Ecology* (1979) and, with Robin Blackburn, *Student Power: Problems, Diagnosis, Action* (1969), a collection of essays by progressive British students published in Britain, as was *Incompatibles: Trade Union Militancy and the Consensus* (1967). (See also MARTIN A. LEE.)

ANDREI CODRESCU (b. 1946), born in Romania, came to the United States in 1966. Known for his sardonic wit, he is a regular commentator on National Public Radio's "All Things Considered." He is a professor of English at Louisiana State University in Baton Rouge and a newspaper columnist for the Baltimore *Sun,* and he edits the zany literary magazine *The Exquisite Corpse.* His NPR essays are collected in two books: *A Craving for Swan* (Ohio State University Press) and *Raised by Puppets Only to Be Killed by Research* (Addison-Wesley). He wrote a long essay on the post–iron curtain world called *The Disappearance of the Outside.* In 1989, Codrescu returned to his native Romania where he covered the dramatic events of the fall of the Ceaucescu dictatorship for NPR and for ABC News's *Nightline.* The story of his return is the subject of *The Hole in the Flag: A Romanian Exile's Story of Return and Revolution* (William Morrow, 1991). Since his return from Romania he completed a two-hour feature film for PBS called *Road Scholar,* which aired in 1993. It documents the contributions of immigrants to American life in the 1990s. He began his career as a poet, and his most recent book of poetry is *Belligerence.* Recipient of an NEA arts fellowship, among other awards, he has published books of stories, poetry, translations, and recorded commentary.

LENARD J. COHEN is a professor of political science at Simon Fraser University in Canada. His books include *Political Cohesion in a Fragile Mosaic: The Yugoslav Experience* (Westview Press, Boulder, 1983), *The Socialist Pyramid: Elites and Power in Yugoslavia* (Mosaic Press, Oakville, Ontario, 1989), and *Broken Bonds: The Disintegration of the Yugoslav State* (Westview Press, Boulder, 1993). All are recommended reading for a better understanding of the ethnic strife and the background of religious prejudices which plague the former Yugoslavia today.

ROBERT COLES (b. 1929) is a renowned child psychiatrist, educator, and widely published author who holds degrees from Harvard and Columbia universities and honorary degrees from other U.S. institutions. He has served as staff physician at many hospitals, directed clinics, and taught at various universities:

Harvard Medical School; Children's Hospital, Boston; Massachusetts General Hospital; Dartmouth College; and Duke University. Widely versed in the humanities and literature, he is the recipient of several humane service awards, among them the Anisfield-Wolf Award in Race Relations, as well as a Pulitzer Prize in 1973 for volumes 2 and 3 of *Children of Crisis*. *The Call of Stories: Teaching and the Moral Imagination* (1989) and *The Spiritual Life of Children* (1990) are among his relevant works. He won a MacArthur Foundation Award in 1981 and served on many foundations. His books and articles deal in part with issues of race and class xenophobia, how prejudice is acquired by children, as well as morals and ethics. He has served as an adviser to the Institute for Nonviolent Social Change of Martin Luther King, Jr., Americans for Children's Relief, and Citizens for Responsive Public Television. A fellow of Yale University, the American Academy of Arts and Sciences, and the Institute for Ethics and the Life Sciences, he is a member of the American Psychiatric Association and a past director of the Academy for Psychoanalysis.

JOSEPH CONRAD (1857–1924), Josef Teodor Konrad Korzeniowski, was born near Kiev in what was then Russian Poland. He spent most of his life at sea, beginning in 1890 with travels to the Congo, fulfilling his boyhood dream to travel in Africa. He became a British subject in 1886 and, though utterly unschooled in English until after the age of twenty, became a brilliant stylist in his adopted self-taught tongue. Conrad was the son of Polish aristocrats and revolutionaries who abandoned his own country and culture to write many novels considered works of genius in English, among them *The Nigger of the Narcissus, Lord Jim,* and *Nostromo*. His best-known novel, *Heart of Darkness* (1903), like the excerpt included here from *The Congo: An Outpost of Progress* (1902)—with *progress* used sarcastically—exposes the ugly decadence of slave trade in Africa and the abuse of African peoples and resources. His description, around 1890, might be of Somalia today, a country in which the "cold war" rages "hot" for the profit of Western arms dealers.

JAYNE CORTEZ, a celebrated poet and lecturer, was born in Arizona, grew up in California, and lives in New York City. Author of eight books and producer of five recordings of poetry, she recently published *Poetic Magnetic* and her latest recording is *Everywhere Drums*. The poem reprinted here comes from her prize-winning collection *Coagulations* (Thunder's Mouth Press, New York). Her work has appeared in journals, magazines, and anthologies such as *Women on War, Powers of Desire, Confirmation, The Poetry of Black America, Free Spirits, Black Scholar,* and *UNESCO Courier*. She is the recipient of several awards: the National Endowment for the Arts grant, the American Book Award, and the New York Artists Foundation Award for Poetry. Her work has been translated into more than twenty-eight languages. She has lectured and read her poetry throughout the United States, Africa, Europe, Latin America, and the Caribbean.

FAZIL HÜSNÜ DAĞLARCA (b. 1914), born in Istanbul, won the Award of the International Poetry Forum, Pittsburgh, Pennsylvania, in 1968. One of Turkey's leading poets, with more than sixty volumes published worldwide, he was honored at the Struga and Rotterdam International Poetry Festivals. Known and translated throughout the world as a "poet of peace," his *Selected Poems* (University of Pittsburgh Press, 1969), *The Bird & I* (Cross-Cultural Communications, 1980), and *Beacon* (1993) are rendered in English by TALÂT SAIT HALMAN, the foremost poet/translator of Turkey, editor of *Contemporary Turkish Literature, Modern Turkish Drama,* and *Living Poetry of Turkey* as well as the bilingual *American Women Poets and Living American Poets* (Varlik, Istanbul, and Cross-Cultural Communications, Merrick, New York). Halman is a professor of Turkish Language and Literature at New York University and has taught at Columbia and Princeton. Bosphorus University, Istanbul, awarded him an honorary doctorate in 1988. In 1971 he was decorated with the Knight Grand Cross, GBE, by Queen Elizabeth II. From 1980 to 1982 he served as his country's Ambassador of Cultural Affairs.

BEI DAO (b. 1949), born in Peking and recently introduced to English readers, is a Chinese poet living in exile since the massacres at Tiananmen Square. His education was interrupted by the "Cultural Revolution," but he is among the most gifted and controversial writers to arise from the massive upheavals of modern China. After Mao's death and the defeat of the Gang of Four, he began with fellow poet Mang Ke to edit *Jintian* (Today), an official journal of the 1978 Democracy Wall Movement. Since 1989, he has lived in West Berlin, England, Iowa, and Oslo, working with the movement to release political prisoners of the Tiananmen uprising. He escaped imprisonment and execution because he was in Germany at the time of the massacres, but his family remains in China, unable to leave under prejudicial threat from the government, which has banned his widely disseminated writing. Bei Dao's work is uncompromising, poignant, and rhapsodic in its advocacy of freedom of the imagination: "The still horizon / Divides the ranks of the living and the dead / I can only choose the sky / I will not kneel on the ground / Allowing the executioners to look tall / The better to obstruct the wind of freedom." The translator of his *The August Sleepwalker* (New Directions, 1988), from which the poem reprinted here comes, is Bonnie S. McDougall (b. 1941), a professor of Chinese at the University of Edinburgh who previously taught at Sydney, Harvard, Peking, and Oslo. She has published many books and articles on modern Chinese literature, including translations of poetry and fiction.

DIANA DER–HOVANESSIAN is a New England–born poet of Armenian ancestry who has authored twelve books of poetry and translations. Her work has appeared in *American Scholar, Graham House Review, The Nation,* the *New Republic, Partisan Review, Yankee* and *The Christian Science Monitor.* She serves on the governing board of the Columbia University Translation Center and as president of the New England Poetry Club. Her awards include the Armand-Erph Translation Award from Columbia, a National Endowment for the Arts grant, and many Massachusetts Poet-in-the-Schools appointments. Her latest book is *Songs of Bread, Songs of Salt* (Ashod Press, New York, 1990).

FREDERICK DOUGLASS (1817?–1895) was born into slavery as Frederick Augustus Washington Bailey near Easton in Talbot County, Maryland. He is believed to be the son of his Black slave mother by her white master. As a young boy, he was sent to Baltimore as a household servant, where he learned to read and write, assisted by his master's wife. In 1838 he escaped from slavery and journeyed to New York City and married Anna Murray, whom he'd met in Baltimore. His abolitionist oratory so impressed the Massachusetts Anti-Slavery Society in Nantucket in 1841 that it inducted him into service as a speaker. Many who heard his impressive speaking refused to believe he had been a slave. He wrote *Narrative of the Life of Frederick Douglass* in part to dispel such disbelief. During the Civil War he assisted in recruiting Black men to regimental service as he consistently argued for emancipation. After the war he was an eloquent activist for the rights of freed slaves. In later years, he served as secretary to the Santo Domingo Commission, marshal and recorder for deeds of the District of Columbia, and U.S. minister to Haiti. Other autobiographical works are *My Bondage and My Freedom* (1855) and *Life and Times of Frederick Douglass* (1881). With W. E. B. DU BOIS he is considered the father of the civil rights movement in the United States.

SIOBHAN DOWD has been program director of PEN American Center's Freedom-to-Write Committee since 1990. Before that she worked for PEN's international headquarters in London as coordinator for the Writers in Prison Committee. She has also published about seventy articles and book reviews in various journals in England and the United States. The piece excerpted here is from a longer one on the plight of imprisoned writers worldwide.

W. E. B. DU BOIS (1868–1963), born William Edward Burghardt Du Bois in Great Barrington, Massachusetts, is often referred to as the father of the Black civil rights movement of the United States along with FREDERICK DOUGLASS. Du Bois attended public schools and graduated with a B.A. from Fisk University in 1888. He received a second B.A., an M.A., and a Ph.D. from

Harvard University and studied at the University of Berlin as well. He taught and lectured at numerous institutions of higher learning, particularly the University of Pennsylvania, where he served for many years as a sociologist, historian, poet, and writer of several novels. Du Bois was an instrumental founder of the National Association for the Advancement of Colored People (NAACP) and a lifelong critic of the evils of U.S. society, its bigotry, and political hypocrisy. He understood the world politics of racial injustice and articulated them well. He died in Ghana, where he spent his last years as editor of *Encyclopedia Africana*. An eloquent and popular speaker since his first widely known publication, *The Souls of Black Folks* (1903), Du Bois is perhaps the best American writer one can read on the subject of racial politics, history, and sociology for a global perspective. Martin Luther King, Jr., put it most aptly when he said: "When a young man William Edward Burghardt Du Bois told himself in his own diary, 'be the truth what it may, I shall seek it on the pure assumption that it is worth seeking—and Heaven nor Hell, God or Devil shall turn me from my purpose till I die.' When Du Bois died in Accra, Ghana, at the age of ninety-five, it could truly be said of him that here was the end of a life unswervingly dedicated to truth." He was a prolific writer. Among his many books and articles in the area of Black history and sociology are *Suppression of the African Slave Trade* (1986), volume 1 in the Harvard Classics Series; *The Philadelphia Negro* (1899), *Black Reconstruction in America* (1941), a work proclaimed as the finest work ever produced on the subject; and three autobiographies, *Darkwater: Voices from within the Veil* (1921), *Dusk of Dawn: An Essay toward an Autobiography of a Race Concept* (1940), and his posthumously published *The Autobiography of W. E. B. Du Bois* (1968, Pathfinder Press, New York). It is a blight upon U.S. history that Du Bois was indicted and tried, though acquitted, of being a "foreign agent" of the Communist party for his leadership in the world peace movement, one of several reasons that he chose to live his final years in Africa as an expatriate. The speech excerpted here was delivered throughout the United States beginning in August 1914, after World War I began. James Weldon Johnson said: "Du Bois showed that when we cut down through the layers of international rivalries and jealousies we found that the roots of the great war were in Africa."

MARGUERITE DURAS (b. 1914), is a renowned French novelist and author of many internationally known books. She wrote of World War II war crimes in *The War* (Pantheon Books, 1984), her critically acclaimed memoir about her life in Paris during those eventful and trying years. The entire book is an insight into what is often women's lot during times of war: waiting in tense anxiety, their lives suspended, for soldiers or loved ones to return from front lines or prison camps.

BARBARA EHRENREICH has a Ph.D. in biology and has written and lectured widely on subjects related to health care and women's issues. She has contributed articles to *The Nation,* the *New York Review of Books,* and *Monthly Review.* She is currently on the editorial board of *Social Policy and Health Right,* a national women's health newsletter. Her books include *Re-making love: The Feminization of Sex,* with Elizabeth Hess and Gloria Jacobs, and *The Hearts of Men: American Dreams and the Flight from Commitment* (Anchor Books). An eminent socialist and political commentator known for her wit and candor in her *Mother Jones* columns, she has authored, with DEIRDRE ENGLISH, classic studies of women and health care issues: *Witches, Midwives, and Nurses: A History of Women Healers* (1972), and *Complaints and Disorders: The Sexual Politics of Sickness* (1974); and *For Her Own Good: 150 Years of the Experts' Advice to Women* (1978).

BUCHI EMECHETA (b. 1944), born in Yaba, Lagos, Nigeria, earned a degree at the University of London in 1972, graduating with honors. Named one of the best young British writers in 1983, she has published several novels rich with autobiographical detail of her Nigerian homeland. Her work is especially concerned with issues of race and the clash of cultures, as Western values impact on the agrarian traditions and customs of Nigerian life. Though she has written for children and has scripted television dramas, she is best known for her novels, among them *A Kind of Marriage; Adha's Story; The Rape of Shavi; Double Yoke, Naira Power; and Destination Biafra,* and an autobiographical work, *Head above Water,* all published 1982 to 1987. The selection printed here comes from an earlier work, *Second Class Citizen* (George Braziller, 1976). Emecheta is the most internationally known of Nigerian writers, and her works deal intensely with the role of women, so crucial and yet firmly subordinate, though full of potential liberation in a changing African culture.

DEIRDRE ENGLISH, coauthor with BARBARA EHRENREICH of *For Her Own Good: 150 Years of the Experts' Advice to Women* (Anchor Books, 1978), from which the excerpt here is taken, is former editor of the award-winning investigative magazine *Mother Jones,* for which she worked from 1978 to 1985. She is currently a San Francisco Bay Area journalist and executive series editor of "America's Women," a documentary series for the Public Broadcasting System. In 1970 she cofounded one of the country's first women's studies programs at the College of Old Westbury, State University of New York, where she taught journalism and women's history until 1976. She has taught and lectured from UCLA and CCNY to Oxford, Yale, and Vassar and was a keynote speaker for the National Women's Studies Association of the United States.

MARTIN ESPADA (b. 1957), born in Brooklyn, New York, is author of three books of poetry: *The Immigrant Iceboy's Bolero* (1982), *Trumpets from the Island of Their Eviction* (1987), and *Rebellion Is the Circle of a Lover's Hands* (1990). His work has appeared in numerous periodicals and anthologies, including the *Kenyon Review, Ploughshares,* and *Under 35: The New Generation of American Poets.* He has been awarded two fellowships from the National Endowment for the Arts, a Massachusetts artist's fellowship, and the PEN/Revson Foundation fellowship, as well as the Paterson Poetry Prize. Espada works as a tenants' lawyer and supervisor of Su Clinica Legal for Hispanic-Americans in Boston. He continues to address the problems of prejudice in the United States and the colonization of his Puerto Rican people's island home, whose culture has been destroyed in great measure by U.S. annexation.

LAWRENCE FERLINGHETTI (b. 1919?), born in New York or Paris, internationally traveled, and orphaned from his cultural heritage, has rediscovered his roots. A worldly poet of progressive ideals, he founded his pioneering establishment, City Lights Books, in San Francisco, which published Allen Ginsberg and other poets of the Beat Generation early in their careers. He holds an M.A. from Columbia University (1947) and a doctorate from the University of Paris (1950). Among his multifaceted books of poetry, travel essays, fiction, and drama are *A Coney Island of the Mind* (poems, 1958); *Endless Life: Selected Poems; Her* (a surrealistic novel); *Landscapes of Living and Dying; Mexican Night* (travel journals); *Over All the Obscene Boundaries; Routines* (plays); *The Secret Meaning of Things; Starting from San Francisco; Tyrannus Nix; Unfair Arguments with Existence* (plays); and *European Poems and Transitions* (1984), all from New Directions, New York. One can't read his cosmopolitan meanderings with their astute sociopolitical observations and remain close-minded or prejudiced about other cultures.

MARILYN FRENCH received her B.A. and M.A. from Hofstra University and her Ph.D. from Harvard. She has taught English at Hofstra, Harvard, and the College of the Holy Cross and in 1976–77 was a Mellon Fellow at Harvard. She has published articles and stories in a wide range of magazines. Her first book, *The Book as World: James Joyce's* Ulysses, was published in 1976. Since then, she has published three very successful novels that have achieved the *New York Times* best-seller list: *The Women's Room* (1977), *The Bleeding Heart* (1980), and *Her Mother's Daughter* (1988). Her fiction has been translated into twenty languages and published worldwide. French's nonfiction includes *Shakespeare's Division of Experience* (1981); *Beyond Power: On Women, Men and Morals* (1985), *The War against Women* (1992), and *From Eve to Dawn: A Woman's History of the World* (1993). The latter is a history of women from the earliest protohuman emergence to the present, and it fully develops the summarizing essay reprinted here and delivered as a reading at Hunter College, New York, in 1990 as the finale of "Women Write to Choose," an event produced by the PEN American Center Women's Committee. Her current novel is *Our Father*.

SIGMUND FREUD (1856–1939), Austrian neurologist and founder of the psychoanalytic movement, was born in Freiburg, Moravia, of Jewish parentage. He studied medicine in Vienna and joined the staff of Vienna General Hospital in 1882, specializing in neurological disorders. He collaborated with Joseph Breuer in the treatment of various forms of "hysteria," by inducing the recall of traumatic experiences under hypnosis. In 1885 he moved to Paris to study under Jean Martin Charcot and changed his focus from neurology to psychopathology. When he returned to Vienna, he developed a conversational technique or "free association" style of dealing with patients, in place of hypnosis, refining psychoanalysis as his method. Against opposition from professional colleagues, patients, and friends, he developed his revolutionary thinking and in 1900 published his seminal work, *The Interpretation of Dreams,* arguing that dreams, like neuroses, are disguised manifestations of repressed sexual desires. While working under a professorship at the University of Vienna, in 1902, he initiated his weekly home seminars with like-minded professionals, Alfred Adler among them, and produced more crucial works—*The Psychology of Daily Life* (1904) and *Three Theoretical Essays on Sexuality* (1905)—which caused great controversy. In 1908, his weekly meetings became the Vienna Psychoanalytical Society, which internationalized into an association in 1910, with Carl Jung as its first president. Both Adler and Jung broke from the mentorship of Freud to develop their own theories. Undaunted, Freud continued and published *Totem and Taboo* (1913), *Beyond the Pleasure Principle* (1919–20), *Ego, Id and Super-Ego* (1923), and a controversial view of religion, *The Future of an Illusion* (1927). He won the prestigious Goethe Prize in 1930, and in 1933 he published *Why War?,* written with Albert Einstein. Under the Nazi regime, psychoanalysis was banned in 1938, causing Freud to escape from Vienna and resettle in London with his family. He died of cancer only one year later, but his profound theories, despite a measure of feminist correction and controversy, remain vital to an understanding of the psychodynamics of prejudice.

RICHARD GAMBINO is Director of Italian American Studies at Queens College of the City University of New York—the first such program in the United States, which he founded in 1973. Having lived his youth among the diaspora, he wrote his acclaimed volume *Blood of My Blood; The Dilemma of the Italian-Americans* (Doubleday, New York, 1974) as a personal interpretation of an immigrant culture based on history, sociology, and scholarly sources. Like the more recent *La Storia; Five Centuries of the Italian-American Experience* (HarperCollins, 1992), by Jerre Mangione and Ben Morreale, his book is an insightful journey that explains and analyzes the problems of and bigotry toward an immigrant culture analogous to many others around the world. Yet his book zeros in on the plight of the Italian-American as a scapegoat for all the evils of society, cruelly stereotyped and maligned without reason. Like MICHAEL PARENTI, he explains the ways of media sensationalizing in creating prejudice.

MOHANDAS KARAMCHAND GANDHI (1869–1948), known as Mahatma ("a great soul"), was an Indian leader famed worldwide for his use of nonviolent resistance, *satyagraha*. He spent a lifetime fighting Britain's cruel colonization of India. Born in Porbandar, Kathiawas, he managed to study law in London and used his legal knowledge for the liberation and unification of India against British occupation. In 1893, he gave up his lucrative Bombay legal practice to live a humble life in South Africa where for twenty-one years he opposed racist laws against Indians who were near to "slave labor" in that social order. He returned to India in 1914 to become increasing involved in leading India's "home rule" movement, *swaraj*. His civil disobedience campaign of 1920 brought violent disorders and Gandhi, like NELSON MANDELA was imprisoned from 1922 to 1924, for his just protest. In 1930 he led a two-hundred-mile march to the sea to collect salt in symbolic defiance of the British government's monopoly on the essential substance. Analogies can be drawn with MARTIN LUTHER KING, JR.'s freedom marches. Again Gandhi was arrested. He had become a powerful symbol of resistance, even from jail, and when released he negotiated a truce between the congress and the government and attended the London Round Table Conference of 1931 on Indian constitutional reforms. Back in India, he renewed his civil disobedience. For the next six years he was periodically arrested and released, employing his "fasts unto death," a nonviolent resistance tactic which became world news. In 1937 he managed some measure of government reforms toward local congressional involvement, and when war broke out, he used Britain's distraction to press for Indian independence. In 1942 he was again arrested for civil disobedience, which allegedly obstructed Britain's war efforts, and was not released until 1944. In 1946 he negotiated a new constitutional structure with the British Cabinet Commission, and finally, in 1947, he was able—with characteristic diplomacy—to hail Britain's decision to grant India independence as "the noblest act of the British nation." The last year of Gandhi's life was darkened by internal strife between Hindus and Muslims, a strife which still continues, rising to a crescendo again in 1992. Some believe that Gandhi's fasts to shame the instigators of India's religious strife helped to avert greater tragedy, but these episodes took their toll on the Mahatma. Ironically, he was assassinated in Delhi by a Hindu fanatic, ten days after another attack on his life. Parallels can be drawn with MALCOLM X's assassination in the struggle for Black equal rights in the United States. Gandhi, like Martin Luther King, Jr., was venerated as a great moral teacher, a reformer who sought to free India from the caste system as well as from the inequities of British control. His many writings include *The Story of My Experiment with Truth,* republished many times and available in many languages. To draw useful analogies in the worldwide and enduring struggles against inequality and prejudice, see SITTING BULL, BARBARA JORDAN, VACLAV HAVEL, LEO TOLSTOY, and ALDOUS HUXLEY, as well as Malcolm X, Martin Luther King, Jr., and Nelson Mandela, whose life parallels Gandhi's in so many ways. Gandhi's example has become a universal symbol of the nonviolent global peace movement and has been an inspiration for the U.S. antiwar and antinuclear movements, embodied in spiritual leaders like Dorothy Day and Father Daniel Berrigan and the Ploughshares Eight, as well as the late Petra Kelly of the Greens of West Germany and Helen Caldicott of Australia.

ENILDO A. GARCÍA. See NICOLÁS GUILLÉN.

FEDERICO GARCIA LORCA (1898–1936) was born to the lyric and gypsy, or *gitano,* traditions of southern Spain's Andalusia, at Fuentevagueros near Granada. He is the most renowned modern poet of Spain, and his works are available worldwide in numerous languages. His famous verse dramas *Blood Wedding, The House of Bernardo Alba,* and *Yerma* tell of the terrors of love, passion, and sexual repression, particularly of women under Spain's most stalwart Catholic traditions. Valued for the incredible Andalusian musical qualities of his subtle surreal and emotional verse, untranslatable into the cadences of English, Garcia Lorca has become a symbol of liberation to artists everywhere who are persecuted for their conscience. He was executed by Falangists of the Fascist movement who were occupying Granada in 1936, and his body was thrown unceremoniously into an unmarked grave. He is, nevertheless, one of the greatest of Spanish-language poets.

GERONIMO (1829–1909) was a powerful and legendary chief and consummate warrior of the Apache Nation. His family was murdered by Mexicans whose government was offering a cheap bounty for the scalps of braves, squaws, and children. For a few dollars, Mexicans had slaughtered his entire family—his mother, wife, and three children—in their own home. A "demon" in his grief, with nothing more to lose, Geronimo was for good reason fiercely committed to revenge upon the Mexican invaders. The natives of the Americas were not the savage aggressors in battle so often portrayed in American history, literature, drama, and film. Rather they were fighting to defend their families and homes from the savagery of the European invaders who were bigoted against the value of their tribal lives and cultures and who were stealing from them their very sustenance. Geronimo died a sorrowful prisoner at Fort Sill, Oklahoma, in 1909, after the Mexican and U.S. invaders who had joined forces against him had treacherously violated the terms of his surrender to save his braves in 1866.

CHRIS GILLESPIE (b. 1968) has been a medical writer and editor for *Clinical Advances in Critical Care, Clinical Advances in Infections,* and *Practice Economics* and is currently editor of *Superconductor Industry.* He has published political commentary and satire in *The New York Times,* the *Bergen Record* and the *Rutgers Review,* as well as other periodicals. As a young child, he suffered from perthes disease, a circulatory disorder of the hip, which forced him to wear a full leg prosthesis for a prolonged period. He was fully rehabilitated and played on the Rutgers University football team as an undergraduate.

DANIELA GIOSEFFI (b. 1941) is a widely published poet, novelist, editor, nonfiction writer, and activist who was born and raised in New Jersey but lived much of her life in New York City. Her writing has appeared in *Antaeus, The Nation,* the *Paris Review,* and *Ms.,* among many periodicals. She won the 1990 American Book Award for her edited and annotated compendium *Women on War: International Voices.* (Touchstone, New York and Frauenverlag Vienna, 1992). She is the recipient of an NEA grant in poetry and a PEN Syndicated Fiction Award. Her books include *Eggs in the Lake* (Boa Editions, Ltd., 1980), *The Great American Belly* . . . (Doubleday Dell, 1977, 1979), *Word Wounds and Water Flowers* (Mosaic Publications, Vienna, New York, and London, 1993), and *Dust Disappears: The Poetry of a Latin American Feminist, Carilda Oliver Labra* (Cross-Cultural Communications, 1993). A professor of Communications and World Literature, she has specialized in Intercultural Communication and lectured and read her work throughout the United States and Europe, broadcasting for NPR, WBAI, and the BBC and CBC. She has been a civil rights advocate since her days in Selma among the Freedom Riders as an intern journalist who helped integrate Deep South television in 1961. She is editor/annotator of this compendium, *On Prejudice.*

AL GORE (b. 1948), formerly a southern Democratic senator, was elected to the vice presidency of the United States in 1993. He has been an environmental advocate for over twenty years and was a U.S. senator when he wrote his best-selling book *Earth in the Balance: Ecology and the Human Spirit* (Houghton Mifflin, Boston, 1992), highly recommended reading for understanding issues of environmental racism and human survival. Vice President Gore graduated with a B.A., cum laude, from Harvard University in 1969, attended the

Graduate School of Religion, Vanderbilt University in 1971–72, and completed law school in 1976. He served as an investigative reporter and editorial writer for *The Tennessean* from 1971 to 1976 and was a member of the 95th–98th Congresses from Tennessee (1977–1985) before being elected to the U.S. Senate in 1985, where he served until his nomination as Bill Clinton's running mate. He has worked as a land developer with Tanglewood Home Builders Co. (1971–1976) and has been a livestock and tobacco farmer since 1973.

STEPHEN JAY GOULD (b. 1941) is a renowned biologist who specializes in paleontology and has written and lectured with clarity, philosophical musing, and infectious enthusiasm on a variety of scientific subjects. Born in New York City, he was inspired by childhood visits to the Museum of Natural History, where he discovered his first dinosaur bones and marine fossils. Educated at Antioch College, he earned his Ph.D. from Columbia University and is now curator of invertebrate paleontology at Harvard's Museum of Comparative Zoology. Most important for our subject, he won the National Book Critics Circle Award in 1982 for *The Mismeasure of Man*. This highly recommended book deals with an aspect of biological determinism, a claim regarding the measurability of human intelligence, which Gould explains is based on fallacies about socially oppressed or disadvantaged groups—races, classes, or sexes. Among Gould's many books and essays is his National Book Award–winning *The Panda's Thumb* (1980), from which the essay here comes. He also won the National Magazine Award in 1980 for his essays in *Natural History* as well as a MacArthur Foundation award in 1981.

PAULA GREEN ventured to the Burma border for the first time in 1990 to teach nonviolence workshops to students. She led an international delegation to the border in 1991 and another in February 1992. She is director of the Daruna Center for Burmese people and is also a psychologist and the coeditor of *Psychology and Social Responsibility: Global Challenges* (New York University Press, 1992). Her selection on the problems in Burma today comes from *The Non-Violent Activist* of the War Resisters League, an international organization, with offices in New York and London. The group publishes and distributes a catalog called "Books That Make a Difference," listing books that deal with issues of prejudice and genocide, as well as war, on a global scale.

NICOLÁS GUILLÉN (1902–1991) was a leading Black Caribbean poet, the best representative of Afro-Cuban poetry. He is famed for using the rhythms of Afro-Cuban music and dance and his Latin American dialect sprinkled with African words in his revival of the folk art of his people. Guillén's is an ardent voice of protest against the racist abuses of sociopolitics—and the struggle against fascism of the Cuban people. A revolutionary poet, he changed the traditional style of "cultivated" poetry with his folkloric spirit of renewal and is symbolic as a pioneering voice for the inhabitants of Black ghettos and slums worldwide. A Communist in the non-Stalinist, idealist mode, he was considered to be a sincere humanitarian whose concern for his people amounted to more than a superficial theme in his poetry. He protested the racism and classism of big business, the military, and Fascist Spain and was part of the post–World War I African cultural renaissance in modern and contemporary art that swept from Harlem to Paris, from South Africa to the West Indies during this century. His works are available in many bilingual translations or from Letras Cubanas, Havana, and make excellent reading on racism. One of his translators herein, ENILDO A. GARCÍA, of St. Francis College, Brooklyn, a graduate of the University of Havana, New York University, and Columbia University, is a world-renowned scholar of Caribbean Literature. Born in Matanzas, he annotated the Harvard Library collection of Cuban letters and published numerous books and articles on the subject of Caribbean letters and theological history.

EDWARD T. HALL (b. 1914) is an internationally known anthropologist and author as well as a partner in Edward T. Hall Associates, a firm specializing in intercultural communication. A foremost pioneer in his specialty, he has authored many books in the field, his most recent being *An Anthropology of Everyday Life* (Doubleday, 1992). He coauthored, with Mildred Reed Hall, *Understanding Cultural Difference: Germans, French, and Americans* (Intercultural Press, 1990). The Halls' widely acclaimed book *Hidden Differences: Doing Business with the Japanese* was published by Doubleday in 1987. Hall's groundbreaking earlier books have been translated into numerous languages. Among them are *The Silent Language; Beyond Culture; The Hidden Dimension,* from which the excerpt herein comes; and *The Dance of Life* (all Anchor/Doubleday, New York). All are highly recommended reading for achieving open-minded communication with and tolerance of peoples of differing cultures. Hall is a fellow of the American Anthropological Association and the Society for Applied Anthropology. He is Professor Emeritus of Anthropology at Northwestern University and in 1987 was named a Doctor Honoris Causa by Université Catholique de Louvain in Belgium. He is the recipient of the first Edward J. Lehman Award of the American Anthropological Association.

TALÂT SAIT HALMAN. See FAZIL HÜSNÜ DAĞLARCA.

BRIAN HAMILTON-TWEEDALE (b. 1953), born in Liverpool, England, has been a member of the Peace and Conflict Studies Development Group since 1986. He lives in Sheffield where he has written a book on the British press in

Northern Ireland. The essay reprinted here first appeared in a recommended compendium: *A Reader in Peace Studies,* edited by Paul Smoker, Ruth Davies, and Barbara Munske (Pergamon International Books, 1990). (For analogous situations with reference to media prejudice, see MARTIN A. LEE, WINONA LA DUKE, GLORIA CHANNON, ALEXANDER COCKBURN, SUSANNA HECHT, and MICHAEL PARENTI.)

A. FRANCES ELLEN WATKINS HARPER (1825–1911) was the most popular Black feminist abolitionist writer and activist of the nineteenth century in the United States. Her works have been edited by Frances Smith Foster, a specialist in early Black women writers and a professor of Literature at the University of California, San Diego, for the Feminist Press at the City University of New York, under the title *A Brighter Day.* Watkins Harper was the best known and loved African-American poet of her time. She wrote movingly of the suffering of slaves, as well as lyrics of freedom, love, and heroism. Among the heroes of her narrative poems are Moses, John Brown, and Aunt Chloe, whose voice paved the way for the use of Black dialect in American literature. Harper traveled before the Civil War for the Maine Anti-Slavery Society and after the war throughout the southern states speaking on abolition, suffrage, temperance, and education. Her oratory and writing earned her international fame.

PHILLIP BRIAN HARPER received an M.A. and Ph.D. in English from Cornell University. He served as assistant professor of English in American Literature at Brandeis University, where he taught twentieth-century English, American, and African American literature and contemporary cultural studies. Currently an assistant professor at Harvard in the same subject areas, he has contributed articles and book reviews to leading journals since 1981 and is on the board of directors of the *Gay Community News,* Boston, for which he coedited the Black History Month issue in 1989. He has worked on a book of essays on representation of African Americans in popular culture.

VACLÁV HAVEL (b. 1936), born in Czechoslovakia, is a noted playwright. In 1989 he helped to found the Civic Forum, the country's first legal opposition movement in forty years, and in December of 1989 he was elected as his renewed nation's first president. In 1979 he was sentenced to four and a half years in prison for his association with the Czech human rights movement. From this experience came a volume of writings to his wife, *Letters to Olga* (1988), which marked him as a literary hero of the Czech resistance and a champion of his people's democratic rights. He published a book-length interview in 1990 titled *Disturbing the Peace,* which brought international understanding of the civil disobedience movement in which he was an active participant. He has written numerous influential essays on totalitarianism and dissent, some of which are collected in his *Open Letters* (1991). Alfred A. Knopf, New York has published much of his work in English. Odeon, in Prague, is his chief European publisher. Paul Wilson of Canada has translated and edited much of his prose writings into English.

ANNE HEBÉRT (b. 1916) is a premier French-Canadian poet who has been brought to the attention of U.S. readers by AL POULIN, JR., a French-Canadian poet of the United States, also a translator and entrepreneur publisher, founder of Boa Editions Ltd., a leading U.S. poetry press. Born and raised in Saint Catherine, a village twenty miles from Quebec, Hebért has written for the stage, film, and television. One of her most common themes is the sadness of women depressed and repressed by their domestic prisons. A bilingual edition of *Anne Hebért: Selected Poems,* translated by Al Poulin, Jr. (Boa Editions Ltd., Brockport, N.Y., 1987), was highly praised by Margaret Atwood, whose own work has been inspired by Hebért.

SUSANNA HECHT is an agronomist who has worked in the Amazon for more than a decade. She is an associate professor at the Graduate School of Planning at UCLA and co-author, with Alexander Cockburn, of *Developers, Destroyers, Defenders of the Amazon* (Verso, 1989) as well as articles on environmental racism and ecology in *The Nation, The Utne Reader, The New Statesman,* and other periodicals. (See also ALEXANDER COCKBURN and MARTIN F. LEE of Fairness and Accuracy in Reporting, N.Y.)

CALVIN C. HERNTON has published eight books. He is a United States poet, novelist, essayist, and social scientist, and has taught Black and African literature and creative writing at Oberlin College for over fifteen years. His widely acclaimed study *Sex and Racism in America* (Doubleday, New York, 1965) was praised by Langston Hughes, who said, "No writer I have come across except Hernton has had the temerity to so frankly tackle that old bugabook S-E-X as it relates to life, liberty and the pursuit of integration." Both European and American reviewers found great validity and sociological integrity in his groundbreaking study, reissued by Anchor Books in 1992.

WILLIAM HEYEN (b. 1940) was born in Brooklyn, New York, of German immigrant parents and raised on Long Island. He is the editor of *American Poets in 1976* and *The Generation of 2000: Contemporary American Poets* and the author of *Erika: Poems of the Holocaust,* in which "Men in History" and "A Visit to Belzec" appear. His most recent books are *Pterodactyl Rose: Poems of Ecology* (Time Being Books, St. Louis, 1991) and *Ribbons: The Gulf War* (1991) described by poet Philip Booth as "the most self-demanding war poem of our century's death-throes." Heyen has received Fulbright, Guggenheim, NEA, and other awards and is currently professor of English and poet-in-residence at the State University of New York at Brockport.

MERLE HOFFMAN is an author, speaker, radio and TV spokesperson for women's rights, social psychologist, publisher, and political organizer, internationally known as an activist for women's medical and political rights. Founder and president of Choices Women's Medical Center, Inc., one of the largest, most comprehensive women's medical facilities in the United States, she started the New York Pro-Choice Coalition, an umbrella organization, and has organized civil disobedience actions. She is publisher and editor of *On the Issues: The Progressive Woman's Quarterly,* Forest Hills, New York, from which her selection comes. The publication has included interviews with Petra Kelly and Andrea Dworkin, as well as ELIE WIESEL, and is recommended reading about social injustices and prejudices, especially those affecting women worldwide. Hoffman has published numerous articles on women's medical and political issues in such magazines as *American Journal of Obstetrics and Gynecology* and *The Journal of the American Medical Women's Associations* and she has run her own cable TV show.

LANGSTON HUGHES (1902–1967) was called the "Poet Laureate of Harlem." One of the first Black Americans to achieve widespread fame as an author, he published ten volumes of poetry and nine works of fiction, essays, plays, and autobiographical pieces, bringing the African American experience to life for his readers. Born in Joplin, Missouri, to a schoolteacher mother and a store-keeper father, he was raised until the age of twelve chiefly by his grand-mother, Mary Sampson Patterson Leary Langston, the last surviving widow of John Brown's raid at Harpers Ferry. His parents divorced, and he lived mostly in Cleveland, but after his graduation from high school he visited his father in Mexico for a year, where he was influenced by Black Latino poets. From Mexico, in 1921 he went to Columbia University for a year and then worked around New York, ending up as a seaman on transatlantic trips to Africa and Holland. He was a cook in a Montmarte nightclub in Paris and a busboy at the Wardman Park Hotel in Washington, where Vachel Lindsay helped attract attention to his work by reading three of Hughes's poems at a recital in the Little Theatre of the hotel. In 1925 Hughes received his first literary award from *Opportunity,* a journal of "Negro" life. Carl Van Vechten became interested in his work and sent it to Alfred A. Knopf, who published *The Weary Blues,* Hughes's first collection. He was then helped by a benefactor to complete his education at Lincoln University, Pennsylvania, from which he graduated in 1929 with a B.A. He began to earn a living as a professional writer, and his play *Mulatto* ran for two years on Broadway. He wrote for motion pictures in Moscow and Hollywood and produced numerous works, among them the stories of "Simple" from which the selection here comes. Simple was a folk hero whose simple wisdom and moral truths, told with Hughes wit, outdo the decadent, learned society around him; *The Ways of White Folks* (1934) is particularly interesting reading on the subtleties and blatancies of race prejudice. His collected works are widely available, as are excellent biographies of his life. Throughout his life Hughes won many plaudits and awards, including a Guggenheim fellowship, and championed the cause of African American writers throughout the Americas, founding, among other projects, the Harlem Suitcase Theater. He wrote extensively in Black dialect as well as eloquent English and was a widely traveled and cosmopolitan intellect—one of the first U.S. writers to translate and bring attention to Caribbean Black poets in North America, as well as pioneering the current renaissance of African American literature and art.

ALDOUS HUXLEY (1894–1963) born in Surrey, England, the son of the author Leonard Huxley and grandson of biologist T. H. Huxley, was a world-famous writer and philosophical essayist from an eminent British family. He became a caustic critic of the technocratic and decadent evils of contemporary society and foresaw much of the folly of our time. Huxley's best-known work, *Brave New World,* a title taken from Shakespeare's *The Tempest,* is a warning, like George Orwell's *Animal Farm,* against the mechanistic dictatorial technocratic takeover of humanity and all its endeavors—so evident throughout the cold war years and now our legacy. In the excerpt printed here he expresses an important point with reference to TOLSTOY and GANDHI and the nonviolent movement against xenophobic oppression.

DAVID IGNATOW (b. 1914) is a venerable Jewish American author of sixteen volumes of poetry and three books of prose. He is President Emeritus of the Poetry Society of America and winner of the Bollingen Prize for poetry in 1977; a Wallace Stevens fellowship in 1972; the Robert Frost Silver Medal in 1992; and the Shelley Memorial Prize in 1968. Recent books include *Shadowing the Ground* (1991), *Despite the Plainness of the Day: Love Poems* (1991), and *Talking Together: Letters of David Ignatow, 1946–1990* (1992). The poem selected here is from *Rescue the Dead* (Wesleyan University Press, 1968).

SHIGETOSHI IWAMATSU (b. 1923) is a survivor of the 1945 U.S. bombing of Nagasaki. He served for some years as a professor of the faculty of economics at Nagasaki University. Like other victims of the atomic bombs dropped on Hiroshima and Nagasaki, he emphasizes the peculiarly brutal effects of nuclear weapons, far beyond comparison with the effects of other weapons. Like so many antinuclear activists throughout the world, he explains that the merciless and wide-ranging cruelty these heinous weapons inflict and the resultant devastation of the environment constitute "war crimes" in their very existence and manufacture. The essay reprinted here is from a magazine of science and public affairs, *The Bulletin of Atomic Scientists,* supported by the Educational Foundation for Nuclear Science (Chicago, Illinois), dedicated to educating against the use of nuclear warfare. Though Iwamatsu deplored the violence of the Japanese regime during the war—its brutal unconcern for its own people—he also explains how U.S. bombings on civilian populations were an act of xenophobic vengeance upon the innocent. He shows how the United States suppressed the free speech of bomb victims in occupied Japan.

GISH JEN (b. 1955), born in New York City, is the daughter of immigrants. Her fiction has appeared in *The Atlantic* and *The New Yorker,* as well as in numerous quarterlies and anthologies, including *Best American Short Stories 1988.* Her first novel, *Typical American* (Houghton Mifflin, 1991), was nominated for a National Book Critics Circle Award. Support for her work has come from the Radcliffe Bunting Institute, the Massachusetts Artists Foundation, the James A. Michener/Copernicus Society, the National Endowment for the Arts, and the Guggenheim Foundation. A graduate of Harvard University and the Iowa Writers Workshop, she currently lives in Massachusetts. The story reprinted here demonstrates, among other problems of interculturalism, the Western tendency to lump all Asian cultures together as one—a tendency caused by ignorance of Asia's history and culture.

BARBARA JORDAN (b. 1936), U.S. congressional representative and educator, was born in Houston, graduated from Texas Southern University in 1956, and received an LL.B. from Boston University in 1959. She subsequently became a member of the Texas bar and then the Texas state Senate from 1966 to 1972. She rose to prominence in the Democratic party during the Lyndon B. Johnson administration and has held influential positions in U.S. government and at the United Nations. She is among the first Black women to hold a seat in the U.S. Congress (1972–1978). The selection here comes from her speech at the 1976 Democratic National Convention. She is the recipient of many awards, including an Eleanor Roosevelt Humanities Award (1984). She remains an important voice within the Democratic party, having served on the House Democratic Caucus Committee and the Judiciary Committee, as well as other government positions. She holds a professorship at the Lyndon B. Johnson School of Public Affairs of the University of Texas, Austin. Her words are echoed by VACLÁV HAVEL, showing the desire for ethical democracy throughout the world as the means to ending the injustices of prejudice.

ROBERT D. KAPLAN (b. 1952), born in New York City, is an accomplished author of books about the famine in Ethiopia, the war in Afghanistan, and the renewal of history in the Balkans. His next book will be about American Arabists. His articles have appeared often in *The Atlantic* as well as the *New Republic*. The term "Arabist" has acquired a pejorative connotation in U.S. political lexicons, now referring to a diplomat who has "gone native" and in the process lost sight of U.S. special interests. State Department Arabists have been criticized for diplomatic blundering preceding the Gulf War with Iraq, for example, and have been accused for decades of animosity toward the United States or Israel, simply for their interest in and empathy with Arab peoples and cultures, regardless of their politics.

EDMUND KEELEY. See YANNIS RITSOS.

DARLENE KEJU-JOHNSON (b. c. 1936) was born on Ebeye in the "Marshall Islands," as colonizers call them, in the Pacific and grew up on the northern islands of Bikini and Enietok. A graduate student in public health, she has spoken in many countries on the devastating effects of nuclear testing among the peoples and lands of the Pacific islands. She bears witness to the evacuation of Rongelop and Utirik after the people were contaminated by radioactive fallout from the 1954 explosion of a U.S. hydrogen bomb more than a thousand times stronger than the Hiroshima bomb. What is happening to the natives of her Micronesian islands is an example of what might happen to all if nuclear waste dumping and nuclear warfare manufacture does not come to a quick halt. It is one of many examples of "environmental racism" that one might highlight. (Also see AL GORE.) The United States is complicit with the continued French nuclear testing in the Pacific region, according to Greenpeace, Worldwatch, and other international environmentalists.

MAURICE KENNY, born in the Saranack Lake area of New York State, is a venerable poet of the Mohawk Nation, now a visiting professor at the University of Oklahoma. He has served as poet-in-residence at North Country Community College and taught at Paul Smith's College as well as En'owkin Center, University of Victoria, British Columbia. Coeditor of the pioneering multicultural magazine *Contact II* and publisher of Strawberry Press, he has written for many anthologies and journals. In 1984 Kenny received an *American Book Award* for *The Mama Poems*. He has published more than twenty-two volumes of verse. His selected poetry, *Between Two Rivers* (White Pine Press), won a wide readership. His most recent volumes are *Tekonwatonti: Molly Brant Poems of War* and *On Second Thought* (1993). He has won a New York State Council on the Arts fellowship with a residency at the Community Writers Project, Syracuse. His poetry has been translated into many languages. His short story collection, *Rain and Other Fictions,* reviewed in *Studies in American Indian Literature,* captures his heritage and explores the value of tradition. He has recently edited *Talking Leaves: Contemporary Native American Short Stories* (Dell, New York).

MILTON KESSLER (b. 1930), born in Brooklyn, New York, is a poet known as a cantor for humane concerns. A consummate teacher of poetry, he has been associated with the State University of New York at Binghamton since 1965. He has also taught throughout the world, in Belgium, England, Israel, and Japan. A precocious scholar in his youth, he has written many books, including *A Road Came Once* (1963), *Called Home* (1967), *Woodlawn North* (1970), *Sailing Too Far* (1974), and *The Grand Concourse (Sulphur* literary magazine) (1990, 1993), from which the poem printed here comes. *Riding First Car,* a collection of forty-one short poems will be reprinted with graphics in 1993. From 1972 to 1980 he coedited *Choice: A Magazine of Poetry and Graphics,* founded by the poet John Logan. He has contributed to numerous publications worldwide.

DR. MARTIN LUTHER KING, JR. (1929–1968) delivered passionate oratory for action in the form of nonviolent resistance to racial injustice from the mid-1950s until his assassination. Under his leadership, civil rights protesters of every color marched, boycotted, staged sit-ins, and faced police dogs and fire hoses, merciless beatings, and murderers, finally winning strategic victories in new civil rights laws. Lawyers like Thurgood Marshall, later Supreme Court Justice of the United States, who died in 1993 at age eighty-four, aided in the struggle by winning historic court cases such as *Brown v. Board of Education* (1954), which desegregated U.S. public schools, at least by law if not in practice. Born in Atlanta, Georgia, where his father raised himself out of poverty to become pastor of Ebenezer Baptist Church and a respected leader of Atlanta's middle-class Black community, King grew up in a comfortable and deely religious family. His mother was an educated woman, the daughter of an influential Atlanta preacher who had been born of a slave and had founded the church. King was a precocious scholar and avid reader who won an oratory contest in high school with the speech "The Negro and the Constitution." He entered Morehouse College in 1944 at age fifteen, graduated at age nineteen with a degree in sociology, and later earned a Ph.D. from Boston University. In Boston he met Coretta Scott, a southerner studying at the Boston Conservatory of Music; she became his wife and the mother of his children and remains an active leader in the civil rights movement. In 1954 he accepted the pastorate at the Dexter Avenue Baptist Church in Montgomery, Alabama, "the cradle of the Confederacy," from which his ministry as a "militant nonviolent resistance" leader spread throughout the world, culminating in his winning the Nobel Peace Prize in 1964. It was in Montgomery that King met Rosa Parks, an elderly Black schoolteacher arrested for refusing to give up her seat to a white man on a public bus. From her initiative, King found himself spearheading a successful boycott of the city bus system to protest racially segregated seating policies. From the Rosa Parks incident grew the renowned sit-ins and "Freedom Rides" and massive marches of the U.S. civil rights movement in which Blacks and whites of the Student Nonviolent Coordinating Committee (SNCC) and the Southern Christian Leadership Conference (SCLC), among other organizations, participated throughout the region along with citizens and lawyers from around the nation. Many collections of King's sermons are available, and a host of articles and essays by him are also widely collected. His famous "I Have a Dream" speech, delivered at the climactic March on Washington in 1963, is a classic speech in many textbooks of oratory worldwide. His birthday, January 15, was declared a national holiday in 1983 in honor of his tireless commitment to justice. There is debate among Black activists of our time about the actual accomplishments of the movement he inspired, but most agree that his work was a great achievement in the continuing struggle for human rights. Gandhi's philosophy, as well as Henry David Thoreau's writings, especially *Civil Disobedience,* were an important influence on King. (Also see LERONE BENNETT, JR., MALCOLM X, MAHATMA GANDHI, LEO TOLSTOY. Studs Terkel's *Race* (Anchor, 1992) contains oral histories of the period.)

WINONA LA DUKE is a nationally known contemporary Native American activist of the Chippewa Nation. She has written many articles and given numerous lectures on the continuing struggle for Native American land rights. She wrote the article excerpted here for *Extra,* the journal of Fairness and Accuracy in Reporting, a nonprofit media watch group in New York City. She serves on the group's advisory editorial board with other illustrious investigative reporters. (Also see MARTIN A. LEE.) La Duke's speech "Indian Treaty Rights Are a Critical Environmental Issue" won the Reebok Human Rights Award (reprinted in *Utne Reader,* January/February 1990). Indigenous peoples are threatened with extinction worldwide because of environmental racism, and their loss of protection of their lands threatens the entire globe with further biospheric degradation. (See also AL GORE, SITTING BULL, JULIAN BURGER, MAURICE F. STRONG, PAULA GUNN ALLEN, JOSEPH BRUCHAC, MAURICE KENNY, BLACK HAWK, CHIEF ANDREW J. BLACKBIRD, GERONIMO.)

ELINOR LANGER (b. 1939), born in New York and living in Portland, Oregon, is a graduate of Swarthmore College. Her literary and social criticism has appeared in publications such as *The New York Review of Books, The New York Times Book Review, Working Papers, Ms.,* and elsewhere for many years. She has held both a Guggenheim and an NEA fellowship in creative writing, and in 1984 received a National Book Critics Circle nomination for her biography of the American radical author Josephine Herbst (Warner Books). She is currently working on *The Death of Mulugeta Seraw,* the story of a skinhead killing of an Ethiopian man in Portland in 1988. She has been a visiting fellow in the Yale University American Studies Program. Research for the article in *The Nation* from which the excerpt in this book comes was supported in part by grants from the Fund for Investigative Journalism and the Dick Goldensohn Fund. Langer acknowledges research assistance from people working with Political Research Association, the Anti-Defamation League, the Portland Coalition for Human Dignity, the Anti-Klan Committee, and the Center for Democratic Renewal—mentioned here as a reminder that there are many human rights organizations working to eradicate prejudice to whom the student or activist can turn for information or to offer commitment.

WENDY WILDER LARSEN. See TRAN THI NGA.

MARTIN A. LEE (b. 1954) is a U.S. journalist, educated at the University of Michigan, who cofounded, with Jeff Cohen, Fairness and Accuracy in Reporting. FAIR publishes *Extra,* from which the selection is gleaned. FAIR is a national media watch group offering well-documented criticism in an effort to correct bias and imbalance in news reporting and commentary. A nonprofit organization funded by citizen contributions, FAIR focuses public awareness on the narrow corporate ownership of the press, the media's allegiance to official agendas, and their insensitivity to women, labor, minorities, and other public interest constituencies. It counts Ben Bagdikian, Helen Caldicott, Noam Chomsky Maggie Kuhn, WINONA LA DUKE, Studs Terkel, and Frances Moore Lappe among the many writers fighting prejudical propaganda on its international advisory board. FAIR invigorates the First Amendment by advocating greater media pluralism and the inclusion of public interest voices in national debates. (See also MICHAEL PARENTI and BRIAN HAMILTON-TWEEDALE.) FAIR has pointed out the dearth of women and minorities called to testify as experts on major media news shows and succeeded in helping to awaken a conscience toward greater equity in journalism. Lee, publisher for FAIR, is known for his recent book *Unreliable Sources: A Guide to Detecting Bias in News Media* (Lyle Stuart, 1990) and his earlier exposé *Acid Dream: The C.I.A., L.S.D., and the 60's Rebellion* (Grove Press, 1986). He works with a host of other journalists and researchers: Jim Naureckas, who edits *Extra*; Ben Bagdikian, author of *Media Monopoly*; Steve Rendall; Janine Jackson; Hollie Ainbinder; and Tiffany Devitt among them. Laura Flanders heads the Women's Desk with Veena Cabreros-Sud, and Joel Washington is in charge of the Racism Desk. Lee wrote the selection in this book with GLORIA CHANNON.

PHILIP LEVINE (b. 1928) holds a B.A. and an M.A. from Wayne State University in the United States. He has published many books of poetry. *Not This Pig* (Wesleyan University Press, 1968), is the volume which contains "Baby Villon." He has translated and published Spanish poetry, as well. Among his many awards are the Lenore Marshall Poetry Prize, two National Book Critics Circle Awards, and The American Book Award in 1980. He has served for many years as a professor of English at Tufts University, and lives in Cambridge, Massachusetts.

ROBERT JAY LIFTON, author with ERIC MARKUSEN of *The Genocidal Mentality: Nazi Holocaust and Nuclear Threat* (1990), from which the selection excerpted here comes, is Distinguished Professor of Psychiatry and Psychology at John Jay College and the Graduate Center of the City University of New York, and serves on the staff of Mount Sinai School of Medicine. Particularly concerned with the psychology of the Holocaust and the omnicidal mentality involved in nuclear warfare, he has lectured worldwide on such subjects as well as issues related to prejudice. Lifton has spent his life probing the psychic roots of drastic collective behavior and the syndrome that underlies and accompanies genocide and the planning for nuclear war. His many books include *The Nazi Doctors* (1986), *Death in Life: Survivors of Hiroshima* (1967), and, with Richard Falk, *Indefensible Weapons* (1982), winner of the National Book Award, all from Basic Books, New York.

GENNY LIM is author of the award-winning play *Paper Angels,* which aired on PBS's *American Playhouse* in 1985. She is coauthor of *Island: Poetry and History of Chinese Immigrants on Angel Island, 1910–1940* (Hoc-Doi, 1980), which won an American Book Award in 1982. Lim was awarded a 1988 fellowship in New Genre by the California Arts Council for her innovative work in multidisciplinary theater. Her award-winning performance piece *XX* premiered at the Lab in San Francisco in 1987, and her one-woman performance piece *Winter Place,* combining sculpture, *banraku,* jazz, and poetry, opened at Hatley Martin Gallery in San Francisco in 1989. *Bitter Cane,* a play set in the Hawaiian cane fields at the turn of the century, received a workshop production at the Bay Area Playwrights Festival in 1989 and was performed in Honolulu as part of the 1991 National Asian-American Studies Conference. Lim teaches at the New College in California, where she coordinates the Performance Program under the Arts and Social Change Department. For the San Francisco Festival 2000, she performed with Sonia Sanchez, Victor Hernandez Cruz, and others in *Sense-Us: The Rainbow Anthems,* a multicultural music and poetry collaboration.

SHIRLEY GEOK-LIN LIM was born in Malacca, Malaysia, to a Nonya (Malaysian assimilated) family. One of ten children, she received a Ph.D. in English and American Literature from Brandeis University in 1973. Her first book of poems, *Crossing the Peninsula* (Heinemann Educational Books), won the 1980 Commonwealth Poetry Prize. She has published two other poetry collections, *No Man's Grove* (National University of Singapore, 1985) and *Modern Secrets* (Dangaroo Press, London) as well as a volume of stories, *Another Country* (Times Books International, 1982). She is coeditor of *The Forbidden Stitch: An Asian American Women's Anthology* (Calyx Books, Corvallis, Oregon), which received an American Book Award in 1990, and of *Reading the Literatures of Asian America* and *One World of Literature.* She has published poetry in leading literary journals, *Asia, Asiaweek, Contact II,* and *Melus* among many.

DEBORAH E. LIPSTADT, the author of *Beyond Belief: The American Press and the Coming of the Holocaust, 1933–45,* is director of research for the Sirball Institute in Los Angeles. A faculty member at Occidental College, she is working on a book on Holocaust revisionism. She is a syndicated columnist who appears in *New York Newsday,* among many sources, and is a widely published nonfiction writer.

CLARENCE LUSANE (b. 1953) is an author, lecturer, and freelance journalist living in Washington, D.C. He has lectured at major universities including Harvard, Howard, Georgetown, the University of California at Berkeley, and Yale. The book from which the excerpt printed here comes, *Pipe Dream Blues: Racism and the War on Drugs* (South End Press, Boston, 1992), is a vital book that offers more documented truth than any other concerning the U.S. establishment and international drug trade, ghetto problems, and the role of racism in drug trafficking. Lusane's writings have appeared in *The Black Scholar,* the *Washington Post,* the *Oakland Tribune,* and other publications. In 1983 his article "Israeli Arms to Central America" won the prestigious Project Censored investigative reporting award (from Sonoma Valley State College, California) as the most censored story. He currently works for the Democratic Study Group, the primary research source for legislative analysis for Democrats in the U.S. House of Representatives. He is completing a doctorate in Political Science at Howard University.

MALCOLM X (1925–1964) was born at University Hospital in Omaha, Nebraska. His father, Earl Little, a Baptist preacher and a Garveyite activist from Georgia with the Universal Negro Improvement Association's Back to Africa movement, married Louise Norton in Montreal—Malcolm's mother, whose mother had become pregnant as the result of a rape by a white man. The couple was run out of their Philadelphia residence by threats from the Ku Klux Klan and settled in Omaha. When the couple moved to Lansing, Michigan, their home was burned to the ground, whereupon they resettled in East Lansing. Soon after, Earl Little was run down by a streetcar. It is believed by many Black activists that he was murdered by the Black Legion, a local white supremacist group. After much harassment by white supremacists and upon her husband's death, Louise Little suffered a nervous breakdown and was institutionalized. Malcolm Little was thereafter raised in various foster homes and finally moved to Boston to live with his sister Ella. He held many jobs, from shoe shining to soda jerking, and then became a porter on the New Haven Railroad. Discouraged by bigotry and the suffering of his parents, he entered the Boston underworld and led a life of crime, which he later said was greatly inspired by the white man's decadence and the impotence of Christianity to achieve more than hypocrisy. He worked intermittently on the railroad and became known on the streets of Boston as "Big Red." For a while he become a nightclub entertainer under the name of Jack Carlton and traveled back and forth between Michigan and Boston, later finally settling in New York City's Harlem. He was arrested in Boston on January 12, 1946, and indicted for carrying firearms, larceny, and breaking and entering. He began serving a prison term during which he educated himself using the prison library. During this period he was initiated into the Nation of Islam and the teachings of Elijah Muhammad. In Charlestown prison, he had access to an excellent library and continued educating himself in history, politics, philosophy, and theology. Upon parole in 1952, he obtained a job as a salesman with the help of his brother, who managed a furniture store in Chicago. In Chicago, he was dubbed "X" in place of "Little" by the Nation of Islam temple he had joined. He worked next on the assembly line of the Ford Motor Company and subsequently at the Gar Wood factory in Detroit. He rose to fame as a minister of Islam and a Black Nationalist, preaching nationwide and settling in New York with his wife, Betty (Shabazz). A charismatic leader and orator of the modern Black Power and Black Is Beautiful movements in the United States and a world traveler for the Nation of Islam, Malcolm X came to believe that all like-minded people of decency must join together against oppression, cruelty, and decadence and stand together for human rights, *regardless* of "race." Malcolm X was assassinated by hired gun, allegedly instigated by followers of Elijah Muhammad, whom Malcolm had begun to expose for his hypocritical ways. His autobiographical article "I'm

Talking to You, White Man," was printed in the *Saturday Evening Post* on September 12, 1964, at the height of his fame. The X surname was assumed as a defiant gesture against the history of slavery which deprived a Black person of his true African heritage. Similarly inspired, many American Blacks changed their names to African ones during the Black Power movement in the 1960s. For example, LeRoi Jones became Amiri Baraka, his African cultural identity. Indeed, it was a known technique of slaveholders throughout history, including during the Roman Empire, to rob slaves of their names and thus their filial identities to demean their spirit and keep them obedient. *The Autobiography of Malcolm X,* written with Alex Haley and published posthumously (1965), was heralded in the *New York Times* as an eloquent statement against racism. To this day there is much suspicion that the hired assassin, Tallmadge Hayer, twenty-two years old at the time of the murder, was acting in league with underground FBI activity. (See *Malcolm X, As They Knew Him* by Alex Haley, James Baldwin, Maya Angelou, William Kunstler, James Farmer, Eldridge Cleaver, and others, edited by David Gallen, Carol & Graf Publishers, New York, 1992.)

NELSON (ROLIHLAHLA) MANDELA (b. 1918) is a famed African nationalist leader, born in Transkei, South Africa. He became a successful lawyer in Johannesburg before joining the African National Congress in 1944. For more than twenty years, in defiance of brutal tactics, he led an insurgent movement among his people against the South African government and its racist policy of Apartheid, organizing three days of national strikes in 1961. His memorable four-hour defense speech, a profound argument for justice, delivered at his 1964 trial, did not save him from a sentence of life imprisonment. As a potent symbol of Black resistance, his imprisonment helped greatly in mounting an internationally coordinated campaign of cooperation between Black activists and moral peoples of all colors, worldwide, against Apartheid. During nearly three decades his wife, Winnie Mandela, also often cruelly imprisoned, restricted, or harassed herself, became a potent symbol of Black resistance, aiding immeasurably in the international campaign for his release—a movement peopled by numerous resistance fighters, many of whom sacrificed their lives. Nelson Mandela was finally set free in 1990, to worldwide rejoicing, his freedom a symbol of hope for the sufferers under Apartheid. He was invited to the United States in 1991 to make the speech to the Congress that is excerpted here. His significant return to the international political arena has accelerated the anticipation of fundamental changes in South African social and political policies, but the battle is far from won as the Black struggle against white supremacist governments continues worldwide. Mandela's life is analogous, in many ways, to CHIEF SITTING BULL's in the Americas or to DR.

MARTIN LUTHER KING, JR.'s or MALCOLM X's in the United States or to MAHATMA GANDHI's in India.

ERIC MARKUSEN, with ROBERT JAY LIFTON, wrote *The Genocidal Mentality* (1990), excerpted here. He is associate professor of sociology at Carthage College, Kenosha, Wisconsin, and coeditor of *Nuclear Weapons and the Threat of War*. *The Genocidal Mentality* attempts to explain what mentalities result when sane minds confront collective madness and explains connections between the psychology of nuclear omnicide and the Nazi Holocaust genocide.

MARIA MAZZIOTTI-GILLAN (b. 1940), cultural affairs director of the Poetry Center and Paterson Poetry Prize at Passaic County College, New Jersey, is editor of *Footwork: The Paterson Literary Review*. She has won two New Jersey State Council on the Arts fellowships. Her books include *Winter Light* (Chantry Press, 1980); *Luce d'inverno* (Cross Cultural Communications, 1988), which won an ALTA Award; *The Weather of Old Seasons* (Cross Cultural Communications, 1989); and *Growing Up Italian* (Malafemina and Chantry Press 1991–92). She has edited, with her daughter Jennifer Gillan, *Unsettling America* (Viking, 1994), an anthology of ethnic poetry that encompasses the struggle of many cultures to survive rejection from the mainstream. Her work is included in *From the Margin: Readings in Italian Americana* (Purdue University Press, 1991) and *Cries of the Spirit* (Beacon Press, 1991), as well as *The Dream Book: Writings of Italian American Women* (Schocken, 1987).

D. H. MELHEM is a poet, author, critic, and playwright, as well as an educator. *Rest in Love,* excerpted here, is a book-length poem about her mother and herself, reflecting her Arab American heritage as the child of immigrants in Brooklyn. *Notes on 94th Street* and *Children of the House Afire* concern her life on Manhattan's Upper West Side. Her books of criticism (from University Press of Kentucky) include *Gwendolyn Brooks: Poetry and the Heroic Voice* (1987) and *Heroism in the New Black Poetry: Introductions and Interviews* (1990), excerpted here. (Also see AMIRI BARAKA and GWENDOLYN BROOKS.) She won an American Book Award in 1991.

EDNA ST. VINCENT MILLAY (1892–1950), born in Rockland, Maine, was a leading classic modern poet of the United States. She lived much of her life in New York City and died in 1952 in northwestern New York State, near the Massachusetts border, where a colony for the arts was established on her estate by her actress sister, Norma Millay. A pioneer for women's rights and a fighter for social justice, she wrote for the stage and was active with the

Provincetown Players, who staged works by Eugene O'Neill and other important U.S. writers. She was the first modern U.S. poet to become a household name, traveling the country reading her works on radio. She sincerely involved herself in social justice causes such as the writers' protest against the imprisonment and execution of the immigrant Italian labor organizers SACCO and Vanzetti. She wrote the memorial poem, reprinted here, concerning the "justice denied" them by the bigoted Judge Thayer, who used ethnic epithets to declaim their labor agitation for decent wages and working conditions. Millay was herself born into poverty. With hard work she attended Vassar College and forged a brilliant literary career. Many eminent critics have written that her craft of the sonnet form in the English language is unparalleled except by William Shakespeare. Her *Collected Lyrics* and *Collected Sonnets* are also in a *selected* edition from Harper Perennial, New York.

ASHLEY MONTAGU (b. 1905), born in London, came to the United States in 1927 and was naturalized as a citizen in 1940. He studied at the University of London and the University of Florence from 1922 to 1929 and received his Ph.D. from Columbia University in 1937. He has received honorary doctorates from various U.S. colleges and universities and numerous prestigious awards throughout his long career. He had already served as research associate at Britian's Museum of Natural History and curator of Physical Anthropology for Wellcome Historical Medical Museum before becoming a professor of anatomy at New York University, a position he held from 1931 to 1938. He has since taught and lectured at numerous universities, Princeton and the New School for Social Research among them. He was responsible for drafting UNESCO's First Statement on Race in 1942. (See Statements III, IV, Appendix.) A prolific writer, he has published numerous works in anthropology and has used science to fight racism and bigotry. His numerous books on racism or issues of prejudice include *Man's Most Dangerous Myth: The Fallacy of Race* (1974), from which the excerpts herein come; *The Natural Superiority of Women* (1953, 3rd ed., 1992); *Race, Science, and Humanity* (1963); *The Nature of Human Aggression* (1976); *Human Evolution,* with Floyd Matson (1977); *What We Know about Race* (1987); *Coming into Being* (1988); and *The Story of People* (1988), all recommended reading. He edited the Natural History Sociology Series, Classics of Anthropology and served as advisory editor on anthropology for Science, Technology and the Humanities, (1936–56). He lives in Princeton, New Jersey.

EUGENIO MONTALE (1896–1981), born in Genoa, was a world-renowned Italian poet who was awarded the Nobel Prize for Literature in 1975. He pioneered the modern "Hermetic" movement in Italian poetry—intensely concerned with language, meaning, and stoic endurance—and his work is extremely difficult to translate. His many books include *Ossi di Seppia* (1925), *Le occasioni* (1939), *La bufera* (1956), *Satura* (1962), and *Xenia* (1966). His many editions and titles have been rendered into several languages by numerous poets and are available worldwide. The scene of "The Hitler Spring," the poem reprinted here, is Florence on the feast of San Giovanni, patron of the city, a festival celebrated with fireworks. The Fuehrer, with his puppet Duce and their henchmen, visits the city, grotesquely perverting the sense of the holy day. The poem epitomizes the intellectual rebellion under fascism in Italy. Its tone is analogous, for example, to much Russian poetry under Stalin, Haitian poetry under Papa Doc, Philippine poetry under Marcos, U.S. or Latin American poetry during the Reagan/Bush years—a way for cultural opposition to share the communality of moral indignation. "A country without meaningful poetry, from and for its peoples, becomes brutish," as MAYA ANGELOU, U.S. Inaugural poet in 1993, explained. A raison d'être for the style of this book.

ROBIN MORGAN is an award-winning poet, novelist, journalist, and feminist activist who has published fourteen books, including the classic anthologies *Sisterhood Is Powerful* (Random House, 1970) and *Sisterhood Is Global* (Anchor/ Doubleday, 1984), from which the selection excerpted here comes. Active in the international women's movement for two decades, she is currently editor-in-chief of the new, no-advertising *Ms.* magazine. A recipient of a National Endowment for the Arts Prize in Poetry and the Front Page Award for Distinguished Journalism, the Woman of the Year in 1990, an award from the Feminist Majority Foundation, and numerous other honors. She lives in New York City, from which she often travels to speak at major universities throughout the world. She has investigated the problems of women firsthand worldwide and recently has assessed the situation of women in Palestinian refugee camps in Jordan, Syria, Lebanon, Egypt, and the occupied territories of the West Bank and Gaza. Her latest books include a novel, *Dry Your Smile* (Doubleday, 1987); a nonfiction work, *The Demon Lover: On the Sexuality of Terrorism* (Norton, 1989); *Upstairs in the Garden and New Poems, 1968–88* (Norton, 1990); *The Mer-Child: A Legend for Children and Adults* (Feminist Press, 1991); and *The Word of a Woman: New and Selected Essays* (Norton, 1992).

TONI MORRISON (b. 1931), formerly Chloe Anthony Morrison, is a celebrated African American novelist, winner of the Pulitzer Prize for *Beloved* (1988), a poignant historical drama about slave life in the United States. A graduate of Howard and Cornell universities, she currently holds the Council of the Humanities Robert F. Goheen Chair Professorship at Princeton University. Since 1965 she has worked as an editor for Random House in New York. Winner of many literary awards for fiction, she has published several acclaimed novels: *The Bluest Eye* (1970), *Sula* (1974), *Song of Solomon* (1977), *Tar Baby* (1983), and *Jazz* (1992). Her current work, an astute analysis of the race factor in American literature and moral life titled *Playing in the Dark: Whiteness and the Literary Imagination* (1992), contains a discussion of the American classic *Huckleberry Finn* by MARK TWAIN in terms of the character "Nigger Jim." The book is recommended as a pointed study of the issues of prejudice in literary culture and racial attitudes in U.S. literature.

DANIEL PATRICK MOYNIHAN (b. 1927) is a senior Democratic senator from New York. A graduate of the City University of New York and of Tufts Fletcher School of Law and Diplomacy (Ph.D. 1949) and a Fulbright fellow at the London School of Economics and Political Science (1950–51), he served as professor of Government at Harvard and as director for the Center for Urban Studies at MIT and Harvard; as a delegate and permanent representative to the United Nations; as an ambassador to India; and in numerous other distinguished posts. Among his writings are books important to issues of prejudice, such as *Family and Nation* (1986), *On Understanding Poverty* (1969), and two classic studies of American sociology and demographics, coauthored with Nathan Glazer: *Beyond the Melting Pot* (1963) and *Ethnicity: Theory and Experience* (1975). (See quotation in "An Extraordinary Bigotry" by RICHARD GAMBINO, in this book.) "A Nation of Nations" is excerpted from an introduction to a series of books from Chelsea House Publishers, New York, on U.S. immigrant culture. (See also RACHEL TOOR.)

BHARATI MUKHERJEE is the author of two novels, *Wife* and *The Tiger's Daughter;* two works of nonfiction, *Days and Nights in Calcutta* and *The Sorrow and the Terror;* and a collection of short stories, *Darkness,* which the *New York Times Book Review* named one of the best books of the year. Born and educated in Calcutta, she earned a Ph.D. at the University of Iowa and has received grants from the National Endowment for the Arts and the Guggenheim Foundation for her fiction. She has taught Creative Writing at many universities, among them Columbia, CUNY, and UCLA. *The Middleman* (Grove Press) was chosen for *Best American Short Stories 1987.*

DAVID MURA is a poet, creative nonfiction writer, performance artist, and playwright. His memoir about a year in Japan, *Turning Japanese: Memoirs of a Sansei* (Atlantic Monthly & Anchor/Doubleday, New York, 1991), won the PEN Oakland Josephine Miles Book Award. *The New Yorker* said: "observations of Japanese humanity and culture . . . more penetrating than what we usually get from Westerners." He has also published *After We Lost Our Way,* a collection of poems which won the 1989 National Poetry Series Contest, and *A Male Grief: Notes on Pornography and Addiction.* Mura has written numerous essays on race and multiculturalism for such publications as *Mother Jones,* the *New York Times, The Utne Reader,* and *The Graywolf Annual V: Multicultural Literacy,* from which the essay reprinted here comes. His poems have appeared in the *New Republic,* the *American Poetry Review, The Nation,* the *New England Review,* and *Crazyhorse.* Among his awards are a US/Japan Creative Artist Exchange Fellowship, an NEA fellowship, a Minnesota State Arts Board grant, and a Loft-Mcknight Award of Distinction.

ARYEH NEIER, who received his B.S. from Cornell University in 1958, is the author of hundreds of articles dealing with human rights issues in prominent periodicals and law journals. Winner of the Gavel Award from the American Bar Association in 1974, he has received many academic honors and is currently executive director of Human Rights Watch, including Africa Watch, Americas Watch, Asia Watch, Helsinki Watch, and Middle East Watch. He is vice chair of the Fund for Free Expression, and an adjunct professor of Law at New York University. From 1978 to 1981 he served as director and fellow of the New York Institute for the Humanities. From 1963 to 1978 he served with the American Civil Liberties Union as a field director, then an executive director, and finally a national director. From 1960 to 1963 he was associate editor of *Current* magazine. Among his books and many book contributions, *Only Judgment* (Wesleyan University Press, 1982) and *Defending My Enemy* (1979) deal with issues related to prejudice and genocide and humane and lawful solutions to conflicts between ethnic groups.

PABLO NERUDA (1904–1973) was a Chilean Nobel Prize-winning poet who first won recognition at the age of sixteen. He served as Chilean consulate in Rangoon, Colombo, Singapore, Batavia, Buenos Aires, and Madrid throughout the 1920s. His active role in politics—beginning in 1936 and continuing until his death—resulted in conflict with the oppressive government, expulsion, and exile from his homeland. He returned to Chile in 1953, surrounded by controversy and firmly established as the world-class poet he had become. In his later works he stressed the political and social uses of poetry. His awards are international and many.

TRAN THI NGA (b. 1927) and WENDY WILDER LARSEN (b. 1940), a Vietnamese and an American woman, respectively, have formed a unique literary and cultural collaboration. Nga is a Vietnamese born in China and educated in Hanoi and South Wales, now relocated to Connecticut; Larsen is an American writer born in Boston, a graduate of Harvard, an English teacher, and the wife of a journalist who covered the Vietnam War from Saigon. Larsen traveled to Saigon to join her husband in 1970 and met Nga, a bookkeeper in her husband's office. The women became friends, Nga guiding Larsen through the culture shock of living in Saigon. After the war the women were reunited in New York City, where they collaborated on *Shallow Graves,* their unusual autobiographical, poetic narrative—a verse novel, or *truyen,* a Vietnamese genre. Their verse novel is a cross-cultural experience, an expression of how war and prejudice affect those who do not actually fight on the battlefields. The two women have given readings from *Shallow Graves* throughout the United States; the poem printed here is from that book. Larsen has published in many leading journals and is on the board of Poets House, New York City.

TESS ONWUEME (b. 1954) comes from Ogwashi-uku, Delta State, Nigeria. Since winning the Drama Prize of the Association of Nigerian Authors with her 1985 play *The Desert Encroaches,* she has been in the literary limelight in Africa, the United States, the UK, Europe, and Canada. In 1988 she won the Distinguished Authors Award at the Ife International Book Fair, Nigeria, and in 1989 she won the Martin Luther King Distinguished Writer's Award at Wayne State University, Detroit, whose press is soon to publish a compendium of her plays. She has a doctorate in drama from the University of Benin, Nigeria, and is on the faculty at Vassar College as professor of African Studies and English. Her plays include *Legacies; The Reign of Wazobia; Mirror for Campus; Ban Empty Barn; In Search of a Theme; The Broken Calabash; A Hen Too Soon;* and *Riot in Heaven,* published from 1984 to 1993. Her epic drama *Go Tell It to Women* (1992) was celebrated at Columbia U.'s School of Foreign Affairs.

JOSE EMILIO PACHECO (b. 1939) was born in Mexico City where his book *No preguntes como pasa el tiempo* (Don't Ask Me How the Time Goes By) won the National Poetry Prize in 1969. In his early twenties he was a prodigy among the great Latin American poets and a friend and student of Octavio Paz. He is an honored member of the Colegio Nacional (Mexican Academy of Arts and Sciences) and author of three collections of short stories, two novels, and ten volumes of poetry. One of his latest is *Ciudad de la memoria* (City of Memory). His work is imbued with themes of ecology, society, philosophy, and history, as well as the lyricism of love and death.

PAULINHO PAIAKAN is Chief of the Kayopo Nation of Brazil where the surviving 200,000 natives of 120 nations, who are one percent of the population of the country, are among the least assimilated peoples left living in the world. The entire region they inhabit is threatened by deforestation, colonization, mining, dam building, land conflicts, and various forms of environmental racism. His words appear in *The Gaia Atlas of First Peoples,* Anchor, NY and Gaia Books, London, 1990. (See: JULIAN BURGER.)

CHAILANG PALACIOS is a Chamorro woman from Saipan in the northern Mariana Islands. A public health education worker, in 1985 she traveled to Britian to speak, on tour with Women Working for a Nuclear Free and Independent Pacific. As a child, Palacios lived through World War II in the Pacific and has been a local witness to the devastation caused by nuclear testing among her island people, who were used as human "guinea pigs." The French nuclear testing—in complicity with the United States, according to Greenpeace, Worldwatch, and other global environmental groups—continues to this day under the reefs of the islands, a gross example of environmental racism as it continues to be practiced around the globe. (Also see AL GORE, ALEXANDER COCKBURN, GLORIA CHANNON.)

GRACE PALEY (b. 1922), Grace Goodside at birth, is an award-winning writer of fiction, poetry, criticism, and commentary. She is best known for her poignant and humorous, cryptic and poetic short stories. Considered the "Chekhov of New York City," she has produced widely acclaimed collections of short fiction: *The Little Disturbances of Man, Enormous Changes at the Last Minute,* and *Later the Same Day.* The story printed here comes from *Long Walks and Intimate Talks* (Feminist Press, New York, 1991). Paley has won a senior fellowship from the National Endowment for the Arts, has served as a New York State writer of the year, and has been a professor at Sarah Lawrence College and CCNY. She now lives in Vermont and New York City and is known as a staunch nonviolent activist for world peace and social justice. She was a member of the Women's Pentagon Action and was instrumental in drafting the Women's Pentagon Action Statement (see Appendix) along with Sybil Claiborne, novelist and chairperson of the PEN Women's Committee, among many other activists who participated in that historic demonstration. In attempts to prevent violence, Paley has been arrested several times for nonviolent civil disobedience and has worked closely with the War Resisters League in New York City. Paley has written two collections of published poetry as well as numerous reviews and articles and was one of the Washington Eleven, arrested for protesting nuclear weapons manufacture in the United States and the USSR. With the artist Vera B. Williams she created *365 Reasons Not to Have Another War* (1989) for WRL and New Society Publishers (New York and California).

MICHAEL PARENTI received a Ph.D. in Political Science from Yale University in 1962 and has taught at a number of colleges and universities. With a charismatic and sardonic wit, he has lectured widely on college campuses and before religious, labor, community, and public interest groups around the nation. His articles have appeared in leading periodicals, among them *The Nation,* the *New York Times,* and the *Los Angeles Times.* Among his books are

Powerless; Democracy for the Few; Inventing Reality: The Politics of the Mass Media; and *The Sword and the Dollar: Imperialism, Revolution and the Arms Race. Make-Believe Media,* from which the brief excerpts printed here come, is the culmination of many years of study of the U.S. media and its sociopolitical effects upon world sensibilities and its fostering of false historical perspectives, bigotry, stereotyping, and xenophobia.

LUCIA MARIA PERILLO is a poet and essayist of mixed Yugoslavian and Italian heritage. She divides her time between the state of Washington and Illinois, where she teaches at Southern Illinois University at Carbondale. Her first book, *Dangerous Life,* was published by Northeastern University Press and won the Poetry Society of America's Norma Farber Award. Her new book, *The Body Mutinies,* won the 1991 PEN/Revson Award.

JACK NUSAN PORTER (b. 1944), born in the Ukraine and raised in Milwaukee, is a sociologist, author, editor, and Jewish activist. He graduated from the University of Wisconsin–Milwaukee and received his Ph.D. in sociology from Northwestern University in 1971. He has served as a research associate at the Ukrainian Research Institute of Harvard University and has taught at Boston University. He has published twenty books and anthologies and more than 250 articles, including *Student Protest and the Technocratic Society, Jewish Radicalism* (with Peter Dreier); *The Sociology of American Jews, The Jew as Outsider; Collected Essays; Kids in Cults* (with Irvin Doress); *Conflict Resolution; Jewish Partisans,* volumes 1 and 2, and *Genocide and Human Rights,* from which his essay on genocide comes. He has lectured widely on American social problems and political/religious movements and has testified before several government commissions. His books are recommended reading on the subject of prejudice and he has edited a curriculum guide, *The Sociology of Genocide/The Holocaust* (1992), for the American Sociological Association. He lives with his wife and children in Boston.

AL POULIN, JR. See ANNE HEBÉRT.

LILIA QUINDOZA-SANTIAGO (b. 1949), born in Lipit Manaoag, Pangasinan, lived for more than twenty years in Baguio City. She currently teaches Philippine literature at the University of the Philippines, Diliman, Quezon City. She has won major awards as a poet, fiction writer, essayist, and critic from the Palanca, cultural center of the Philippines. She won the title of "Poet of the Year" *(Makta ng Taon)* for 1989 by winning first prize in the Talaang Ginto of the Linangan ng mga Wika ng Philipinas. She is mother to four children, and her husband, Jesus Manuel Santiago, is also a poet. She spent years in prison as a resistance fighter and writes in the indigenous language of her people. Her book of poetry *Kagampan at iba pan tula (Pregnant and Other Poems)* (1989), is available in a bilingual edition from Kalikasan Press, Sampaloc, Manila.

ROCHELLE RATNER (b. 1948) lives in New York City where she is executive editor of *American Book Review*—strong on issues of multicultural literature— and a poetry editor of *Israel Horizons*. She reviews regularly for *Library Journal*. Her books include two novels, *Bobby's Girl* (1986) and *Lion's Share* (1991), both from Coffee House Press. She has published twelve books of poems, including *Practicing to Be a Woman: New and Selected Poems* (Scarecrow Press, 1982) and *Someday Songs,* BkMk Press, University of Missouri–Kansas City, 1992), from which the poem selected here comes. The letter collection offers an understanding of Jewish ritual customs and holidays throughout.

DIANE (SILVER) RAVITCH (b. 1938), born in Houston, Texas, is a historian, educator, author, and government official in the area of education. With a B.A. from Wellesley College and a Ph.D. from Columbia (1975) and honorary degrees from several other institutions of higher learning, she teaches at Teachers College of Columbia University and has served as assistant secretary to the Office of Education Research and Improvement of the U.S. Department of Education and counselor to the Secretary of Education. Among her books, all useful reading about the battle for multiculturalism and a curriculum of inclusion, are *The Great School Wars* (1974); *The Revisionist Revised* (1977); *The Troubled Crusade* (1983); *The Schools We Deserve* (1985); and, with others, *Educating an Urban People* (1981); *The School and the City* (1985); *Against Mediocrity* (1984); *Challenges to the Humanities* (1985); *What Do Our Seventeen Year Olds Know?* (1987); *The American Reader* (1990); and a coedited volume, *The Democracy Reader* (1992). Though her view is particular to U.S. education, it is analogous to problems of education wherever there are so-called minority cultures within a majority culture. The target of angry Afrocentrists of late, Ravitch can be viewed as a moderate in the area of education and is considered too progressive by those conservatives who are angry Eurocentrists. For an interesting revelation of culture and history, see Martin Barnal's *Black Athena* (1987), a controversial but factual view of the issues. Ravitch here presents a moderate humanistic view for all sides. The problem with such views is that they cannot correct heinous wrongs with enough passion and intensity to satisfy the avengers, even as they may cause less conflict and destruction in the present. And so the heated argument between the Afrocentrists—with their justifiable anger—and "threatened" Eurocentrists continues. (Also see W. E. B. DU BOIS and AMIRI BARAKA.)

ISHMAEL REED (b. 1938), born in Chattanooga, Tennessee, is president and a founder of the Before Columbus Foundation, publisher of a review dealing with various matters of "ethnic" American literatures, and founder of the American Book Awards for the advancement of multicultural literature in the United States and throughout the world. A fellow of Calhoun House, Yale University in 1983, he now serves as an associate editor for the *American Book Review*. He is a recipient of an award from the National Institute of Arts and Letters (1975) and the National Endowment for the Arts (1974) and was a Guggenhiem fellow in 1975. He has served as chair for the Berkeley Council on the Arts and the Coordinating Council of Literary Magazines. A major force in the advancement of African American literature as well as other ethnic literatures, he has written many astute and controversial novels, collections of poetry, and essays, among them the highly recommended *Writin' Is Fightin'* (Atheneum, New York, 1988), from which the essay herein is garnered. Also see *Mumbo Jumbo* (1972); *The Flight to Canada* (1976); *Terrible Twos* (1982); *Cab Calloway Stands in for the Moon* (1986); *Catechism of the Neo-American HooDoo Church* (1970); *Ishmael Reed: New and Collected Poems* (1989); and *God Made Alaska for the Indians* (1981). He is a senior lecturer at the University of California at Berkeley and a member of the language usage panel of *The American Heritage Dictionary*.

EDWIN O. REISCHAUER (b. 1910), born in Tokyo and raised in Japan, is University Professor Emeritus of Japanese and a historian of Harvard University, where he received his doctorate in Far Eastern Languages in 1938. After being graduated Phi Beta Kappa from Oberlin College, Ohio, in 1931 and receiving a graduate degree in History from Harvard in 1932, he went on to study at the universities of Paris, Tokyo, and Kyoto. He served as U.S. ambassador to Japan in the 1960s and has written and lectured widely on Japanese culture and Asian affairs. The excerpt printed here is from *The Japanese Today: Change and Continuity* (Belknap Press of Harvard University Press, 1977). Among his other titles are *Japan: Past and Present* (1946) *The United States and Japan* (1950), and *Wanted: An Asian Policy* (1955). To counterbalance what Reischauer says here concerning Japanese xenophobia, particularly toward the Koreans, one must be aware of the xenophobia of U.S. Americans toward the Japanese. (See SHIGOTOSHI IWAMATSU, DAVID MURA, and EDWARD T. HALL.)

ALAN RIDING (b. 1943), born in Brazil's Rio de Janeiro, is an internationally known journalist and correspondent who works for the *New York Times* among other publications worldwide. Winner of the Maria Moors Cabet prize from the Columbia University Graduate School of Journalism in 1979, he has served as a bureau chief for South America and has been based in Rio as well as Mexico City. "Called to the bar" at Grey's Inn, London, in 1966, he has worked with the *New York Times* News Service in London, as a foreign correspondent at the United Nations, in Buenos Aires, and for the *Financial Times* of London.

YANNIS RITSOS (b. 1909) was a premier resistance poet of Greece who suffered great hardship, misfortune, exile, and censorship, most notably in 1936 when his classic work *Epitaphios* was burned along with the works of other resistance writers. Ritsos was exiled from his homeland for four years in the murderous turmoil following World War II. His poem is translated here by eminent U.S. author Edmund Keeley, president of American PEN Center since 1991. Keeley's third Ritsos collection, *Yannis Ritsos: Repetitions, Testimonies, Parentheses,* was published by Princeton University Press in 1990. A graduate of Princeton and Oxford, Keeley has published six novels and fourteen volumes of poetry in translation, as well as five volumes of nonfiction. Among his works are *The Libation,* which won the Rome Prize of the American Academy of Arts and Letters; *The Gold Hatted Lover; Cavafy's Alexandria; A Wilderness Called Peace; The Salonika Bay Murder: Cold War Politics and the Polk Affair;* and *School for Pagan Lovers.* He has won numerous literary and translation prizes and has been awarded many distinguished grants. In 1992 he was elected a fellow of the American Academy of Arts and Sciences. In the translation printed here, the Greek poet's main theme is crystallized—the search for a humanity which extends compassion to others.

JAN ROGOZIŃSKI is a historian who lives in Florida and publishes with Facts on File of New York and Oxford, U.K. His *Brief History of the Caribbean,* from which the chapter "The World of the Slaves" is excerpted, provides factual understanding of much of the racism in that region of conflict. See in particular his explanation of what occurred in Haiti as well as with the career of Toussaint, liberator of the first Black African nation of the Caribbean, and his chapter on runaway slaves and slave rebellion, which demonstrates how active slaves were in the struggle for their own liberation. There is a tendency to think of Blacks under slavery as acquiescent and accepting of their fate, when the opposite was the rule. Recent films from Hollywood depicting the struggle of Black American troops for their own liberation during the U.S. Civil War have finally captured the popular imagination, but W. E. B. DU BOIS and FREDERICK DOUGLASS, fathers of the civil rights movement in the United States, have written much about the activities of freedom-fighting "slaves." See also the career of Harriet Tubman, among so many others, including MALCOLM X, MARTIN LUTHER KING, JR., Chief Justice Thurgood Marshall, SOJOURNER TRUTH, and A. FRANCES ELLEN WATKINS HARPER. Many narratives written by slaves, such as Douglass's, provide good firsthand accounts on the subject.

DOROTHY ROWE (b. 1930) is an eminent psychologist of the United Kingdom who was born in Australia. She worked as a teacher and child psychologist in Sydney, before coming to Britain in 1968 as a clinical psychologist researching depression. Upon completing her Ph.D. from Sheffield University, she moved to North Lincolnshire to head the Department of Clinical Psychology there. In 1986 she returned to live in Sheffield and devote herself full-time to writing, research, and teaching. Her work concerns questions of cognitive meaning and communication. She has written eight successful books, including *Depression: The Way Out of Your Prison* (Routledge, 1983), which won the MIND Book of the Year Award. Rowe writes regularly for national newspapers and magazines in England and appears frequently on television and radio. Her studies into aggression and creating enemies were important to her writing of *Living with the Bomb* (Routledge, 1984). Others of her books include *Wanting Everything, Beyond Fear, The Courage to Live,* and *Breaking the Bonds.*

NICOLO SACCO (1891–1927) and Bartolomeo Vanzetti were two unschooled labor union activists and political "anarchists" who were active among beleaguered working-class immigrants, particularly Italians and Jews, agitating for decent wages and working conditions in the United States during the 1920s. They were executed in 1927 by the order of Judge Thayer of Massachusetts for a crime they did not commit. Judge Thayer is known to have called them "dirty dagoes" and other ethnic epithets. In 1891 Italian immigrant workers had been the object of the largest mass lynching in U.S. history in New Orleans. Writers like EDNA ST. VINCENT MILLAY, Edmund Wilson, Katherine Anne Porter, John Dos Passos, Maxwell Anderson, and many others protested their innocence and their unfair trial. For a historic account of bigotry against U.S. working-class immigrants, with a detailed account of Sacco and Vanzetti, see *La Storia* by Jerre Mongione and Ben Morreale (HarperCollins, New York, 1992); Richard Schon's *A History of the Jews in America* (Knopf, 1991); or Howard Zinn's *People's History of the United States* (Harper, 1986). For analogous contemporary accounts of bigotry against immigrants worldwide, see RACHEL TOOR, RICHARD GAMBINO, MICHAEL PARENTI, DANIEL PATRICK MOYNIHAN, ALAN RIDING, EDWIN O. REISCHAUER, FRANK THALER, JOSE EMILIO PACHECO, and DORA YATES.

HARVEY SHAPIRO is author of *National Cold Storage Company; The Light Holds; This World;* and *Lauds and Nightsounds,* among other books of poetry. His ninth book is *A Day's Portion* (1993). He is deputy editor of the *New York Times Magazine,* which he joined in 1957. From 1975 to 1983 he was editor of the *New York Times Book Review.* He lives in Brooklyn, has two sons, and served in the 15th Air Force in World War II.

SITTING BULL (1834–1890), Tantanka Iyotake, was a great Dakota Sioux warrior chief born near Grand Rapids. He was a medicine man, or healer, widely respected and admired among all native tribes except for those relatively few who had become agents of the European invaders. He was a leader in the Sioux War of 1876–77 and defeated General Custer at the Little Bighorn in 1876. White propaganda portrayed Sitting Bull as an evil monster and ambitious savage, though he was considered a great savior and organizer among his people, exemplary of intelligence, wisdom, and generosity. He escaped to Canada but surrendered in 1881 and was put into the reservation at Standing Rock. He was made a spectacle attraction of Buffalo Bill Cody's "Wild West Show" in 1885 but, still rebellious, was killed attempting to escape the police in the "Ghost Dance" uprising of 1890.

SHARON SPENCER has been active in human relations activities and multicultural curriculum development throughout her career as a professor of English and Comparative Literature at Montclair State College, New Jersey. A fiction writer and literary critic, Spencer has published books, articles, short stories, and poems. She has directed seven faculty development grants in multicultural literatures; one of these was funded by the National Endowment for the Humanities. Originally from Colorado, Spencer settled in New Jersey after completing her education at New York University.

CAROLE STONE, born in Newark, New Jersey, is the recipient of three fellowships from the New Jersey State Council on the Arts and has won many literary prizes. She is a professor of English and Literature at Montclair State College, New Jersey, and has published numerous poems and critical commentary in magazines and anthologies. Her latest book of poetry is *Giving Each Other Up* (Andrew Mountain Press, Connecticut).

MAURICE F. STRONG, secretary general of the 1992 United Nations Conference on Environment and Development, has held top positions in numerous organizations concerned with environmental and humanitarian issues and has won several international awards. The selection printed here is from his Foreword to *A Gaia Atlas of First Peoples: A Future for the Indigenous World* (Anchor, 1991), edited and composed by Julian Burger with campaigning groups of native peoples worldwide, important reading for an understanding of the severity of environmental racism and cultural destruction on a global scale. It offers an understanding of how this issue affects us all. (See also AL GORE, ALEXANDER COCKBURN and GLORIA CHANNON, JULIAN BURGER, WINONA LA DUKE.)

FRANK THALER, a foreign correspondent worldwide, is a freelance journalist currently working in Germany. This article appeared in the *New Republic,* Washington, D.C.

HUGH TINKER (b. 1921), was born in Westcliff, England, and gained his M.A. at Cambridge University. He has been a professor of Asian Government and Politics at the University of London and a professor of Politics at the University of Lancaster, where he is now Emeritus Professor. Other responsibilities have been as director of the Institute of Race Relations; a member of Z Council, Minority Rights Groups; chairman of the Advisory Committee of SSRC Unit on Ethnic Relations; and vice president of Ex-Services Campaign for Nuclear Disarmament. The article printed here is adapted from the original in *International Journal,* Vol. 34, No 3., reprinted by the author and the Canadian Institute for International Affairs, in *A Reader for Peace Studies* (Pergamon International Press, Oxford, UK, 1990).

SANDY TOLAN (b. 1956) has written for the *New York Times Magazine,* the *Boston Globe,* the *Miami Herald, The Village Voice, Audubon,* and *The Nation.* A regular contributor to National Public Radio, he received broadcasting's Columbia-DuPont Award in 1986 for an NPR series on the sanctuary movement for Central American refugees. Tolan, a 1992–93 Nieman Journalism fellow at Harvard, is executive producer for Homelands Productions. During 1991–92, he collaborated with ALAN WEISMAN on the NPR and Soundprint series *Vanishing Homelands: A Chronicle of Change across the Americas,* excerpted here.

RACHEL TOOR received a degree in English from Yale University and currently serves as an editor at a major publishing house in New York City. She lives in Brooklyn. *The Polish Americans* in the Peoples of North America Series (1988) was her first book. The series from Chelsea House also includes the Afro, Indian, Amish, Arab, Armenian, Bulgarian, Carpatho-Rusyn, Central, Chinese, Croatian, Cuban, Czech, Danish, Dominican, Dutch, English, Filipino, French, French-Canadian, German, Greek, Haitian, Hungarian, Iberian, Indo, Indo-Chinese, Iranian, Irish, Italian, Japanese, Jewish, Korean, Mexican, Norwegian, Pacific Islander, Arctic, Puerto Rican, Romanian, Russian, Scotch-Irish, Scottish, Serbian, Slovak, South Swedish, Turkish, Ukrainian, and West Indian Americans—giving an idea of the ethnic diversity which makes up the United States. The series is introduced by DANIEL PATRICK MOYNIHAN, the sociologist/political scientist/senator of New York.

LEO TOLSTOY (1828–1910), Count Leo (Lev) Nikolayevich Tolstoy, world-renowned Russian author and moral philosopher, was born in Yasnaya Polyana, near Tula, Russia, to a family of aristocratic landowners. He was educated at the University of Kazan, which he left without finishing his degree. One of his early and enduring influences was the French philosopher Rousseau. He attempted to improve working and educational conditions of the serfs on his estate. Frustrated in his task, he left in 1851 to join the army in the Caucasus and wrote his novel *The Cossacks* (1854, published 1863) among the Cossack settlers, where he also finished his first important work, the autobiographical *Childhood,* followed by *Boyhood* and *Adolescence.* His stories written during his participation in the Crimean War won him his popular reputation for frank realism. He lived in Moscow and traveled extensively abroad, where he became increasing disappointed with the materialist and militaristic trend of Western civilization, fostering in him a growing sympathy for the peasant masses whose simple way of life he extolled. In 1869 he finished his masterwork, *War and Peace,* followed by many books read with rapt attention by the European public, including *Anna Karenina,* a novel sympathetic to women's plight in a male-dominated society. In 1897, in *What Is Art?,* he condemned art that failed to foster the moral good among humans, as he had come to embrace the Sermon on the Mount and "brotherly love" as the only true meaning of life. During his last twenty years he became not only the most widely read literary figure in the world but a major moral force. He was able, because of his fame and nobility, to escape censorship of the repressive czarist regime. He died from pneumonia in a small railway station, in flight from his home and quixotic quarrels with his wife and children over his desire to give away all his worldly goods and land to the peasants who had worked his estate. Among the important works of his later years are *The Resurrection, The Power of Darkness,* and *The Live Corpse* (1911). He was a seminal influence on the slowly but steadily burgeoning nonviolent activist movement, his banner having been taken up by such important civil rights leaders as GANDHI and MARTIN LUTHER KING, JR. His *Writings on Civil Disobedience and Non-Violence* is available from New Society Publishers, Santa Cruz, California.

SOJOURNER TRUTH (c. 1797–1883) was an abolitionist and freed slave originally called Isabella. Born in Ulster County, New York, she left domestic employment in New York City in 1843, named herself Sojourner Truth, and traveled throughout North America preaching emancipation and women's rights with great eloquence, despite her lack of schooling. This quote was a public answer to a heckler.

MARINA TSVETAYEVA (1892–1941) is considered by many to be among the finest poets Russia has ever produced. Pasternak among others offered praise for her passionate work. She led a tragic life, disrupted by wars and political turmoil, caught between her loyalties to the White Russian Army and to the Bolshevik Revolution. She experienced war's resultant poverty and periods of political exile. She wrote many verses in a spirit of opposition to "The Terrible Years"—as Russia's great poets call them—of purges under Stalin's dictatorship. She lost her youngest daughter to starvation during the Moscow famine of 1919 and suffered great despair when her husband, accused of being a Soviet agent, was arrested and shot. In 1941, harassed and destitute, she committed suicide.

BISHOP DESMOND TUTU (b. 1931) is an internationally renowned Civil Rights Activist of South Africa who was born in Klerksdorp and ordained an Anglican priest in 1961. He received his degree in divinity and theology from Kings College, London, and was an educator throughout the 1970s, becoming Anglican Dean of Johannesburg in 1975. He was among those to appeal for an international boycott of South African business and trade in an attempt to end apartheid. He received the Nobel Prize for Peace for his nonviolent campaign against apartheid, and in 1986 he became the first Black to be elected Archbishop of Capetown. He heads the Anglican Church of South Africa in Nambia, Mozambique, Swaziland, and Lesotho, and served as Bishop of Lesotho in 1976 and of Johannesburg in 1984.

MARK TWAIN (1835–1910), born Samuel Langhorne Clemens, was an American journalist, essayist, and novelist, avant-garde in his day and still read as an American classic for his astute wit, folkloric style, and wry political commentary. He began his career, which included freelance lecture travels, as assistant to his brother, who was secretary to the governor of Nevada. He tried his hand at gold mining before becoming a journalist with the *Virginia City Territorial Enterprise*. In 1864 he moved to San Francisco as a reporter and also worked for a time as a correspondent in Hawaii. After the success of his early writings, he visited Europe, traveling throughout France, Italy, and Palestine, and finally settling in Hartford, Connecticut, with his wife and family. While in Europe he gathered material for his *Innocents Abroad* (1869) and *Roughing It* (1872), which established his reputation as a humorist. Famous for his popular *Huckleberry Finn,* characterization, Twain, as did William James and other writers of conscience of his time, sought to expose the brutal excesses of American colonization of the Philippines, facts still unknown to the general American public. The public at the time was fairly ignorant of the genocidal prejudice and xenophobia practiced abroad by U.S. military enterprises and multinational corporate ambitions—just as people of the Soviet Union during the cold war years were prevented from knowing the evil committed abroad by its government which sought to hold its expansionist line against U.S. expansionism.

SHARON VENNE of the Cree Nation is of a group of 70,000 indigenous peoples of Canada. There are 326,000 registered natives organized in 577 bands surviving in the country. These Indians, threatened by varying forms of colonization and environmental racism, make up 4 percent of the Canadian population. Her words appear in *The Gaia Atlas of First Peoples* (Anchor, New York, and Gaia Books, London, 1990). (See JULIAN BURGER.)

ROBERT VISCUSI is executive officer of the Wolfe Institute for the Humanities at Brooklyn College of the City University of New York. He is the author of *Max Beerbohm, or the Dandy Dante: Rereading with Mirrors* and has edited the volume *Victorian Learning for Browning Institute Studies*. His work in literary theory and Italian-American writing has been widely published. He is founder of the Italian-American Writers Association in New York and is an accomplished poet. He serves on the advisory board of *VIA: Voices in Italian Americana* (Purdue University), and Italian-Americana (SUNY, Buffalo).

VOLTAIRE (1694–1778), born François Marie Arouet Voltaire in Paris, was the son of a notary and of Marguerite Daumard, of the lesser nobility of Poitou. A philosopher who gained entry, through his father's social climbing, to the aristocratic circles of the Richelieus, Voltaire was well educated in literature at the Jesuit College of Louis-le-Grand. His wit, irreverence, and skepticism toward aristocratic society led him to compose satiric verses that landed him for the year of 1717 in the Bastille. He lived from 1726 to 1729 in self-exile in London, where he met Pope and Swift. His progressive works, celebrating Newtonian physics among other new ideas, were condemned by the French government. Voltaire, a symbol of the "Enlightenment," was an implacable enemy of ignorance, religious superstition, bigotry, ethnocentrism, and hypocrisy, which he satirized well in his famed harrowing and comic adventures of Candide, an optimistic idealist who suffers the xenophobic miseries of the real world.

ALAN WEISMAN (b. 1947) collaborated with SANDY TOLAN on a documentary series produced by National Public Radio and Soundprint titled *Vanishing Homelands. A Chronicle of Change across the Americas,* on which the article excerpted here is based. With their colleagues Nancy Postero and Cecilia Vaisman, they won a Robert F. Kennedy Journalism Award for international reporting on the disadvantaged. Weisman and Tolan are currently writing a book called *Vanishing Homelands* and producing a sequel series titled *Searching for Solutions.* Weisman, a former Fulbright Senior Scholar in Colombia and a 1986 Bread Loaf fellow in nonfiction, is a contributing editor to the *Los Angeles Times Magazine* and associate producer for Homelands Productions. His books include *We, Immortals* (1979) and *La Frontera: The United States Border with Mexico* (1986). He has written stories for leading magazines as well.

WALT WHITMAN (1819–1891), the most renowned of American poets for his authorship of the essay *Democratic Vistas* as well as his poetry collection *Leaves of Grass* (c. 1865), was born in West Hills, Long Island, New York, the son of a radical, free-thinking carpenter. Brought up in Brooklyn from the age of four, he served as an apprentice in a lawyer's, a doctor's, and a printer's office before becoming an itinerant teacher in country schools and turning to editing, in 1846, on the *Brooklyn Eagle*. During the U.S. Civil War, he served as a nurse among the wounded and was read and applauded by Abraham Lincoln, if scorned and dismissed by Secretary Harlan and others as the author of "an indecent book"—that book being *Leaves of Grass*, now thought of as the most important and original of U.S. classics. His curiously irregular free verse forged the way for modern U.S. poetry and is known for its humanizing sentiments against racism, sexism, sexual repression, and oppression. Though his writing had to struggle for acceptance in his lifetime, today Whitman has become known worldwide as the voice of the mosaic of American culture and democracy struggling to born from government corruption. Whitman had a profound influence on many progressive poets of our time, particularly Allen Ginsberg.

ELIE WIESEL (b. 1928), born in Sighet, Transylvania, was a child when arrested from his home and imprisoned at Auschwitz concentration camp and subsequently Buchenwald. Though he survived, he witnessed the murder of his family. After the Holocaust, he was taken to Paris where he worked as a journalist and writer. He has been a U.S. citizen for many years. Winner of the Nobel Prize for Peace in 1986, he lives with his wife in the Boston area and is on the faculty of Boston University. He has established an international foundation, the Institute for Humanity, based in New York City, which holds global conferences on the study of human rights issues and the search for world peace. He is a renowned spokesperson for the worldwide Never Again movement against anti-Semitism. His many writings are available in numerous languages and examine human suffering, injustice, guilt, and the mentality of genocide as it was practiced in Nazi Germany's systematic murder of Jews. Among his many suggested books are *One Generation After* and *A Jew Today* (Random House, New York), translated from the French by Marion Wiesel.

VIRGINA WOOLF (1882–1941), an English novelist and essayist, was a successful innovator of modern fiction. She was a member of the Bloomsbury group, which included Dora Carrington and Lytton Strachey, John Maynard Keynes, E. M. Forster, and others. Author of many books, and a pioneer for women's rights, she wrote two feminist tracts, *A Room of One's Own* (1930), and *Three Guineas* (1938), from which this quotation comes.

CAROLYNE WRIGHT (b. 1949), born in Bellingham, Washington, received her doctorate in English and Creative Writing from Syracuse University. In 1971–72, she held a Fulbright study grant in Chile, during the presidency of Salvador Allende. Her investigative memoir-in-progress about her experience, *The Road to Isla Negra,* received a 1990 PEN/Jerard Fund Award. Four collections of her poetry have been published, plus a volume of translations from Chilean Spanish: *In Order to Talk with the Dead: Selected Poems of Jorge Teillier* (University of Texas Press, 1993). From 1986 to 1988, Wright was in Calcutta on an Indo-U.S. fellowship; and from 1989 to 1991 she was in Dhaka, Bangladesh, on a Fulbright senior research grant to collect and translate, with the assistance of natives, the work of twentieth-century Bengali women writers. She was a 1991 fellow of the Bunting Institute/Radcliffe College and in 1992–93 was an associate of the Department of Sanskrit and Indian Studies at Harvard, where she completed two anthologies of Bengali women poets and fiction writers.

JAMES WRIGHT (1927–1980) was born in Martin's Ferry, Ohio, the son of a factory worker and was graduated from Kenyon College with assistance from the GI Bill of Rights for his service in Japan with the peacetime army. He was a Fulbright fellow at the University of Vienna and received an M.A. and Ph.D. from the University of Washington. He taught in Minneapolis and at Hunter College, New York, from 1966 to 1980. His *Collected Poems* won the Pulitzer Prize in 1972. He was winner of a Rockefeller Foundation grant and a fellowship from the Academy of American Poets, as well as two Guggenheim grants. He traveled often, with his wife Anne, to Europe, especially Italy. *This Journey* and *Above the River,* his complete poems and prose pieces, were published posthumously.

DORA E. YATES, (c. 1910–79), was secretary of the Gypsy Lore Society in London. She wrote the essay reprinted here for that association in 1949 and it was later published in *Commentary.* It has also been reprinted in Jack Nusan Porter's *Genocide and Human Rights* (University of America, Maryland), which contains essays on genocide against Armenians, Jews, Cambodians, Tibetans, Bengalis, and Paraguayan Indians as well as a selected bibliography on the issues of genocide. The bigotry against Romanian gypsies, and gypsy culture in general, persists today, as neo-Nazi skinheads demonstrate for their expulsion from sanctuary in East Germany. Gypsies might again be forced back over the border where they will likely perish in starvation and exile. (Also see the works in this book by JACK NUSAN PORTER and the ZORYAN INSTITUTE.)

WILLIAM BUTLER YEATS (1865–1939) is the consummate modern poet of Ireland. Born in Sandymount, a Dublin suburb, to an artist father of some accomplishment and educated in his youth in London, he returned to Ireland in 1880 to attend Howth High School near Dublin. His first lyrics were published in *The Dublin University Review* in 1884. Very concerned with Irish folklore and mythology, he edited *Fairy and Folk Tales of the Irish Peasantry* in 1888, after publishing his own volume of verse and contributing to various reviews. Inspired by Maud Gonne, an ardent Irish nationalist, he wrote poetry and dramas rich in Celtic imagery and founded the Irish Literary Society to foster the culture of his homeland against British cultural repression. In 1896 he met Lady Gregory, the mistress of an estate at Coole in Galway, where he set and composed many of his finest poems. He published a plethora of books, and his life was a tangled twine of political and cultural involvement. He played an important role in developing the Irish Renaissance with his move to the Abbey Theatre in 1904. His play *Cathleen ni Houlihan* (1902), with Maud Gonne in the title role, is said to have helped spark the Easter Rising in 1916. Yeats wrote a memorial poem for those executed as a result of that uprising, titled "Easter 1916." After many books of poems and much political involvement, interrupted by the Irish Civil War, he became a member of the Irish Senate in 1922 and in 1923 was awarded the Nobel Prize for Literature. A titan of twentieth-century literature, he moved in 1928 to Rapallo in Italy, where he completed his final works, including the controversial anthology *The Oxford Book of Modern Verse, 1892–1935*. He died in self-exile in Cap Martin, Alpes Maritimes, in 1939. His experiences are collected in *Autobiographies* (1955).

YEVGENY YEVTUSHENKO (b. 1933), a famed Russian poet, was born in Sima in Siberia and moved with his mother to Moscow in 1944. His work attracted attention with the publication of *The Third Snow* (1955) and *Chausse Eutuziastov* (1956). *The Promise* (1957) made him a popular spokesperson for the post-Stalinist generation. He became a controversial celebrity with the publication of *Zima Junction* and "Babi Yar" (1962), an attack on anti-Semitism in Russia as well as on Nazi Germany. He has often expressed his beliefs and opinions even at risk of official disapproval, and in 1974 he publicly supported Solzhenitsyn upon the occasion of his arrest. He has spoken out for a post-Stalinist spiritual revolution. His later works include the collections *Love Poems* (1977), *Heavy Soils* (1978), and *Ivan the Terrible and Ivan the Fool* (1979) and the novel *Berries* (1981). Dmitri Shostakovich composed his Thirteenth Symphony for the lyrics of five of Yevtushenko's poems, including "Babi Yar." Yevtushenko published his *Precocious Autobiography* in 1963.

HARRIET ZINNES, Professor Emerita of English, Queens College of the City University of New York, is the award-winning author of six books of poems; a volume of short fiction, *Lover* (Coffee House Press, 1989); translations, *Blood and Feathers: Selected Poems of Jacques Prevert* (Schocken, 1988); a book on art, *Ezra Pound and the Visual Arts* (New Directions, 1980); and articles and reviews in such publications as *Hollins Critic, The Nation,* the *New York Times Book Review, Parnassus, Newsday, Philadelphia Inquirer,* and *Washington Post Book World.*

ZORYAN INSTITUTE is an international center for Armenian research with affiliates in Cambridge, Massachusetts, Toronto, and Paris. Its purpose is to document the Armenian experience in relation to culture, history, and thought, seeking to understand the dynamics of Armenian social, political, and cultural life, particularly in terms of the changing environment which defines the diaspora. The institute sponsors colloquia, public presentations, and publications in Genocide Studies, Diaspora Studies, and Republic of Armenia Studies. Comparable institutes can be discovered for many cultures, especially those which have suffered unparalleled genocide in their histories. The institute maintains a library of monographs, tapes, oral histories, photographs, newspapers, bibliographies, and books from around the world and is a nonprofit organization. (Also see Resource List.)

Resource List of Organizations

UNESCO
United Nations Plaza
New York, NY 10017
*Various publications: international law,
human rights documents, as herein.*

Amnesty International, USA
322 Eighth Ave.
New York, NY 10001
Human rights issues
Publications and Action

Greenpeace
1436 U St. N.W., P.O. Box 96128
Washington, DC 20090
Environmental racism
Newsletter: *Greenpeace*

The Center for Defense
  Information
1500 Massachusetts Ave.
Washington, DC 20005
Combats military spending overkill
Newsletter: *The Defense Monitor*

Anti-Defamation League
823 United Nations Plaza
New York, NY 10017
Training and curriculum materials
Handbook: *Extremism on the Right*

Educators for Social Responsibility
490 Riverside Dr., Room 27
New York, NY 10027
*Conflict resolution materials;
publications for teachers*

NYC Commission on Human
  Rights
Bias Prevention/Response Team
280 Broadway, Room 311
New York, NY 10007
*Biased crimes laws and information;
most cities have a unit*

People for the American Way
2000 M St. N.W.
Washington, DC 20036
*Defense of constitutional rights
and religious freedoms*

Foundation for Humanity
803 Third Ave.
New York, NY 10022
Elie Wiesel, Founder
International peace conferences

Center for Democratic Renewal
P.O. Box 50469
Atlanta, GA 30302
Source of references
Newsletter: *The Monitor*

John Brown Anti-Klan Committee
220 9th St., #443
San Francisco, CA 94103
An activist group

Searchlight
37B New Cavendish Street
London, WIM 8JR England
*Information about neo-Nazi
movement in Europe;
British anti-fascist monthly magazine*

National Institute against Prejudice
31 South Green St.
Baltimore, MD 21201
Study of violence in media;
research in laws and policy

Southern Poverty Law Center
400 Washington Avenue
Montgomery, AL 36104
KKK Special Report, history, etc.
Newsletter: "Teaching Tolerance"

Louisiana Coalition against Racism
and Nazism
806 Perdido Street, Room 205
New Orleans, LA 70112
Information on David Duke
and other issues

National Gay and Lesbian Task
Force
1517 U St. N.W.
Washington, DC 20009
Variety of publications
concerning hate crimes

Data Center
464 19th St.
Oakland, CA 94612
Archives of newspapers;
on-line search capability

Political Research Associates
678 Massachusetts Ave., Room 205
Cambridge, MA 02139
Research institute on right-
wing & authoritarian groups

World Council of Indigenous
Peoples
(International Secretariat)
555 King Edward Ave.
Ottawa, Ontario, Canada KIN 6NS
International information and support

Indigenous Survival International
Dene National Office
P.O. Box 2338, Yellowknife
N.W.T.
Canada XIA 2P7
Support group for North America's
natives

International Work Group for
Indigenous Affairs (IWGIA)
Fiolstraede 10
DK-1171 Copenhagen K, Denmark
Support group for native peoples

Cultural Survival
11 Divinity Avenue
Cambridge, MA 02138
Indigenous peoples' survival

Sahabat Alam Malaysia
(Friends of the Earth)
37 Lorong Birch
10250 Penang, Malaysia
Support group for Asian natives

Survival International
310 Edgware Rd.
London W2 1DY United Kingdom
Information and support for
indigenous peoples

Acknowledgments of Copyright

APPLEMAN, PHILIP, "And Then the Perfect Truth of Hatred," from *Let There Be Light,* © 1991 by Philip Appleman. HarperCollins, New York. Reprinted by permission of the author.

BALDWIN, JAMES, "If Black English Ain't a Language, Then Tell Me What Is?" © 1979, James Baldwin Estate and the *New York Times,* Jul. 29, 1979, Op-Ed. Reprinted by permission of The New York Times Company.

BARAKA, AMIRI, "Brought Up on Right-Wing Anthologies," from an interview by Bertrand Mathieu, editor, *The Noiseless Spider,* Vol. 8, No. 2, The University of New Haven, Connecticut, 1978. Reprinted by permission of the publisher. "Nationalism Is Always Oppressive," excerpted from an interview with D. H. Melhem, from *Heroism in the New Black Poetry,* © 1990 by D. H. Melhem, The University Press of Kentucky, Lexington, KY.

BARKAN, STANLEY, "From the Garden of Eden," from *Biblical Broadsides and Bubbes and Bubbemeises,* © 1990, Stanley H. Barkan. Reprinted by permission of the author and Cross-Cultural Communications, Merrick, NY.

BAROLINI, HELEN, excerpts from "Literary Hegemonies and Oversights" Introduction to *The Dream Book: Writings by Italian American Women,* © 1985 by Helen Barolini, Schocken Books, New York. Reprinted by permission of the author.

BASHO, Matsuo, "Curiosity about My Strange Neighbor," a haiku, 1694, translated and adapted by Daniela Gioseffi, © 1993. Printed by permission.

BENNETT, LERONE, JR., "There's Been a Misunderstanding about the Sixties," An Overview from *Race,* by Studs Terkel. © 1992, Studs Terkel. Reprinted by permission of the New Press, W. W. Norton, New York.

BISCHOF, PHYLLIS, "African Language Writing," from *Before Columbus Review,* Spring/Summer 1990, Vol. 1, Nos. 3 & 4. © 1990 Phyllis Bischof, Berkeley, CA. Reprinted by permission of the author.

BONNER, ELENA, "Ethnic Tensions Split the Commonwealth," from "Looking to the Future [of the Former U.S.S.R.]" *Current History,* Vol. 91, No. 567, October 1992, © 1992 by Current History, Inc. Reprinted with permission.

CONRAD, JOSEPH, excerpt from *The Congo: An Outpost of Progress,* c. 1899, London.

CORTEZ, JAYNE, "Everything Is Wonderful," from *Coagulations,* © 1984 by Jayne Cortez, Thunder's Mouth Press, New York. Reprinted by permission of the author.

DAO, BEI, "Language," from *The August Sleepwalker.* Translated by Bonnie S. McDougall, © 1988, Bonnie S. McDougall and New Directions, New York. Reprinted by permission of the publisher and translator.

DAĞLARCA, FAZIL HÜSNÜ, "Worldwide" and "Awake," from *The Bird & I,* translated by Talât Sait Halman. English translation © 1980 by Talât Sait Halman. Reprinted by permission of the translator and Cross-Cultural Communications, Merrick, NY.

DER-HOVANESSIAN, DIANA, "Songs of Bread" and "An Armenian Looking at Newsphotos of the Cambodian Deathwatch," from *Songs of Bread, Songs of Salt,* © 1990 by Diana Der-Hovanessian, Ashod Press, New York. First appeared in *Graham House Review* and *Nantucket Review.* Reprinted by permission of the author.

DOUGLASS, FREDERICK, excerpt from "Fourth of July Speech to a White Audience, 1852," and Chapter One from *Narrative of the Life of Frederick Douglass: An American Slave* by Frederick Douglass. Text found in an edition © 1973, 1989 Anchor/Doubleday, New York.

DOWD, SIOBHAN, "Religion Is Known to Be a Dangerous Topic for Writers," from *Sentenced to Silence* from *Poets & Writers Magazine,* Vol. 20, Issue 6, Nov./Dec. 1992, New York. © 1992 by Siobhan Dowd, International PEN's Freedom-to-Write Committee. Reprinted by permission of the author.

DU BOIS, W. E. B., "On Being Crazy" and "The Souls of Black Folks," from *The Souls of Black Folks,* first published 1903 by A. C. McClurg & Company. "Africa, Abused Continent," from a public speech, "The African Roots of War," delivered in August 1914 at the outbreak of World War I.

DURAS, MARGUERITE, "We Must Share the Crime," translated by D. G. Luttinger, © 1992. From *La Guerre* (original French), © 1986 by Marguerite Duras, Paris. Reprinted by permission of the translator.

EHRENREICH, BARBARA, and DEIRDRE ENGLISH, "The Witch Hunts," from *For Her Own Good,* © 1979 by Barbara Ehrenreich and Deirdre English, Anchor/Doubleday, New York. Reprinted by permission of the authors.

EMECHETA, BUCHI, "Sorry, No Coloureds," excerpted from *Second Class Citizen,* © 1977, Buchi Emecheta, George Braziller, New York. Reprinted by permission of the publisher.

ESPADA, MARTIN, "Trumpets from the Island of Their Eviction," from *Trumpets from the Island of Their Eviction,* © 1987 by Martin Espada and Bilingual Review/Press Hispanic Research Center, Arizona State University, Tempe, AZ. Reprinted by permission of the author and publisher.

FERLINGHETTI, LAWRENCE, "The Old Italians Dying," © 1979 by Lawrence Ferlinghetti, City Lights Books, San Francisco, CA. Also from *Wild Dreams of a New Beginning,* © 1988, New Directions Paperback #663, New York. Reprinted by permission of the author.

FRENCH, MARILYN, "A Brief History of Women in a Man's World," summary of a forthcoming book: *From Eve to Dawn: A Woman's History of the World,* © 1993, Marilyn French, Little, Brown, New York. Delivered as a reading for the PEN Women's Committee, Hunter College, New York, 1991. Reprinted courtesy and permission of the author.

FREUD, SIGMUND, "Man Is Endowed with a Strong Aggressive Nature," from "A Reply to a Letter from Einstein: What Makes Hate?" and *Civilization and Its Discontents.* This version translated and adapted by D. G. Luttinger. © 1993 by D. G. Luttinger. Reprinted by permission of the translator.

GAMBINO, Richard, "An Extraordinary Bigotry," from *Blood of My Blood: The Dilemma of Italian-Americans,* © 1974 by Richard Gambino, Doubleday, New York. Reprinted by permission of the author.

GARCIA LORCA, FEDERICO, "The Small Mute Boy" and "The Small Deaf Boy," translated and adapted by Daniela Gioseffi. © 1993. Reprinted by permission of the translator. Original Spanish texts from *Poeta en Nueva York,* © 1940 Federico Garcia Lorca.

GILLESPIE, CHRIS, "Prejudice against the Handicapped," © 1992 by Chris Gillespie of Rutgers University, N.J. Reprinted by permission of the author.

GIOSEFFI, DANIELA, "Lampshades of Human Skin" from *Word Wounds and Water Flowers,* © 1993 by Daniela Gioseffi. Mosaic Publications, Vienna and New York. Also appears as "Unfinished Autobiography," in *Unsettling America: Race and Ethnicity in Contemporary American Poetry,* edited by Maria Mazziotti-Gillan and Jennifer Gillan, Viking Penguin, New York, 1994.

GORE, AL, excerpts from *Earth in the Balance,* © 1992 by Senator Al Gore, Houghton Mifflin, Boston, MA. Reprinted by permission of the publisher. All rights reserved.

GOULD, STEPHEN JAY, "Women's Brains" from *The Panda's Thumb: More Reflections in Natural History,* © 1980 by Stephen Jay Gould, W. W. Norton, New York, © 1981 by Stephen Jay Gould. Reprinted by permission of the author.

GREEN, PAULA, "Burma: A Nation of Prisoners," from *Non-violent Activist: The Magazine of the War Resisters League,* Vol. 9, No. 2, March 1992. © by WRL, 339 Lafayette St., New York. Reprinted by permission of the War Resisters League.

GUILLÉN, NICOLÁS, "Stain of the Blood of the Master," translated by Daniela Gioseffi and Enildo A. García. © 1992 by Daniela Gioseffi and Enildo A. García. Original text © by Lettras Cubanas, Havana, Cuba. Reprinted by permission of the translators.

HALL, EDWARD T., "Proxemics in a Cross-Cultural Context: Japan and the Arab World," © 1966, from *The Hidden Dimension.* Anchor/Doubleday, New York. Reprinted by permission of the author and publisher.

HAMILTON-TWEEDALE, BRIAN, "Reporting 'Terrorism': The Experience of Northern Ireland," from *A Reader in Peace Studies,* © 1991 Pergamon Press Ltd., Oxford, England. Reprinted by permission of the publisher.

HARPER, A. FRANCES ELLEN WATKINS, letter to John Brown and "Bury me in a Free Land," from *A Brighter Day,* edited by Frances Smith Foster, © 1990, The Feminist Press, New York, NY.

HARPER, PHILLIP BRIAN, "Racism and Homophobia as Reflections on Their Perpetrators," from *Homophobia: How We All Pay the Price,* edited by Warren J. Blumenfeld, © 1992. Reprinted by permission of Beacon Press, Boston, MA.

HAVEL, VÁCLAV, "True Democracy Demands Moral Conviction," quotations from public speeches, c. 1990–1992, Prague, Czechoslovakia. Also see original Czech in *Letni premitani,* © 1991 by Odeon, Prague. Translated by Sophia Buzevska, © 1992. Reprinted by permission.

HEBÉRT, ANNE, "The Offended," translated by A. Poulin, Jr., from *Anne Hebert: Selected Poems,* © 1987 by Al Poulin, Jr., Boa Editions, Ltd., 92 Park Ave., Brockport, NY 14420. Reprinted by permission of the translator and publisher.

HECHT, SUSANNA, and ALEXANDER COCKBURN, "Amazon Rain Forest: Missing the People for the Trees," from *Extra,* Summer 1989. © 1989 by Fairness and Accuracy in Reporting, Inc., New York. Reprinted by permission of FAIR.

HERNTON, CALVIN C., "The Sexualization of Racism," from *Sex and Racism in America,* © 1965, 1988 by Calvin C. Hernton, Doubleday and Anchor Books, New York. Reprinted by permission of the publisher.

HEYEN, WILLIAM, "Men in History" and "A Visit to Belzec" from *Erika: Poems of the Holocaust,* by William Heyen © 1991, Timeless Press, Saint Louis. "Men in History" also appears in *Falling from Heaven: Holocaust Poems of a Jew and a Gentile,* by Louis Daniel Brodsky and William Heyen, © 1991, Time Being Books, Saint Louis. Reprinted by permission of the author and publishers.

HOFFMAN, MERLE, "I Am a Child of the Holocaust," from *On the Issues: The Progressive Woman's Quarterly,* Summer 1990, © 1990 by Choices Women's Medical Center, Queens, NY. Reprinted by permission of the author and publisher.

HUGHES, LANGSTON, "Name in Print!" from *The Best of Simple* by Langston Hughes. © 1961. Copyright renewed by George Houston Bass, © 1989. Reprinted by permission of Hill and Wang, a division of Farrar, Straus & Giroux. British and Canadian rights: Harold Ober Associates, New York. Reprinted by courtesy and permission of the publisher and Harold Ober Associates. All rights reserved.

HUXLEY, ALDOUS, excerpt from *Science, Liberty, and Peace,* a pamphlet published by the War Resisters League, Lafayette St., New York. A. J. Muste Memorial Institute Essay Series, #9. Originally published in 1944.

Elinor Langer. Research for the essay was supported, in part, by grants from the Fund for Investigative Journalism and the Dick Goldensohn Fund. Reprinted by permission of Georges Borchardt, Inc., New York, on behalf of the author.

LARSEN, WENDY WILDER. See TRAN THI NGA.

LEE, MARTIN A. and GLORIA CHANNON, "Invisible Victims: The Press and Human Rights," *Extra, A Newsletter of Fairness & Accuracy in Reporting,* © 1991 by FAIR. All rights reserved. Reprinted by permission.

LEVINE, PHILIP, "Baby Villon," from *Not This Pig,* © 1968, Wesleyan University Press, CT. Reprinted by permission of the author.

LIFTON, ROBERT J., with ERIC MARKUSEN, "Genocidal Ideology: Trauma and Cure," excerpt from *The Genocidal Mentality: Nazi Holocaust and Nuclear Threat,* © 1990 by Robert J. Lifton and Erik Markusen, Basic Books, a division of HarperCollins Publishers, New York. Also © 1990 by the authors and Macmillan London, Ltd., London, and Verlagsgemeinshaft Ernst Klett, Stuttgart, Germany. Reprinted by permission of the publishers.

LIM, GENNY, "Children Are Color-Blind," from *Forbidden Stitches: An Asian American Women's Anthology.* © 1989 by Genny Lim and Calyx Books, Corvallis, Oregon. Reprinted by permission of the author.

LIM, SHIRLEY GEOK-LIN, Modern Secrets: "Last Night I Dreamt in Chinese . . . ," © 1989 by Shirley Geok-Lin Lim, Asian-American Studies Program, University of California, Santa Barbara. Reprinted by permission of the author.

LIPSTADT, DEBORAH E., "Beyond Belief: The Press and the Holocaust," from "The American Press and the Coming of the Holocaust, 1933–45," from *Extra: A Newsletter of Fairness and Accuracy in Reporting,* © 1989 by FAIR, New York. All rights reserved. Reprinted by permission of the publisher.

LUSANE, CLARENCE, "Racism and the War on Drugs," excerpts from *From Pipe Dream Blues: Racism and the War on Drugs,* by Clarence Lusane, © 1991 by Clarence Lusane, South End Press, 116 Botolph St., Boston, MA 02115. Reprinted courtesy and permission of the author and publisher.

MALCOLM X, brief quotations from various public speeches and public media interviews, 1959–1965. These words and ideas were repeated many times, nationally, in the course of Malcolm X's life of public oratory.

MANDELA, NELSON, excerpted from a public speech, "Address to the U.S. Congress," Washington, DC, 1991, by Nelson Mandela.

MAZZIOTI-GILLAN, MARIA, "Public School No. 18: Paterson, New Jersey," from *Winter Light,* Chantry Press, Box 144, Midland Park, NJ 07432. © 1985 by Maria Mazziotti-Gillan. Reprinted by permission of the author.

MELHEM, D. H., "say french," from *Rest in Love,* © 1975, 1978 by D. H. Melhem, Dovetail Press, New York. Reprinted by permission of the author.

MILLAY, EDNA ST. VINCENT, "Justice Denied in Massachusetts," from *Collected Poems,* HarperCollins, New York. © 1928, 1955 Edna St. Vincent Millay and Norma Millay Ellis. Reprinted by permission of Elizabeth Barnett, Literary Executor, Steepletop, Austerlitz, NY.

MONTAGU, ASHLEY, "Ethnic Group," "Race," and "The Term Miscegenation" from *Man's Most Dangerous Myth: The Fallacy of Race.* © 1974 by Ashley Montagu, published by Oxford University Press, 1974. Reprinted by permission of the author, Princeton, NJ.

MONTALE, EUGENIO, "The Hitler Spring," translated by Daniela Gioseffi, © 1993, Daniela Gioseffi. Italian text © 1943, Eugenio Montale, Arnoldo Mondadori Editore, Italia. Reprinted by permission of the translator.

MORGAN, ROBIN, "Planetary Feminism: The Politics of the 21st Century," excerpt from the Introduction to *Sisterhood Is Global,* © 1984 by Robin Morgan, Anchor/Doubleday, New York. Reprinted by permission of the author.

MORRISON, TONI, excerpt from "A Bench by the Side of the Road," © 1989 Tony Morrison. An interview in *The World: The Journal of the Unitarian Universalist Association,* January/February 1989, Vol. 3, No. 1. Boston, MA. Reprinted by permission of the author.

MOYNIHAN, DANIEL PATRICK, excerpt from "A Nation of Nations," from *The Polish Americans,* the Peoples of North America Series, © 1988, Chelsea House Publishers, New York. Reprinted by permission of the publisher.

TOOR, RACHEL, "Extreme Prejudice Toward Polish Americans" from *The Polish Americans,* the Peoples of North America Series, © 1988, Chelsea House Publishers, New York. Reprinted by permission of the publisher.

TRUTH, SOJOURNER, "Ain't I a Woman," from a public speech by Sojourner Truth, c. 1851, Akron, Ohio.

TSVETAYEVA, MARINA, "Poets of Truth," excerpted from "Poem of the End," translated and adapted by Daniela Gioseffi with Sophia Buzevska. © 1992 by Daniela Gioseffi. Reprinted by permission. Original Russian text of "Poem of the End," written in Prague, 1924.

TUTU, BISHOP DESMOND, from a public speech delivered in South Africa in 1986.

TWAIN, MARK, "Massacre and Murderous Butching," quotations reprinted by Howard Zinn in *A People's History of the United States,* © by Howard Zinn, Harper & Row, New York.

UNITED NATIONS GENERAL ASSEMBLY: The Universal Declaration of Human Rights. Reprinted by permission of UNESCO, The United Nations, New York. Also, Statements on Race, III. and IV., The United Nations, New York, UNESCO SCHOLARS. See end of texts for credits.

VISCUSI, ROBERT, "Breaking the Silence," excerpt from an essay, © 1990 by *VIA: Voices in Italian Americana,* Vol 1., No. 1., edited by Anthony Tamburri, Paolo A. Giordano, and Fred L. Gardaphe, Purdue University Department of Foreign Languages, West Lafayette, IN 47907, and by Robert Viscusi, the Wolfe Institute for the Humanities, Brooklyn College of the City University of New York. Reprinted by permission of the author.

VOLTAIRE, "The slave he met   " from *Candide* Translation; anonymous, 1896. Original French, 1759, Paris.

VENNE, SHARON. See JULIAN BURGER.

WEISMAN, ALAN, AND SANDY TOLAN, "Central America: Vanishing Forests, Endangered Peoples," excerpted from a longer essay, © 1992 by Alan Weisman and Sandy Tolan, Box 3032, Tucson, AZ 85702. First appeared in Audubon, Nov./Dec. 1992, National Audubon Society, New York. Reprinted by permission of the authors.

WHITMAN, WALT, "I Sing the Body Electric," from *Leaves of Grass,* c. 1855 by Walt Whitman. Originally printed by Walt Whitman, Long Island, New York.

WIESEL, ELIE, with MERLE HOFFMAN, "I Am against Fanatics," from an interview conducted by Merle Hoffman, *On the Issues,* Vol. 18, Spring 1991, © 1991 by Choices Women's Medical Center, Forest Hills, Queens, NY. Reprinted by permission of Merle Hoffman, Publisher/Editor-in-Chief.

WOOLF, VIRGINIA, "My Country Is the World," excerpt from *Three Guineas,* © 1938 by Virginia Woolf, London.

WRIGHT, CAROLYNE, "English Revisited," from *Before Columbus Review,* Spring/Summer 1990, Vol. 1, Nos. 3 & 4. © 1990 Carolyne Wright. Reprinted by permission of the author.

WRIGHT, JAMES, "In the Face of Hatred," © 1983 by James Wright, from *The Branch Will Not Break,* Wesleyan University Press, Wesleyan, CT. Reprinted by permission of Anne Wright, executrix of the literary estate of James Wright, New York.

YATES, DORA E., "Hitler and the Gypsies: A Genocide That Must Be Remembered," from *Genocide and Human Rights,* The University Press of America, MD, © 1982, by Jack Nusan Porter, editor. Reprinted by permission.

YEATS, W. B., "The Leaders of the Crowd," © 1903 by William Butler Yeats, Dublin and London.

YEVTUSHENKO, YEVGENY, "The Song of the Slaves," translated by Daniela Gioseffi with Sofia Buzevska. © 1993. Original Russian copyright by Yevgeny Yevtushenko, Moscow, 1966. Reprinted by permission.

ZINNES, HARRIET, "Orange: Hiring," © 1991 by Harriet Zinnes. Reprinted by permission of the author, New York.

ZORYAN INSTITUTE for Contemporary Armenian Research and Documentation, Inc., "The Armenian Experience of Genocide," © 1984 by the Zoryan Institute, Laura Yardumian, director, Cambridge, MA. Reprinted by permission of the Zoryan Institute.

Index of Authors

ADILMAN, MONA ELAINE, 561

ALLEN, PAULA GUNN, 343

ANGELOU, MAYA, 574

APES, WILLIAM, 40

APPLEMAN, PHILIP, 196

BALDWIN, JAMES, 372

BARAKA, AMIRI, 427, 559

BARKAN, STANLEY, 315

BAROLINI, HELEN, 429

BASHO, MATSUO, 518

BENNETT, LERONE, JR., 585

BISCHOF, PHYLLIS, 379

BLACKBIRD, CHIEF ANDREW J., 43

BLACK HAWK, 48

BONNER, ELENA (YELENA), 236

BORTON, LADY, 562

BOSMAJIAN, HAIG A., 356

BROOKS, GWENDOLYN, 470

BRUCHAC, JOSEPH, 44

BRUTUS, DENNIS, 572

BURGER, JULIAN, 195, 259, 376, 567, 589

CASTAN, FRAN, 565

CHANNON, GLORIA (MARCHISIO), 415

COCKBURN, ALEXANDER, 312

CODRESCU, ANDREI, 418

COHEN, LENARD J., 244

COLES, ROBERT, 298

CONRAD, JOSEPH, 3

CORTEZ, JAYNE, 134

DAĞLARCA, FAZIL HÜSNÜ, 612

DAO, BEI, 355

DER-HOVANESSIAN, DIANA, 98, 99

DOUGLASS, FREDERICK, 56, 583

DOWD, SIOBHAN, 197

DU BOIS, W. E. B., 26, 271, 468

DURAS, MARGUERITE, 83

EHRENREICH, BARBARA, 125

EMECHETA, BUCHI, 205

ENGLISH, DEIRDRE, 125

ESPADA, MARTIN, 401

FERLINGHETTI, LAWRENCE, 385

FRENCH, MARILYN, 115

FREUD, SIGMUND, 288

GAMBINO, RICHARD, 180

GANDHI, MOHANDAS KARAMCHAND, 545

GARCIA LORCA, FEDERICO, 235

GERONIMO, 45

GILLESPIE, CHRIS, 227

GIOSEFFI, DANIELA, 301

GORE, AL, 306

GOULD, STEPHEN JAY, 118

GREEN, PAULA, 260

GUILLÉN, NICOLÁS, 25

HALL, EDWARD T., 521

HALMAN, TALÂT SAIT. See FAZIL HÜSNÜ DAĞLARCA.

HAMILTON-TWEEDALE, BRIAN, 404

HARPER, A. FRANCES ELLEN WATKINS, 54, 55

HARPER, PHILLIP BRIAN, 273

HAVEL, VACLÁV, 606

HEBÉRT, ANNE, 1

HECHT, SUSANNA, 312

HERNTON, CALVIN C., 266

HEYEN, WILLIAM, 65, 73

HOFFMAN, MERLE, 75, 546

HUGHES, LANGSTON, 409

HUXLEY, ALDOUS, 542

IGNATOW, DAVID, 588

IWAMATSU, SHIGETOSHI, 110

JEN, GISH, 451

JORDAN, BARBARA, 605

KAPLAN, ROBERT D., 189
KEELEY, EDMUND. See YANNIS RITSOS.
KEJU-JOHNSON, DARLENE, 129
KENNY, MAURICE, 220
KESSLER, MILTON, 213
KING, MARTIN LUTHER, JR., 575
LA DUKE, WINONA, 402
LANGER, ELINOR, 159
LARSEN, WENDY WILDER. See TRAN
    THI NGA.
LEE, MARTIN A., 415
LEVINE, PHILIP, 291
LIFTON, ROBERT JAY, 281
LIM, GENNY, 609
LIM, SHIRLEY GEOK-LIN, 450
LIPSTADT, DEBORAH E., 412
LUSANE, CLARENCE, 215
MALCOLM X, 199
MANDELA, NELSON (ROLIHLAHLA), 569
MARKUSEN, ERIC, 281
MAZZIOTTI-GILLAN, MARIA, 483
MELHEM, D. H., 411
MILLAY, EDNA ST. VINCENT, 479
MONTAGU, ASHLEY, 591
MONTALE, EUGENIO, 174
MORGAN, ROBIN, 316
MORRISON, TONI, 584
MOYNIHAN, DANIEL PATRICK, 155
MUKHERJEE, BHARATI, 484
MURA, DAVID, 188, 434
NEIER, ARYEH, 153
NERUDA, PABLO, 225
NGA, TRAN THI, 226
ONWUEME, TESS, 608
PACHECO, JOSE EMILIO, 84
PAIAKAN, PAULINHO, 589
PALACIOS, CHAILANG, 399
PALEY, GRACE, 203
PARENTI, MICHAEL, 394
PERILLO, LUCIA MARIA, 339

PORTER, JACK NUSAN, 67, 143
QUINDOZA-SANTIAGO, LILIA, 199
RATNER, ROCHELLE, 64
RAVITCH, DIANE (SILVER), 498
REED, ISHMAEL, 537
REISCHAUER, EDWIN O., 182
RIDING, ALAN, 175
RITSOS, YANNIS, 582
ROGOZIŃSKI, JAN, 6
ROWE, DOROTHY, 292
SACCO, NICOLO, 480
SHAPIRO, HARVEY, 352
SITTING BULL, 590
SPENCER, SHARON, 471
STONE, CAROLE, 372
STRONG, MAURICE F., 305
THALER, FRANK, 170
TINKER, HUGH, 135
TOLAN, SANDY, 221
TOOR, RACHEL, 177
TOLSTOY, LEO, 541
TRUTH, SOJOURNER, 339
TSVETAYEVA, MARINA, 611
TUTU, BISHOP DESMOND, 573
TWAIN, MARK, 99
VENNE, SHARON, 378
VISCUSI, ROBERT, 381
VOLTAIRE, 1
WEISMAN, ALAN, 221
WHITMAN, WALT, 602
WIESEL, ELIE, 546
WOOLF, VIRGINA, 338
WRIGHT, CAROLYNE, 388
WRIGHT, JAMES, 169
YATES, DORA E., 103
YEATS, WILLIAM BUTLER, 536
YEVTUSHENKO, YEVGENY, 37
ZINNES, HARRIET, 431
ZORYAN INSTITUTE, 86